BASEBALL

P9-ELF-873

BASEBALL:

THE PEOPLE'S GAME

BASEBALL:

BASEBALL

THE PEOPLE'S GAME · HAROLD SEYMOUR, Ph.D.

New York   Oxford
Oxford University Press
1990

Oxford University Press

Oxford   New York   Toronto
Delhi   Bombay   Calcutta   Madras   Karachi
Petaling Jaya   Singapore   Hong Kong   Tokyo
Nairobi   Dar es Salaam   Cape Town
Melbourne   Auckland
and associated companies in
Berlin   Ibadan

Copyright © 1990 by Harold Seymour

Published by Oxford University Press, Inc.,
200 Madison Avenue, New York, New York 10016

Oxford is a registered trademark of Oxford University Press

Library of Congress Cataloging-in-Publication Data
(Revised for volume 3)
Seymour, Harold, 1910-
Baseball.
Contents: [1] The early years.
[2] The golden age.   [3] The people's game.
1. Baseball—History. I. Title.
GV863.A1S48   1960
796.357'09   60-5799
ISBN 0-19-503890-8

9 8 7 6 5 4 3 2 1
Printed in the United States of America
on acid-free paper

$\mathbf{T}$his book of baseball history is unique. It is the first one devoted entirely to those players and teams who played baseball outside so-called Organized Baseball—that is, the professional major and minor leagues—up to World War II. For baseball may be likened to a large house containing many rooms occupied by a wide variety of baseball tenants—college players, members of the armed forces, industrial players, semipros, blacks, women, Indians, town team players, and softballers. Five chapters are devoted to blacks before segregation compelled them to form their own professional leagues. The story of women has also required an equal number of chapters. Organized Baseball is mentioned only incidentally, when necessitated by the account of those outside it. Other writers on baseball have almost completely ignored these tenants of the house of baseball. *Baseball: The People's Game* fills the void created by this long-time omission.

While Organized Baseball depends on all these tenants of the house of baseball for the source of its strength and appeal, the various tenants do not require Organized Baseball for their existence. For the professionals of O.B. are like the *Schlag*, the whipped cream, on a piece of Sachertorte, the famous Viennese cake of several layers, which can be relished "mit oder ohne"— with or without the *Schlag*. So can baseball be enjoyed without the professionals, as it was played throughout America regardless of geographic location—on the sandlots, cow pastures, playgrounds, and parks, or in connection with various institutions like schools, colleges, prisons and reformatories, industries, churches, town organizations, and other sponsors, who promoted the game, confident of the benefits it conferred on their institutions as well as to the players involved. The book reveals that women, Indians, blacks, convicts, and even the handicapped played baseball earlier or more extensively than heretofore recorded.

In the last analysis the foundation of baseball's house with its heterogeneous occupants ultimately draws its strength and vitality from a foundation of boys' teams, for only in boyhood and youth can skill in playing the game and, more important, love of it, be developed. This affinity of youth for

baseball carried over into manhood as boys continued to be players or spectators, or both, and in the doing created the many types of teams revealed
in this book and the countless spectators eager to attend their games. It is
this layered structure of amateur and semipro play below the top story of
baseball's house that made baseball for more than a century truly the national
game.

It is difficult today to appreciate the omnipresence of baseball in the past—
its countless teams, multitudes of spectators, and even its spread both in
war and peace to some foreign shores. The material in this book, lengthy
though it is, could have encompassed several volumes. Yet this volume is
the first to present a comprehensive account of baseball outside of Organized
Baseball. Few scholars have ventured to give any attention to this need.
Many topics included herewith warrant separate monographs.

I trust readers of this volume will feel rewarded for their long wait for
what they expected would be a chronological continuation of my first two
volumes. Actually, I had started volume three with that intention, but it
occured to me that the game outside Organized Baseball had been scanted,
so I then decided to discountinue work on Organized Baseball and prepare
this book instead. When I suggested this different approach to Sheldon
Meyer, my long-time Oxford editor, he agreed with my decision and exercised great patience during the book's long gestation.

For that matter, although trained professional historians have come a long
way they even ignored professional baseball until after I opened the subject
with my Cornell University doctoral dissertation almost fifty years ago, the
first one on professional baseball, later rewritten and expanded into *Baseball:
The Early Years* and continued separately with *Baseball: The Golden Age*,
the first scholarly works published on the history of the game, which were
reprinted in softcover last year. The faculty where I taught in the late 1940s
voted a hundred percent against a course in baseball history that I proposed,
but since then courses in sport history have become widespread in American
colleges. Still, as recently as the mid-seventies one doctoral candidate who
wanted to write his dissertation on an aspect of baseball history fecklessly
kept quiet about it because, he said later, baseball was not normally the
stuff of a successful career in history. He chose a more "conventional" topic
and came out of hiding only after being safely nestled in a teaching position.

As in my two previous volumes, I have omitted footnotes, since they
inhibit the general reader, even the so-called intelligent layman—a rapidly
disappearing species—and consume space, especially a consideration in this
lengthy work.

A book of this length and range of topics is bound to invite some honest
criticism, which is to be expected but I scorn the nit-pickers and scrap
nibblers, not to mention a few plagiarizers, who, without citing me as their
source, like yipping jackals snatch chunks from the disdainful tiger's kill.

One even had the gall to complain of the taste of a chunk he gulped from one of my books.

In the course of writing the text I have cited as many helpful sources as possible without cumbering the story and I included many more in a lengthy bibliographic note. I am most grateful to all who helped, especially to the many librarians who aided the work. The assistance of my wife, Dorothy Zander Seymour, needs only one word: indispensable.

Big League Camp   Harold Seymour, Ph.D.
Keene, New Hampshire

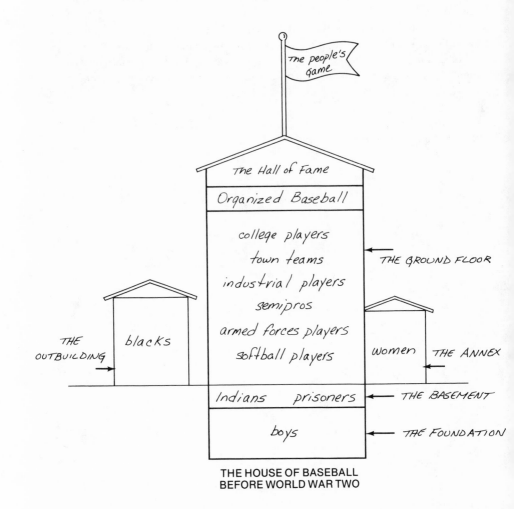

**THE HOUSE OF BASEBALL
BEFORE WORLD WAR TWO**

CONTENTS

Illustrations between pages 212 and 213 and between 362 and 363.

PART ONE

THE HOUSE OF BASEBALL:
THE FOUNDATION

1

SANDLOT AND COW PASTURE

"**G**et the leading lady!" "He swings like a rusty gate!" "Right over, batter, waddaya waitin' for?" "Two out, run on anything!" "A walk's as good as a hit!" "He runs like an old lady with wet drawers!"

Cries of encouragement and derision like these have been shouted by generations of boys playing baseball on the sandlots and cow pastures of America. They also experienced sounds like the satisfying thwack of the ball into a glove, the click of spikes on concrete or wood, the sharp crack of the bat hitting the ball. And they knew smells like the scent of oil on a glove, and feelings like the raw inner skin on the thumb that comes from gripping the bat.

Boys who have experienced such sounds, smells, and feelings formed the foundation of the entire structure of baseball, which may be likened to a rambling, old-fashioned boarding house. Small at first, the House of Baseball gradually grew larger, not according to a preconceived architectural plan but pragmatically and often laggardly. New rooms were added, old ones renovated or abandoned, and a second story that dominated the structure built on.

The crowded ground floor of the House of Baseball housed a bewildering assortment of amateurs and quasi amateurs, including collegians, town team players, industrial players, semipros, soldiers and sailors, and softballers. In the basement resided Indians and prisoners. An annex lodged women players. In an outbuilding almost hidden from view were squeezed black players, segregated by the occupants of the big house except when it was advantageous for them to have dealings with the outcastes.

The upper floor of the House of Baseball came to serve professional teams and leagues in a form eventually known as Organized Baseball. This relatively small minority, in turn controlled by a handful of major-league clubs, has dominated the House of Baseball for the best part of a century. Purveyors of the best brand of play and organized down to the number of stitches on the baseballs they use, the professionals have received the major share of the media coverage and public attention. Indeed, those who own and control

3

the closely-knit combine of professional leagues and teams known as Organized Baseball see themselves as holders of the title-deeds of the game and tend to equate their commercialized operation with the whole of baseball—the one word BASEBALL inscribed on the office door of their commissioner says much for the attitude of the professional hierarchs and their retainers. Consequently, they are prone to believe their interests and policies good for baseball and anything they disapprove of bad for it, forgetting that the other tenants of the House of Baseball vastly outnumber the professionals and may have quite different interests and objectives.

The superstructure of baseball, professional and nonprofessional, is only as strong as its foundation, boys' baseball, on which it ultimately depends for a continuing supply of players, to say nothing of future customers. Baseball begins with boys because to play it with skill one must begin in boyhood. To learn any sport an early start is desirable; to learn baseball it is essential. Perhaps no other team game demands of an individual more physical skills, mental alertness, steady nerves, and calm courage as does baseball. And only in the long springs and summers of his formative years can one gradually develop the quick, spontaneous movements involved in catching, throwing, and hitting a baseball. Only by starting then can he hope to acquire those fielding techniques unheard of in cricket but commonplace in baseball: an outfielder's ability to gauge instantly the flight of a towering fly ball, race to get under it, and catch it on the run, or the dexterity of an infielder in scooping up a ground ball and in the same fluid motion throwing it to the proper base.

The necessity for an early start applies doubly to batting. All team sports lay claim to the necessity for high skill, but none equal that of hitting a pitched ball with a small round length of wood: this may be the most difficult feat in all of sport. To gauge the speed and trajectory of a ball not more than 9 1/4 inches in circumference coming toward you from less than 60 feet 6 inches away, and to hit it into a prescribed space with a round bat not more than 2 3/4 inches at the fattest part takes quick reflexes, perfect coordination, and precise timing.

Even these are not enough. Another crucial ingredient is courage. In baseball the batter stands alone; on his own he faces the pitcher and the eight other players who support him.* A pitched ball thrown at a speed up to a hundred miles an hour is a projectile capable of maiming or even killing. When facing such a missile the natural impulse, instead of striding into the pitch and putting one's body into the swing, is to "bail out"—pull away, particularly from a curve ball, which usually starts toward the batter only to break, or curve, down and away just before it reaches him. Building the confidence needed to suppress this impulse demands constant practice com-

---

*In cricket, too, the batter stands alone, but he defends the wicket with a broad, flat bat, whereas in baseball he attacks.

menced in boyhood and kept up season after season. Many otherwise good ball players never succeed in doing it. An indelicate report on a rookie written in 1913 by a major-league scout contains the classic thumbs-down verdict that has ended the baseball dreams of countless young men: "Butcher won't hit over .250 in [the] National League. He pulls his ass away on a curve ball. . . . " (The report predicted accurately; he never did.) One of the oldest anecdotes in baseball lore tells of the rookie who writes his mother from spring training camp telling her not to rent his room because the pitchers have started throwing curves.

In the case of the pitcher alone, the necessity for an early start might be qualified, because if he throws too much or attempts curve balls too soon he risks ruining his arm.

Baseball also emphasizes team play. One of the game's attractions is its pleasing blend of teamwork with highly refined individual skills. Each player must be alert to act instantly, almost instinctively, in combination with his teammates, depending upon the situation at the moment. One does not acquire this "baseball sense" overnight. Only by playing the game as a boy does he develop it together with those other faculties that Jacques Barzun called the "American virtues that shine in baseball," namely "accuracy and speed, the practiced eye and hefty arm, the mind to take in and readjust to the unexpected, the possession of more than one talent and the willingness to work in harness without special orders. . . . "

Boys and baseball are closely associated in the minds of many Americans, to whom a sure sign of spring is a noisy sandlot game, and they speak of the so-called baseball heritage of America's boys as though youngsters began playing the game as soon as the first immigrants stepped off the *Mayflower*. Actually, the bond between boys and baseball is less hoary than some imagine. Boys did enjoy various bat and ball games from Colonial times onward, ranging from the simplest, like barn ball, which could be played by only two boys, to town ball, which accommodated large numbers. Even the name *base ball* has long been in common usage. But the game as now understood did not arrive on the American scene until 1845 when Alexander Cartwright of the New York Knickerbockers formulated the playing rules followed in the main ever since. So the period of unstandardized or folk ball playing in America prevailed for more than two hundred years, a considerably longer span than that of the formal game with written rules, and in fact lingered in many communities until much later. Town ball, for instance, survived in northern California into the 1870s and in Xenia, Illinois, until after the turn of the century. Boys in Benton Harbor, Michigan, played rounders as late as 1908.

After professionalism infiltrated the ranks of the early teams they did not die, although many became tinctured with the professionalism of the commercial clubs. The "amateurs" own group, the National Association, survived until 1874, and the pioneer Knickerbockers continued active until 1882.

Meanwhile, teams that preferred to call themselves amateur had spread the game all over the country, and even before the Civil War baseball had already won acclaim as the National Game.* Before long the Knickerbockers' style of play had conquered the old Massachusetts Game of New England, the variant that was its closest rival, and secured a foothold in the South before the Civil War. Cartwright himself aided its march across country when he took a ball with him on a long overland journey to the West Coast and thence to Hawaii in 1849, demonstrating his version of baseball at every opportunity along the way.

Baseball's appeal and spread democratized it, changing its character from a polite and gentlemanly pastime to a popular sport for the masses, whose urge to play it was astonishing. Some young Detroit men who, prevented from playing during the day by jobs in stores and offices, rose at daybreak to practice until 7:00 A.M. and formed the Early Risers Base Ball Club in 1859. The Detroit *Free Press* encouraged them. Playing baseball, it claimed,

> will . . . occupy their leisure time in healthy exercise counteracting the growing tendency to visit saloons and other places of resort with which the city abounds, thus saving them from early immorality. . . . Those who hang around the billiard saloons and liquor shops, constantly complaining of a lack of exercise and consequent loss of appetite, would do well to join one of the base ball clubs, and take regular exercise with them.

Other newspapers also endorsed the physical and moral value of ball playing for young men and boys. "No parent," said a New Orleans paper in 1865, "will object to his son taking up bat and ball in preference to the dice, the cards or the glass." A few years later the New York *Clipper* called baseball clubs "missionary organizations preaching the new gospel of health" and "arousing an interest in physical exercise" among youth. Thus adult amateurs carried all over the country the "baseball fever" of the 1870s that made the game the number one outdoor sport of America.

Boys easily caught the fever. Because of their long familiarity with bat-and-ball games they could learn the new one about as easily as switching from plain vanilla to multiflavored ice cream, especially with so many adult teams to serve as models. In fact, most of the early clubs had a membership large enough—frequently 60 or 70—to field a junior nine for boys in addition to their first and second teams. As early as 1858 at least sixty such junior teams played in the New York City alone, and two years later junior teams formed a national association. Boys played baseball early on the New England commons and in Washington, D.C. During the Civil War Abraham Lincoln intervened on behalf of several boys who had been ordered by the Building Officer to stop playing on the White House grounds, as one of those boys recalled many years later. *The Spirit of the Times* observed in 1867, "the

---

*For a detailed account of the early evolution of the game, see *Baseball: The Early Years*, Chapters 1–6, and "How Baseball Began," *The New-York Historical Society Quarterly* (October 1955), pp. 300–323.

schoolboy may join a junior club at a mere trifling expense, and the gamin can and does play ball for nothing."

Baseball adapted itself easily to boys. With the possible exception of soccer, size and brute strength count for less in baseball than in other team sports. Small, agile players with quick reflexes often hold their own with big, hulking ones—"piano movers," as Ty Cobb contemptuously called them. The game requires only minimum equipment and some space, and its essentials are simple. It can be played on any level, from the most elementary to the highly complex. Most boys could play it, and most of them did. In 1881 A.G. Spalding and Company stopped printing the rules of baseball in its annual guides because every boy knew the rudiments of the game. A decade later a French visitor, impressed by the baseball skill of children as young as six and seven, wrote that "the entire nation bears witness to the enormous interest taken" in baseball. The game became the favorite, often the only, team sport of American boys and held this position into the 1920s if not longer.

Even so, not every boy romped carefree on sandlots and pastures. A glance at reality dissipates any such idyll. More than 100,000 children in the early 1870s toiled in the factories of New York City and neighboring districts, and an additional 15,000 drifted from one factory to another. A paper-box factory worked children ten hours a day for three dollars a week and permitted take-home work after hours. Children aged nine worked in New Jersey in the eighties for two dollars a week. Boys in the coal regions entered the mines as soon as they could carry a lunch bucket, nine-year-olds putting in ten hours a day picking slate from coal. Major-league pitcher Stanley Coveleskie, who worked from seven to seven, six days a week, as a boy in the Pennsylvania mines, said he had little opportunity to play ball, but in the evenings he threw stones at cans. Southern cotton mill operators hired boys of ten or twelve to remove filled bobbins and replace them with empty ones, working from six to six for five days a week and six to five Saturdays, at a quarter a day. Some children even preferred work to school, and many parents needed their pay. At the turn of the century one out of every five boys aged ten to fifteen was gainfully employed, and for them baseball was at best a sometime thing.

Other boys had to curtail their ball playing out of the necessity of working part-time, as lines from a 1912 poem, "Songs of the Alley League," attest:

> There's gloom over Hooligan's Alley today,
> They're sorer than Hamid the Turk;
> There's a crimp in the ragged stars rally today
> As they gather to warm up for work,
> For Micky O'Brien the star of them all who
> Furnished the brains and intrigue
> From the lineup has passed, signed and drafted at last,
> By his Dad for the Grocery League.

In the depression years several boys of promise as ball players on my own teams were forced to forego playing in our Saturday games because they had to work that day.

Some parents saw no sense in ball playing. Joe Di Maggio's father wanted him to make something of himself and thought ball playing a waste of time and no way to bring in money. A farmer quoted in 1915 refused to let his son have Saturday afternoons off to join other boys in forming a team: "Baseball!" he shouted, "What in tarnation do you want to play baseball for? Don't you get enough exercise during the week?"

How did boys play baseball during the six or seven decades before World War II? Boys rarely leave documentary evidence of their baseball days until youth passes. Then a few of them, the author of this book included, peer through the soft mists of memory and record their boyhood baseball experiences. As the Irish writer James Greer expressed it:

> Childhood and home and youth they come again,
> Take shapes and hues and play in clouds at even.
> And Deering woods are fresh and fair,
> And with joy that is almost pain
> My heart goes back to wander there,
> And among the dreams of the days that were
> I find my lost youth again.

Scanty as they are, baseball reminiscences are prototypes of what thousands of others could have written about the way they played ball. To peruse them is to sense how much baseball meant to so many for so long.

The old American trait of improvisation guided the sandlot players of earlier generations. In those bygone days before an affluent society showered boys with costly ready-made and child-size equipment, boys had to exercise contrivance and frugality. Ready-made baseballs were often hard to come by. Before the Civil War only two or three manufacturers made them, largely to order, and sold them singly or at most by the dozen. Many a lad made his own. Early in the nineteenth century boys of New York made balls out of cork or shreds of india rubber wound with yarn from a stocking and covered with pieces from an ordinary glove. *The Boy's Treasury of Sports* helped by recommending cutting two small india-rubber bottles into long strips, winding them around a piece of cork, covering the rubber with some worsted, and sewing a piece of leather over the whole. Parents sometimes lent a hand. In the 1850s James Lovett's father made him a ball out of yarn wound around rubber and quilted with twine—a "mushy, pulpy-feeling" thing.

Even after the Civil War when each city soon had at least one factory turning out bats and balls, ready-made baseballs long remained scarce among youngsters. Seldom did they boast a big-league ball, although once in a while a youngster who lived near a major-league park could grab one hit out of the park. One day outside Ebbets Field I was lucky enough to get two! The poet Carl Sandburg, a baseball enthusiast in his youth, recalled that on rare occasions when the boys he played with got a chance to use a Spalding big-league ball they gathered around it "in wonder." Their more usual implement was a five-cent rubber ball wrapped around with grocery string. That son of the middle border, Hamlin Garland, remembered that his mother sewed covers on the boys' baseballs. In Nebraska around 1890 Sam Crawford, later a Detroit Tiger star, and his friends could not afford regular league baseballs, so they collected string and yarn, used a little rubber ball for the center, and had their mothers sew on a cover to hold the lump together. Crawford's future teammate, Ty Cobb, wound yarn around a rubber ball and got a leathermaker to cover it for the price of a few errands. The father of Earle Combs, later a big leaguer, made a baseball by cutting a center for it from an old gym shoe, winding it with unraveled socks, and making a cover from an old high-topped woman's shoe. Dizzy Dean, an Arkansas country boy who pitched for the St. Louis Cardinals of the 1930s, claimed that the first ball he ever owned was fashioned out of string wound around a walnut and held together with a cover made of tongues cut from shoes. Charlie Finley, later a big-league club owner, said that as a boy in Alabama he and his friends made a ball of cottonseed wound with friction tape.

A roll of heavy black friction tape became standard equipment for sand-lotters. One of the group usually managed to have a roll in his pocket or knew where to find one in his house. For when the cover of a proper baseball came off, as it did sooner or later from constant batting and use on rough ground, one of the boys grown expert with practice taped what was left, then rubbed it with sand to remove the stickiness, after which play resumed. George Toporcer, the first big-league infielder to wear glasses, performed the taping job when he played with the boys of New York's Yorkville section. As late as the 1930s the boys who played on Warren Street in Newburyport, Massachusetts, never had more than one ball, often taped.

For boys of Flushing, Michigan, around 1920, the biggest problem was to get a ball to start with. If they succeeded they never knew when another would materialize, so after the cover came off they taped over the exposed string. If the ball became lopsided they stopped the game and pounded it into shape. At last, when the ball became so small they could hardly see it, they combined it with the remains of another ball to make a new one. At best, a taped ball was a makeshift, lacking the smooth, satisfying feel of a covered ball and harder to throw than a new one because of the added weight of the tape.

City boys faced several major risks to their ball. A game might be ended by an irate grownup who would keep a ball hit into his or her yard. Or the ball might escape from the lot and roll down a sewer, in which case the iron grating that covered it was quickly lifted off and one daring—or foolhardy—boy allowed himself to be lowered by the heels into the sewer to salvage the ball before it could sink into the black water. Country youngsters had a similar though less dangerous problem. One wetting in the old pond, and their rock-hard homemade ball would, as one put it, "forever after remain about as springy and light as a round piece of pig iron sewed up in one thickness of mosquito netting."

The network of trolley tracks that once crisscrossed cities posed another problem for youthful ball players. Whenever the ball landed on a streetcar track the boy closest to it had to dash out and snatch it up before an oncoming trolley ran over it and squashed it. If a trolley won the race, there were two sickening thumps as its wheels passed over the ball, and the game ended abruptly as a bunch of downcast boys stared at a once-precious baseball reduced to a misshapen lump exuding the warm smell of friction.

One field near Avenue H in Brooklyn posed a greater hazard. A short distance beyond home plate the tracks of the Brighton subway line ran in the open through a cut, and a ball hit foul back of the catcher often fell between the tracks. To retrieve it one of the boys would clamber down the embankment, negotiate a chain fence, and then step carefully over the third rail, all the while making sure that neither a train nor a railway policeman was approaching.

Store-bought bats were rare among most boys, even though around 1880 a Willow Wand with "Home Run" printed on it in red letters cost only fifteen cents. In 1912 bats cost a dollar, and in the 1920s those with facsimile signatures of big-league stars cost $1.50 or $2.00. Ford Frick, former commissioner of Organized Baseball, who played in the stubble fields and pastures of Indiana, said that whoever owned a readymade bat was captain of the team.

Sometimes one bat had to serve both sides in a game. If it broke, the game ended. So a bat had to last. The shouted warning, "Hold the label up!" revealed both anxiety to preserve the bat and the belief that failure to hold the label up while hitting would split it on contact with the ball. For a special game a boy might bring out, as one in my neighborhood used to, one or two of those old-fashioned, hefty, thick-handled models called Wagon Tongues, with their faded paint, handed down from his father or grandfather. The size and weight of these clubs did not daunt us because until we learned better we thought the heavier the bat the farther it would drive the ball.

Often as not, sandlotters made do with old broken bats by carefully tacking the split handles together and then taping them over for added strength and smoother grip. Probably the best bat I ever had was a Jake Flowers model that the big-league infielder himself gave me one day after he split it in a game at Ebbets Field, where I was batboy. When it was tacked and taped it proved better than a new storebought bat because the wood in it was of better quality and better seasoned than in the cheap mass-produced bats. Later in high school I had some bats made to order with my name imprinted on them. Now it is nothing unusual even for very young boys to have their own names on their bats, but in those days it was a source of much attention.

Boys who lacked even a repaired bat made their own from the handle of a broom, rake, or shovel. In the nineteenth century boys of Cincinnati were seen using barrel staves as bats. About a century ago a group of sandlotters batted with a fence picket whittled down at the sharp end to make a rounded handle. In the twenties the DiMaggio brothers, three of whom made the major leagues, supposedly used a sawed-off oar from their father's fishing boat.

Years ago a boy felt privileged to have a glove of his own. Carl Sandburg said that some of his group played barehanded while others stuffed a large man-sized glove with cotton, wool, or hair to take the sting out of the batted ball. The McDaniel brothers, Lindy and Von, who grew up in a small Oklahoma town and later pitched in the major leagues, made their first gloves out of sacks crudely sewn to the shape of their hands. Bing Miller's first glove cost a dime and had a piece of cardboard for padding! George Toporcer's mother saved soap wrapper coupons to get him his first glove, and Ty Cobb traded two of his father's books for his first one. My mother bought me my first glove, in the firm conviction of the value of sports, for fifty cents. She did not realize that some baseball positions had their own glove styles. I was a first baseman; the glove was a catcher's mitt.

In a game there were seldom enough gloves to go around; those without them simply borrowed from players on the other side. Sometimes this compelled a right-handed lad to play with a left-hand glove or vice versa. In either case he simply wore it in reverse.

Before a boy put his glove away at the end of the season he oiled it. To preserve the pocket, he placed a ball in it, folded the fingers of the glove over the ball, and slipped rubber bands around them to hold the ball in place. One of the rites of spring was to remove the glove and ball from the closet or drawer and slam the ball repeatedly into the glove, supposedly to make sure the pocket was in shape but really more in eager anticipation of the new baseball season. Boys in fact sometimes rushed the season: Phil Rizzuto, later a Yankee shortstop, played catch on Long Island before snow left the ground, and in my neighborhood we played in the street while snow was still piled high, using a pincushion donated by my mother.

Not many youngsters owned baseball shoes, and country boys might even play barefoot. Some boys managed with an older brother's hand-me-downs. The shoes of others were apt to have worn-down spikes and torn uppers held together with strips of tape. To protect against constant scuffing a boy who fancied himself a pitcher often wore a copper toeplate or had a piece of heavy leather stitched into the toe of the shoe for his pivot foot. But most parents did well to put up with having street shoes scuffed from ball playing, let alone buying special shoes. As a solution to their desire for baseball shoes some boys bought a fifty-cent set of spikes and got the shoemaker to fasten them onto a pair of old street shoes with the heels knocked off. My first spikes were of this kind and, as I soon learned, they were apt to come loose and could trip a boy into a hard fall if a spike broke away from his shoe when he was running full speed.

A juvenile catcher could dream of a chest protector and shin guards, but at most he usually possessed a glove and perhaps a cheap, old-fashioned "birdcage" mask of wire mesh bordered with leather-covered padding and held to his head by elastic straps. At times a boy might foolishly go behind the bat without a mask, but if none was available he usually stood a safe distance back, as professionals used to before the invention of the mask. In such cases the two sides agreed that there would be no stealing of home, or no stealing at all.

Only boys on organized teams experienced the thrill of wearing baseball uniforms. Country boys or city neighborhood groups restricted to "choosing up sides" and playing scrub games among themselves had none. Hans Lobert, playing with a team in a town near Pittsburgh about 1895, got his first uniform at age 15. "Boy, I'll never forget it," he told Lawrence Ritter later. "I slept in it that night. They couldn't get that thing off my back." Columnist Herb Caen told of being the only boy on his sandlot team with a complete uniform newly given him by his father and being stripped of it by his jealous teammates after he struck out in a game. They tied it in knots and threw it up in a tree! Sometimes the first-flush-of-spring enthusiasm inspired a group to buy a set of caps and an equal number of felt letters to be sewn on them. Once a bunch in my Brooklyn neighborhood decided upon bright red caps and a white letter A for "Amity Club." Some teams added a set of white sweat shirts. But ordinarily boys dressed in motley, an odd cap here and there and perhaps a few old baseball shirts.

The boys who lived on Sterling Street, Brooklyn, and several others like me from adjacent blocks who usually played choose-up games among ourselves occasionally arranged for a game against an "outside" team, like the altar boys, sponsored by the nearby Catholic church. For such an occasion Red Kirkland, the lad who could produce Wagon Tongue bats, donated a supply of old-fashioned baseball caps and shirts and divided these among us as far as they would go. The thrill of wearing even a piece of baseball regalia and the sight of each other in such togs gave each of us the marvelous feeling that he was a real ball player among other real ball players.

Boys had to rely mostly on themselves to convert whatever play space they had into a tolerable ball field, since the complete diamonds laid out by latter-day parents and communities did not yet exist. Open fields, prairies, and cow pastures beckoned country lads, although fences and disturbed farmers sometimes presented hazards. Boys had only to pace off distances between bases, or, as some did, fix more precise ones with a tape measure. Most anything served as bases—rocks, tin cans, grain bags cut to size, pieces of shingle, or certain by-products of cows. For a home plate a California group sank an old enameled roasting pan upside down in the dirt. In the Hill District of Pittsburgh in the 1900s, a participant recalled, home plate was a pile of shavings from an abandoned bushel basket, first base an old derby hat, second a used beer bottle, and third "the discarded corset of a female relative." In New York City on Rivington Street in the same era George Burns remembered that home was a manhole cover, first was a fire hydrant, second was a lamp post, and third was "Mr. Gitletz, who used to bring a kitchen chair down to watch us play."

Village and small-town boys in the early decades of the country could usually find open land on the outskirts or open lots in town or in an old apple orchard, as they once did in such far-flung communities as Haverhill, Massachusetts; Ford City, Pennsylvania; Brimfield, Indiana; Wichita, Kansas; and Flagler, Colorado, as boys of those places remembered later. Those of Honesdale, Pennsylvania, after getting chased from the field they played on, simply found another, cleared it, and made it into a diamond that they used for years.

City boys transformed many empty lots into playgrounds. Rocks, weeds, and stickers did not stop such teams as the Cinders, the Brickyards, and the Crickets from playing on the sandlots of St. Paul before 1920. Out in Sacramento in the twenties a group of boys chopped down weeds in a vacant, rocky lot, carted off boulders, and sprinkled the dusty infield with watering cans. The vacant lots of old Brooklyn were for Brooklyn boys, as David Boroff has written, "what the Mississippi was for Huck Finn, an escape from adults and a school of experience."

Although such lots constantly grew more scarce, they were still available in the twenties particularly to boys willing to walk far enough or to make them into ball fields. In our Brooklyn neighborhood we played in "the lumberyard," an abandoned lot that formed a narrow rectangle covering the block-long stretch alongside Nostrand Avenue and what is now Empire Boulevard. One spring we organized ourselves into a cleanup squad. Those who could brought rakes and shovels; one even furnished a wheelbarrow and another an unwieldy pickax. Some could supply only their labor. For several hours we collected papers, cans, bottles, and rocks, dumped them into the already-trash-filled ditch that ran next to one side of the lot, pried out many of the more exposed cobblestones that still lay beneath a thin covering of dirt in some places, chopped out weeds, and raked the rough, stony ground as smooth as we could. For a backstop we piled an old bedspring and other junk against the lower part of a billboard that faced the boulevard. After a morning's labor we had a passable ball field, although, as in the case of so many sandlots, our field was misshapen. It was more like a lozenge than a square. Actually, this design better suited the throwing ability of youngsters because it pushed first and third bases closer to each other and prompted us to move second base closer to home than on a regulation diamond. On the other hand, the narrower field gave less scope to the batters and resulted in more foul balls. An academician, Robert Streeter, played his first baseball in a back alley "so narrow that we brought up a generation . . . who hit only to center field, because if we hit more than fifteen degrees off a straight line to center field, we were in serious trouble."

Other city boys with a will to play baseball likewise found a way. New York boys on Manhattan's lower West Side developed their own diamond in the thirties on the former site of the New York Central Railroad's freight buildings. Boys without open space used the streets. *Frank Leslie's Illustrated Newspaper* reported in 1869 that New York boys playing baseball in the streets "seem utterly unconscious of other persons. No cars nor trucks, no apple-women nor fire-engines, can interrupt their games . . . they . . . fire away in spite of all travel and obstructions." Boys playing in the streets endangered themselves. Once around 1907 in Chicago on a Saturday afternoon when a group of boys were playing ball in a street, one had his back to an approaching team of horses and wagon, whose driver reprimanded the boy and then cut him with a lash of his long whip, eliciting a "cry of rage and resentment." Many children were killed in city streets, some while playing.

On Sundays in the 1920s some New York youngsters took advantage of the deserted streets of the wholesale business district to play ball there. Joe Garagiola, former big leaguer, has recorded how he and others of his St. Louis neighborhood converted the street into a diamond by painting bases on the pavement. Countless others in congested city areas invented adaptations of baseball, such as stickball, to suit conditions.

The spontaneous, unguided character of the sandlot scrub games of past generations contrasts sharply with that of the over-organized, over-supervised, and overindulged youngsters of recent times. Formerly, a clearer distinction existed between the world of adults and that of boys. Fathers had no disposition to be "pals" of their sons, and sons did not expect them to be. Besides, parents had too much to do. Most fathers worked at least a half-day on Saturdays, and mothers had to look after the house and do the weekend grocery shopping. On their part, boys did not want meddling parents interfering with their play. In former days boys played in their own style, made their own mistakes, settled or failed to settle their own arguments.

The typical scrub game—after a little preliminary batting, fielding, and throwing—began with the two best players "choosing up sides" according to what might be called a picking order based on how good a player each boy was. The favorite method of picking sides was an important ritual. One leader among the boys held the bat vertically and tossed it to another, who caught it with one hand at or slightly above the middle. The first boy then gripped it just above the other's hand. They continued alternating in gripping it until there was little or no space left at the top of the bat handle. The boy with the last hold won first choice among the players crowded around watching. But if the losing boy insisted that there was still enough room between the other fellow's fist and the end of the bat for him to squeeze in the last hold, he had to "stand a rock" (let one of the boys strike hard on the top of the handle with a stone) to back up his claim. The winning boy chose one player for his side, the loser chose the next, and so on until two teams were picked. A variation required the boy with the last handhold to toss the bat backward over his shoulder. If he succeeded in throwing it ten paces, he won first pick; if he failed, the other boy did.

Another way of choosing sides, called "odds and evens," though more common in street games, was sometimes used for baseball. In this method, as the two leaders who were to do the picking faced each other the one who first shouted "Odds!" or "Evens!" received his choice, and the other took the opposite. Then three times in rhythm each boy raised his clenched fist and brought it down while snapping out one or more fingers. If the extended fingers matched twice, the boy with "evens" won; if not, the boy with "odds" had first pick of the assembled talent.

As Zane Grey remarked in 1909, the choosing-up ceremony, conducted on "every green common and vacant lot and public square," attested to "the ruling passion of the youthful generation of Americans." He believed that because boys were chosen according to ability, sandlot ball marked one place "where caste is lost. . . . Ragamuffins and velvet-breeched, white-collared boys stand in that equality which augurs well for the Stars and Stripes."

Whatever the choose-up games lacked in skill they made up for in gusto. The players' cries of encouragement and derision sounded like a magpies' convention. The comment of the New York *Times* in 1920 that a boys' baseball game rendered life in the neighborhood "impossible" no doubt contained much truth.

Rarely did a choose-up game last nine innings. Most of the time there was no umpire, so an over-particular or timid batter could slow up the game by allowing pitch after pitch to go by until at last under the impatient urgings of disgusted players on both sides he would swing at the ball. Lack of an umpire also encouraged lengthy arguments. Education authority Elwood Cubberly was dismayed at the "constant quarrelling" and "profanity" of the corner-lot ball game. Disputes over whether a runner was safe or out or a batted ball fair or foul might be settled by agreement to "do it over," or by the eventual willingness of one side to "give," but if neither budged the game ended then and there. Or an individual player might simply stalk off the field if a decision was not to his liking. But a boy who made a habit of this won a reputation as a sorehead or a quitter. Sometimes one of the boys served as an umpire, but if his decisions failed to satisfy, one side or the other might force him out. A ball lost in the weeds brought long delays while everyone searched for it, hardly helped by the inevitable facetious suggestion to "pick it up and look for it after."

If a game got too boisterous a neighborhood adult (a crank, in the boys' estimation) would complain or even call the police to break it up. A New York City ordinance forbade baseball, and every day in the spring many boys wound up in Children's Court for the crime of playing ball. Wichita preachers petitioned for such an ordinance in 1913 because they heard boys swearing as they played on vacant lots. On the lower East Side of New York in the 1880s, recalled Isidore Kanowitz, "Sometimes we'd get chased by a storekeeper who was afraid we'd break a window. Some of them thought they owned the street." George F. Johnson, in an upstate New York town, played on a team about 1867 and did break a window, after which he disappeared as fast as he could. As late as 1938 Judge Jenkin B. Hochert heard a complaint by a Queens, New York, housewife who lived next to a lot from which boys sometimes knocked balls into her livingroom. The judge examined the lay of the land himself and after going up to bat and striking out, restricted the lot to boys from six to eight years old. Moreover, in the days when laws banning Sunday ball playing were still in force, boys were frequently arrested for breaking them.*

Whenever there were not enough boys to choose up sides for a game, boys reverted to the timeworn folk forms of ball, such as one-o'-cat, two-o'-cat, and fly-a-lick. There were no standard rules for these games: groups in various localities played them in their own way, even under other names, but they were all variations on the same theme. For one-o'-cat, four or five boys sufficed. One boy would suggest the game and without pause would shout, "One-o'-cat one!" in order to win the right to bat first. Cries of "One-o'-cat two!" ". . . three!" and so on, following in rapid succession, determined the rest of the batting order and the fielding positions of each boy: one-o'-cat two was the catcher, three the pitcher, four the first baseman—at the only base used—and five roamed the rest of the field. To remain at bat the batter tried to hit the ball (there was no base on balls) and get to first and back home safely. When he "made out" he moved to the field, the bottom of the five-rung ladder, and began his upward climb to batter again. At the same time each of the others advanced in regular order: the catcher to batter, pitcher to catcher, first baseman to pitcher, and fielder to first base. If more than five boys participated they could bat in pairs (two-o'-cat), and in this case one of them had only to reach first safely and wait for his partner to drive him home. Boys kept no score, and the game continued round and round indefinitely.

Aside from offering the chance to learn to field and throw a baseball, much of the pleasure of games like these lay in the opportunity they provided to do plenty of batting, as compared with the small amount of it afforded boys of recent years, their play so controlled by adults that they may get to swing at a ball only a few times a week, thus missing out on both the fun of batting and the practice needed to become good at it.

Games against boys from a different neighborhood required some preparation. Negotiations were held on where and when to play, most likely a

*See *Baseball: The Golden Age,* p. 359.

Saturday morning, and the stake, usually a specified type of baseball to be put up by each team, the winner to keep both. Differences of opinion over which boys would make up the best team had to be argued out. Sometimes two equally weak players were permitted to play a half-game each in right field, where presumably they could do the least damage, but there was no nonsense about giving everyone a chance to participate. The worst players simply did not play. The boys had no coach, but an older fellow might be on hand for the game to give advice.

The week before "the big game" the boys practiced after school, and excitement and anticipation grew. As the group broke up after Friday afternoon practice they admonished each other to be out early the next morning, but when the time came someone usually had to be sent to ring the doorbell of a laggard who had overslept or whose "old lady" had made him do some chores before allowing him out. Meanwhile came the exhilaration of "warming up" on a cool, sunlit morning: experiencing the satisfying sound of the ball smacking into a glove and smelling the pungent oiled leather, thrilling to the chance to stop a ground ball or pluck a line drive out of the air with one hand, and best of all listening to the sharp, clear crack of the bat and watching the flight of a well-hit ball, all the while wondering if the other team would show up.

At last they arrived, a few shouldering a bat with glove looped casually over it, others with a glove fastened by its strap and button to their belts, and two already having a running catch as the squad straggled along. They took their turn practicing, usually prolonging it until the home-team boys began shouting "Cut it out!" and "Get the game started!" Then agreement had to be reached on a few ground rules, such as how many bases a runner could take on a passed ball, the two baseballs had to be inspected to make sure one side did not try to palm off a Kiffe or some other ball cheaper than the type agreed upon, and finally an older boy or adult had to be persuaded to act as what we called the empire. Then the game was on.

Such adaptations of baseball as stickball, punch ball, and stoop ball were played in city streets with a rubber ball or tennis ball, not only by boys in slums with no place to play baseball but by others who enjoyed them. In stickball, home was a manhole cover—called a sewer—in the middle of the street; second was the next sewer, or a chalked square at an appropriate distance beyond it; and first and third bases might be a sidewalk flagstone, tree trunk, fire hydrant, or, when automobiles began to choke the streets, the fender of a parked car. In an earlier day if a parked horse and wagon interfered with the game a youngster just grabbed the reins and walked the horse down the street, much to the later displeasure of the driver, especially if he emerged from a building with a heavy bundle and had to "jackass it" quite a distance to his wagon. In stickball the pitcher delivered the ball on a bounce, and the batter swung a broomstick. He was allowed only one swing, hit or miss, and there were no bases on balls. Like many basically simple games, stickball contained the potential for skilled play: pitchers learned to fool batters with tricky bounces, and batters to drive the ball a long distance, always measured by the number of sewers roughly 75 feet apart. To be a "four-sewer hitter" conferred distinction.

In Flatbush, my section of Brooklyn, punch ball was a popular after-supper game on the long evenings provided by Daylight Saving Time when teams from different blocks, five or six to a side, played close, low-score games before audiences of other youngsters and many grownups sitting on their stone stoops. Punch ball was essentially stickball minus the stick and the pitcher. The "batter" bounced the ball or tossed it in the air and punched it with his fist. Many of the boys developed the ability to punch the ball with surprising accuracy to selected spots, and some of the big, strong fellows could send it remarkable distances.

In stoop ball one boy played another, or two played against two. The boy or boys at bat stood close to the stone stoop of a house and threw the ball hard against it, usually aiming for the edge of the second step in order to make it rebound sharply on the fly. The field was the area from the near curb all the way to the house or wall across the street, bounded by two chalk lines drawn perhaps ten or twelve feet apart. If the ball rebounded on the ground from the stoop or was caught on the fly, it was out. If it rebounded on the fly and, before being caught, landed beyond the near curb and inside the chalk marks, it was a single, double, triple, or homer depending on the distance from the curb at which it struck the ground. The boys kept track of phantom baserunners and advanced them according to the performance of succeeding batters.

A game that called forth the boys' knowledge of big-league batting orders required two boys on a side, pitcher and catcher, along with a tennis ball and a broom handle or the handle of a shovel cut to a suitable length. The pitcher threw in the same manner as in regular baseball from the tree lawn on one side of the street to the batter standing directly across the street from him. The catcher crouched up close and also called balls and strikes. There had to be a clearing behind the pitcher, because the ball could be sent much farther than in stoop ball, and the zones for determining the type of hits needed to be proportionately larger as well. Ordinarily, each side chose a major-league team to represent, and as the boys batted they acted out "their" team's batting order, pretending each time they came to bat to be the appropriate big-league hitter, batting right- or left-handed as the case required, and even sending in make-believe pinch hitters. The nearness of the pitcher and the ease with which a tennis ball can be made to curve placed the batter on his mettle and sharpened his batting eye.

Whatever the gap between these games of truncated baseball and the real thing, boys bridged it on the wings of their imagination. In so doing they unwittingly laid the groundwork for an attachment to baseball that for many of them lasted a lifetime. Aside from training in baseball, the great value to this kind of independent, self-organized play lay in its development of children's ability to reason, to judge what is appropriate, to weigh arguments, and to learn how to reach a consensus, as Bruno Bettelheim has explained in "The Importance of Play." John Updike said that vacant lots were places where "the spirit can find exercise." And Clarence Darrow, remembering his youth, said baseball was "the only perfect pleasure we ever knew."

DOUBLE CURVES AND MAGIC BATS

Appetite for baseball spurred boys to watch and read about the game as well as play it. Because of the abundance of town, college, industrial, and semipro teams, and Organized Baseball's low-classification minor-league professional clubs that once honeycombed the land, even boys in remote areas had little difficulty in finding some kind of ball games to watch. But as for major leaguers or high-minor leaguers, youngsters outside large cities had little chance of seeing them except in spring exhibition games played in their own or a nearby town by teams barnstorming their way north from training camp, or by groups of professional players on post-season exhibition tours.

For boys who lived near enough—and their number grew as automobiles began to shorten distances—a trip to see a major-league game was an experience to remember. Editor Frank Brookhouser wrote that in the 1920s his biggest thrill came when his father said, "Well, son, let's go down and see the Pirates." The journey, about forty miles each way, was "a day's adventure." The best trips author Ed Love took as a boy were to see the Tigers of the twenties with his grandfather, traveling first to Flint, Michigan, and from there to Detroit on the interurban railway. Johnny Keane, who later managed big-league teams, recalled that his father used to take him to the old Sportsman's Park in St. Louis two hours before game time to watch the Cardinals practice: "It was the greatest show on earth." When the future Cardinal executive, Bing Devine, was a boy his father would collect the whole family in the car and spend his vacation driving them to see the Cardinals play on one of their road trips.

Many boys in major-league cities could get to games on their own. Sportswriter Jimmy Breslin understood their anticipation and excitement: "Did you ever watch a kid coming up out of the subway to go to a ball game? The whole wonderful thing of being young is there. Eyes shining, feet running, pushing through those adults to get the first look at the ball park." And what adult who could not contain himself as a youngster can deny that his pace still quickens ever so little as he heads for the ticket window of a ball park?

20

Not John K. Hutchens, whose baseball conditioning started at age eight when he saw his first big-league game and never forgot the afternoon, "golden and exciting," that left him "exhausted, limp with vicarious excitement." Long afterward, in 1946, he wrote, "Some of my early fanaticism . . . has passed with the years. . . . Still, when I know that I am going to spend an afternoon at what sportswriters used to call the ball orchard, I feel a touch of the old excitement."

Such days inside a big-league ball park were "very heaven." Robert Smith has described with fine flavor what this meant years ago for boys in knickerbockers and long black stockings, to whom professional baseball was dearer than meat. ". . . to climb to the very top of the hot splintery bleachers among the men in straw hats and shirt sleeves, with handkerchiefs tucked inside their collars," to see on the field below "the owners of those names that were almost holy to us, . . . to crack peanuts joyfully between our teeth and scatter the shells without regard," and to "watch prayerfully, as a fly ball came right into the seats among us and rolled there for any boy to grab and take home"—this "was ten times to us what good food was, or even clothes and a bed." The words of another will bring equally warm memories to many: "Going to the ball game was always an occasion. We felt a tinge of excitement when we first glimpsed the stadium, looming over the clustered tenements like a medieval castle. . . . we took our place at the end of the ticket line" and "when our turn came, we shoved our money through the opening. The owlish figure behind the glass thrust out two tickets." Then came climbing "an Everest of steps," viewing at the top

> The panorama of baseball . . . always impressive at first sight. . . . the tiny figures in the bright-billed caps completed their pre-game rituals and disappeared into the dugout . . . the home team jogged to their positions on the field. The crowd came to life. . . . The watcher was transported to a world apart—an understandable, orderly world that ran strictly according to the rules. There were all sorts of emotions to experience. . . . We loved it.

The author of this book was among those fortunate boys who lived in major-league cities. Ebbets Field, Brooklyn, was only a couple of blocks from my home. Rarely did any of us have 35 cents for a space on a backless bleacher bench, to say nothing of $1.10 for a seat in the grandstand. Yet some of us managed to see many games. We had more ways of sneaking in than convicts have of getting out of prison. Some boys, at considerable risk of injury, climbed one of the fences. Sometimes we succeeded in prying up an unused side gate, one of those metal doors that opened upward from the inside by a chain-pull, until it was high enough to shove some bricks beneath so it would stay up while we squirmed under. Or we might stand outside the pass gate and ask men going in, "Got an extra pass, Mister?" on the chance of finding someone whose friend had failed to show up. Once in a while a couple of us took our lunches and slipped into the park in the morning while some of the gates were open, hiding until it was safe to emerge and mingle with the crowd. A favorite hiding place was the men's room, where we would stand on toilet seats hoping that the special police searching the park would do no more than glance under the doors. Another good place to hide was behind the last row of seats in the extreme right-field corner of the upper tier, because the park police sometimes forgot or were too lazy to climb that far to search. Success depended on the patience to lie low for hours and then, resisting the temptation to come out of hiding at the first sounds of players emerging, stay put until the grandstand filled up enough for us to escape detection. Boys in other major-league cities used the same method. Writer Nelson Algren and a friend, as boys, once hid for three hours under the bleachers before slipping into the stands, there to watch Eddie Cicotte of the White Sox shut out Carl Mays and the Yankees.

Sportswriter Wells Twombly recalled how he and two other boys once crept out of school and sneaked into old Bulkeley Stadium, home of the minor-league Hartford, Connecticut, Chiefs. The truants had just settled into seats when the team's general manager, who had seen them sneak in, tapped them on the shoulder and asked for their ticket stubs. What, no stubs? To let them work out the $1.05 admission price the general manager put them to sweeping concessions stands, stacking boxes, and supplying men's rooms with toilet paper. Just before the first pitch he relented and permitted them to watch the game.

In Brooklyn we also availed ourselves of more legitimate means of getting into the ball park. Picking up papers in the grandstand mornings before a game earned a pass to the bleachers; turning the stile at one of the gates paid fifty cents and the opportunity to watch the game after a few innings; working on the old manually-operated wooden scoreboard afforded a view of the game from the open slots of the board.

Once George P. Cross, later an engineer, emerging from his Chicago high school in 1915, encountered Federal League representatives handing out tickets to a game then in progress at nearby Washington Park. The "Feds," an outlaw league challenging Organized Baseball's monopoly, merely wanted to fill the stands to show how well they drew. But to Cross and his fellow students, the tickets meant something else, as he wrote this author: "Imagine the thrill to baseball-minded kids to have grandstand seats, no less, to a major league game. We would tear down and get there about the second or third inning. We were in seventh heaven."

Harry Golden and his pals on New York's lower East Side took turns delivering a supply of pretzels to the Polo Grounds' concessionaire for a local bakery. They earned 25 cents and could stay to see the game. To see the big leaguers at League Park in Cleveland in the thirties, George Solomon or one of his friends would lie on the sidewalk next to the fence, peek under it, and give a play-by-play description of the game to the rest. Leo Norris, later a big leaguer, worked as ball boy or sold peanuts to see the local New

Orleans Pelicans play at Heineman Park. Win Karlson, to see pro teams in Boston, cleaned the stands or turned the stiles or helped roll the field. Charley Grimm, later of the Pirates, got into the park of the St. Louis Cardinals by selling peanuts. In a 1958 article Jack Kofoed recaptured the "glorious days" early in the century when he got permission to clean up around the clubhouse at the Philadelphia park or help the groundkeeper, because these jobs brought him closer to the ball players. On summer evenings he and other boys used to go to a decaying hotel called Junction House, where they could talk to and run errands for the unmarried players who stopped there and who sat outside on the pavement in a row of wooden chairs talking, chewing tobacco, and ogling. Kofoed recalled that the players had few intellectual interests; some refused even to read for fear of straining their batting eyes. Their amusements were saloons and burlesque shows, but the boys did not care about the players' social, intellectual, or recreational limitations.

The glamour job for a youthful fan was that of batboy, so remote that it seemed unattainable. However, one Sunday in 1924 I was standing near the press gate at Ebbets Field hoping to get in on an extra pass when the Brooklyn clubhouse man, Babe Hamburger, happened along and asked if I wanted to mind the bats for the Cincinnati team, which was playing a doubleheader with the Robins, as they were then called. I accepted instantly, despite misgivings about my ignorance of the job—soon forgotten as I was put to work at once, in my everyday clothes. These and a baseball cap of my own continued to be my uniform. I learned as I went along, and after the games the visiting teams' clubhouse man, Johnny Griffin, told me to come back again the next morning. Thus began three memorable summers among the big leaguers, the first two with visiting clubs and the last with the Brooklyn team itself.

The duties of the batboy required reporting to the clubhouse by late morning to run errands, mostly to buy chewing tobacco and snacks for the players and otherwise make myself useful until time for practice. Then I had to pile the bulging bat bags on a hand truck and push the heavy load along a dirt passageway under the stands all the way from the clubhouse on the far right field end of the grandstand around to the visitors' dugout on the third base side. The bats could not be wheeled the entire distance because the passageway ended about ten yards from the dugout in a tunnel too narrow for the hand truck, so they had to be unloaded and laboriously lugged by the armful through the tunnel and up the steps of the dugout, where they were dumped on the field. Cincinnati, as it happened, always brought the most bats, about ninety of them, including those of Edd Roush, who used the heaviest bats in the league. Since there were no bat racks or trays in those days, the bats had to be laid out on the ground in a row in front of the dugout. To fetch the pails, towels, catchers' gear, and other sundries meant a second trip to the clubhouse. On hot summer days this work soaked my clothes with sweat. After the game I had to gather up the equipment, reload the hand truck, and return everything to the clubhouse.

One day this last task inadvertently caused me to violate one of baseball's pet superstitions. The visiting team held a big lead as Brooklyn came to bat in the last of the ninth. With the outcome of the game apparently a foregone conclusion, I began to collect the bats, but a chorus of shouts arose from the players: the bats must be let alone until the final out for fear of jinxing the result! Two other superstitions about bats soon surfaced. Once the players shouted for me to uncross the handles of two of them, because otherwise they could be rendered impotent. Another time when the team seemed helpless against Brooklyn's pitcher, some players suddenly jumped up and scattered the neatly-arranged bats in all directions. I was dumfounded and not a little miffed at having to pick them all up and realign them until enlightened by the assurance that "shaking up" the bats would "put some base hits into them." At the time I did not realize that many baseball superstitions are not indigenous but derive from ancient folk beliefs.

Between the trundling of bats to and fro stretched the long, delicious interval of pre-game practice followed by the game itself. Except for an occasional fast trip to the clubhouse on an errand, my time during practice was largely free, so it was usually possible to borrow a glove and horn in on a pepper game with the players or catch balls returned to a fungo hitter and toss them to him. Once I even warmed up a young pitching prospect before he pitched batting practice, and another time I volunteered to hit grounders to some utility players working out in the infield when the player hitting to them was called away.

When the game started, my responsibilities were to kneel in the on-deck circle near home plate while "my" team was at bat and be ready to run up and recover each hitter's bat the moment he dropped it and broke for first base (or flung it aside after striking out) and return it to its place; to retrieve foul balls hit into the screen back of home plate; and to keep the home plate umpire supplied with baseballs.

Boys now receive pay for acting as batboy and may, if their team wins the pennant, even receive a substantial share of the prize money. But in my day the job paid no money. The daily wage was a baseball. In the afterlight such scanting can easily be regarded as callous exploitation of a youngster's love for baseball. Nevertheless, I remain content. Besides measureless psychological income, I picked up considerable inside baseball by observing, listening, and, whenever opportune, asking questions. And presumably benefits flowed from being introduced early to the world of men, although some of these were of doubtful value, such as achieving fluency in a second language: profanity. Moreover, associating with big leaguers in closest propinquity was to put them in an aspect more human than heroic, and after a time I began to see them as men engaged, howsoever they loved what they were doing, in fierce daily competition for a livelihood, not only with their

opponents but with their own teammates, rather than as sportsmen up-
holding the glory of a city or as paragons of virtue for American youth to
emulate.

I was privy to much that did not appear in the press and fans did not see.
Before one game Cincinnati infielders Babe Pinelli and Sammy Bohne exchanged hard words on the bench and then suddenly sprang at each other,
flailing and pummeling like gamecocks. Teammates quickly screened them
from the stands and tried to separate the two as Jack Hendricks, the portly
manager, dithered over the lot of them, pleading, "Stop it, boys! Not out
here, right in front of the public!" One afternoon Bill Sherdel was pitching
a good game for St. Louis when his team's left fielder muffed a fly ball that
should have been an easy out. Several Brooklyn hits followed, and the
Cardinals' manager removed Sherdel from the game. Furious over his teammate's error, which he blamed for being taken out, Sherdel stalked to the
dugout mouthing epithets about the fielder, picked up the drinking glass,
and hurled it against the dugout wall, shattering it.

Other incidents stick in my memory. It was amusing to see a notice posted
on the Brooklyn clubhouse door one morning to the effect that hereafter,
players who reported after 10:00 A.M. would be fined $100.00, and then to
watch as they straggled in and read it, some of them bleary-eyed and squint-
ing. It was absorbing to listen to the sharp barbs and often coarse humor of
the bench jockeys directed at opposing players, and the inevitable cries of
"No! No!" from the bench when the players disagreed with the umpire's
call on a pitch. Once the Cardinals enjoyed a small triumph over the plate
umpire. They were riding him so hard after what they believed to be a
particularly bad call that he decided to oust the player he thought was his
chief heckler: he called time, whipped off his mask, strode toward the bench,
and shouted, "Get off there, Stewart!" only to be met with jeers because
Stewart happened not to be there. The umpire gamely swallowed his embarrassment and proceeded with the game.

If proximity to the big leaguers diminished them as heroic figures it magnified them as professional experts put to the proof anew each day in open,
measurable fashion. Such looks behind the scene helped lay the foundation
for a sensible, more mature attitude toward them. To witness the action
close up deepened appreciation of the intensity and single-minded purpose
with which nearly all the professionals approached a game, and it left impres-
sions that remain fresh and vivid of what playing major-league ball was really
like: the hot fits of Adolfo Luque, the Cuban pitcher, whenever he thought
the umpire had called one of his pitches wrong; the wild expression on a
runner's face, arms and legs pumping like pistons, as he tore past third base
straining to score, and his desperate, dusty, sliding collision with the shin-
guarded catcher attempting to block him off and tag him at home plate; a
pitcher drenched with sweat sprawled on the bench, gasping, "Get me some
runs, Goddammit!" as two teammates alternately snapped towels in his face

to cool him off; batters without helmets standing up to the fearsome speed of a high, tight fast ball whizzing past and smacking into the catcher's mitt with a bang like a pistol shot, or to the approach of a swift curve ball that suddenly darts sharply down and away from the hitter as though rolling off a table.*

The next best thing to playing and watching baseball was reading about it. Just as most boys managed to locate some type of ball game to watch, so too did they usually find some kind of baseball material to read. Small-town newspapers did well to report on the local team, but boys could usually lay hands on the sports section of one of the big-city dailies and feast on its copious supply of baseball stories and special features, as did Ty Cobb, who as a Georgia country boy read his favorite writer, Grantland Rice, on the sports pages of the Atlanta *Journal*. In the days before radio and television, boys who lived near enough to a telegraph office could get news of the World Series, which was carried on all the wires. Farm boys might go to the village general store, where the post office was located, and there hear the news read aloud by a local subscriber to a city paper. After the turn of the century the farm boy's opportunity to read about baseball increased immeasurably with the completion of the federal government's rural free delivery system that brought city dailies and magazines to his family's own mailbox.

On summer evenings boys in the major-league cities often waited at the newsstand for the final edition, which contained the complete play-by-play account of the day's game. When it arrived they gathered around asking, "Who won?" "Who pitched?" "How many hits did Wheat get?" At times one read the account aloud while the others listened and pictured the game mentally. Those who, like Dave Stanley, a Brooklyn boy, were too impatient to wait for the newspaper, stood around some dim poolroom anxious for the magic ticker to begin chattering as the scores came over a leased wire, then watched the results being chalked up on a large blackboard out front. The thrill of seeing the scores go up, said Stanley, equalled seeing serials twice a week at the neighborhood movie house.

In Brooklyn Steve McKeever, who eventually became owner of the Brooklyn National League team, read "for hours" about the triumphs of the best local club of the 1870s, the Brooklyn Atlantics, and often sneaked away from the nuns and priests at Assumption Parochial School to watch the Atlantics practice.

Boys sent in questions to sportswriters who conducted question-and-answer columns on baseball like those in (Dan) "Daniel's Dope," for many years a widely-read feature. Those who had access to copies of the monthly *Baseball Magazine* devoured its many feature stories. Some cut out and pinned up or even framed the two close-up photographs of major-league

*See Harold Seymour, "Big-League Batboy," *Sports Heritage*, Spring 1988, pp. 13–17.

players that appeared inside each issue's front and back covers. Boys also gathered to discuss their favorite players, or pretended, as Hal Borland did, to be one while playing ball. For pretense I enjoyed a metal board game in the shape of a baseball diamond, played by releasing a ball from a spring mechanism, after which the idea was to try to hit it to various fields with a bat-shaped lever. We also played surrogate baseball through a dice game with cardboard players formed into regular lineups—anticipating Robert Coover's Universal Baseball Association.

In those pre-television days, when youngsters read more and gaped less, books constituted staple entertainment for many. Clyde Brion Davis and his friends collected their sports books in a barn, where any member of the gang could borrow one by recording its title and date in a notebook. One summer in the 1920s a group of boys in my neighborhood conceived the idea of temporarily pooling our books. One fellow volunteered his cellar to house the collection, and shortly some fifty or sixty books materialized. For a time passersby viewed the uncommon spectacle of a band of boys congregated on stoops and lawns in various grotesque postures, quietly reading. Many of the books dealt with baseball.

As we enjoyed and shared the exploits of Baseball Joe, Frank Merriwell, and Lefty Locke, we did not realize that we were dipping into what was part of an outpouring of baseball fiction for juveniles that by then had reached the proportions of an entire subliterature, countless volumes written by a hundred authors over the previous half-century and read avidly by millions of boys like ourselves.

Although boys could read juvenile fiction even before the Civil War, sports literature for boys had a slow growth. As far as is known, baseball books for boys trace from an 1868 novel, *Changing Base*, by William Everett, a story influenced by the English novels about Tom Brown at Rugby. *Changing Base* is about a boys' school resembling Boston Latin, where the boys form a club rivaling a nine of Irish fellows. Imitating the Harvard "tone," the club develops "discipline" and "spirit." The writer's class bias comes through as he depicts an Irish player as a bully, having the hero, Edward Rice, call him a "blackguard" and a "brute." Rice gets in trouble by throwing a baseball in the classroom, and after punishment by the school he is reinstated in the club. Performing well in games, Rice scorns cheating by some opponents. Baseball is shown to be of value when Rice saves a man's gold by catching large bags of it thrown from a beached boat, and an observer comments, "I never liked base ball before, but I see what it's good for now." Rice's father, too, praises the boy, who asks him to "allow base ball did good for once. How glad I am I can catch!" In other adventures the author boosts the work ethic as Rice is made to realize that he must perform in order to succeed.

In Everett's second book, *Double Play* (1870) a group of high school boys are challenged by the Wide-Awakes, a team in a nearby town, a "hard, tough-looking lot." They plan a nine to respond to the challenge and engage in highly ethical play, teach a cheater a lesson, and help a disliked fellow get along better with others through his baseball experiences.

An 1880 novel entitled *The Fairport Nine*, by Noah Brooks, a Civil War correspondent and friend of Abraham Lincoln, centers around the social gulf and rivalry between the Fairport club and the White Bears. Like the Everett books, *The Fairport Nine* reeks of middle class bias. The Fairport boys come from "better families" and have never been accused of being "ruffianly" or "destructive," yet they are not "goody-goody." The White Bears, mostly sons of fishermen, longshoremen, and men who "did chores" about town, are known for their "rough mischief" and their disrespect for law, order, and the rights of others. The two teams engage in a seesaw struggle for baseball supremacy. Entwined in the story are instances of competition between the two groups in spheres other than baseball. An unusual feature for those days is the inclusion in the narrative of a black youth, the only one in town and the son of a former slave, as a respected member of the Fairport nine. Brooks's other juvenile, *Our Base Ball Club and How It Won the Championship*, written in 1884, focusses on baseball in a small town and opposition to it on the part of some townsfolk because of game-throwing.

After Brooks's books, practically two decades would pass before baseball-centered fiction blossomed out on a wide scale. Stories published in the intervening years used baseball more as a vehicle for carrying other themes. A case in point is Charles Munroe Sheldon's 1882 short story, "The Captain of the Orient Nine," which subordinated baseball to the moral dilemma of the Orient captain: should he confess that he had not really made the game-saving shoestring catch of a fly ball credited to him, that the ball had touched the ground first? The captain struggled with himself until, as Robert Cantwell put it in a *Sports Illustrated* article, "he looked like a character in *Pilgrim's Progress* chasing a fly ball into the Slough of Despond."

Authors of dime novels, which began in the 1860s, especially enlisted baseball to their ends. Edward Wheeler, who ground out many successful ones, used the game, of which he knew next to nothing, as a medium in *High Hat Harry, the Baseball Detective* (1885), but Wheeler's depiction of baseball in the game Harry pitched was so palpably ludicrous that the book flopped. On Wheeler's premature death George Jenks, an Englishman, took up where he left off at the publishing house of Beadle and Adams and produced a series of dime novels with baseball settings starring Double-Curve Dan, so named because he could pitch a ball that curved in two directions. In the first of the series, *Double-Curve Dan, the Baseball Detective, or Against Heavy Odds* (1888), when the regular pitcher refuses to play in a game at the Polo Grounds Dan leaves his seat in the stands and volunteers to pitch, winding up in the usual way: "Then with a peculiar round-arm movement, he lets it go. It flies straight as an arrow for about half the distance; then it takes a sudden twist to the right, and again another to the left!" Jenks's series did poorly, but soon another would successfully employ the double-curve device.

Two other titles, both of them popular, underscored the dime novel as the leading source of early baseball fiction, Tom Teaser's *Muldoon's Baseball Club in Philadelphia* (1890), a humorous description of games played by Muldoon's Irish team against such opponents as the Germantown Guzzlers, and Bill Boxer's *Yale Murphy, the Great Shortstop, or The Little Midget of the Giants* (1892), an account of a Yale man's career from college ball to the New York Giants. Even Horatio Alger paid his devoirs to baseball with an opening chapter about it in *Frank Fowler, The Cash Boy*, first serialized in 1875 and published as a book in 1887.

As the dime novel faded, baseball expanded from an incidental in stories to a subject for them. Often as not, authors reversed the earlier pattern: instead of having detectives posing as ball players, they had players turn to sleuthing, with the result that many a villain of deepest dye found himself foiled in his dastardly deeds by a baseball player. The debut in 1896 of one of the most famous players in the game's history, Gilbert Patten's fictional Frank Merriwell, signalled the change. Patten serialized his Merriwell stories under the pen name of Burt L. Standish in Street and Smith's *Tip Top Weekly*. By the early 1900s sales of the periodical at five cents a copy reached 135,000. Mail stoppage from the San Francisco earthquake of 1906 brought anxious inquiries from West Coast subscribers. Grownups read *Tip Top*, too, as they had dime novels. A soldier stationed in the Philippines reported that "The boys here nearly fight for it every time the mail comes in, and it is pretty well worn by the time all have read it." For 17 years Patten turned out 20,000 words a week on Merriwell. Sales eventually rose to 300,000, and a million readers read the magazine each week. Merriwell stories continued into the 1920s and were later serialized on radio. In book form they totaled more than 200 titles and sold a spectacular 125,000,000 copies.

Not all Merriwells were about baseball; Frank starred at other sports, too, but his reputation as an athletic titan rested largely on his baseball exploits. Patten knew something about the game, having briefly managed a bush league team, but that did not deter him from investing Frank with a Superman quality: the ability to pitch a "double-shoot" reminiscent of Double Curve Dan's, which started to curve outward and then took an "in-shoot." More than anything else this device established Merriwell's fame. Long after, Patten told how he hit upon the idea. In the course of working on a Merriwell story and at a loss for something new for Frank to do, he went to a ball game where he saw a pitcher throw a fast ball that curved sharply inward and caromed off the bat before the surprised hitter could even swing. A fan jumped up and shouted that it was the first time he ever saw a ball curve two ways on one pitch. Thereafter, Patten said, Frank threw that "amazing and impossible double curve" on dangerous batters in pinches, and "over the country boys almost ruined their arms trying to throw it."

Patten's publisher outlined a plan for the series beforehand, and Patten ground out plain, fast-moving, action-packed narratives to flesh it out, drawing his heroes and villains in sharp blacks and whites and using stilted dialogue. Cliches encrusted his descriptions: "the sphere" (ball), "the old orchard" (ball field), "slab-man" (pitcher), "initial sack" (first base). And in a day when ethnic stereotypes formed a part of the mental dross of the dominant Anglo-Saxon population, Patten, at the instigation of his publisher, worked in such characters as a clownish German or a "crazy dago" speaking in heavily accented English, for what passed as comic relief. Patten also injected large doses of moralizing into his stories, equating virtue and morality with discipline in sport. At the same time he did not shrink from frequent mention of betting by spectators at his ball games.

In these stories Frank Merriwell himself came off as a clean-living, clean-minded athlete who played fair, never quit, and always rose to the occasion both on and off the field. He epitomized, as Professor Tris Coffin, the folklorist, has well said, "Everyman's dream of himself—secure, resourceful, capable; fair, if unrelenting; cool under fire; respected, often eventually loved, by his enemies." But Frank also conformed to the American ethos in his readiness to solve problems pragmatically and if need be violently. More than once he was prepared to strike the villain, and in one story Frank shows himself willing to break the rules if his opponents do: "As long as they are on the level, we'll stay so"; if, however, the other team goes "back on the agreement, putting in better players or professionals, I know where to get hold of a few good men myself."

On the baseball field Merriwell's skills bordered on the unbelievable. His tremendous pitching and batting feats together with his theatrical penchant for turning defeat into victory at the last moment sealed his fame and slipped into the language the phrases "a Frank Merriwell play" and "a Frank Merriwell finish" to describe a sensational performance of any kind. Frank's knowledge of baseball proved uneven, however. He was familiar with such playing techniques as "working on" a batter by varying his pitches and throwing "waste" pitches, as well as hitting "behind" a runner on first base into right field in order to advance the runner to third, but he lacked understanding of even elementary team strategy. In one game alone he three times violated the cardinal principle that a team trailing by more than one or two runs strives for a "big inning"—scoring a cluster of runs rather than playing for a run at a time. At such times it does not take chances on the bases. It plays safe: players refrain from trying to "stretch" a hit or steal a base, because even if such a gamble succeeds and leads to a run's being made, that lone run makes no appreciable difference in the score, whereas if the gamble fails and the runner is put out, the possibility of a batting rally and big inning are reduced or completely quenched.

Frank proves oblivious to all this in *Frank Merriwell at Yale*. Only one instance need be described. With Harvard leading 7–0 in the sixth inning, Yale runners reach first and third with none out. In this situation—it makes one wince—Frank, who is on first, gives the sign for a double steal. This is a compound blunder, for on top of the principle set forth above, Frank was ignoring another canon of baseball strategy: that under no circumstance does a runner attempt to steal home with none out. Had the Yale players employed the play-it-safe strategy instead of Merriwell's atrocious tactics they may well have had a big sixth inning and a victory instead of the one-run loss they suffered in the story. Perhaps Frank's ignorance of such fundamentals explains why his creator lasted only one season as a minor-league manager.

In Frank's senior year at Yale, Patten's publisher suggested that he introduce another character closely related to Frank. As a result, a half-brother Dick turned up. Dick Merriwell's acceptance among boys never equalled Frank's, and the series began to decline. After Frank finished at Yale and married, Frank Merriwell, Jr., appeared on the scene, at which point Patten quit doing Merriwells, although others carried on for him a while longer. Patten blamed Merriwell's finish on the motion pictures: instead of buying books, boys spent their nickels on movies.

After dropping the Merriwell stories Patten wrote two sets of baseball novels. *Lefty o' the Bush*, which appeared initially in *Top Notch* magazine, became the first of fourteen books, dating from 1914, in the "Big League Series." The set chronicled the career of Lefty Locke from bush-league pitcher to major-league star and finally clubowner. These novels were more realistic than the Merriwell tales but contained the usual baseball cliches (runners "prance off the hassock" and "dive back to the cushion") and some absurd baseball strategy in game descriptions.

Patten wrote his "College Life Series" under his own name. It featured another Yale athlete, Roger Boltwood, who eventually becomes playing manager of a minor-league team. Although Patten had never attended college— to his intense regret—in *Sons of Old Eli* (1923) he realistically reflected the dilemma of college players who desired to keep their "amateur" status in college while still accepting money for playing as a professional. Patten also emphasized what he believed to be "college spirit" by having his characters play for the college rather than for themselves. He also upheld clean and ethical play. Declares Roger Boltwood, "It's the desire of every true Yale man that our athletics should be kept clean and unsmirched."

Patten's shortcomings should not cause us to lose sight of his significance. Apart from being the first to make baseball more than a backdrop to his narratives on an extensive and continuing basis, in the Merriwell stories Patten fathered a hero who awakened the public to the value of athletics for boys. And for young readers, as Russel Nye, a biographer, has pointed out, Patten opened a world of school and college life and athletics, one that Alger heroes scarcely knew. Like William Everett before him, Patten grasped the spirit of the emerging cult of mass sport and made athletics seem exciting and glamorous, and instead of the rather stiff, life-is-real, life-is-earnest Alger heroes, who all strove to be merchants and bankers, created more carefree characters who both reflected and nourished boys' desire to become big leaguers. Patten also tried to motivate all action from character, as his biographer John L. Cutler explained, and this peopled his stories with characters more believable than most.

Patten soon had company. From the turn of the century onward a swarm of writers entered the field, and what had been a trickle of baseball fiction swelled into a torrent. Two writers, Ralph Henry Barbour and William Heyliger, both of whom broke out of the confines of series books, stand out among the many. Barbour, a newspaperman before he turned to writing boys' books, published in 1899 the first of about 150 such books and quickly became one of the most widely read and prosperous writers of his time. He usually set his stories at mythical, romanticized prep schools or colleges and, as Cornelia Meigs states in the authoritative *A Critical History of Children's Literature*, emphasized "the right school spirit, good sportsmanship, the triumph of those who are right-minded over those who are not."

Barbour dealt with sports for all seasons at his schools until the publication of *Weatherby's Inning* (1903), which concentrated on baseball. When seventeen-year-old Jack Weatherby, a "clean-cut, manly-looking" freshman at Erskine College, makes no attempt to rescue a drowning boy, he is branded a coward and ostracized by the students. Little do they know that Jack has a dread of water and cannot swim. At first he plans to leave but decides instead, "No, I'll stay and—and fight!" He makes the baseball team, but many of the players refuse to eat at the same training table with him. Weatherby's gradual acceptance by his fellows is complete when they discover him taking swimming lessons, and at the climax he saves the final big game in the ninth inning by catching a line drive, hit with the bases full, turning it into a triple play that ends the game. But Jack is by no means finished. The story concludes with the team's triumphal return to the campus. One of the horse-drawn hacks carrying the players becomes a runaway. Jack leaps from his carriage and, as he fearlessly halts the runaway, cries, "It's my inning at last!"

In *Billy Mayes's Great Discovery*, considered by some to be his best, Barbour departed from his usual pattern and introduced some delightful fantasy. The book tells the story of a lad who is not much of a ball player until he obtains a bat made of wood from the hoki-moki, a tree with the property of drawing horsehide, alive or dead, to it like a magnet. Armed with this magic bat, Billy cannot miss. All he does is close his eyes and swing, since the horsehide-covered ball is unable to resist the pull of hoki-moki.

Barbour's descriptions of fictitious ball games were so interesting that some maintain they were instrumental in enlivening sports writing. Barbour's ball games also served a greater purpose: character portrayal. His hero, as Professor Henry Steele Commager has said, was always "a little democrat." Conversely, his villain was surly and sallow, or fat and pasty-faced—a sneering toady or sneak. Needless to say, the "honorable player," as Commager noted, "won out over the sneak, the poor over the rich, the boy with the school spirit over the one who derided it." In a scholarly analysis Professor Fred Erisman sees in Barbour's books a reflection of the philosophy of progressivism that pervaded the climate of opinion in those years: in his emphasis on physical prowess, which he equates with morality, and on sportsmanship in the sense of teamwork and absolute honesty, Barbour expressed through the idiom of sports the two principal articles of the progressive faith, which Professor Rollo May argues were "the reality and eternity of moral values and the inevitability of progress toward a better world." Erisman points out, however, that Barbour differed with progressive ideology in one significant way: whereas the latter advocated acceleration of man's forward march by changing the rules if necessary, Barbour wished to reach the goal by re-establishing the old ones. If Erisman is correct, and bearing in mind the great popularity of Barbour's books—for thirty years none ever failed—among the impressionable ten- to fifteen-year-olds who read them, his influence in spreading the gospel of his version of progressivism must have been substantial.

Like Barbour, William Heyliger was a newspaper reporter until his first book, *Bartley, Freshman Pitcher*, published in 1911, launched him into the field of juvenile fiction, where he would match Barbour in output and eventually surpass him in popularity. Heyliger's books were more down-to-earth than those of others in the field. He decried stories of "impossible persons who do improbable deeds in improbable ways." Heyliger realized that the problems of boyhood were not mythical. The reader did not want moralizing, he wanted "a hero matched in possibilities to himself . . . not a prodigy or a caricature . . . a book that will have, within limitations, the forms and depth of the adult novel. . . ." At the same time, however, Heyliger declared in *High Benton*, his best book, that there was only one type of success, the kind that comes from hard work. His formula was: first education, then work, then the reward for work. Obviously, the work ethic had not died with Alger. And in such books as *The County Pennant* Heyliger implicitly admonished his readers to be loyal and determined, to give their best always, never to quit or shirk, to accept discipline, and to play fair.

Like the others in this genre, Heyliger's books projected virtues that parents could admire. The strongest swear word in *Against Odds* (1915) is

"Thunder!" In *The Captain of the Nine*, second baseman Mellen violates high principles in his efforts to undermine pitcher Bartley out of resentment over Bartley's election as team captain. "You heard me," a friend of Bartley's tells Mellen, "You threw the game. As for shaking hands with you, I have no use for your sort." Apparently out of team loyalty, the players and coach keep to themselves Mellen's machinations and the dissension he creates, and Mellen continues to scheme. Finally, when Mellen is revealed to have sent a fake telegram, Bartley benches him, but his rascality is kept from the public, and Bartley also accedes to Mellen's pleas not to report him to the school principal and prevent his graduation.

The players in Heyliger's stories took baseball more seriously, and the outcome of games loomed more important, than in Barbour's books:

> Of course, there were one or two fellows who kept digging knowledge from their books and who did not seem to know that the ancient enemy, Rockton, had such a dangerous baseball nine. But they were the wonder and the shame of the school.

Heyliger's game descriptions, which sometimes included questionable baseball tactics along with some strategy borrowed from Christy Mathewson's *Pitching in a Pinch*, were more detailed than Barbour's, too. But like Barbour, Heyliger translated into words boys' feelings and memories about what it meant to play baseball. As Robert Cantwell wrote, Heyliger "put into images the confused and nebulous sensations that come to life when the games started in the spring." Here is an example:

> "Tomorrow?" they [the players] demanded.
> "Tomorrow," [Coach] Jenkins laughed, "we start the outdoor practice. Are you glad?"
> They shrieked their joy, and pounded their fists on each others' backs. The wide free field, the smell of early grass, the ripple of soft breezes over flushed faces, the damp give of springy turf—They fell to cheering again at the prospect.

The remarkable success of Barbour and Heyliger can hardly be ascribed solely to the comparative superiority of their craftsmanship. Popularity and financial success also smiled on such low-grade materials as the Baseball Joe series by Lester Chadwick, and another series with alliterative titles—*First Base Faulkner, Second Base Sloan, Third Base Thatcher*—supposedly the work of Christy Mathewson, the famous pitcher of the pre–World War I New York Giants. "Lester Chadwick" was one of the sixty-five pseudonyms of Edward Stratemeyer, a hack who with his assistants spewed forth approximately 800 books, including the well-known Rover Boys and the Tom Swift series. Stratemeyer dominated the juvenile field until his death in 1930 and, according to Arthur Prager, who studied his career, had "almost as great an effect on the pre-teens of his days as the invention of television . . . on a later generation." Himself capable of whipping up a book in two or three days, Stratemeyer eventually organized a syndicate whose stable of writers mass-produced books as if they were canned goods on an assembly line. By 1908 Stratemeyer had at least ten juvenile series in operation under as many different names. The fourteen-volume Baseball Joe series, which began in 1912, conducted its hero, Joe Matson, on a journey similar to Lefty Locke's: from the sandlots all the way to major-league club ownership, with a college stop (*Baseball Joe at Yale*) en route.

Baseball Joe, as both a superlative pitcher and matchless batter, was even less credible than Frank Merriwell; nevertheless, he soon rivaled Merriwell in the pantheon of youngsters. Joe combined the brash but refreshing self-confidence that once typified big leaguers ("I'm the boy that can do it") with the cloying self-effacement affected by latter-day professionals ("The team's the biggest thing on earth to me outside of my home and folks, and it's always a pleasure to give it my best efforts") who, as Heywood Hale Broun observed, attribute their success "to their mothers, their ministers, and the wise old bullpen coach" and leave their interviewer with "the feeling of being pelted to death with marshmallows."

To read one Baseball Joe story was to read them all: Joe always extricates himself from a precarious predicament in time to perform unbelievable deeds in the crucial game. And at the end of every Stratemeyer story, everyone acclaims the deeds of the hero, as Carol Billman's study of the syndicate remarks, and the writer of the story, showing that crime never pays, underlines the conservative theme of the preservation of order.

Baseball Joe in the World Series illustrates the formulary plot. To prevent Joe from pitching the final game in the World Series the villain and his henchmen kidnap Joe and hold him, chloroformed and tied, in Boston until after the last train for New York has left. But Joe revives, loosens his bonds, overcomes his captors, rushes to the railroad station, and quickly arranges for a special locomotive that takes him on a wild ride to New York. He reaches the Polo Grounds just before game time:

> . . . he was fighting against odds. His head was still aching from the effects of the [kidnapper's] blow and the chloroform. The rocking of the engine had made his legs unsteady. And the only food he had had since the night before was a sandwich he had sent for while slipping into his uniform. But it is just such circumstances that bring out the thoroughbred strain in a man, and as Baseball Joe took his place in the box and looked around at the enormous crowd and realized the immense responsibility that rested on him, he rose magnificently to the occasion.

Discarding his cap (its band hurt his head where he had been struck) Joe pitches a no-hit game topped off in the ninth inning with a leaping, barehand catch of a line drive, which he converts into a triple play. For youngsters, this made heady reading!

Midst thickets of such cliches as "one cushion jolt" (a base hit) and some defective game strategy, the Baseball Joe books planted an idealistic impression of professional baseball and its players. On receipt of a telegram in *Baseball Joe, Pitching Wizard*, to report for spring training with the Giants,

> Joe's nostrils dilated like those of the war horse that sniffs the battle from afar, and in his eyes was a light of one who sees a vision.
>
> A vision of green baseball parks with white lines leading to first and third and out toward the posts that marked the foul lines; great stands and bleachers black with excited spectators; the thunderous roars of applause for a brilliant play; the crack of the bat as the ball soared into the air and winged its way toward the fence, the struggle of baseball gladiators where all were straining every nerve to win; the countless thrills that for so many people make baseball the greatest sport in the world.

Joe, always a faithful student but not a "natural scholar," went in for baseball only after convincing his mother that whatever might have been true of baseball in the early days of the game, many "high-class men" now turned to it. Once in professional ball Joe becomes familiar with the "great currents of the world." He and his teammates, with the example before them of "Bugs" Hartley, whose career was ruined by "dissipation" (a character based on the real-life player "Bugs" Raymond, one of the supposed exceptions among men of irreproachable character), pour gifts of wine and whiskey down the drain! Joe also respects the opposition: his pitching opponent is "worthy of his steel."

More clues to American mores and assumptions appear in the Baseball Joe books. Joe frequently uses violence to settle issues, although not in the presence of "ladies." He thrashes villains with receding chins whose faces show unmistakable signs of dissipation, fellows who are sons of the idle rich and whose money "makes their path easier." Personal bias determines a policeman's actions, regardless of civil rights: in *Baseball Joe in the World Series* an officer arrives during an altercation between Joe and a character called Fleming, and because he recognizes Joe, the officer accepts his explanation and ignore's Fleming, telling him to "beat it" and poking him in the back with his stick. The racism of American society comes through as one player, describing a manager, says "he's as white as they make 'em." Joe is one of those who says he has nothing against Jews—"Our shortstop, Levy, is a Jew, and he's as fine a fellow as there is on the team"—but Russnak, a gambler, is a Jew and a "low, greasy specimen that makes a decent man feel a crawling in his spine whenever he looks at him."

The Matthewson series was ghosted by John N. Wheeler, another syndicate hack. The undistinguished stories in this series resorted heavily to inning-by-inning, play-by-play accounts of games. However, *Won in the Ninth*, another Matty book, contained two unusual sequences, one on baseball as seen through the eyes of a visiting Japanese student in his letters home, and another in which the editor of the school paper translates his jargon-studded account of a game for his mystified professor of English. The book upheld traits of character believed desirable in those times and lauded the supposed democratic spirit of college athletics that permitted rich and poor boys to receive the same treatment, as "Crossley," the "spoiled son of a very rich man," learned. Crossley had a car and a servant, thought he could have everything he wanted, and was furious to find that "merit alone counted" in athletics, which put boys on common ground as nothing else did. It is worth adding that the "Matthewson" books showed no compunction either about throwing in such phrases as "Mexican greaser" or having a Japanese or Italian character use dialect for purposes of "humor." In view of what really happened in the major leagues at the time, it is also revealing that *Won in the Ninth* (1910) included a character named Hal Case (a thinly-disguised Hal Chase), who is accused of stealing but is exonerated.*

Another of several players credited with books written by ghost writers was Frank Chance, of "Tinker to Evers to Chance" fame. His *The Bride and the Pennant* (1910) employed the same device used by Stratemeyer and Mathewson's ghosts, that of using contemporary big-league stars as characters under such names as Hagner (for Wagner) and Robb (for Cobb).

Zane Grey belongs on any list of authors of baseball fiction for juveniles. Grey himself was an outstanding ball player at the University of Pennsylvania and afterwards entered professional ball as an outfielder for Fort Wayne of the Western League, where he batted .374 in 61 games. When he began writing he sandwiched several baseball novels in between his better-known westerns. Except for *The Redheaded Outfield and Other Baseball Stories*, in which he attempted some characterization, Grey's plots conformed to the well-worn prescription, but because of his intimate acquaintance with college and professional ball his books imparted a good deal of sound playing instruction and offered authentic vignettes of minor-league life. Grey pointed up the disparate values and codes of the collegians and the professionals— the way the former stressed the "pleasure and glory" of playing baseball and the importance of school and college spirit, whereas the latter regarded baseball as serious business. In *The Shortstop* he describes a rookie's professional debut:

> ...when he went out upon the field he was conscious of a difference in his feelings. ... The joy of playing the game, as he had played it ever since he was big enough to throw a ball, had gone. It was not fun, not play before him, but work,—work that called for strength, courage, endurance.

Hazed by veterans on the team, the rookie decides to strike back, and at the next opportunity he delivers a knockout punch to the toughest of his tormentors and wins his teammates' respect and acceptance.

Grey belonged to the rough, tough school of letters of the Roosevelt-Kipling era, as Frank Luther Mott put it. But books of baseball fiction on the whole fed youngsters a diet somewhat more bland. In broad composite

*See *Baseball: The Golden Age*, pp. 288–290, for Chase's misconduct.

they held up to readers a neat, clean youth with a "strong" face of "the manly, honest sort" who shunned drinking and smoking, especially cigarettes, had nothing "coarse or common" about him, and was of modest demeanor, devoid of pomp or show, never arrogant or swollen-headed; possessed nerve (pluck, sand, or grit) and was always "game"; never shirked, but did his best at all times regardless of ridicule or adverse conditions; believed that determination compensated for lack of brilliance and that success resulted from hard work; was "cool, alert, and heady" on the ball field; was fair and "on the level," a good sport even in defeat, never a "knocker" or a "mucker"; was loyal to his coach or captain and followed orders, realizing he must play not for himself but for the team; was not a "soft molly," a "quitter," or "yellow," and, because he was "made of the right stuff," could "pull himself together" after a bad play and rise to the demands of the occasion. Above all, the books implied that success on the ball field enabled one to cope with life after it—to rescue a drowning person, stop a runaway horse, or earn a livelihood. With a mix of melodrama and moralism they touted values and traits of character that parents, teachers, clergymen, and the middle class in general could and did endorse.

No one can tell the extent to which these books influenced the attitudes of their readers. Perhaps they did help inculcate ideals of sportsmanship, as some have claimed. But many boys fell under the pervading influence of the professional ethic of "win without being overly concerned about methods." In my circle, I freely admit, the ethic of the pros prevailed. In any case, reading these baseball novels constituted part of the tribal rites of passage from puberty to adulthood for countless boys of the pre–World War II era, gave them further incentive to play baseball, and left them with a deepened devotion to the game.

3

EVERY MOTHER OUGHT TO REJOICE

The forces of industrialism and urbanization that spurred the growth of amateur and semiprofessional baseball after the Civil War simultaneously obstructed it by reducing the number of open lots that served as ball fields for American boys. The city youth saw his play spaces disappear steadily under brick and mortar as manufacturers and real estate promoters, intent on erecting plants, warehouses, and residences, gobbled them up. The doubling of land values in Chicago within the last quarter of the nineteenth century plainly showed the space shrinkage.

The implications of this change for recreation did not go unnoticed. As early as 1838 Horace Mann, the Massachusetts schoolman, expressed fear that lack of space for outdoor recreation would lead to physical deterioration of Americans. In 1862 the Brooklyn *Eagle* noted that vacant lots were getting scarce as the city grew and baseball teams increased. Swollen in number and pressed for space, city youths in search of playing fields were compelled to travel farther out by foot, horsecar, or ferry, and later by electric trolley, subway, auto, or truck. Following in the wake of the pioneer Knickerbocker team, who forty years before paid the thirteen-cent round trip ferriage to play on the Jersey shore, hundreds of shirt-sleeved New York youth crossed the Hudson on Saturday afternoons and Sundays in the 1880s to play dozens of games in the open spaces between Hoboken and Guttenberg. The same problem occurred in other urban centers of the East and even in the South, where in New Orleans, as Professor Dale Somers has shown, city expansion was swallowing up so much space that ball players were using the streets or taking long trolley rides to find a place to play.

Appreciating baseball's appeal to boys, private and public agencies began in the nineteenth century to boost boys' baseball and subsidize it. As well, they exploited it as an instrument for fostering desirable social attitudes and mitigating social problems, such as ill health and juvenile delinquency, that arose from or were magnified by the headlong rush of industrialism and urbanization. In short, boys' baseball became the beneficiary of attempts to solve broad social problems. Aid for city players resulted largely from an effort to steer boys into "wholesome" recreation, to "housebreak" or socialize them according to prevailing middle-class criteria. Such aid was also the initial step toward the adult intervention that would eventually make boys' baseball less and less the affair of boys.

A prerequisite to the assistance rendered young ball players was the gradual transformation in the public's view of sports. Much of the early Calvinistic antipathy to sport eroded even before the Civil War as a climate of opinion favorable to sports and outdoor recreation materialized. Americans gradually awoke to the threat to their physical and mental well-being posed by the increasingly confined and sedentary life of the city. Walt Whitman wrote in 1846, "In our sun-down perambulations, of late, through the outer parts of Brooklyn, we have observed several parties of youngsters playing 'base,' a certain game of ball. We wish such sights were more common among us. . . . Let us go forth awhile, and get better air in our lungs."

As baseball spread, more merits were claimed for it as a healthy activity counteracting the effects of city life, and these supposed merits in turn fed its growth. Even the New York *Times* in October of 1859 urged editorially the greater participation of citizens in sports for physical fitness. Articles on physical culture appeared in periodicals like *Lippincott's*, *Atlantic Monthly*, and *Appleton's Journal*, and special magazines on physical culture began publication: *Health*, *Good Health*, and *Health and Home*.

The generally brightening view of sports reflected plainly in the schools, where for a long time schoolmen had held sports in low esteem. The once contemptible status of scholastic sports stands in sharp contrast with their exalted position nowadays, when schools spend thousands each year for equipment, coaches, bus rentals, and maintenance of fields and stadiums, and when parents seem less concerned with whether Johnny can read than whether he can play during school hours.

How did sports entrench themselves so deeply in the schools? The process began before the Civil War, and many elements shared in setting it in motion, among them the influence of European ideas of education bringing in fresh views of childhood; advocacy of exercise by physicians and reformers; criticism of schools for neglecting health; the example of immigrant sportsmen, such as the German Turnvereiners; and increased newspaper coverage of sports.

William A. Alcott personified the changing attitude toward school sports. Alcott's New England upbringing had instilled in him the belief that fondness for play indicated foolishness rather than wisdom in a child, and he admitted in 1839 that this notion led him to cheat his pupils of as much time as possible out of the fifteen minutes allotted them at noon for sports, until he realized that "sports are as indispensible to the health of both bodies and minds of children as their food, their drink, or their sleep. . . . " Alcott himself became addicted to sports: "Our most common exercise was ball playing. In this, I was not very expert; but I believe had all the healthful advantages which pertain to it, notwithstanding. It is really an excellent sport."

Academic sponsorship of sports not only opened additional opportunities for boys to play ball, it persuaded many parents that sports benefited their children because scholastic sanction invested it with legitimacy. Still, relatively few children had school baseball opportunities in the nineteenth century. Although most towns outside the South maintained some kind of primary school, generally such institutions were poorly financed, and relatively few attended regularly or for long. As for their baseball, until the eighties and nineties it usually came in the shape of informal, intramural games in the schoolyard during recess or lunch time. The children played ball in whatever style was familiar to them. One octogenarian of 1900 remembered playing with his country schoolmates in Erie, Pennsylvania, according to the early style of "soaking" base runners—putting them out by hitting them with the ball.

By 1850 the principle of state-supported schools for all children regardless of social status had been established, but the practice still fell far short. By that time only half the children of New England, the pioneer in the field, received a free education. Besides, some diehard pedagogues continued to fight a delaying action against sports. So despite growing recognition of the value of exercise and play, only a minority of boys could avail themselves of the little baseball that primary schools afforded.

Baseball fared better on the secondary level, where the privately-endowed academies dominated. They spread rapidly to all sections of the country and reached full bloom by the first half of the nineteenth century, by which time they totalled about 6,000. Although they catered primarily to the rich, they sometimes received public subsidies and, especially in rural districts, admitted poor boys. The presence of boarding schools and adequate land and facilities enabled academies to respond to the schoolmen's growing approval of sports.

Round Hill School in Northampton, Massachusetts, introduced sports as early as 1826, although Governor Dummer School in Byfield, Massachusetts, may have done so even earlier. Wallkill Academy in upstate New York fielded a baseball team that played outsiders, the Stars, in 1866. St. Paul's developed a baseball team in the sixties, too. Students at Groton, St. Mark's, and many other elite way stations on the road to college played baseball before the turn of the century. As for private military academies, Virginia Military Institute had interscholastic baseball in 1867, Hyatt Military Academy in Pennsylvania in the 1870s, and Staunton and Texas Military at least by the 1890s. At Exeter, the boys first played rounders and early ball games like one-o'-cat, but soon they graduated to the "new" game of baseball, and in 1878 Exeter and Andover began playing annual baseball games. At the academies the students generally organized and controlled the games. They arranged matches both between classes and with outside teams, but some academies went so far as to accept sports as an integral part of their education programs. A notable example is The Gunnery, whose founder, Frederick Gunn, converted early to the idea that sports developed morals and character.

As a nationwide system of public education emerged soon after the Civil War, scholastic sports expanded. Urban growth created the populations that made mass public education economically practicable while industrial growth produced the wealth to pay for it. Grammar school teachers might play ball with the children at recess. Clarence Darrow, teaching at a country school in the 1880s, lengthened the noon hours and recess periods to provide more recreation time, despite the irritation of parents, and joined in the students' games and sports, "including, of course, baseball," he wrote in his autobiography. In Missouri, visiting county superintendent Hervey Vories always joined in the baseball games, along with the teacher. Once in the middle of an exciting game, with Vories pitching, the teacher looked at his watch and reported, "Time for books." "Oh, heck, we can't stop now!" cried Vories. "This thing's got to be settled." And it was, his team winning by a narrow margin. The teacher, Millard Kennedy, wrote later that "the rural male teacher of those days who didn't play with the boys didn't get very far."

Free secondary education accelerated in the sixties and seventies, the number of high schools reaching about 6,000 by the end of the century, stimulated in part by the promise to businessmen of trained clerical help and of citizens with "sound" economic views. Baseball would in effect become an appurtenance to these goals insofar as the game was encouraged by those who believed playing it would teach youngsters respect for the rules and subordination of self to the team. For baseball in public high schools, Worcester, Massachusetts, may have set a precedent. In 1859 some of its pupils formed a team on their own but got into difficulties with school officials by calling it the Worcester High School Baseball Club. Soon, however, they won over the administration, who began to see value in their endeavor and gave school sponsorship to the team.

Penetration of baseball into the schools owed something to those teachers who encouraged games as a result of belief in John Dewey's doctrine of "progressive" education. Important too were outside influences like the comments of Walter Camp, Yale's prominent coach, who declared in 1889 that:

> base-ball is for every boy a good, wholesome sport. It brings him out of the close confinement of the schoolroom. It takes the stoop from his shoulders and puts hard, honest muscle all over his frame. It rests his eyes, strengthens his lungs, and teaches him self-reliance and courage. Every mother ought to rejoice when her boy says he is on the school or college nine.

Jacob Riis reported with satisfaction that the New York state legislature had passed a law requiring every new public school being built to include a playground in its plan.

Gradually, most white children anywhere from fourth grade through high school had some kind of chance at school sports, either to play on a school team or to learn sports techniques that readied them to compete outside school. In Buffalo, Central School and Heathcote School both had baseball teams in 1868. A student athletic association formed in Providence in 1876 and concentrated largely upon baseball. In Brooklyn, teams of several prep schools, such as Polytechnic and Pratt Institutes and Adelphi Academy, along with Brooklyn High School and the Latin School, rated among the "prominent" baseball clubs, most of them playing their championship games at the Parade Grounds or at abandoned professional parks, such as Washington Park in South Brooklyn. A Boston area Interscholastic Baseball League operated in the 1890s with teams from several towns. Cook County, Illinois, also conducted a high school championship series in the 1890s. In the Midwest, too, associations were forming. In 1895 Illinois and Wisconsin organized state high school athletic associations, which of course included baseball teams. In 1891 the Detroit High School team played interstate ball, boarding a boat for Cleveland to play its Central High School, which reciprocated the following year. Detroit school administrators even that early were becoming concerned by students' use of ringers in school sports. The Honesdale High School, in the Pennsylvania coal mining district, where baseball was the rage, proved skilled enough in 1897 to defeat St. Thomas College 18–7.

A word of caution about the number of school ball players is in order, however. In 1870 about six and a half million young people enrolled in schools, but daily attendance averaged only four million, with just 78 days per year for each pupil. So a great many missed out on scholastic baseball, having to work or being unable to attend school for other reasons. But enrollments climbed steadily, and by 1900 public schools counted fifteen and a half million pupils. Outside the South, most states passed some form of compulsory attendance law that they gradually extended and strengthened. At the end of the century, therefore, the public school stood poised to exert strong influence on baseball.

In time, an infant park and playground movement also matured into a source of aid for city ball players. The *American Journal of Education* had called attention back in the 1820s to the need for city playgrounds, but in a society that accented individualism, public responsibility for recreation came no more naturally than public operation of other city services. After all, major American cities failed to wrest control of their water supplies from private hands until the eve of the Civil War, and then only because the ravages of fire and epidemic forced the change. Even more loath were public authorities to concern themselves with seemingly frivolous matters like play and recreation.

In 1853, however, New York City set a new trend by purchasing a huge tract of land for a park and, a few years later, appointing Frederick Law

Olmsted supervisor of the proposed Central Park. Before the Civil War Olmsted completed his plan, and afterward he also began work on Brooklyn's Prospect Park.

From the first, a fundamental difference of opinion arose over the purpose of these parks and those that followed. Olmsted and other conservative reformers conceived Central Park primarily as a place for contemplation in simulated rural serenity, a place where working people and their families could stroll quietly to escape from the tensions and ugliness of the city. They also hoped the park would serve as a "remedy for the dangerous problem of discontent among the urban masses," as Geoffrey Blodgett has expressed it, and an inspiration to "communal feelings among all urban classes, muting resentments over disparities of wealth and fashion." In short, the park would be a safety valve for those who could not, like the wealthy, flee to the mountains, the shore, or their elegant, park-like estates. But others saw Central Park as a place for active recreation, where games and sports could be played. Olmsted, typical of his class, underestimated the desire for vigorous sports among boys and workingmen. He and his collaborator, architect Calvert Vaux, felt that the ballplayers in particular were the most demanding and the least capable of grasping their concept of the park's purpose:

> It seems difficult for them [the ballplayers] to realize [Olmsted wrote] that the large open surface of turf that, to the cultivated taste is among the most attractive features of the Park, can have any other use than that of a playground, and nothing is more certain than that the beauty of these lawns would soon be lost, and that they would be rendered disagreeable objects, if these games were to be constantly played upon them. . . .

In their plan, Olmsted and Vaux limited active sport to a few specified spots such as the Ball Ground or Play Ground. But they did not take sufficiently into account the intrusion of politicians who, with their eyes on votes and patronage, were keen to load the park with projects and to honor the multiplicity of park purposes pressed upon them, including more areas for baseball play.

As a result of the wrangle over the park's purpose, Olmsted was dismissed in 1878, but by then his position had already begun to erode. In the sixties children were allowed to play in Central Park, although only after supplying a statement from a teacher and making application to the park commissioners! Before he left Olmsted himself had conceded to the extent of preparing plans for more active recreation. By the eighties Brooklyn's Prospect Park permitted a few sports, and the Parade Grounds adajacent to it had already been opened in 1870 to use for baseball, other field sports, and military exercises.

After leaving New York Olmsted responded to park enthusiasts in Boston who for some time had sought his services. Ball players had used the lower end of the Boston Common, near Charles Street, for baseball since the

1850s, and there is still a baseball diamond there. At one point in the 1860s, according to a contemporary baseball player, James D.W. Lovett, the ball ground was ploughed up and games discontinued, so the ball players got together and, under the insignia of a red ball, campaigned for and managed to elect a new city administration more sympathetic to sports, especially on the Common. A rhyme in the 1868 novel *Changing Base* by William Everett reflects this dispute:

> The Common is the place—a pasture wide,
> Which civic fathers oft to close have tried;
> But bravely still the citizens have withstood,
> Thinking their children's sport is for the general good.

When Olmsted arrived in Boston he found that the topography of the city inspired him to girdle it with a six-mile belt of greenery extending from the Public Garden, which abuts the Common, to Franklin Park. In the face of growing public demand for active recreation he unbent to the extent of providing areas for baseball diamonds, tennis courts, a children's playground, and the like, around the rural center of the park proper. The Playstead, a thirty-acre field reserved for schoolboy sports, opened in the eighties.

Slowly the idea of playgrounds for youths and adults, ones either connected or unconnected with public parks, spread. An outdoor play center established in Boston in 1885 and equipped with a sandpile is generally taken as the birthdate of the playground movement in America. By 1887 the city had ten such centers in operation. Boston's park and recreational program expanded in the nineties well beyond Olmsted's prescription with the state-created metropolitan park commission. Many cities, including Pittsburgh, Baltimore, Milwaukee, Cleveland, Minneapolis, St. Paul, and Denver, as well as smaller communities like Brookline, Massachusetts, had made a start on playgrounds by the close of the century. Chicago provided a "recreation park" early, and the new Audubon Park in New Orleans included a baseball field. In some places, however, as in Johnstown, Pennsylvania, Worcester, Massachusetts, and in parts of Chicago, park administrators posted "keep off the grass" signs, and people who wanted to play or wanted their children to play continued to fight for city space.

These new measures to set up parks with play spaces left many dissatisfied. Women's groups and civic-minded organizations put pressure on city governments to furnish separate play spaces outside parks. In Brooklyn the *Eagle* reported in 1896 that a Women's Health Protective Association was plumping for baseball grounds for boys. In Boston the Massachusetts Emergency and Hygiene Association, a private group, established playgrounds near schools, furnishing toys and balls, and reported in its minutes that when a playground opened on North Bennet Street "a hundred children rushed in, wild with delight." The first playground in California opened in 1898 as an experiment of the women of the California Club. Sarah Josepha Hale, editor of *Godey's Lady's Book*, appealed for playgrounds in Philadelphia. Acts like these set the stage for a larger play movement in the twentieth century.

In addition to the nucleus of a play movement, the nineteenth century saw the beginnings of other allies for boys' baseball like the Young Men's Christian Association, the settlement houses, and the boys' work movements. Although different in approach and objectives, these forces, at first privately-financed and staffed by volunteers, shared a concern for the welfare of youth caught up in the onslaught of industrial-urbanism. Their interest would prove conducive to furthering boys' baseball.

The YMCA, a Protestant organization transplanted from England in 1851, aided baseball both directly and indirectly. By 1900 it had more than 1,400 branches throughout the country and 250,000 dues-paying members. It owed its growth largely to the backwardness of churches in attending to the troubling social problems of the changing times. The "old-time religion" that in a rural age may have been "good enough for pappy" left many city youth cold. The Y, which at first served the poor but soon began appealing to the lower middle class, took a practical route to carrying out its evangelistic mission. Perceiving the need for "wholesome" recreation to counteract "the allurement of objectionable places of resort," and wishing to temper the largely feminine aspect of American Protestantism by means of the idea of "muscular Christianity," Y leaders capitalized on the mounting interest of the young in athletics by adding sports, baseball included, to the Y's many-sided program as bait to lure youth into the fold. Beginning with gymnastics in the 1850s, the Y had by the seventies moved into athletics for young men and boys. Out of 327 Y branches that offered athletics in the 1880s, 180 offered baseball teams—Christy Mathewson played on one, the Scranton Y, in the nineties—and in 1895 the Y established an athletic league of North American Ys under Dr. Luther Gulick, a missionary's son, who intoned, "Christ's kingdom should include the athletic world."

YMCA athletics expanded quickly. The New York City Y sponsored a thirty-club baseball league in 1889, according to *Harper's*, and Brooklyn Ys competed in baseball in 1892. When the Boston Y leased outdoor grounds in 1888 for baseball and other sports, one of the Boston newspapers commented that on the Y grounds, "Base-ball will be played just as enthusiastically as of yore, but the crowd will not be allowed to swear at the umpire." Besides sponsoring athletics themselves, Y branches encouraged Sunday schools, public schools, colleges, and business firms to sponsor baseball and other sports, and they furnished trained leaders to help. The Y's imprimatur had the side effect of winning doubting Protestant parents' approval of ball playing.

The settlement house movement's aid to boys' baseball, though significant, was less direct than the Y's. Like the YMCA the settlement house was an English import, patterned on Toynbee Hall of London's East End. The first settlement in America opened on New York's lower East Side in 1886. Thereafter, the number of such houses increased rapidly, and by the end of the century about a hundred were operating, mostly in northern and midwestern cities. The most famous were Chicago's Hull-House, Boston's South End House, and New York's Henry Street Settlement, founded respectively by Jane Addams, Robert A. Woods, and Lillian D. Wald. In accordance with the movement's rather condescending motto, "elevation by contact"—reminiscent of Olmsted's attitude—dedicated social workers left their middle-class homes and moved into poor neighborhoods, where they set up multifarious programs in efforts to narrow the enormous gulf between the largely immigrant masses and the upper classes.

The settlement leaders and their co-workers got more than they bargained for. Shocked by the squalor around them and swamped with practical problems, they soon realized the job was not as simple as mere "elevation," that they must attack the unspeakable slum conditions themselves and deal with the inability of immigrant families to cope with the new conditions of their lives. Led by a remarkable corps, mostly female, the settlements agitated for a variety of social laws, but it was their stress on child welfare, recreation included, that redounded to the benefit of boys' baseball.

The attitude toward their young charges of settlement workers and others who helped children has been much criticized as patronizing, and their views do have an arrogant flavor. Jane Addams has been quoted as saying that immigrants lacked the "social energy which makes for progress, . . . [and] the inherent uncleanliness of their minds prevents many from rising above the ranks of labor." In Boston the Massachusetts Emergency and Hygiene Association, which worked for playgrounds, regretted at the end of the 1887 season that the poor Boston neighborhood in which it worked was "not wholly reformed and Christianized," but at least the children showed "less wildness" and more interest in "healthy games and sports," and moreover, "these waifs, who have no standards," know now that while at the playgrounds "they must speak the truth and be clean." Yet these workers merely expressed their attempts to impose the kind of order and discipline they were used to from their own background, so from their perspective the children they worked with lacked restraint and tidiness. By their own lights they were improving the children by requiring what they believed to be the kind of behavior needed for middle-class success.

The settlement workers were aware of the latest educational theories about the treatment of children and their need for play. They also recognized the strong grip of baseball on boys. In their work they utilized this knowledge by enlisting sports and recreation as weapons against the "demoralizing amusements" of the city. Many settlements, like Hull-House in Chicago and East Side House in New York, themselves established small playgrounds in the slums out of private funds; they lacked the resources and space for large playing fields. Lillian Wald of New York and Julia Lathrop of Chicago urged women's groups and city administrations to set up playgrounds. Even the University of Chicago in 1888 established a playground where "The bigger boys play, as usual, at nothing but baseball." The push of the settlements for school and public playgrounds and their endorsement of sports and games in time benefited young ball players.

Boys' work, a new category of welfare work undertaken by volunteers in the 1890s, constituted another movement that quickly fastened on baseball as a tool to help accomplish its basic purpose of keeping youngsters off the streets and out of trouble and "evangelizing" them by providing healthy spare-time activities. In the main, two conditions gave rise to this attempt to fit children into society: greater appreciation among parents, teachers, librarians, and social reformers of the needs of children, gained from the child study movement, and the growing worry among citizens over the increasing number of delinquent, poor, and neglected children bred by industrial-urbanism and immigration.

Some boys' work took place under the auspices of social welfare agencies: for instance, Robert A. Woods organized boys' clubs to keep Boston boys off the streets, and Hull-House began a club for boys about sixteen years old, all of whom were eager to come and "very respectful," although their habit of wearing hats indoors and spitting tobacco on the floor exasperated the young Victorian ladies in charge of them. Other boys' clubs, however, were autonomous organizations, founded by civic-minded women and men as early as the 1860s and 1870s in Hartford, Connecticut, for example, and in New York City.

Boys' work strategy sought to replace neighborhood gangs or at least pull their fangs by establishing clubs through which to divert youngsters into more "wholesome" activities. Among these, sports, and of course baseball, ranked high in keeping with the credo that, as Lillian Wald put it, "clean sport and stimulating competition can replace the gang feud and even modify racial antagonisms." When Wald's settlement in New York moved from Rivington Street to Henry Street she retained the name of the former building, Nurses' Settlement, until, as Irving Howe relates, the boys' athletic club could no longer bear the teasing of opponents on the baseball field: "Hey noices! Noices!" whereupon she gave in to their pleas and changed the name to the Henry Street Settlement.

The experience of Marion Lawrence furnishes an illustration of boys' work strategy in action and its sometimes unpredictable results. Lawrence, a member of a prominent Massachusetts family, ran the North Bennet Street Boys' Club in Boston around the turn of the century as one of her "charities." The club numbered some forty to fifty "underprivileged" teenage boys, mostly Irish and Italian. An essay could be written on the implications of the club's rules as an effort to impose upper-class standards upon these sons of immigrants: the boys "mustn't get excited, chew gum, spit, swear, cheat or talk Italian"—or, presumably, Gaelic, had any known it. Baseball quickly became one of the boys' favorite activities. During a day's outing in the country they played an intraclub game, Irish against Italians. It broke up in a fight. So much for baseball as a civilizing force.

Soon the Bennet Street lads had their own baseball uniforms and played teams in one of Olmsted's parks. Miss Lawrence, who was nothing if not game, ventured to arrange a match between her Lawrence Club, as the boys named themselves, and the elite Groton School team. To prepare for the match the boys practiced daily for weeks in their spare time, and Miss Lawrence constantly impressed on them "one essential thing": to play "a clean, sporty, gentlemanly game and to take a licking cheerfully." "This they did," she reported, "to a remarkable degree." Imagine then, she went on, the "disgust and surprise" of all when the Groton first baseman deliberately tripped up Tom McHugh, who was "running very hard" on a long hit, causing him to fall heavily. The Lawrence Club boys instantly showed "a general expression of 'So that's what you call gentlemanly playing!' " So much for elevation by contact.

To be sure, the Groton alumni were "furious"; they stopped the game and got the umpire to send the "blackguard" off the field. Groton won that game, but it is only right to add that in a rematch the following year the Lawrence boys, in the words of their mentor, "all batted like a streak," and even though one of her boys had worked on a "watering cart" all morning and had had no food since 6:oo A.M., they "wiped up the ground with Groton."

4

SCRUB BALL IS NOT ENOUGH

As the twentieth century unfolded, boys' baseball entered a new phase.
Aid for it increased and broadened. Government assistance rose markedly
while private organizations already supporting boys' baseball remained steadfast and others joined them. The twin offspring of this aid, adult intrusion
and control, pointed boys' baseball toward highly organized competition that
entailed selection of the best players, devotion of substantial amounts of
spare time to formal practice, and contention for awards and honors. Co-
option of boys' baseball by adults also led to use of boys' games for their
own ends. All the while, the baseball cult solidified as the unslackened
popularity of the game and the lengthening list of reputed benefits from
playing it reinforced each other.

These developments were in part offshoots of the so-called progressive
movement, that groundswell of exposé, protest, and reform that gathered
in the latter part of the old century and attained full force in the first two
decades of the new. The progressive movement—complex, moderate, al-
truistic and selfish, often naive, and never unified—constituted an essentially
middle-class effort to cope with the distressful economic and social consequences of unbridled industrial expansion and over-rapid urban growth that
helped transform America in less than a generation.

Despite conflicting goals and mixed motives, the progressives were in
general accord on certain interrelated themes, three of which etched a clear
imprint on boys' baseball: solicitude for the welfare of children, belief in the
necessity for and efficacy of social action, and disposition toward bureaucratic
precepts. In their zeal to better the lives of children, humanitarian progressives aimed not only at such obvious targets as getting children out of
factories and sweat shops and into schools, but also at improved schools and
greater opportunities for recreation and games, especially baseball, in keeping with heightened public understanding of the needs of youngsters and of
environmental hazards to them. Concluding from the research of social scientists and from firsthand experience that the causes of poverty and other
social evils were more environmental than personal, and that traditional

50

reliance on private philanthropy and charity (like that of the Marion Law-
rences) no longer sufficed, the progressives meant to enlist the power and
wealth of government to bring about reform through social legislation. And
in what Robert A. Wiebe termed a search for order, a new middle class of
young professionals and business people that had emerged would ensure
the effectiveness and continuity of such reform measures by extending the
civil service or creating appointive jobs and filling them with experts. Thus
municipalities began to spawn departments, commissions, boards, and bur-
eaus of parks, recreation, and playgrounds, with squads of superintendents,
supervisors, directors, and groundkeepers—products of the progressives'
view of bureaucratic, more sustained solutions to urban-industrial problems.

Around 1900 the stage was set for the full flowering of the movement.
The country had just about climbed out of the depression of the misnamed
gay nineties, but vexatious problems ranging from corporate monopoly to
play space in which city youngsters could play baseball persisted or worsened. Ambitious young middle-class progressives scrutinized the deficiencies of municipal services, and the reform wave that emerged affected boys'
baseball, for, as Wiebe put it, if progressivism had a central theme, it was
the child. Progressives soon injected new vigor and better organization into
the drive for playgrounds. Jacob Riis, author of *How the Other Half Lives*
(1890), the classic exposé of slum conditions in New York City, made the
point strongly in another book, *The Making of an American*:

> Probably all thinking people subscribe today to the statement that it is the
> business of the municipality to give its children a chance to play, just as much
> as to give them schools to go to. Everybody applauds it. The authorities do
> not question it; but still they do not provide playgrounds. Private charity has
> to keep a beggarly half-dozen going where there ought to be forty or fifty, as
> a matter of right, not of charity.

Advocacy like this soon produced results. In the first six years of the new
century twenty-six cities established playgrounds. Chicago's leadership in
these years influenced the subsequent development of recreation: in 1903
Chicagoans voted a five million dollar bond issue for the construction of
recreation parks on the crowded South Side, and ten of them opened in
1905. Theodore Roosevelt called them "the most notable civic achievement
of any American city." Large sections of these parks provided year-round
active recreation for children and adults on fields for games and sports,
including baseball, as well as playgrounds and outdoor gyms for children.
In harmony with the progressive approach, park administrators also supplied
trained leaders. Other sections of the city soon followed the South Side's
lead under various park commissioners and park boards.

Favorable publicity about these parks strongly affected other cities. Los
Angeles, after appointing a Board of Playground Commissioners in 1904,
built a number of small parks on Chicago's model. Boston also stayed among

the van. By 1905 Boston was spending a half million dollars annually for parks and playgrounds. In 1901 it opened a fourteen-acre site, Charlestown Playground near Sullivan Square, primarily for baseball playing.

More far-reaching even than the opening of Chicago's South Side parks was a three-day meeting held in April 1906 at Washington, D.C., to consider the nation's play needs, particularly those of city children. The party, one of several reform groups that descended on Washington during those years, included such progressives as Jacob Riis; Luther H. Gulick, who for many years had headed the physical training department of the YMCA's training school at Springfield, Massachusetts, where he reputedly suggested that James Naismith devise the game that became basketball; and the ubiquitous Jane Addams. Gulick, who at prep school in Oberlin reportedly "threw a swift underhand ball," believed in the social and moral value of athletics and once observed that boys with nothing to do could be a "menace to the social order," and that training them in athletics pointed them to "social loyalty." The meeting, one session of it held at the White House, resulted in the formation of the Playground Association of America—a title later broadened to include recreation—whose main purpose was to work for the "establishment of playgrounds and athletic fields" headed by professional administrators and directors and supported by the communities. President Theodore Roosevelt, the foremost propagandist for sport in the progressive era, heartily endorsed the association and became its honorary president.

The Playground Association mirrored the progressive style, and its formation placed the recreation movement on a national footing. The association acted as a clearinghouse for recreation information, published a monthly magazine, *The Playground* (later, *Recreation*), prepared a course in play that schools and colleges adopted for training play leaders, and employed traveling field workers who went from city to city enlisting support for playgrounds and advising how to get them.

The sharp increase in the number of cities that established playgrounds in the years immediately after 1906 attests to the association's effectiveness. By 1911 more than 500 cities had playgrounds or were campaigning to secure them.

The election of "reform" administrations in many cities contributed to the growth of municipal playgrounds. In Toledo, Ohio, Samuel M. Jones created parks and playgrounds for children during four administrations as mayor, and on his death in 1904 Brand Whitlock, his disciple, succeeded him and carried on his policies. Cleveland matched this idealistic duo. There Mayor Tom L. Johnson (1901–09), whose brother Albert had been a key figure in the major league players' revolt of 1890,* encouraged the building of playgrounds and reputedly remarked that he hoped one would be made above his grave, because he preferred romping children to monuments over him.

*See *Baseball: The Early Years*, pp. 221–250.

After he left office Spalding's baseball guide praised him for having provided Cleveland with one of the finest systems of park baseball grounds anywhere. Johnson owed much of his success to his readiness to appoint progressive specialists like Newton D. Baker, a lawyer and tax expert, to key positions and to listen to their advice. Baker, who himself became mayor, believed in public taxation as the support for recreation, arguing in an address before the Playground Association in 1912 that the city should furnish whatever country life provided that the city lacked. He reasoned that if the city's social functions included providing courts, jails, and insane asylums, it must also offer the chance to avoid using them by establishing playgrounds. In the course of his mayoralty Cleveland submitted a million-dollar bond issue for playgrounds.

Frederick Law Olmsted, on the other hand, still dithered on the question of supplying baseball grounds in public parks. He wrote Gulick in April of 1909 that the Playground Association should consider a "perplexing practical point": "the question of what attitude to take in regard to baseball." Setting aside enough land for a diamond to accommodate only eighteen players seemed to him "of very doubtful propriety," but "to cut out baseball altogether or to confine it to very small boys is apt to make a playground unpopular." E.B. DeGroot, director of playgrounds, on seeing Olmsted's letter, thought otherwise, commenting that "it is worth while to make every effort to prolong the life of a game [baseball] that has American origin and tradition back of it." At Chicago, said DeGroot, each baseball site consisted of twenty acres, for "it costs no more to equip and operate twenty acres than ten acres." He recommended the introduction of park police, as in Chicago's parks, to keep order and prevent betting, and the use of permits for play to reserve use of a diamond in advance.

Permits mitigated somewhat the perennial park problem of fighting over diamonds. Letters flooded into *Baseball Magazine* about older children taking over diamonds from little ones, who were thus prevented from completing their games. Sometimes "adult loafers" drove boys from a diamond and used it themselves. Facing this problem, Dallas, Rochester, and Worcester, Massachusetts, as well as many other cities had by 1909 developed permit systems for baseball diamonds and hired guards to protect small boys against "rowdies."

Solid gains in playground construction during the progressive era did not end the remorseless shrinking of space for play. Joseph Lee, the "father" and "philosopher" of the playground movement and one-time president of the Playground Association, wrote in its journal in 1913 that lack of space still presented a problem and that America stood in danger of losing its play tradition because of crowding. In the past, he said, the small village green had furnished a place for everyone to play, but today's city did not.

New York certainly fit his description, as George Wingate, of whom more later, made plain:

There is nothing more needed in the city than places where children attending our schools can have an opportunity to practice athletic exercise and to play.... That many additional playgrounds are needed... is too clear for argument.

In the press for space in New York the Dock Commissioner permitted tenement boys who lived too far from athletic grounds to use the city's recreation piers for spring baseball practice. Fifteen diamonds in Central Park were reported "very extensively used" in 1905, and authorities even opened the park to baseball on Sunday afternoons in 1910. But in 1915 Henry S. Curtis of the Playground Association, visiting Central Park, saw "two or more [baseball] games going on in practically the same space, one being played across the other." The police in New York and other cities created a little more play space by closing some streets to traffic, a step welcomed by Lillian Wald, a champion of the playground movement.

Meanwhile, the number of playgrounds in the country grew. Parks with space for baseball and other active sports availed in Buffalo, Los Angeles, and St. Louis. By 1909, 267 cities operated 1,537 playgrounds, and the end was not in sight. In some cities, where park authorities resisted accepting playgrounds, municipal administrations established separate recreation commissions to open up playgrounds elsewhere. In addition, park baseball leagues, some of them conducting interpark competition, operated in several cities.

In the course of the progressive era city governments also enlarged opportunities for children to play baseball in the public schools. Given the child-centered point of view of progressives, it is unsurprising that reformers placed educational reform high on their list. To progressives, school improvement was part of restriction on child labor: keep the child out of the factory and sweat shop, educate him properly, and he would create the better society they envisioned. So progressives advocated a longer school year, stricter attendance laws, and a curriculum better suited to an industrial society and to children of immigrants. Most important for boys' baseball, they pressed the schools to apply new ideas about child psychology, including the need of school children for play.

Jane Addams, the settlement house worker, illustrated this mutual reinforcement among different child welfare programs by voicing her impatience with schools that "lay all stress on reading and writing" (a fault more than rectified since!) and offer a type of education that "fails to give the child any clew to the life about him." Addams, Lillian Wald, and settlement workers in general supported the playground movement in the conviction that sports prevented juvenile delinquency. The Playground Association also recommended more "directed play" in the schools and the allotment of at least three acres for grade school playgrounds and five for high schools.

A continued boom in public school enrollments between 1900 and 1914 assured plenty of clients for partisans of scholastic sports. As state after state

lifted the school-leaving age, the nation's high school enrollments in particular increased phenomenally, more than doubling in fourteen years. To
absorb the flood of students, communities constructed high schools at the
rate of one a day! The South especially struggled to climb out of its public
education slough by spending its meager funds much more generously.

Baseball and other sports had already made headway in the schools by
the time enrollments began to boom, yet they occupied a peculiar position.
Run mostly by students with what coaching help they could scrape up from
teachers or other adults, scholastic sports programs in the main operated on
the educational periphery, associated with the schools but rarely an integral
part of them. As a result of lack of adult supervision, schools heard complaints
of abuses like the use of ringers and the hiring of nonfaculty coaches by
students. In one 1912 high school game a player insulted an umpire and,
because the situation soon got out of hand, the police had to be called in.
In Brooklyn in 1901 the *Eagle* reported that Queens high school discipline
was said to be "injuriously affected" by the baseball "craze."

Consequently, in Boston, as in some other high schools, the administration
began to take over athletics. In Cleveland in 1904 the Board of Education
approved a new High School Athletic Senate to control athletic events and
foster "good sportsmanship." In a study reported in 1907 in the *American
Physical Education Review*, about a quarter of high schools queried said
they had taken at least partial control of athletics. Those who replied also
gave evidence that baseball did not pay its way, and that poor scholarship
sometimes resulted from concentration on baseball to the exclusion of study.
Nevertheless, most of the schools replying considered athletics of benefit to
the school. In Nebraska in 1909 its seventy-five leading high schools declared
that, because boys could not participate unless they kept their grades up,
school athletics had helped "remarkably" in raising the standard of academic
work.

In this period some boys developed high school baseball skills that helped
get them to the big leagues. Jack Knight, later of the New York Americans,
came to the attention of the professionals while playing on the championship
high school team in Philadelphia in 1905 and signed with Connie Mack of
the Philadelphia Athletics. Morris Rath went from the same school to the
big leagues. Frank Frisch starred at Public School Number 8 in the Bronx
as well as at Fordham Preparatory School. Pie Traynor played shortstop on
his high school team in Framingham, Massachusetts; he had decided at age
eight that he would become a major leaguer. Lou Fonseca played at Sacred
Heart in San Francisco, which encouraged athletics. Al Schacht pitched his
high school team to a New York City championship. Casey Stengel likewise
pitched his Kansas City high school team to a state championship in 1909.
Carmen Hill's exploits for his high school in Corry, Pennsylvania, caused
him to quit school (to his everlasting regret) within three months of graduation to join the majors. "I was a boob," he said later. "But that Big League

offer floored me. The temptation was too strong." Other good scholastic players entered different fields: Leverett Saltonstall of Boston and Newton schools, later a politician; Earl Warren of Kern City Union High in California, later a judge; and Francis Spellman, first baseman of Whitman High School, Whitman, Massachusetts, eventually a priest.

In many schools sports remained outside the physical education curriculum, which at the time generally featured body building through exercises in the European tradition. First introduced here in the 1820s by German refugees, gymnastics proved too regimented and boring to win more than a sporadic acceptance in American schools and colleges until redesigned by Dio Lewis of Auburn, New York, into a different system performed with light implements and set to music. Lewis popularized the gymnasium and brought it into the school as never before, paving the way for the broader, more substantial physical education work of a later day. In the late 1880s the German Turnvereiners succeeded in getting their system of physical training into the public schools of many midwestern cities, and soon thereafter a Swedish system received broader interest in the Northeast.

The paucity of sports in physical education classes resulted largely from the fact that the women who taught most of them had less contact with sports than males and often proved unqualified to handle them. Consequently, sports and physical training usually remained separate entities.

So when sports education enthusiasts founded the Public Schools Athletic League in New York City in 1903, they organized it as a private corporation rather than as a branch of the physical education department, although the board of education cooperated closely with it. The girls' branch of the PSAL, however, when it organized in 1905, became from the beginning part of girls' physical education.*

The initiator of the movement that brought about the PSAL was Luther Gulick, then director of physical training in the city's public schools. He believed in athletic competition for the average as well as the skilled boy. The PSAL offered elementary as well as high school ball players an opportunity to play on organized teams under scholastic auspices.

Gulick's idea became a reality through the cooperation of the heads of the public schools as well as New York's City College and leaders of the Amateur Athletic Union and the Intercollegiate Athletic Association,** as well as the endowment of George Wingate of the National Guard, a Civil War veteran and New York City lawyer who had helped organize the National Rifle Association in 1871. Wingate became the PSAL's president, and soon Brooklyn's new public school athletic field took his name. Additional operating funds came from a few memberships of various types, beginning with annual

*See below, Chapter 30.
**The Intercollegiate Athletic Association became the National Collegiate Athletic Association, for which see below, Chapter 11.

ones at $10.00, and contributions from such capitalists as S.J. Guggenheim, Harry Paine Whitney, J.P. Morgan, and John D. Rockefeller.

President Theodore Roosevelt, advocate of the "strenuous life," who seldom overlooked a chance to trumpet the value of sports as a builder of "virile, moral manhood" and a "manly race," congratulated Wingate on the founding of the PSAL, observing that crowded streets, especially in the tenement districts, deprived New York City children of an opportunity to exercise. It is "a great disadvantage to a boy," Roosevelt went on, "to be unable to play games; and every boy who knows how to play base ball or football, to box or wrestle, has by just so much fitted himself to be a better citizen." Thus did the blessing of Wingate and Roosevelt lend a certain nationalistic overtone to the birth of the PSAL.

Gulick took care to enlist the support of the local newspapers. The *Sunday World* and the *Journal* furnished prizes and other assistance; the *Herald* supplied trophies and arranged final championships for PSAL competition.

New York's PSAL conducted a comprehensive program of indoor and outdoor athletics in day and evening elementary and high schools. Its leadership held intramural and interscholastic events in many sports, for which the children were classified according to grade, weight, or skill. It sponsored huge annual field days to encourage participation in sports that its backers believed would teach "fairness, cheerfulness, pluck and skill—the true sportsmanlike spirit of honorable competition."

Baseball was the most popular of the team games. Varsity and junior varsity teams competed for the championship of their boroughs, and borough winners played each other for the city championship. Already in 1907 PSAL teams numbered 106, and as many as 15,000 persons attended a single game. In 1912 every high school in the city entered a baseball team in the PSAL. City and borough champions received trophies, and the *Herald* even presented them to the elementary and high schools that scored the greatest number of runs and those that had the fewest runs scored against them. At a Brooklyn *Eagle* special day for the schools at Ebbets Field in June 1913, fully 24,000 watched track and field and saw the baseball champions of Brooklyn and Queens compete for the grade school championship of Long Island.

The PSAL could not have essayed such an ambitious program without the cooperation of the city's bureaucracies, especially the park department and playground commmssion. By 1912 the PSAL could count six playing fields at its disposal, with from 600 to 800 schools trying to use each one daily between April and mid-October. The PSAL also prevailed on the Board of Education to open its fields to working boys Sunday afternoons and summer evenings and secured the use of diamonds in Prospect Park for PSAL practice and competition. But because of a cut in the Board of Education budget, playing fields remained open Sunday afternoons for only two seasons.

By the end of the PSAL's tenth year 350,000 New York school children

were competing in organized PSAL athletics, and in that year it spent almost
$17,000.00. Wingate in his address before the ninth annual meeting asserted
(correctly) that the PSAL was "too firmly rooted" in the school system "ever
to be disturbed." The New York PSAL is still in existence, and although it
remains a privately operated group, it is for all intents and purposes, said
its assistant director in 1978, "an integral part of the New York City Board
of Education."

The PSAL gave thousands of pasty-faced, chicken-chested youngsters who
might never have had sports experience a chance to test themselves physically. Wingate believed that by the end of its first decade the children of
New York schools were stronger and healthier, had improved ethics, better
discipline, and more esprit de corps. He claimed success for the PSAL in
keeping boys away from smoking and out of gangs, not by preaching but by
interesting them in athletics. Even those who merely joined the Saturday
morning walking clubs gained: as Wingate pointed out, walks outside the
slums opened a new world to children who could not afford ten cents' carfare
and "whose lives are spent in the little squalid circle of crowded streets and
tenements and to whom a few trees and a little grass are a mysterious wonder
and delight." What impressed Professor Charles W. Larned of the United
States Military Academy was the "wonderful morale" that PSAL athletics
developed "in this heterogeneous mass of undeveloped children" of the
"tenement class." Thus PSAL athletics may have raised their spirits and
given them a broader view of the possibilities of life.

Such organizations as the PSAL marked the real beginning of highly organized mass sports competition under adult direction for school-age youngsters. Although not new, interscholastic competition under the PSAL system
became much more firmly entrenched, as casual matches between schools
and competition that happened one year and not the next gave way to
sustained interest over a long period, with a consequent tendency toward
greater emphasis on winning. The soon-familiar baggage of such organized
competition followed: extensive newspaper publicity, crowds of adult spectators, annual selection of individual and team champions plus all-star teams,
and a flood of prizes—trophies, cups, plaques, medals, and badges. (One
year I received "honorable mention" in the press as a PSAL baseball player
at Alexander Hamilton High School.) A.G. Spalding and Company, the
leading sporting goods manufacturer, quickly traded on the PSAL by offering
trophies of its own, and its subsidiary, the American Sports Publishing Company, donated to the leagues 5,000 free copies of the PSAL Handbook,
which it printed, featuring photos of winning school teams.

Like Roosevelt, Wingate regarded competitive athletics as beneficial, declaring that nothing else developed "the robust, manly qualities of courage,
nerve and hardihood" as they did. He pointed out that the main purpose of
the league was to encourage the average boy and even the boy who was
"physically below average" to develop health and strength, but he also saw

the emergence of "star athletes" as the natural result of competition. To guard against abuses the PSAL established eligibility rules: players must maintain satisfactory grades, nobody could bet, transfer students encountered restrictions, and pupils could not at the same time represent such outside organizations as YMCAs and settlement houses, although they could represent their churches.

In view of the way ex-servicemen later took hold of boys' baseball, the strong vein of nationalism in the PSAL program must be noted. Students engaged in such external rituals as pledging allegiance to the flag and marching in review at athletic meets before politicians, prominent citizens, and military officers. Rifle shooting, one of the most popular PSAL activities, was close to Wingate's heart. He thought it could lead to "a force of sharpshooters" that could guarantee national peace. Rifle and ammunition companies were permitted to sponsor tournaments and supply prizes, and their representatives, along with National Guard officers, participated in meets.

For a time the New York PSAL represented the epitome of highly organized scholastic sport, but it did not measure the full extent of sport popularity in the schools. A survey of 555 cities in 1905 revealed that 360 supported school baseball, although most, especially outside the Northeast, still lacked organized leagues. But the New York PSAL helped change that. It became a pattern for other cities to copy: first, volunteers set up an organization tailored to fit the local situation, with the New York organization's rules as a base; later, school authorities granted it recognition.

Baltimore, inspired by New York, formulated an even more comprehensive recreational plan, the Public Athletic League, out of concern over studies indicating that blue collar workers, especially in factory towns, were below average in height and weight, so Baltimore's PAL planned playgrounds, gyms, and games not only for school children but also for working boys and young men. Even parochial schools joined in. Tournaments in baseball and track capped the season.

By 1910 nineteen cities, including Chicago, Cleveland, New Orleans, Boston, and San Francisco, had all established similar organizations, and more embraced the idea in the following decade. The rise of parochial schools as an adjunct to the tremendous growth of the Roman Catholic Church in large cities led eventually to the formation of separate Catholic School Athletic Leagues, although sometimes public and Catholic teams did play "practice" (nonleague) games against each other. PSAL baseball teams also played private high schools, prep schools, and the school teams of different PSAL leagues.

The speedy success and far-flung acceptance of the PSAL idea helped make the separation of physical training and sports in the school curriculum an increasing anomaly. By 1906 the issue could no longer be ignored by physical education teachers. That year the question came before the American Physical Education Association when George J. Fisher, a prominent

YMCA leader and a physician, called on the convention to take a stand on competitive athletics and to recognize that within proper limitations they were a legitimate part of physical education. Flabby muscles, Fisher declared, could result in flabby thought and action, and he knew of nothing to equal competitive athletics for developing "endurance, grit, self-confidence, self-control, [and] courage." One physical training specialist, looking back at these days, put a slightly different cast on the matter:

> Seeking a way to stimulate interest in physical education, . . . we began to see a light . . . [when] we discovered that the sports which the young men like are usually good for them.

A year after Fisher's plea a founder of American psychology and pioneer of the child study movement, G. Stanley Hall, lent authority to the proposition that team sports had educational value for adolescents. He contended that baseball and other sports could satisfy an adolescent need for group loyalty and organization and become sources of mental and moral training. Like Fisher, Hall could not refrain from a finishing coat of gilt: the group loyalty fostered by Anglo-Saxon games, he asserted, could be utilized "to develop a spirit of service not only to town, country, and race, but to God and the Church." Equally extravagant claims came from the director of religious education at Boston University, Norman E. Richardson, who maintained that a well-conducted high school athletic program supplied an antidote to the "soft sensuality" of the age, a stimulus to school loyalty and scholarship, and a broadening influence through the attendant opportunities for travel and business experience.

And that was not all. C. Ward Crampton, a medical doctor and secretary of the New York PSAL, rationalized his support for organized school sport by claiming that, contrary to the assumption of no interrelation between mental and physical training, qualities required for supremacy in business duplicated those primitive man depended on for survival and were the same as those taught through vigorous play: "alertness, precision, coordination, . . . courage, fairness, and courtesy." James Naismith, M.D., a professor of physical education generally credited with the invention of basketball, contributed to a book about high schools with a chapter claiming that athletics developed application, loyalty, self-control, self-sacrifice, and obedience to laws, among other virtues. Thus did medical, educational, psychological, and religious pundits expound the educational value of athletic competition and fertilize the sport cult.

Toward the end of the progressive era the educational value of play became so widely accepted by the schools and public that George E. Johnson, Pittsburgh superintendent of recreation and later teacher at Columbia and Harvard, could write in his book, *Education Through Recreation*, that it was now "universally admitted" that "the play interests of children and youth answer to deep seated needs and are essential for fullest development and education." Those play interests, including "great games" like baseball, Johnson explained, foreshadowed adult interests, and for "the physically sound American boy" never to have played baseball meant "losing an important element in his education." Then Johnson came to the crux of the matter as he saw it. For boys just to play ball in their own way was not enough. In a presage of what may be called the "organized boy," Johnson declared that "Boys should not only play baseball, . . . they should play on well-organized teams. Scrub baseball is not the real thing. A scrub team has scarcely half the social value of a regular team."

By then athletics and the old-line physical training had begun to merge in the schools. The New York PSAL, for instance, had found that gym work lacked the appeal of competitive athletics. Many schools had no gyms anyway and so could not easily conduct physical training. Besides, a surprising number of children were not required to take physical training. But the New York PSAL had an idea for a new kind of physical education designed to interest pupils. To induce as many as possible to compete in athletics, it conducted training in athletic skills—running, jumping, and chinning— offering medals, badges, or buttons to those who met certain simple standards. (I still have the bronze medal I won at Public School 92, Brooklyn, in the early twenties.) It also introduced into the physical education curriculum a new course for grammar school boys consisting of training in athletic skills that could be put to practice in team games—leadup games, as they were called, simpler than baseball and other sports but leading up to them— even though the physical director of the Minneapolis YMCA reported in a meeting that these leadup games were unpopular and "the boys want the real game." But the PSAL went ahead, dramatizing its new program in June 1913 when a mass of 10,000 New York school children put on an "exhibition of Physical Training and Applied Athletics" on the Central Park Playing Green. What would Olmsted have thought had he seen it?

Still, inclusion of athletics in the physical education curriculum of school came about only slowly. Until 1910 at Athens, Ohio, for example, a student athletic association still sponsored the high school teams and raised money for them any way it could; the faculty had no control over athletics. Nationwide, the general shortage of teachers competent in both physical training and sports retarded any change, although colleges had gradually begun to alter their physical education requirements in ways that would lead to preparation of teachers versed in athletics.*

School baseball and playground baseball were supplemented in the progressive era by private donors, such as factories, whose owners sometimes established playgrounds for children of workers, as at the Amoskeag Company, in Lawrence, Massachusetts, and the National Cash Register Company of Dayton, Ohio. The boys' work movement, engaged in by various private

*See Chapter 5.

agencies, along with the work of the settlement houses, the YMCAs, and such relative newcomers as the church, furnished boys' baseball, too.

In the first decade of progressivism's high tide, 1900–1910, the number of settlement houses quadrupled and their facilities and influence expanded. As their workers became professionalized they worked for more playgrounds, especially in the slums. West End House in New York, reported its sponsor Mary Simkhovich, cherished sports and featured baseball beginning with its first summer, 1906. Such organizations even established an intersettlement athletic league. Intersettlement baseball games "form a bond of union among clubs of the settlement," said an observer at a settlement in a Yiddish-speaking section of New York in 1904. In 1908 more than 10,000 boys participated in the various sports of the intersettlement league, and A.G. Spalding and Company published an Intersettlement Athletic Association Handbook claiming that in five years the settlement houses had "accomplished wonders."

After 1900 the YMCA, still growing, increased the number of its gyms, athletic fields, physical training programs, and athletic directors until by 1915 almost 500,000 participated in Y sports on 307 athletic fields. When the Reverend Dr. S. Edward Young preached before the Y baseball leagues in 1911 he declared that if St. Paul were preaching in America that summer he would attend baseball games and use the experience in his sermons, because baseball quickened the intellect, taught teamwork, and inspired honor. A 1901 writer describing the Y's physical program announced, "We are soldiers of Christ, strengthening our muscles, not against a foreign foe but against sin, within and without us."

A relatively new arrival to the world of boys' baseball during the progressive era was the church. Although some Sunday school teams and leagues had organized and played earlier, not until the flowering of the social gospel movement after 1900 among some Protestant clergymen did many churches pay much attention to sports as a means of improving the lives of the young. Until this awakening, many Protestant clergy, instead of emulating settlement house workers by going into the slums to live, fled them to tend middle- and upper-class flocks in greener pastures. But in harmony with the new social gospel's effort to reconcile Christian ethics with capitalism, in the 1900s a number of Protestant clergymen began offering sports as part of their social services. Even in tiny Chesham, New Hampshire, the Baptist Church in 1903 showed what the Keene *Sentinel* called "the growing liberal tendency in religion" when a Chesham Baptist minister was observed umpiring a baseball game.

One of the earliest clergymen to support sports was Thomas K. Beecher of the famed reformist Beecher family, who when he took up his pastorate at Elmira, New York, himself joined a baseball team. In the 1880s and 1890s with the development of the so-called institutional church, which sponsored physical culture, sports classes, children's clubs, and baseball received some impetus. St. George's Episcopal Church in New York and Berkeley Temple in Boston were among churches conducting baseball and other sports in that era.

The Roman Catholic Church lagged even farther behind, guided by Pius IX's anathemas against modernism and all its works in his 1864 encyclical, *Syllabus of Errors.* Only with Leo's *Rerum novarum* in 1891 did the Roman Church adopt a somewhat more liberal view, expanding its ministrations to the poor beyond charity and by implication putting its imprimatur on sports for youth. Perhaps reflecting this change, in Woonsocket, Rhode Island, in the nineties parish teams played regular baseball games, and the Brooklyn *Eagle* of July 1891 headlined a story, "St. Patrick beats St. Peter."

The steady rise in the popularity of sports moved both Protestant and Catholic to take them into account. Looking back on this era later, Pius XII commented frankly,

> With the beginning of the present century sport assumed such proportions, for the numbers of amateurs and professionals, for the crowds which gathered in the stadia, and for the interest aroused in it by means of the press, as to become one of the typical phenomena of modern society. The increased importance gave rise, in its turn, to new repercussions and problems in the field of education, of religious practice, of morality, and even in the social order, so that it could not be overlooked by the Church, always anxious to promote organizations corresponding to the needs of the time.

When the churches began a more wholehearted involvement in boys' sports, Catholics regarded them more as a wholesome diversion from naughtier pursuits, whereas Protestants sometimes employed them as bait, a tactic that resulted in the production of what might be called sport Christians: boys and young men who joined a Sunday school to obtain a baseball uniform and play on an organized team. In 1913 a religious education director found reason to condemn the "shameful trickery adopted by some workers in using a temporary or superficial play program as the means of baiting young people." But, gloated one Illinois pastor in 1912, "There is many a one who comes to play and remains to pray."

By the 1900s churches were building athletic fields, equipping teams, and finding coaches. Church athletic leagues formed in Chicago, Kansas City, and New York, as well as in smaller communities. In 1907 Baltimore was reportedly "ablaze" with Sunday school baseball. The boys' choir of a Medfield, Massachusetts, church, on a visit to the rich Boston heiress Mrs. Jack Gardner, at her home in Fenway Court, informed her that they wanted uniforms for their baseball team, and when she had them made they were "delighted."

Some church baseball teams formed leagues of their own denominations, such as the Protestant Church League and Diocesan Union League in New York; others joined interdenominational church leagues or even city leagues in which clubs representing religious groups mingled and competed with secular teams. In 1914 Chicago had a separate citywide organization of church baseball teams, the Church Athletic Association. Henry S. Curtis, author of *Play and Recreation for the Open Country*, observed that even many village pastors were serving as baseball managers.

A number of young men who later became professionals got their early baseball experience on church teams, somewhat as choir singers sometimes graduate to opera careers. Bucky Harris, a major-league player and manager, played for St. Peter's Lutheran Church in the Sunday School League of Pittston, Pennsylvania; Beans Reardon, a major-league umpire, played and umpired for St. Benedict's Church in Los Angeles; Ossie Bluege of the Washington Senators got his first uniform at age fifteen from St. Mark's Lutheran Church in Chicago; and New York Giants infielder Blondy Ryan played with the Altar Boys' Club of Lynn, Massachusetts, his first team. Big-leaguer Pepper Martin, who pitched for the Second Presbyterian Church in Oklahoma City, "got canned because I didn't go to Sunday school." An unlikely church star was Moe Berg, who became a major league catcher. Someone persuaded Berg, a Jew, to play for the Rose Methodist Church in Newark, where he starred in a game against the Presbyterians.

Summer camps, just coming into popularity as a means of working with boys, featured baseball, too. The city of Trenton sponsored them in 1908 and 1909 for 1,500 boys, reporting afterwards that juvenile crime was practically nil those summers. Marienfeld Camp at Silver Lake, New Hampshire, opening in 1899 as one of the first camps in the nation, had a baseball team. So did Camp Roosevelt, at Muskegon, Michigan, established by the Chicago Board of Education in the teens. On Lake Champlain the Catholic Summer School of America, where boys of ages 13 to 20 lived in tents, they devoted themselves to sport. There, Father Talbott Smith of the Summer School praised baseball as developing character values and "an instinct of solidarity." At one camp in 1911 baseball play was carefully organized into first and second teams, intermediate first and second teams, and a junior team, not to mention informal teams. The Educational Alliance, a self-help agency set up by New York Jews, sponsored camps for children from the lower East Side, and although the boys objected to helping remove rocks from the ball field because of what the writer believed to be traditional antipathy to manual labor, at least they got a chance to play ball. Even juvenile literature reflected the emergence of camp baseball with "Frank Merriwell's Summer Camp; Or, The Athletic School in the Woods," a story in *Tip Top Weekly*.

The boys' work movement operated in the 1900s through a variety of agencies, such as the Boys' Club of America, started in 1906 by Jacob Riis, along with older ones like the United Boys' Brigades of America (1893) and Children's Aid Society (1853). Members of the Boys' Club of New York City engaged in ball games. A representative of the Boys' Club of America boasted later that the organization's systematic training in sports had produced five major league baseball players. In describing how he lured boys to the Chicago Boys' Club, a 1907 writer, in a chapter baldly entitled "Bidding for the Boy," advised using baseball and other games as a "pretext," a way to "break the ice" and "get acquainted," in competing with commercial attractions for the interest of boys. National boys' clubs themselves became commercialized by such groups as the "Knights of the Holy Grail," which through its publication *The Young Knight* offered baseball equipment as premiums for getting subscribers and publicized its members who organized baseball teams. *Baseball Magazine* used the same device.

There was yet another facet to boys' baseball: a place for organized boys' teams to play in an organized way among adults. Many of the adult teams forming in these years all over the country joined forces to form municipal associations, and although dominated by the older groups these associations often included some boys' teams and leagues. Municipal authorities cooperated with these associations. Motivated by the logic of making functional the diamonds and facilities they had constructed, the appropriate city departments began to furnish varying degrees of service and supervision, frequently including provision for boys' or "junior" teams.

Private sponsors joined in. In San Francisco in 1908 when the *Examiner* started a competition for boys, 75 independent teams applied, and a permanent league formed with backing from leading citizens and business houses. In 1914 the St. Louis Municipal Baseball Association organized two divisions, one for those under 18 and another for those older. In 1916 the association increased from 68 to 115 teams, and in 1917 the St. Louis city champions planned to compete against municipal players in other cities. In Trenton, New Jersey, the city council appropriated money for baseball competition among boys from 8 to 16, and one July day nearly 150 uniformed teams, 1,500 boys, marched in a parade.

Notwithstanding this continuing trend toward regimentation, uncounted numbers of independent boys' teams, long- and short-lived, uniformed or tatterdemalion, still vied for city diamonds or scrounged for sandlots. Boys continued to play scrub games as the spirit moved them wherever they could find space and to form their own teams, arrange their own games, and even raise money for uniforms, largely oblivious of the "benefits" and "values" adults attributed to play and unaware that private and public agencies, gradually making boys' baseball their province, had started it on a journey from which there was to be no return. "Play specialists" spoke of the value of "directed play," "organized play," "supervised play," and of "using play as an educational force." A few, however, began to lament the passing of "free play." A religious writer in 1912 thought "undirected play" superior in that it developed initiative, imagination, and resourcefulness. G. Stanley Hall mused that directing a child's play made it a form of work. Another writer commented in 1909 that "Games constantly accompanied by a teacher make play a parody." An eleven-year-old boy on a Worcester playground expressed most directly of all a child's disdain for the efforts of adults in teaching boys how to play: "with so many men and women around telling you what to do," he said irritably, "they get on me nerves."

FROM SANDLOT TO MUNICIPAL DIAMOND

From the conclusion of the Great War to the resumption of war in scarcely more than twenty years, the dominant feature of boys' baseball was its further expropriation by adults. Whether in the prosperous twenties or the depressed thirties, the drift toward organization and adult direction gathered force.

In the first of these two decades the trend coincided with unprecedented popular pursuit of sports by adults. For the first time in America, asserted social scientist Jesse F. Steiner, play "took its place alongside work and was recognized as one of the major interests of life." In the same vein Professor Preston W. Slosson wrote that "Next to the sport of business the American enjoyed the business of sport." Even the somnolent Calvin Coolidge took enough notice to call a National Conference on Outdoor Recreation in 1924.

The postwar years proved propitious for sports. Urban population surpassed rural for the first time, and still-growing cities and towns increased the need for participant sports as well as the market for spectator goods. The belief that sports participation benefited people, especially the health and morals of children, and made them good citizens enjoyed wide acceptance. Promoters of professional sport and organizers of amateur groups also played a part, as did plentiful newspaper and radio publicity.

Undoubtedly, these and other elements would have assured a continued but gradual rise in the popularity of sports in the years to come, but of themselves they would not have triggered the overnight boom in sports that occurred. The more immediate explanation of the approbation for sports, as Professor Guy M. Lewis demonstrated, lies primarily in the federal government's massive sports program of World War I, which in his words provided the "catalyst for the sudden burst of popular interest in sports" after the war and, one might add, for its effect on boys' baseball. The War and Navy Departments had used sports lavishly during the conflict,* and afterward sports gained more adherents as millions of men, thousands of

*See Chapter 21.

whom had received their sports baptism in uniform, carried the sports message home in their kit bags. In the twenties, government officials, influential community leaders, and the private agencies that had marshalled the recreational resources of some 600 war camp communities under the aegis of the Playground Association's War Camp Community Service urged that wartime gains in sports and recreation be preserved and extended to additional cities in peacetime. Public opinion favored this proposal, so as the training camps closed, Community Service, Incorporated, a national organization, replaced the War Camp Community Service.

Community Service encouraged communities to carry on those sports and recreation programs established in wartime and helped other communities start them. Local governments stood the cost of buildings (often designated as war memorials), equipment, and management; then, as each program, such as a boys' baseball program, became viable, local agencies took over and Community Service withdrew. By 1920, about 450 communities had established recreation programs for people of all ages, many of these programs consisting primarily of sports for children and adults.

This scheme launched sports and recreation into unprecedented growth in the twenties, a growth nourished by the heightened realization that in the city, where home and neighborhood had lost much of their former roles in recreation, leisure had become commercialized, and play often turned into crime. The concept of sports for all, not just for the young or the privileged, took hold in the conviction that the community had a responsibility to provide recreation for those without the means of doing so on their own. So in this era when the Playground Association published its annual figures on the thousands of playgrounds established all over the nation, those figures referred not just to playgrounds for children but to playgrounds for everyone. As the national game, baseball received a large share of this playground space.

A graph of the expenditures for organized community recreation, meaning mostly sports, from the end of the war to the depression would show a constantly rising curve. The 1924 outlay alone amounted to twenty times as much as it had back in 1907. A report of the Department of Commerce that year revealed that 250 cities of 30,000 or more spent almost 136 million dollars on all types of recreation, including playgrounds. City departments of recreation multiplied as one state after another authorized local governments to create playgrounds. The budget of the Playground Association in 1930 amounted to about 240 times what it had expended in its first year. Numbers of full-time, part-time, and summer recreation leaders, paid and volunteer, also rose: there were nearly 16,000 of them in 1924 and 25,000 in 1930. Many leaders came from the YMCA college at Springfield and from a school established in Chicago by the Playground Association. Urged continually by the association to accept financial and administrative responsibility for recreation, cities conducted formal surveys of their facilities and in the resulting reports recommended improvements.

The association told cities how to lay out their playgrounds: fields for those over 15 should measure at least 10 and preferably 24 acres, with space for baseball and other active sports, and one of these grounds was needed for every 8,000 to 12,000 people or for every 500 high school age youngsters. Playgrounds should also be located no farther than three blocks from children's homes, said these authorities. By 1924, 460 cities already counted more than 2,500 baseball fields, and by 1930, 510 cities had more than 4,300 municipally controlled diamonds.

As cities encroached relentlessly on old parks and built new ones in their hunt for playing fields, the Olmsted vision of the park as a serene public environment for rest and contemplation practically disappeared. Many cities sacrificed some of their scenic park perfection to make way for playgrounds, although New York police sometimes confiscated baseball bats when boys played in restricted spaces. In Chicago's West Side Parks, however, a judge ordered rules against playing ball on the grass interpreted less strictly, for, he said, "It is either the grass or humanity."

All the while, empty lots continued to vanish inexorably as streets became paved and rendered unsafe for youngsters under the growing tyranny of the automobile. Nevertheless, the increase in ball fields furnished some relief. A number of boys who became professionals, such as Ted Williams and Jack Burns, began their baseball careers on public playgrounds. Burns spent his boyhood hanging around his local Cambridge, Massachusetts, playground, where he joined a "sub-junior" team at age ten. Later he said, "I am actually a product of the public playground system." More important, the public playground supplied many boys with a green island of baseball in an urban sea of concrete and asphalt.

The great depression propelled government—federal, state, and municipal—into recreation and sports on a scale unforeseen by the most ardent reformers of the progressive era. Millions thrown out of work or reduced to part-time employment had thrust upon them the leisure time they lacked the means of using, except perhaps for an occasional splurge on a ten-cent ticket to a double feature movie. With a commendable regard for the spiritual as well as the material needs of citizens, the New Deal appropriated funds not only for artists and writers but for recreation and play. Thus it sought both to provide jobs and to maintain morale.

As the depression worsened a sharp rise in the use of playgrounds, athletic fields, and baseball diamonds in 1931 over the previous year's record indicated that people found in them a temporary release from their cares. And when Franklin D. Roosevelt took office and the severity of the depression compelled drastic remedies, the government did not neglect recreation in its diversified plans for relief. By 1937 the Works Progress Administration

(WPA) had spent a half billion dollars, about ten percent of its total expenditures, on new parks and recreation. Before it finished the New Deal invested more than a billion and a half dollars on recreation, about half of that in sports.

The government's program naturally included construction of baseball diamonds. Federal funds filled the gap left when capital expenditures in cities fell off sharply. By 1937 the WPA and other government agencies had built 3,600 baseball and 8,800 softball fields. The federal government paid most of the bill between 1935 and 1941 for the construction of nearly 6,000 athletic fields and the renovation of almost 12,000 others. Chicago's recreation survey showed that the city's 4,000 baseball fields in 1937 included 156 tax-supported diamonds. These gains provided space for both adults and children.

The federal funds affected communities differently. Some never had a public recreation official until the national agencies moved in, and a number of citizens questioned whether public funds should be used to "teach people to play," but in other parts of the country it proved impossible to keep pace with demands for this kind of aid. In Manhattan, Kansas, the WPA built a fine public baseball park to house the local team of the Ban Johnson League, a three-state organization of 1,000 youngsters under age twenty-one. With an eye to the sale of equipment, Julian Curtiss, chairman of A.G. Spalding and Company and head of the playground committee of the Athletic Goods Manufacturers Association, urged all communities with a park director to apply for federal funds as a "chance that is offered to give boys and girls health and recreation."

During the depression a number of cities paid special attention to baseball-minded youngsters by conducting baseball "schools" for them. In a typical program of this kind, one city's recreation department offered 4,000 children indoor sessions weekly in four social centers plus eight weeks of outdoor training, conducted by residents and big-league players. Santa Monica sponsored a daily summer baseball school with Arnold "Jigger" Statz and Jimmy Reese, then Pacific Coast League stars, as instructors. Milwaukee, Houston, and Spokane were among cities conducting such baseball schools, and Louisville held sixteen separate ones in 1936. During 1937–38 the WPA ran a school at Sherman Park, St. Louis, with Cardinal players Terry Moore and Enos Slaughter as teachers, and among the boys who attended, future major-league catchers Yogi Berra and Joe Garagiola appeared. Under WPA auspices in Connecticut "Big Ed" Walsh, a former star pitcher, conducted a baseball school that over four months treated 70,000 boys to talks on baseball, sportsmanship, and good health habits.

As intended, these sports and recreation projects provided jobs for a small army of adults, many of whom knew little or nothing about supervising a playground. Some cities used WPA or NRA (National Recovery Act) money to hire jobless persons as play leaders, although in the case of some former white collar workers, they often felt that the job caused them to lose respect among their former peers. Some former professional ball players, a few of them ex-major leaguers, became playground instructors, too, and the question arose as to whether these men knew how to work with boys. An authority on boys' work, Walter L. Stone, deplored the widespread practice of hiring "good fellows" and star athletes instead of trained workers for such duties. But special classes made it possible for many to train while on the job, and by 1933 the number of trained leaders exceeded 43,000. These adults, trained or not, represented a further extension of organization and adult supervision of youngsters.

Another New Deal agency, the Civilian Conservation Corps, also provided opportunities for boys of high school age to play baseball, and out of a total of about two and a half million youths who joined the CCC, many thousands played ball. A *Guide to the CCC* published in 1936 urged the "red-blooded enrollee" to play "for fun and for finding friends," as well as for learning "teamwork, fair play, [and] sportsmanship." The camps were reportedly "sports crazy" and soon became hunting grounds for big-league scouts, who signed a number of players for trials with professional clubs. Two of my own players, Bill Durkin and Sonny Selmer, joined the CCC one fall, returning bigger and stronger in time to play on one of my teams the following spring.

Sometimes baseball at CCC camps suffered delay when equipment failed to arrive until winter, or when bats became available and no baseballs could be found, as some Cleveland boys reported later. But the boys at a Bear Mountain camp in the northern Adirondacks found two complete "baseball sets" among recreation items furnished them by the United States Army. Players at CCC camps in Pineville, West Virginia, at Hayward, Wisconsin, at Tupper Lake, New York, and at Salem, Virginia played baseball against local town and village teams. A camp at Cresco, Iowa, even entered a state tournament in which twenty-one other CCC camps competed. Some camp administrators gave winning teams prizes purchased with profits from canteens. And in 1939 the CCC's publication, *Happy Days*, selected an all-American honor team of fifty star CCC ball players and tried to get them jobs in major, minor, and semipro leagues.

More palliative than curative though they were, the increased expenditures of local governments and the large sums pumped into communities by the New Deal for playgrounds changed the character of boys' baseball; for as their sandlots were eaten up many boys turned to municipal, "muny," or "park" ball, as it came to be called. Boys in increased numbers went to the city-run playgrounds for a place to play ball, and in 1926 the National Amateur Athletic Federation, a collection of nationally organized agencies interested in sports, found that muny ball was actually supplanting sandlot ball.

With more ball fields and players than ever to look after, city authorities took a direct hand in baseball organizations. They recognized and in some instances organized and supervised separate muny leagues not only for adults but also for boys of different ages. Cleveland, Buffalo, Pittsburgh, Detroit, St. Paul, Indianapolis, Washington, D.C., and Portland, Oregon all had comprehensive organizations of this type. In the thirties many associations began to line up on a statewide basis and by 1932 topped off the trend with a Municipal Baseball Association of America.

Although gallimaufries of leagues had always characterized muny ball, after World War I cities made greater provision for boys' leagues. In Cincinnati, for example, boys of 15 were at first the youngest amateurs in muny ball, but when the city's Community Service learned that 12- and 13-year-olds were having trouble scheduling games because they came from tough neighborhoods, the Service arranged tournaments for them, enlisted the support of local newspapers and the help of old-time players as umpires, and established rules for competition and eligibility. Children from all parts of the city responded, some even using the birth certificates of younger brothers to gain entrance. That year (1922) 240 teams competed on six diamonds, and so constant was the interest that the Service renewed the program annually. By 1931 the number of boys' teams entering Cincinnati's annual tournaments had reached 107.

Other cities operated similar programs for boys in the twenties. Community Service in Boston embarked on its boys' baseball league in 1926 on learning that big boys often kept smaller ones from playing ball. In Greenville, South Carolina, local daily papers published scores of the city's juvenile pennant season, and in St. Paul, the *Pioneer Press and Dispatch* presented prizes to the champion boys' team. At Allentown, Pennsylvania, reported the Allentown *Record*, youngsters of the city's Junior Division "fought with the friendly rivalry that will teach them the lessons of life."

Johnstown, Pennsylvania, ran an elaborate city recreation program that included boys as part of its six-league baseball setup playing on municipal diamonds. The Minneapolis baseball program of 25 divisions included boys aged 12 and older. In Oakland, California, 75 teams of boys under 16 played muny ball in 1935.

Although muny ball and recreation generally lagged in the South, one of the most complete baseball programs for boys operated in Columbus, Georgia, where in the mid-twenties the city's recreation department organized four leagues, six teams for high school age boys, four for "smaller" boys, and eight in a "Ne-Hi" league for "little fellers."

With the flowering of muny ball a clearer pattern of its operation emerged. A check of 20 representative cities disclosed a tendency for those with fewer than 100,000 people to organize both boys and adults but for larger cities to organize only the boys, even paying umpires, while leaving adult baseball for private groups to handle. Cities usually provided the fields, which included a backstop, regulation bases, home plate, and foul lines. More than half those responding to the survey reported skinned or semi-skinned infields. Most cities furnished about one diamond for every 15,000 persons. Many offered seating, ranging from park benches to regular bleachers, and most supplied dressing rooms, toilets, and showers. Cities had learned that players and fans no longer felt satisfied with poorly maintained sites, old sacks for bases, and fields without places to change into uniforms.

The Cleveland Baseball Federation, an agency completely independent of the city, provided free medical attention for all players from age 12 to 36. The Federation hired a physician to care for injured players and provided hospital treatment for serious cases. William T. Duggan, later president of the National Amateur Baseball Federation, conceived the Cleveland medical plan as a result of an accident he had himself sustained as a youngster in a game in Chicago when he was hit on the shinbone by a ball but paid no attention to the injury, until after five years of neglect the bone had to be scraped and two tumors removed, at heavy expense to his parents. Even more comprehensive medical plans came into use in the thirties, notably those in San Francisco and Oakland, and the local Pacific Coast League teams played an annual game to raise funds for the scheme. Medical provision removed parental objections and made team sponsors easier to find.

Supervision of a city's muny ball facilities rested in the person who took up the permits issued at a central office and assigned dressing rooms and diamonds, taking care of league games first and independent or nonleague games after. Services and facilities ordinarily entailed no charge, although at the Brooklyn Parade Grounds teams that wished to could rent regular canvas bases for fifty cents a game. Money for equipment, uniforms, and other expenses was raised in a variety of ways. In Buffalo, sponsors gave the boys caps and sweat shirts only. Detroit's muny ball commissioners solved the problem of supplying uniforms to newsboys by letting local clothing shops provide them. The Cleveland Federation raised money by holding "amateur days" that charged admission and once staged a boxing show that brought in $10,000.00. A New York Baseball Federation dinner realized the same amount. New York's group, a voluntary organization formed in 1933 and supported by Governor Herbert Lehman, former Governor Al Smith, and some local big-league executives, provided baseball for boys, especially the poorer ones of the city.

Occasionally a major-league club would lend a muny organization its park for a benefit game played behind closed gates. The Cleveland Club began doing so in 1925 with "Boys Day," originated by Ban Johnson, president of the American League, and more than 12,000 boys under fifteen turned out as guests of the club to see two boys' teams play before the regular game started. In Boston Bob Quinn of the Red Sox served as honorary president of the Park Department's Amateur Baseball League, and its chairman wrote in 1935 thanking him for having "put the Park Department League on the map."

Demand for permits to play on public diamonds far exceeded the supply, and many applications had to be denied. When I first applied to the Park Department for a season permit for my team to play Sundays on the Brooklyn Parade Grounds, all I received was a couple of two-hour permits for two Sundays out of the entire summer. But political "pull," no stranger in Organized Baseball circles, also counted in muny ball. One of my players, Bill Kuhlke, told me that his grandmother belonged to the local Democratic Club and would "talk to Hesterberg," the district leader; thereafter, John O'Brien, the man in charge of the Parade Grounds, supplied my team with a dressing room and regular permits, usually two every Sunday, for morning and afternoon games. Who said playing baseball did not teach citizenship? Then, as my ball clubs became established as regular, uniformed teams attracting crowds, often as many as 3,000 people, they also received more chances to play on one of the best diamonds, Number 1 or Number 21, located nearest the clubhouse, set off more from the others, somewhat better maintained, and equipped with stands. The Brooklyn *Times Union* reporter watched our games and published the box scores.

Other cities found equal demand for diamonds. The Chicago Recreation Survey of 1937 concluded that the number of baseball teams "still overtaxes all facilities." In Pittsburgh so many boys were being forced off corner lots that city officials in 1932 laid out ball fields in the city's two large parks.

As muny ball waxed and sandlot ball waned, the voice of the bureaucrat sounded across the diamond. Said John C. Henderson, an Oregon Community Services director: "better results, more evenly balanced competition, and a more efficient use of fields are obtained by requiring all teams to organize into leagues and eliminating the independent team." This policy, he allowed, should not prevent "games at picnics or scrub games." Henderson's prescription would eventually be filled beyond his highest expectation, for where once boys played when they wanted, where they wanted, the way they wanted, for as long as they wanted on scattered fields, relying almost completely on their own resources, with little or no adult intrusion or help, in muny ball their play was "assigned on a schedule basis" by adults to "accommodate a maximum number of games" (as though baseball, of all games, could be governed by a clock) and bunched on diamonds laid out close together to the point of hazard.

Of course, whenever adults took a hand in boys' baseball, they maintained that playing the game ingeminated certain "values." The rationale for junior muny ball expounded by Charles J. Birt, in charge of municipal athletics in Cincinnati in the twenties, hewed close to the orthodox line. He declared that baseball benefits not "merely from a physical point of view" but through junior tournaments it also provided "training in discipline [and] the opportunity to develop the spirit of cooperation, loyalty, and fairness." As evidence, Birt related how in Cincinnati before the games the umpire and tournament director lectured the boys on "the fundamentals of fair play" and "how athletes should conduct themselves." Birt claimed that this reminder played a large part in the boys' "splendid behavior": only one fight occurred in three years. On close plays that would have brought "hot arguments" among professionals, he said, the boys stayed in their positions on the field or bench while the captain "consulted" the umpire—proof of "splendid training in self control and recognition of authority"—and, I might add, indication that they were a docile lot compared with my players and their opponents. Earnest to uphold the traditional amateur code, Birt declared that supervisors should stress the "honor and joy" that goes with playing the game rather than the awards. He cautioned against the effect of commercialization on "easily spoiled" boys, advising that prizes volunteered by merchants be declined and that only gold medals be awarded. At the Parade Grounds, however, John O'Brien spouted none of this verbiage. He merely watched the games from his office in the clubhouse.

Awards and trophies continued to be presented to muny players, however. Joe Cronin's exploits on San Francisco's playgrounds in the twenties entitled him to receive an "athletic diploma" at city hall one day at 2:00 P.M. He arrived breathless at 11:00 A.M. and waited nervously until two, when he heard the preliminary oration in a daze, mumbled incoherent thanks, and ran home as fast as he could: "I was the happiest and most excited boy in the nation." As for whether organized baseball or other athletic games really develop "character" (honesty, obedience, citizenship), attempts at experiments in the twenties and thirties showed only equivocal results.

The hammer strokes of World War I also left their impress upon scholastic baseball. Fear that the federal government might impose compulsory physical or even military training on the schools and public shock over figures showing thirty-five percent of draftees unfit brought the long-debated issue of athletics in school curriculums to high pitch. The United States Commissioner of Education convened representatives of various agencies to deal with the poor physical condition of youth, with the result that a campaign started to require physical education in the schools. Opinion on ways to go about making youth physically fit was divided. Some leaders favored more calisthenics and others military drill, but those who wanted sports won out, largely because of the support of Secretary of War Newton D. Baker, the former Cleveland progressive. The Playground Association led the drive for state physical education laws, supplied financial aid, and worked for new physical education curriculums that stressed sports.

But placing laws on the books—and seventeen more states did between 1919 and 1921—proved easier than putting enough coaches in the schools. Still faced with a severe shortage of teachers capable of conducting athletics, the schools were frequently reduced to recruiting college graduates and others versed in sports but inadequately trained in teaching. Consequently, physical education programs tilted further toward sports, to the advantage of baseball, still the leading scholastic game, particularly in New England.

During the twenties the sports camel worked practically all the way into the public education tent. Many drivers guided and encouraged it. One was the National Amateur Athletic Federation (NAAF), an association produced by a meeting, called by the War and Navy Departments in 1922, of almost twenty national organizations ranging from the Boy Scouts and the Y to the National Education Association. Although short-lived, the NAAF effectively promoted sports by means of "educational" campaigns and by studies of amateur athletics, including baseball. Another camel driver, the National Committee on Physical Education, with financial backing from the Recreation Association, dispatched field representatives into the schools to win over lukewarm physical training teachers and to persuade school officials to incorporate sport into the curriculum. "The American system of physical education," pronounced Professor Elmer Mitchell of the University of Michigan, "must be built around games." In truth, the camel by then needed no great assistance, enticed as it was by the scent of "progressive," extraintellectual, and so-called social engineering aspects of education that pervaded the tent's interior and by the example of the worshipful welcome accorded his older brother in the tent of higher education.

As gymnastics and calisthenics paled before the popularity of interscholastic competition, administrators strove to control sports by placing physical education directors instead of student athletic associations in charge of them, and once sports became firmly ensconced, physical education teachers rationalized the fait accompli by finding them educationally beneficial. The NEA's utilitarian "Cardinal Principles of Education" began not with learning but with "health" and never mentioned intellectual development, and because the sixth principle was "worthy use of leisure," physical training specialists could claim sports educational.

Sports instruction became part of the preparation of physical training teachers, and coaches received faculty status. In the upshot, the schools, reflecting society as they usually do, mirrored the sports-oriented twenties while at the same time contributing to the sports boom. By the end of the decade all but two states required physical education, and by the time sports merged with physical training and hygiene into a broader program of physical education, such programs consisted almost entirely of sports instruction. The "baseball throw," for example, became part of many physical education tests.

Competitive high school athletics were the most palpable part of scholastic sports programs. By the mid-twenties no fewer than 45 states had established athletic organizations of some kind to deal with interscholastic competition. A national organization of high school athletic associations formed in 1922 as varsity teams in public, parochial, and private high schools multiplied and vied for league, city, and even intercity championships. By 1925 it had spread to every state. In an intercity high school championship a boy named Lou Gehrig attracted wide attention by winning a game for New York against Chicago with a home run driven out of Wrigley Field.

The New York *Times* reported that baseball thrived in the schools, and the NAAF estimated that sixty percent of all schools participated in inter-scholastic baseball. "The trend," advised a White House conference on health in 1930, "is away from formal gymnastics to the more natural activ-ities," and it recommended games as part of daily physical education classes. By then public schools enrolled more than 25 million, or about 42 percent more than in 1910, with most of the rise in the high schools, where the gain over the twenty years was 400 percent, and nearly every school had a uni-formed baseball team.

At Keene High School, Keene, New Hampshire, the varsity team played three games a week in 1924 under coach Ronald Darby, who used road work and calisthenics as well as hitting and bunting practice to build physical ability and "fighting spirit." Darby "explained the psychology of baseball and impressed on the fellows," said *Salmagundi*, the school yearbook, "that more than just ability was needed to win games." The varsity played ball in the Connecticut Valley League with other nearby towns and in 1936, not slowed by the depression, won the state championship with a record of 14–2.

Large high schools attracted far more candidates than varsity and junior varsity squads could use. The crowd that reported to the big new gym at my high school, Brooklyn's Erasmus Hall, in the late twenties could have filled a whole league with teams, and the weeding out process began im-mediately. Infield candidates were directed to line up at one end of the gym and take turns fielding grounders and throwing across to first base, where about ten of us, including a "veteran" of the previous season, were trying out. After I finished catching my share of the allotted throws the coach, Max Croohe, a physical training instructor, asked what year I was in, but when I told him "freshman," he said, "Go out for J.V."

Junior varsity candidates, at Croohe's direction, assembled at Wingate Field the morning of the first day of Easter vacation and busied themselves aimlessly with bats and balls. Not until noon did Croohe saunter onto the field and, after a few minutes of looking us over, tell us in effect, "Nice work, boys; report the same time tomorrow." This farce was repeated the next day, so I stopped coming and soon changed schools.

But at Alexander Hamilton High the baseball competition proved at least as keen. Even before the call for candidates went out we knew that some positions were almost certainly taken by boys who had played the previous season. Nearly a hundred tried out for infield alone—a very considerable number, even after discounting those who, as we used to say, "couldn't stop a pig coming down a gangway." The coach stationed us around the infield in four groups according to the position we were trying for, and each in turn had three ground balls batted to him; those who failed to field all three were eliminated right away. To attract more notice in the crowd and to indicate having had some experience I had rushed home beforehand to don the cap and shirt of the "outside" team I played on.

When those of us who survived the Alexander Hamilton fielding trials underwent batting practice a couple of days later, casualties among us mounted sharply. The handful still in the running after that did not know whether we had made the team until some of us were told to report for the trip to Long Island on the morning of the opening game with Jamaica High. Even then one could not count on actually playing until the coach announced the starting lineup, where I was listed as batting fifth—a thrill tempered by the prospect of facing pitcher Roy Alpert, who was said to have had a trial with the Yankees. In the game I proved satisfactory at my position, for I continued to play during succeeding seasons.

New York City's PSAL continued to epitomize scholastic competition in the twenties. By 1927 it listed 27 high schools in three divisions competing for the city championship. The evening high schools also supported athletic teams, playing twilight ball between six and eight P.M. during Daylight Saving Time. By then the PSAL still possessed only six playing fields, although some of them had more than one baseball diamond. Six smaller fields next to school buildings supplemented the big ones, and as new high schools opened, like James Madison and Samuel J. Tilden in Brooklyn, they generally had their own adjacent fields. Neighborhood boys could avail themselves of these fields when not in use by the schools, as Hank Greenberg, the major-league star of the thirties, did. As a boy he often ran over to the PSAL field, Crotona Park, near his home in the Bronx to get into pickup games with other youngsters.

As scholastic sports became highly organized, problems arose, particularly in the larger school systems. The fact that some teams began to charge admission necessitated working out a formula for sharing receipts that took into account the cost of travel, printing tickets, and payment of umpires as well as income at the gate. Harvard's William A. Geer in 1924 expressed disapproval of the high school state and national championship "mania" because of absences from class, expense of travel, overstrenuous schedules, and undue showering of honors by townspeople. In 1923 an article in *School Review* reported that some athletes attended high schools "for years" and only for sport. "They are never ineligible, . . . shifting from school to school in order to conform to the letter of the rules." In the late twenties the New York City Board of Education decided feebly that post-season intercity contests should be "discouraged." Even rules banning "professionals" became necessary. As publicity for interscholastic sports swelled—some games were actually broadcast—business firms attempted to trade on their popularity. "High school teams must cease to be town teams to bring glory upon the Chamber of Commerce and an ad for the town," remarked James E. Rogers, Director of the National Physical Education Service, an NEA department. New York finally barred schools from accepting trophies that private organizations tendered. A.G. Spalding and Company still held a favored position, though. Its trophy remained the only one that New York high school champions received permission to accept, and the American Rifle Association and various gun and ammunition companies were allowed to continue with what PSAL leaders called "generous" contributions.

To counteract what some began to look upon as the over-organization of interscholastic baseball, Professor Frederick R. Rogers of Boston University proposed a plan to partly restore the high school game to the players. Hailed by John Dewey as "the greatest advance step yet taken" in schoolboy athletics, the Player Control plan devised by Rogers called for the boys to assume responsibility for directing the games after they had begun. Although the coach could "instruct" during practice, once the game started he must sit in the stands and leave the captain in charge. Coaches in general condemned the plan, but it lasted for a few years throughout New York state and in some other cities, although with little success. What sounded appealing to some on paper failed in practice. The coach of my high school, for example, chose three of us to run the games. After consultation with the other two, the ceremonial captain was supposed to decide on the play to be tried, and one of us would then give the necessary sign—an impossible arrangement to begin with. Ball games cannot be run by committee. To make matters worse, our captain proved over-cautious, reluctant to take any risk for fear of making a mistake, so one of the two "advisors," losing patience, would give the sign himself. For example, one of us standing up meant the "steal" sign was on, so when I thought a runner should try to steal I just stood up. To remedy the situation, the coach finally decided that he himself would give us the signs from his seat in the stands, and we would then merely relay them to the players. Thus our lesson in how to play according to the rules of Player Control.

The school directors of the Junior Baseball League of Shreveport, Louisiana, attempted another witless scheme: to score games according to something other than the actual results of play—50 percent for sportsmanship, 25 percent for reliability, and 25 percent for the winning runs! Similar attempts to award season championship trophies in Detroit and in Reading, Pennsylvania, on the basis of "sportsmanship" rather than scores drew criticism by Theodore Gross, superintendent of playgrounds in Chicago, who said it simply could not be done and merely penalized the winning team. "Character cannot be developed by legislation," he added.

As for playing instruction on the part of high school coaches, at the risk of sweeping generalization I will say that scarcely any was forthcoming. To coach baseball well is not simple, and coaches rarely possessed the competence to do it. They lacked knowledge of the techniques of playing the different positions on a ball team, as well as batting, pitching, and team play, to say nothing of team strategy or even proper sliding, so important in reducing the risk of injury. To be sure, a great many fellows who later became professionals, such as Jimmy Foxx, Chuck Klein, Lefty Gomez, Wally Berger, Dizzy Dean, Joe Bowman, and Charlie Devens, had played high school or prep school ball, but it is safe to say that most of these players were not really products of school baseball. No doubt high school competition helped them, but it merely supplemented experience on the sandlot and outside teams through which a boy with baseball potential usually developed his skill in those days.

Elementary schools, too, conducted interscholastic competition. In New York, for example, sixty-eight elementary schools competed in its 1926 baseball tournament. Competition at the elementary level occurred on a lesser scale, however. Uniforms and equipment cost too much for most school budgets, and coaches of any kind were difficult to secure, particularly since most of the teachers were women, who seldom had a baseball background. In my grade school in Brooklyn, P.S. 92, the administration and all of the teachers were members of the fair sex, some of them charter members. Miss Zabriskie, who taught seventh grade and remained popular with the boys despite her rooting (or pretending to root) for the hated New York Giants, handled the team one spring until the administration found a man with some baseball experience to take charge. Besides, not all teachers approved of playing baseball during school hours. The virago who taught an eighth grade class in our school became so annoyed when the principal's monitor came in with a list of boys to be excused early for baseball that before complying she gave me (the only one in her class on the list) an angry reprimand about the foolishness of putting baseball before school work. It would not be long before other instructors would begin objecting, and rightly so, to organized competitive sports for elementary school children, not because they were taking pupils out of classes but because they were inappropriate for young children.

The effect of the depression on school baseball varied from system to system. Some schools were hard hit, but high schools fared better than elementary. The New York PSAL still held city and intercity championships, although not every school operated a team. Large crowds turned out for games of those that did. An estimated 25,000 came to a contest at Ebbets Field for the city high school championship staged through the cooperation of the city, the *World-Telegram,* and the Brooklyn Baseball Club, which donated the use of its park. In Chicago the high schools, both public and private, played complete league schedules.

Most of the regular interscholastic games of the thirties took place on school properties. Seventeen of Chicago's public diamonds lay on school grounds, thirteen on other fields set aside for interscholastic competition. Some of New York's 168 diamonds were located on school property, too. Otherwise, pupils in these cities played school games in the public parks or in commercially owned stadiums. Chicago, for example, could use eight enclosed fields for a nominal rental, $15.00 minimum, or twenty percent of the gate. Even in such comparatively small cities of the West and the South as Memphis, San Antonio (which had its own stadium), and Columbia, South

Carolina, schools fielded teams in the thirties. Ted Williams claimed that his first "strong baseball influence" was that of his San Diego high school coach, who used a switch to encourage the players to run faster!

On the other hand, the depression forced some schools to forego baseball. A Dallas editor reported in 1934 that schools there featured football, golf, tennis, and other sports, and had practically dropped baseball. The results of an investigation in 1935 claimed to show that boys preferred basketball and football over baseball. Even in Chicago, where for a time teachers were paid in scrip, some schools came close to discontinuing the game for lack of funds or equipment. A *Sporting News* editorial in 1936 blamed the decline in participation on high school athletic directors, who were often football men uninterested in baseball, as well as on the indifference of Organized Baseball. At the 1933 New York Baseball Writers dinner Branch Rickey of the St. Louis Cardinals, with enlightened self-interest, scored the major leagues for their lack of interest in amateur baseball: "Above all, we should use our influence to prevent baseball from being abandoned because of the depression by high school, college, and semipro teams." Far from abandoning high schools, by 1940 Organized Baseball was actively recruiting from them. When the Wisconsin Interstate Athletic Association appealed to Judge Kenesaw M. Landis, Organized Baseball's commissioner, to have major league clubs stop approaching high school boys to sign with them, Landis demurred:

> Baseball is justified in dipping as low as high schools for talent—but only when a boy is confronted by the necessity of making a living for himself or under the obligation of helping to support his family. Why should baseball be closed to him when other livelihoods are open?"

The most obvious need of school teams in the depression was equipment. A baseball coach at Grand Rapids, Michigan, wrote that the equipment cost too much for "the slender financial set-up under which the schools must operate. It is because of the expense of maintaining a team that many high schools have passed up the game." The previous year, he said, the Detroit Tigers had sent him two dozen balls and the Chicago Cubs a dozen, but in asking clubs for used balls this spring he received only one reply, from a minor-league team offering to sell them for a quarter apiece. A few other major league clubs made some effort to help high school teams. At a Memphis prep school where Bill Terry, Jr., son of the New York Giants' manager, captained the team, the club used discarded Giant uniforms donated by his father. The high schools of Los Angeles were the beneficiaries of an exhibition game played in 1934 between the Cubs and their Los Angeles farm teams during spring training. In Detroit the Tigers gave local high schools equipment that made possible the continuation of baseball there.

After the worst of the depression passed, high school baseball showed signs of picking up. Lou Fonseca, former major leaguer who carried on public relations work for the American League, while showing a publicity film at schools and colleges saw evidence of revival by mid-decade. During film showings at two Chicago schools, students contributed dimes to help prevent baseball's being dropped.

Haverstraw, New York, self-styled as "the most baseball-minded spot in the United States," presented an instance of strong interest in scholastic ball and the ease with which abuses could creep into it. In 1935 when school authorities ordered the high school team to disband, more than 700 townsfolk signed a petition to restore school baseball, and more than half the pupils went on strike. The superintendent explained that the action had been taken because the athletic director, instead of devoting his time to the student body as a whole, spent most of it on the baseball team, which he used as a "feeder" for the local professional nine.

In the elementary school interscholastic competition shriveled during the thirties, although probably not solely on account of the depression. Most likely, want of funds nudged matters along, but the main reason lay elsewhere. Hints of a coming change in the attitude of school people toward sports for young children appeared toward the end of the twenties in the schools' abortive Player Control plan and in the PSAL's halfhearted rule limiting to seven innings New York's elementary school baseball games if played on a day before a school day, unless both competing schools agreed to another arrangement. Then in the thirties, as Professor Jack Berryman has shown, physical education teachers and playground leaders reversed themselves with regard to organized competitive sports for children below high school age. What they once condoned they now condemned, on the ground, since become familiar, that competition for league championships, with its inordinate emphasis on winning, restricted participation to the best players and placed too heavy a physical and emotional strain on youngsters— conclusions that still have force today. They advocated, and on the whole successfully, intramural sports for youngsters instead.

Meanwhile, a teacher in a one-room country school in remote Pazo Nuevo, Arizona, where children of vaqueros on ranches of the area were bussed in, really made baseball an educational experience. In an interschool game she arranged, teacher Eulalia Bourne discovered that the boys needed practice and instruction. Their victorious opponents acted cool and scornful before-hand, skillful and enthusiastic in the game. "The desert resounded with their rude shouts and insults . . . in Spanish—a language rich in invective and obscenities." They had brought along their whole school, which cheered them on effectively. Afterwards, when Bourne's beaten students filed disconsolately into the schoolroom, she met them with a pep talk.

> "Boys and girls, *let's get 'm!* Let's work until we are *good* ball players and go to their school and beat the socks off them. And with none of the rudeness and insults they gave us. . . . It won't be easy. . . . We can't neglect our lessons. We owe the state that. . . . But somehow we'll *make* time. Are you with me?"

She had to tap the bell for order.

With this goal ahead of them the children worked as they never had before. "I truly believe," Bourne wrote later, "that no school ever put more activity into short fall days." Following the game in which they vindicated themselves, students wrote for their school paper, *The Little Cowpuncher*, such compositions as the following:

Little Cowpunchers Win a Baseball Game

Tuesday we took the pleasure of redeeming ourselves playing ball with Three Points. . . . Everybody was full of joy and we had lots of enthusiasm in playing them ball. We played politely. . . . We felt sorry because one couple of their boys was gone from their district. . . . It would have been more fair if everybody had been there who came to play us here.

Anyway we defeated them just as they did us when they came down here. The score was seventeen to six. . . . We all enjoyed ourselves and we were very polite to the losers.

NEW SPONSORS AND OLD

A midst the remarkable growth and popularity of sports in the twenties arose an anxious belief that baseball, among boys in particular, teetered on the brink of downgrade.

Ever since the game's rise to prominence and popular appeal in the latter half of the nineteenth century, assertions of its decline had been made. In the 1870s gambling became the supposed culprit, but predictions that the game was already "petering out" proved false. Baseball also recovered quickly from the bruises inflicted by the Black Sox scandal of 1919 and in the 1920s still possessed almost universal regard as the national game. Contemporary studies, notably one published in the *International Labor Review of 1924*, found baseball the most popular amateur sport. Several years later the New York *Times* presented a more qualified opinion: "After some nine decades of existence [baseball] continues to hold its supremacy as the game Americans most like to see others play."

Nevertheless, disquieting claims in the early twenties that American boys were forsaking the game disturbed many Americans. According to a nationwide survey in 1924 by the National Amateur Athletic Federation, participation of boys had fallen off by fifty percent. A cascade of magazine articles and newspaper editorials chorused that "The old-fashioned spontaneous game of baseball, played for the fun of it, has disappeared"; "corner games" and "catch" during recess had ended; on the playgrounds, boys played tennis; the sale of baseball equipment lagged; sporting goods manufacturers reported boys as shifting to other sports; baseball was in "devastating" decline.

Among the reasons advanced for the alleged deterioration of baseball among youngsters, the shrinking of available space ranked first. "It is necessary to realize," wrote the Secretary of Cincinnati's Community Service in 1925,

> that conditions are changing, open spaces are disappearing, streets are becoming crowded with traffic, and most municipalities are in poor financial

condition. Who is going to accept the responsibility of seeing that such a game as baseball is not stamped out in our lives, or limited to a chosen few?

Gas stations, parking lots, and grocery shops, as novelist Irwin Shaw wrote of Brooklyn, stood on "remembered fields, where you shagged flies and slid home with the winning run."

The other reason most often pointed to was the rise of other team games. Football had spread from the ivy league colleges to become a national favorite as universities caved in to the demands of alumni and public for teams of hired oafs. High schools, in imitation, also introduced or expanded football. Basketball showed signs of increased popularity in colleges and schools, too, particularly in the midwest, where it had in some places driven baseball out. Golf, fast losing its aura as a game of the leisure class, made great gains, and schools had begun to conduct tournaments. Tennis stood not far behind. No longer a sissyish, lazy summer afternoon game for "flanneled fools," it was becoming the province of the populace. Although baseball maintained its position as the national game, the conclusion of Foster Rhea Dulles that it lost ground relatively seems safe; whether as well it had suffered an absolute decrease in interest and play among youngsters appears less certain. The point is that many believed it had.

One of those convinced that baseball had decreased in popularity among boys was Major John L. Griffith, executive vice president of the NAAF. Griffith pounded away at his theme, particularly in a series of articles in *The Athletic Journal*, a new monthly magazine founded in 1921, of which he became editor in 1925, and that year he instigated a NAAF survey of amateur baseball.

What is more, Griffith also belonged to the American Legion. He told Frank G. McCormick, state commander of the South Dakota Legion, about the results of the NAAF survey and suggested that the Legion do something to save baseball. McCormick responded by instituting an experimental youth baseball program in his state.*

From the time of its founding in 1919 the Legion had taken active interest in sports and had at first promoted for its own members a nationwide athletic league. But the success of the South Dakota baseball program with boys convinced the state convention to urge the Legion to adopt a national program of summer baseball for teenagers. At its national convention in Omaha in the fall of 1925 the Legion enthusiastically passed a resolution to inaugurate and conduct junior baseball leagues and tournaments for local, state, sectional, regional, and "world" (national) championships.

The Legion established Junior Baseball not as part of a boys' program but under its "Americanism program" as a counter to the so-called Red Scare

*Some sources credit George Maines, a member of Oakley Trainer Post, Flint, Michigan, as the first to conceive the idea for Legion ball.

that permeated America at the time. In fact, McCormick launched the project with the idea that the Legion should "promote athletics as a means of teaching Americanism," and in the convention proceedings of 1928 stated its purpose as "to teach . . . concrete Americanism through playing the game." Russell Cook of Indiana, quoted by Marquis James in *The American Legion Monthly* in 1932, said that the program represented a means to combat "subversive elements."

The obscurantism of the term "Americanism" is best illustrated by the story of Boies Penrose, the Republican senator from Pennsylvania, who solemnly predicted that the key issue in the 1920 presidential election would be Americanism. Asked what that meant, he allegedly replied, "How in the hell do I know? But it will get a lot of votes."

Spokesmen for the Legion have offered various definitions and interpretations of the term "Americanism" since the organization passed a resolution at its first national convention to establish an Americanism Commission. At the 1925 convention the Commission itself admitted that it was "in a sense, a sales unit . . . to sell the ideals of the American Legion to the nation." In practice, the program led these self-appointed guardians of America to try to impose a public orthodoxy, a kind of civil religion, on everybody. To this end the Legion advocated strictures on immigration, tried to suppress those it considered "subversives" and "radicals," infringed on the civil rights of those who disagreed with the Legion, and, in time of domestic crisis, lent encouragement to fascist movements or solutions.

To get its ideas across the Legion relied on dissemination of what it called "American propaganda," employing two approaches, direct and indirect. Unlike its direct penetration of the schools, in which it sought to persuade teachers and pupils of its principles, the baseball program formed part of the Legion's indirect approach, which it concluded in 1926 was "very frequently more effective." For in 1925 it had already recognized that

> a popular athletic program would afford the American Legion the best possible medium through which to teach the principles of Americanism. Under cloak of a sport code, we would inculcate more good citizenship during one year than would be possible in ve years of direct appeal.

Promotion of community athletics by the Legion therefore came under the jurisdiction of Frank Cross, head of its Americanism Commission, which advised Legionnaires in 1927 to "Take an active, friendly interest in the boys of this country—teach them leadership and loyalty . . . and clean sports, and there can be no doubt as to their reaction to the approach of the economic fiction from the communist tongue and pen."

Legion Baseball proved as successful as the sponsors had hoped. At the Legion's eighth convention the Americanism Commission reported that the baseball program had not only "solved the problem of [a way to] approach . . . the red-blooded American boy who has no time for preachments or

studious application to the doctrines of good citizenship," it had also established "direct contact with upwards of a million people who are connected
with the families of these boys" and brought home "the same lessons to
[their] brothers and sisters and to [their] parents."

Major Griffith praised the militaristic implications of the Legion's program:

> Legionnaires know the value of national physical fitness in war. . . . Army men
> appreciate . . . that the qualities of character stressed by athletic training are
> the same as those needed in the making of a soldier. . . . initiative, aggres-
> siveness, poise, courage, co-operation, unselfishness, willingness to serve and
> the ability to carry on when punished.

The Legion also understood the self-serving value of conducting junior
baseball. A passage from the minutes of the seventh convention paraphrases
a comment about the program:

> Even though it did not have great possibilities for the promotion of good
> citizenship, it would provide the American Legion with a most desirable and
> effective type of publicity. Sport invites almost universal interest. It is not
> unreasonable to predict that many capable men . . . would be attracted to our
> ranks by the program. . . .

The Legion's Americanism Commission likewise appreciated the useful-
ness of Junior Baseball in sharpening the organization's own bayonet, as it
were, for by the time of its sixteenth convention in 1934 it reported that
the Legion was "receiving more publicity through the promotion of the junior
baseball program than through any one of its activities." The Commission
went on to say that the good will created by the program was "in great
measure responsible for the Legion's legislative victory in Washington,
D.C."*

William Gellerman put all this more bluntly. In his well-documented
doctoral dissertation, *The American Legion as Educator*, from which quo-
tations from Legion conventions are taken, he summarized the purpose of
Legion baseball as having

> as its basic objective the training of soldiers for future wars and the rearing of
> citizens who will accept the status quo without criticism or objection, willing
> to play the game according to the rules prescribed by the American Legion
> and the group in American society from which the leadership of the American
> Legion is drawn.

The quick acceptance and spread of Junior Baseball bears out the Legionnaire who said, "Junior Baseball was not just sport. The sport was bait
which the young ballplayers readily took." The number of teams participating
increased from 750 in 1925 to 9,000 (some 122,000 boys) in 1928. A year

---

*This remark probably referred to the Legion's success in persuading the Senate to pass a
bill that in effect limited most employees to a thirty-hour week.

later every state in the union had Legion teams, and the work of the Americanism Commission had doubled.

Originally, only boys from 14 to 16 could join, but by 1937 Junior Baseball opened itself to those who reached 17 as of March 31. The program's competitive system also underwent revision from time to time, but broadly speaking teams that survived district, state, and regional championship playoffs qualified for the national tournament, the first of which the Cook Post 321 of Yonkers, New York, won.

The Legion dropped its tournament in 1927 because of financial difficulties, perhaps brought on by the expense of holding its annual convention in Paris that year. But a fresh source of funds materialized the next year when Dan Sowers, then head of the Americanism Commission, appeared before Organized Baseball's executive council and asked for financial assistance. Actually, the Legion had benefited from Organized Baseball even before it began its boys' program when in 1932 it collected a $20,352.00 windfall from Commissioner Landis, whose political views harmonized with the Legion's, after the second game of the World Series ended on account of darkness and Landis ordered gate receipts distributed to various organizations, including the Legion. Thus Sowers had reason to expect a sympathetic reception by Organized Baseball, and he was not disappointed. Landis and the council agreed to an annual contribution of "up to $50,000.00."

At the end of the twenties Junior Baseball became well established, and whether by coincidence or otherwise Legion membership rose each year from a record low of about 609,500 in 1925 to almost 1,154,000 in 1931.

A foretaste of things to come occurred in 1928 when Margaret Gisolo starred in the national tournament. She had received little attention as a female among male players until she helped her Blanford, Indiana, team win the county championship by stealing three bases and in the twelfth inning driving in the deciding run. The losing team, Clinton, then protested the game on the ground that girls were ineligible for Legion ball. Then the buck-passing started, from tournament officials to the state baseball chairman to the national Legion chairman to the Americanism Commission and finally, of all places, to Commissioner Landis of Organized Baseball, who ruled that nothing in the Legion rules kept the girl out. She continued, and in the game for the district title against Terre Haute scored the winning run. Blanford then went on to win the sectional and state championships. In the national finals, however, Blanford lost to a team from Chicago, but Gisolo got three hits and accepted three chances without an error. She also pitched an inning in the sectional game, and tournament officials awarded her the sportsmanship trophy. The next year the Legion hastened to correct its oversight by barring all girls.

During the thirties boys played Legion ball in greater numbers than ever, and by 1935 as many as 500,000 joined. By then the final championship series commanded national attention. The Legion invited every youngster in Chicago to the 1934 tournament between the champions of the East and the West, and 18,000 "howling" children came. Two major-league umpires officiated as Post 13, Cumberland, Maryland, defeated New Orleans two games out of three. Even in 1928 the National Broadcasting Company had carried the national championship on a nationwide radio hookup, and by 1938 more than 3,000 radio stations broadcast the finals.

Organized Baseball backed the Legion's Junior Baseball program with its $50,000.00 annual contributions until the depression dampened its support. Sources conflict on details, but contributions, cut considerably for 1933, resumed with a small sum in 1934, and for a number of years thereafter amounted to only $20,000.00. But other private donors picked up the slack.

Legionnaires supported boys' baseball, wrote the sports editor of the St. Louis *Globe-Democrat* in 1937, for a program of "wholesome recreation, expert instruction and character building." The Legionnaires, he stated, supplied equipment and instruction to "help prepare boys for good citizenship." Equipment might not always be of the best quality, however. The coach of one Legion team grumbled that the local post furnished him only with an assortment of broken bats and a dozen or so cheap baseballs that he believed ruinous to a boy's arm. He thought Organized Baseball ought to give used balls to Legion teams.

Sportsmanship proved lacking both on the part of the Legion and of Organized Baseball. O.B. had an understanding that Legion players would not be signed until they had passed the Legion's age limit, so when a minor-league club signed a Legion player anyway, Landis voided the contract, pointing out that signing such players would injure the Legion's program and "discredit the financial and other assistance we extend to the Legion's baseball program." On the other hand, Legion teams were not above using questionable tactics, either. Detroit high school coaches complained in 1938 because American Legion teams allegedly took many of their best players who, the coaches felt, should be "giving their undivided [sports] attention to their alma maters."

But the relationship between the Legion and Organized Baseball proved durable. George Trautman, president of the minor leagues' National Association, once claimed that Legion ball "produced incalculable benefits for the youth of America" and added that many professionals had "commenced their baseball careers" with Legion posts. Trautman came closest to the mark, however, when he avowed that Organized Baseball's association with the Legion "has been a most happy one for both parties."

Organized Baseball did receive value from its investment. As Ford Frick, one-time commissioner, acknowledged, the Legion's program proved a valuable source of talent for professional ball. By 1946 about one in five major leaguers, including outstanding players like Bob Feller, had had Legion ball experience. On its part Organized Baseball helped the Legion finance a project that became the largest segment of its national youth program and possibly the Legion's greatest source of publicity. In addition, each organization could transfer to itself some of the other's patriotic and nationalistic stereotypes.

Boys' baseball suffered no letup in other private sponsorship, either, and by the early thirties an estimated fifty to seventy-five percent of boys' work consisted of athletics. The YMCA, besides fielding its own teams, sometimes on its own diamonds, also helped city governments, churches, and industries organize baseball programs. The Y even ran entire leagues, as in Lynn, Massachusetts. In Williamsport, Pennsylvania, it handled a Sunday school association of twenty-four teams divided into three leagues. Like other supporters of baseball, the Y believed in its character-building propensities: speaking in Hazleton, Pennsylvania, the local Y secretary called the "wholesome interest" of boys in baseball "a vital influence in producing clean-minded, peaceloving citizens in our democracy."

The churches themselves embarked upon an even more robust sponsorship of boys' baseball after World War I. Shaking off their former hesitancy they allocated funds, built facilities, supplied equipment, and secured coaches and umpires for church teams and leagues as never before. The Methodist Episcopal Church, for example, decided in 1921 to erect playgrounds and organize athletic teams and classes. It appointed a committee to visit rural ministers and teach them how to direct games, supplying money for equipment from the Church's twenty-two million dollar centenary fund. Bishop William T. Manning of the Episcopal Church proved a vocal advocate of sport, including Sunday baseball, provided it was not commercialized. He wrote that the "instinct for play" is "divinely planted in human nature" and "The Church must not merely tolerate clean sport and recreation, but give them its glad and open blessing." A 1925 survey of eighty ministers of various denominations found a majority of them favoring greater church recognition of the importance of sports and recreation.

The Roman Catholic Church kept pace with Protestant churches in backing boys' teams, greatly extending its participation when in 1930 the "labor priest" Bishop Bernard Sheil of Chicago founded the Catholic Youth Organization (CYO), a parish-based program for training elementary and high school youth in sports, among them baseball. The diocese of Los Angeles and San Diego sponsored 160 baseball teams, and in San Francisco the Church backed 250 squads organized into midget, junior, and senior divisions. A priest at St. Francis Monastery in St. Paul, Kansas, had a more concrete objective when he wrote Garry Herrmann of the Cincinnati Reds in January, 1925: first praising baseball for building morals, character, and health, he declared that "The boy who will fight for his team's pennant will never refuse to fight for his Country's Flag." He then concluded by recommending a young player to Herrmann.

By the late thirties both Protestant and Catholic church leagues boomed.

Chicago's church baseball leagues separated some players by denominations, with a Lutheran Baseball Association, a Northwest Baptist League, a Polish Roman Catholic Union, and one general West Side Church League. In addition, the CYO reported 3,000 Chicago boys playing in 96 locations. The winner of Chicago's Church Athletic Association frequently competed for a church championship against the winner of the Walther League Tournament, a Lutheran youth organization.

Some good ball players performed on church teams: Billy Herman helped New Covenant Presbyterian win the Louisville Church Championship in 1927, and Pee Wee Reese, once his church team's batboy, in 1937 played for New Covenant in the city's annual amateur elimination series. Both players became outstanding major-league infielders.

Although many church teams played on their own fields, others used city diamonds and facilities and entered their teams in muny leagues. In Chicago 24 churches used 45 city parks for baseball in 1937—a practice that might have raised a nice constitutional question of separation of church and state, but apparently, in the craze for public baseball, did not.

By sponsoring boys' baseball in a big way the churches indicated that they had resigned themselves to utilization of the game for sustaining the interest of young members of their flocks and for adding if not new souls then new bodies to the fold, as well as ordering the personal lives of boys. Church leagues generally required Sunday school attendance and often demanded restrained behavior of participants in their baseball leagues. Chicago's Church Athletic Association, one of many that set such requirements, demanded two attendances monthly at Sunday school, and its umpires enforced rules against the use of tobacco and "bad language."

Some of the boys in these church leagues, as usual, were baseball Christians, who did not necessarily accept the religious doctrine of their sponsors. Jake Banks, a Jew who later signed a professional contract, played on a Catholic Church team in Hartford, Connecticut, in 1934 after assuring the priest that he attended nine o'clock mass every Sunday morning. Another fellow later described his New England town's church league as a marriage of convenience: the youngsters needed equipment, and the church leagues represented one place to get it. Religious beliefs could be overlooked when churches organized teams. Unitarians might snap up a Baptist if they needed a shortstop, or a pastor's influence could be used to snare a player.

Churchmen did profess belief, some of it doubtless genuine, in the benefits of sports. With Canada already in World War II the Reverend Harold J. Martin, president of the Canadian-American League, declared warmly:

> We can thank Almighty God we have such an institution as baseball to take our minds off the tragedy of the world. I know of no institution outside the church that can accomplish what baseball has and will continue to do for the good of God, country and fellow men.

Other institutions furnished boys' baseball a measure of support between the wars. The Helms Athletic Foundation, a nonprofit organization founded in 1936 by the retired president of the General Baking Corporation, annually presented awards to the best high school, prep school, and junior college baseball players in southern California. In fact, according to a study by Harold Coffman, in the 1920s twenty-two philanthropic foundations spent more than eight million dollars on recreation and sports. Contributions from such foundations to groups like the Playground Association and to cities for recreation surveys, for example, redounded to the benefit of boys' baseball. Gifts and subscriptions aided the growth of boys' clubs, too, and provided the means to form more teams and occasionally their own leagues. The Boys Club of Little Rock, Arkansas, in the twenties sponsored a series of leagues graded by age, including Knee High, Midget, and Intermediate. A boys' club figured in Joe DiMaggio's career, too. A story has it that Joe lost interest in baseball at age fourteen and took up other games, but when older brother Vince signed with the local minor-league club in 1932 Joe joined the San Francisco Boys' Club and returned to baseball.

In the thirties the Boystown Clubs, formed to work with boys who "formerly roamed the streets," operated baseball clubs and leagues as part of their physical education program. And a political group, the Young Communist League (YCL), operated baseball teams in the Bronx. What would the American Legion think of Communist baseball?

The settlement houses lost force in the 1930s as the depression overwhelmed their backing from private sources while civic-supported groups expanded. Nevertheless, settlement and intersettlement baseball continued in some cities, despite the intrusion, as Robert A. Woods of a Boston settlement commented, of a "lust for prizes." Nevertheless, asserted *A Manual of Settlement Boys' Work* in 1935, "the settlement which has good facilities for sport has an assured following."

Support for boys' baseball from older sources became supplemented in the twenties and thirties by a stronger infusion of interest on the part of business and business-related organizations. Even before the war, of course, individual companies had begun to furnish play facilities for boys. United States Steel and the Goodyear Tire & Rubber Company, for instance, sponsored recreation programs for children of their employees. After the war business cast about more energetically for strategems to place itself in a favorable public light. In a sports-crazy, child-centered society, what better way for a company to win approval than to associate itself with boys' baseball, either through direct sponsorship or via such business-oriented civic and fraternal organizations as Rotary and Kiwanis and the zoo group: Lions, Moose, Eagles, et cetera. A number of these associations dated from the nineteenth century, but in the twenties they experienced such barrelling growth as to make unexceptional the increase in Kiwanis clubs from 205 in

1920 to 1,800 in 1929. So the means and manpower for baseball sponsorship presented itself. Perhaps the successful promotion of Junior Baseball by the pro-business American Legion did not go unnoticed by business groups, either.

Although they kept no central records of their participation, articles in periodicals show that civic, fraternal, and service clubs provided the main channels through which business aided boys' baseball. Major Griffith of the American Legion, who also belonged to Rotary, reported in the mid-twenties that many individual service clubs took the initiative in organizing local baseball clubs and leagues for boys. In 1925, for example, the Rotary Club of Fargo, North Dakota, appointed an athletic director and sponsored teams in the city league. Civic and fraternal groups backed teams in the leagues of the Minneapolis Playground and Recreation Association, too. In 1920 Kiwanis operated an entire league for young New York players and another in East Chicago in 1935. In Cicero, Illinois, a combination of Rotary, Lions, and businessmen's associations formed a committee to foster boys' baseball there. Many of these civic and fraternal groups also contributed money to the American Legion for its Junior Baseball program.

Business also sponsored boys' baseball directly. One of the largest programs for teenage boys came under the auspices of the Remar Baking Company of Oakland, California, where in 1937 fourteen divisions (104 teams) competed, and over a three-year period about 12,000 boys participated. In Remar's league members of winning teams in each age division received gold baseballs as awards and played for a divisional trophy in the local minor-league park. The fact that only three of the boys got into serious trouble with the law, said the writer who prepared the story, evidenced that "baseball is America's good-citizen building sport." Business houses also sponsored teams for their own employees, many of whom, as high school dropouts, were very young men.

Commercial summer camps opened a new era in the thirties, for by that time going to camp in summer had become "the thing to do." Porter Sargent's 1935 camp handbook listed more than 3,500 summer camps for youth. At many of them the directors, often college athletes or coaches, featured sports, particularly baseball. In Sargent's list some camps that featured baseball described themselves as Catholic, Jewish, or Episcopal, but most listed no religious affiliation. Sargent himself thought some camps over-emphasized athletics. One of the so-called sports camps was Camp Kill Care in Vermont, for boys from eight to sixteen, where the campers selected one minor and one major sport for a two-week coaching session. Camp Munsee in Pennsylvania even awarded camp letters to boys who excelled in athletics. But other camps offered more balanced programs, including opportunities to enjoy nature, Sargent noted. Despite his disapproval of sports overemphasis at camps, Sargent still thought that baseball, "beloved by campers of all ages," represented "the ideal team game" for "friendly" intramural contests as well as the "natural method" of planning competition with some neighboring camp.

About the same time, business and other private sponsors of boys' baseball received an additional stimulus. Ironically, it resulted from a drumfire of condemnation from education and recreation people aimed at organized competition for preadolescents. Teachers and recreation workers spoke up about possible physical and psychological hazards of highly organized sport for youngsters as well as against the exploitation of youth by commercial interests. Their criticism, although instrumental in causing elementary and junior high schools to pull back from such competition, had about as much effect outside the schools as BB pellets on the hide of a rhinoceros. So far from curtailing organized sport for boys below high school age, such criticism actually helped increase opportunities for them to play ball, because with the blessing and support of most community leaders, business and other private sponsors simply occupied the territory vacated by the schools. The nationwide devotion to sports, along with the firmly imbued belief in their benefits for children, which school and recreation people had themselves done much to create, were too powerful to turn aside, and outside groups, which had no educational theories to inhibit them, used baseball and other sports programs to advertise themselves, attract new members, or demonstrate that their organizations served the community.

High on the list of benefits attributed to the game stood baseball's influence in teaching children to behave like Americans, although usually that meant the narrow, nationalistic American Legion brand of "Americanism." Wearing his Legionnaire's cap while wielding the editorial pen of *The Athletic Journal* in the early twenties, Major John L. Griffith opined that coaches should "contest anti-patriotic tendencies" by teaching "loyalty and respect for the institutions which have made this country great." Every coach and player, he declared, should "consider it his duty to combat the foreign propaganda" that blames society or the government for problems and wants to revamp them. Others attributed to baseball the power of "Americanization" in the sense of assimilating youngsters, especially those of foreign parentage, into the culture. Baseball's power to Americanize received endorsement in 1925 from the New York *Times*: next to the public schools, it was to sports that "we must look for the principal molding force of a sense of kind. . . . The baseball diamond, which is the nation's great playground, has long reflected this assimilative process." *Collier's* appeared to support this theory in 1911 in its description of a game in New York between two gangs of ragged hoodlums on a rocky, rubbish-strewn vacant lot, where the boys played together amidst cries of "Clancy!" "You Dutchy!" and "The dago!" until at the approach of a policeman they all ran. In the thirties Franklin D. Roosevelt and the *Sporting News* also subscribed to baseball's assimilative propensities.

The notion that children could become assimilated by playing baseball did not originate with the boys' work organizations of the twenties and thirties but came from superAmerican zealots. Preoccupation with "Americanism" and "Americanization" reached back decades into the reaction of the dominant white Anglo-Saxon Protestant (WASP) society (ASP would be more accurate, since white is redundant, and more fitting, since the asp is more venomous) to the shift of American immigration about 1890 from western to southern and eastern Europeans. This so-called new immigration, composed mostly of Slavs, Italians, and Jews, formed the major part of the wave of more than eighteen million foreigners that poured into the country between then and 1915, settling in squalid urban ghettos that bred grievous social problems. To swallowers of the myth of ASP superiority, these newcomers, jabbering in outlandish languages, observing strange customs, and practicing questionable religions, seemed to pose a menace to the American way of life. Moved by suspicion, fear, and hostility, zealots among Americans of older stock, assisted by organized labor seeking to protect jobs and wages against more poorly paid immigrant workers, and reformers struggling to shut off the flow of immigrants as a step toward eliminating slums, called for the assimilation of immigrants already here and exclusion of others to come.

To these zealots it appeared that home and church could no longer be entrusted with the task of imparting community (ASP) ideals and mores, so the job fell largely to the public schools, where, as chief custodians of the "melting pot," teachers fueled it with everything from flag saluting to checks for head lice, and from homogenized history to instruction in baseball, all calculated to produce a conformist blend of children indoctrinated with "Americanism."

A widely held view of immigrant children and the intent of school athletics in relation to them comes through in George Wingate's summary of the results of the New York PSAL's program at the organization's ninth annual meeting in 1913:

> There is no way in which the robust, manly qualities of courage, nerve and hardihood are developed as much as in competitive athletics, and our games are having this result, particularly upon the school boys of foreign birth whose ancestors for hundreds of years before them have been so oppressed as to have been almost slaves in the countries from which they came. . . . [T]he manly qualities which these boys are acquiring through our athletic contests are changing their natures, or rather the mental habits forced upon them by their oppression. This cannot but be fully equal in value to the intellectual information they attain in school. . . .

He overlooked blacks, who for decades had been slaves in America, to say nothing of the treatment of Indians.

Then the Yankee Doodle Dandy patriotism of World War I and the hysteria of the red scare immediately following opened the way for ASP racism and anti-immigration sentiment to surface with renewed strength. Sweeping laws drastically limited all immigration and settled on quotas heavily weighted in favor of the "old" and against the "new" stocks. Those of foreign birth or parentage already here became prime targets of superpatriot demands for total conformity. The schools floated on the tides of intolerance: Americanization, declared the superintendent of New York's public schools, meant "absolute forgetfulness of all obligations or connections with other countries because of descent or birth," while outside the schools private sponsors of boys' baseball, like the American Legion, reflected this climate by proclaiming that playing baseball "Americanized" or instilled "Americanism."

Fortunately, "ethnicity" survived, although in time it became less significant than class in establishing social distinctions. Clinging to their heritage, immigrants established their own schools, churches, newspapers, and social clubs to preserve and perpetuate their own cultures, while at the same time they strove to assume the outward aspects—in dress, speech, work, and play—of those whose ancestors had arrived on earlier ships.

One way children of foreign birth or parentage could fit into the new culture was to take part in baseball, and early on, many of them perceived in it their badge as Americans. "You see that Filipino?" asked a Catholic priest of his visitor at a summer camp in 1908. "He is looked upon as a good American because he plays a first class game of baseball." An Italian boy named Nick, the subject of a case study by an education writer in the thirties, played baseball despite his parents' disapproval, since "it was the one thing above all else that could make him an American and give him status. Because of his ability to play baseball the boys quit calling him 'dago.'" Sons of Italians, Slavs, Jews, and other newcomers increasingly took up the game in the large cities, mining towns, and steel centers where they concentrated, thus following in the steps of the earlier English, Irish, and Germans. Brooklyn, for instance, was marked by a polyglot population from way back, and as Robert P. Smith's study of the borough in the nineties demonstrated, many children of the poor, because of distance and lack of carfare, could not avail themselves of the recreational pleasures that the Brooklyn press assumed they did, so the streets became their playgrounds and baseball, or versions thereof, their most popular game.

The immigrants' own sport and social clubs also sponsored baseball teams. Their newspapers gave the game support and space, and their children learned baseball at local settlement houses established to help them get acquainted with American life. Italian boys quickly became proficient in baseball, and by the twenties and thirties many cities had entire teams of boys whose parents had come from Italy. New York had these juvenile teams, and even out in the small town of Weed, California, a well-equipped Sons of Italy team played. Once in 1907 on New York's lower East Side, a boy named Edward Corsi, an Italian immigrant who eventually became head of immigration at Ellis Island, wanted, with his gang, to form a baseball team. "The police would not tolerate our presence on street corners and persist-ently chased us. . . . We needed a club room," he recalled. Mustering the courage of a Catholic boy warned to avoid Protestant establishments, Corsi and his gang applied at the local settlement. Encouraged there, Corsi organized his baseball team, "caught the spirit of the settlement and entered into its program."

The various Slavic peoples supported baseball almost from the first, particularly in Chicago, where so many of them settled. By 1927 the American Bohemian Alliance there was sponsoring a fifteen-team league of nine senior and eight junior teams, furnishing their equipment, and charging an admission fee to the games. Young men of Slovak descent in Bethlehem, Pennsylvania, founded in the 1900s several athletic associations that fielded baseball teams. In 1931 the small town of Struthers, Ohio, had a Slovak League and a Magyar League. Perhaps owing to a small population, the Magyar League in Struthers allowed each team seven "outsiders"—English, German, French, Italian, and others—along with ten Hungarians. Children of smaller immigrant groups, such as Greeks and Swedes, also turned to baseball. In the 1930s the Independent Order of Vikings, composed of immigrants of Swedish descent, operated baseball leagues in Chicago. Sport could thus play a dual and often conflicting role, preserving ethnic identity on ethnic teams and at other times mixing nationality groups while its practitioners played an American game.

Sons of immigrants sometimes played baseball in their parents despite, but Jewish lads often had to overcome stronger parental objections than most because of the longer intellectual tradition in Jewish culture, which varied somewhat from American pragmatism. "Ah, the atheistical baseball!" moaned Charles Angoff's great-grandfather when the Boston boy became preoccupied with the Red Sox and the Braves instead of his studies. Although the Talmud contained favorable references to ball playing and some Jews had played certain types of ball games even in Europe, the average American synagogue had little in the way of social, athletic, or recreational facilities, so boys who wanted to play ball had to go elsewhere.

Jewish groups themselves agonized over the problem of reconciling the two cultures. In New York, German Jews, who had left the ghetto and moved uptown as a stable, "Americanized" middle class, tended to patronize the "new" Russian Jewish "greenhorns" of the lower East Side, and, to Americanize them, German Jews founded the Educational Alliance, patterned after the settlement houses. In its first annual report the Alliance observed that nothing would more effectively remove the impression of Jews as lacking in physical courage than athletic training. Russian Jews, naturally, resented an organization foisted upon them from outside and set up their own Jewish Center more attuned to their heritage. Thus more than most first-generation youngsters of immigrant parents, Jewish lads found themselves torn between efforts of parents to preserve the old way of life and the pressure and pull of American surroundings.

The dilemma of Jewish boys can be glimpsed through their experience
with baseball. Irving Howe's *Land of Our Fathers*, for example, describes
how the show business star Eddie Cantor recalled that in his boyhood the
worst name his grandmother could call a child was "you baseball player,
you!" because to orthodox Jews of the East Side ghetto a ball player was
"the king of loafers." Howe also tells of a mother who berated her boy for
playing ball in the street because he could end up a "street bum," and a
father who asked, "what is the point of this crazy game?" adding that "the
children can get crippled. . . . I want my boy to grow up a mensch, not a
wild American runner." In 1934 Hank Greenberg, the major-league star,
recalled for *Sporting News* the trepidation with which he played ball as a
youngster because he dreaded to bring down the wrath of his parents on
himself for "idling."

But Jewish boys interested in playing ball were not without allies. The
editor of the influential *Jewish Daily Forward*, Abraham Cahan, urged that
they be allowed to play baseball "as long as it does not interfere with their
education" because "the body needs to develop also. Baseball is played in
the fresh air." He maintained that unlike football, baseball was not dangerous. "Let your boy play baseball," he advised readers, "and become excellent
in playing the game," not only for a healthy body but "Mainly, let us not
so raise the children that they should grow up foreigners in their own birthplace." Rabbi Charles Fleischer, in a 1908 article in *Baseball Magazine*,
avowed his own love for baseball and proudly displayed his fingers deformed
from playing the game, a common condition of men's hands in the United
States, he declared, that represented a worthier symbol of virility and athleticism than the ugly dueling scars across a German student's cheek.

As a practical matter, immigrant families coped with the question "to play
or not to play" in their own way, as did the Jewish family in which the son,
knowing he could not tell his father he played baseball, got his mother to
"sneak out my baseball gear and put it in the candy store downstairs." In
my own case my father, whose family immigrated from England when he
was a child, at first mildly opposed my playing ball, but he never tried to
stop me. My mother, on the other hand, firmly believed in the value of
sports for keeping boys out of trouble. Moral reinforcement came from my
"Irish" grandfather (American-born, as he always made clear), who constantly
sang the praises of Honus Wagner and Christy Mathewson, whom he had
seen play at the Polo Grounds as a boy, and also from my mother's oldest
brother, a rabid Giants fan and a truant officer for the New York Board of
Education, who somehow found the Polo Grounds the best place to hunt
for truants once the baseball season started.

In the upshot, the game proved irresistible to many immigrant and first-
generation American boys, including those who were Jewish. Howe said
Jewish boys of New York became "fanatics of baseball" and resented losing
to after-school religious education the time that might be spent at baseball.

Many played in Tompkins Park on the lower East Side. The *Alliance Review*, published by the Educational Alliance, recorded their baseball clubs' "fierce athletic rivalries," as another writer described them. In the early 1900s a Jewish boy named Albert Stark, who lived in a Henry Street tenement, got up at three every morning—hungry, cold, skinny, and undernourished—to push a peddler's cart; nevertheless, he played ball every chance he got and eventually became a well-known major-league umpire.

Jewish adults also succumbed to baseball. The candy stores, those miniature social centers that once dotted neighborhoods, appeared in Jewish ones as well, and there the men talked baseball. A Jewish writer described young New York Jews of the twenties as "thoroughly 'Americanized.' They are a jolly crowd, know the batting averages to a 'T'. . . . " The Young Men's Hebrew Association (YMHA), which took root in the 1870s and by 1880 numbered about fifty branches, by copying the YMCA in emphasizing sports clearly showed that Jews had turned to athletics. Baseball appealed so much to Jews that in 1910 statistician Louis Heilbroner wrote a confidential letter to Garry Herrmann recommending that he arrange big-league games on the Jewish New Year and the Day of Atonement, pointing with admiration to the 28,000 attendance in New York at an Atonement Day game. By 1920 the big new Central Jewish Institute in New York, although focussed on the Talmud Torah, included provision for sports as well. The YMHA of Scranton, Pennsylvania, in 1927 fielded one of the strongest baseball teams in the area. In Baltimore in 1936, 700 young Jewish fellows came to the local Educational Alliance to hear the general manager of the Orioles Baseball Club answer questions about baseball and to watch an American League publicity film.

While sons of immigrants formed teams of their own nationality, these teams often belonged to leagues with squads of other or mixed ethnic origin. Particularly at school, boys who played with ethnic outside teams might find themselves on the same team with "others." Most of my teammates in Brooklyn high school ball were Jewish, but one year we also had two players of Spanish background, one of whom, Ernie Rojas, captained the team (before the incident of the Player Control plan). One season the coach was an ASP, Leslie Wood, and another a Jew, George Zuckerman, both equally ignorant of the fine points of baseball, and come to think of it both seasons I was the only Anglo-Irish in the regular lineup. None of this, it seems, made any difference in our playing.

Once I had the adventure of playing for an all-Italian team against another all-Italian team in an Italian neighborhood. I had struck up an acquaintance with Johnny Dee, an older Italian fellow who delivered groceries in our neighborhood and always took time out from his rounds to watch our ball games. One day he said his team needed a first baseman for a Sunday game and invited me to fill in. Dee came from a nearby section called Pigtown, where poor Italians, many of them squatters, lived and into which none of us ever ventured, since we knew that all Italians carried stilettos—except, of course, for those in our own neighborhood. But flattered at being asked, I put aside fear and the next Sunday morning found myself walking with some apprehension through Pigtown. My teammates of the day accepted me matter-of-factly, I quickly felt comfortable, the morning passed pleasantly, the more so because I got three hits, and the experience proved unforgettable, as this telling of it bears out.

On teams I organized and ran on the Brooklyn Parade Grounds, ability and attitude represented the only requirements for membership, and at one time or another over the years I brought in players who were Protestant, Catholic, and Jewish, and second generation Swedish, Italian, Irish, French, German, Spanish, and Polish boys. For a short time a Chinese boy, George Lee, played with one of my teams. Once I offered a black player a tryout, but although he agreed to come he never showed up, probably diffident about going out for an all-white team. I did have some black friends speak at a team meeting, though. My teams in turn played not only those of mixed origins but also such ethnic teams as the Polish Falcons, the Celtics (Irish Catholics), and the Lafayette Triangles (Italian). Although the point is rarely made, playing on mixed teams may have enabled boys of different ethnic groups to temper if not overcome some of the old animosities and suspicions passed down from their parents as much as it aided their assimilation into the dominant culture.

Toward the end of the twenties, aid of sorts for young ball players opened up from a new source, the commercial baseball "school." Unlike such institutions as churches, the Y, the Legion, and various conventional businesses that sponsored boys' baseball, the baseball schools were enterprises organized by professional ball players and ex-players, sometimes in conjunction with professional ball clubs. Those who opened such schools hoped to find and develop good players for the professional leagues, or at least make some money.

Sessions at commercial baseball schools varied from two to seven weeks in length, and tuition ranged from $25.00 to $85.00, not counting room and board. Professional players or ex-players acted as instructors. Operators of the more permanent schools that opened year after year probably made a living from the tuition fees, and, if they uncovered any youngsters worth signing, modest cash bonuses from pro clubs. As the schools became popular in the thirties, a few conventional business firms sponsored them free of charge for public relations purposes, and occasionally city and federal governments lent a hand. The regimen of the schools combined classroom lectures with outdoor work similar to that of the spring training routine of major leaguers.

The first really permanent commercial baseball school was Jess W. Orndorff's National College of Baseball, established at Burbank, California, in 1923 but later moved to Los Angeles and renamed the National Baseball School. Orndorff, who had played briefly in the big leagues, began by soliciting Organized baseball for students, claiming he could develop recruits quickly at low cost and offering reports on recruits upon completion of a three-month course. Evidently, this plan failed, for his ads in *Sporting News* indicated the year 1927 as when he actually began giving instruction. By 1935 Orndorff reportedly was receiving applications from as far away as Cuba, Panama, and Japan, and that year he placed twenty-five of his students with minor-league teams. Then he came up with an idea to use with boys unable to come to his school: a six-week mail order course, followed by a week of personal instruction at some central location, all for $25.00.

In 1933 Ray Doan opened another well-known baseball school at Hot Springs, Arkansas. Doan had started as a promising semipro pitcher, who, after his arm went bad, turned booking agent and publicity man for a famous independent club. He had also been an athletic director in the United States Army and a coach at Springfield College, the outgrowth of the Y's school there. This background in both promotion and instruction evidently made an effective combination, for his school soon outstripped Orndorff's, although the latter continued to operate up to the time of World War II.

As many as 325 boys attended Doan's four-week session in 1936 at a cost of $40.00 plus room and board in town at about $7.00 a week. Boys as young as thirteen signed up, and well-known professionals like Lynwood "Schoolboy" Rowe, Dizzy Dean, Rogers Hornsby, and George Sisler instructed the boys on four diamonds that the city put at Doan's disposal. The program included a separate section for umpires conducted by major-league umpire George Barr, who shortly opened his own school. Doan placed a hundred boys from his class of 1937 with professional clubs. One year, two minor-league clubs recruited their entire teams from among his students. All told, he claimed to have placed about 500 boys by 1939. By then he had shifted operations to Jackson, Mississippi, but in 1940 he moved to Palatka, Florida and merged with the All-American School.

The depression spawned many other such schools, run mostly by big-league or former big-league players as a way to pick up some extra money for several weeks' pleasant work in the off-season. Most such schools were one-time ventures. In the mid-thirties Jack Onslow began what became a popular radio version of the baseball school, his "Baseball School of the Air," teaching fundamentals of the game to New England children. The National League even voted in 1936 to conduct such a radio "college" of its own, and President Ford Frick of the National League reportedly wanted every league club to operate a baseball school, but nothing came of either scheme.

Giants' manager Bill Terry, in conjunction with the New York club, ran one of the largest temporary schools at Pensacola, Florida, in 1936, in hope of finding prospects for the club. About 165 boys paid $25.00 tuition for the month-long session, bringing their own equipment and rooming with private families for two dollars a week or five with board. Terry and his nine assistants shared the $4,000.00 profit. *Sporting News* praised them for their efficient instruction: no experienced Y secretary, welfare worker, camp counsellor, or physical education instructor could have done as good a job in handling the boys, asserted the writer, and although the instructors never had any training in teaching they plunged into the work "with no psychological theories."

It could be said that these schools exploited the consuming interest of youngsters in baseball. New York Yankees owner Jake Ruppert reproached ball players who associated themselves with such schools for taking money to show boys how to play: "You would think they would say to themselves, 'nobody ever asked me to pay money to learn baseball, so why should I take money from these youngsters who want to learn.'" To which Ray Doan replied that as long as Organized Baseball ran no schools, those who filled an obvious need should not be criticized. Others agreed with Doan. The sports editor of the Shreveport, Louisiana, *Journal* believed that the schools gave baseball-minded youngsters an opportunity to get the best instruction, and the editor of *Sporting News* thought they filled a need neglected by "short-sighted educators" and that the "educational system is remiss in this respect." Granted, most boys, after incurring the expense of travel, board, and tuition, went home unsigned, and the relatively few who received contracts rarely got beyond the lowest minor leagues; but those who attended may have acquired a memorable experience and learned something from failure.

Other baseball schools sponsored by business firms, government agencies, and newspapers generally charged no tuition and catered only to boys in their local areas. They offered short sessions and accepted boys as young as ten. The Kellogg cereal company, advertising "the Serious Business of Boy Building," sponsored such schools in several cities and claimed that 45,000 boys received instruction in 1937 from such baseball luminaries as Walter Johnson and Johnny Evers. Socony-Vacuum Oil Company backed similar schools in Boston and nearby communities in the thirties. The Coca Cola Bottling Company of Minden, Louisiana, sponsored one under the former big-leaguer Kid Elberfeld in 1940 and equipped several teenage teams, one called the Coca Cola Giants. The Elks of Spokane, Washington, conducted schools in six city parks for a thousand boys from twelve to seventeen in 1941. Attendance at such schools indicated the steadfast popularity of baseball among youngsters and their eagerness to learn more about it.

Private groups also obtained the aid of government agencies to sponsor baseball schools. One such school in Hazard, Kentucky, in 1939 found backing from the WPA and the local schools as well as private business, giving ten days of free instruction to youths up to age twenty-two. Hillerich & Bradsby Company donated bats, and the Cincinnati Reds offered baseballs and trials to promising youngsters, finally signing five of the boys for their farm team—not a bad return on a modest investment. Sports departments of newspapers entered the baseball school business, too. The New York

Daily Mirror, the Chicago *Daily News* and Chicago *American*, and the Dallas *News*, along with papers in Schenectady and Omaha, sponsored instructional classes, some in combination with local businesses. *Sporting News*, ever ready to encourage interest in baseball among boys, regularly offered them "scholarships" to commercial baseball schools as prizes for selling a certain number of subscriptions to the paper. A 1936 winner of such a *Sporting News* prize, John Grodzicki, developed into a major-league pitcher.

Boys could take advantage of another new baseball opportunity, the tryout camp. Several major-league clubs operated such camps in the late thirties, either directly or through their farm clubs and in some cases with the co-operation of government agencies or universities. Although they sought primarily to acquire young talent cheaply and efficiently, the camps brought incidental benefits to the boys who attended. Before the advent of the tryout camps, each spring during the depression throngs of older boys hitchhiked or "rode the rods" south to major-league training camps uninvited. They arrived hungry and without funds, in no condition to show their talent even if they had any, and the clubs turned virtually all of them away. The tryout camps cut down on this traffic. Located in cities and towns all over the country, they were much more accessible than spring training camps. And instead of peremptorily chasing boys away, the tryout camps welcomed them by the hundreds free of charge. A boy could write in for a tryout or just appear with a glove and spikes and get a chance to show his stuff to professional scouts assigned to look him over. Most tryout camps conducted by Organized Baseball, like the commercial baseball schools, generally made no pretense of offering anything but plain, straightforward, meat and potatoes baseball free from humbug about building character, developing citizenship, or instilling Americanism.

In contrast, camps conducted in cooperation with city recreation departments, the WPA, or universities went beyond uncovering prospects and accepted very young boys. These more educational camps emphasized instruction sufficiently to be called schools or clinics, like those run by the St. Louis Cardinals and Browns in the late thirties. Beginning in 1937 the Cardinals held one-day clinics at the University of Rochester, and at the 1939 session the Cardinals' general manager, Branch Rickey, along with Cardinal and Rochester Red Wing players, did the teaching. On the last day of a clinic under Rickey, a high school player named Marty Marion showed so much promise that he received a professional offer, and he eventually became a star shortstop with the Cardinals.

Sometimes sponsors combined a tryout camp and a school, as the Cardinals and Browns did in 1940. Perhaps the most elaborate camp-school program was the one sponsored jointly by the Philadelphia Athletics and the Atlantic Refining Company in 1939, with Atlantic funding more than two dozen centers from New England to Florida. Possibly 200,000 boys aged ten to twenty registered. On completion of the instructional sessions the best players from each city competed in a tournament, and an estimated 35,000 fans attended the final championship game at Shibe Park.

Was Organized Baseball doing all it could for boys? In the view of important baseball men like Branch Rickey, Ban Johnson, and Taylor Spink, editor of the *Sporting News*, it should have done more. The only undertaking that entailed a sizable financial outlay by the big leagues came from the annual contribution to the American Legion. Other gestures toward support emanated from whichever individual clubs chose to make them, often at an insignificant outlay or none at all. Like the Organized Baseball donations to the Legion, most forms of aid were to a degree self-serving, in some instances granted with strings attached. Even the well-publicized "knothole gang" introduced by the Cardinals in an earlier era originated as an incentive to St. Louis citizens to buy stock in the club.* Clubs that adopted the knothole idea and admitted boys free on certain slow weekdays required them to sign a pledge promising to abide by a code of behavior that made the Boy Scout prescript seem indulgent by comparison. Boys had to promise not to skip school in order to attend, not to attend against the wishes of parents, teachers, or guardians, and not to use profane language (presumably, boys got seats out of earshot of players), or in any way conduct themselves at the ball park in a manner unbecoming a "sport." Violation of a rule meant cancellation of membership for as long as warranted. The Salem Club of Oregon admitted children free if they pledged to refrain from profanity, do a good deed at home daily, attend one Boy Scout, YMCA, Sunday school, church, or boys' or girls' meeting each week, and act like gentlemen and ladies inside and outside the ball park! They must also have the signature of a parent or sponsor, who could suspend the privilege as a punishment by simply telephoning the clubowner's wife.

On occasion the knothole gang could become burdensome. In 1933 Judge Emil Fuchs, president of the Boston Braves, discovered belatedly that he had promised free admission to his knotholers on the same day the paying customers were prepared to knock down the fences to see a doubleheader with the Giants. Faced with a choice of postponing the boys' entertainment or losing an estimated $5,000.00 in gate receipts that the club could ill afford to pass up, Fuchs decided to "keep faith" with "the gang" and settle for good will.

Other assistance rendered by clubs to baseball players proved mostly token: passing out some free tickets to elementary school children, inviting orphans to a game, or taking a few outstanding players on a road trip with the team or to spring training camp. Some baseball men gave talks on baseball. Clubs also occasionally allowed school and boys' teams to use their parks for championship games. The San Francisco Seals of the Pacific Coast League, however, made a real effort: annually they opened their games to

*See *Baseball: The Early Years*, p. 61.

nine or ten thousand children and gave away thousands of miniature bats or other mementos. They also staged benefit games for the CYO and donated the use of their stadium to many groups that sponsored boys' teams. The Seals' president, Charles Graham, even encouraged boys to play on their own by organizing some boys' teams.

Still, Ban Johnson asserted that Organized Baseball did "nothing" to meet the competition of other sports for boys' attention, and he recalled nostalgically the days when "baseball was the one outlet for all athletic aspiration, and every youngster's dream was to be a major leaguer." The *Sporting News* editor, Taylor Spink, too, kept charging Organized Baseball with doing nothing to help scholastic and municipal ball regain their former high place. Knothole gangs were not enough, he said; boys wanted to play, not just watch. Spink urged ex-professional players, with financial support by Organized Baseball, to get into the high schools and community recreation centers to help arrest the alleged decline in boys' baseball. In New York, sports writer Jimmy Powers criticized club officials for failing to teach baseball fundamentals to boys and asserted that some clubs had cut back on their assistance. The Giants, he charged, when asked to repeat a tryout session at the Polo Grounds said it was too much trouble, and the Dodgers, after learning that $32.00 worth of baseballs had been used in a few morning workouts for boys, stopped them.

The interest of Organized Baseball in boys sometimes proved something less than enlightened. In a letter to the Cincinnati ball club in 1923 the assistant director of the local public schools' attendance department complained that the Reds illegally employed truants in and near the park and that some truant officers' rights to legally enter the park had been questioned. Neatly sidestepping admission of illegal employment, Garry Herrmann replied that he would admit the officers any time and would rather pay more wages to adults than have the kind of annoyance with children that "we are experiencing right along," especially when they are truants. And in the thirties some high school officials protested to Commissioner Landis about major-league clubs recruiting their players. One school spokesman in St. Louis declared that the situation had reached the point where "Baseball seems to be more important than . . . studies to many of our students, and I feel that the best way to curb this interest . . . is to discontinue the high school league."

Thus borne on old and strong new currents during the twenties and thirties, boys' baseball journeyed ever further from simplicity and autonomy as, more and more, adults bestowed their attentions and ministrations on it.

A SURE WAY TO A BOY'S HEART

Boys institutionalized for supposed transgressions against society played baseball as eagerly as did those outside such institutions. For despite assertions of boys' work authorities that baseball made good citizens, boys who played ball might very well end up on the wrong side of the law, become separated from their parents, and find themselves incarcerated in juvenile institutions, or even jails or prisons, as delinquents.

Ironically, the institutions that housed these unfortunates frequently utilized baseball in programs aimed at rehabilitating them. Like school authorities, directors of these agencies came to believe in the idea that sports participation could inculcate the kind of middle-class behavior that prepared their charges to rejoin society.

The ostensible motive of juvenile institutions was to redeem children; at bottom, however, they sought to protect society from disorder. Particularly did these institutions sting immigrant and poor parents, since many thought them wanting in the moral qualities necessary for being fit preceptors to their children.

From earliest colonial days the states exercised parental authority to remove recalcitrant or unsupervised children to institutions, and those conducted for juveniles resembled school and penitentiary combined. The earliest of these establishments, the so-called houses of refuge, privately funded and founded mostly in Eastern cities between 1820 and 1850, imposed strict discipline. Some allowed a little play as well.

Earliest of the type, the New York House of Refuge, stood in 1824 on Madison Square, a neighborhood stamped with baseball history by the Knickerbocker ball club and later by meetings of the National League. Henry Curtis, a businessman interested in benevolent activities, superintended the House of Refuge. To discipline the children Curtis employed a carrot-and-stick method, putting them in cloth handcuffs and whipping them but also allowing boys who finished their work to enjoy marbles, running, kite flying, and in summer, swimming. Holidays also included sports and amusements. Curtis joined the children in their games, including playing ball with them.

Proof of Curtis's use of ball games lies in an unsigned letter from a friend
of Curtis's assistant, dated November 1857, a year after Curtis's death,
who stated that he had seen the superintendent playing some form of pre-
Knickerbocker baseball with the boys. But in 1826 Curtis resigned or was
fired for alleged leniency.

A similar institution, the Boston House of Refuge, opened the year Curtis
left the New York House. Its motley clientele, according to Stanley Schultz
in *The Culture Factory* (1973), comprised stubborn servants, orphans without visible means of support, youthful street idlers, vagrants, pilferers, and
children who refused to attend school. They could be incarcerated on flimsy
evidence given by parents or anyone "of position." Inmates lived under a
strict regimen, rising at 4:30 A.M. in summer and 6:00 in winter and retiring
at 8:00 P.M. According to a study by the Swedish writer Torsten Ericksson,
inmates worked for five and a half hours, attended school for four hours,
spent an hour and a half at devotion, and enjoyed recreation for two and a
half hours daily. Like Curtis, their superintendent, an Episcopal priest
named E.M. Wells, advocated games and played with the children. On
Christmas, Thanksgiving, and the Fourth of July he permitted "innocent
and agreeable recreation." And like Curtis, Wells did not last long as superintendent. A commission appointed to investigate "excessive recreation"
and other faults led him to resign, and the institution did not long survive
his departure.

Refuges came of age as a national phenomenon, according to Professor
Robert S. Pickett, by 1857, the year delegates from every major "child-
saving" institution in the United States gathered in New York for the first
national convention of refuge and reformatory representatives. But like a
consumptive in remission, the movement of the refuges proved retrograde.
Careful scrutiny uncovered use of severe physical coercion characterized by
unsparing application of the rattan, little or no instruction, and rife corruption. By 1870 refuges were judged, in Pickett's words, markedly deficient
and at the turn of the century "a subject for exposé."

In the meantime a new institution, the reform school, had entered the
dismal picture and by the 1850s had become "the rage." The new name
connoted a more constructive atmosphere and objective, but the institution
still presented a miasmic environment. In the course of time, as Homer
Folks pointed out in 1902, discharge from a reform school attached a stigma
to its products. To avoid this, authorities emphasized industrial features of
the reform institutions and adopted the name *industrial school*, only to have
an unfortunate effect on genuine industrial schools whose purpose was not
reformatory. So the name *training school* came into use as well, or institutions hedged by naming themselves after persons or places. To simplify
matters this account sticks to the term *reform school*.

Reform schools, unlike the houses of refuge, were usually located in the
country in order to remove inmates from the "corrupting" environment of

the city. They received more state support than the refuges and attempted to instill morals and habits of industry rather than simply providing a refuge for homeless street boys. However, as Joseph Kett has written, they were essentially prisons, often brutal and disorderly ones. The liberal judge Ben Lindsey claimed he saw the water cure administered to boys in Colorado's State Reform School in the 1890s. And in her 1916 book, *Society's Misfits*, reformer Madeline Doty brought to light many shocking stories of children in pre-1900 institutions having been beaten with rubber hoses or rattans. Frustrated and enraged, she said, they learned only anger and on their release turned to lives of crime. Nevertheless, evidence can be found that some of these early institutions made efforts to provide play, including baseball, for their young charges.

The first state reform school of its kind opened at Westborough, Massachusetts, in 1847 or 1848 (even official reports differ on the date). This school represented the first state-sponsored institution for juveniles in the United States, according to relevant documents, but it also received more than $60,000.00 from Theodore Lyman, a shipping magnate and former Boston mayor, and by 1896, taking his name, it had become the Lyman School for Boys.

As a manual training school, the 1894 Report of the Trustees stated, Lyman purposed to employ, instruct, and reform juvenile delinquents. At first it accepted boys as old as seventeen, many of them hardened criminals, but after the Massachusetts Reformatory at Concord opened in 1884, older boys could be sent there, so Lyman lowered the age of admission to fifteen. Boys might be committed to Lyman for such infractions as stubbornness, idleness, disorderliness, vagrancy, malicious mischief, possessing obscene books, and trespassing. Most of those committed had been truants.

The Lyman regimen consisted of studies along with shop, house work, and farm work, but even in winter, according to the superintendent's report, the children had an hour of recreation. In summer they enjoyed two recreation periods, from 2:30 to 3:00 P.M. and from 6:00 to 7:30 P.M. They were also permitted brief recesses during the day. In addition, the school fitted up a gym and bought skates, footballs, dumbbells, and fireworks for the Fourth of July. The administration took "great care," said the 1863 annual report, for the proper cleanliness, good diet, and exercise of the boys. In 1862 the superintendent, referring to efforts to "provide sources of amusement for the young" and "remove outward evidence that this is a place of punishment," mentioned that the directors had graded a large playground for the use of the boys.

The trustees of Lyman asserted in their 1880 report that they recognized a need for "the gratification of the innocent desire for recreation and amusement" and had therefore "provided games and the opportunities for playing them" and "encouraged athletic sports of various kinds." Apparently, this declaration carried weight with the superintendent, for in his report of 1879

under "Petties" (petty disbursements) he mentioned purchase of three baseballs for $2.00. In 1880 the school bought 27 baseballs for $16.00 and four
bats for $2.12. The following year it purchased 41 more baseballs for $25.00,
and by 1895 Lyman school owned baseballs and bats worth $39.66.

By that time Lyman, under an instructor named Alliston Greene, conducted physical training, which included both gymnastics and sports. The
big day for field sports came on July Fourth, which always featured baseball.
The best performers received prizes. During summer vacations Greene ran
a baseball tournament. Lyman, like many similar institutions, used the cottage plan, so the residents of its cottages vied with each other in baseball
for a silver cup. Greene explained in his 1896–97 report that he used "games
of recognized educational value" and in his next report stated that "baseball
contests were entered into with zest." Lyman's superintendent, Theodore
F. Chapin, supported Greene's work in his own 1898 report: "Sports and
amusements are not neglected and are entered into enthusiastically."

Among the sampling of schools discussed below, those that mention sports
only, rather than baseball specifically, doubtless offered baseball. In fact,
the recognition of baseball's supremacy as the national game in the second
half of the nineteenth century changes such probability into virtual certainty.

One of these institutions, a Massachusetts primary school for paupers
called Monson, had playgrounds in addition to its recreation rooms containing games and magazines. Letters of Monson children, reported principal
Eugenia M. Fullington in 1894, expressed their interest in sports as well as
studies and work.

A playground also availed at a school in Lansing, Michigan, at first called
the House of Correction for Juvenile Offenders. There, said an observer in
1875, "the lads of the school can comfortably spend the hours allotted to
them for recreation and sport." By 1891 the State Board of Corrections and
Charities could report an expenditure at the Lansing school of $906.17 for
"Amusement and instruction." The Lansing school reflects well the evolution
of institutional names, for within a span of about fifty years its name shifted
from the original "House of Correction" to "Reform School" and finally to
"Industrial School."

Records of the Minnesota Reform School in St. Paul revealed it as a no-
nonsense institution. The work plan outlined by Superintendent J.G.
Richeldaffer in his annual reports disclosed that inmates did all the institution's labor. They made, washed, ironed, and mended clothes, they baked
and cooked, they washed, scrubbed, and cleaned the premises, and they
labored on the farm or in the shops as well, except that some lads between
seven and thirteen were too young to do much. They also studied a half-
day. Punishments included bread and water for one or more meals, the
lockup, and the rod. A few, said Richeldaffer, "had to have a good whipping."
Generally, however, the boys stayed "cheerful and contented," no doubt in
part because Richeldaffer, sensible to the need for recreation and sports,

had assigned regular hours for play. Early on (1869) he recommended construction of a new building with a basement, part of which could serve as a
playroom in bad weather. He got it.

Holding that public holidays should be devoted to children's "pleasure
and training," Richeldaffer saw to it that each Fourth of July his charges
spent the day on the prairie outside the school grounds indulging in "such
games and amusements as may best please them." He also set aside Christmas, New Year's, and Thanksgiving holidays and a day at the State Fair for
the pleasure of the inmates.

In his annual reports Richeldaffer reverted repeatedly to the theme of
recreational value:

> We recognize the necessity for recreation and fun. The pleasantest home needs
> the spice of variety and change, and the most agreeable occupation becomes
> drudgery without occasional seasons of rest and amusement. Play is therefore
> a part of our daily business. We make the best use we can, to this end, of all
> our light holidays, giving them up to such sports and plays as are most pleasant
> to the young.

In another report Richeldaffer maintained fervently,

> Playfulness is a prominent characteristic of youth; ours are not stinted in their
> allowance of fun and frolic. There is in this school none of that dejected, self-
> deprecatory, and hang-dog look, too often to be seen in institutions where
> youth are confined, whether for correction or in compliance with the behests
> of pity and benevolence.

Upon Richeldaffer's retirement J.W. Brown, his assistant and successor,
continued Richeldaffer's liberal policy toward play. On all holidays and during the three daily recreation periods (the evening period was lengthened
in summer), the boys enjoyed full freedom, Brown reported in 1880, in
playing, on "the fine large playground," "base-ball" and "all other games of
which only boys can think."

As the century neared its end, the numbers of incarcerated youngsters
grew. The United States census of 1880 reported almost 11,500 children in
juvenile reformatories. Ten years later the count was higher by more than
3,000. During the 1890s authorities founded approximately 240 new institutions and, in the first decade of the twentieth century, more than 200
more. Even so, the census report of 1896, *Crime and Pauperism*, revealed
that the states still "put away" children for vague offenses like "incorrigibility"
and mixed the unfortunate with the criminal. More odious, many juvenile
offenders continued to find themselves in adult prisons.

Some progressive spokesmen tried to alleviate the plight of troubled children. At the 1901 annual conference of Charities and Corrections in Ohio
a Miss Rogers recommended games as an antidote for lawlessness and a
producer of order. At the same conference Superintendent Ira Otterson of
the State Home for Boys in Jamesburg, New Jersey, expressed his belief in

sports and urged reform school officers to "guide the sports in lines that are manly, healthful and pure," suggesting blandly that "By showing an interest in the sports of the pupils" these officers could increase the pupils' esteem for them. Institutions for wayward youths also heeded G. Stanley Hall's ideas about play as a means of occupying spare time, holding interest, and preventing outbursts against authority.

Others in the progressive era contributed a modicum of concrete aid to hapless youth. Denver Judge Ben Lindsey got a law passed in 1901 establishing in Colorado the first special court for juveniles, and by 1910 the boys he sent to the Colorado Industrial School (formerly the Reform School) at Golden, according to their *Industrial School Magazine*, instead of being subjected to the water cure were being taken to Denver to see baseball games. President William Howard Taft appointed Julia Lathrop as the first head of a Children's Bureau in 1912, and she pressed various boards and agencies for separate facilities for juveniles. The International Prison Association, too, passed resolutions in 1910 suggesting improvement in the treatment of young delinquents by making "vast additions" to playgrounds and athletic fields "as the surest preventives of juvenile mischief and crime."

The most innovative of progressive era reformers was William R. George, a businessman and philanthropist with a unique approach to boys' work. George believed that the standard institutions for juvenile delinquents did nothing to help the boys learn to regulate their own conduct, so he developed a noninstitutional approach that featured self-rule, eventually establishing what he called the George Junior Republic.

George began work with boys in New York's toughest neighborhoods, gaining the boys' confidence by organizing them into gangs and playing baseball and other sports with them. Then he started to take groups of teenagers camping annually, but soon the children got into trouble with their country neighbors by begging and stealing. By the fifth summer he realized their problem: the children took charity for granted. So he decided they must earn their way instead.

At Freeville, New York, on a forty-acre farm George therefore formed in 1890 a utopian community in which the children gradually took over their own government, creating their own laws and courts and electing their own leaders, although George retained veto power. The boys remained free to work or not, as they chose, at vocational training or at farm or house work, but if they had not earned the price of a meal or bed they went without. Besides this serious side of life the boys could have plenty of fun at the Republic, especially through sports, with baseball and football taking center stage. Teams not only played local schools on their own grounds, they toured the area, defeating nearby high school teams.

George gave the following example of the enthusiasm for baseball at the Republic. Once the children learned of the eight-hour day movement and enthusiastically persuaded the president of the Republic to sign a "law" establishing it. Then the boys marched off to the hayfield, bringing their bats, balls, masks, and mitts along. Said one, "We'll work until four P.M. and then we'll have a great old game down there in the field until supper time." At six they were heard returning, "discussing the sundry merits of the eight-hour law and the great game of baseball they had just finished playing. One allowed that the eight-hour law was "OK," and so was baseball, but "grub is best." When they arrived they found no dinner ready: the girls, too, had worked only an eight-hour day. All went to bed without dinner. The eight-hour bill got repealed.

Other reformers, including Washington Gladden, the Congregational minister, visited the Republic, Gladden witnessing a "very exciting" baseball game against a team from a neighboring village, umpired with scrupulous fairness by "Daddy" George, as the children called him. Another important reformer who visited Freeville was Thomas Osborne of nearby Auburn, who eventually tried out George's principles of self-government in prisons.* Osborne furnished his own local urchins with uniforms; they formed the Osborne Athletic Club and played baseball against many teams, chiefly the George Junior Republic team. Once Osborne offered a cup that would become the permanent possession of the first team to win it three seasons in a row. To celebrate the opening of the season Osborne invited the two teams to play at Willow Point, his summer home on Lake Owasco, and enjoy a repast afterward. The game ended in a fight, so the food was rushed on to quell it.

Other similar groups, some of them affiliated with George's, copied his idea of a junior republic. In 1906, for example, Homer Lane organized the Ford Republic near Detroit. Lane, like George, believed that the typical child-saving institutions failed to train the children to regulate their own behavior. J.M. McIndoo, just completing his Ph.D. under G. Stanley Hall, superintended the Ford Republic from 1912 to 1922. Like other progressives McIndoo hailed the role of team sports as a device for teaching youngsters to "give up much for the sake of the group" and instilling "many valuable lessons of self-control." And like leaders in the play movement he wanted those sports conducted by trained experts.

George's Junior Republic, despite criticism by the State Board of Charities and threats of legal action under the child labor laws, continued into the thirties at least, and a George biographer claims most graduates became good citizens.

During the 1900s other reform institutions, new and old, endorsed the palliative properties of play, including baseball. The Rochester, New York, State Industrial School had by the 1890s and 1900s already turned to baseball and other sports as "a sure way to a boy's heart" and a means of "securing and holding" the boys' interest, according to the reports of Samuel D. Bow-

*See Chapter 25.

den, Protestant chaplain and acting sports director. Yet the 1898 report stated that the boys got only ten minutes a day for recreation, except for an hour and a half on Saturdays. But Chaplain Bowden obviously made the most of his time, furthering sports in his work "by every means at my disposal." In his reports he claimed that, although the difficulties of securing equipment created a serious obstacle, baseball and other sports influenced the boys toward "clean sport" and "cleaner lives."

Acknowledging some opposition to his policy, Bowden remarked, "It may seem to some that our boys are not sent here for a play-time and that it is needless expense to provide foot-balls and base-balls and bats and catcher's gloves," so he assured critics that sport was not "given first place" at Rochester and that he used it as a means of "getting in touch" with the boys. He thought sports brought them to believe him "their friend" and that his presence as umpire had given him a "more respectful hearing in the preaching service" and made for increased interest in religious events. Then, letting the doctrinal cat all the way out of the bag, he said that through sports he demonstrated by personal example that "the manliest manhood is Christian manhood." An observer from the New York Prison Association noted in a 1913 report, *Prison Progress*, that the Rochester institution used the cottage plan, and that every cottage (there were 32 at the time) had its own baseball diamond. Because the school operated both a farm and an industrial department, the boys played in two baseball leagues, one for the farm workers and the other for those who performed industrial work. The best team in each league received a banner.

On Rainford Island, Massachusetts, a successor to the aforementioned House of Refuge had emerged: the Boston House of Reformation. By 1898 the new institution's trustees were reporting special attention to instruction in sports and athletic games given by a new yard officer capable of combining his regular law duties with a knowledge of sports, thus keeping in "better touch" with the boys. Apparently, he did a good job, for the boys received regular coaching in athletics outside of school hours. Reports of the superintendent, school principal, and physician for 1900 through 1912 described baseball games and other athletic competitions for prizes, activities in which many boys of all ages showed "a surprising proficiency." In 1901–02 the principal declared that the staff recognized the value of "rightly directed play" carried out through regular classes conducted in both indoor and outdoor games and athletics. Like other institutions, the Boston House observed holidays appropriately with patriotic exercises and athletic sports. By 1906–07 the House of Reformation had taken a new name, the Suffolk School for Boys, but it still sponsored "the usual athletics," according to its official reports.

St. Mary's Industrial School, founded at Baltimore in 1866, remained relatively obscure until George Herman "Babe" Ruth, its former resident (1902 to 1914) called public attention to it by his unprecedented performance in major-league baseball parks and his licentious behavior away from them. Few, however, realized that even before Ruth's matriculation, St. Mary's had built a long and stout baseball tradition. As Marshall Smelser, a Ruth biographer, has written, no fewer than forty-four teams, organized by age, played daily intramural and interscholastic games on good fields from March through September.

St. Mary's, an institution founded to shelter wayward or helpless street boys, orphans, paupers, and some boarders, at once served as orphanage, boarding school, detention home, reform school, and vocational school. It had been founded by the Congregation of St. Francis Xavier, usually called the Xaverian Brothers, who offered vocational training and extracurricular activities of which baseball ranked the highest. St. Mary's won its first interscholastic championship in 1897. According to another biographer, Ken Sobel, at least three future major leaguers besides Ruth passed through its gates.

Lyman School in Westborough, Massachusetts, continued after the turn of the century its program of gym exercises combined with games and sports because J.A. Puffer, then its principal, appreciated that boys, especially the smaller ones, preferred play and games to routine gym exercises. "The play instinct," declared Puffer in his 1904 report, "is the strongest instinct of a boy's life." In his own report that year the boys' physical training instructor carried the point further:

> The boys in playing these games improve not only along the physical lines but along moral lines as well, [and] the boy who learns to play fairly ... has made a great stride towards the formation of a strong character.

As already noted, before 1908 boys too old for acceptance by Lyman had to be sent to jail or the reformatory at Concord, where they mingled with mature offenders, but, according to the Report of the Massachussetts Training Schools for 1912, the state did in 1908 establish the Industrial School for Boys in Shirley, to take in delinquents over fifteen. The leaders of this school gave much attention to baseball and other sports. "Properly supervised recreation and amusement are tremendously important," asserted George P. Campbell, Shirley's superintendent in 1913. Shirley operated on the cottage plan, and each cottage fielded a baseball team. In addition, an all-school team made up of players chosen from the cottage nines played neighboring high school and academy teams.

Other reformatory leaders in the early twentieth century likewise affirmed their faith in the salutary powers of baseball. At the same time, the response of the boys demonstrated the popularity and familiarity of the game even among boys in institutions. In or out of trouble, in custody or free, all were susceptible to the lure of baseball. In the Bronx, at the Catholic Protectory, inmates played baseball on the home's own athletic field with seats for more than 500. And upstate in Valhalla the Children's Aid Society operated a farm home for "criminal" and homeless youth, where the boys could play ball during their recreation hours. The Home for Neglected Children, operated by the New York Female Benevolent Society, employed a Columbia University student to serve as companion and sports leader for the boys. In the summer the Home sent youngsters to Oceanport, on the Jersey coast, and one year a Captain Parsons, the boys' friend from Red Bank, organized two baseball teams called Harvard and Yale, which played "most exciting" games.

Boys played baseball on the Saturday half-holiday at the Indiana Reform School, about a mile west of Plainfield, a compound of thirty-two separate buildings where children lived on the cottage system, each cottage with its own playground. The sight of three or four baseball games going on simultaneously among cottage teams, said an observer in describing the Indiana prison system in 1900, "is a sight which once seen will never be forgotten."

The problem of truancy led to the establishment in the mid-nineteenth century of another type of institution. Many children roamed Boston streets without any supervision, as David Nasaw has explained, thereby becoming criminals in the eyes of the law, so the police apprehended them as truants. Judges sentenced offenders to special institutions for truants known as parental schools, some of them day schools but most boarding. They housed boys from ages 7 or 8 to 16 or 18 convicted of truancy or other criminal offenses, according to James Hiatt's 1915 bulletin on the subject from the United States Bureau of Education. By that time, thirteen cities in all parts of the country had established such truancy schools, many on the cottage plan. Those within city limits stressed gymnastic work, Hiatt said, as much as fourteen hours a week of gym in Buffalo and in Butte. The country schools, on the other hand, with more space in which to function, turned to outdoor farm and gardening work as well as athletic sports. The Parental School in West Roxbury, Massachusetts, adjacent to Boston proper, for example, permitted many sports and games after school hours and especially on holidays. Its superintendent, D.F. Dane, made a point of mentioning in his 1903–04 report that the cottage baseball teams had played a series of games for the school championship.

The shoals of incarcerated children grew larger, meanwhile. By 1910 the count of institutionalized children had swelled to approximately 100,000, although this figure included orphans, half-orphans, the homeless, the neglected, and the indigent as well as juvenile offenders.

This growth seems related to the progressives' trust in the powers of the state. They apparently felt no compulsion to limit the discretionary power of officials and wanted to give the state all the authority that seemed necessary. Probation officers needed no warrant to enter a home and dictate to the family, and juvenile judges often overlooked laws of evidence, leaving child care agencies literally to assume complete parental powers over youngsters. In short, as Ira Glasser has pointed out, the Bill of Rights did not apply to children.

Worse yet, such institutions, despite their baseball programs, often proved ineffective in preventing children from becoming criminals after their release. Progressives did recognize the ineffectiveness of many institutions, although they attributed failures not to the plan of institutionalizing children but to lack of funds and incompetent administrations. More recently, however, many have questioned the system, calling it social control and declaring that "doing good" masks motives of self-interest. Some sociologists do not even think incarceration helps and point out that children from affluent families who get into trouble are perceived as merely "mischievous" and receive individual attention, such as their own private psychologists, whereas poor children are viewed as habitual troublemakers and relegated to institutions. As recently as 1972 the Provo Experiment showed graphically that boys committed to a state industrial school were almost three times as likely to get arrested after their release as boys kept in the community under peer group supervision.

Even after the progressive era the faith of reformers in incarcerating children did not abate. Neither during the flourishing twenties nor the collapsing thirties did conditions for incarcerated children change appreciably. A letter of Grace Abbot, Chief of the Children's Bureau, dated November 1921, stated that federal law still made no distinction between adults and children: juveniles were still being arrested, detained in jail, and indicted by grand juries. The Department of Labor reported in 1922 that most local institutions that received children also accepted adults. Crime statistics revealed that even in the 1930s large numbers of youngsters were committed not merely to reformatories but to state prisons.

Nor did the sports programs of such institutions appear to deter crime. The Wickersham Commission found in 1930 that nearly 55 percent of criminals had been under 21 when committed, and an additional 20,000 under 18 went to juvenile institutions every year. Investigators like Sheldon and Eleanor Glueck demonstrated statistically in the thirties that imprisonment of children, far from being a success, indicated failure: children who had spent time in training schools (even though they played games there) displayed very high rates of subsequent arrest.

Yet reform schools of the twenties and thirties continued to use baseball as a child-saving agent. "Recreation is as necessary for the boy as oil for an engine," asserted C.H. Lewis, general superintendent of the State Reformatory for Boys in Pontiac, Illinois. "Supervised play develops poise, self-release and balance. It also develops character." A few examples betoken the continued presence of baseball in such institutions. The State Reform School at Greendale, Kentucky, organized ten boys' baseball teams as part of its recreation program in 1921. Inmates at Children's Village in Dobbs Ferry, New York, regarded baseball as the most popular activity in its spring and summer program, and several baseball diamonds served senior boys, those over twelve. Baseball, together with football and basketball, proved popular at the Topeka, Kansas, Industrial School, but the paltry funds for sports commonly allocated to such institutions led its superintendent, Samuel G. Clarke, in his biennial report of 1926 to urge more ample appropriations for equipment because games "teach boys fairness and help them physically and mentally." Two years later, the Topeka school still starved for sports gear. Clarke's successor, Louis D. White, said he had capable instructors but they needed $1,000.00 for equipment. "We have bought a few balls and bats with donated money," White said, and installed other equipment for games made from material at hand, but it was not enough. By the late thirties, however, the Topeka boys had their own baseball ground and even played "extramural" games with teams from outside the institution.

The depression swelled the number of boys who left home for the open road. A 1935 study of a group of 347 boys adrift in southern California, for instance, found that seventy percent of these wanderers, euphemistically called "transient boys," had once been active in organized recreation: sixty-eight percent had belonged to athletic teams, particularly baseball and football, and thus came from "normal" recreation backgrounds; but "obviously," concluded the researcher, the experience had "not met their needs."

Baseball also found its way into orphanages. Girard College, as one Philadelphia orphanage was called, accommodated in 1915 some 1,600 orphaned youngsters aged seven through twelve. A generous endowment allowed Girard to furnish several playgrounds for the boys. Nevertheless, its chief weakness, according to an article in *Playground*, lay in neglecting to organize play for all the boys. Instead, Girard concentrated on the few talented athletes and produced some "very superior" baseball (and football) teams, counting among its alumni Harry Davis, an infielder who played for years with the Philadelphia Athletics; Ben Houser, a first baseman who also made the Athletics; and John Lush, who pitched for the Philadelphia Nationals.

Orphanages often had to scrape for equipment. Bob Quinn, president of the Boston Red Sox in 1926, said that he sent old and "real torn" uniforms to the orphans at the House of Angels Guarding. Garry Herrmann, president of the Cincinnati Reds, usually contributed a few baseballs annually to the local General Protestant Orphan Society.

In the late teens St. Elizabeth Orphan Asylum in New Orleans summoned a policeman named Hereford to lie in wait several nights for a "scoundrel" who had broken into the place. During his vigil Patrolman Hereford became friendly with the children and noticed that they wasted their leisure hours. "A little tot came to me and said, 'Mister, can you get us a ball and a bat?' 'Why,' said I, 'haven't you anything to play with here?'" When the child said no, "That set my mind working. The next afternoon I brought them a half dozen balls and a couple of bats." He also solicited help from others to erect some playground equipment and purchase more bats and balls. Hereford even persuaded members of the local Playground Commission to teach the inmates some games and donate still more baseballs and bats. Whether he also caught the "scoundrel" is unknown.

The Hebrew Orphanage of New York City, situated on thirteen acres of fields and playgrounds, cared for 1,150 children, about 40 percent of them sent by the juvenile court on charges of having "improper guardianship" and 75 percent of them already branded as "incipient juvenile delinquents." Superintendent L.J. Simmonds, who believed in play as a method of instilling "moral stamina" into these neophyte transgressors, spent as much for recreation, about $1,500.00 annually, as for religion. Simmonds encouraged his play leaders to get every child to participate, and during the summer of 1922 thirty orphanage teams played baseball. He favored the annual baseball game of orphans versus faculty as giving the boys a chance to test the sportsmanship of their elders!

A Passaic, New Jersey, orphanage made news in July of 1933 after six of its inmates discovered a dangerous washout on the Erie Railroad tracks and flagged down the oncoming train, thereby averting much damage. Grateful passengers asked the boys what reward they wanted. They requested that Babe Ruth hear of their act. As a result, Ruth visited the school and invited the lads to Yankee Stadium as his guests. Yankee owner Colonel Jacob Ruppert sent a bus to bring them and some of their schoolmates to his ball park, where their orphanage baseball team took the field, Ruth hitting fungoes to their infield and Herb Pennock to their outfield.

Special institutions that looked after handicapped youngsters might also include baseball in their programs. At one, the Massachusetts State School for the Deaf in Hartford, Millard Phillips, who had lost his hearing because of scarlet fever, caught for the school, then taught baseball to his son, who eventually became a good semipro player. The school's best-known alumnus, William E. "Dummy" Hoy, played outfield in the major leagues from 1888 to 1902.*

In one school for "mental defectives," where baseball was popular, "there were several nines among the boys," disclosed a committee from the Playground Association in 1911, but the "crack nine" comprised some inmates and some employees. "The foreman of a shop at the bat, one of his inmate workers in the box, and another feeble-minded boy as umpire made an ideal combination," averred the committee members, making the report more humorous than intended. Warming to the subject, the committee went on,

> It was more fun to "strike out" the foreman than anyone else, except perhaps the superintendent himself. . . . In such institutions the gains that come from happy play are by no means confined to inmates. The esprit de corps that is promoted on the diamond carries over into the schoolhouse and to the shop.

*See *Baseball: The Early Years*, pp. 287, 326, and 336.

The committee concluded, "It is just as necessary to promote the happiness of the employees as it is that of the inmates."

Blind children, too, played a form of baseball. After undergoing training in listening for the ball, they took their places on a diamond a third the regular size. Upon the umpire's signal the pitcher, who was partly sighted, threw overhand at a consistent speed, and batters swung at every pitch, hitting the ball on the ground so that the fielders could try to find it. A 1923 story in *Playground* averred that such games offered a valuable means of enabling blind children not only to "learn about the physical world" but also to "take their places" in a "normal social environment."

Boys in these special schools, together with those in the reform schools, constituted a less noticed but substantial part of the foundation of baseball.

BOYS' BASEBALL IN MIDPASSAGE

The onset of World War II found boys' baseball in transition. The traditional boys' game was on the way out. Adult sponsorship and intrusion had run the gamut from private to public agencies and various combinations of these, a sponsorship that reflected the mix of private and public enterprise that characterized the nation's economy and would continue to do so.

The organization of boys' baseball had also fanned out from local teams and leagues to state and nationwide scope. It had drifted ever farther from the impromptu, self-directed, unfettered pastime of the sandlot toward the directed, highly organized and supervised game of adult intervention and control for adult purposes. Once a folk game played for fun and transmitted culturally—"picked up" haphazardly and informally from other boys and from watching young men—it was now explicitly taught not only in public and private schools but in commercial baseball "schools."

Recreation leaders tirelessly iterated, in keeping with bureaucratic doctrine, that the game must be supervised by "experts." Play could no longer be left in the hands of children, warned reformers, if American ideals and morals inculcated through play were to withstand the corrosion of urban-industrialism and the flood of immigrants unfamiliar with American traditions. The magazine *Outlook* in 1912 even praised the influence of professional ball players on boys as "on the whole thoroughly wholesome" because it stimulated them to play "proficiently."

The rationale for all this adult involvement was rooted in the child study movement that brought about an evolution in the concept of play from a time waster to a useful activity through which youngsters learned and developed. Seizing upon these revelations, adults endowed ball playing with more beneficial qualities than seem possible: it fostered good health and morals, deterred juvenile delinquency, Americanized children of immigrants, and taught youngsters loyalty, cooperation, obedience, discipline, self-sacrifice, teamwork, fair play, sportsmanship, recognition of authority, and acceptance of defeat. In a word, boys' baseball became a panacea for the eradication of social problems and the answer to the puzzle of ways desired traits of character and behavior could be inculcated.

The chief proponents and promoters of this bundle of goals and ideals, the private and public sponsors and supporters of boys' baseball, were closely intermeshed. Business and fraternal organizations sponsored boys' baseball directly or contributed financially to agencies like the American Legion and the PSAL. Organized Baseball helped subsidize the former, and A.G. Spalding and Company supplied the latter's trophies and other awards. Service clubs formed by businessmen, Legonnaires among them, supported boys' teams that played on public grounds and availed themselves of public services.

Government also fostered boys' baseball through the schools, which in turn responded readily to the requirements and requests of business. In the late thirties a private group called the Athletic Institute, formed by sporting goods dealers to promote sports equipment, went so far as to devise a plan to back baseball outright in grade schools as well as in high schools. And as we have seen, the newspaper business lent powerful support and publicity to all these kinds of sponsorship.

The careers of individuals also evidenced the interlock among sponsors of boys' baseball. Luther Gulick moved easily from YMCA executive work to PSAL and playground leadership. Jane Addams proved equally mobile, and Major John L. Griffith, who belonged to the American Legion and Rotary, also served as executive vice president of the NAAF and editor of the *Athletic Journal*.

This power structure, purveying basically conformist, conventional goals and ideals for baseball play, sought to socialize youngsters, especially those of foreign parentage, to mold them into compliant citizens, and to prepare them to fit into an increasingly bureaucratized political and economic environment. Progressive Newton D. Baker acknowledged as much when in 1918 he wrote that children's play, particularly team games for adolescents, created a new "system of social constraints" to replace those once imposed by the rural village.

With the change to urban life, the vaunted individualism of rural Americans was to be exercised only within the context of larger social goals. So too with boys' baseball. Reformers and social workers fastened upon the game as a vehicle for cultivating in boys those attitudes appropriate to life in a bureaucratized industrial-urban setting—cooperation, teamwork, and obedience to the rules—rather than those requiring individual discretion. That side of the game must be subordinated, for the good of the team. In short, they submitted a recipe for preparing well-oiled functionaries to fit into the growing bureaucracies of business, industry, and government.

Underpinning for these objectives came from an impressive group of psychologists, among them, of course, G. Stanley Hall, who in 1905 wrote that baseball, football, and cricket, by teaching "the subordination of each member to the whole and to a leader, cultivate the social and cooperative instincts" that he appeared to favor. William McDougall, too, stressed the value of play as a socializing force, "molding the individual and preparing him for social life, for cooperation, for submission, and for leadership, for the postponement of individual to collective ends. . . . "

Henry S. Curtis of the Playground Association approved of these social objectives and suggested how playing baseball furthered them: "A long hit or a daring run may not be what is needed," and deciding to strike out "in order that the man on third [may] run in" (to sacrifice) is a "social judgment" affecting the success of the team. (Obviously, Curtis knew little about baseball.) "This type of loyalty," he said, "is the same thing we call good citizenship."

Many ideals and goals put forward by reformers and promoters were not unworthy, and many well-intentioned sponsors conscientiously interested themselves in the welfare of boys and genuinely believed ball playing benefited youngsters morally as well as physically. Others, capitalizing on baseball's hold on Americans and on the widespread presumption of the game's benefits to boys, exploited boys' baseball in their own interest, sometimes enlightened and often selfish. Most programs contained a mixture of both purposes.

W.I. Newstetter observed in the *Encyclopedia of the Social Sciences* that the line between a club promoting a cause and one with the object of substituting desirable for undesirable behavior is often blurred; the real purpose may be disguised in a program of ostensible value. "Under the cloak of objectivity and detachment," he pointed out, "many subtle influences operate in the implanting of ideas and ideals in the minds of boys and girls through group activity." Some organizations, he went on, make their appeal through sports, and "The interest thus stimulated is used to develop a variety of specific behavior patterns" often expressed through slogans or glittering generalities like "good citizenship" and "character building."

Nor was America alone in sponsoring extensive youth programs like baseball. In their own way and for their own objectives authorities in other countries in the twenties and thirties attended to boys through such organizations as Russia's Young Pioneers, which in 1928 had millions of members aged six to sixteen; Italy's Balilla, which numbered thousands of young Fascists; and Republican Germany's Youth Association, ten million strong, the largest and most vital movement of the kind in the world, replaced by the Hitler Jugend, composed of children aged six to eighteen. Some sports figures in this country viewed such developments benignly. Avery Brundage of the Olympic Committee, speaking before the German-American Bund in 1937, declared, "We can learn much from Germany. . . . We, too, if we wish to preserve our institutions, must stamp out communism. We, too, must take steps to arrest the decline of patriotism."

Others were not so sure. Lotus D. Coffman, president of the University of Minnesota, writing in *Educational Record* in 1936, saw danger in the co-opting of youth by government agencies, "who, even though their motives may be laudable enough, nevertheless indoctrinate students with their special creeds and philosophies."

Probably, the new course set for boys' baseball in America was inevitable. With urban-industrialism bent on large, highly organized and bureaucratized entities in so many other segments of society, boys' baseball and sports in general could hardly escape similar corporate trends, particularly since boys' baseball got caught up in attempts to solve a host of social problems, such as juvenile delinquency, child labor, and poor schooling, made acute by burgeoning city life.

There is no gainsaying that the reform efforts, government action, and sponsorship by private organizations bestowed advantages on boys' baseball. They provided space and better diamonds to play on; more stable, orderly, and dependable playing conditions; greater safety with less chance of injury; and in some cases equipment, uniforms, and coaching. More important, adult intervention afforded a chance to play ball to many boys who under the circumstances would probably have been deprived of the opportunity. But succor came at a price, one that would mount as time went on.

Not that the sandlot game of simpler days was idyllic. The past is seldom as good, the present as bad, or the future as hopeless as they often seem. Sandlot ball too had grating features. Yet despite its drawbacks informal baseball, in its spontaneity and freedom from adults, possessed a vitality and pungency much of which the evolving new order in boys' baseball would drain from it.

Even so, surrender of some sandlot advantages might have been warranted or at least tolerable if the assumption that playing ball imbued boys with desirable attitudes and traits of character had proved indisputable. It did not. Even in those earlier times, critics sniped at such claims. In *The Book of Athletics and Out-of-Door Sports* (1895) Norman W. Bingham discerned possible harmful effects of athletics. He believed they tended to occupy too much of boys' time to the neglect of schoolwork and caused boys to value physical over intellectual and moral abilities. And in contrast with those already heaping encomiums on boys' baseball at that time, Bingham singled it out for dispraise because it disposed boys to trickery and dishonesty: "in baseball, boys who in most things are the soul of honesty will cut across from first to third base" or will claim "to have caught a ball 'on the fly' which they know to have touched the ground. . . . " Similarly, Thorstein Veblen believed that sport taught "chicanery," "falsehood," and "brow-beating," habituating players to fraud. A well-known champion of progressive education, Professor George Counts, had reservations, too, reportedly holding baseball responsible for "the degradation of American morals in public and private life," since it taught that applause falls to those who can steal and get away with it! In 1925 a psychologist, Mary A. Brownell, offered what seems like a balanced view:

> There is nothing inherent in the activity of baseball which *in itself* would make a participant develop along social, physical, or mental lines. One can be made a cheat and a poor sport just as well as one can develop the desirable character traits.

More recent scholarly studies have cast doubts better founded than Veblen's or Counts's on the gospel of boys' baseball and athletics in general. Bruce C. Ogilvie and Thomas A. Tutko, for example, discovered "no empirical support for the tradition that sport builds character." They concluded that "athletic competition has no more beneficial effects than intense endeavor in any other field." Apparently, athletics afford only an opportunity for participants to exercise certain traits they possessed to begin with. In any case, it appears that the mind-cast of athletes and coaches in general is "conservative"—a term that is often a euphemism for "reactionary."

Then, too, the ever-present gap between code preached and code practiced made ideals like sportsmanship, fair play, and respect for rules somewhat unrealistic in a highly competitive society where sponsors looked upon competitive sports as a training ground for success in the adult world. Besides, athletics themselves are nothing if not competitive. Winning is of course not everything, except in war, but in athletics it looms large, and, notwithstanding its disparagement by the counterculture of the 1960s, is surely preferable to losing. Small wonder, therefore, that abuses, some of which have been instanced, crept into boys' baseball particularly where schools and private groups sponsored highly organized athletics for older boys.

One aspect of baseball's purported effect on juvenile delinquency is seldom emphasized: the fact that boys got into trouble with the law simply for playing ball in the place most convenient for them, the street. In big cities like New York, Washington, and Boston, as well as in small towns like Shenandoah, Pennsylvania, well into the twentieth century ball playing in the street was illegal. Policemen not only chased boys, they broke up games, arrested boys, and haled them into court for this crime. In July 1909, for example, police arrested 128 children in New York for playing ball. In Prospect Park in 1913 police took four lads into custody for tossing a rubber ball around; a newspaper reporter said their parents were not notified, and they were put into a cell so crowded they had to stand for nearly twenty-four hours. On Thanksgiving Day, 1897, a New York policeman actually shot a boy running from a ball game that broke up when he appeared. In the 1930s, by ironic contrast, the New York City Police Athletic League (PAL) encouraged boys to play ball; instead of trying to catch the baseball mice who played when they were away, police cats began to aid and abet the mice.

Despite the earlier arrests for the crime of ball playing, no benefit ascribed to baseball was more highly touted than its value as a deterrent to juvenile crime. This claim enjoyed long currency. Since early in the century police chiefs and other authorities in New York, Newark, Chicago, Cincinnati, and San Francisco habitually submitted figures to "prove" an equation that read: more baseball equals less juvenile delinquency. The appeal and apparent validity of this claim furnished powerful ammunition for reformers and social workers seeking support and public funds for supervised ball play. The president of the National Probation Association in 1928 declared organized play to be "the best preventive that has ever been discovered for juvenile wrong-doing." Evidently, no one thought to ask why so many good ball players played on prison teams.*

Herbert Hoover, an officer of the Boys' Clubs of America, added his prestige, or what was left of it in the thirties, to bolster this belief. Through sports, he said, we "channel" boys' desire for exercise and "let off their explosive violence without letting them get into the police courts." Ford Frick recited this litany in the 1950s before a Congressional committee.

The equation linking baseball with crime prevention never proved out. Frederick Thrasher's 1927 study of Chicago gangs revealed that delinquents loved baseball, so much so that they not only had their own teams but played hooky from school to go to games, thus bearing out G. Stanley Hall's earlier observation that "If hoodlums play at all, they become infatuated with baseball and football." Thrasher concluded that it was erroneous to assume juvenile delinquency problems could be solved by a "multiplication" of playgrounds and social centers in gang areas because "gangland" territory already provided adventure with which no playground could compete. The solution, he thought, lay in finding leaders who could "crystallize the bellicose propensity of the gang into some sort of athletic team . . . [because] Through conventionalization the gang may become accommodated to society." Apparently, even good leaders might make no difference. A four-year study of a well-housed and -financed boys' club in a criminal area of New York City conducted in 1927–31 by New York University showed that the club exerted no appreciable influence in preventing juvenile delinquency. Despite a broad program of activities, including athletics, the delinquency rate of the boys enrolled still exceeded that of the general community, and besides, the club failed to reach a large number of the boys it was designed to serve.

Dominick Cavallo's doctoral study provided the clincher on the argument that baseball playing did not remedy delinquency. He presented persuasive evidence that playgrounds (and hence ball playing) were ineffective against such serious juvenile crime as assault and substantial theft. Playgrounds did diminish the juvenile arrest rate—something quite different, because when slum children had only the street to play in they were arrested for petty

*See below, Chapter 25.

acts: truancy, begging, selling papers, pitching pennies, throwing stones, singing, shouting, overturning trash cans, or anything the police and magistrates chose to interpret as juvenile crimes. In the late twenties I was myself yanked up, shoved, and threatened with being "locked up" for refusing to "move on" with the others because I said I had a right to play there after a policeman broke up our punch ball game on a middle-class street in Brooklyn. Once a place to play was provided, Cavallo showed, arrest for this type of "crime" dropped markedly. Meanwhile, however, serious juvenile crime persisted.

The most regrettable defect in the looming new order of things in boys' baseball lay not in what youngsters learned or allegedly learned but in what they were hindered from learning. G. Stanley Hall sensed this when early in the century he decried the "propensity to codify sports, to standardize the weight and size of their implements, and to reduce them to . . . regimentation," an inclination he regarded as "an outcrop of uniformitarianism" working against "that individuation which is one of the chief advantages of free play" and leading to "specialism and professionalism." The goals for boys' baseball pointed in the same general direction. Conspicuously absent among them was encouragement of such qualities as imagination and a critical attitude of mind. As Isaac B. Berkson remarked in *Theories of Americanization*, the attempt was to adjust individuals to conditions, with no thought of what those conditions should be. Indeed, a boys' work leader's reason for recommending "expert" supervisors was that boys could no more be left to themselves than they could be turned loose on city streets—in effect, saying "Let us get boys to adjust to an admittedly inhospitable environment."

Adult obtrusion, however necessary and well-intentioned, on balance ran athwart boys' nature and in the long run very likely their best interests. Already held in tight ligature at home and at school, as at least they once were, boys increasingly found their domain of play invaded too. They were robbed of what sandlot ball in large measure provided: time to escape, to be let alone, to be themselves, to experience and learn on their own at their own pace and through informal play in free association with their fellows, where they could test themselves, gauge their friends, make decisions, commit mistakes, exercise imagination, improvise, give and take (lumps included), and experience a lot more that comes under the rubric of social, emotional, and moral growth. In short, adult intrusion cramped boys' style. It contravened their simple but supreme need to play ball, or anything else, just for the fun of it without adults constantly standing over them.

Up to World War II, adult intrusion had not thoroughly encompassed boys' baseball. Uncounted numbers of boys still played ball independently. A prodigy of teams, organized and operated by themselves, played for the most part under the professional code of "take all you can get away with in order to win," a code that probably prepared them more realistically for later success in a capitalistic society than some of the preachments listed earlier. At least, this approach had the virtue of being less hypocritical than that professed by many teams under adult sponsors, who were not always above stooping a bit to conquer. Teams I formed and coached on the Brooklyn Parade Grounds in the late twenties and early thirties, as well as most of their opponents, made no bones about following the "win" ethic, as exemplified by the following incident.

Just before an away game against a team we knew would be tough to beat, especially on its home grounds, I arranged with my catcher to conceal in his pocket a potato shaped as nearly as possible like a baseball and explained the plan he was to execute. To insure that the play would be as realistic as possible, we kept our other players in the dark about it. Late in the game, with the score tied or close, the opposing team filled the bases with only one out. The time had come to carry out our stratagem. When I gave the sign, my catcher called for a pitchout and threw the potato high and far over the head of our first baseman who, naturally thinking the potato was the ball, leaped high in a vain effort to catch it. Our right fielder, equally deceived, raced frantically to retrieve it as an exultant shout went up from the home crowd. The opposing baserunners immediately began to run, but those racing joyously in to score from third and second were met at the plate by our catcher holding the ball and were gently tagged out. Great confusion followed. The other team argued that we had used two baseballs until one of the spectators came running in with several pieces of broken potato. Then the opposition's argument switched to "You can't do that!" My reply was, "Why not? Our catcher happened to have a potato in his pocket and it interfered with his play, so he got rid of it, just as he would throw a stone aside if it were in his way. It isn't our fault that your base runners are so stupid they don't know a potato from a baseball." After a long wrangle, during which the umpires could produce no rule against throwing a potato away, we won the decision: a "double play" had retired the side, and the inning was over.* Unfortunately, we lost the game anyway.

The incompleteness of adult intervention in boys' baseball applied in particular to youngsters below junior high school age, who were still relatively exempt from it. But in the late thirties, a new breeze stirred. No one realized then that it would gather gale force sufficient to transport boys' baseball the rest of the way on its journey toward almost total organization of youngsters of all ages. It began when in 1939 a group of boys in Williamsport, Pennsylvania, were having difficulty trying to play ball because older boys kept them off the diamond. The uncle of two of the lads, Carl Stotz, a minor executive in a local bottling plant, saw what was happening one day and decided to help his nephews and their companions. With the aid of a couple of neighbors Stotz organized a three-league team of boys aged twelve and under and helped them lay out a diamond that he considered suited to

*See Chapter 36 for another team that used the potato play.

their size and ability—a 40-foot pitching distance and 60-foot baselines. Equipment, including the ball, was also scaled down, and some rules were imposed to ensure balanced competition and protection of the boys' well-being. Thus was born Little League Baseball.

The idea of organized baseball play for very young boys was not brand new. It had been germinating for some time. Several sports for young children—football, boxing, and tennis—had already been organized regionally and nationally. Other people had previously miniaturized the adult regulation diamond and adapted baseball play for children. In fact, in the twenties Spalding's guide printed rules and specifications for a child-size ball and diamond adapted by Organized Baseball's Joint Rules Committee. And in East Akron, Ohio, in 1939 some Y clubs belonged to what was called the U.S. Juvenile Baseball League. But the Little League augured the future. Soon to be backed by a commercial firm, in time it would become the quintessence of boys' baseball.

PART TWO

THE HOUSE OF BASEBALL:
THE GROUND FLOOR

BASEBALL GOES TO COLLEGE

A mong the first to take up residence in the House of Baseball were college players. Together with early gentlemen and businessmen amateurs, they proved instrumental in popularizing the "New York game" in its formative years. As early as the eighteenth century college students, like other boys and young men in America, played folk ball games. They indulged in such informal play among themselves on their own campuses, often at the displeasure of college authorities.

At Princeton the earliest recognition of ball playing came in 1761 from the board of trustees in the form of a ban on playing ball against the president's house under penalty of five shillings. A Princeton student's diary mentions playing on campus in 1786: "A fine day, play baste ball in the campus but am beaten for I miss catching and striking the ball," but the following year the faculty ruled out ball playing because it was "low and unbecoming gentlemen" and constituted "great danger to the health by sudden alternate heats and colds and as it tends by accidents . . . to disfiguring and maiming those who are engaged in it . . . "

In time, however, colleges found that if students worked off surplus energy in ball games, mischief and disorder decreased. Perhaps with this in mind Harvard in the second half of the eighteenth century allowed a limited time for sports, but on campus only. Oliver Wendell Holmes said he played ball there in the 1820s, and Edward Everett Hale reported playing in the 1830s. George F. Hoar, who in his boyhood in the thirties had played various kinds of ball games including old-cat and base, continued to take pleasure in "the old-fashioned game of base" as a Harvard undergraduate in the forties. Harvard students kept the ball and bat in the buttery, presided over by the butler, and played in silk hats and long, tight-fitting trousers held in place with a strap beneath the instep.

At Bowdoin College authorities themselves initiated ball games in 1824 as a means of reducing sickness—a decision pleasing to students, wrote Henry Wadsworth Longfellow. As an undergraduate that year he explained that ball playing communicated such an impulse to our limbs and joints, that there is nothing now heard of, in our leisure hours, but ball, ball, ball. I cannot prophesy with any degree of accuracy concerning the continuance of this rage for play, but the effect is good, since there has been a thoroughgoing reformation from inactivity and torpitude.

At Dartmouth, too, students early indulged in forms of ball games. Daniel Webster wrote in 1797 of "playing at ball" in his free time there, and David Cross, later a judge, claimed a dozen or more students played it in 1837. The University of North Carolina banned several sports in 1799, but baseball remained one of the games permitted there.

Students played at Brown University in the early nineteenth century. Williams Latham, in residence from 1823 to 1827, explained that he did not enjoy the games at Brown as much as he had at Bridgewater because only six or seven played on a side, a style of play that wasted too much time chasing the ball. He also complained of the pitching, because pitchers "did throw so fair [a] ball, They are affraid [sic] the fellow will hit it with his bat-stick." And in 1831 the Reverend Mr. Alvin Hyde wrote one of his sons at Williams College, "I hope you will not be seen with the ball club in your hand this summer." He did advise exercise, by walking and woodchopping. At Princeton by the forties at least, students used a portion of the campus for town ball and cricket on half-holidays.

In those days literary and debating societies, not sports, dominated extracurricular activities, and many students, indifferent to exercise, sur-rendered to "intense physical indolence." Those who played ball did so in rudimentary form on their own, without college supervision. In thus shrug-ging off athletics, American colleges lagged behind the English, which at this time already fostered athletic sports, believing them conducive to the development of leadership, whereas gymnastics, which some American col-leges began to consider, were in England thought suitable only for the lower classes. Not until mid-century did colleges really awaken to baseball and, because of their prestige and association with gentlemen, contribute out of proportion to their numbers to the rise and spread of the game described in an earlier volume of this history.* At this time students began to establish baseball clubs, arrange interclass games, and, on campuses with more than one college, intercollege matches. At first they played the old Massachusetts or New England game, an improved form of town ball, and then, as it gained popularity, the new-style New York game.

At Princeton in the fall of 1857 a few freshmen of the class of '61 formed the Nassau Baseball Club, complete with officers and a standing committee to clear a field of bricks and stones. They challenged the sophomores to a Massachusetts-style game and lost in five innings. A year later some freshmen of the class of '62 from Brooklyn, accoutred with bats, balls, and uniforms,

*For a description of the early styles of play see *Baseball: The Early Years,* pp. 7, 26–28.

taught their fellows the New York game, from which modern baseball is directly descended. In the spring of 1859 the freshmen formed a formal club with a constitution and by-laws that, like those of the earliest formal clubs in New York, required a ten-cent fine for "profane or impious language while assembled for field exercise" and a three-cent fine for expressing an opinion on a close play before the umpire's decision. The club made only members of the freshmen class eligible, but upperclassmen could be honorary members. That fall the freshmen began regular play against Princeton seminary students, and the following year some of them organized another Nassau Club, of which the best players became Princeton's varsity.

While in the fall of 1858 Brooklyn freshmen introduced the New York game at Princeton, some thirty-five Harvard students, graduates, and possibly some nonstudents formed the Lawrence Base Ball Club to play in Cambridge. The club's records, extant among the papers of Professor F.W. Putnam, included a constitution specifying that the club would play only the New York game. Rules demonstrated that the club emphasized the social side of play, and a member wrote later that its meetings were "very jolly affairs." Any member, however, who behaved in an "ungentlemanly manner, or rendering himself obnoxious to the Club" faced expulsion. The club played Mondays and Thursdays at 2:30 P.M., and after each game the president appointed two captains to choose sides for the next one and direct it. The secretary's girlfriend made the bases and flags. Members practiced on grounds opposite Divinity Hall but played regular games on the Cambridge Common against a team of Law School students. Apparently, the club enjoyed the approval of at least some of the faculty, one of whom accepted honorary membership, and it continued active until the outbreak of the Civil War, when so many members joined the Army that games were suspended.

College ball took a major step at Amherst, where students and often faculty had for some time played various forms of baseball, when in 1859 Amherst students challenged Williams College to a regular game. Williams not only accepted but countered with a challenge to a chess match, an arrangement headlined in the Amherst *Express*:

> Williams And Amherst
> Baseball and Chess!
> Muscle And Mind!

Student committees from each college worked out arrangements, and the student body of each college chose participants by ballot. On July 1, 1859, the first intercollegiate baseball game of record was played under the Massachusetts rules at Pittsfield, where the town's baseball club had proffered its field. Each team (thirteen men to a side) provided its own bat and ball, the latter a lead pellet wound with yarn and covered with calfskin. Neither team wore uniforms, but Williams sported club belts. Although only one out constituted an inning, the game lasted from 11 A.M. until 2:30, but that included a cricket-style recess between the fifth and sixth innings. Amherst won 73–22. The Amherst "thrower," Henry D. Hyde, pitched the entire game, and the *Express* said he "threw every ball at the beck of the catcher with a precision and strength which was remarkable." The Williams pitcher, Robert E. Beecher, developed a sore arm and had to switch places with a player at another position, since the rules prohibited substitutions unless a player was disabled. An excited crowd rooted mostly for Williams, because the Amherst faculty had refused to grant students a holiday, believing they had already had enough time off for the year, but spectators acknowledged good playing on both sides. After the game the "ladies" of Pittsfield's Maplewood Institute Academy across the road presented flowers to James Claflin, the captain of the victorious team. Late that evening, when news of the victory reached Amherst, students went about the streets ringing bells and shouting the score. They also lit a bonfire and set off rockets. When the Amherst players returned the next afternoon, a coach-and-four met them and drove them through town amid marching students waving pennants and setting off fireworks. The following day, the Fourth of July, students lengthened the celebration when the news arrived that Amherst had won the incongruous doubleheader, having triumphed in chess as well.

During the 1850s other colleges in New England, New York, and the upper South had already begun to play baseball: Yale, Middlebury, Trinity, Fordham, Hamilton, Rochester, and Georgetown. Even in the Midwest, Northwestern, Kenyon, and Capital University had started teams. At Rutgers ball playing became "quite the rage," as the students' quarterly had it, in 1860.

In October of 1860 the "first nine" (varsity) of Princeton's Nassau Club ventured off campus at the invitation of a team of older men at Orange, New Jersey, but with the score tied at 42, the umpire called the game on account of darkness. The Nassau Club's captain also challenged Yale, Columbia, and Rutgers at baseball, but the students there replied that they were still playing the New England game.

The Civil War left college baseball largely unscathed. Its ravages hit southern colleges hard, but most college ball was confined to the Northeast, and in the North higher education actually expanded. Congress passed the Morrill Act, the number of colleges increased, and losses in enrollments were negligible, so except for players who joined the colors, college ball was hardly affected—as at Princeton, where baseball thrived. Two more clubs formed there, and the Nassaus became "champions of New Jersey" by twice defeating the former champs, a team called the Brunswick Stars. The second game with the Stars marked a "great affair" in the college's history because President John MacLean granted the student body permission to accompany the team to Brunswick. Speeches and a "jolly supper" followed the game. In May of 1863 the Nassaus traveled to Philadelphia, where they lost to the Athletics and won over the Olympics, both famous teams. The success of this trip emboldened the club to once more challenge Columbia, Rutgers, and Yale, and for good measure Williams, but those colleges had still not adopted the New York game.

That fall the Nassaus played the Athletics at Princeton and this time beat them. A Philadelphia newspaper lamely attributed the Athletics' loss to weakness from empty stomachs and unfamiliarity with the peculiar terrain of the Princeton field, on which "To get to first base you ran up a hill, down to second base, up to 3rd base and home base. The first field[er] played on the top of a hill, the center at the bottom and the left field[er] in a gully." Afterwards the Nassaus made amends for starving the Athletics, treating them to a "hearty supper," an occasion "marked by an interchange of many delicate courtesies."

The next day the Princeton team beat one from Irvington, New Jersey, and, paying their own expenses, boldly set out for Brooklyn, where most of them lived anyway, to take on some of its strong teams. For the trip they had secured uniforms of blue pants and white shirts with white ribbon badges bearing the word "Nassau." They defeated the famous Resolutes, Eckfords, and Stars, but, having left for last the strongest team, the Atlantics, so-called champions of the United States, they lost. They had, however, accomplished what no other visiting team had done: won three out of four against Brooklyn clubs. With good reason a reporter for the Philadelphia *Enquirer* found Princeton students suffering from "Baseball on the brain."

The season of 1864 left fresh imprints on Princeton ball: intramural play began, and the Nassaus played their first intercollegiate game. They also defeated the New York Mutuals and won a "fly game," in which outs had to be made by catching the ball on the fly only, against the Brooklyn Stars. But again the Atlantics drubbed them, 42–7, in a game for which ten cents admission was charged—an indication of the professionalism seeping into amateur ranks. As for the club's maiden intercollegiate game, that took place at Princeton against Williams College, where the students, after losses to Amherst in 1859 and again in 1860, had taken up the New York game. The Princeton-Williams game of November 22, 1864, constituted the first inter-collegiate game of New York-style ball, played before an audience of "passionate lovers of manly sport." The Nassaus for some reason had no uniforms but won 27–16, leaving the Williams players, who wore blue outfits, chagrined at being "beaten by a crowd of 'countries' in shirt sleeves." Nevertheless, the game ended with three cheers for each club and was followed by "bountiful refreshments" including turkey, snipe, tongue, chicken, oysters, scallops, lobster, ham, beer, plum pudding, three kinds of pie, ice cream, fruit, nuts, cakes, candies, and cigars!

In a return match at Williamstown in 1865, however, the Nassaus lost before a crowd of 500, among them "large numbers of ladies, who lent their grace and beauty to the occasion." This time both teams wore uniforms and again found the tables afterwards "loaded" with "delicate viands." This victory marked the beginning of an upward baseball climb for Williams, which concentrated so much on improvement that the following year it even downed Harvard.

At Harvard baseball withered for a spell during the war, and the *Harvard Magazine* in 1863 deplored the little attention to sport among the students, making the case that "football, base-ball and cricket... are truly manly sports, crushing out effeminacy and laziness..." But change had already commenced, because in 1862 when a group of students from Phillips Exeter Academy entered Harvard they revived the New York game, and that December George Flagg and Frank Wright organized the '66 Baseball Club. Next spring interest in baseball rose so high that students petitioned the Cambridge city government for the use of part of the Common on which to play. The city granted permission and, with the advice of some members of the Lowell Club of Boston, students laid out a diamond there. Flagg and Wright, along with players from Boston clubs, coached, and the Harvard players invited other colleges to play. The Yale class of '66 replied that although its members did not yet play the game, it hoped soon to meet Harvard on the ball field. The Harvard men did, however, play the Brown University class of '65 at Providence in June, cheered by a brass band and the smiles of the "fair ones." Harvard won in this, its first intercollegiate match. Interclass games played during fall of 1863 took place on the Common, but in the following spring, with permission of the faculty, students laid out a field on a piece of campus land called the Delta, although they staged important games on the Common.

To unite the best players of the various class teams, students formed the Harvard University Base Ball Club in October of 1864, and for the next two years Flagg and Wright controlled this emerging varsity. The club adopted a grey uniform, the caps perversely trimmed by a Boston seamstress not in Harvard crimson but in magenta. The pantaloons had drawstring bottoms for freedom of movement and for ease of tucking into high-top spike shoes. The shirts, fastened in front with buttons to give the appearance of a shield, and with a large *H* embroidered in the shield's center, resembled those of the earlier firemen. Each man outfitted himself, kept uniform and equipment in his room, and dressed there. He also paid his own traveling expenses. The club levied fines for absence, lateness, and broken training rules, and its members practiced on the field every afternoon as well as in the gym in winter. The club formed a second nine in spring of 1865 to enable the varsity to play a practice game daily.

This first Harvard varsity played its first game in June 1865 in Boston with the Trimountain Club, the first New England team to forsake the Massachusetts game for the New York, and won 59–32. The varsity also played a long-anticipated game against the Lowell Club of Boston, holders of a silver ball representing the championship of New England, and won it 28–17. Later that month the Harvard varsity played its first intercollegiate game against Williams and won that one, too. After futile attempts to arrange games with other colleges, Harvard styled itself "Champion of College Nines." The following year, however, Lowell regained the silver ball from Harvard, and the college won only six games out of fourteen.

At Bowdoin some students learned about the New York game during the summer of 1860 and that fall introduced it on campus, where it met with much enthusiasm as being "scientific." Each class organized a baseball club with two nines, and by the time the season ended in November Bowdoin players totaled 109. The seniors laid out a diamond on campus for interclass games that, according to the *Bowdoin Orient*, "attracted the attention and curiosity of the non-comprehending passers-by and . . . [drew] crowds of intelligent loafers."

After a month the Bowdoin seniors were challenged at baseball by a local team called the Sunrise Club, whose members worked in Brunswick and had to play before breakfast. The seniors felt reluctant to accept, since the Sunrise Club had been practicing the new-style game since spring, but finally decided that losing would not hurt them, and they would at least have a good time. A large gathering watched the game, pressing in on the players so that the police had to force spectators back to give more room to play. As the Bowdoin players feared, the Sunrise club won 46–42. As the historian of the college stated, "The teams were well matched, one was nearly as bad as the other." Although baseball interest at Bowdoin decreased somewhat afterwards, students formed a college nine in 1864.

Other colleges turned to baseball during the war: Union, Fordham, Tufts, and Seton Hall, for instance. Yale's first varsity formed in 1865, and the university marked its first intercollegiate game by defeating Wesleyan 39 to 13. By the end of the Civil War baseball had a good foothold in Northeastern colleges and had already begun to radiate to other sections of the country. At Columbia in 1867 Hamilton Fish, Jr., served as vice president of the university's Baseball Association. Dartmouth's first baseball club organized in the early sixties and played intercollegiate ball against Amherst. The Dartmouth *Aegis* in John H. Bartlett's college history declared in 1868,

Our national game, base-ball, is a manifold blessing to our college. It has performed an important mission in bringing the classes to a better feeling toward each other. It is an absorbing and exciting exercise.

Harvard's varsity undertook its first extended trip during the spring recess of 1866, journeying to New York for four games. A New York paper, reviewing Harvard's first game against the Atlantics, paid tribute to catcher Flagg: "With both hands used up, a battered face, and a half blinded eye, he stood up to his post as unflinchingly as if he had been Casabianca on the traditional burning deck." That year Williams graduates hired a professional coach for $300.00, drawing sneers from Harvard men: "Our Williams friends learned baseball from New York professionals and that is where they got their manners." But Williams defeated Harvard 39–37.

At Princeton the faculty refused permission for the Nassaus to play Columbia at Bordentown, New Jersey, but some of the best players organized another nine, the Pickwicks, and went anyway. The Nassaus also played a club in Princeton made up of alumni, tutors, and a few undergraduates, that was better financed than the Nassaus and for a time overshadowed them. On campus students bet heavily on interclass "muffing matches." Princeton sophomores did play and beat Yale after the students won faculty approval to bring the New Haven team to the campus despite the president's reservations about having such a large group of visitors there for the weekend. In 1868 Princeton students took up a collection throughout the college to support the team. And the newly inaugurated president, James McCosh, watched approvingly as the college trounced the Philadelphia Athletics 25–17.

Bowdoin baseball picked up in 1866 after the club reorganized and joined an association of local clubs in competition for the Maine championship, which offered a silver ball and $100.00 in cash. Bates and Colby took up baseball in this era as well. Tufts inaugurated intercollegiate ball in the sixties, losing two games to Brown.

Over in New York state Cornell reputedly had a baseball team since the first nine men registered in the year of its founding, 1865. When Andrew D. White became president in 1867 he recommended the construction of a gym and the preparation of baseball diamonds. Little that furthered the game occurred, however, until spring of 1869 when "anxious applicants for positions on the 'first nine'," according to a college publication, sent "balls innumerable . . . flying across the campus." Daily practice games and hotly contested scrub games took place, and that year Cornell's varsity won its first game, against an Ithaca club. In its second, against the Owego Amateurs, the opposition threatened to overcome Cornell's big early lead, and when an Owego batter sent "a tremendous fly" into center, "Everything depended upon Belden. He caught the ball and won the day!"

The Cornell varsity secured its uniforms by subscription, with the varsity and President White contributing liberally. A local paper, sounding like *Godey's Lady's Book*, rhapsodized over the suits:

> The shirt is white flannel, with carnelian trimmings, and the pants of light gray flannel. The cap will be white with a carnelian star in the center of the crown. The *tout ensemble* will be very pretty . . .

That first season the varsity in its pretty ensemble won three out of four games and supposedly became "the champion bat for three counties." At Cornell nearly every autumn until the mid-eighties a regularly organized team played as long as weather permitted, since baseball at Cornell, as at

Harvard and many other colleges, was both a spring and a fall sport until football appropriated the fall.

In the seventies all prominent colleges played intercollegiate baseball according to rules established by the professionals. By then the club of Dickinson College in Pennsylvania had twenty members. Ohio teams played at Otterbein, Geneva, and Antioch as early as the sixties. The Oberlin Resolutes played teams in nearby towns. A varsity formed at Northwestern in the late sixties. At Lafayette the faculty permitted a baseball club a day's absence for an intercollegiate game. In Illinois when Monmouth College's Classic Club played the College City Club of Galesburg in 1867, a local paper praised the latter as "having few superiors in this popular game." Two teams formed at the University of Kansas in the sixties and played a Thanksgiving Day game. All four University of Michigan classes fielded teams by 1867. Normal schools in the Wisconsin towns of Platteville and Whitewater played baseball by the seventies.

The war had left southern colleges in poor condition, but the University of Georgia had three clubs in 1867, with others following, and it seemed to a campus observer that "the business would not end until the whole body of students . . . [was] divided into groups of nine." At the University of Virginia town ball had been played before the war, and so many baseball clubs formed in the Charlottesville area afterwards that the contagion spread to the campus. In 1866 University of Virginia students formed the Monticello club, which really amounted to the varsity and was often called the "first nine" or "great nine" to distinguish it from campus scrub teams. The Monticellos played clubs in the national capital as well as Washington and Lee University, their recruits coming from lesser nines called the "Bum Stingers," the "Hell Busters," and the "Pill-Garlics."

College students organized and controlled their own teams through their own student associations, supplying their own equipment and paying their own expenses. College administrations at most furnished places to play, sometimes reluctantly. Students or local team members coached the nines. Games occasioned social intercourse, as in the amateur clubs of the period, especially since, like members of the early amateur clubs, ivy league students came from the middle and upper classes. As professionalism filtered into both amateur and college baseball in the seventies, a few colleges began to show professional symptoms: playing a team that charged admission, competing for a cash prize, or hiring a professional coach. These practices met with some criticism. Richard Henry Dana let Williams College know he disapproved of employing a professional coach, declaring that the students should instead have employed an educated and respected gentleman, preferably a graduate or friend of the college. But when Yale offered the New York Knickerbockers, prime purveyors of amateurism in the fifties, a $50.00 guarantee and a share of its gate receipts, the Knickerbockers accepted.

As amateur teams outside the college began to turn professional in the

1870s, college players engaged in games with the pros as well as with amateurs and each other. After playing more than forty games in 1870, Harvard toured the North, West, and South, playing mostly professionals and winning most of its games. In 1876 Harvard even defeated the Boston Red Stockings of the new National League. Fred Thayer, Harvard captain, invented the catcher's mask, adapted, he said, from a fencing mask worn by his teammate James Tyng in a game at Lynn in 1877. Other colleges like Brown, Tufts, and Fordham also played the pros, but Spalding's college guide rated Harvard foremost in college ball in the era before 1880.

Baseball exerted a great pull upon its devotees, distracting them from other activities. At Brown in the seventies student players in the French recitation hall, on the ground floor, would sit one at a time on the window seat, and when "Frenchie's" attention seemed fully engaged elsewhere the student would swing around, put his legs out the window, let himself down to the ground, and go off to practice with the club. Soon the whole club had left, and the instructor, although he seemed to suspect something, never figured out what had happened. At Vanderbilt University the students rashly took it upon themselves in 1877 to arrange a baseball schedule against the University of the South, whereupon the faculty forbade any further "foolishness" of this type. At Dartmouth students explained repeated absences from classes as for athletic training and practice "for the good of the college." In contrast, at the University of Illinois students tried to manage, but could not get away with, class absence for baseball practice. At Allegheny College in Pennsylvania, Clarence Darrow said he "found baseball an important adjunct to school life . . . I came back a better ball player for my higher education." Interest in baseball might distract students from harmful activities, too. Harvard Professor N.S. Shaler, recalling in 1889 the era of the sixties, said that drunkenness among students was not unusual then, but since about 1870, when the athletic motive for sound health developed, "this vice has been rapidly diminishing." Despite this approval, administrations did little to support baseball. At the University of Pennsylvania in the seventies the administration gave no help and arranged no clubhouse or field for the players, who had to practice on a trash-filled triangle of land and keep their equipment at players' homes or with the porter.

At Cornell, however, at least the student publication Era encouraged baseball throughout the decade of the seventies, and its appeals brought about organization of a Baseball Association numbering more than a hundred and charging a membership fee to provide team expenses, since there were as yet no gate receipts. Most Cornell games were still informal and played on campus, which was also the Cornell family cow pasture and, as one alumnus recalled later, "thus presented its particular hazards." Before an important game the Cornell cows had to be driven off the diamond and locked up. Once the Ithaca Journal, as cited by a college history, reported, "The main feature of the game occurred in the seventh inning when the visitors' captain slid into what he thought was first base." Betting reigned at interclass and interfraternity games. Faculty and graduates participated in the games, too.

By then Boston College in the East and Ohio University in the Midwest, among others, had entered intercollegiate competition. Birchard Hayes no doubt expressed the feeling of many students in his 1873 letter to his father, Rutherford B. Hayes, then Ohio's governor, that "one reason for my dread of life after leaving College is because I will be unable to play ball."

Once at Northwestern University in 1871 two teams played a game that attracted many fans who thought they were about to see women play baseball. In 1870 Northwestern set up a new Ladies College, headed by Frances Willard of temperance fame. She needed to raise money, so she organized a Fourth of July celebration with a cornerstone-laying, a regatta, a play, orations by politicians, drill by a Zouave regiment, and a silver ball, contributed by a local jeweler, for the winner of a baseball game by two nines called the Northwestern University team and the Ladies College Nine. "Quite a number of persons," said the Chicago *Tribune*, "paid the admission fee" under the impression that a women's team would play, but when they entered the enclosure they saw two teams of young men. Judging by the score—Northwestern won 57 to 8—a women's team could hardly have done worse. Teenagers played the second game, between a Chicago and an Evanston team. Nevertheless, the one-day extravaganza netted $30,000.00 for the building fund of the new college.

Another midwestern game, one that Northwestern played against Chicago University in 1879, is reminiscent of a Cornell occasion. The teams played on low, swampy ground next to Chicago University's campus and, said a Northwestern reporter, "The grounds were in miserable condition." As well, "The game was frequently interrupted by cows and innocent-looking females strolling leisurely through the field." Nevertheless, Northwestern won 30–13.

Southern colleges, still feeling the effects of the war in the seventies, lagged behind other sections because of small enrollments, scarce funds, and a shortage of coaches. But soon baseball thrived at the University of Virginia, where each spring the college magazine's reporter noted "the festive sphere flying around campus" and "many sprained fingers and other pleasant attendants of base ball." A lot of "rollicking students" accompanied the varsity to games on the Washington and Lee campus, where local schoolgirls "swarmed like bees" and where the administration suspended classes and residents of the area came to the game. A banquet or dance followed. Until 1878 Virginia won these games; its comeuppance came in the form of a Washington and Lee pitcher named Sykes who "threw curved balls," as a Virginia reporter expressed it, and "wiped up the face of the earth" with the Virginia team, 12–0. At the end of the decade the University of Virginia's varsity, seeing the need for more organization, adopted eligibility regulations for the team, in a move that proved prescient.

Other southern institutions found baseball exciting in the seventies. Baseball was "all the rage" at Randolph-Macon (men's) college in Virginia, where two clubs blossomed, and at the University of North Carolina baseball and football were "vigorously adopted," according to Angela Lumpkin's research.

Like Birchard Hayes in Ohio, Josephus Daniels in North Carolina was greatly attached to baseball. Daniels, later secretary of war, said of his baseball experience at Wilson Collegiate Institute in the seventies:

> My passion was baseball, which I played from early dawn until nightfall when not in school or at work. We had two good teams, the Swift Foot and the Red Hot . . . my greatest honor was to be captain of the Swift Foots when we played match games in near-by towns.

The game with Snow Hill, reached by a day's wagon ride over sandy roads, said Daniels, "was great fun, particularly since we won despite the fact that two of our best players became intoxicated at the dance the night before the game."

The Far West had baseball in the seventies, at the universities of Washington and Oregon. In California's warmth baseball flourished, and St. Mary's of Oakland began in 1870 making a reputation in baseball that lasted for at least a generation, while at Santa Clara College baseball "went on forever, winter rains merely postponing the playing long enough for the clay yard to dry out," as explained in a college history. At the University of California class teams held tournaments for the university championship.

The advancing professional ethic led college teams to adopt more professional techniques, not only in play on the field but in administration of the game. To raise money for uniforms and equipment a team might pass the hat, or enclose the field and charge admission. Or a team might use a "ringer," a skilled nonstudent, or even a professional, in an important game. At Harvard in the early seventies the team charged admission of fifty cents, but only for the annual Yale game. Members raised money for costs by subscription, and one season they spent $862.00 on baseball.

Once a ringer caused a game cancellation. In 1871 Amherst and Dartmouth had arranged a three-game series. When the Amherst team arrived in Hanover, New Hampshire, for the first game, a good crowd had already gathered, but suddenly, after pregame practice, the spectators learned that no game would be played. It came out that Dartmouth's manager had challenged the status of an Amherst man, saying he was not a bona fide student. President Stearns of Amherst, replying by telegraph to the Dartmouth manager, admitted that the player was a "townie" and had no connection with the college. But because the Amherst players refused to proceed without him, the game was cancelled.

In 1879, in a story told by Professor Ronald Smith in a 1986 article,

Harvard, embarrassed by defeats by Brown and Yale, secured the services of two alumni, one in the university's medical school and the other studying law. Although Harvard's opponents expressed their indignation at this anomaly, no eligibility rules forbade the practice, so the alumni played.

Just before this incident, in the game Harvard played with Brown, the latter's fine pitcher, Lee Richmond, had already pitched a game for a professional team, Worcester of the National League, against Cleveland, a game in which he registered Organized Baseball's first "perfect game" (no hits and no runs made against him). So when Richmond played for Brown against Harvard, he was already a professional, and his eligibility to continue as a college player came into question. These events caused the important eastern college baseball clubs to come together to try to agree on eligibility rules, as well as on schedules, postponements, money matters, and the settlement of disputes. Student representatives from Harvard, Yale, Princeton, Brown, Dartmouth, and Amherst met in Springfield, Massachusetts, in December of 1879 and formed the American College Base Ball Association, but Yale soon withdrew because the other members refused to rule out alumni like the ones Harvard had used or professionals like Brown's Lee Richmond.

As the guidon of amateurism began to fall from the failing hands of amateur baseball clubs, another institution picked it up: the elite athletic club. Lineal descendants of the pre–Civil War amateur baseball and other single-sport clubs, athletic clubs sponsored a variety of sports, including baseball. Their ascendancy dates from the establishment of the New York Athletic Club in 1866, but others soon formed in the New York area and in major cities throughout the country. Until the eighties the New York A.C. stood supreme among them in athletic competition and influence. Their exclusiveness safeguarded by stiff initiation fees and blackballing, the athletic clubs at first consisted of small memberships of young gentleman and businessman athletes of middle- and upper-middle-class standing organized to compete as amateurs. They did much to promote and popularize amateur athletics, spurring the development of college sports, college athletic associations, and national amateur associations to regulate athletics. Their baseball clubs also frequently played college nines.

In the same year that eastern college baseball teams met to try to solve their eligibility problems, eight of the exclusive athletic clubs met for the same reason and set up a formal organization. An earlier such group had formed to regulate track and field, and the new one in 1879 lasted only until the New York A.C. withdrew its support in 1886. Even before that, it had little influence and no power. Group influence would have to wait until more pressure for solution of problems built up.

10

THE PRINCIPAL COLLEGE GAME

In the 1880s baseball reigned as the foremost sport on college campuses. The factors that contributed to its growth included the students' enjoyment of the game and the colleges' faith that it benefited students' health and character. In addition, the expanded railroad network facilitated scheduling of intercollegiate contests. President William J. Tucker of Dartmouth thought no healthier agent of "moral development" existed than organized athletics. President Charles Eliot of Harvard believed they transformed a "stooping, weak, and sickly youth into one well-formed, robust, and healthy." President James McCosh of Princeton saw sports as "gentlemanly contests for supremacy."

In staging these "gentlemanly contests" college men could for a time look to the elite athletic clubs as models. In the eighties many members of these clubs came from the same social breed as the college men, and their conduct of elaborate sporting contests, including baseball games, helped make sports reputable on college campuses. In the eighties, at least, as Joe Willis and Richard Wettan show, athletes for the elite clubs were the members themselves. Some former college athletes, too, joined these clubs: Arthur Hunnewell, Harvard pitcher, for example, became one of the incorporators of the Boston Athletic Association formed in 1887.

Many college authorities also viewed baseball and other sports as a unifying influence on campus, countering the fragmentation caused by the founding of professional schools. This unifying influence, however, on the part of many spectators soared to exaggerated heights of chauvinistic pride in one's alma mater, whose reputation and honor seemed to rest on the outcome of intercollegiate contests rather than on intellectual distinction, as illustrated by the wild celebrations that followed baseball victories. As instance is the following description by a Dartmouth alumnus, William Byron Forbush, '88, of the aftermath of his team's win over Williams, quoted in Bartlett's history of Dartmouth:

> ...the diamond is full of maddened forms dancing up and down; some are yelling, some weeping, all are hatless. One great student seizes another, who

144

is leaping in the air for joy, and, as he strains him in his arms, discovers that he is a professor. And now the victorious champions are lifted on a score of willing shoulders and carried to their rooms, the college bell is rung, and the great green pennant is raised to the belfry tower. After supper the celebration is begun by songs on the campus fence, and as soon as it is really dark a bonfire is built in the campus, and every man's unprotected woodpile is levied on for the purpose. The whole college is out again. Soon a procession is formed, with a band at the head of it, and the ball nine is dragged in a great chariot by three hundred pairs of hands around the diamond. The man who made the winning hit wears a new silk hat, just presented to him. Every player has to make a speech and be cheered, and everybody is happy. Then a line is formed again and marches through the principal streets. A stop is made at the house of every member of the faculty, and he must make a speech and be cheered also. At length the bonfire burns low, and the cheering ceases, and it is the dead of night. That college cheer—how much it brings back to me! Its savage "wah-hoo-wah" rings in my ears, even as I heard it when last I gave it to bid my classmates farewell, in those days when college dreams were all there was of life and when BASE-BALL was its noblest conflict.

Similar merrymaking events took place all over the nation. Following a game in 1889, described in a college history, in which Northwestern played off a tie with Wisconsin to take the championship of the Northwest, a "howling mob" of Northwestern students paraded the streets of Milwaukee carrying the school colors of purple and gold. The student paper added that the team "painted Milwaukee" and that the cheer "Rah! Rah! Rah! Zip! Boom! Bah! N.W.U. Champions!" greeted (or assaulted?) the ear at every train station between Milwaukee and Evanston. Similarly, in 1886 when Columbia beat Harvard the New York students celebrated for a full twenty-four hours.

Players also held their own private festivities. After a game in Ohio in which Marietta College defeated a strong town team 5–3, the players staged such a party in the bandwagon on the way home that the college president, hearing of it, suspended three of them for three weeks. Players became important personages on campus, where leadership in athletics, not grades, was the criterion for status.

Extravagant appreciation for the victories of the institution's baseball team set the tone for the character of the eighties. The year 1880 might well be taken as a dividing line between college baseball's simple, formative period and the highly organized intercollegiate extravaganzas to follow. Further, the failure in 1879 of several eastern ivy league colleges to agree on common eligibility rules so that they could arrange a championship foretold the frustrations of the period to follow.

Using nonstudents, especially semipros, professionals, or even professors in college games became common despite attempts to rule out such dubious capers. In 1886–87 the baseball association of Tufts College in Boston hired two nonTufts men to play in a five-game schedule, but the team captain and the manager, hearing of the action, resigned in protest. The practice, as revealed by the college historian, or hiring an occasional player continued at Tufts until 1891.

In 1880 Northwestern, in a league with some local colleges, drew a fine for playing an ineligible man in two games with Racine College. Northwestern refused to pay and withdrew from the league, which immediately broke up.

Young faculty members who like to play often took part in varsity games. Among the best players on the Illinois College varsity in the 1880s, as shown in the college history, *Pioneer's Progress*, were Professors Harold W. Johnstone of the Latin Department, second base, and Samuel W. Parr of the Agricultural Department, first base. And David Starr Jordan, later named president of Stanford University, while on the faculty at Lombard University in Illinois pitched for the student team.

Another practice that began to cause concern involved the activities of varsity ball players who took jobs playing ball during their summer vacations and so, from the point of view of the college, turned into professionals. A spectacular example, Frank W. Olin, paid his way through Cornell by summer work in teaching, repairing agricultural machinery, and playing professional baseball, not only for pro clubs but for the major leagues. Nevertheless, he also played on the Cornell varsity in his freshman, sophomore, and senior years. Anyone who had at any time received money to play ball was branded a professional. The Cornell *Daily Sun*, which may not have been objective, asserted in 1884 that the Hamilton, Hobart, and Union college baseball teams employed professionals, five of them by Union alone. Samuel Eliot Morison, writing of Harvard, states that its 1888 team included four pros, but that Yale used five and Princeton six!

College athletic or baseball associations also hired professional coaches to bring their teams to a higher level of skill. Princeton in 1882 engaged John M. Ward of the New York National League Club to coach its team. Northwestern hired Billy Sunday, the Chicago pro, to coach before the season of 1881.

Loss of time from studies because of baseball presented a problem for colleges. At the University of Georgia the faculty deliberated over whether to permit the varsity to travel to a nearby town on Saturday for a game. After finally granting permission, the faculty told students that future absences would require applications from parents to the chancellor. At the University of Missouri in Columbia the team asked at least once a year for permission to travel to Fulton to play the Westminster College nine. Usually, the faculty agreed. Once, however, the team members arrived home in Columbia in such a "hilarious mood" that the police held them under arrest until they identified themselves.

Long athletic trips and the consequent loss of study time caused President Frederick Barnard of Columbia University to consider prohibiting intercollegiate games. Oberlin, however, strictly prescribed the time students could spend at ball playing and other sports on college grounds, and the varsity could not leave the campus during the term.

Some deplored the growing influence of the professionals on college games. President Eliot of Harvard thought the curve ball a "low form of cunning" and a college pitcher who looked at one player and threw to another "ungentlemanly." Some administrators believed playing professionals made a bad influence on the college students, exposing them to an ungentlemanly model. About 1883 Harvard, Brown, Princeton, Dartmouth, and Amherst agreed to stop playing professionals, although Yale refused to go along with them. After a few years, however, Harvard rescinded its restriction as tending to increase irritation between faculty and students, since the students ascribed every defeat to lack of practice playing against professionals. The captain of the Princeton team hit upon a way to demonstrate to his college that even nonprofessionals could be "ungentlemanly." He scheduled a game with a New Jersey industrial team. The faculty came and witnessed the worst "ruffianism" yet displayed on campus, with attendant quarreling and howling. The Princeton faculty then rescinded the rule against playing professionals, apparently convinced that worse people than professionals existed!

Varsity ball definitely affected the quality of college work. President McCosh of Princeton, suspicious that his university was producing not the gentleman-scholar-athlete but just the athlete, checked the college records and reported to the trustees in 1885, as his biographer has written, that Princeton's best athletes were no longer, as they had been earlier, its best students.

Finances loomed larger in the eighties, too. The athletic budget at the University of Illinois in 1884–85 reportedly came to an incredible $19.40, covering the cost of some baseball suits and laundering them plus a bat, ball, and bases, as well as traveling expenses for the team to Lincoln, Illinois. That amount, if correct, would not nearly suffice for other colleges. The Oberlin team laid plans in 1881 to raise money through gate receipts, so before a game against Michigan, as reported in the *Oberlin Review*, the students worked to enclose the field so that the team could charge admission. When 600 spectators came to the Michigan game, Oberlin collected $128.00 in gate receipts. Others devised imaginative moneymaking schemes: in 1881 a party of Dartmouth undergraduates toured the country giving concerts to raise money for the college baseball nine. At Yale one year in the eighties income from baseball came to $7,255.15 but cost only $6,863.38, so the baseball association realized a profit.

As a further byproduct of the extravagant emphasis on intercollegiate sport, one more applicable today than ever, President Ezekiel G. Robinson of Brown lamented in 1884,

only a small portion of our students receive any personal benefit from our athletic sports. Those who take part in them merely to fit themselves for the match games, too often run into hurtful extremes; others, engaging in them fitfully and unintelligently, fail of the good they might otherwise receive; while the majority, content with merely looking on and applauding, get no real benefit whatever from them.

To defend college athletics Professor Eugene L. Richards of Yale's Math Department countered such complaints in a fatuous 1884 article in *Popular Science*. He wrote that grumblers exaggerated the amount of time students supposedly devoted to college athletics. To the argument that the excitement of play distracted from study he replied that sport was excitement of a healthy kind. Some remarked, he said, upon the betting at games, but betting was not peculiar to athletics and if banned would only increase. As for student disorders stemming from victories, these were seldom serious, Richards claimed. Others pointed to the limiting of athletic benefits to the few while others merely watched; to this the professor replied that the exploits of the few inspired others to exercise. The system, complained some, made "brutes" out of athletes because it set a physical standard only; to which Richards retorted that the standards of good conduct and good scholarship remained. As for those who disliked the expense, he argued that, at least at Yale, subscriptions covered half the cost and alumni covered the rest. Besides, costs were more than met by earnings. Professor Richards, in addition to teaching math, surely qualified to teach a course in sophistry.

Such rationalizations about the undesirable accompaniments of college athletics failed to mollify college administrations, who began trying to contain the explosive growth and commercialization of athletics, to bring order into eligibility rules, and to govern competition among members of particular college groups. Some worked through regional college baseball associations like the Western, the New York State, and the New England. Other broadened their approach to include athletics in general.

Harvard and Princeton led in the effort to reach agreement on rules for conducting athletics. In the spring of 1882 the Harvard faculty, alarmed at the number of games the varsity baseball team proposed to play away from Cambridge, appointed a committee to study athletic sports. Its concern resulted in President Eliot's writing to other New England colleges suggesting a conference on institutional control of athletics. At the meeting, held in 1883, Harvard accepted resolutions against playing professionals and employing pro coaches, agreeing to limit students' play to four years, requiring faculty committees to supervise intercollegiate games, and restricting contests to the home field of one of the contestants.

This agreement aroused students who, fearing their own colleges might adopt such rules, believed that their rights were being infringed upon. The following year they held a protest meeting in New York City, where student representatives from twelve colleges met to discuss Harvard's ban. At the meeting, as reported in the New York *Times*, the Lehigh student representative deplored this "interference" on the part of college faculties as having "caused bad feeling," adding that while his athletic association did not believe in "much" professionalism, a little (like partial pregnancy) was essential, and professional trainers in particular were needed. A Columbia student declared that the faculty had little or no right to control off-campus student activities if these did not seriously interfere with students' college duties. Princeton students, too, opposed interference by faculties in student athletic affairs. Representatives from Amherst, Cornell, Lafayette, Stevens Institute, Yale, and the University of Pennsylvania stated that in general their students opposed the resolutions adopted by Harvard and Princeton at the meeting the year before (1882). These protestations amounted to a desire to have the sailors, not the captain and officers, run the ship. Only City College representatives said students at their colleges accepted all regulations.

Harvard's actions inspired faculty discussions of athletics at other colleges, notably Princeton, Dartmouth, and Union, although the latter decided to permit its baseball team to use two professional players. In 1886 Princeton urged interadministration cooperation, but Yale, the dominant athletic school at the time, refused, and that ended the matter. Instead, each college tried to impose its own restrictions, beginning with Harvard's innovative formation of a new nine-person athletic committee of three faculty representatives, three alumni, and three undergraduates. This imposition of college control, although weak, would in years to come stand as a prototype for later organizations on many college campuses.

Despite its problems, the eighties also opened an era of new ideas. The seventh-inning stretch, a practice that became traditional throughout baseball, may have begun at Manhattan College in 1882 when Brother Jasper, who had ruled that students could not leave or move about during games, noticed them becoming restless in a long, drawn-out contest, so in the seventh inning he ordered everyone to stand and stretch. Since the stretch eased the tension, he repeated the tactic in the next four games. After that, the seventh-inning stretch became a habit, and when it reputedly spread from Manhattan College to the nearby Polo Grounds, it became a part of baseball.

Another new idea in college ball appeared in 1883 when 2,000 people came to an evening game in which some students at Fort Wayne Methodist Episcopal College (later Taylor University) played a team that included some professionals on the Quincy, Indiana, club. The Jenney Electric Company, which arranged the game as a promotional stunt, provided seventeen arc lights for the outfield fences. The Fort Wayne *Sentinel* reported that the lights burned brilliantly but cast shadows, so the ball was difficult to see. Twice the lights went out, plunging the park into darkness, a condition that "loving couples" took advantage of. The reporter pronounced the experiment "fun" but "impractical."

A third new notion of the era, one that heralded similar ventures to come, entailed sending a few college players abroad. A group of ivy league collegians, financed by A.G. Spalding and Company, visited England to play ball, mixing on teams with English players and taking part in games at the Bootle grounds in Liverpool. Members included the captains of the Harvard, Yale, and Princeton varsities along with another Harvard player and another from Yale. Dudley Dean, the Harvard player, said that to play in England he was paid $4.00 a week plus expenses.

In the 1890s football began to dispute the supremacy of baseball in the colleges. Some later attributed football's challenge of campus baseball to the lack of pro football leagues, which left the college football players as the prime exemplars of the sport, whereas in baseball interest diffused more widely among many groups, and the major leaguers, not the collegers, represented the models for the best play. A more likely explanation is that football as a spectacle epitomized the ruthless business ethic and martial spirit of American society even more than did professional baseball and seemed to develop the qualities necessary for survival later in business or war. But even though football surpassed it in popularity, baseball kept growing in the nineties. Each year large crowds attended baseball games, for instance, between the teams of Harvard, Yale, and Princeton. At the University of Illinois the student paper noted that "once the literary society held the palm" but "it is now being fast relegated to obscurity by the sports of the diamond or the quadrangle." Well might Duncan Edwards write in Scribner's in 1895 that undergraduate life "is imbued with the spirit of athletics."

This expansion of college ball may be seen in the steadily lengthening schedules and greater distances traveled by varsities and the widening variety of opponents played, among them the growing number of intercollegiate games as compared with noncollege opponents taken on. Records at Rutgers University, for instance, show that the number of games its varsity played yearly jumped from 23 in the seventies to 73 in the eighties and to 87 in the nineties. Out of 15 different Rutgers opponents in the 1870s only 5 were college teams, all of them fairly nearby; but in the eighties the total number rose to 34 teams, of which college nines numbered 13; and in the nineties Rutgers again played 34 teams, this time 18 of them collegiate, some located as far afield as Virginia.

Cornell's schedule expanded as substantially as any. From only a few games per season with local amateur teams and small nearby colleges the schedule had by 1900 enlarged to as many as 33 games, including one against the Brooklyn major league team played on a southern trip during the spring recess.

In the South baseball became a mounting activity at Tulane and the universities of Alabama, Mississippi, Vanderbilt, Texas, and North Carolina. The University of Georgia, whose varsity essayed a fairly ambitious schedule, in 1897 won a signal victory over the University of Pennsylvania at Atlanta.

This last and well-advertised game played during Pennsylvania's spring trip was also the first one played by a northern college in Atlanta. The crowd of 3,000 included many local University of Georgia alumni. The game, said the correspondent of the Philadelphia *Public Ledger*, became a society event, and "sponsors," as they were called—"the creme de la creme of the Southern queens"—were selected for both teams to preside over the game. The substitute players of the teams attended these sponsors "most gallantly." In the game Sanford, Georgia's pitcher, held the Philadelphia hitters helpless. He not only shut them out but pitched a no-hit game and in the second inning scored Georgia's first run with a homer over the left-field fence. Afterward, the Atlanta *Looking Glass* hailed the southerners' "glorious victory," explaining that "Heretofore the haughty athletes of the great universities of the North have labored under the delusion that their Southern brethren were 'farmers'. . . the University of Georgia nine covered itself with glory." The Atlanta *Journal* editorialized, "The complete and overwhelming victory of the Georgia team marks an era in the history of athletics at the State University. The institution now takes rank with leading universities of the country in athletics." The press made no mention, however, of the Georgia players having been coached by a Yankee, the professional star Hughey Jennings of the Baltimore Orioles. And unfortunately for them, the following year Pennsylvania returned and defeated Georgia 11–2.

The flavor of southern college baseball as well as southern attitudes toward women may be gleaned from the account in the Richmond *Times* of a game that the University of Virginia played in Richmond in June of 1893, where

> many pretty girls . . . clad in their most fetching gowns and broad-brimmed hats . . . smiled . . . and almost split their dainty gloves applauding the plays. Some of them didn't know what it was all about, but their ignorance is bliss. Girls have funny ideas about base-ball anyhow. They always imagine something is about to happen to the umpire. Sometimes they imagine rightly. Sometimes they don't. . . . Every maid borrowed a lead pencil and kept the tallies on the back of a visiting card

Even small denominational colleges found baseball irresistible. At Brigham Young Academy, which became a university, President Benjamin Cluff, Jr., viewed sports as complementary to academic life, and baseball soon became a main athletic attraction. A school publication, *The Normal*, supported the formation of an athletic club in 1893 even though some Mormon leaders still maintained that sports damaged the respectability of educational institutions and destroyed their religious tone.

While some southern fans remained bemused at the demureness of female fans, midwesterners tried more colorful tactics. Spectator behavior at a game in Champaign, Illinois, between the University of Illinois and Northwestern drew comment from the Chicago *InterOcean*, quoted in a history of Northwestern:

A new method of guying was resorted to at the game which proved effective. Quite a few Illinois students brought revolvers loaded with blank cartridges and kept up a desultory fire during the game. This is much more convenient than yelling, and has a better effect on the visiting team.

A more sober occasion took place farther west when in one of the University of Wisconsin's games in 1892 it came up against Eau Claire, a club of "husky men," according to the Wisconsin *Daily Cardinal's* account, but the Wisconsin captain, "with his usual confidence, told the boys 'not to be scared,' that they were only practicing." Although just before the game the team had been treated to a "hearty dinner" at Galloway House, run by two alumni, it won, thanks to the pitching of Palmer, who, one of the Eau Claire players remarked, "had a ball which when you strike at it, it is not there."

Eastern fans could act about as wild as those in Illinois, according to a contemporary account reprinted in a history of Brown University:

> When Brown wins a ball game the students are prone to suffer temporary aberration of the mind. The usual flight of intellect or a supper of hasheesh led about 300 of the university children to array themselves in the garments of sleep and parade down College Hill and through Westminster and Weybosset streets. Of course they yowled and blocked the street-cars . . . blew horns and yelled. . . .

All this while posting on a monument a placard that read "Brown 6, Princeton only 3."

Earnestness, however, reigned during the training of an important varsity team. The training methods employed by leading college teams leave no doubt about the overseriousness with which they had come to regard the game. Take Princeton, for example. In 1893 the captain of the previous year explained that to train the team, work began early in January for the more than sixty candidates who turned out hoping to be selected. After three weeks of drill and running they practiced for several weeks in the indoor cage, half the size of a diamond. By this time most of the culls had been eliminated, and a professional ball player coached the survivors. Daily their trainer sponged the men with salt water. About mid-March, outdoor practice games began between the first team and the reserves, and in early April the varsity commenced playing professional teams. No fried food and few sweets appeared on the training table; no smoking, drinking, or chewing was allowed, and parties and social dinners were forbidden for three months. Skull practice took place the night before big games: difficult plays underwent review in the captain's room on a board containing a miniature diamond on which checkers indicated positions. When the schedule called for an open date, the team practiced three hours a day. Endurance was stressed. The main object of all this? To defeat Harvard and Yale.

Meanwhile, up at Yale, the varsity's training, as described by its captain, proceeded along lines similar to Princeton's. Directly the football season ended the captain and manager of the baseball team made plans for the coming baseball season—the number of games at home and away, the Easter trip, the selection of a pitching coach. Training, which began in February in the gym, consisted of running, exercising, and fielding grounders. The men practiced sliding on a strip of heavy carpet stretched across a wooden frame, a piece of equipment invented by a former Yale captain. After March first the coach arrived and took charge of the pitchers, preferably four of them. The team might get in a week of outdoor practice before the Easter trip, on which the fifteen or sixteen men played a game every day, usually against professionals. On their return they played two or three games a week for the rest of the season. For about two hours each off day they practiced batting, fielding, sliding, and team plays. Yale's training table menu might have been planned for Sumo wrestlers: breakfast consisted of fruit, oatmeal, steak, omelet, and potatoes; lunch meant steak, cold beef, or chicken, and more potatoes; dinner included soup, chicken, beef, mashed potatoes, bread, peas or corn, and tomatoes, with tapioca or custard pudding as dessert, and ice cream twice a week. Toast, milk, and a concoction called oatmeal water appeared at every meal.

The baseball association backed up the athletes. At Yale, students organized all activities to an unusual degree. They set up their athletic teams, even the freshman nine, like their fathers' business organizations, with a president (who acted as manager), vice president, and secretary, in addition to the captain and team members. These association officers reputedly enjoyed even more importance on campus than did the athletes.

Sport in English institutions did not assume such an air of serious business as it did in American colleges. British colleges spent much less money on paraphernalia or training, yet the proportion of students who took part in athletics at Oxford exceeded that of Harvard, where the emphasis fell upon the few who played for the varsity. This anomaly could be defended. The president of the Massachusetts Institute of Technology, Francis Walker, speaking before the Phi Beta Kappa Society at Harvard in 1893, ventured the highly questionable view that athletics by the few stimulated interest in gymnastics among others. Moreover, he declared, college athletics taught habits of discipline, perseverance, and courage that might be applied in later professions. "The college athletics of to-day," he maintained, "do wonderfully light up the life of our people."

Similar defenses of the American college sport system appeared in the nineties. W.M. Sloane, a professor at Princeton, wrote in *Harper's Weekly* in 1890 that the "rivalry and ambition" embodied in sports "are part of a liberal education." President Walker of M.I.T. and president Eliot of Harvard also hint subtly at an advantage sport may bestow that they cannot bring themselves to name. Walker said hearty physical exercise "may diminish and uproot vicious desires . . . [for] what is bad and degrading." As Eliot expressed it, athletics "supplied a new and effective force for resisting all sins which weaken or corrupt the body" and help constrain "forces toward immorality."

The embodiment of sport advocacy in the 1890s was William Rainey Harper, the University of Chicago's first president. His ludicrous idea of a great university—and he planned to make Chicago great—included the notion that a strong athletic program was just as necessary as scholastic achievement. He hired Amos Alonzo Stagg as both coach and faculty member, an unusual combination for those days, and directed him to "develop teams which we can send around the country and knock out all the colleges. We will give [our varsity players] a palace car and a vacation too." Stagg on his part, as college histories agree, saw coaching athletics as an opportunity for Christian character training, and he at once complied. Under Stagg the University of Chicago rapidly developed strong varsity teams.

In order for Stagg to offer a complete sports program immediately, he found himself obliged to play on the university baseball and football teams the first year. But other colleges engaged in or permitted practices just as questionable. A historian of Dartmouth has shown that the Dartmouth alumni proposed to raise funds for a gym and athletics and to promote interest in athletics—if the administration gave them complete control of the college athletics program! Incredibly, in 1892 the college agreed to these conditions, and the alumni built an athletic field, including a baseball field with a grandstand. That year Dartmouth played baseball successfully against athletic powers like Princeton, Georgetown, Harvard, Amherst, Williams, and the University of Pennsylvania. That same year, however, *Harper's Weekly* castigated Dartmouth for playing the professional battery of O'Connor and Ranney who, the article charged, went to Dartmouth not to study medicine but to play ball.

Gate receipts increased in importance in college sports in the nineties. At Tufts the college finally came to the embarrassed realization in 1894 of the necessity for a fenced baseball field so that admission could be charged for intercollegiate contests. At Northwestern, too, the new athletic field of 1892, financed by contributions from students, alumni, and local businessmen, was fenced in several years later with money contributed by a wellwisher. At the University of Virginia the board of directors that controlled the varsity gave up trying to support it through voluntary student contributions and instead borrowed money to enclose the field in order to charge admission. Of course, stated a Harvard representative, spectators at games should be limited, as far as possible, to college men, but "it is impracticable to abolish gate receipts altogether." Less wealthy colleges had to scrape up every little bit they could for athletics. At Whitewater Normal School in Wisconsin at the end of the century the students and faculty played each other at baseball in order to raise money for the athletic association. Princeton's baseball team, on the other hand, experienced a self-supporting season in 1891, and Yale's realized a profit of $12,000.00 the previous year.

A common tactic of baseball teams to elevate their level of skill remained the old standby, use of a ringer. The University of Virginia, to round out its team in the spring of 1890, persuaded a skilled pitcher and recent graduate to return. He strengthened the team so that it won eleven out of fifteen games of a schedule that listed front-rank colleges of the North as well as several athletic clubs and independent teams. Before two years were up the club also hired a professional coach.

Even at tiny Mars Hill College in North Carolina, according to an account in the college archives, interested parties raised money to pay travelling expenses for two ringers from Wake Forest to play for Mars Hill in an important game against neighboring Weaverville College.

At Otterbein in Ohio, Ernest S. Barnard, later president of the American League, appointed himself coach and manager of the baseball team. Once he found himself without a battery, so he borrowed pitcher John Cooney and catcher Bob Quinn from a noncollege team in Columbus, collecting them himself with a horse and wagon. With these ringers in tow, Otterbein scored a series of successes—until the team faced Capital University in Columbus. Capital's manager spotted catcher Quinn as a ringer, whereupon Barnard loudly declared that Quinn was taking a course in business, thus informing Quinn on what he supposedly was studying. Capital's manager then challenged Quinn to give the college yell, but Quinn replied that he had been too busy studying to learn it! Otterbein got away with the deception. Quinn, consonant with the abilities shown in this incident, later entered baseball as an administrator, and Cooney became a big-league pitcher. All this took place within the Ohio Intercollegiate Athletic Association, to which Otterbein belonged, with its reputedly "strict eligibility rules" that prevented any except undergraduates from participating in intercollegiate contests.

At Illinois College, too, as a college history shows, it was common to see men on the baseball team that could hardly be regarded as bona fide students. The college magazine also arraigned the Illinois College Athletic Association for its use of athletic scholarships, by which it paid "specialists to be our athletes . . . [a practice that] discourages honest, hard training on the part of the genuine college students." College use of the athletic scholarship proliferated in the nineties. Zane Grey received one to attend the University of Pennsylvania after a college scout saw him perform for a town team. Grey starred as a pitcher and outfielder in 1896 when the Pennsylvania varsity won 16 out of 22 games, among them victories over Lehigh, Johns Hopkins, Cornell, Harvard, and even the New York Giants. Grey made the team while still a freshman, according to a story told by Robert D. Parker, when the baseball coach saw him holding off a band of sophomores bent on hazing him by throwing potatoes at them from a basketful being delivered to the college kitchen. So well aimed were the missiles that the coach asked him to come out for the varsity.

At Harvard, representatives admitted that the varsity athletes received free athletic clothing and better food than the rest of the students, "but we do not think they are paid directly or indirectly." Such students might be too busy with athletics to study as they should. At Yale, according to M.I.T. President Walker, some of the athletes "have been at the foot of their classes and had to be hounded to keep them up to the mark." The Rutgers administration cancelled nine of the twelve baseball games scheduled for 1897 because of "Players Scholastic Conditions," the records show. Well-known Professor Albert Bushnell Hart, in a blistering reproval, wrote later that the professional spirit of the 1890s in athletics made evasion of the rules common, and "men who had no serious purpose of study . . . were . . . brought into the colleges."

The question of whether varsity ball players should play summer ball began to cause ever more difficulties in competition. In 1897 the visiting Michigan team refused to play a game with Northwestern unless it dropped Arthur Sicles, first baseman, claiming Sicles had played semipro ball for Oak Park the previous summer. Northwestern refused to cast off Sicles, so the Michigan players packed up their gear and left. James Wadsworth, Yalie and later a United States Congressman, played ball every summer in Geneseo, New York. In his third summer at Yale Wadsworth's father, a baseball fanatic, collected a team of college players from Cornell, Wesleyan, Princeton, Brown, Dartmouth, and Lafayette, and his Geneseo Collegians toured the Northeast, playing ball successfully, just before Wadsworth's final year at Yale. With this intensive practice behind him Wadsworth as a senior led the college team in fielding, came in second in batting, and won selection by Walter Camp as a member of his All-American baseball team.

Colleges usually permitted professional players to coach teams. Tim Keefe of the New York National League club coached Harvard in 1892 while Robert Caruthers coached at Princeton, and John McGraw and Hugh Jennings both studied and coached at St. Bonaventure for several years.

Some college baseball men became professionals. Dave Fultz of Brown University played seven years in the majors and later acted as president of the Baseball Players' Fraternity of 1912.* Another Brown student, Fred Tenney, became an accomplished Boston National League first baseman. A few acquired big names in other fields. Herbert Hoover, treasurer of the Stanford University Athletic Association, got its accounts itemized and organized for the first time in the association's history. Stephen Crane, a varsity player at Syracuse, became a writer, and Robert Wagner, shortstop for the City College nine, entered politics.

In this period some faculties maundered on in a fiddle-faddling effort to control athletics. At the University of Illinois, for example, professors met to discuss a policy on absence for games, ways to make up absence, and

*See *Baseball: The Golden Age*, pp. 194 ff.

minimum grade requirements for participation in athletics. At Amherst, by contrast, the faculty set no eligibility requirements, gave the schedule little supervision, and permitted the participation of players of questionable academic status in the university. At the University of Wisconsin, too, the Athletic Council permitted open recruitment by captains, coaches, and alumni, with promises of social favors or nominal employment. Colleges did attempt joint action in a meeting at Brown University in 1898 attended by faculty, alumni, and students of ivy league colleges, but the various proposals made there for dealing with professionalism proved impossible to carry out. Meanwhile, colleges in particular geographic areas did set up localized "conferences" (athletic associations) that gradually made some feeble headway in setting eligibility rules that its members were supposed to uphold. Even the Amateur Athletic Union, formed in the late eighties by elite athletic clubs, tried to impose some rules on college sports, but by 1899 it had dropped any effort to control college baseball, football, and certain other college sports.

Concurrent with the rise of professionalism in colleges, a similar development among the elite athletic clubs took place. With many of their older members retiring, they began to find the supply of active athletes drying up. To replenish the field the New York A.C., for example, established up to a hundred "special athletic memberships" for men who, barred from voting and holding office, in effect were janissaries assigned to compete for the club in athletics. In baseball the New York A.C. went to even greater lengths. Its April 1893 *Journal* predicted that the club would field one of the strongest teams of "strictly amateur players ever got together," and the squad soon set out on an extended trip. But in the *Journal's* next issue, after hailing the team's "brilliant victories," the magazine revealed that because "our college players will not be available until July 1 . . . a . . . professional battery has been engaged to play in games prior to that date," adding blandly, "the nine will otherwise remain strictly amateur."

11

HUSKY MUCKERS INTRUDE

By the turn of the century baseball was a fixture on American college campuses. But it represented only an important branch of the sapling of intercollegiate sport. That sapling, already firmly rooted, underwent sturdy growth in the decade and a half or so prior to America's entrance into the Great War. Assiduously cultivated by students, alumni, and the public, it thrived in soil watered by enrollments that climbed from 157,000 in 1890 to 600,000 in 1920. State universities in particular attracted students.

Intercollegiate sports also expanded because an increasing number of young people appeared to be going to college not to learn, as Marion Talbot mentioned in a 1910 book, but for "a good time." A writer in the University of Washington's student magazine went so far as to assert that indulgence in athletics or support of them was "as important as obedience to instructors." A national preoccupation with health and manliness contributed to the accretion of sports.

The actions—and inaction—of college administrators themselves proved crucial in the expansion of college sports. Physical training specialists led an effort to incorporate athletics, which had germinated largely outside the educational sphere, into the college proper. Where this worked it gave sports academic recognition and merged them with the physical education program. At the University of Missouri and at Tufts, for instance, the administration placed sports under the jurisdiction of the physical training department. At some institutions, as at the University of California, men could substitute certain sports for the required calisthenics or gym. Consequently, athletics gained a legitimate place in college and university curriculums. Legitimizing athletics enabled the college administration to justify expenditure on them and publicity for them, allowing presidents to argue that sports contributed to the educational goals of the institution. The resulting college curriculum, called "the new physical education," provided a place for sports and games and stimulated the preparation of college instructors trained to conduct them.

Another support for college sport lay in the frequent expression by prominent persons of its supposed benefits. G. Stanley Hall, the influential psychologist, praised sports as an aid to health and to character building. Theodore Roosevelt, although he deplored "excessive devotion to sports and games," said that any sport, such as baseball, if treated as "good, healthy play . . . is of great benefit, not only to the body, but in its effect upon character." Athletics were also said to bring students together, thus inspiring "school spirit," a presumably laudable objective. President A. L. Lowell, in his Harvard inaugural address in October of 1909, declared stoutly that "such contests offer to students the one common interest, the only striking occasion for display of college solidarity." That college spirit, observed Thorstein Veblen wryly, "as inspired by athletics," merely represented a reversion to a proclivity for "youthful exploits of ferocity." Sports might, however, serve as a kind of escape valve, as President Alston Ellis of Ohio University pointed out in 1907, "for a certain amount of animal activity that might be employed in more questionable directions." This could be a veiled reference to an observed decline in rowdyism, hazing, and vandalism that, Jacques Barzun noted, reportedly coincided with the rise of intercollegiate sport. Another academic support for athletics came from the director of the Yale gym. William G. Anderson studied 807 Yale athletes over the period 1855–1905 and concluded that athletes lived longer than nonathletes, their death rate emerging as little more than half the rate of the student body as a whole. Whatever the reasons, college athletics commanded much prestige. *Baseball Magazine* in 1911 instituted a new column to cover colleges, "in compliance to growing interest in college athletics throughout the country." A.G. Spalding and Company as usual lost little time in taking advantage of a trend and issued a college baseball guide in 1912.

At the same time its promoters disseminated the benefits of college athletics, its detractors exposed its deficiencies. "Overemphasis," a frequent complaint, found in Woodrow Wilson an apt interpreter. In a 1909 piece for *Scribner's*, Wilson, then the president of Princeton University, stated,

> Amusement, athletic games, the zest of contest and competition . . . are wholesome means of stimulation. . . . But they should not assume the front of the stage where more serious and lasting interests are to be served. Men cannot be prepared by them for modern life. . . . The side shows need not be abolished. They need not be cast out or even discredited. But they must be subordinated . . . put in their natural place as diversions . . . .

Another flaw in college athletics, the pressure to win at any cost, created invidious practices like special aids to athletes: bestowing athletic "scholarships," paying students (and nonstudents) to play for varsity teams, and reserving the scorecard concession at the park for student athletes. College athletics became large commercial ventures that brought attention and therefore attracted business (students) to the institution, thus subtracting from its educational purpose. Furthermore, the excitement of contests distracted students from their studies, as G. Stanley Hall pointed out.

Student athletes in effect became semipros or professionals, and indeed the major and minor leagues recruited them avidly (Christy Mathewson, Jack Coombs, Charles Bender, and Eddie Collins, to mention standouts) into professional ball. And colleges in turn recruited athletes from high schools. George Wingate warned young high school athletes in 1910:

> I know some of you are receiving all kinds of inducements to go to this or that [college], that offers of support are practically being made. You want to remember that the man who does this [accepts such an offer], when he leaves his college, is regarded by his associates very differently from the regular collegian. They are all glad to make use of your services but they look down on you. When they have college meetings you won't be asked.

Another result of the overweening importance of college athletics was the acceptance into college of "husky muckers," men who, wrote G. Stanley Hall, "belong outside academic circles."

Overemphasis also meant that many colleges and universities in the new century built huge athletic plants involving more than ten percent of their total capital investment. To finance athletics, administrators imposed compulsory athletic fees, most of which they expended upon the varsity teams; charged admission to varsity games; raised funds from alumni; and applied some athletic expenditures to advertising. An investigating committee of the National Collegiate Athletic Association found that 150 institutions spent $1,090,000.00 on intercollegiate sports, thus averaging $7,266.66 each, but they spent probably not a tenth as much on intramurals, which could benefit the student body as a whole rather than a few members of varsity teams.

Institutions did, however, encourage intramural sports, for educational reasons. At Williams the college undertook an elaborate intramural program to mitigate the system in which only a few highly trained competed. Some colleges merely used intramurals as a feeder for varsity teams, but others turned them to educational account by promoting "athletics for all."

Both the successes and the failures of college athletics moved administrators to step in and take more control in the 1900s. Successes because athletics had become too valuable an enterprise to be jeopardized by part-time or careless student supervision; failures because abuses made for problems in scheduling games with other institutions or permitted athletics to get out of hand. If not student athletic associations, then alumni might gain the ascendance and use athletics for their own entertainment and ego satisfaction.

Various systems of athletic control sprang up, but the most popular became a three-part committee with a few representatives each from faculty, students, and alumni. Especially after football, which had become the foremost college sport and also the most brutal, killed forty-four students in 1903 alone, a cry for reform in college athletics arose. A few institutions abolished football, and the others came close to doing so. The football crisis in the first decade of the century helped some college authorities screw up the courage to impose stricter controls on all college athletics. Gradually, however, the zeal for reform waned, but while it lasted it spawned national college associations and sports "conferences" in various areas of the country that continued to press for general agreement on elimination of abuses. The only lasting national-level association, the National Collegiate Athletic Association, an advisory group, "suggested" rules that might keep players and institutions in compliance with eligibility rules, but it had no enforcement powers.

The elite athletic clubs continued to influence colleges. The large, wealthy ones developed their property holdings until each important club, like the New York A.C., owned buildings, fields, and sports apparatus worth between a half million and four million dollars each. The 156 members of the American Athletic Union, the athletic clubs' association, together owned property valued in 1910 at twenty-five million dollars. Many of these clubs fielded baseball teams that competed for a yearly "amateur" championship, but for these "amateur" teams they often hired college athletes and YMCA players to represent them in important games, offering them inducements like free club membership, athletic clothing, and special training. The AAU ruled against the practice, but as late as 1918 the future major leaguer Frank Frisch, while a Fordham student, enjoyed such privileges as a baseball player for the New York A.C., which permitted him to practice at beautiful Travers Island, the club's private athletic facility, where after practice he and the other players were treated to a "luxurious meal" and permitted to row over to another island for a swim. Frisch also enjoyed the Sunday games he played. Players could bring their girl friends, who would share the ample meal that followed. "We could hardly wait till the game was over," Frisch said, "to dig into a thick, juicy steak, mashed potatoes, corn on the cob, and as many heaping plates of ice cream as we wanted."

The elite athletic clubs, besides serving as models for colleges, also inspired the formation of hundreds of lower-class boys' and young men's amateur and semipro organizations all over the country that used the name "athletic club" but organized primarily to play baseball.

In such an athletic setting college baseball burgeoned after 1900. *Sporting News* boasted in 1905 of the familiarity of every college with baseball. *Baseball Magazine* claimed in 1909 that it had a special correspondent ("stringer") in every American college to furnish information for its college department.

The style and flavor of college ball in this era is conveyed especially in fiction, in books like Christy Matthewson's *Won in the Ninth* and Zane Grey's *The Young Pitcher*. On the fictional college teams described by Matthewson and Grey the young men on the varsity take their participation in baseball with "intense seriousness," dining at a special training table, with the coach at its head, and sometimes living together in a special training house, with training rules that included a ten P.M. bedtime rule, although rules in these stories are occasionally broken by fellows who smoke, drink, or eat the forbidden pie or cake. The college athlete is admiringly portrayed in such books as a fellow with an erect form, a lithe and springy stride, and assurance in every move. Two real, not fictional, coaches, W.J. Clarke of Princeton and Frederick T. Dawson of Union College, in their instructional 1915 book, charge college players to adhere to high ethical principles:

> Remember that when you are chosen to play on a college team you represent not only your particular student body but the whole host of alumni and the friends and benefactors of the college. Therefore do not perform one act which will prevent you from being absolutely at your best—worthy of the trust placed in you.

Of course, as Dudley Sargent remarked in 1906, the advantages of rigorous and systematic health rules (if they were advantages) accrued only to the varsity. The majority of the students on any campus received no such personal attention to their health and were on their own when it came to health training.

Hiring former professional baseball players as coaches helped make the training of college athletes resemble that of the professionals. Fred Pfeffer, former National League second baseman, coached baseball at the University of Wisconsin; Art Devlin of the New York Giants came over to Fordham to coach; and Fred Mitchell of the Boston Braves coached at Harvard—all despite the NCAA's recommendation that part-time professional ball players be replaced as coaches by full-time faculty members with strong educational backgrounds. In 1913 Yale, Harvard, and Princeton agreed to remove their coaches from the bench, according to *Outlook* magazine, but that hardly ended the influence of professional coaches. College coaches often did well financially. John W. Heisman at Georgia Tech in 1904 signed a contract to teach baseball and football for $2,250.00 plus thirty percent of the net gate receipts of all varsity games. His later contracts, although they dropped the gate receipts proviso, all raised his salary.

College teams aped the professionals in other ways: tripping opponents, shouting to disconcert them, gibing "in ungentlemanly fashion," as Dean Lebaron R. Briggs of Harvard described it, and even having the pitcher throw directly at the batter, as illustrated in Zane Grey's fiction. Pro players even invaded college campuses. One year at Northwestern University, according to the 1903 baseball captain, the Chicago Cubs did not send all their men south for spring training, and the leftover professionals worked out with the Northwestern team. Colleges also played pro teams from time to time. Faculty complaints concerning these contacts with the pros evoked sarcasm in 1912 from Tom Rice, writing in *Sporting News*. He called the denouncers "snobbish" and "milk soppish." If they were so easily contaminated, asserted Rice, they should go back to their monasteries.

Training varsity baseball teams and hiring professionals to coach them cost money. Harvard spent $10,634.45 on varsity baseball in 1903, but the varsity earned $14,954.68 that year, thus turning a neat profit of $4,320.23. The following year the team did well again, spending $12,638.89 but earning $16,674.08, thus profiting by $4,035.19. Princeton was making about the same amount of profit on baseball. The University of Pennsylvania, another baseball power, and Cornell University each spent around $10,000.00 in 1909, and Yale expended a whopping $29,041.00, but Columbia only $3,475.00.

The best college players often turned professional after their academic careers were over, or even before. A number of them became major league fixtures. Holy Cross College produced many pros, some of them (like Jigger Statz, Eddie Collins, Joe Dugan, and Bill Carrigan) leaving college before graduation to sign professional contracts. Larry Gardner quit the University of Vermont after three years to sign with the Boston American League club in 1908. Jack Coombs stayed to graduate from Colby College in Maine, helping it win the New England championship in 1908 and playing semipro ball every summer. Eppa Rixey, although he left the University of Virginia after his third year to sign with the Philadelphia National League club, returned to get his degree and after that kept returning in the major-league off seasons to earn a master's degree in chemistry. Jakie May would have completed his degree at Oak Ridge Business College in Tennessee but the administration expelled him as a senior for a practical joke; he stabled some calves overnight in the president's room. After his expulsion one of the professors helped him get a professional baseball position for 1914, and by 1917 he was with the St. Louis Cardinals. At Fordham, Francis Spellman, a good fielder, did poorly at bat and found the competition too keen, especially from first baseman Jack Coffey, later a well-known coach. Spellman became not a St. Louis Cardinal but a Roman Catholic Cardinal. The University of Alabama produced Derrell Pratt, Luke Sewell, and Riggs Stephenson, all of whom became big leaguers. Zack Taylor, in the majors during the twenties and thirties, confessed in 1927 that when attending Rollins College in Winter Park, Florida, for two years, he "learned little there except baseball." In the midwest Notre Dame, Villanova, Concordia, Dickinson, and Michigan all produced players who made the professional ranks. At Southwestern University in Texas Curt Walker theoretically studied "a literary course," but actually his major interest was baseball, and he left after two years, when the professionals signed him.

California's good weather meant plenty of baseball at colleges like Sacred Heart (Joe Cronin and John F. Kerr studied there), Santa Clara, which supplied many players to the Pacific Coast League, and St. Mary's, by 1910 bearing the reputation as the leading producer of major league ball players, including Harry Hooper, who joined the Boston American League club, Charles Enright of the St. Louis Cardinals, and Joe Oeschger, who went to the Philadelphia National Leaguers. St. Mary's even shut out the Boston Red Sox in a 1911 game.

In all this preparation of what sometimes amounted to semipro teams of college men, college administrators compromised amateur principles whenever they believed they could do so. The athletic "scholarship," a misnomer that meant paying a player's tuition and expenses while he played ball for the college, became a favorite method of attracting and keeping good players. Dixon College in Illinois gave Davy Jones, later a National League outfielder, such a "scholarship" in 1900. Alma College in Milford, Michigan, gave one to George Brilmeyer. Harvard awarded one to a C student, "Home Run" Frantz, in 1903, with the support of President Eliot. Southern Kentucky Union College paid Gabby Street, later a big-league catcher and manager, to play there at a rate he claimed to be better than he could have received in the minor leagues. The University of Alabama granted Riggs Stephenson free tuition in exchange not for playing ball, he asserted later, but for "seeing to it that prankish boys didn't throw rocks through armory windows." Even a small college like Mars Hill in North Carolina hired both a coach and a pitcher in 1913, although college records are not clear as to whether either studied there.

Paying students to play revived the old breed of early professional baseball's "revolvers"—players who switched from one college to another that offered more pelf, as did one called Lolly Gray who, according to *Sporting News*, played in succession for Clemson, Wofford, Furman, and Virginia Polytechnic Institute. Another abuse was the use of noncollege men on the team. Henry Needham wrote in *McClure's Magazine* in 1905 of two known semipros that Harvard, "with all her smug self-righteousness," had enlisted on the baseball nine. The opposite occurred as well: college varsity members might play temporarily for professional teams, as did "Bodwell, the well known University of Chicago athlete," when he caught for the semipro Nebraska Indians in a game in Iowa, as related in Guy Greene's 1903 book on the Indians.

By far the biggest problem, from the point of view of college administrations, arose from "summer ball," the practice by varsity members of taking jobs playing baseball during vacations on teams formed by summer resorts, or on professional, semipro, or industrial teams. As Professor Albert Bushnell Hart commented in 1890, when the practice was already noticed, players thus "honorably" acquired the means to pay their college bills. But in the opinion of many college administrators their paid play impaired the students' amateur standing. As a result, student athletes resorted to the subterfuge of false names when they played summers for pay. Jimmy Doyle of the Chicago National League team of 1911 admitted that as a student and crack shortstop at Niagara University, he played summer ball for money in Utica, New York. Eddie Collins played as "Eddie Sullivan" for Rutland, Vermont, in the Northern League to get spending money while he attended college in New York. Ed Reulbach of the 1905 Chicago Cubs, as a Notre Dame member 1901–1903, also played summer ball under names variously reported as "Lawson" and "Sheldon." Art Nehf of the Boston Braves and New York Giants, while in attendance at Rose Polytechnic Institute in Terre Haute, played one summer for the Iron & Copper League of Northern Michigan. He admitted in 1915, ". . . if it got out we would be ineligible for college ball. But as this place was a long way from home I thought I would take a chance." It worked for Nehf, and he graduated in 1914. Others used the same subterfuge at Princeton, Tufts, and Harvard Law. As one transgressor said, "Nobody asked any questions in those days." The most famous summer ball case involved Jim Thorpe, the incomparable Indian athlete whose Olympic medals were withdrawn when someone discovered he had played summer ball while in college.*

Proof of violation of rules against summer ball, if indeed a college passed such a rule, was difficult to produce. Henry Needham in *McClure's* listed in 1905 the names of Dartmouth, Princeton, Cornell, Yale, and Pennsylvania men who for want of conclusive evidence retained their college standing despite having played summer ball. In 1901, however, some Yale and Andover men injudiciously allowed themselves to be photographed in their college uniforms while playing for an Adirondack team. A Yale professor saw their pictures, and the college removed them from the varsity. Some college players claimed, however, that they played in summer without pay and only to keep in practice—an explanation difficult to verify.

Faculties found themselves divided on the issue of summer ball. Some thought that perhaps they should not bother about what students did summers. Physical training people like Clark Hetherington and George J. Fisher, along with coaches like Alonzo Stagg and professors from Dartmouth and Pennsylvania, discussed the problem intermittently between 1906 and 1909 in the *American Physical Education Review. Baseball Magazine* published an article implying that permitting a college man to earn money in summer by selling stereoscopes or bibles but not by playing ball was silly. The National Collegiate Athletic Association found in 1909 that a majority of its members permitted summer ball, but in the classic faculty dodge it recommended only more study of the problem.

In 1911 Captain Palmer E. Pierce of the NCAA tried to grip the issue. He called the summer caper a violation of amateurism and a disgrace, and he challenged colleges to agree on how to handle it. But as usual, nothing collective could be decided. In the spring of 1913, in fact, George Huff, athletic director of Illinois University, along with sports writer Hugh Ful-

*See below, Chapter 24.

lerton and supported by American League president Ban Johnson, decided to throw out the rule themselves and proposed a summer league of eight or ten clubs made up of college athletes, paying the players a stipend to perform. Interestingly, this is essentially what took place about fifty years later. *Sporting News* supported summer ball and maintained that no stigma should attach to making money in summer by playing ball, adding that it was safe to say that a quarter of all college players engaged in the practice, especially at resorts.

Two summer ball "scandals" erupted in 1915. Five University of Michigan players were discovered to be pros, and upon further investigation the university learned that practically every member of the varsity team had received money to play summer ball. That fall Yale declared five of its ball players ineligible because they had played summer ball in exchange for room and board.

Conferences and committees continued rehashing the problem, and articles in popular journals like *Saturday Evening Post*, *Outlook*, and *Baseball Magazine* discussed it. The chief concern of many, as the New York *Times* noted in 1915, seemed to be that trying to rule against summer ball simply made hypocrites of the players. Public opinion, the *University of Chicago Magazine* believed in 1916, unquestionably lay on the side of permitting the athletes to play summer ball. Professors and athletic directors, in another sludge of irresolution, made pompous public pronouncements that came to no conclusions but employed catchwords like "vexatious" and "inalienable right." Colleges and athletic conferences imposed their own restrictions, some rigid, others loose, attempting to narrow the conditions under which students could legitimately play, or else they had no restrictions at all. Even if players violated such rules, according to Harold Wolf's thesis on college sport, some faculties ignored the violations.

Near the end of the teens the University of Chicago's Amos Alonzo Stagg moved that the NCAA ask a foundation that studied educational questions to survey the problem, but, probably in part because of World War I, more than a decade passed before such a study was published. Meanwhile, the summer ball question persisted. In Zane Grey's story, *The Young Pitcher*, for instance, he portrays the entire varsity of a university as disqualified for having played at resorts like Cape May or Atlantic City, where expenses were usually covered and the players paid for their services. But the story has a happy ending. As a result of the varsity's disqualification the hero, although a mere freshman, becomes the college's star pitcher.

While colleges contemplated what to do about summer ball, Organized Baseball acted to obtain desirable college players by secret means. College athletes got Organized Baseball's club officials to conceal their signing with big-league clubs so that they could keep their amateur standing at their institutions. The major-league clubs benefited by such undercover arrangements because the signed player, as an active member of his college varsity, continued to obtain playing experience. Some big-league clubs also paid players' tuition. This subversion of college rules sometimes involved the connivance of the college coach.

In 1906 the chairman of the University of Michigan's Board of Control of Athletics, V.H. Lane, wrote Garry Herrmann, chairman of the National Commission and president of the Cincinnati Reds, saying that his board felt "much troubled" by problems of amateurism and asking if Herrmann could occasionally give advice on the subject. Herrmann was a poor one to ask. As revealed in his correspondence, Herrmann was conducting his own subversion of college rules. In 1905, for instance, Leo Hafford asked Herrmann to conceal his signing with Cincinnati for 1906:

> The college where I am going is giving me my tuition for running and therefore I must be careful to have myself protected and also not to have the college blacklisted from its place among the other colleges.

And in 1911 Herrmann agreed to suppress the news that Davis Robertson, another college player, had signed with the New York National League club for 1912. Robertson feared his faculty might object, so he got the secretary of the New York club to write Herrmann about keeping his signing quiet. In addition, a scout named Thomas F. O'Hara signed James McLaughlin, captain of the Colgate team, for Herrmann's Cincinnati club, but O'Hara told Herrmann that the matter had to be kept secret, because, he said, he would not be able to sign another college player if the news got out. One tempted player changed his mind. J.T. Sullivan, a medical student at the University of Michigan, signed with the Cincinnati Reds but decided to return the advance money the Reds had given him and asked Herrmann to keep his name out of the papers, explaining that he had just been elected captain and knew his signing would hurt his amateur standing.

Herrmann was not the only violator among club owners. Frank Navin of the Detroit American League club wrote coach Hugh Lanigan of the University of Virginia in April 1912 of his willingness to sign Eppa Rixey while still in college and give him a bonus, assuring Lanigan that "his signing with our club will not be made public until he is ready to report to our team." That year, however, Rixey chose to go with the Philadelphia Athletics and pitched twenty-three games for the team.

Playing for an Organized Baseball club under an assumed name could be accomplished in those days before televised games. Andy Coakley played in 1902 for Connie Mack's Philadelphia American League team under the name "McAllister." Lew Malone of Mount St. Joseph's played for Mack under the name "Ryan." Eddie Collins joined the Philadelphia Athletics while a Columbia law student just before he was slated to captain the team in his final year, but a faculty member discovered his picture in a newspaper. His removal from the team followed, although he obtained his degree.

Some college men drew a fine line between membership on a professional team and actually playing for it, as did Johnny Ogden, who belonged to the New York Giants for three years before his public signing in 1918, but since he did not play for the Giants during those three years he felt he could still pitch for Swarthmore. Or the line was drawn between playing for but not actually signing a contract with a pro team, as did Harry McIvain when he played summers for Steubenville, Ohio, while at State College, Pennsylvania, claiming that he broke no rule because he did not sign a contract. The height of futility occurred when the team of Santa Clara College, California, discovered that St. Mary's of Oakland, their next opponent, harbored a player named Nealon Lynch, who had already signed with the New York American League club. Santa Clara disputed St. Mary's right to use Lynch. To obtain a ruling on the player, Brother Joseph of St. Mary's wrote to Ban Johnson, president of the American League! Johnson, of course, decided that Lynch could play.

A new development for American college baseballists presented itself in the 1900s when Asian college players took advantage of opportunities to come to the United States to play and American college teams reciprocated. The skill and success of Asian teams constituted a revelation to American college athletes.

The series of foreign exchanges in baseball began when the baseball team of Waseda University in Tokyo, founded by Count Shigenobu Okuma, a government figure and prominent reformer, came to America in 1905. Waseda had been playing ball since the 1890s and by 1905 fielded one of Japan's best teams under Isoo Abe, head of its baseball department, who had studied at Hartford Theological Seminary. Abe said that he first saw baseball in London, played between American and British teams, and "was extremely impressed with its sportsmanship and fair play." Abe had promised his Waseda players he would take them to America if they ever achieved a perfect season. When they finished the 1904 fall season without a loss, Abe obtained the consent of Waseda's founder, Count Okuma, as well as that of its president, Kazuo Hatoyama, who had himself studied at Columbia and Yale. Since the Japanese war with Russia was still in progress, many of those asked for an opinion believed a visit to America might convey a favorable impression of "a surplus of national strength," as Ki Kimura claimed in his book, *Japanese Literature*.

Despite popular belief, the Japanese government did not, according to Waseda archives, finance the trip. Instead, the team received two gifts, 5,500 yen (about $11,000.00) from the university and 700 yen (about $1,400.00) from private sources, and the rest had to come from gate receipts, of which the team would get two-thirds. The baseball players trained for their American series on an island south of Yokohama, and there in the evenings Abe instructed the players in American manners and etiquette in order to prevent any unforeseen embarrassment in the United States. The team carried two players now in the Japanese Hall of Fame, Atsushi Kono, pitcher, and Shin Hashido, captain and shortstop, who later also wrote a book on baseball.

Coached in part by Fred Merrifield, formerly of the University of Chicago, Waseda displayed its prowess initially against Stanford University at Palo Alto in late April of 1905 before 2,000 fans. Stanford won 9–1. Abe, disappointed, wrote in his diary that the loss probably stemmed from the arduous Pacific crossing. But Waseda again lost to Stanford, 3–1, as well as to the Naval Academy at Goat Island, 11–8. I May Waseda finally defeated an American team, the Encina Club, at Palo Alto, and beat the Stanford University faculty.

Waseda next journeyed to San Francisco, where it lost 16–0 to St. Mary's College, the California students' yearbook gloating about the win over the "little brown men" and proclaiming its own team intercollegiate champions not only of California but also of Japan! Waseda continued losing, to such teams as the University of Oregon, Pomona College, and the University of Washington, although it won 13–6 over the University of Southern California and an Indian school team, Sherman Institute. It also lost to some semipro teams. All told, Waseda won only 7 of 26 games. The competition turned out to be tougher than expected, but Abe said his players never despaired.

After the game with the University of Washington the Seattle *Post Intelligencer* reported the Japanese players were "especially strong in their fielding, and if they could bat as well, they would make any of the collegiate teams of this country hustle to beat them." The Seattle *Times* declared that "The sympathy of the crowd was all with the Japs, and there was an oriental tinge to the grand stand, given by a few hundred Seattle Japs who smoked cigarettes, cracked peanuts and rooted for the Waseda bunch." Because the Japanese proved "woefully weak with the bat," the Washington boys outhit and therefore beat "the little brown men."

After the Waseda trip and until the onset of World War I, hardly a year passed without an exchange of visits between American college teams and Asian teams, or at least a visit by one side or both to the intermediate ground of Hawaii.

In 1907 the Keio University team of Tokyo hit upon the idea of playing "nearby" Americans, the Hawaiians. Hawaii was then an American protectorate. Keio University invited a team called St. Louis University to play in Japan, discovering only later that it was the strongest semipro team in the islands. However, Keio managed to take two of the five games played. The following year Keio paid a return visit to Hawaii, playing fourteen games, one of them against Santa Clara College of California.

Santa Clara's five-week trip to Hawaii proved memorable. Met on the wharf by 1,500 cheering people, including the students from Keio in caps and gowns, then bedecked with flowers, the California players marched to the hotel to the music of a twenty-five-piece band. In Hawaii the Santa Clara team won six out of eight games, including the one with

Keio. "The little Japanese players made a sturdy fight," reported the Santa Clara college magazine, and the game "was by no means a poor game to watch."

In 1908 Waseda University of Tokyo invited University of Washington to visit Japan and play a series there—the first mainland college team to visit the Orient. Financial arrangements for the trip, according to Waseda archives, came from gate receipts.

For their trip to Japan the twelve University of Washington men, their manager reported, enjoyed pleasant weather on the *Tosa Maru*. They spent most of their time on board reading and even "occasionally discussed" college studies. At Yokohama the travelers were received by their advance agent, a Japanese and former Washington student, and carried to their hotel by ricksha. During the days of sightseeing that followed, the American players found their visit treated by reporters as almost as important as the impending visit of the so-called White Fleet of American battleships.

To their surprise, about 2,000 people attended the first baseball practice of the American players in Tokyo. Nearly 7,000 came out for the first game on a cold, wet, and cloudy day, some of them giving the Washington team yell. The American team won the first game but lost the second. Later it won twice more over Waseda. It lost, however, three times to Keio, which the Washington shortstop Walter Meagher said "had the strongest team we met in Japan." During the trip the Americans attended Japanese theatre and visited the shrines of Nikko as the guest of a Japanese silk merchant, owner of two stores in Seattle. Finally, Count Okuma, the Waseda founder, showed the team around his garden and "magnificent mansion," after which they attended a banquet. Meagher reported in the college magazine that the team returned home "feeling we had had one of the greatest trips that any college team had ever taken."

In 1909 the University of Wisconsin baseball team received an invitation to visit Japan as guests of Keio University and to play other teams. The invitation, largely through the efforts of a Wisconsin alumnus, Genkwan Shibata, came from Professor Matsuoka of Keio, who had taken his master's degree in political science at Wisconsin in 1906. Wisconsin received a contract guaranteeing 8,000 yen, about $4,000.00, for expenses, and in turn Wisconsin offered to pay half of all expenses above that amount. The invitation created excitement at the university, where students and faculty regarded it, the Wisconsin *Daily Cardinal* exclaimed, as "the greatest proposition that had ever been offered to a Wisconsin team." The college paper also quoted professors as calling the invitation one of "exceptional educational advantages," "a good thing for the university itself," "a great scheme," and "a splendid opportunity." Keio University was reported to be especially eager to entertain the Americans "to dispel rumors of enmity between the U.S. and Japan." Dr. Charles McCarthy realized the players would miss part of the fall semester's work, "but I don't think that the time missed will be enough to make much difference." Other American colleges, notably Pennsylvania, were ready to take Wisconsin's place if the university should decide against it, but Wisconsin accepted the offer.

Professor Matsuoka, in order to act as Wisconsin cheerleader at the Japanese games, wrote Genkwan Shibata for the words of the Wisconsin yell, the words and music of the college song, and 500 cardinal-colored armbands, to be used by Japanese students who were to represent Wisconsin fans at the games!

Dr. McCarthy warned in the Wisconsin Daily *Cardinal*, "Of course, there must be no trouble, and the men must leave for home having all the Japanese proud of them as gentlemen and students." McCarthy accompanied the thirteen players as coach and university representative, while Genkwan Shibata went as manager and interpreter. One reporter went along. The group took a train to Seattle, where the Wisconsin players lost two games to local teams and then visited the Alaska-Yukon-Pacific Exposition.

Arriving in Yokohama at the end of a "cold and disagreeable" sixteen-day sea trip, the team was besieged by reporters and Keio students. Idealized sketches of their determined-looking faces appeared in Tokyo *Punch*. During the social affairs that introduced them to Japan, Captain Douglas Knight, after listening to geisha girls play an unfamiliar instrument, commented, "Often you couldn't tell whether they were playing tunes or tuning up." Knight also marveled, "We took off our shoes at the door and sat on the floor."

After watching a Keio University baseball practice, Knight worried, "The Keio bunch are awfully fast fielders and look like fair hitters." Knight's observation was prescient: his club dropped the first two games to Keio, 3–2 in 11 innings and 2–1 in 19 innings, and lost to the same team again later 5–4. All told, although Wisconsin lost 3 out of 4 to Keio, it won 2 out of 3 from Waseda, and it defeated two other Japanese teams as well. Wisconsin players claimed they lost the first two games out of inability to grasp Japanese field rules and because some players suffered from the hot, damp climate. Despite the frequency of rain, crowds at the games averaged 20,000, many fans bearing banners complimentary to the Wisconsin team.

On the Americans' return home, Dr. McCarthy claimed that his players had kept up with their college work by studying on board ship. A homecoming celebration for the team at the university furnished entertainment for all, including speeches by local politicians. The university president congratulated the players on their gentlemanly conduct and added, "The class room is not all of the university education." Wisconsin Secretary of State William A. Frear boasted that by this trip "Wisconsin unlock[ed] the door of social fraternity with Japan in a manner never before equalled." Dr. McCarthy declared that the American consul had informed him that the trip did more for the United States in Japan than any visit previously made by any organization.

Not to be outdone, the University of Chicago baseball team sailed for the Pacific in 1910 as a result of an invitation of two years' standing from Waseda to play that university and Keio. The Chicago faculty, unlike Wisconsin's, granted permission for student players to miss part of the fall semester only on condition that they attend college in the summer session. In Japan, the powerful Chicago team swept all nine games played before the large crowds of from 6,500 to 12,000. Whole schools attended, dismissing for the day. The club was invited to return every fifth year until 1930! And the University of Chicago invited Waseda to return the visit in 1911. After leaving Tokyo the Americans continued to China and the Philippines, where the team played soldiers and foreign residents, losing only one, to the Marines in Manila.

Both Keio and Waseda university teams visited the United States in 1911. Keio won three quarters of its games, beating such colleges as Fordham University. When Keio played Georgetown in Washington, D.C., the Japanese Embassy came out in force to support the team, and Japanese singing and cheering could be heard above the din despite Keio's loss. When Waseda played the University of Chicago that year in Chicago, the Japanese were beaten 6–4, but in playing some of the strongest American college teams it made, according to *Baseball Magazine*, a "very creditable showing."

As an outgrowth of Waseda's original 1905 trip to the states, during which it lost to Stanford University, Stanford's team traveled to Japan in 1913. Keio University sent Stanford a contract offering to cover expenses up to $3,500.00, and Stanford agreed to stay 30 days and to finance a return trip of Keio to the States. In Japan Stanford won only half its eight games with Keio, but the Americans also beat Meiji, another Tokyo university. Stanford's captain, Zeb Terry, later became a professional and spent seven years playing shortstop in the majors.

That fall (1913) the University of Washington set out upon another Japanese trip to play several universities. A dispute marred this trip. In a game with Keio, the Americans alleged an unfair decision against them and left the field during the game, thus causing "considerable discussion" among the Japanese over their behavior, as the New York *Times* wrote. The difficulty was, however, overcome, and the series continued, the Washington team winning some and losing some against Japanese colleges like Meiji, Waseda, and Shoyyo. As many as 15,000 saw the University of Washington defeat Meiji. Graduate Manager Ralph Horr wrote later about the "unusually courteous treatment, clean sport on the field," and the enthusiastic rooting that "reminds one of a Bull Moose convention."

The University of Chicago team came to Japan for the second time in 1915. American Ambassador George W. Guthrie and the president of Waseda University were among the 20,000 who saw the university win its first game, 5–3, against Waseda. Chicago made another clean sweep of its Japanese series, taking Waseda twice and Keio three times.

Cross-cultural college baseball contacts also took place among Hawaiians and mainlanders, with fertilization from Japanese college teams. After the St. Louis University team of Hawaii visited Japan in 1907, Keio made a visit to Hawaii in 1908, playing various local teams. In Hawaii, besides multiethnic teams there were also Japanese and Chinese teams. Beginning in 1910 the Chinese team of the University of Hawaii began making trips to the States to play American college teams and others. In its 1910 trip the Chinese team won 66, lost 49, and tied 4. Among its college hosts were the universities of California, Utah, Colorado, Chicago, Wisconsin, Syracuse, Georgetown, and Fordham.

On the 1912 trip of Hawaii University's Chinese team, it lost to the Wisconsin Badgers, the champions of the Western Conference, 8–7 in 10 innings and 5–4 to Williams College, the Eastern champions. According to S.H. Hoe, a member of the Chinese team, the team made a "wonderful showing in some games and miserable in others." During its 1913 trip it played an amazing total of 144 games, winning 105, losing 38, and tieing 1. Of that total, 54 games were played against colleges, and of those it won 49! Its victories that year included ones against strong teams like St. Mary's College, Stanford University, Ohio University, Oberlin College, Ohio State, and Duquesne. At Urbana, Illinois, the Chinese played a group of students at the University of Illinois called the Ineligibles—players who could not participate in varsity games either because of their professional standing or their deficiency in scholarship. The Chinese were told this team was much stronger than the varsity. The Ineligibles beat them 5–4, but the Chinese took the second game 9–4. During this 1913 trip the Chinese were defeated by a famous semipro team, the Ridgewoods of Brooklyn, and by strong industrial teams like the Telling Company of Cleveland and the Strawbridge-Clothier Company of Philadelphia, as well as by the black team called the American Giants. The Chinese returned to America again in 1914, 1915, and 1916.

After the 1913 trip S.H. Hoe, a team member, told some of the hardships of the venture: eating "quick-order" dinners at crowded railroad stations and "dog-houses," for example, with "many curious eyes staring." The cold bothered the players: some had never seen snow. But they were impressed by "the true sportsmanlike spirit displayed by the American college students and fans" who always applauded good plays, even those of "the invaders." One welcoming college president, speaking before a student assembly, remarked "The Yellow Peril! We have seen it here this evening. That's the only kind of yellow peril that I know. Let Providence give us more of this kind."

On their 1914 tour the Chinese team defeated both Lafayette University and Columbia. At the former game, said the New York *Times*, the "Celestials" (the Chinese) "drove the ball with terrific force." In fact, "The Orientals played all around the Blue and White, both in the field and at the bat."

When the University of California team visited Hawaii in 1914, the most successful opponents among the different teams it played were the Chinese teams of the Chinese Athletic Union, winners of two games against the Californians. After the second the Hawaiians set off 20,000 firecrackers.

World War I put a temporary halt to these Pacific baseball contacts with American colleges, but on many American campuses baseball continued. President Wilson supported college athletics during the war for the students' physical development. The United States government thought intercollegiate sport should be continued, to provide what Colonel Palmer Pierce of the NCAA called "training and experiences that helped develop leadership qualities in the young men the military needed as officers." Some colleges dropped varsity schedules or shortened them during the war. The University of Pittsburgh eliminated intercollegiate baseball, citing interference with military drill and general lack of interest. Harvard suspended all intercollegiate sport, although Williams and Wesleyan tried to keep theirs going. Many institutions emphasized intramurals instead, mouthing the theme "athletics for the service of the nation." Eligibility rules suddenly seemed no longer a matter of deep concern; colleges modified or discarded them at will. But the prewar activity had set the stage for a postwar boom in college sport both intercollegiate and intramural—and a revival of the same problems.

12

COLLEGE OR KINDERGARTEN

During the prosperity of the twenties, enrollment in colleges and universities expanded from more than a half million at the beginning of the decade to double that ten years later. The general American sports mania of the era solidified into an appanage of college life characterized by virulent spectatoritis. At the University of Chicago, for instance, most students spent two hours or more each week not participating in sports but watching and cheering at college games and rallies, where their athletic association or fraternity expected them to demonstrate allegiance to their institution and solidarity with their peers by expressing "college spirit." Athletes themselves loomed large in importance and prestige on college campuses. The president of Yale marveled in a 1927 *Harper's* article that students' parents often preferred their offspring to win distinction in athletics rather than in science or letters.

Football, the campus king, dominated athletic budgets and athletic news, just as professional football threatened to do on national sports pages. Baseball, no longer the pre-emininent college sport, fell to second or third, after football and perhaps even behind basketball. Major John L. Griffith of the NAAF believed that summer ball—really, the impossibility of enforcing rules against it—had contributed to the decline of college ball because some colleges had even eliminated intercollegiate baseball in their despair over inability to control their players' summer professionalism. Other commentators thought football's drama or basketball's speed had elbowed college baseball aside. Some institutions, such as Michigan and Bowdoin, turned to intramurals to counteract overemphasis on intercollegiate sports, but in intramural athletics a lower standard of skill prevailed, so participants in men's college intramurals could not obtain the same college status from taking part in them. Attention in most institutions centered upon intercollegiate exploits, especially football, which spawned huge stadia that a student of architecture thought resembled those of indulgent Roman emperors and represented "a new and vital note in American architecture." Colleges of the twenties, in the words of Professor Harvey Wish, gladly went into debt even to the point of "starving" the regular academic departments in order to build these "magnificent" stadia.

Yet baseball still attracted many. In 1923 a three-game series in Boston between Boston College and Holy Cross drew 80,000 paying customers, including one crowd of more than 30,000. And in the spring of 1925 Major Griffith estimated that eighty percent of American colleges would play intercollegiate baseball that year. Fifty men turned out as candidates for Harvard's varsity baseball team in February of 1921, and Yale sent its baseball players south for ten days of spring training in 1920, establishing headquarters at Macon, Georgia.

The military academies emerged as popular college opponents in the twenties. Baseball strongholds like Lafayette, Harvard, Amherst, Swarthmore, New York University, Penn State, Fordham, and the University of Pennsylvania often scheduled games with Annapolis and West Point teams, and Columbia scheduled an annual baseball game with the latter. Less well-known institutions competed among themselves. In 1928 three colleges fought out the annual championship of the Minnesota State College Conference, and the Wisconsin Normal Schools held a similar competition.

Sport in Catholic colleges developed a little differently. According to a history of Catholic higher education by Edward Power, baseball bulked large in Catholic institutions after World War I. At first, Catholic colleges permitted play on campuses only but, as the number of (Catholic) colleges increased, they allowed intercollegiate games as well. Although each college itself did not officially sponsor matches, it permitted them, so it assumed "some remote responsibility" for their conduct. Teams had no coaches, but some had faculty "moderators," whose purpose lay not in instruction but in discipline. For Catholic colleges, according to Power, baseball and other sports gained popularity partly because they furnished good recreation and also because they theoretically developed a moral sense in the students. Baseball remained the major college sport at Catholic colleges, in Power's view, until the institutions altered their school year to exclude the months when baseball stood at its height and thereby shortened its season so much that the game declined greatly as a college sport, whereupon football replaced it. Seton Hall in 1920, however, still played an elaborate schedule not only with other Catholic colleges like Fordham, Cathedral, St. Francis, St. Anselm's, Manhattan, Holy Cross, and Villanova, but also such non-Catholic institutions as Tufts, Colby, Lehigh, Cooper Union, CCNY, and even West Point and the Crescent A.C.

At John Carroll University, a Catholic College in Cleveland, baseball did not begin to fade from the sport scene until 1923, and up to then, as the college history has it, the baseball varsity attracted "good turnouts." Once the John Carroll nine got carried away in a game with local Case Institute of Technology. John Carroll, winning 14–1 in what Case had scheduled as a "practice game," claimed the city championship of Cleveland, since John Carroll had already defeated the other local college, Western Reserve. The Case coach, Pat Pasini, expressed intense irritation at John Carroll's claim, stating that since the match was designated only as a practice game he did not use his regulars, and he himself pitched the first inning, lobbing the ball over the plate and giving up eleven runs to John Carroll. But the John Carroll nine left the field declaring themselves city champs.

The sport ethic of the 1920s, as remarked in 1926 by writer Percy Marks, appeared to be "win at any cost." Each side used every available tactic to secure superiority over the other. Unrealistic entreaties like those of coach Albert Ben Wegener to "be a good sport," "compete for pure love of competition rather than for prizes, pride, or excessive desire to win," and "treat opponents as guests rather than as enemies" fell on deaf ears. "If I play a game," asserted drama critic George Jean Nathan in *American Mercury*, "I play it to win. . . . The best sportsman is out to demonstrate his superior skill and to lick his opponent. Any other view is sheer sentimental buncombe." Many coaches, observed Robert Angell in his 1928 book, *The Campus*, taught that players should do whatever they could get away with—an injunction hardly in line with assertions that athletics developed favorable character traits. More likely, as Angell noted, if young men had not developed such qualities by the time of their college years, they were unlikely to acquire them thereafter.

The requirement of winning placed the coach in the position of needing to produce a champion team or be fired, as Frederick Rand Rogers observed in a 1929 book, instead of preparing young college men able to play fairly and sportingly. The pressures of winning came out graphically in 1921 when Coach George Sawtelle of Northwestern University, as described by one of his players, told the team in a mindless pregame pep talk, "Listen, you guys, the man who doesn't get a hit doesn't eat tonight; now go out there and show me how the game should be played." As a result, recalled the player, "We hit like demons that day; every man got a hit, and when they finally added up the score we had beaten Notre Dame, 13 to 2."

Coaching, although it came with pressures, paid well, better than university teaching. The highest coaching salary in the twenties amounted to $14,000.00, the average $5,095.00; for professors, the maximum was $12,000.00, the average $5,158.00. And coaches often had a free hand in their work. At the University of Chicago, presidents who succeeded William Rainey Harper in the twenties supported Coach Amos Alonzo Stagg's heavy emphasis on varsity athletics. Not until Robert Hutchins arrived as president in 1929 were restrictions placed on Stagg's activity and intramurals elevated. In the late twenties, after much criticism of coaches as turning athletes into "puppets" on the field, a few ivy league colleges tried the new "coachless" games in which the coach remained on the bench during the game and permitted the players to run it. This plan paralleled the equally farcical PSAL plan.* But spasmodic trials of the coachless plan hardly eliminated the ethic of winning at any cost. Boston University continued the coachless plan until 1934, when the coach decided it was better to conform to the traditional practice. And that ended the experiment.

The vital importance of winning, to support the elaborate sports structure that had sprung up, meant bringing in professional baseball players as coaches, like Ray Schalk at the University of Wisconsin, Jack Barry at Holy Cross, Jack Slattery and Hugh Duffy at Boston College, and Derril Pratt at the University of Michigan. At the same time more institutions installed sports in the curriculum itself and made their physical training departments nominally responsible for sports. Most college students of the twenties could even substitute sports participation, either varsity or intramural, for classroom work in physical training. Physical training teachers rationalized the inclusion of sports in their curriculum with the piffle that they developed "moral and social values" and provided "physically wholesome, mentally stimulating and satisfying, and socially sound . . . situations" for students. Instead of pressing for elimination of continued abuses by athletics, physical training departments concerned themselves with such matters as tests and measurements, teaching techniques, and "philosophical" matters related to the general field of education. Most directors of athletics in colleges of the twenties were football coaches, many with only bachelor's degrees or none at all.

For building strong teams, recruiting became common. At Muskingum College in Ohio, the institution produced excellent teams in baseball, football, and basketball in the twenties and, according to the college history, never remunerated athletes, although "there were cases of tuition remission"! Some student athletes performed small jobs in exchange for tuition, as Russell Van Atta, later an American League pitcher, did at Penn State, where he made the beds in his fraternity house and tended the furnace while also engaging in sports. "Russell," wrote *Baseball Magazine* later, "really majored in baseball."

Summarizing the abuses in college athletics of the twenties, Upton Sinclair wrote in his hard-hitting *The Goose-step* (1922):

> College rivalries have been [elevated] into the dignity of little wars, enlisting an elaborate cult of loyalties and heroisms. The securing of prize athletes, the training of them, the exploiting of them in mass combats, has become an enormous industry, absorbing the services not merely of students and alumni, but of a whole class of professional coaches, directors, press agents and promoters, who are rapidly coming to dominate college life. . . .

In short, the athletic tail began wagging the academic dog, as it has continued to do so ever more vigorously to the present.

*See above, Chapter 5.

Instead of attacking these major evils, colleges continued to concern themselves with summer ball. Policing players in summer proved frustrating and indeed impossible. Such eventual major leaguers as Bib Falk, Bill Watson Clark, Charles Gehringer, Bump Hadley, Luke Appling, Horace Ford, Mickey Cochrane, and Bill Werber all played with professional or semipro baseball teams while in college. Five Princeton players performed with an industrial team in Hamilton, Ohio, in 1920. Even a minister's son, Victor Keen, while at Maryland University, accepted a job playing for a Virginia League team under the name Unglaub. That deception "might look a little shady," admitted Keen later, "but you see it wasn't so bad, because I had an uncle by that name and I just borrowed it for the occasion."

The colleges' great concern over their athletes' summer ball playing sometimes backfired. When his college discovered that Ernest Wingard had played semipro ball one summer and disqualified him from future college play, he lost interest in his studies and signed to pitch for the St. Louis Browns. The same thing happened to Mace Brown, who left the University of Iowa and signed with Pittsburgh, and to Oral Hildebrand, who quit at Butler and joined the Indianapolis club and then the Cleveland Indians.

Organized Baseball in the twenties still signed college players secretly so they could continue to play on their college teams until graduation without interfering with their amateur standing. Detroit owner Frank Navin signed Owen Carroll of Holy Cross by at least 1923, admitting the action in a letter to Garry Herrmann. Navin said he kept the signing quiet so as not to jeopardize Owen's college standing. Carroll did not pitch for Detroit until 1925. A college coach might serve as a go-between or paid bird dog (unofficial scout) for major league clubs that desired to sign players who wanted at the same time to continue their college careers. As revealed in Herrmann's correspondence, Billy Disch, a University of Texas baseball coach, represented St. Louis and New-York major league clubs in this way and also offered to help Garry Herrmann obtain for Cincinnati a player still in college.

Jake Ruppert, owner of the New York American League club, admitted at a major league meeting in 1929 that he paid some players' way through college and said he saw no harm in doing it. Moreover, he declared that others there in the room with him had done the same. As for the minor league clubs, "they all do it. They are lying about it."

Major league clubs even carried on their underground recruitment among high school seniors while they were planning their college careers. Nelson Schlegel, only sixteen, of Warsaw High School, Warsaw, New York, confided to his high school physical director, H.A. Burgess, that he had received an offer of $100.00 a month from a big-league team and asked Burgess's advice: would taking the job bar him from college athletics? Burgess, in a quandary, wrote in turn for counsel to R. Tait McKenzie of the physical education department at the University of Pennsylvania. McKenzie replied that playing professional ball would prevent Schlegel from playing for the college he planned to attend in the fall; moreover, "The atmosphere of a professional team is not the kind of atmosphere that prepares a boy for college life. . . ."

The issues in college athletics boiled down to the matter of who controlled the athletic system. At the beginning of the decade George Meylan of Columbia checked 194 institutions to ascertain their method of athletic control. He discovered that in only 40 of them did the institution itself control its own athletics; in 108, faculty and students together supervised them; in 40, faculty with students and alumni did; and in 6, the students handled them alone.

But the trend of the twenties was toward more alumni control. Alumni supported their colleges anyway, particularly private colleges. These institutions exploited the alumni's nostalgic memories of the supposedly happiest years of their lives by soliciting graduates' participation in fund drives and by offering opportunities to support prospective athletic stars. In return the colleges proffered athletic victories as entertainment and the chance for puerile boasting of their alma mater's winning teams as well as a large voice in the control of the college's athletic program. In 1928, in fact, one New York university even offered its alumni increased proportional representation on its athletic board so that graduates would be able to "exercise a larger voice in the deliberations, policies, and programs of athletics" and thus end the former "lopsided" representation "favoring faculty domination."

In his 1928 book of higher education, *College or Kindergarten?* Max McConn, dean of Lehigh University, delivered a searing indictment of college sports, pointing out that all college athletes, paid or not, were professionals because of the other practices that enveloped them. He advocated letting the "kindergarteners" proceed but also establishing a "real" college on campus for serious students, who could participate in sports intramurally in their own manner, directed as they wished.

Near the end of the decade the Carnegie Foundation, at the request of the NCAA and its affiliates, began a survey of athletic practices in American colleges and universities under the direction of Howard Savage, a Harvard Ph.D. The resulting report, *American College Athletics* (1929) constituted a scathing condemnation of the college athletic system, revealing a sordid story of evasions, fraud, deceit, and warped intellectual values. *Baseball Magazine* commented insightfully that the report failed to stress what represented the chief indictment of college athletics: the hypocrisy that lingers in the almost meaningless word *amateur*, because "intercollegiate athletics is half professional without daring to confess as much."

Despite heavy publicity the report had little discernible, much less lasting, impact on the college athletic scene, for, ironically, *American College Athletics* appeared on the day the stock market crashed, and colleges soon faced something even more urgent.

The depression meant cuts in funds for all colleges, especially state institutions, which lost 31 percent of their income; private institutions lost 19 percent. On top of this, enrollment declined more than 8 percent. Students who did attend seemed to observers more sober and conservative than their predecessors of the twenties.

The depression affected college baseball as it did everything else. In the first part of the decade interest in baseball declined as some colleges dropped it altogether. At Santa Clara College in California, intercollegiate ball was almost forgotten in the depression, but other important institutions like Harvard, Yale, Holy Cross, Michigan State, and Georgia Tech continued to play other colleges. By 1931 baseball began showing signs of renewal, and that same season several New York University games on Saturdays attracted an attendance of between 4,000 and 5,000. In South Carolina three colleges abolished baseball, but five others organized a financially successful league in 1932 in which each team played sixteen games. *Sporting News* announced in 1932 that college ball had revived and in 1933 reported that the Eastern Collegiate Baseball League had started playing again; in 1934 that league played a full season with six clubs as members. In 1932 Boston College cut its regular baseball schedule in half, and many teams cancelled games that had been scheduled, but in 1933 the team played 17, winning 10. At Keene State College in New Hampshire, varsity ball, revived in 1934 after an absence of two years, proved successful, and, according to the student year-book, the *Kronicle*, Keene State took the New England Teachers' College Championship several times during the decade. In an innovation, George Washington University planned a complete schedule of night benefit games in 1933 for the national capital's civic fund. The Middle Atlantic States Conference planned to start night ball, too, in 1935.

By mid-decade, sources agree, baseball showed new life on American campuses. Assumption College in Worcester, Massachusetts, which had abandoned baseball in 1929, for example, returned it to the campus in 1935. The year following, a survey by a major-league representative showed that 380 colleges, or 70 percent of the country's 539, had scheduled intercollegiate baseball contests. About a hundred colleges, however, had still not restored baseball by 1938. But publications reported many success stories. At North-western the baseball teams had in 1929, 1930, and 1931 taken enjoyable and successful training trips to Texas; these had to be discontinued for a while, and players felt the lack of the valuable early-season practice, but in 1937 the trips were restored. At Taylor University in Indiana the college presi-dent's sons, who had keen interest in athletics, persuaded their father for the first time to permit intercollegiate baseball and other sports beginning in 1932.

For the truth was that athletics even in the depression still drew many supporters. President William M. Lewis of Lafayette College advocated more college baseball leagues. The well-known coach Glenn "Pop" Warner expressed the general feeling for sports straightforwardly:

Love of sports is normal; distaste for athletic competition is abnormal. The youth who doesn't thrill to the strain of struggle and the joy of victory isn't much of a lad.

Athletics, said Professors Jesse F. Williams and William Hughes in a more staid pronouncement, had a legitimate place in education, if they could be made to further educational goals and if they were directed by the physical education staff—big "ifs," because these conditions expressed an ideal seldom attained. Athletics did not, after all, begin on campuses as part of the curriculum, and attempts of professors to force it into an educational framework never quite worked. Yet by the thirties nearly all colleges had accepted sports and games into their physical education programs—albeit with separate faculty—stressing what educators declared to be the social and psychological benefits to be obtained from them.

College baseball coaches in the thirties remained quite different from the rest of the faculty. During cutbacks of the depression the baseball coach in less wealthy colleges was merely the assistant football coach. But institutions like Yale, Cornell, Syracuse, Dartmouth, and the University of California hired professional baseball players to coach their varsity ball teams. Clever coaches could still supplement their salaries by selling their best players to the big leagues, some of them acting as regular agents for certain clubs, diverting their best products to those clubs alone. In one case a coach asked $5,000.00 for permitting a student to sign with a particular club. Coaches defended their actions by pointing out that through their work they had developed the athletes to the point that they became valuable property, conveniently forgetting that they already drew salaries from their colleges for that work.

At the University of Chicago, the new chancellor, Robert M. Hutchins, made sweeping changes in the sports program. He believed that a university should promote intellectual leadership, not produce professional athletes. Besides eliminating football completely, he so restricted the actions of Amos Alonzo Stagg that the latter eventually left. Hutchins expatiated on his ideas in an article, "Gate Receipts and Glory," in 1938, in which he declared, "Biceps are not substitutes for brains." He described colleges' use of sports for publicity and profit as not athletics but "athleticism," attacked the notion that sports developed leadership, asserted that most college sports systems focussed attention on those who needed it least of all, and exploded the myths that college sports developed well-rounded, healthy men who played fair and that college gate receipts for big-time sports built laboratories and paid for carrying on minor sports. "I'm running a university, not a circus," he declared.

In blasting the commercialized sports system Hutchins underlined points already made in the Carnegie Report. Another critic, Abraham Flexner, a Ph.D. who reformed the medical schools, also backed up the Carnegie

Report. Flexner, author of *Universities: American, English, German* (1930) declared that colleges spent more money on athletics than on any legitimate college activity and were "too timid to tell their respective alumni that excessive interest in intercollegiate athletics is proof of the cultural mediocrity of the college graduate. . . . " John Tunis, sports writer, laid the reluctance of college administrations not to timidity but to the desire to continue the good publicity accruing from sports.

Hutchins stood among those few administrators who attacked head-on the problem of control in college athletics. A group of the larger colleges also agreed to an eligibility rule designed to eliminate the "tramp athlete" by preventing any student from playing for his institution for more than three years; some athletes had played as many as five. Other colleges wrestled with the problem of whether to permit alumni to secretly pay an athlete's tuition and expenses. At Mars Hill College in North Carolina in 1930 the Board of Trustees recommended that such gifts to athletes either be eliminated or be made public—"frank and above-board." Colleges had less to gain from alumni in the depression anyhow; many students had graduated from college not to jobs but to unemployment—2,097 at Ohio State, 1,798 at the University of Chicago, and 750 at Princeton among them.

Summer ball weighed less upon college administrations in the thirties. The depression had weakened the grand old resort hotels that used to hire college players for the entertainment of guests, although athletes could still obtain summer jobs playing with independent or semipro clubs, and some colleges (although not Harvard) legalized play for pay. The Ohio Collegiate Conference, a group of colleges playing each other, permitted their student athletes to play with professionals in summer without harming their amateur standing. After all, argued a writer in the Ashland, Ohio, *Times Gazette*, "Did you ever hear of a drummer bounced out of the college band because he played in a professional dance band?" Professors Williams and Hughes stated similarly, "Surely to earn $500 playing baseball two months in the summer is better economics, more healthful, and generally of more educational worth than to earn $100 . . . by acting as night clerk in a railroad Y.M.C.A. or by 'waiting on table' at a summer hotel." In fact, a separate semipro league for outstanding college players formed in Vermont in 1936 and played successfully each summer until World War II.

With a more lax college policy generally concerning summer ball, Organized Baseball had more leeway in signing players, although at least two, Sol Hudson of the University of Michigan and Forrest Twogood of the University of Iowa, were ousted from their perspective varsity teams when their summer ball became known. As a result, they left college and signed with pro cubs. Joe Medwick, a high schooler in 1929–30, agreed to play for a St. Louis Cardinals farm team for the summer of 1930 but only under the name Michael King, since he planned to enter Notre Dame. After he hit

.419 with the Scottsdale, Arizona, club, Organized Baseball persuaded him to return to the use of his own name, and within two years he was in the majors and an outstanding hitter.

Organized Baseball's forays into the colleges proved an irritant to institutions who were trying to keep their students. In 1930 the major leagues, although they agreed to leave other good performers to the minors to sign, stated outright that they were going to sign any college players they could. The colleges protested the recruiting of players before their graduation, stating that the students should be given the opportunity of completing their education, but Organized Baseball remained adamant, and when the University of Chicago remonstrated at the Chicago White Sox's signing of athlete Lefty Feiber, Harry Grabiner of the White Sox retorted, "Both the boy and his father signed the contract with us willingly, and we can't see what the university can do about it." The major-league clubs also signed some students to their minor-league farms, then brought them up to the major clubs whenever they desired.

Some efforts were made to assuage the growing bad feeling between colleges and Organized Baseball. In the fall of 1934 Branch Rickey of the St. Louis National League organization proposed that major-league clubs agree not to sign students until they completed their college educations, but nothing definite came of the idea. Affluent clubs even paid students' way all through college, as the New York Yankees did for Tom Kelly (Tom Holmes), who studied at Duke for four years under coach Jack Coombs before graduating to the majors.

Irritation of Judge Kenesaw Mountain Landis, commissioner of Organized Baseball, over a case at St. Mary's College in California may even have retarded solution of the problem. St. Mary's Athletic Director E.P. "Slip" Madigan protested the signing of sophomore Francis Kelleher by a Yankee scout, Joe Devine. St. Mary's claimed an unwritten understanding that Organized Baseball would not recruit a player until he graduated. Professional football did have such an agreement with the colleges, and, as *Sporting News* editorialized, Organized Baseball should perhaps have had one too, but it did not. On the other hand, Madigan went about his protest in a way calculated to draw no sympathy from Landis, releasing his protest to the press before submitting it to the commissioner and issuing a tirade against Landis in which he accused the commissioner of interest only "in the big, fat check he receives for protecting the moneyed interests of baseball." Landis refused to consider the case on the ground that Madigan merely sought publicity. The Pacific Coast League, too, protested to Landis that major-league scouts were making big offers to high school and college students on the West Coast, thus preventing students from playing on their institutions' teams, whereupon they lost interest in their studies and soon quit.

In the case of Lou Boudreau, it came out during his parents' divorce that the Cleveland Indians were paying his parents $100.00 a week as a reward for giving the club a verbal contract with Lou. So his college, the University of Illinois, ousted him from the varsity team, and the NCAA began a survey of 500 colleges asking what alliances their coaches had with professional clubs for recruiting players. After the survey *Sporting News* published various facts and figures about college play, but nothing about those alliances. In 1938 college and Organized Baseball representatives finally met to try to thrash out the problem, but they could come to no compromise.

During all this furor over athletes as valuable properties, some institutions remained relatively untouched by commercialism in sports. In one of them, my own undergraduate college, Drew University, sports, including intercollegiate baseball, remained simple and restrained, carried out on a small scale.* Varsity ball at Drew dated from fall 1930, when I entered as a freshman. Dr. Sherman Plato Young, professor of Latin and Greek, brought together the group who came out for the team. Doc Young, as he was called, knew little about the way baseball should be played—much less than I did. He could give no real instruction, and he frequently consulted me on strategy during games. But he exerted an influence on us in other ways, lifting our intellectual sights and giving guidance and counsel on our education. At Drew, classroom and library took precedence over sports, which stood on a par with other extracurricular activities like dramatics. Drew handed out no athletic scholarships, built no stadium, charged no admission to games, allowed no lengthy playing schedule or long road trip, and gave no special perquisites to athletes. In fact, some professors, hostile to intercollegiate competition and bearing the Carnegie Report freshly in their minds, probably graded athletes more strictly than others. As a result, athletes worked as hard and achieved as much scholastically as other students. In baseball, direction of the team fell to me as a freshman and player when Doc Young, stricken with appendicitis, was hospitalized for some time. Drew baseball therefore represented a throwback to earlier times, with student control and noncommercial development. We did, however, I am glad to say, play to win.

Other colleges, to remove some of the commercial onus from athletics after the publication of the Carnegie Report, turned to intramurals. At Southern Illinois Normal, the third largest teachers' college in the United States, students took intramural baseball seriously, watching a bulletin board for statistics of their active sixteen-club league.

In the wake of the Carnegie Report, although it pertained largely to football, a number of institutions did, however, report that they were passing through a time of readjustment relative to control measures for athletics in general. Alumni still sat on many athletic boards, nevertheless. The NCAA appointed committees to look into recruiting and subsidization, especially

*See "Books Before Baseball, A Personal History," *The National Pastime* (Fall 1982), pp. 70–76.

of football, but this organization was merely advisory, although some members tried to persuade it to assume the regulatory power that college administrators seemed unwilling to exert in their own institutions. Major Griffith commented in 1936 that there was nothing the NCAA could do for institutions that presidents and faculty could not do for themselves. Meanwhile, by mid-decade colleges that supported intercollegiate baseball could join regional associations like the Western Conference, Big Six, Pacific Coast, Southeastern, Southern, Southwest, and Eastern Intercollegiate, and compete by whatever rules the other association members had agreed upon.

The big leagues had by the twenties and thirties taken in many college players. In 1927 those who played in the majors represented some fifty colleges, as reported in *Baseball Magazine*, and in 1935 the same publication listed about the same number of institutions. That year the American League estimated that nearly a third of its players had some college experience. One varsity player at the University of Arizona, Abelardo L. Rodriguez, was such a good second baseman that the Los Angeles Club of the Pacific Coast League scouted him, but his parents would not permit him to accept the offer. In 1932 he became president of Mexico.

American college teams continued their baseball exchanges with Japanese colleges in the twenties and even during the depression of the thirties. Waseda, Meiji, and Keio Universities alternated in inviting an American team to Japan; the host college paid for visitor's expenses, but each of the other colleges agreed to play a series with the guests for a percentage of the gate. The baseball team of the University of California visited Japan at least three times during this era, but its 1921 and 1927 trips were unsuccessful against strong Japanese university teams. The Universities of Washington, Indiana, Illinois, Yale, Chicago, Harvard, and Stanford all visited in these years. Harvard lost six out of ten games against the Japanese in 1934, and Yale had the same dismal result in 1935.

Japanese teams also visited the States. Waseda, Meiji, Keio, and Rikkyo all made trips. In 1936 Waseda won over Yale, Princeton, Harvard, and the University of Chicago! Meiji made its trip in 1924 despite the fact that its university had just been destroyed in an earthquake.

These exchanges presumably taught American players some lessons. First, the Americans learned respect for Japanese ball playing. Being able to defeat a top Japanese university team became something to boast of, as did a player on the 1929 Northwestern team, which, he said, "was a hustling ball team . . . [and] we beat one of the last Japanese teams to visit this country." When the University of Michigan lost to both Meiji and Waseda in 1929, Ray Fisher,* the American coach, observed that although the Michigan students had the advantage pitching, the Japanese in their general playing

---

*For Fisher's background see *Baseball: The Golden Age*, pp. 117, 172, 373–4.

ability were "right up with the American university teams, and in catching [fielding] possibly superior."

Japanese politeness was also a revelation to the Americans. Before the game, Japanese players lined up and bowed. "The courtesy of our opponents," said Fisher, "was almost beyond belief. In fact, it grew painful at times. . . . We had first privilege in everything. . . . " Once a small Japanese player was thrown aside in a violent collision with a Michigan player; he apologized to the American who had collided with him, tipping his cap to him. When a Japanese faculty member noticed that a Michigan player had a bleeding spike wound in the toe, he dropped to his knees and prayed for quick healing.

American students were probably unaware of one other unique aspect of Japanese college ball that contrasted with the American system. When Japanese college ball began to show signs of becoming commercialized in 1932, the government cracked down, imposing strict student eligibility rules and restricting the use of rooters and of players' photos.

Such college contacts as those with Japan may not have advanced international relations, but some participants thought they did. In 1921 Japanese alumni of the University of California gave a dinner in Tokyo to the visiting California team, and expressions of Japanese-American friendship were exchanged. "All Japanese love peace," said Bunshiro Ito, a University of California alumnus, "and never will dare to dream of fighting America. . . . If some people say there may be trouble, tell them we want to settle it on a baseball field"!

Besides playing such international games, some thought of playing an American national championship series in college baseball, especially after basketball successfully initiated a similar championship in 1938, but this idea waited until after the war for fruition. Meanwhile, other landmark occasions presented themselves. On May 13, 1939, two college teams, Boston College and Fordham, played a game at Cooperstown, New York, to celebrate the mythical hundredth anniversary of the invention of baseball there. The game was billed as the "Centennial Game." Intercollegiate ball itself, of course, had been going on for only about eighty years. Five days after, a more significant event occurred: Princeton and Columbia played a game before a television audience. This was the first sports contest ever televised. Princeton won in ten innings.

In 1938 Boston University compiled some statistics about the game preferences of American students. Although most students, rather than playing, watched, the survey revealed that when it came to games students enjoyed taking part in, the national pastime stood at the head of the list, with basketball second and football third. So despite the commercial spectacle that the colleges had made out of athletics, especially football, baseball remained the students' favorite participant game.

13

DOWN-HOME BASEBALL

For most young men past high school age who wanted to continue playing ball, opportunities to join the collegians in the House of Baseball had little practical meaning. At best, colleges and universities can absorb only a relatively small quota of players, and for a long time college admission fell mostly to those who could afford to pay. So the vast majority of young men did their playing outside academe.

Young men who lived in small towns and villages or on farms did, however, find room in baseball's house. For them, the town team offered the possibility of playing ball on a regular basis. It also became a step onto the steep staircase from which some clambered all the way to the top into successful major-league careers: for example, John McGraw started pitching for his home town of Truxton, New York, at 16; Branch Rickey caught for the town team of Lucasville, Ohio, when he was 18; Smokey Joe Wood was 16 when he pitched for the Ness City, Kansas, town team; and Christy Mathewson was only 13 when he began pitching for the Mill City and Factoryville, Pennsylvania, teams. Other town team players made their marks in different fields: poet Robert Frost pitched in Salem, New Hampshire, in his early youth; and Frank Merriwell's creator, Gilbert Patten, caught barehanded for the second team of the Corinna, Maine, town team in the 1870s, suffering a broken finger from a foul tip. Those fellows who quit playing on reaching manhood often exchanged a place on the field for a seat in the stands to cheer on the local team.

The town team amounted to more than a means of reaching the big leagues. It evolved into an American institution meriting a place alongside such other symbols of America's past as the little red schoolhouse, the fervid revival meeting, and the old-fashioned Fourth of July celebration. And understandably so. Before the twenties America remained mostly rural, and baseball, like other early bat-and-ball games, had long been played in the countryside. After the Knickerbockers of the metropolis polished its folk character by rubbing away some of the rough edges through rules that made it more appealing to city folk, the game returned to the provinces, where rural people welcomed it in its more standard-ized and sophisticated form.

To communities lacking a public library or Rural Free Delivery, let alone a movie house, where the comparatively sparse population dwelled on iso-lated farms or in widely separated settlements, baseball was a welcome diversion. Conditions in small-town and rural America have often been ro-manticized. It is easy to conjure up a vision of serenity midst tree-shaded streets of comfortable houses sheltering families of skilled workers and professionals who diverted themselves with jolly church socials. But towns might also harbor intellectual stagnation, Babbittry, and abysmal slums. The countryside around them often proved worse, with poor, malnourished, illiterate families living on exhausted farms. Life down home might not be as attractive as it has sometimes been remembered.

Towns lacked not only elaborately organized sports and public recreation but awareness of the need for them. Men and boys found recreation in hunting and fishing and in informal cow pasture ball games and old-fashioned town ball until after the turn of the century, when YMCA field secretaries, women's clubs, the Playground Association, and other city-based organiza-tions began to offer encouragement and support for more elaborate play, recreation, and entertainment through granges and rural churches.

In the meantime, the town's baseball team helped refresh the often parched social landscape of rural America. In all parts of the country in the late nineteenth century, and in some areas well into the twentieth, the local baseball team represented for many towns the only athletic organization and nearly the only entertainment, as many accounts of small-town and country life make clear. For instance, in Oklahoma right up to World War I, as Harold Keith has related, nearly every hamlet had a team, although it had little else in the way of amusement. In Watonga, a village of 1,500, town baseball became "the annual summer dementia." Local people built their summers around "their" team and discussed it up and down Main Street or around the square. In Geary, another Oklahoma town, despite an ordinance against Sunday ball a local minister who liked baseball and counted six Geary ball players among his flock regularly excused them and their wives or girlfriends in the middle of his sermon so they could drive to nearby towns in time for a road game. At Prague in 1907, fans at a game rooted so loudly that the horses one young man had rented with a buggy to take his fiancee to the game bolted and ran off, wrecking the buggy, and it cost him all the money he had saved for her engagement ring to pay the damages. They married anyway, but it was not until 38 years later that she finally got her ring. The local baseball park must have been a favorite place to court, because small-town resident Harry Truman several times in 1911 invited Bess Wal-lace, his future wife, to go out with him in his auto to a baseball game.

Even in the South the growth and multiplication of towns, together with the gradually improving transportation and the general material prosperity that accompanied the rise of the cotton mill, had by the twentieth century permitted small towns to maintain ball diamonds where town teams competed with those representing business firms and social and civic groups.

Town teams playing standardized baseball served a number of functions in the hinterlands. For adults they offered a lively diversion that interrupted the dullness of daily routine and the deep quiet of bucolic life. For youngsters they supplied local flesh-and-blood heroes, sometimes members of their own families, to watch, talk to, and emulate. As Ford Frick, former commissioner of Organized Baseball, said of a boyhood hero, Ed Morley, pitcher for Brimfield, Indiana (population 250), he was "handy-by" and could be seen "in the flesh. We could touch him. We could talk to him. He was our own personal property." Although Frick and the other boys appreciated the famous big leaguers their elders discussed, Ed Morley could be admired close up. In Hooper, Nebraska, about the turn of the century boys would hang onto the hitching posts and watch town team players practice evenings after work right out on Main Street, and when balls rolled under the board sidewalks the gossoons would crawl underneath to retrieve them. Town teams also gave youngsters greater incentive to play ball by providing a tangible goal: the possibility of playing on the town team themselves one day. Or they might try for the junior town team, which formed in some communities as a feeder for the first team, and move up from it.

A town team could furnish a young player with ineradicable moments. In 1893 when William Lyon Phelps, who often struck out in the ninth, came up with three men on in the last inning with his team, Bad Axe, Michigan, three runs behind Sand Beach, the enemy catcher hollered, "Put one right over; the big stiff can't hit it!" But Phelps remembered that he,

> with the strength of despair, swung my bat with all my might. To my amazement I saw the ball going on a line over the centre fielder's head. It brought in four runs and won the game, and as I crossed the plate, I had the greatest single thrill of my life.

Most of all, the town baseball team acted as a cohesive agent in the community. Symbolizing as it did the town's quality and providing a clearcut means of demonstrating it, the town team ignited local pride and furnished a channel for its frequently violent expression. Most teams, at least at the outset, were composed wholly or in part of home town players, the fan's own neighbors and even relatives, and so made for a close bond between team and residents.

If baseball brought much to the hamlets of an earlier day, some also credited it with bringing more, claiming that baseball helped absorb the frontier and tie West to East. As for its connective action between North and South, a sports writer asserted in 1912 that baseball accomplished more to bridge the sectional gap left by the Civil War than all the speeches of politicians. Local teams may also have contributed to the assimilation of those of immigrant parentage who settled in the ethnic enclaves of steel and mining towns. And as voluntary associations, such teams may have softened severe social disorder, as Don H. Doyle of the University of Michigan believed such associations did in Jacksonville, Illinois, before 1900. Finally, town teams may even have helped ameliorate the despair and even madness for those unable to cope with the isolation of rural life.

Town teams playing standard baseball or an approximation of it began appearing on the eve of the Civil War, by which time the Knickerbocker style of play had begun to spread from the New York area to other sections of the country. After the war the mushroom growth of baseball from the confines of middle-class Eastern clubhouses caused *The Spirit of the Times* to report in 1873 that "in every little town and hamlet throughout the country we find a ball club, generally two. . . . " Baseball appeared early in Newburgh and other large towns in upstate New York and in the smaller Hudson Valley communities in the vicinity, such as Goshen, whose Monitor Club played nearby teams with names like Quickstep, Union, Ne Plus Ultra, Eagle, and Hudson River. In western New York state the Niagaras of Buffalo played the teams of Lockport and Auburn as well as the Excelsiors and Alerts of Rochester. By the mid-seventies other teams in towns like Monticello, Port Jervis, Binghamton, Owego, Norwich, and Oneonta fielded teams. Farther north, town teams dotted the New England states of the 1870s all the way to Maine, especially in the industrial centers of Lowell, Fall River, Lynn, New Bedford, and Providence.

Across the Hudson in Paterson, New Jersey, an 1867 newspaper commented on the "baseball frenzy," and beyond Jersey, neighboring Pennsylvania as early as 1865 boasted an estimated 48 ball clubs. No area of that state outdid the coal mining region in baseball enthusiasm. By 1890 Honesdale alone had teams in every section of the town, and its baseball rivalry with Carbondale would soon become the "hottest" one in northwestern Pennsylvania.

In Indiana, Fort Wayne in 1862 formed its first team from the best players in town, and a decade later after its professional club collapsed, dozens of amateur teams replaced it and played each other and neighboring community teams evenings and weekends. Toledo, Ohio, had four ball teams as early as 1866, and by the seventies such towns as Akron, Orrsville, Garretsville, Elyria, Norwalk, Seville, Ravenna, Mansfield, Portsmouth, and Kent all had teams. Zane Grey observed after the turn of the century that in Ohio "Every small town . . . as well as every large one, supported a ball club."

Baseball gained a foothold in some western communities before the Civil War. Settlers in the new territories formed teams even before the areas achieved statehood. The first organized ball club in Minnesota Territory appeared in 1867, and within a decade every village and town in the young state reportedly had a team. The same held for territories like the Dakotas, New Mexico, and Arizona. The Deseret Club of Salt Lake City, trying to make its club acceptable to Mormons in 1877, discouraged smoking and drinking in public. An opposing club, the Red Stockings, composed mostly of Mormons, included a second baseman, Heber J. Grant, who became a Mormon apostle. In 1896, only three years after the Cherokee Strip Run, teams appeared in Oklahoma Territory. Especially were the mining camps and towns of the West and Southwest hotbeds of baseball early on, and after the mines played out, the game survived as a leading sport of the region. In Nebraska the first recorded game took place in 1870, and as towns sprang up on the prairie with the advent of homesteaders and the railroad, many teams like the Striped Stockings, Blue Belts, Bug-eaters, and Close-cuts formed there and began competing with Iowa teams. One of the latter included a father and several sons, among them Adrian Anson, the future star player-manager of the Chicago White Stockings.

California, particularly its San Francisco area, led the Pacific Coast in number of teams. Baseball played New York style got started there before the Civil War, and after the war Coast teams proliferated, flourishing in Sacramento, Oakland, and such northern settlements as Yreka, Little Shasta, Weed, Etna, Gazelle, and Hilts, as well as in Eugene and Portland, Oregon, towns that doubtless received inspiration from the visit of the expert Cincinnati Red Stockings to the latter two cities in the fall of 1869.

Southern baseball resurged after the Civil War. Baltimore teams had played frequently even in 1861, and New Orleans's baseball reputution dated from before the war, but baseball in the South lagged until after the surrender, when in the next decade the game captured the southern imagination as those from all walks of life, from clerks to gentlemen, participated. Lynchburg, Virginia's, first organized club began playing in the spring of 1867. Ball teams began to form in Tennessee, Alabama, Georgia, and North and South Carolina. In the Palmetto State, where games often linked with dinners or picnics, the gentlemanly ambiance continued well into the seventies. In San Antonio, Texas, too, many teams played in the same decade.

The profusion of town teams that once covered the country all had their tales to tell, and some local and regional history journals have begun to publish reminiscences and scholarly articles about them. Such nostalgic pieces show that forming a town team was at first a rather simple matter. Participants chose teams from the best local players, who genuinely represented their towns because they lived there or in an adjacent area. Few players received any money: they were satisfied just to play ball. Equipment posed no great problem, either. Its solution resembled that of the boys described earlier. The two essentials, a bat and a ball, cost little. A ball could be had for a quarter. Some teams economized by saving their regular baseballs for "match" games and practicing with a solid rubber ball or homemade rag ball—the usual twine-wrapped core covered with a piece of leather. Players used makeshift bats, too, either homemade or inexpensive readymade ones. Before the famous Louisville Slugger came into favor, they purchased simple hickory or willow bats sold under a name like "favorite Wagon Tongue," and players who found them too long or heavy simply sawed them off.

Gloves and catcher's masks did not enter the picture until the second half of the seventies, and then only slowly, because much as players might want to wear them their fear of public ridicule or their own notions of manliness deterred them. And even after gloves and masks won acceptance, down-home catchers did not adopt them immediately. A former catcher for the Little Jokers, a San Antonio, Texas, team of the seventies, remembered catchers still disdaining gloves even though after a game their hands swelled up like pillows. The first primitive fielder's gloves, of thin leather with the fingers cut off to the second joint, sold for a dollar, but the reason for their tardy adoption in far parts cannot be attributed only to cost or embarrassment. Before national advertising blanketed the land, it took time for players in the hinterlands to become aware of such equipment and the protection it afforded, flimsy though it was.

Recollections of men who played in remote areas in the seventies, eighties, and nineties invariably mention the lack of fielding equipment. Although some ex-players' statements are contradictory and sometimes even belied by contemporary photos, they agree generally that fielders' gloves did not begin to appear in distant places like California until the nineties. Catchers, for obvious reasons, were the first to take protective measures, as was the case in baseball centers of the East. At first they wore a glove on each hand. Then they settled for one glove with a thin strip of padding across the palm at the base of the fingers that left the fingers themselves uncovered. The wire mask and what were called belly pads followed.

Accounts of play based on catchers' recollections supplement the evidence of swollen hands, fingers knocked crooked, and nails torn off so common in those days. A surgeon, C.W. Nutting, who started a team in Etna Mills, California, and played second base, quit after three years in order to save his hands for his work. It took courage to catch a hard ball barehanded, and even after the first protective equipment became customary, it remained so crude and inadequate that for years one could detect a former player, especially a catcher, by the condition of his fingers. As the saying went, to shake hands with a catcher felt like grabbing a handful of walnuts.

Many teams wore no uniforms. They played in the clothes on their backs. Some teams devised homemade suits, and others simulated uniforms with storebought clothing. When the Fort Jones, California, players, who were mostly farmers wearing overalls and black shirts, arrived for a game about 1896 against the Yreka team wearing fine new uniforms, Yreka greeted the visitors with cries of "Hayseeds!" and "Cowsappers!" Others sported flashy outfits. In 1863 the Goshen, New York, Monitors played in rather elegant uniforms of peg-topped pants, a blouse with voluminous sleeves, and a hat with a stiff leather visor. The junior team of Hooper, Nebraska, by contrast, wore white mason's overalls with the bibs tucked in and legs rolled up, and sweaters of various hues. Some baseball pants of the 1870s, like those of a century later, were "close-fitting, without baggy knees," as one old-timer recalled. Red and black seemed to be a favorite color combination. The McAdam Creek, California, team of 1883 displayed red shirts with black velvet trim, and the so-called Schoolboy team of Little Shasta wore suits of red flannel trousers with black sateen shirts. In Nebraska around the turn of the century the Hooper team presented themselves in brilliant red uniforms with the name of the town printed in large black letters over the front of the shirt. After Hooper's red shirts faded and wore out, new green ones and later blue ones replaced them.

By the latter decades of the century, thanks to the gradual introduction of Rural Free Delivery, the mail order catalogue business picked up, and town teams began ordering sporting goods from mail order houses and department stores. Sears, Roebuck's 1895 catalogue, for example, devoted some eighty pages to sports items, including baseball paraphernalia, and around the same time A.G. Spalding and Company advertised a complete baseball uniform including shoes and toeplates, all of first quality, for only ten dollars. Even at that price, the cost of outfitting an entire team remained beyond the means of many farming and working class young men. To raise funds for uniforms they began to pass the hat among spectators. From this practice it became only a short step to soliciting local shopkeepers for contributions. Some backers even got to choose the color of the team's suit.

The contours and evolution of town team baseball fields depended on local topography, as did the location and shape of city fields, and their character and distinctiveness surpassed that of early big-league parks. Spirited play often offset crude grounds and lack of amenities. The Summit Club of Fort Wayne played in 1862 on a piece of land donated by a local banker. Out in Yreka, California, following the "great fire" of 1871 citizens cleared many lots of burned buildings and used them for town team games. Communities with race tracks often laid out baseball fields in their centers, as, for instance, some did in the Red River Valley. In large towns, when electric streetcars came into use after 1895, the fair grounds or a recreational park at the end of a trolley line commonly included a baseball field.

New settlers on the frontier could hardly wait to play ball. Homesteaders marked out on the prairie rude diamonds that in time would give way to "skinned" ones. The Darlington, Wisconsin, town team played at a spot called "the Strawberry Diggings." At Virginia City, Nevada, teams played on the grounds behind the gas works, at what locals called "the dunghill." Helena, Montana, used a field pockmarked with holes and ditches left by prospectors. In a South Dakota camp ball ground someone discovered a bed of ore under home plate, so the field was moved, a shaft sunk, and the ore strike named "Homerun."

The largely fortuitous location of fields often made polished play impossible, but it added to the excitement. In Dunsmuir, California, the swampy center and left fields of the local diamond compelled outfielders chasing balls to keep an eye out not for fences but for mudholes. Local fans long remembered an outfielder on a club in Elkhorn, Nebraska, where the first recorded games took place in 1870, for the one-handed catch he made while leaning over the back of a cow that had wandered across the field. During a game in Utah, with two runners on base and none out, a batter reputedly hit a ball high into a tree, where it stuck; as the runners dashed around the bases the resourceful fielder frantically shook the tree, dislodged the ball, caught it before it hit the ground, and turned a three-run homer into a triple play!

Another baseball yarn worked its way into the local lore of Roanoke Rapids, North Carolina. A variation of the old baseball story of "batter makes homer by hitting ball onto a passing train," the tale relates that during a Saturday afternoon game on a field adjacent to the railroad tracks a player hit a long fly ball just as a train passed, and the ball landed on top of the coal car. According to the local grounds rules, if a hitter drove a ball beyond the reach of the fielders, the batter could keep circling the bases and scoring runs until the other team recovered it. To retrieve the ball one of the fielders jumped on his horse and galloped to nearby Enfield, where the train stopped. Meanwhile, the batter ran, walked, then staggered around and around the bases, finally sitting down to rest before the mounted fielder could return with the ball. The team at bat won the game by a margin of 150 runs.

Chickenwire backstops were so common on country diamonds that they became recognized photographic symbols of small-town baseball fields, the way a bottle of milk on the dining table once indicated a poor family in the movies. On village diamonds well into the twenties the pitcher still toed wooden slabs or simply threw from a bare spot worn in the grass. Home plates might be pieces of wood, marble, or rubber. Bases, just strapped to a spike in the ground, often wobbled dangerously. Uneven outfields might include a ditch, stream, barn, or other obstacle that required special ground rules.

Many fields provided no seats: spectators just stood around or sat on the grass, or on logs, boxes, nail kegs, and improvised benches. Some towns provided wooden stands, and fans could also view the game from their buggies. Pictures still extant show fields partly ringed with horsedrawn buggies from which fans watched. With changing times after 1900, autos began to ring the field instead, and their honking horns added to the rooting and cheers of the spectators. In North Dakota drivers pulled the windshields of their Model Ts down to protect them from fly balls.

When teams started to charge admission, they fenced fields to systematize the collection of money. San Francisco built the first enclosed park on the Pacific Coast in 1868. As usual, youngsters found ways to overcome such barriers. In one park so many boys got in under the fence that its owner pastured his vicious bull near the opening to keep them out. In the 1890s

Carl Sandburg and other boys from his neighborhood in Galesburg, Illinois, saw games in the time-honored way: through knotholes in the fence. Or they watched from high in the crotch of a tree behind home plate. In Butte, Montana, in 1892, a bitter dispute between the local athletic association and one Enoch Johns and his wife over ownership of the baseball grounds led to the brandishing of shotguns, the conversion of the team's fence into kindling, and finally a court battle.

Erecting fences also made it possible for a home team to adjust a fence to its own advantage, a practice still indulged in by the professionals. When the Sisson, California, team came to play at Weed in 1912 they found that to accommodate the seven left-handed batters on the home team, Weed had moved the right field fence in to only 125 feet back of first base. Sisson suffered double frustration, since all its hitters were right-handed. In the unsurprising outcome, the Weed players hit nine home runs over the short fence and won 24–0.

The evolution and pace of town team competition corresponded somewhat to that of the early gentlemanly and college teams. Such factors as the proximity of other teams and the type of transport available governed a town team's baseball schedule and the kind of association, if any, it entered into with other teams. Ball clubs in large towns that clustered in the most populated districts of the Northeast and Midwest experienced little trouble in finding other teams to play, but those in small settlements or embryonic towns in isolated areas often found themselves hard up for competition, as were some players in Vicksburg who complained just after the Civil War that they had to get up games among themselves because they could find no clubs on the Mississippi River south of St. Louis. Teams in this predicament might split into two and play each other. But as soon as more interesting competition offered itself, teams exchanged challenges and arranged games.

A visiting Japanese government official, Arinori Mori, noted this baseball ardor, especially in the countryside, in 1871:

> The young people have it all their own way, and there is no end to the variety of their amusements. . . . Ball-playing and Sleigh-riding are two pastimes in which the Americans indulge with rare gusto. By the rural population, Saturday afternoon is usually assigned to the former, on which the young men are as active and expert in throwing and catching or striking the ball as if they had been idle all the previous week instead of having had to work in the fields. . . .

Albert G. Spalding knew of young men whose urge to play ball caused them to "tramp four or five miles to play with the team of a neighboring town and walk all the way home after the game was over." One young man, John McGraw, according to one of his biographers, was offered $2.00 a game to pitch two games for the East Homer, New York, team in 1889 but held out for and received $5.00 plus transportation costs; he then walked both ways both times, won both games, and pocketed the transportation money. Early Wynn, growing up in Hartford, Alabama, said later, "We'd ride mule wagons many a mile for a town game."

If circumstances prevented or limited games with other town teams, it might be possible to play a military post nine, college varsity, or high school nine, since such teams were equally happy to get games with whatever opposition they could find. The presence of a college team might even inspire the college town itself to form a team, as it did in Athens, Ohio, where local enthusiasm over a successful Ohio University team in 1906 led to the formation of a team to represent the town.

Local newspapers often reported down-home games. As early as 1869 newspapers recorded games among the Eclipse team of Cheyenne, the Alerts of Fort Laramie, Wyoming, and a team of cavalrymen stationed at Fort Russell. The Richmond *Times*, in reporting a game between a team of Richmond citizens against the University of Virginia in June 1893, tried to describe in breezy terms the motley team of citizens that called themselves the Virginias: "some are embryo railroad presidents; some dally with the ledger and cash drawer; some sing 'After the Ball' to the merry hum of machinery; some don't use much effort to get through this vale of care." The game description included such passages as, "Timothy West, forgetting the intricacies of typewriters for the nonce, singled." In Rockport, Massachusetts, a newspaper called the *Gleaner* noted primly, after the town's two teams played in 1878, "It is a pity if we cannot have good honest ball playing without swearing," but the following month it announced that "entire games have been played with hardly a profane utterance." The Winona, Minnesota, *Daily Republican* obviously enjoyed reporting in 1869 that "The Passagassawaukeag base ball club of Belfast, Maine, was beaten in Augusta the other day by a club bearing a name one quarter as long."

Some early-day town teams had the temerity to take on professionals and invariably suffered defeat. Professor Robert E. Barney has detailed a notable instance of these one-sided encounters in his description of the Cincinnati Red Stockings' journey to the West Coast in 1869, the first transcontinental trip by a ball club. Feverish preparations to receive the Reds followed their acceptance of an invitation to San Francisco, where local teams formed an association to plan hospitality for the visitors, arranged a pavilion seating 1,000 for "ladies" and their escorts at a dollar a person, and saw that local newspapers gave the event front-page publicity. The Reds played six games, five in San Francisco and one in Sacramento, easily winning all by lopsided scores, but the losers learned some new playing techniques, and enthusiasts achieved their purpose, stimulating renewed interest in the game, by inviting the famous club.

The West Coast visit of the Red Stockings also fanned baseball interest in Nevada, where baseball rivalry between Virginia City, the gold-mining center, and neighboring Carson City, the capital, had begun to catch fire.

Both teams invited the Reds to stop over on their return East and made plans for games with the famous team. But for the Red Stockings to reach Carson City or Virginia City would necessitate long, rough wagon rides overland from the railway station at Reno, a side trip the Red Stockings chose to pass up. Although disappointed, Nevada clubs' enthusiasm for baseball did not decline. Reports of the California expedition increased and deepened ardor for the sport, as reports in local newspapers showed. One, the Carson City *Daily Appeal*, announced,

> The rage for baseball is very apparent hereabouts. Old fellows whose hair and teeth are going and gone, and young ones who have just got their first breeches and boots on are knocking, tossing, and catching balls on the plaza and the streets from daybreak to dark.

By the seventies Nevada baseball had spread to other towns like Reno, Genoa, and Gold Hill, and teams frequently traveled by train to California to play teams there.

The allurement of down-home baseball soon led to even more elaborate forms of competition.

14

WIDER HORIZONS DOWN HOME

As soon as conditions permitted, town teams began to arrange more regular playing schedules and to sharpen competition by holding tournaments and organizing leagues. Even before the Civil War California teams dramatized their natural rivalry by holding a tournament. In western New York several town teams, at Auburn's instigation, staged a tournament in 1866 among the Buffalo Niagaras, Albany Knickerbockers, and two Rochester teams. According to researcher Joseph M. Overfield, "chicanery" on the part of the two Rochester clubs resulted in victory for the Niagaras, who also won the following year. By 1877 teams in New York had convened to set up a state championship, deciding that for a ten-dollar fee participating teams would play four games with each other. That same year Iowa town teams held a convention at Cedar Rapids to form a state league and play for a championship. Georgia teams arranged a championship in 1883, and Alabama town teams formed a league in 1888.

The cooperative trend continued well into the twentieth century. Around 1900 anthracite coal town teams in Pennsylvania like Nolan's Carbondale Independents, the Scranton Choctaws, and the Honesdale Reds took part in a Wayne County League. A Northern California League operated at least as early as 1912, and in 1914 town teams from all over California's Siskiyou County competed in a county league.

No set pattern to these groupings can be discerned. They might be based on local area, county, region, or state, and alignments did not necessarily remain fixed year after year. They might fall apart, become defunct, or regroup in different combinations of teams, after the fashion of Organized Baseball's early minor leagues. Indeed, occasionally a town team joined one of those leagues.

Saturday afternoon marked the time for ball games in rural areas, as the aforementioned Japanese visitor observed, but so did Sunday, where the law allowed or where the authorities looked the other way. Teams also got around local ordinances by playing on open fields just outside town limits. Richard Lingeman in *Small Town America* related one compromise of the

1890s on Sunday play: allowing ball games so long as the band played hymns between innings!

Baseball also became part of the festivities of holidays and special celebrations. Harold Keith tells of some teams that used movable stands easily bolted together and set up anywhere that a team of horses and a scraper had gouged out an infield and that could be as quickly dismantled and hauled away by wagon. A county fair usually occasioned a ball game, along with other sports and livestock showings. At Raleigh, North Carolina, in the seventies, Fair Days included baseball, as did Cape Cod fairs in the 1920s. Memorial Day, which used to be more of a festival than it is now, generally featured town team baseball, too. A special week-long celebration held in Honesdale, Pennsylvania, in August of 1919 to welcome servicemen home from the war featured a ball game on each of three different days. One game was rained out, but Honesdale defeated Port Jervis and Carbondale in the others.

A ball game between town teams ranked with parades, patriotic orations, and firecrackers as a Fourth of July must. "Nothing more picturesque, more delightful, more helpful" had ever arisen out of American rural life to relieve "the sordid loneliness" of the farm, Hamlin Garland fondly remembered, than the picnics and the ball games that usually accompanied them on July Fourth in Iowa and Wisconsin during the 1870s and '80s. "No community event pulled together the straggling farms of the frontier like the Fourth of July," commented Robert Hine in *Community of the Frontier*, and the day, he said, was full of flags, speeches, cold chicken, races, and baseball. The local grange often played its annual ball game at the July Fourth picnic. As far back as 1885 the tiny Beech Community in Madison County, North Carolina, celebrated annually at the settlement's baseball field with a pet parade, athletic contests, bands, homemade ice cream, lemonade, good dinners, and of course a ball game. Early in this century the small sheep-raising town of Caldwell, Idaho, generally staged a ball game on the national holiday. In Wayne County, Pennsylvania, where the Fourth had been special for town teams since the 1880s, a sumptuous choice in 1911 of three double-headers and six single games were available to county fans.

Authors of baseball fiction did not overlook the affinity between the game and Independence Day. The Fairport Nine of Noah Brooks's novel by that name, having defeated all towns "roundabout," played on the Fourth the game that decided the championship. Zane Grey in *The Shortstop* gave an account of a Fourth of July home-and-home doubleheader between two neighboring town teams, the first played at one team's park in the morning, the other played in the afternoon at the second one, in which fans, annoyed at the opposing pitcher for striking out two batters, threw firecrackers at him.

Sellers of baseball suits reflected this holiday demand for baseball. In its 1905 catalog Sears, Roebuck felt constrained to advise customers that delivery of uniforms ordinarily took from four to ten days "except just prior to Decoration Day and Fourth of July, when we require orders for suits to be furnished on these days to be placed two weeks in advance . . . on account of the enormous demand for suits at this time of the season."

In New England a holiday called Fast Day, celebrated in different states on various spring days since colonial times for religious reasons, had long been associated with baseball. In Keene, New Hampshire, residents used the town common for the Fast Day ball game in 1844. Henry David Thoreau's journal mentions in the 1850s the association in his mind between baseball and Fast Day. A town's centennial represented another excuse for a ball game. When Meriden, Connecticut, celebrated its hundredth year in June 1906 the town spent $268.35 on baseball and recouped $50.00 of it in a game at Hanover Park featuring former members of the Meriden town team who had graduated to a professional league.

During the second half of the nineteenth century and beyond, town teams in order to play distant towns utilized the railroads whenever they could, for travel represented an experience that held promise of adventure and sometimes kept it. Fans often chartered one or more cars on a train and accompanied their heroes, or the railroad itself would run an excursion train. All-day excursions were popular in North Carolina during the nineties. For one trip from Raleigh to Tarboro, about sixty miles, the train became so crowded that everyone who wanted to could not get on it. The line provided a servant and lots of ice water at a total excursion cost of $1.50 a person. On arriving, the travelers went sightseeing, picnicked, and then topped off the day by watching their team beat Tarboro.

Early in the 1900s the Sisson, California, team chartered a railway car for a game with Kennett in the next county. Most of the town's citizens went along, accompanied by a band. The train left very early in the morning, and "the band marched through the whole train playing anything but music and waking up the folks in the sleepers," a participant recalled. One time the Sisson team went by train to play Cottonwood, a trip that entailed an over-night stay at a hotel. The players slept three or four to a room, and despite the hot night they finally got to sleep, only to be awakened by loud thumping. Discovering one of their teammates using a baseball bat to kill bedbugs on the ceiling, they left him to his task and took their mattresses out on the veranda, where they passed the rest of the night. During the game next day a Sisson player who hit a homer collapsed from the heat between third and home, but a couple of his teammates solved that problem by carrying him across the plate to make the score 24–4 in Sisson's favor.

Another time the Sisson team ran into difficulty at the start of a trip to Hilts. The players gathered at the station, but when the time came to board the train their pitcher had not shown up. The conductor held the train while they went to look for him. Finding him drunk in a hotel bed, they wrapped him in a blanket, carried him aboard, and dressed him on the way. At the ball field they had to locate the pitcher's box for him, but after he warmed up he did all right, and Sisson won.

Adventures of a sort also befell the Sand Creek, Oklahoma, team. For one game they walked fifteen miles to meet their opponents, spurred on by the business manager's promise that if they won, their percentage would be enough for them to return by train. They did win and immediately rushed to phone their girlfriends to meet them at the railway station when they arrived home, but their call elicited bad news, for they learned that the business manager had taken off on a date and squandered the money, so they had to trudge the fifteen miles home.

Of all technological factors affecting intertown baseball competition, the railroad contributed the most stimulus. But railroads were built more to create new towns than to connect existing ones, and countless communities remained bypassed and isolated. If the road passed close enough, a farm boy could go to town by horseback or buggy to catch the train or a livery rig, and go on from there to the ball game. Other transportation might be found. For an important game in September 1900 between two northern California teams, one side summoned a player who worked in Oregon, and he came down by bicycle. As late as 1919 Carl Hubbell, who would star for the New York Giants in the 1930s, rode a horse nine miles from Meeker, Oklahoma, to pitch for the Spark town team.

The advent of the electric street railway in 1895 eased the travel problem not only in large cities and towns but in the adjacent countryside, where its rapid extension greatly increased the mobility of rural people. Soon one could travel great distances on hard rush seats or wooden benches by taking each line to its terminus and transferring to the next. Streetcar lines connected many New England towns, and one could go all the way from New York's lower East Side to Boston for about $2.50. Trolley tracks branched out from Cleveland to many nearby towns, and other states built long-distance lines, among them New Jersey, Pennsylvania, Illinois, Missouri, and Wisconsin.

The trolley provided cheap transport to and from the baseball grounds, generally for a nickel, collected at stated intervals. Thousands who rarely got away could now enjoy a visit to one of the great recreation grounds operated as profitable subsidiaries by the streetcar companies. At Middletown, New York, to cite only one example, baseball was a prime attraction up through the early twenties in the Wallkill area near an amusement center named Midway Park, where it created additional business for the street railway that owned it. Later the company built a new diamond and gave ball games special advertising in an effort to keep the trolley going in the face of growing competition from the automobile, which enabled people to go even farther afield for recreation. In 1906 autos already numbered 100,000, a figure that increased tenfold by 1913.

Early on, some venturesome fans and players undertook motor cars for baseball. Once the Alva, Oklahoma, team and some 500 fans embarked on an auto trip to Fairview for a game. On the way the travelers stopped to quench their thirst with some wine. Shortly, a man came down the road driving an elephant. The fans, having relieved their thirst copiously, spent the rest of the trip wondering whether they had actually seen the beast. On the way home the caravan of fans had to halt at a river bridge, where they found the elephant cautiously testing each plank in the bridge before taking his next step. Although they were held up for hours, the travelers felt comforted to learn that their earlier view of the animal had not been a hallucination.

But the coming of the auto did not appreciably alter small-town baseball until the twenties. Particularly in remote or hilly country, people continued to rely on the horse and buggy. In Nebraska's Elkhorn Valley around the turn of the century the first means of transport to neighboring towns, wrote a 1925 observer, remained a team of horses and a spring wagon or surrey. The town team would crowd into one wagon until the springs rested on the axles, drive to its destination, play a game, and return late in the evening. Carriages remained prominent at games after 1900. Both players and fans used them to get to town team games, and a mixed collection of vehicles continued to ring playing fields.

Once in the late nineties a band of youths set out on a three- to four-week baseball expedition in a lumber wagon drawn by two horses. This group of teenagers included Sam Crawford, the future Detroit Tigers star, who re-called the trip to Lawrence Ritter. The itinerants traveled from one Nebraska town after another playing such town teams as Fremont, Dodge, and West Point, passing the hat, sleeping in the open, and living on steak and bread supplemented with apples picked from orchards along the way. Such ca-maraderie could be duplicated by other town teams. Players might have their own private celebration after a game: Sherwood Anderson recalled the young fellows of the team of Clyde, Ohio, "having won a game from some neighboring town, [and] having got a keg of beer," going off to the woods "to drink there in the darkness, to sing ribald songs."

The great expanse of America retarded uniform dissemination of knowl-edge of the latest playing techniques and of rules changes made frequently during the game's formative years. Technological improvements gradually reduced the lag, but on the West Coast pitchers had to release the ball from below the belt even after a rules change in 1884 permitted them to throw from any position. In time, though, up-to-date styles of play spread as better communication brought in baseball books, magazines, guidebooks, and out-of-town newspapers that helped keep country teams and fans abreast of baseball doings. Spalding's guides, with their annual records of major-league stars, furnished inspiration to youths dreaming of becoming big leaguers and even to grownups. In his boyhood, recalled E.G. Brands, an editor, the most important man at town team games was the local storekeeper, who kept score from where he sat under a big umbrella along the baseline. So revered was he for his knowledge of the game that even umpires appealed to him on disputed decisions. One day Brands discovered that the great man had a folded newspaper in his hip pocket, and when it fell out Brands picked it up and read it before handing it back. The paper was *The Sporting News.* By selling five subscriptions the youngster obtained a free copy for himself and soon rivalled the storekeeper as a baseball authority.

At the crest of this rising flow of baseball information in small frontier towns and rural areas floated the general country store, where baseball continued after the playing season ended. Fans gathered there in the off-season to operate the Hot Stove League, a venerable institution that could function in the country barbershop as well. In this store or barbershop fans gathered for sociable winter afternoons or evenings at a warm stove, where chairs and whiskey awaited them, to smoke, chew, and spit while they talked baseball. Youngsters came to drink in the words of baseball wisdom of their elders as they looked over the books and periodicals sold there. Thus was the oral tradition of the game, embellished and constantly refurbished, carried on from one generation to the next.

When the government's Parcel Post Service came along in 1913, with its direct deliveries to farm and home, it dampened but did not destroy the Hot Stove League. During the depression of the thirties, when Willie Morris returned to Yazoo, Mississippi, he found The Store still the principal center of ferment. It sold everything from drug supplies to whiskey, and while white workingmen congregated on one side to talk of the day's batting averages and baseball scores, the blacks gathered on the other to do the same thing.

Whatever the differences in towns, one constant ran through down-home baseball: the fierce rivalry between towns and the prominent role of town teams as an instrument of this rivalry. American townsfolk used baseball games to sublimate temptation to open warfare against neighboring towns. Ford Frick recalled that these villages, "intensely proud and violently competitive, were the battlegrounds of our baseball wars." And Smokey Joe Wood marveled,

> The smaller the town the more important their ball club was. Boy, if you beat a bigger town they'd practically hand you the key to the city. And if you lost a game by making an error in the ninth or something like that—well, the best thing to do was just pack your grip and hit the road, 'cause they'd never let you forget it.

Baseball thus crystallized town rivalries through exciting head-on confrontations that came to definite conclusions.

Since residents believed that a town's showing in baseball reflected its worth and character, a winner was imperative. Writing from his own experience, Gilbert Patten in *Boltwood at Yale* had a small-town newspaper editor declare that a first-rate team

> would be of incalculable value in the way of attracting favorable attention. Outsiders would say that a town that could support such a team must be a wide-awake, hustling place.

So towns exerted themselves to put together winning teams, thus soon shrinking the initial phase of town team development in which teams comprised local youths content to play for enjoyment plus perhaps some beer, or a special supper prepared by a local housewife, or a small prize or contribution to pay for suits. Instead, the compulsion to victory led townsmen to employ outside talent and to indulge in increased betting and violence, often with an alcoholic assist.

Hiring ringers usually began on a modest scale with the employment of a pitcher. Like the queen in chess, the pitcher is the most important actor in any ball game, and his relative effectiveness often increases inversely with the class of ball being played. Teams usually added a catcher next and might hire a battery (pitcher and catcher) as a unit. Towns even employed minor and major leaguers, if the opportunity arose, usually in October after the professional season ended. The Geary, Oklahoma, team imported a Class D minor leaguer to pitch for them one autumn day before World War I, but to their dismay found that their opponents had secured none other than Walter Johnson, who beat them 2–1 without even removing his warmup sweater. The Sisson, California, team once found it possible to enlist Dolly Gray of the Washington American League team because he had left the club in mid-season to bring his sick wife to the Coast to recover. Sisson also had to add another ringer to catch, because the regular catcher could not cope with Gray's pitches.

A raid on a rival town's talent could make assurance doubly certain, because it strengthened the raider and weakened the raided in one fell stroke. The celebrated trial lawyer Clarence Darrow remembered his and his friends' boyhood shock when they learned that some men cared "nothing whatever" for "local patriotism" and would permit themselves to be hired by "a natural enemy," a "rival town."

How much money a player could get from a town depended on the importance of a particular game, the size of the crowd anticipated, and a player's skill and reputation. A player could earn anywhere from a few dollars to a few hundred for a game, with the pitcher, the key man, generally commanding more than the rest. But a player might increase (or lose) part or all of his take by betting on the game. Besides, he might literally pick up additional money for an exceptional performance, such as hitting a homer, for which fans might throw quarters, half dollars, and silver dollars to him. Local merchants offered prizes: a pair of shoes, for instance, to a batter who hit a shoe advertisement displayed on an outfield fence. At the end of the season local backers might treat the team to a banquet, a purse, or the proceeds from a benefit game, plus a suit of clothes for each player and a pair of shoes or cash award for the leading hitter. In addition to a monthly stipend of, say, $15.00 or $20.00, some towns offered room and board or a sinecure during the week.

Other town teams played certain games for a fixed sum, winner-take-all, the players having the option of placing side bets in addition to playing for the pot. Depending on the outcome, teams could make as much as a hundred dollars or else have to borrow money for fare, or hitchhike home. Outfielder Edd Roush gave early sign of the hard bargainer he would become as a major league star. Playing for nothing on the Oakland City, Indiana, town team in 1911 he learned that some players on the team were getting $5.00 a game, so he quit and went to play for the nearest town. Ed Hamman, who later ran the Indianapolis Clowns, as a high school senior made five dollars Sundays playing with a town team, but when school officials learned of it they banned him as a pro. Then the town team dropped him because he had not graduated!

Gate receipts helped towns defray expenses. Teams that played on open fields had to rely on passing the hat and other schemes to make ends meet. In McLean County, Illinois, teams could count on several hundred fans to watch a Sunday afternoon meadow game, but one season, to raise enough money to pay some imported players from $5.00 to $25.00 a game, community officials ran a raffle with a trip to Europe as first prize. Other towns staged benefit games—the Fats against the Leans, Married against Single— or put on a Grand Ball to help finance the team. Often club officials and other backers had to put up extra money at the end of the season to cover losses. This burden would become increasingly heavy as teams slithered deeper into debt caused by hiring ringers.

So anxious were some towns for a top-flight team that they scorned gradual immersion and chose to dive all the way into the ringer business, hiring an entire team in the hope of coming up with an instant winner. Professor Duane Smith's detailed account of the Leadville, Colorado, Blues illustrates this method. Leadville had in the 1870s become the "silver queen of the country" when rich deposits came to light, but in 1880 two of the best mines failed and a bitter strike left ill feeling in its wake. To help restore harmony in the community and attract new investors and settlers through a refurbished town reputation, Leadville leaders decided to form a team capable of defeating all rival nines in the area and perhaps of winning the state championship. In 1882 they formed the Leadville Baseball and Athletic Association and collected funds from $12.00 membership fees and other sources. Backers brushed aside local players regardless of ability, and a hired manager rounded up a squad of professionals that included four past or future major leaguers. Members of the association worked to raise money, prepare an enclosed field, erect a grandstand with a dressing room, and outfit the team with uniforms from Spalding's. The local newspapers and townspeople rallied around, and the Blues not only won the state championship but embarked on a strenuous post-season trip in states to the east of Colorado. All told, the Blues won 34 games, lost 8, and tied 1. In a district of only 15,000 people and with tickets priced at 25 cents for general admission, 50 cents for grandstand, and five dollars for the season, home attendance at Leadville's games reached 1,000 a game.

Hiring players and betting worked together: the ringer business stimulated the urge to bet, and betting heightened the desire for ringers to safeguard the wagers. As anxiety about their money grew, the bettors' conduct deteriorated and often flared into fisticuffs. Teams usually bet a lump sum, perhaps $500.00, on an important game, their financial backers much more. Players made individual side bets. Even boys risked their "two bits." Spectators bet on any aspect of the game, not just the final score: "Betcha a dollar he gets a hit"; and if his neighbor refused, "Betcha a dollar he *don't* get a hit!" Taken together, wagers on a big game could amount to as much as six or eight thousand dollars.

They could also cause wrangling and quarreling over almost every play, with fans rushing on the field to join in, particularly if a team had put up a lump sum on the game as a quick way to reimburse its backers. Heated arguments and drunken scraps among spectators became so common that games played without fights were exceptions. Writer Hal Borland recalled fist fights after every game between Flagler and Hugo, Colorado, in the years around 1915. Ab Evans, an old-timer, remembered a game at Hilts, California, in the early 1900s after which some fans, angry over a "rotten decision" in the game, tore down the wooden fence and attacked others with the boards. Fortunately, the melee was stopped before anyone got hurt, but the home team players, still nursing their wrath, would not allow the outsiders to eat in town.

For poor performance players suffered expressions of fan displeasure ranging from booing to refusal of a ride and thus being forced to walk home. Because the home team usually supplied the umpire, he might be either very good or very poor depending on the point of view. One recourse of visitors to raw decisions on the part of a home umpire was to walk off the field. Or, if a home team became displeased with the decisions of its umpire, he might be fired in the middle of a game and replaced with a more sympathetic one. If a single umpire presided, players tried to get away with taking short cuts around the bases, or punching the ball from the glove of fielders about to tag them. Once an umpire took up his position at the start of a game packing two big pistols and announcing he wanted no trouble!

Use of hired players changed the character of down-home ball and caused occasional complaints that it was on the downgrade. Such assertions reached crescendo in the 1920s and emanated from the same sources then proclaiming that boys were forsaking baseball for other sports: the National Amateur

Athletic Federation (NAAF), along with many playground and recreation leaders, physical education teachers, and coaches. Complaints in the *Athletic Journal* even laid on the town teams some of the responsibility for boys' alleged drift away from baseball.

Galloping professionalism had certainly become rampant. Town businessmen in Shelburne Falls, Massachusetts, for instance, hired out-of-state professionals to fill key positions on the town team and went so far as to import skilled teams to play against them. Once the town of Ossining, New York, hired Clarence Mitchell, a left-handed spitball pitcher, of the Philadelphia Phillies, and paid him $500.00. When the team of Stockbridge, Michigan, arrived at the town of Jackson to play the State Prison team in October of 1931, it brought along Guy Bush of the Chicago National League Club. In 1919 and 1920 two towns in Massachusetts, Attleboro and North Attleboro, discarded all pretense of a representative team and brought in a bevy of topflight major leaguers, among them Babe Ruth, Rogers Hornsby, George Sisler, Grover Alexander, and Walter Johnson, for a post-season series, spending $3,400.00 for the last game of the 1920 series alone. Special charter trains brought interested New England fans from Boston and even farther away.

Not only in October were big leaguers hired. In major-league cities where Sunday ball remained illegal after World War I, professional players took advantage of idle days caused by the Sunday ban to slip away and make extra money playing for a town team. Selling their services outside of Organized Baseball made them liable to fines, but the town teams customarily paid the fines. Sometimes Ring Lardner induced big leaguers to play Sundays on the town team of his home town, Niles, Ohio, which paid up to $250.00 plus the player's fine.

Once in 1920, when the oil was flowing in Yenango County, Pennsylvania, and the townspeople of Franklin felt flushed with money for wagers, they hired Bert Gallis of the Philadelphia Phillies to pitch against their rival, Oil City. The Phillies president, William F. Baker, hearing of it, sent his business manager, James Hagan, to Franklin to serve the player with an injunction or subpoena. His mission accomplished, Hagan spent the evening before his train time in a pool room until, learning that local fans were in an ugly mood over his act, he sneaked back to his hotel room. But a crowd of fans discovered his whereabouts and came to heckle him. When they finally left Hagen crept out the back way and stayed in hiding until his train arrived.

Critics objected to the use of ringers on several counts. They argued that outside the majors, baseball did not amount to a paying business, and paid teams represented an unwarranted burden on local backers. Teams ran up debts that could not be covered and gave up, perhaps to try another year. The result was on-and-off baseball, which depressed local interest. J.A. Butler, a NAAF man writing in the *Athletic Journal*, blamed "improper administration" for the difficulties of town ball, and the New York *Times* agreed, declaring that those who backed town teams were not always the "best citizens." Other critics contended that promoters, seeing everything through "mercenary eyes," looked upon the game only as a spectator amusement and cared nothing for the town. Or they complained that rivalry caused towns to employ ringers regardless of their character. Swede Risberg and Happy Felsch, for example, two of the Black Sox expelled from Organized Baseball for crookedness, had been hired by such teams. The whole system, critics declared, undermined community morale, dried up financial support, repelled nongamblers, disgusted potential "angels," and impelled parents to discourage their children's interest in the game.

This indictment of paid town teams requires a caveat, however. Allowance must be made for the bias of its authors, many of whom belonged to a group that felt uneasy with the increased leisure falling to working Americans as the twenties unfolded. Because of their religious views, the pronouncements of recreation leaders had a moralistic and even self-righteous cast. Many such critics found professionalism in sports distasteful. They tended instead to favor recreation initiated, controlled, and directed by trained experts. Yet who is to ordain what "good" and "bad" recreation is? Kenneth Clarke of Community Service, Inc., thought he could. Apparently serious, he declared that one of the things Carol Kennicott of Sinclair Lewis's *Main Street* should have done in Gopher Prairie was to get Community Service to arrange games between children and between adults on playgrounds, because then a local town baseball team would have developed.

In many communities the reproofs and remonstrances of critics fell on receptive ears. In one Wisconsin town when the players, mostly outsiders, asked for a pay increase, they were reportedly shown the "shortest way out of town" and told "We'll build a golf course first." In the Elkhorn Valley, Nebraska towns that had formed an amateur league discontinued the rule that had permitted each team to hire one man and instead required all players to make affidavit of residence in the towns they played for. Thereafter, the caliber of ball and number of youngsters playing supposedly improved annually, and the town of Fremont, Nebraska, used its gate receipts for boys' baseball. In Texas the towns of Eagle Lake and Moulton boasted successful teams entirely of "home town boys" without any "hired help."

About a dozen areas of Wisconsin also reportedly returned to home-talent or near-home-talent baseball. In Janesville, businessmen tired of footing the bill for imported players now bought only uniforms, and in return could advertise on the backs of them. Although the Southern Wisconsin League still paid pitchers at the rate of ten or fifteen dollars a game, local baseball leaders claimed their plan remained "amateur in spirit" and that fans showed more interest in players they knew personally.

Amherst, Massachusetts, came closer to amateurism. Its rules restricted teams to fifteen local unpaid players. Clubs charged no admission and depended for funds on passing the hat. They used receipts to pay umpires, buy equipment, and cover team expenses. Sponsors supplied uniforms. Here too, fan interest and excitement reportedly increased.

In 1927 the *Athletic Journal* published a survey indicating a decline in the number of paid town teams. Of nearly 2,000 reporting clubs, most stated they had recently quit trying to maintain them (although figures showed that for some, "recently" meant as far back as before 1916). More than half said they would promote amateur clubs for the 1927 season, although about a fifth adopted a compromise policy under which a few players would still be paid. Most compromisers would pay the pitcher or catcher only, or would divide any post-season surplus among all. NAAF declared successful its effort to reawaken amateur ball among town teams, and the New York *Times*, too, thought amateur ball was re-establishing itself in small towns.

But with the rapidly accelerating technological changes in America of the twenties, even small villages felt outside influences as never before, and their long encasement in provincialism began eroding. Untold numbers turned to a greater variety of recreational pursuits, sufficiently in fact to warrant the conclusion that like boys' baseball, down-home ball probably lost ground relatively. Whether it lost absolutely, there seems no real way to determine.

Yet amidst all the external changes of the twenties, much remained the same. Rural folk clung to old folkways, including their ball teams. The fact that the Playground Association and some government agencies felt it advisble to increase aid for hitherto neglected rural recreation indicates that large areas of the country remained little affected by urban inroads. Besides, if radio diverted rural fans from baseball, it also stimulated their interest in it; if advertising created new wants, it also confirmed the value of a town team as an advertisement; if cars carried fans away from town team games, they also brought people to them. Greater prosperity and leisure plus the gradual breakdown of old Sunday ball inhibitions permitted larger attendance and more support for teams. In many villages of the twenties ball games remained an integral part of the celebration of the Fourth of July and Old Home Day, and nostalgic reminiscences show that fierce town rivalries of old lost none of their intensity or vehemence.

The pile-driver blows of the depression blunted and reshaped but did not obliterate developments that affected home-town baseball. Although competition from other sports remained keen, town baseball benefited from the athletic fields, baseball parks, and other recreational fields built by the federal government, and mass unemployment provided leisure for recreation and sports.

Even in the depression, teams varied as to type. A Pure Home Talent League operated in a Wisconsin county, while in North Carolina Ray Scarborough, a future big leaguer, got paid $12.50 a week for "playin' and pickin'"—pitching two days for the Aberdeen town team and picking peaches on the other days. Twenty-one-year-old Earl Averill, before he became an outfielder for the Cleveland Indians, secured a job playing ball for the town of Bellingham, Oregon, where he did so well that the county highway department hired him to paint bridges.

Nor did the atmosphere surrounding town team games change appreciably. Games lost none of their seriousness. In Jefferson County, Wisconsin, for instance, after a disputed decision in a game between Newville and London, Newville fans went to court, and when Judge Jesse Earle, himself a former town team player, in effect found for London, Newville appealed all the way to Commissioner Landis, who held for the umpire. In a game in a Kentucky coal mining district pitcher Bob Bowman found the miners, having just drawn their pay, "bettin' their shirts on their home team," so he had to win "or else." Jeering fans rattled him, and his pitches hit the first two batters. Home fans thought he had hit the batters purposely and tried to attack him, fighting with each other as well. One fan who had drunk too much pulled out a six-shooter, but an alert player knocked it out of his hands with a bat. Finally, state troopers rode their horses into the crowd, walled off Bowman, and escorted him from town with the mob at his heels.

Whether down-home baseball succeeded or failed during the depression depended on local conditions. Town games in Nebraska died down in the thirties, according to Robert Scott, a resident, because of competing sports and the growth in the number of cars and highways. An unnamed person interviewed for the study of "Mineville," a small anonymous town, said baseball became "almost a thing of the past," for young residents would "rather take a car and go swimming... or have a petting party." No such decline was noticeable in northern Wisconsin, according to a letter to the editor of *Sporting News*. There "Every little town and hamlet has a team, and most of them are in Sunday leagues. . . . baseball is thriving." Berwick, Iowa, a tiny community with fewer than a hundred residents and no street lights, provided an electrically lit ball field for its team, the lights purchased by raising funds at dances and ice-cream socials. The even smaller settlement of Heaton, North Dakota, fielded a team that defeated the county seat, Fessenden, during the Wells County Fair, even though half Fessenden's players were ringers from a club in Minnesota.

To Willie Morris in Yazoo, Mississippi, baseball remained "all-meaning" and "the link with the outside."

> On Sunday afternoons we sometimes drove out of town and along the hot, dusty roads to baseball fields that were little more than parched red clearings, the outfield sloping out of the woods and ending in some tortuous gully. . . . One of the backwoods teams had a fastball pitcher . . . who didn't have any teeth, and a fifty-year-old left-handed catcher. It was a wonderfully lazy way to spend those afternoons—my father and my friends and I sitting in the grass

behind the chicken-wire backstop . . . listening at the same time to a big league game on our portable radio. . . .

In spite of change and pitfalls, down-home ball was a vibrant part of small-town life.

1. Brooklyn, New York, boys' team 1936, on Saturdays the Creston Baseball Club, Brooklyn Amateur League Champions, average age 17, youngest in league; on Sundays the Camden Minor Leaguers, a semipro team. (Note ambiguous *C* on shirts.) Harold "Cy" Seymour, organizer and field manager. *From the author's collection.*

2. Tenement boys in New York City playing baseball in an alley, about 1910. Photo by Lewis Hine. *The Granger Collection and George Eastman House.*

3. The North Bennet Street Nine, Boston boys of Italian and Irish background, with Harold Peabody, future husband of Marion Lawrence, who organized the team around the turn of the century. *From Marion Lawrence Peabody,* To Be Young Was Very Heaven. (*Boston: Houghton Mifflin, 1967*). *Courtesy of Gertrude Peabody McCue.*

4. Baseball Joe, hero of Lester Chadwick's series of juvenile novels in the 1900s, has just escaped from kidnappers and is about to pitch a no-hitter in the World Series. *From the author's collection.*

5. Dan Vinton, the hero of Ralph Henry Barbour's juvenile novel *Double Play* (1927), leaps into the air to spear a ball and save the game for his school. *From the author's collection.*

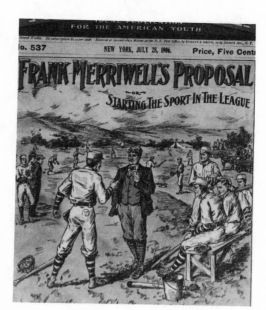

6. Cover of popular boys' periodical, *Tip Top Weekly*, July 28, 1906, featuring a Frank Merriwell baseball story for youngsters. *From the author's collection.*

7. Baseball in the schoolyard at West Branch School, Geneva, New York, in the 1870s, photographed by J. G. Vail. *Courtesy of the New-York Historical Society, New York City.*

8. This serious, tough-looking team is the Hornbrook Grammar School Baseball Club of Hornbook, California, 1901. The coach is Gordon Jacobs, seated at left rear. *Courtesy of Gordon Jacobs. From the Siskiyou County Historical Society, Yreka, California.*

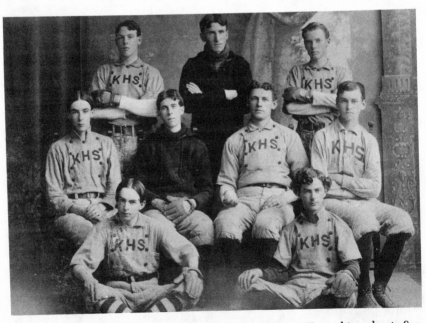

9. The baseball team of Keene High School, Keene, New Hampshire, about 1899. *Courtesy of the Historical Society of Cheshire County.*

10. Amherst College, Amherst, Massachusetts, baseball team of 1873. *By permission of the Trustees of Amherst College, Amherst, Massachusetts.*

11. Bleachers at a baseball game between Cornell and Princeton, May 2, 1903, at Percy Field, Cornell University, Ithaca, New York. Cornell won 10–3. *Department of Manuscripts and University Archives, Cornell University.*

12. The 1866 Dartmouth College baseball team, Hanover, New Hampshire. *Courtesy of Dartmouth College Library.*

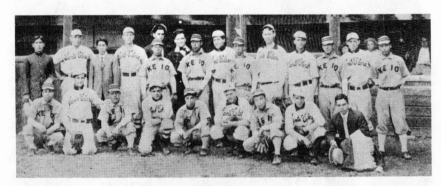

13. Baseball team of Santa Clara College of Santa Clara, California, in Hawaii to play the Keio University baseball team of Tokyo, Japan, on August 8, 1908. Santa Clara won, 9–4. *The Cooperstown Hall of Fame and Museum Library, Cooperstown, New York.*

14. The 1902 baseball team of Seton Hall College, South Orange, New Jersey. Professor Gannon, in the second row, second from left, played shortstop. George H. Gleeson, manager, is at center. *Courtesy of Seton Hall University.*

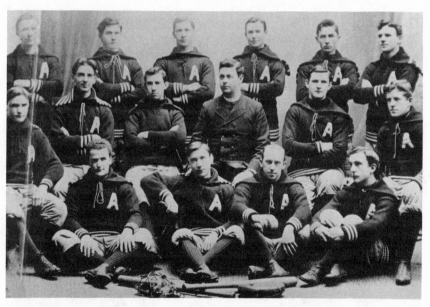

15. Saint Bonaventure University's Allegheny Baseball Club of about 1892. At extreme right, top row, is John McGraw, and at extreme left is Hugh Jennings. In center is Father James Dolan, who founded athletics at Saint Bonaventure. *Courtesy of Saint Bonaventure University, Saint Bonaventure, New York.*

16. A game between the seniors and the faculty of Whitewater Normal School, now University of Wisconsin at Whitewater, June 7, 1900. *University of Wisconsin at Whitewater*.

17. The Yreka Baseball team of Yreka, California, setting off for an away game at Klamathon about 1892, after renting a Concord coach and team. *Courtesy of the Siskiyou County Historical Society. Lent by Frank Herzog, one of the Yreka players*.

18. Steel company baseball team, Buckeye International, Columbus, Ohio, about 1915. *Courtesy of the Ohio Historical Society, Columbus.*

19. Baseball players of the Butler Colliery, near Pittston, Pennsylvania. Stanley "Bucky" Harris, office boy for the coal company, is the youngster at right holding the ball. *From Stanley Harris,* Playing the Game: From Mine Boy to Manager *(New York: Frederick Stokes Company, 1925).*

20. Railroad baseball team of McCloud River, California, 1914. *Courtesy of the Siskiyou County Historical Society, California.*

21. Baseball team of the Mount Shasta Milling Company, Mount Shasta, California, about 1900. *Courtesy of the Siskiyou County Historical Society, California.*

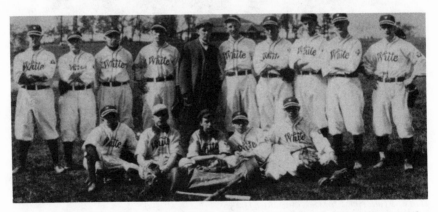

22. Baseball team of the White Motor Company, Cleveland, Ohio, that won the 1914 championship of the city's industrial league with a record of 18 victories and no losses. *From the company's house organ,* The Albatross. *December 1914.*

15

TIME OFF TO PLAY BALL

In the nineteenth century baseball playing sprang up and thrived in the very institution where those in command once forbade play: the workplace. How could such a thing happen? Why would the institution that most completely separated play from work change from forbidding play to becoming one of its most prominent sponsors?

The answer lies in changing views of life, work, and leisure that developed during and after the technological revolution. Before that sweeping change, work included and spawned leisure and entertainment, and life was organized around alternating rhythms of work and play, with the two often combined, as in early barn-raising celebrations and cornhusking bees. When industrialism urbanized life, work and leisure at first separated. Communities formed as appendages to factories, and there life revolved around machines and the business offices they depended upon. Recreation then arose in and clustered about these business and industrial plants.

The nature of the new kind of work itself affected the evolution of leisure. Modern students of industrialism have expatiated upon the degrading effect of the factory system on workers. First, as commentators like Stuart Chase and Carol Aronovici said, the factory system destroyed the creative element in work that had formerly been furnished by handcrafting. Second, as Richard C. Edwards and others explained, the repetitive, routinized, monotonous, and stultifying type of work most factories offered had a regimenting and dulling effect on workers, thus increasing tension and fatigue. In brief, as the motion picture *Modern Times* with Charlie Chaplin graphically demonstrated, the machine ruled and set the pace. With no creative or entertaining features available in their daily work, factory operatives sought leisure elsewhere, and by Saturday night they were more than ready to search for relaxation, which commercialized entertainment increasingly supplied.

Industrial supervisors reacted to their workers' need for better lives not by altering the industrial system and making work more satisfying, as Robert L. Goldman has shown, but by directing the workers' leisure into approved channels outside of the workplace or in connection with it. Business did this

213

through what became known as "welfare capitalism," an attempt to improve morale and to increase production by adding recreation and other programs and services to the work day. Industrial and business baseball thus grew as part of this paternalistic and manipulative system of recreation set up as a method of social control by businesses for motives of enlightened self-interest, such as increased production, less employee turnover, and, above all, prevention of unionism and strikes.

Another aspect of leisure that concerned businessmen was the shortening work week and lengthening time available for leisure in the late nineteenth century, accomplished through the efforts of reformers and unions. Work hours decreased from about 66 a week in mid-century to more like 60 in 1890. Businessmen, according to a seminal article by Robert Goldman and John Wilson, fearing the consequences of the shorter work week, sought to control workers' time off the job, changing it from "leisure" time to "controlled" time. Both business baseball and industrial baseball grew in this environment.

In the decades before 1900, baseball play among workers changed all the way from self-generated play to company-sponsored semipro teams. With factories and their neighborhoods replacing extended families as the centers of allegiance, factory or neighborhood friendships might form the basis for a worker's social life. That meant the possibility of factory or neighborhood ball teams.

At first, during the "baseball fever" of the 1850s and 1860s, an employer might oppose after-work and lunchtime baseball because they took employees' time and attention from the job.* Accordingly, some employers began asking prospective employees if they belonged to baseball clubs, intending to eliminate such applicants. Young men took to getting up at 4:00 or 5:00 A.M. to practice before going to factory or office. At the same time newspapers like the New York *Clipper* and writers like Henry Chadwick urged employers to encourage baseball as healthful exercise. Charles King Newcomb, Philadelphia intellectual, wrote in his journal in 1867 that baseball furnished a great respite, a welcome escape from factory work. By practicing for hours even under a hot summer sun, workers "attest that they mean to be men & not machines." In Chicago in the 1860s some employers, wrote Stephen Freedman in 1978, proved willing to give ball players company time to play on teams containing their fellow workers. As well, some employers, even that early, realizing that company teams made good advertising, started sponsoring them, although sometimes more than one company chipped in to back a team.

After the Civil War, with the economic revolution greatly accelerated especially in the North through the application of science and invention, the way opened for the development of great industrial firms. In this quickening

*See *Baseball: The Early Years,* pp. 23–24.

business atmosphere, baseball thrived. By the 1880s the company team was so well established in large factories and offices that city newspapers published many stories about the employees of one company defeating at baseball those of another in the same trade, or two teams representing different divisions within the same firm battling each other for baseball supremacy. *De Witt's Baseball Guide* revealed the heights to which such rivalry could reach by reporting a message sent in 1883 by one mercantile firm in a western city to its neighbor:

> Gentlemen: It is creditably reported to us that some of your employees frequently use the roofs of buildings extending from yours to ours to play baseball thereon. We are ever desirous to help elevate the national game, and this altitude seems to be about as high as it ever will get, yet there are also a few objections to this special location of the game.

The variety of sponsors in the early days of company baseball is striking. Every kind of establishment imaginable, from druggist to city government, from department store to railroad, from mine to mill had its team in the era prior to the twentieth century. White collar and blue, small business and large, all participated.

The earliest amateur teams like the New York Knickerbockers were made up mostly of young businessmen, but their clubs tended to resemble later "athletic clubs" in that many did not represent particular businesses or trades. The Frontier Baseball Club of Leavenworth, Kansas, and the Lowells of Boston, both of the 1860s, represented that type—various business and professional men mixed on the same team. But teams of workmen employed in the same line, such as the Brooklyn Eckfords, who were shipwrights, as well as teams representing individual companies, formed early, too. Bullard and Foster, druggists of Keene, New Hampshire, fielded a team some time between 1875 and 1885, that even defeated the town team, the Keenes, 11 to 7, winning the local championship plus all gate receipts and a $50.00 wager. Two company teams in Jacksonville, Florida, as told in Bess Beatty's article on Florida ball, the Nonpareils of Kuhn, Furchgott and Company, and the Clerks of Cohen Brothers, played, as the Florida *Times* put it, "until their tongues hung out of their mouths and their bones and muscles felt as if an epidemic of the dengue fever had raged among them for a week."

Sporting goods houses proved to be natural sponsors of baseball teams. Johnny Kling, later a star catcher for the Chicago Cubs, pitched in the 1890s for the Schmeltzers, a sporting goods house in Kansas City, and worked in the store when not playing. J. Leslie Wilkinson, who later owned the black pro team called the Kansas City Monarchs, signed after college with a team backed by the Hopkins Brothers Sporting Goods store in Des Moines, Iowa.

A department store sometimes organized a league within the company, as did Marshall Field's in Chicago. Other stores formed "varsity" teams and played each other. The Jordan Marsh store of Boston, for example, competed with R.H. White's in an unusual game played at night on the lawn of a resort hotel at Nantasket Beach, Massachusetts. O. Eddleton, who checked newspaper accounts of the game, found that three wooden towers bearing electric lamps furnished just enough light for the 300 interested spectators to view the 16–16 tie game.

The latter game also exemplifies another type of business ball game: intratrade baseball. In this type, employees in a particular line of work challenged others in like occupations. Insurance companies in New York, Detroit, and Chicago played each other from the 1870s onward. Newspapermen representing various papers in Chicago played each other; New York newsmen did the same. Politicians took part, too. The Democratic Executive Committee of Hudson County, New Jersey, beat the one of Essex County 19–9 in 1883. Government workers likewise tested themselves against each other. Fire companies competed in baseball at least from the 1860s onward. New York policemen challenged those of Brooklyn in 1883. And the same year, in Washington, D.C., the team of the Government Insane Asylum arranged a game with one from the Interior Department, to be played on the asylum grounds, after which the inmates planned to give the visitors a dinner. The New York *Times*, not specifying which team it referred to, headed the story, "Lunatics to Play Ball."

Other games matched unlikely teams against each other. In Brooklyn, New York, the *Eagle* reported that Wall Street had lost to the Pharmacy College, and the brokers in turn defeated both a milkmen's team and the Bank of New York. The New York Stock Exchange, reinforced with college players of the Staten Island Athletic Club, nearly won over the Brooklyn professional team in 1883. Members of fraternal groups like the Kismets, LuLus, and Boumies fought out a series of baseball games in Brooklyn in the 1890s.

But it was among blue collar workers, including skilled operators, that baseball often received extensive notice and backing by large, well-established industrial firms. Such companies might actually recruit ball players in order to develop a team or teams that would enable it to make a good showing against other companies in industrial leagues.

Railroads at first lagged behind their European counterparts in paternalistic social benefits, as Professor Walter Licht explains in *Working for the Railroad*. But finally American railroad owners, concerned about the tendency of the men to spend their evenings drinking and carousing when compelled to stay in unfamiliar cities overnight, decided the workers must be distracted with Bible study and recreation. In 1868 the Union Pacific, an E.L. Harriman railroad, arranged with the YMCA to supply simple comforts, including recreation, in towns that its workers stopped in. In 1872 the first "railroad Y" organized formally in Cleveland, Ohio, and the idea spread to New York and throughout the nation. To get railroad support, the Y promised owners that their investment would pay dividends in "sober, efficient, uncomplaining, and nonradical workers," as researcher Paul McBride expressed it. Early services to railroad men moved the Y to organize similar programs among lumbermen and miners. These programs led the Y to develop an industrial department to arrange recreation for industrial workers.

Railroad workers, from construction gangs to freight office employees, played baseball from the 1870s on. One, Henry Fabian, labored as a railroad construction worker for the Queen & Crescent Railroad, one of J.P. Morgan's lines, building the road between Cincinnati and New Orleans. He said later in *Sporting News*, "It was with these tough lads that I really learned to play baseball. . . . We worked pretty hard, but when we had any time off we always played baseball. . . . " Later, Fabian became groundkeeper of the Polo Grounds and was credited with designing the turtleback baseball diamond used in the majors. Baseball teams also formed on the Union Pacific line in the 1880s.

Printing represented a line of skilled work in which employees organized baseball teams. Printers played in Chicago, New York, and Boston in the 1860s and 1870s as members of trade teams. Printing was a highly unionized trade, so teams of printers probably formed on their own. Paper manufacturing workers, too, played similar workers at home and away. The New York Paper Trade Club in 1883 planned a visit to Philadelphia to play a paper trade club of that city.

Trade-team baseball in Boston grew into a series of city championships in the summer of 1888 when the local YMCA rented sports grounds and invited young employees of certain trades to play for the championship of their trade. *Leisure Hours*, a Y periodical, published news of the resulting champions of the drug trade (Cutler Brothers Company) and of the sporting goods companies (John P. Lovell Arms Company, which sold baseball goods). Dry goods and leather trade employees also participated in the competition. Two games featuring the woollen workers furnished an opportunity to attempt humor using terms common to the trade. Printed on the scorecard was the slogan, "Never mind about free wool; give us free batting," along with the statement, "No 'Unmerchantable,' 'Pulled,' and 'Fleeced' methods were used to secure players, though the trade was well 'scoured.'"

Employees took advantage of the lunch hour for informal play. Newton Crane, returned to America after having lived in England, noticed factory hands and warehouse clerks "employing the noon hour" by practicing throwing and catching "in nearly every open space and in the side streets of America." Factories built in suburbs made ball playing at lunchtime more inviting: when Procter and Gamble built a new plant in the suburbs of Cincinnati about 1883 it established a playing field adjoining the building. The annual company "outing" (picnic), with one department playing a baseball game against another, became traditional. At the Endicott Johnson Shoe

Company's annual picnic in New York state in the 1880s, recalled founder George F. Johnson, the keg of beer on third base meant that "after a few innings every batter who hit the ball ran straight to third."

New England factory employees had played ball since the 1870s at least—the French-American textile mill workers in Woonsocket, Rhode Island, for instance, and those of Ludlow Manufacturing at Ludlow, Massachusetts. The latter formed their own athletic association in 1896. Bill Klem, while employed as a timekeeper at the American Bridge Company in Berwick, Maine, began a baseball umpiring career that brought him to the National League, where he was for many years a mainstay. In Jewett City, Connecticut, Hugh Duffy, soon to become one of the famous Boston Red Sox outfield trio, worked for a factory during the week and received $30.00 a month extra playing baseball for its team.

Companies soon recognized the promotional value of a "varsity" baseball team. At least four drug manufacturers sponsored teams in the nineteenth century, naming them the Hop Bitters, the Sultan Bitters, the Home Comforts, and the Paregorics. Some company teams developed sufficient skill to play pro clubs, as did the nine backed by the White Sewing Machine Company of Cleveland in 1881. Another sewing machine firm, the Demarest Company of Williamsport, Pennsylvania, charged a dime admission to its games, although Hans Lobert, later a colorful National League third baseman, the man who once raced a horse around the bases, as a boy avoided the fee by crawling under the park fence to see the game.

Miners played ball in the far-western mining towns of Utah and Colorado and in the midwestern Pennsylvania coal fields, a region that produced a number of major leaguers. In Shreveport, Texas, Alvin J. Gardner, working for a local oil company, captained the company baseball team at age seventeen. Later he became president of the Texas League.

In the large industrial firms, company recreation programs that included baseball sprang up from a mixture of humanitarian and self-serving reasons as part of a business policy soon to become widespread and known as welfare capitalism. John Patterson, president of National Cash Register Company in Dayton, Ohio, backed recreation extensively in the 1890s as part of his desire to improve workers' lives in ways that would at the same time benefit the company. Patterson introduced calisthenics and sports programs and a children's playground, which included provision for baseball. Physical recreation for employees started at NCR with the formation of a company ("varsity") baseball team in 1895. Patterson justified expenditures for such programs on the ground that they cut production costs and increased profits by improving workers' health and attitudes. "There is no charity in anything we do," he said. "Isn't it just good business?"

A company town provided an especially receptive venue for baseball. Often the company owned the land and buildings surrounding the factory and used the space for parks and playgrounds, which included baseball diamonds. Owners did not establish such facilities primarily for aesthetic or philanthropic reasons but to attract and retain skilled workers. At Hopedale, Massachusetts, a town controlled by the E.D. and G. Draper Company, the owners in 1888 leveled a field for its Hopedale baseball nine. In Utah, company towns sponsored clubs and recreation, with baseball frequently the chief pastime, according to James Allen in the *Utah Historical Quarterly*, and sometimes put professional players on the payroll during the ball season, not to work in the mine or plant but to make sure the company team made a good showing against others.

George Pullman's company town in Illinois for 5,000 workers, called Pullman, represents the epitome of paternalism. The Pullman Palace Car Company had organized baseball teams in the early seventies, before the town was built, but when George Pullman built his town on 300 acres at Lake Calumet near Chicago he planned to use baseball and other recreation to control his workers. For the company town was a device to restrain absenteeism, lateness, and the spending of money and time outside the area, as well as the insulation of occupants against unions and liquor. Pullman owned the workers' houses as well as the land they were built on, and he collected the rents. In short, Pullman's town resembled a medieval fiefdom.

Studies of the town of Pullman and of Pullman athletics by Stanley Buder and Wilma Pesavento, as well as an 1888 book on amateur athletics by Frederick Janssen, agreed that Pullman believed athletics developed character as well as health. For his new town he organized the Pullman Athletic Association, which sponsored teams in baseball and other sports. He had a park built with about ten acres for baseball and other field games. After work as well as Saturdays the fields were soon crowded with players and spectators. Baseball nines played not only each other but teams of other towns and even those from Chicago. And the nines competed fiercely among themselves to be named the Pullman company team.

Pullman purposed to keep his workers happy, healthy, and contented, but within three years after employees moved into the attractive but controlled environment of Pullman, trouble began. The absence of democracy in the town, according to Almont Linder in *The Pullman Strike*, showed its basic weakness. In 1883 workers struck for an eight-hour day. When they struck again in 1894 after Pullman refused to discuss grievances, National Guard and federal troops were called in, the latter unnecessarily. On the first day of the strike, May 12, a warm, sunny day, young men were out playing ball. But the troops shot thirteen strikers dead and crushed the protest. In the aftermath of the strike, the company restricted athletics, although the Pullman Athletic Club still fielded baseball teams until Pullman died in 1897 and the town was dismantled.

Concentration of industrial power in the early twentieth century led industries to form the giant supercorporations that divorced ownership from management. Although the movement toward concentration slowed or ceased in 1904 with actions of Theodore Roosevelt and William Howard Taft, by then the tendency was clear. Great industrial plants like Henry Ford's in Detroit became the model for others, with owners separated from employees by foremen and other layers of management. Although small business continued, all work, as D.T. Rodgers pointed out in *The Work Ethic in Modern America*, grew more like work in the large industrial plants, with subdivision of the tasks of labor into smaller and smaller units bearing only tenuous relation to the final product.

Such changes in the performance of work came partly from Frederick Winslow Taylor, efficiency expert, who in the nineteenth century advanced his principle of "scientific management." Taylor proved to the satisfaction of many important industrialists that with reorganization of work, use of standardized tools, institution of differential wage incentives (piecework), and application of the results of time-and-motion studies, the execution of even the smallest operation could be improved. Early in the century, Taylorism rode high in industry.

Taylor applied the same principles to the development of sports equipment. As the American tennis champion of 1881, he knew sports and believed that the essential characteristics of both industry and sports was cooperation. But although great increases in production resulted from the application of Taylor's techniques, worker morale declined as employees began to suspect Taylorism of causing "the speedup."

Taylorism, although it bore some relationship to welfare capitalism in that both systems proposed to enhance production and therefore profits, focused less on the worker than on the job the worker did. Although industrialists found that Taylorism raised profits through "scientific management" of the worker and his tools on the job, at the same time they increasingly introduced programs like recreation, especially baseball, that could extend their domination of the worker's life away from the job. Industrialists could also use welfare capitalism to deflect the charges of critics like "the muckrakers" that corporations operated only for their own benefit, because employers could claim that through welfare capitalism they were exercising "social responsibility." So despite the intrusion of Taylorism, welfare capitalism developed still further in industries in the early twentieth century as industrialists elaborated upon it with refinements like public recognition for athletes, athletic awards, and athletic sweaters.

With continued reduction in the hours of work (by 1910, to around 50.3 hours a week) as a result of pressures from unions and reformers, social scientists began, in contravention of the traditional work ethic, to justify leisure for workers. Most industrial critics in the progressive era, as Rodgers points out, concluded that creativity was no longer possible in one's work and must be found instead in after-work leisure activities. People like Joseph Lee of the Recreation Association rationalized these activities as a restorative for work. A. G. Spalding, the sporting goods manufacturer, in one of his usual self-serving statements, declared in his 1906 guide that the mercantile community of the larger cities realized that employees worked better with time out to play ball. Anthropologist Margaret Mead seemed to agree when she said that man must work, then take some recreation so that he might work again. Thus workers' free time would no longer be free. It had to be purposeful: it must prepare them for more work.

With labor now considered a "factor of production" instead of a group of people, employers tried to regulate employees' total environment, including their leisure. As William Tolman expressed it in his 1909 book, *Social Engineering*, "industrial betterment" is "a cold business proposition and is undertaken commonly to get the best results out of labor." Baseball, therefore, was no longer considered just a game. It became a device to improve production.

The idea of industrial betterment for the sake of profits received support from other groups like the National Association of Manufacturers, the National Civic Federation, the YMCA, and the Playground Association. The National Civic Federation, noted Bruno Ramirez in a 1978 book on labor relations, helped employers implement and improve their welfare programs by providing a clearinghouse where they could compare problems and consider solutions. An NCF survey in 1914 showed that 2,500 employers had adopted welfarism. A few critics, like Thorstein Veblen, attacked welfare capitalism, and the Y did point out that welfare programs imposed from above produced poorer results than did those in which workers shared responsibility. And although successful athletic teams could result in a sense of pride even in nonparticipating employees, preferential treatment for athletes sometimes brought resentment on the part of the rest of the work force.

To reduce such resentment and bring employees into the planning of recreation, industries sponsored the formation of athletic associations similar to Pullman's. Many large firms, such as Ford, General Electric, the Metropolitan Life Association, and the Wanamaker department store instituted such sport associations. But even if employees participated in running an association, owners of course kept control. Elbert Gary, who organized United States Steel, baldly told his associates in a company meeting to

> make the Steel Corporation a good place for [employees] to work and live. . . .
> give them playgrounds and parks . . . , and recreation, treating the whole thing
> as a business proposition, drawing the line so that you are just and generous,
> and yet at the same time keeping your position and permitting others to keep
> theirs, retaining the control and management of your affairs, keeping the whole
> thing in your own hands.

Another United States Steel officer, quoted by Ramirez, declared early in the century that welfarism reduced employee turnover and made for a stable work force. In the town Judge Gary founded (Gary, Indiana), the new school superintendent, William Wirt, built a curriculum designed to condition youth to this sort of industrial system. According to Hal Lawson's and Alar Lipping's study of the Gary Plan, it was a work-study-play system developed in part around the idea that sports should be incorporated into the industrial system.

Good citizenship also became part of the rationale for welfare capitalism in an era when the employee population was shifting from the native white Americans of the 1890s to the immigrants of the early 1900s. Buckeye Steel Casting Company of Columbus, Ohio, built a baseball field in 1903 on land next to the plant and took up welfarism in part to ensure that employees would develop into "loyal, patriotic Americans imbued with middle-class values," as explained forthrightly in Mansel Blackford's company history.

Industrialists frankly admitted fear of unionism as a prime reason for welfare capitalism. After a series of strikes and customer complaints, John Patterson of National Cash Register in Dayton, Ohio, embarked in the 1900s on a series of "loyalty-building" projects that included recreation. In 1904 he opened a large athletic field for baseball and other sports. The following year an NCR representative said that welfare work had proved very effective in combating workers' attempts to restrict output. In Dayton, employers like NCR fought unionism both with welfare capitalism and by requiring that a new employee present a card from a previous employer. When unionism became an imminent danger at International Harvester's McCormick works, according to Robert Ozanne, the company improved its athletic and baseball fields but cancelled a planned employee recreation association and retained control of all welfare activities.

Baseball, the supreme American game, seemed an ideal instrument for gaining the objectives of industrial paternalism and the cooperation needed in industrial work because it combined teamwork with individualism, each team member having been trained to do a specialized task for the common good. Baseball, therefore, usually starred in company athletics. Baseball could also give the impression of comradeship with the boss. Simon Mandel, head of Mandel Brothers Clothing Company in Chicago, played ball with the company team, an aggregation that was considered semipro and took part in a Sunday league. In Philadelphia, Joseph B. McCall, president of the Philadelphia Electric Company, according to the company history, in 1910 pitched a victorious game for the Executives against the District Managers. Many departments of that company formed baseball teams playing on leased grounds under the auspices of the company athletic association.

"Wholesomeness" was thought to be an additional virtue of company ball play. The Cleveland Recreation Survey regarded as "wholesome" the experiences of some individual employees it named who played ball with their shop teams in the early part of the century, even entitling its report *Wholesome Citizens and Spare Time*.

Encouragement of ball playing by employers meant the eventual development of players so skilled that they became professionals. Dixie Walker began work at age fifteen for the Tennessee Coal and Iron Company in Birmingham, Alabama, which boasted a strong company league. Walker, who played for the Open Hearth team, took part in the game to decide the company championship. To boost its power the team took on Ben Chapman, then with the Furnace Tenders team, and won the championship. The two men became friends as well as big leaguers. Casey Stengel, later a player on various big-league clubs and eventually a famous manager for the New York Yankees, received $3.00 a game as pitcher for the Parisian Cloak Company in Kansas City while he was still in high school, noted his biographer, Robert Creamer. George Moriarty, player, umpire, and manager, was playing for the Oliver Typewriter Company at Woodstock, Illinois, at age seventeen when scouted by a big-league manager.

Many other jobs gave players a chance to develop their ball-playing skills. Grover Cleveland Alexander, soon to be an outstanding major-league pitcher, played baseball in 1906 for a telephone company, where he worked as a lineman, although the company fired Alexander after he failed to return to work following the baseball season. Rube Marquard pitched for an ice cream company in Cleveland at age seventeen; there he got $15.00 for his work, along with all the ice cream he could eat, plus $10.00 when he pitched for the company team. Eddie Cicotte and Chief Meyer both played in the "copper leagues," baseball organizations set up for the operatives in copper mining country. Earl Well, pitcher for the Ravenscroft mining town team in Tennessee around 1917, said later, "I was born to the coal mines and escaped only because of my ability to play ball."

Railroad teams developed many big-league players: Johnny Wauhap (Warhop), Charles "Butch" Smith, Phil Douglas, and Oscar Vitt all played on railroad teams, each with a different line. In 1907 a league of railroad teams operated in Ohio, with five lines and an express company as members. Its president, W.W. Martin, wrote Garry Herrmann, president of the Cincinnati Reds, trying to get him to buy ten tickets to a vaudeville entertainment for the league's benefit. Trolley leagues formed, too; a group of them around St. Louis put together a sort of superleague in 1909 and 1910.

In a small community the town team might be company backed. Saloonkeepers (and few towns suffered from a shortage of saloons) took the lead in sponsoring teams, thereby extending to small communities the lasting relationship in major-league cities between baseball and beer. Sponsors advertised their businesses on the backs of uniforms, and names like "Kentucky Taylor Whiskey," "Hop Gold Team," and "M.J.B. Coffee" soon decorated uniform shirts.

Some large industrialists extended their paternalism to the families of workers by providing children's playgrounds.* In the early part of the twentieth century, as Stuart Brandes's study, *American Welfare Capitalism*,

*See above, Chapter 6.

shows, United States Steel operated more than 125 such playgrounds. The National Tube Company provided playgrounds, too, according to Professor Joel Spring. So did Patterson at National Cash Register and also The Solvay Process Company in Syracuse, New York.

Some of the most elaborate development of baseball took place in the company towns early in the century, for despite Pullman's failure other such towns arose. Milton Hershey broke ground for his chocolate factory in Pennsylvania in 1903, completing it in 1905, and in 1906 the town name changed to Hershey. Unlike George Pullman, Hershey did not own the employees' homes, but he did help them buy their own. A Hershey baseball team played as early as 1906, as information published by the town explains, and in 1907 a new athletic field opened, featuring a baseball game.

In New York state Walter W. Law adopted the same policy at his 6,000-acre company town named Briarcliff, encouraging and helping employees to buy their own homes. Baseball, played there on graded grounds in a wire-screened grandstand, represented the chief diversion at Briarcliff Manor. Unlike the situation in many large industries, baseball players at Law's company town got no extra pay, and Law reimbursed the team only for expenses of its few away games.

Mill towns continued to furnish examples of extensive company ball. At Ludlow, Massachusetts, the town and the athletic association had by early in the new century become so intertwined that the village recreation association used the company's athletic field and the company athletic association was opened to all who lived and worked in the town. "Labor troubles," commented Edward Titus in *World's Work* in 1905, "have been remarkably few, and the workers are satisfied."

Southern textile mills, as shown in a study by William H. Phillips in the *Journal of Economic History*, invested in welfare activities in order to create a corps of dependable workers and thus lower turnover costs. Team sports proved popular at Dixie Mills, in La Grange, Georgia, and at Eagle and Phoenix Mills in Columbus. Carolina textile mills in particular developed hot baseball competition among mills in the same area. In Greensboro, North Carolina, the White Oak Cotton Mill and the Proximity Mill played each other and teams from neighboring towns on ball fields provided at every mill. The mills around Greenville, South Carolina—Pelzer, Brandon Mills, and Victor Mills in Greer—soon competed for players among their young employees. Joe Jackson, one of the many children employed at Brandon Mills, joined the mill team at age thirteen. As Donald Gropman's biography of Jackson explains, players at Brandon got $2.50 for an afternoon game, and owners often gave players choice jobs and let them practice on company time. But money collected when the team passed the hat, plus coins thrown to Jackson when he hit his home runs, enabled him to net as much as $30.00 a Saturday. In a poor-paying industry like textiles, where only about three percent of the workers belonged to unions, this amounted to more than a month's salary.

Unions, like industrialists, themselves employed baseball to engender loyalty. In Cincinnati in 1908 when the steamfitters and the plumbers tied for first place in the Trades Union Baseball League, the steamfitters' manager even tried to obtain the use of the local professional club's park for the playoff. No union sponsored more enthusiastic ball play than the newspaper typographers' union, which in 1906 formed a league called the Union Printers' International Baseball Federation. That year the typographers' Boston *Globe* squad traveled to New York to play the team of the New York *American*, but lost. In 1907 the Boston players invited the New Yorkers to New England, where the winner of the New York Morning Newspaper League defeated the Boston team and carried home a trophy donated by John I. Taylor, owner of the local American League club. Then in 1908 the typographers took the next step, putting together an eight-club league—Boston, Philadelphia, Washington, Cincinnati, St. Louis, New York, Chicago, and Pittsburgh—and planning to meet yearly in alternate cities for a week-long tournament. Boston took the 1908 championship at New York. Then Garry Herrmann, himself a former typographer, offered a trophy to the next winner. New York won it in 1909 at Chicago and Washington, and Chicago took it in 1911 at St. Louis.

White-collar workers, such as insurance clerks, newspaper writers, and government officials, continued their interest in baseball in the early part of the century. Congressmen Nicholas Longworth and John K. Tener (later president of the National League) played in a Washington game in 1909 when Republicans defeated Democrats and Speaker Joe Cannon cheered them on. Actors and vaudeville players developed well-known teams, and in 1908 a four-club Actor's Baseball League included the White Rats, the Vaudeville Club, the Red Mills (after a popular musical show), and the George M. Cohans. Tom Clarke and Jean Dubuc, both soon to be Cincinnati Reds, and George Chalmers, shortly to join the Philadelphia Nationals, belonged, according to *Sporting News*. Musicians in the band of John Philip Sousa, the composer, formed a team, as did some Victor artists, who reportedly engaged in impromptu games between concert dates.

As a result of all this industrial and business play, cities, towns, and large corporations early in the century formed baseball leagues representing trades, industries, or factories. New York had a Transportation League, an eight-club Factories League, and a fourteen-firm Commercial League. In Brooklyn, the Factory, Transportation, and Commercial leagues operated. Chicago swarmed with 60 commercial, mercantile, bankers', wholesale, manufacturing, and stockyard leagues. Detroit's Automobile League included baseball teams from Ford, Packard, De Luxe, Aerocar, Morgan-Wright, and Northern. In Baltimore five large corporations combined in a league with stringent rules, an eligibility list, and even a reserve clause to guard against stealing players from each other. A business and manufacturing league in Columbus, Ohio, called the Saturday Afternoon League, likewise inserted a reserve clause into its player contracts. Even small Warren, Ohio, ran a league of factory teams. Some such baseball leagues, as in Fort Wayne, Indiana, had company backing; others operated fairly independently.

In the second decade of the century industrial baseball felt the impact of a new interpretation of leisure: commentators on American life, instead of regarding leisure as an asset, still considered it a problem, although of a different sort. Critics saw Americans as victims of "spectatoritis" and in need of instruction in the proper use of recreation. Increased leisure, some said, led to more crime and less participation in recreation, with a consequent growth of commercial recreation, including places of ill repute.

Well might critics rail against spectatoritis, for many aficionados of factory baseball, instead of playing it, attended weekend factory games in large numbers. Some workers had gained a day or a half-day off Saturdays, and it seemed that on weekends some people went amusement-mad. A Chicago park commissioner believed that young folks of the day had "substituted passive pleasure for the active play and recreation" their parents had enjoyed in youth. A Pittsburgh journalist, observing local workers on their free half-holiday, reproached,

> They have work to do—for the most part—and they should be sleeping or eating. But they would rather do without sleep or without a square meal deliberately eaten, than miss a minute of a ball game . . . even if they go on their "night turn" in mill or factory minus the rest that should be theirs.

Thousands of workers turned out for weekend factory games. Plants in the steel mill towns of Pennsylvania held their matches on Sundays, although in Wilkes Barre ministers objected to Sabbath ball, so at least for a time Sunday games had to be called off. In Homestead, Pennsylvania, the Business Men's League could play late afternoons, since their work day was not so long as that of factory employees. In Cleveland the team of the White Auto Company played Saturdays, even though some of its players worked the night shift and some the day. At General Electric in Nela Park, of the same city, the plant operated an after-work Twilight League of from four to eight teams. Textile Field at the great Amoskeag Mill in Manchester, New Hampshire, seated 4,000 spectators. According to the *Amoskeag Bulletin* of 1919 the plant's "varsity" games "were well patronized by fans." When the team won an eleven-inning thriller for the 1919 manufacturing league championship against McElwain, a shoe company, a crowd of 2,500 cheered. Big games between the United States Rubber teams of Millville, Massachusetts, and the rival Blackstone Company attracted as many as 3,500. At Anaconda Copper Mining Company in Montana, two baseball leagues used the company grounds, in the heart of town, four evenings a week, and fully 5,000, many from the surrounding countryside, saw one Anaconda game, described in *Playground* in 1916.

Other criticisms of company athletics in general and company baseball in particular reflected the reality of the overblown athletic development in many large industrial firms, where the varsity nine far outweighed inter-departmental teams in importance and employee interest. Moreover, sports news often dominated all news in company organs, often much exceeding the space and emphasis allotted to employees' production records. Many industrial "varsity" teams became semipro and vied in leagues with similar industrial semipro teams.* Owners padded teams with college stars and other ringers, gave soft jobs or part-time work to athletes, and spent thousands of dollars to equip and maintain teams, as described later by A.H. Wyman, Director of Welfare Work for Carnegie Steel, in the proceedings of the Athletic Research Society.

The Playground Association, responding to critics of industrial athletics, devoted more and more space in its publication to activities suitable for industrial recreation, implying that the intramural, nonprofessional baseball leagues it described represented praiseworthy efforts and were preferable to the development of semipro teams. The Association urged corporations, as Dominic Cavallo noted in his thesis, to build recreation facilities and permit employees to use them during the work day, hoping that such recreation would contribute to industrial peace and productivity.

But baseball earned praise as well as criticism for its domination of the industrial workplace. Ida Tarbell, a leader of the "muckrakers," in particular extolled factory baseball. She did not seem to recognize that many employees were spectators rather than players. Baseball, she declared in a 1915 article, was "easily the favorite factory game," and "It is a poor management indeed, these days, and a thoroughly soured [work] force which does not support departmental nines." In a subsequent article Tarbell asserted that so vital had the athletic field become that "no intelligent employer of labor familiar with advanced practices thinks of building a new shop in factory or town without some provision for an out-of-doors field or an indoor equivalent." In fact, the factory athletic field "is coming to be almost as much a matter of course as the sanitary drinking fountain."

Tarbell recognized that an owner established these fields for the firm's benefit and found them "skillful advertising," but their chief advantage, she thought, remained "the health, efficiency, and social pleasure of the workers." Moreover, she stated, "What the game [baseball] is doing for health and sociability in American industries cannot be estimated." Tarbell also approved of favoritism for athletes in employment. Many owners, she said, consider baseball skill "a sound reason for employing a man, and why not, if it is considered a sound reason for admitting a boy to college?" Thus she

*See Chapters 17 and 18.

condoned hiring accomplished players before other workers on the basis of comparison with the college abuse known as athletic scholarships.

Jane Addams, the social reformer who pioneered the settlement house movement, joined in the praise for factory baseball. To her the sight of city factory workers playing or cheering their baseball team in a game against another factory showed the power of recreation to bring together all classes of society. She thought "organizing work and failing to organize play" was "stupid."

Other praise for company paternalism in sponsoring athletics, especially baseball, blossomed in such serious journals as the *Annals of the American Academy, Industrial Management, Industrial Arts Journal, Journal of Applied Psychology,* and *American Physical Education Review,* as well as in popular periodicals like *American City, Outlook, Recreation,* and *Baseball Magazine.* House organs naturally boosted the game, like *The White Albatross* (later called the *White-Book*), published by the White Auto Company in Cleveland; the *Amoskeag Bulletin,* put out by the Amoskeag Mill; the *Russell Company Bulletin,* published by a textile mill of that name, with headquarters in Boston; and *Fire,* the official magazine of the Chicago Fire Department. Laudatory company histories acclaimed industries for promoting baseball, like George W. Browne's 1915 book on Amoskeag and others devoted to John H. Patterson of National Cash Register Company in Dayton, Ohio.

As Tarbell observed, an interest in playing baseball, instead of being a detriment to a job applicant as it had been during the baseball fever of the 1860s, now proved a decided advantage. By 1917 many firms, said C.B. Lord of the Wagner Electric Company of St. Louis, hired men for their athletic abilities and kept them for the same reason. Baseball could also mean job promotion. In the teens, for instance, Charley Root of Middleton, Ohio, later a pitcher for the Chicago National League club, took a job as patternmaker at the American Rolling Mill and pitched for the maintenance department's team Thursdays and Saturdays, but after three years his baseball skill got him an offer from the company's engine works at Hamilton, Ohio, where his pay rose to $50.00 a week plus $35.00 per game pitched. Like Tarbell, C.B. Lord thought there was no reason athletic teams could not help companies as ads, just as they did schools. He cited his own organization, claiming that a company representative found that recruitment ads mentioning athletics at Wagner "received five times as many answers" as other ads the company ran for the same kind of jobs. A 1917 article in the *Journal of Applied Psychology* approved of the company spirit stimulated by celebration of athletic victories because it caused "an immediate increase in the number and quality of applicants for jobs." As a result of so many amateur players being hired to play ball for companies, remarked *Sporting News* in a 1915 editorial, most supposedly-amateur baseball men had been "taken care of with jobs" and in wearing the signs of their sponsors on the front and back of their uniforms had all become "sandwich men."

Companies no doubt pampered baseball players. Amoskeag owners, as related by Tamara Hareven in *Family Time*, enticed ex-professionals to work in the mill, assigning them to soft jobs and corporation housing in the overseers' section. Hack Wilson, later a National League outfielder, performed only "nominal" duties in a silk mill where he worked in his youth and where what he did on the baseball diamond counted as more important. A former worker in the coal mining country of Harlan County, Kentucky, recalled:

> The companies would employ men who could play baseball and could do something in the coal camp, and I'll have to admit that many of these jobs were more or less what we would call "made jobs." There was a great rivalry with baseball teams, competition became great and there would be pressure put on the officials: "Why don't you hire so-and-so, he's a good player?" and it was done. I can remember when Drift, Kentucky, had a baseball team that hardly had a native on it. It was equally true of Wheelright, Weeksbury, or any other coal camp.

At the many Carnegie Steel plants that featured varsity baseball teams, some professional players not even employed in the mills bolstered the teams—and caused trouble in the company. But Tarbell praised the Steel Corporation for spending thousands annually for the upkeep of baseball teams. Steel Corporation workers, however, made substantial financial contributions of their own to the maintenance of these teams, as did other employees. At Wagner Electric, too, the men and the company went half and half on uniforms and other expenses. At Brown and Bigelow, a carpet factory near St. Paul, Minnesota, an employees' club furnished all baseball equipment out of the treasury, which accumulated from funds employees had to contribute, since all employees belonged to the club by virtue of being workers at Brown and Bigelow. Employees of the German-American Button Company of Rochester, New York, too, had to support the company baseball team through enforced membership in an employees' club. Not until the thirties did some unions object successfully to enforced contributions to company athletic associations. The Southern Pacific Railroad, on the other hand, paid baseball players' expenses, including those for away games; but to the umpires it gave only a pass on the line.

Owners' expenses in maintaining athletic fields could be offset by charging admission to ball games. Endicott Johnson Shoe Company in New York State spent $30,000.00 just to maintain its various athletic fields, but in the Lestershire stadium, at least, the company charged admission to games, although the owner donated proceeds of Sunday games to charity after coming under fire from Sabbatarians. The Actors' Fund of America charged admission to its 1919 game at the Polo Grounds in which the Thespians, with

Mike Donlin, sometime actor and former pro ball player, defeated the Song-writers, thus earning $15,000.00 for the Actors' Fund. Owners' expenses might include prizes, too. Yearly athletic awards in the steel mill at Home-stead, Pennsylvania, totalled more than $250.00, at a time when mill hands were making only six to eight dollars a week.

At the Illinois Steel Company in Gary, Indiana, rivalry even among in-terdepartmental teams reached such a pitch that rules against imported players and other forms of professionalism became urgent by 1914, according to the local YMCA secretary. The national Y, incidentally, often organized interfactory leagues, with the financial help of the corporations. Between 1916 and 1921 Buckeye Steel Casting Company in Columbus, Ohio, ac-cording to the company history, contributed $20,000.00 to the local YMCA and YWCA. Some industries paid for baseball in which none of its employees took part: they hired big-league teams to put on exhibition games for workers. Willys Overland of Toledo, Ohio, hired the Detroit Tigers and the New York Giants to play each other. The Amoskeag Company brought the Boston Red Sox up to Manchester, New Hampshire, but the Red Sox did play factory workers: an all-star aggregation from the local factory league.

Company teams instilled pride in the hearts of nonplaying employees, who talked admiringly of the company baseball players. When the Amoskeag team won the championship of the local Manufacturers' League, each player received the gift of a traveling bag. At White Auto, the team's record of 28 won and 4 lost in 1914 "is a source of pride to the whole White organization," the company organ announced. Interest reached such heights at White Auto in 1915 that employees organized a Rooters' Club that attended each game and gave enthusiastic support. No wonder: that year the team featured Tommy Atkins, former pitcher for the Philadelphia American League Club. At Endicott Johnson, George F. Johnson purposely used baseball teams to instill company pride and "spirit," sometimes called "patriotism" but really meaning company loyalty.

Promotion of baseball could especially be used to counter the potential penetration of unionism, for example in the steel industry, where low wages, long hours, and the open shop prevailed. Andrew Carnegie, according to Robert F. Wheeler in the *Journal of Contemporary History*, established varsity baseball and football teams at the Bessemer works in Braddock, Pennsylvania, after a violent strike there. Welfarism did not always work, however. The strong paternalistic program at Amoskeag designed to instill loyalty, curb labor unrest, and prevent unionism, as Tamara Hareven and Randolph Langenbach observe in their study of Amoskeag, did not prevent the major strike of 1922 that originated from pay cuts and a longer work week. At Ludlow, Colorado, striking miners played baseball on their own even while out on strike, just before the massacre in which the militia killed about fifty men, breaking the union.

Factory baseball may have had a hand in integrating recent immigrants into American society. Amoskeag's company history declared that the Textile Club, which sponsored sports teams, aided in the adjustment of employees, which had formerly been "people at home" and now were "aliens from strange lands." At the United States Steel works in Homestead, Pennsylvania, the worker population represented two waves of immigrants, stated Margaret Byington's 1910 history of the mill town, first the Teutonic and Celtic and later the Slavic, but these differences seem not to have affected athletic team participation. The only noticeable characteristic of Homestead baseball players is that most were young. Among the forty teams of miners at the Frick Coke Company, Connelsville, Pennsylvania, "It is doubtful if there are ever more than two or three men on a team who speak the same tongue, but that seems not to interfere either with their efficiency or their enthusiasm," Ida Tarbell marveled.

Efficiency, of course, remained the business ideal. The *Amoskeag Bulletin*, in commenting on the formation of the Textile Club, pointed out that "The principal object in all forms of business is the search for efficiency." How reminiscent both of Taylorism in 1900 and Robert Wiebe's theme of the "search for order." One sign of this search is the formation in Akron, Ohio, in August of 1918 of a governing body, the American Industrial Athletic Association, to foster and oversee industrial athletics. Prominent members were largely midwestern: Firestone, Goodrich, International Harvester, Carnegie Steel, National Cash Register, Standard Parts of Nela Park, and Clothcraft (Joseph & Feiss Company) of Cleveland. Industrial sport was by this time so embedded that Spalding's 1919 guide devoted thirty-three pages to "Industrial Athletics," most of it baseball. One of the national surveys of industry found only what Ida Tarbell had already asserted: baseball was the most popular physical activity in industry.

In the late teens a national trend toward organizing a city's or a town's industrial baseball leagues into a city federation became noticeable. Some such city organizations included other sports, too, such as indoor ball and basketball. Oakland, California; Jackson, Michigan; New Haven, Connecticut; Paterson, New Jersey; Cleveland, Ohio; Lawrence, Massachusetts; Carlisle, Pennsylvania; and Milwaukee, Wisconsin all contained such superleagues. Milwaukee's city championship of 1915 included the early baseball exploits of Joe Hauser, who became a home run hitter in the minor leagues; an injury destroyed his major-league career. As a boy Hauser pitched for the only uniformed team on Milwaukee's west side, the Zunker Comers, backed by a saloonkeeper named Zunker, who after each game gave sixteen-year-old Joe fifty cents a game and all the soda pop he wanted. At the end of the season the Zunkers challenged a team known as the Goodlows for the city championship—and lost. But Joe could content himself with knowing that the only other game he lost with the Zunkers was one with the West Point A.C., with Rooster Keitenbeil pitching.

Occupational or craft team leagues formed, too. The Cincinnati leather concerns paid Garry Herrmann $50.00 to rent the Reds' park for their annual game on Decoration Day of 1911. And the New York *Times* printed the 1913 standings of the Building Trades Industrial League clubs. The national organization of baseball-playing typographers not only continued playing in the new century, it issued its own periodical, *The Typo-Athlete*, published in Boston, and added Denver and Indianapolis to its league. After each game, both victors and vanquished drank from the perpetual challenge cup donated by Garry Herrmann.

Company-organized baseball teams and other recreation, far from falling victim to World War I, picked up momentum during the war. Industrialists, backed by the government, stepped up welfare capitalism in order to heighten production, prevent possible work stoppages caused by labor discontent, and maintain maximum worker efficiency. To aid war workers the government pressed into service the same organizations it used to provide recreation for soldiers.* The Playground Association also arranged for recreation leaders to serve war workers' communities. In mid-1918 the War Camp Community Service began expanding recreation facilities in towns with new war plants, and before the armistice the WCCS had organized recreation in about fifty districts. The YMCA, too, through its industrial department, provided recreation for industrial workers.

W. Irving Clark, a physician who served with the Red Cross in World War I and was a company surgeon both before and after it, described the way industries adopted college practices during the war in order to spice competition, organizing workers into athletic associations, hiring athletic directors and coaches, and awarding sweaters with factory letters. The interest aroused by such devices relieved the tedium and fatigue of overtime mass production work, Clark declared, but he admitted that wartime industrial athletics were "overdeveloped" and that large companies spent "extravagant sums" on competition—"more than it was worth."

The paternalism of Goodyear Tire and Rubber Company in Akron, Ohio, showed how extensive wartime industrial recreation could be. Akron's phenomenal wartime growth meant that its city recreation facilities, like parks, were overtaxed, so, according to an article in *Playground* in 1916, the company management provided recreation for no fewer than 16,000 employees on various shifts, as well as for their children, on fifty acres of company land. Goodyear offered facilities for many sports and other activities, including a baseball diamond with seats for 9,000, and set up a City Industrial League for baseball and other sports. It also furnished a trained physical director and two trained assistants, a male and a female, along with a superintendent of grounds.

In the munitions, steel, and shipyard industries particularly, athletic rivalry among companies gave rise to corruption that sometimes reached scandalous proportions. The steel industry was the first source of industrial

_____

*See below, Chapter 21.

trouble over athletics. Because professional baseball players had either to find war work or face the possibility of being drafted, many sought refuge in the large steel and shipyard companies.* The team roster for 1918 of the Reading, Pennsylvania, Steel Casting Company included Babe Ruth and Del Pratt of the New York Yankees, Lefty Williams and Joe Jackson of the Chicago White Sox, Frank Schulte, recently of the Washington Club, Rogers Hornsby of the St. Louis National League team, and players from the Brooklyn club as well as the New York Giants. "From this line-up," boasted the Steel Casting Company's vice president, M.G. Moore, "you will realize that we had the best industrial Base Ball team in the United States."

That statement might have been disputed by the Bethlehem Steel Company of Pennsylvania. With some pro players moving from team to team, at one time Bethlehem's Lebanon branch had twelve professionals, including Ruth and Hornsby. Its Steelton plant had such well-known players as the pitcher Eddie Plank of the Philadelphia Athletics; its Bethlehem team included Jeff Tesreau of the Giants; its Fore River club had Dutch Leonard, pitcher of the Boston American League Club, and Al Mamaux, Pittsburgh pitcher; and its Wilmington team listed Joe Jackson. E.G. Grace, the company president, gave gold watches to each member of the Steelton team, which won the championship among its various plants. Working and playing ball with Bethlehem steel in 1919, Jimmy Wilson, later a big-league catcher, earned between $300.00 and $400.00 a month for his work, plus $30.00 a game playing ball two or three times a week—and still more playing for an upstate team Sundays, on the side. At not quite twenty years of age, he said later, "I was making more money than some bank presidents"—almost $1,000.00 a month.

When it became clear that the steel companies were luring big-league players away from the majors with high salaries, President Ban Johnson of the American League went to Charles Schwab, president of Bethlehem Steel, to protest. Schwab claimed he was unaware of the problem and would remedy it. Meanwhile, in the spring of 1918 the government, searching for an executive to see that warships would be built quickly, came up with none other than Charles Schwab, naming him director of the Emergency Fleet Corporation, a government agency. Schwab moved to stimulate enthusiasm and rivalry among shipyard workers, offering prizes to the best producers and introducing competitions in riveting.

During the war shipyards rivaled steel companies in hunger for baseball teams of spectacular professionalism. The yards on both coasts hired any big leaguers they could, along with prospective big leaguers. On the West Coast the McCormick Shipyards of St. Helens, Oregon, employed eighteen-year-old Willie Kamm, later an outstanding big-league third baseman, to work and play company ball, but he soon left for San Francisco and another

*See *Baseball: The Golden Age*, pp. 258–251.

shipyard company, the Union Iron Works, to play on its team. So good were shipyard ball clubs in the Northwest that in 1919 Organized Baseball admitted a four-team league of shipyard players as a Class B league in the National Association. *Sporting Life* explained that the shipyard clubs would play only the last three days of each week so that the players would lose only one day from their jobs. The men would earn both their weekly pay as shipyard workers and extra compensation for playing ball. They would also be signed to regular baseball contracts, the newspaper said, with rules prohibiting signing after August 5 in order to prevent teams from being "loaded up" near the end of the season. Members of the winning team would get five percent of the receipts of the final series.

Ball players on East Coast shipyard teams also did well financially, earning as much as $500.00 a week. Shipyard teams in cities like New York, Newark, Baltimore, Boston, and Wilmington built strong aggregations containing professionals and other skilled players. In 1919 the Federal Shipbuilding Company at Kearny, New Jersey, near Newark, boasted seven members of the New York Giants and had even hired the Giants' black trainer, Ed Mackall. The Harland Shipbuilding Company in Delaware employed a White Sox battery plus Joe Jackson and seven other major leaguers. In 1918 Harland defeated the Standard Shipbuilding Company, which had its own long roster of major leaguers and had won the championship of a New York Shipyard Baseball League, thus deciding the so-called championship of industrial ball.

Paying big-league players to play ball for the shipyards did not sit well with many regular shipyard workers, who saw the athletes given nominal jobs and being excused from hard work while they carried the load. An article by F.C. Lane in the August 1918 *Baseball Magazine* commented on the luring of professional players of draft age to war work in steel and shipbuilding companies ostensibly to work but actually to play on professional teams. He thought the move unfair to both professional club owners and to the government, yet he also felt that the players should not be blamed for accepting the jobs, implying, although not stating outright, that the companies were at fault. *Baseball Magazine* itself defended the players after the war, claiming that most of those who sought shipyard employment did so not to avoid military service but to accede to frequent requests of the government to choose this form of employment because they had dependents and had already been classified as deferred.

An investigation, not entirely unbiased, by the vice-president of the Emergency Fleet Corporation, described by Professor Eugene Murdock, proved to the investigator's own satisfaction that most professional ball players gave the government a full measure of work, praising baseball as a fine recreation for shipyard workers. But in September of 1918, 2,000 shipyard workers struck against favored treatment for ball players. A hurried investigation found complaints to be exaggerated and that individual abuses had been corrected. The strike ended in a day, but criticism of "shipyard slackers" did not stop until the war ended.

Wartime workers' baseball affected another group that one would hardly think of as being susceptible: the Russians. In 1919, just after Russia surrendered to Germany, American railroad engineers, along with YMCA and Red Cross representatives, made up part of the force of 8,000 Americans entering Siberia through Vladivostok, in part to help Czech troops escape. These Americans worked along the route of the Trans-Siberian Railroad, playing ball at Harbin, their field headquarters. Russian youths, exposed to so much baseball, took to it, especially since it resembled *lapta*, a game of their own, and a decade later baseball still enjoyed popularity in that city.

16

BUSINESS PREFERS BALL PLAYERS

From post–World War I to about the mid-twenties, welfare capitalism reached its greatest heights. Industrialists still found it effective in staving off organized labor. Seeking to consolidate their position, large and stable firms, in addition to offering athletic fields and sponsoring athletic teams, co-opted employees with theatres, bowling alleys, cafeterias, and sun parlors as well as old-age pension plans and profit-sharing plans. Unionism declined in the 1920s as many strikes failed, and owners of large corporations gathered support for their nationwide drive for the "open shop," euphemistically called "the American plan," a term inferring that opponents of the open shop were unAmerican. Strikes failed partly because of the courts' readiness to grant injunctions against them.

Welfare capitalism held sway in southern mill towns in particular, where the mill owners not only owned the workers' houses, they also supplied many other components of life, especially social outlets. A commentator in the *American Mercury* in 1925 professed himself amazed at the amount of "welfare work" carried on in southern company towns. "Not merely lodging, but clubrooms, drug stores, YMCA buildings, churches, and funeral parlors are sometimes supplied by the mills. Teachers of the Bible, boxing, and aesthetic dancing are on the company pay-roll." The owners, the writer ascertained, believed that they were public benefactors. Employees, who doubtless would rather have had decent wages, recognized the owners' "good intentions" and "try to be grateful," the researcher declared. A survey of North Carolina plants made in 1926 showed that most of them contributed to the support of churches; 40 offered group insurance plans, 40 employed community workers; 28 supplemented school incomes—and 127 supported baseball teams. In other words, the mill owners controlled a feudalistic system in which they hired and fired clergy, social workers, and mill hands if they strayed from the views of the establishment.

With the further decline in the work week for most employees to about forty-six hours, the literature on "the problem of leisure" increased markedly in the twenties, and concerned intellectuals held international conferences in 1924 and 1930 to discuss it, but the conception of leisure as a difficulty to be overcome was giving way to its definition as an opportunity for "self-expression," an E.R.A. Seligman of Columbia University put it, or "self-investment," as Joffre Dumazedier expressed it, or the chance to do "some lovely thing for its own lovable sake," as Erwin Edman explained it in *Harpers Magazine* in 1928. Probably, the mass of workers seldom cast their minds towards these individualistic views of leisure, for in the "Middletown" of 1925 Robert and Helen Lynd noticed that leisure was "becoming more passive, more formal, more organized, more mechanized, and more commercialized." Commentators like Clarence Rainwater and James Truslow Adams noticed that commercial amusement dominated Americans' leisure hours. Baseball, as a prominent and popular business- and industry-sponsored activity, was part of this manipulation of workers' leisure.

Industrialists still believed in the benefits of recreation for keeping workers satisfied and thus blocking unions. William Butterworth, president of Deere and Company in Moline, Illinois, writing in *Nation's Business* in 1924, thought company recreation promoted "healthier citizenship" and increased efficiency. William B. Cornell in his 1928 textbook on industrial management opined that the worker with the opportunity for companionship in recreation and social life was unlikely to listen to "corner orators painting for him fancied wrongs."

Radical trade unions, however, especially the Industrial Workers of the World, flourished in the early twenties and recommended "direct action" (sabotage and the general strike). Industrialists, fearing "foreign radicalism"—the so-called red menace—and believing they needed to "Americanize" European immigrant workers, viewed recreation as a way to integrate workers into the community of interests they supposedly shared with owners. When industrial league scouts tempted major leaguers to leave their clubs and join industrial ball teams, they could and did give concerned big-league fans the excuse that in bringing excellent players into their plants to counter radical unionism, they were uplifting community spirit. According to *Sporting News*, industrial scouts rationalized their recruiting by asserting that they were merely using baseball to "suppress bolshevism."

Employers also believed recreation improved worker attendance. A 1924 survey of employee turnover, absenteeism, and days lost to accidents and illness at a textile mill claimed that the company's extensive recreation program cut all these figures by about two thirds. Since most company recreation came in the form of athletics, and since baseball dominated athletics, baseball could be considered the source of these perceived advantages to the company.

The Playground Association continued its support for company recreation, praising organized programs. The association's Howard Braucher asserted in 1922 that men engaging in "wholesome recreation . . . will render more efficient service [and] increase the industrial output. . . . " Industrialists could also obtain aid from the Amateur Athletic Union, which published a supportive pamphlet, "The Value of Athletics in American Industries." Employers gave a researcher preparing a master's thesis a summary of the benefits of industrial recreation that transformed recreation into a magic elixir far stronger than the potion of Dr. Dulcamara in "L'Elisir D'Amore." They declared that company recreation made workers come to the job "in good spirits," built cooperation, permitted workers to meet owners on equal terms, cut labor turnover, built physical strength, prepared "better citizens," made routine tasks enjoyable through "anticipation," and taught the character values of initiative, self-control, responsibility, fair play, team spirit, and loyalty, as well as ways to spend leisure.

How did industrialists administer and finance these vast recreation programs of the twenties? Some not only paid for all land, buildings, and athletic fields but also managed the entire program alone. Athletic expenses might be charged to a company's advertising budget. In other programs, as with Filene's Department Store in Boston, employees and owners managed the program jointly. Some employers, like the United Shoe Machine Company of Beverly, Massachusetts, which charged employees a dollar a year membership, financed recreation in large part and allowed workers to manage it. Others, like Marshall Field in Chicago, paid half the membership fee in all clubs. Some firms simply deducted the money to pay for recreation from employees' pay envelopes.

In the Ironbound District of Newark, New Jersey, a triangular section of the city bordered by railroad tracks on all sides and enclosing Newark's most important industrial plants as well as many workers' homes, employees paid $2.50 and their employers a matching $2.50 for recreation services that included baseball and other sports. The Strawbridge and Clothier Company of Philadelphia charged male employees a dollar and females fifty cents, a fee that also admitted them to all company baseball games. At the Norton Company the athletic expenses to the employer in one year amounted to about $34,000.00, but the workers contributed heavily for equipment and expenses of out-of-town trips by turning over gate money to the two athletic associations. A Metropolitan Life Insurance Company report declared that at most of the 67 firms it surveyed, employees usually paid half the cost of recreation, and in some they paid all expenses themselves. Thus the employees themselves helped pay for the device that assisted in staving off unionism.

Industrialists in large cities often secured help in covering expenses by appealing to city authorities. In Cleveland, Ohio, the Community Fund financed industrial ball in large measure. Owners could also find assistance in managing recreation programs from the YMCA and YWCA, so they might not have to pay sports leaders themselves.

Unionized labor generally opposed industrial recreation. The exception, the American Federation of Labor, indicated by its public statements its acquiescence in management's views of leisure and sport. One A.F. of L. vice-president, Matthew Woll, formed a management-labor sport organization, the Sportsmanship Brotherhood, ostensibly to foster and spread the spirit of sportsmanship throughout the world, as *Playground* announced in December of 1925, but, according to Goldman and Wilson, the Brotherhood really represented an effort to integrate the trade union movement with the political economy of the nation. *Literary Digest* the following year published the Brotherhood's "code," admonishing athletes to play fair and keep a clean mind in a healthy body. Besides Woll, members of the Sportsmanship Brotherhood's directorship included such conservative and pro-establishment figures as representatives of sports governing bodies like the National Collegiate Athletic Association, together with the chairman of General Electric, the vice-president of American Telephone and Telegraph, and New York's governor, Franklin Delano Roosevelt.

But Woll and the A.F. of L. represented only a small segment of labor; its view of the workplace had become outdated. It was still wedded to the idea of craft unions, thereby limiting its membership by requiring long apprenticeships. Mechanization was making old craft distinctions obsolete, and most welfare work centered on mass production industries outside the A.F. of L.'s purview. Other unions viewed welfarism differently. The Amalgamated Clothing Workers Union opposed industrial recreation as tending to shackle labor with gratitude and curtail labor's bargaining power. The 1924 repeal of wartime laws against Communists meant that the American Communist Party could organize openly, and it tried to form a workers' sports movement, but instead of concentrating on baseball it emphasized activities familiar to recent immigrants, like soccer and gymnastics. One of its publications, *Young Worker*, attacked giant nonunion corporations for setting up large sports programs as efforts to ensure working class loyalty to capitalism. The leftist Workers Sports League of America, proposing a labor sports movement free of company control and publishing its own periodical, *Sport Call*, also emerged in the late twenties.

Where unions became successful, as in the garment industry, a union like the International Ladies Garment Workers itself took over recreation. A slightly different organization, probably a cross-company union, formed in Flint, Michigan as the Industrial Mutual Association, which grew out of a benevolent society that employees themselves established in 1901 for sick workers and their families. By the late twenties the association had, with the help of donations by General Motors and others, become a workingmen's club with nearly 12,500 members owning an auditorium, gyms, and an athletic park with what researcher Rosalind Graham called a "splendid base ball diamond and seats for 3,000." Members paid fifteen cents dues every week, taken from their paychecks by local factory employers.

Organized athletics, especially baseball, became the centerpiece of industrial recreation programs because of the special benefits that industrialists believed they bestowed. In the twenties many employers cited teamwork in particular as an advantage of company athletics because of its presumed parallel with the cooperation needed for business efficiency. "We talk the language of the team," said the recreation director for Bell Telephone's Hawthorne Works near Chicago. "We believe this team spirit is fostered by athletics," and baseball "calls out the greatest interest." One year the Hawthorne Works' varsity won the championship of the industrial league that the Chicago Association of Commerce sponsored. The Hawthorne Works also supported interdepartmental baseball. Its recreation director believed that executives who played ball were better able to win employees' cooperation and understanding. The secretary of the Illinois Manufacturers' Association made the same point in 1924.

Commentators on industrial athletics in this period, among them writers in *International Labor Review* and the government's *Monthly Labor Review*, agreed that baseball remained the most popular sport. A 1926 government survey revealed that of 319 companies reporting, most listed one or more baseball teams playing at noon and after work. Some teams even played in concrete stadiums seating as many as 4,000. A French visitor to Chicago in 1921, writing in *Revue de Paris*, observed that factory athletic contests were "passionately attended and followed" and that workingmen and small-business men went to the athletic fields near their factories or in the public parks right after work and on Saturday.

Textile mills proved the number one sponsor of baseball among firms listed in the 1926 survey. Thirty-two of the companies reporting baseball were textile mills. Woollen mills in and around Passaic, New Jersey, competed with each other in a league, according to the Forstmann Woollen Company's house organ, *T.F. & H. News*, of December 1920. The American Woollen Company of Lawrence, Massachusetts, in its organ, *A W Employees Booster*, published copious amounts of news about mill baseball games among teams at its various plants. *The Booster's* descriptions of team standings in American Woollen's six-team twilight league at its Riverside Mill in Waterbury, Connecticut, included some written in this chummy tone:

> Charlie Noke of the Electrical Department is on the Worsted team. Charlie's team had to win or his wife, who is a great baseball fan and attends all the games, would not let him come in the house again and Charlie would have to sleep out with his Lizzie Ford. The Office team is playing good ball but this old vacation stuff hurts them badly, and Manager Kenyon has to go in once in a while and play himself and show the younger players up.

The Booster also published tidbits about baseball among teams at Assabet Mills in Maynard and Washington Mills in Lawrence, Massachusetts.

When employees at Bancroft Mills in Wilmington, Delaware, solicited donations for their Industrial League team, the company's organ announced, they got enough money to equip not only their main team but a junior team in another league. Bancroft Mills also supported interdepartmental teams and a women's league. At Whitinsville, Massachussetts, the Whitin Machine Works, through its organ, *The Whitin Spindle*, reported news of its team in the Industrial Triangle League against the other two league members, Hamilton Woollen Company and American Optical Company. The Whitin team also played baseball outside the league, including games with Chase Mills and the Draper Corporation. The Whitin Company entered another team in the six-club Blackstone Valley League and sponsored an interdepartmental league as well.

Employees of three woollen mills at East Douglas and Milbury, Massachusetts, all owned by Schuster & Hayward Company, played ball on a company field, but their baseball interest centered on a pro team that Walter E. Schuster hired to represent the company. Its games, most of them played at home in the company park at East Douglas, began at 5:15 P.M., and many workers who watched had supper at the park. Attendance at these games in 1928 averaged 4,300 paid admissions, which covered part of Schuster's operating costs. For important games Schuster added a player from the majors or minors. Once Schuster guaranteed Lefty Grove $300.00 plus ten dollars for every batter Grove struck out. He made $490.00 on the deal, so he must have fanned nineteen men!

Southern textile mills also continued their sponsorship of baseball. At Danville, Virginia, the Dan River Mills Company, as described in the company history, helped enlarge the Schoolville YMCA, which not only supported clubs and societies but trained athletic teams that collected many prizes and trophies. In Alabama the Lincoln Cotton Mill of Huntsville and nearby Merrimac and Dallas mills featured former professional and college players on their baseball teams.

A 1929 study of welfare work in North Carolina mill villages estimated that more than two-thirds of the Piedmont mill village companies sponsored baseball. Usually, the mill workers formed their own teams, then went to the office for aid and support. Such company backing, customary for at least three decades, began with furnishing bats and balls and expanded into supplying uniforms, which seemed necessary when small leagues formed during and after the World War. Mill companies kept fields in shape by collecting a small admission fee of a dime or fifteen cents, low enough for everyone to afford, and the whole community enjoyed and supported the team, sometimes with bake sales. Employment ads seeking workers who played ball had fallen off, the study added, although sometimes a mill did pay players above the normal wage scale. Few mill executives expressed any concern over problems caused by professionalizing industrial teams. They believed baseball promoted plant and village morale, and all spoke of their teams with pride. Some executives, in fact, let interest in baseball overcome their business acumen. In Roanoke, North Carolina, after a mill ball club lost $4,000.00 because of unusual amounts of rain, the owner, Sam Patterson, president of three local mills and "an ardent baseball enthusiast," made up the loss himself. Patterson often brought in a ringer at a hundred dollars a week to play in an important game, but admission for such games cost seventy-five cents or a dollar instead of the usual dime.

The steel industry persisted in the twenties with sponsorship of extensive recreation that included baseball teams in companies in the Midwest, New England, and the South. Until 1923 many steel workers still toiled twelve hours a day and even endured a seven-day week, so the owners used company recreation to offset this grueling regimen. The American Chain Company in Bridgeport, Connecticut, another steel company, supported a team mostly of major- and minor-league players who were given jobs by the company and played against minor-league and independent teams; bona fide employees of American Chain played in a league of their own. In Middletown, Ohio, the engine works of the American Rolling Mill Company in 1920 reportedly included five star athletes from Princeton, who in a game against Dartown helped American Rolling Mill win what was considered the championship of southern Ohio. The company league of the Tennessee Coal and Iron Company in Alabama, another steel firm, developed big-league players in Joey and Luke Sewell, who worked there about the same time as Phil Douglas and Ben Chapman.

Some companies purloined ball players from others. Gabby Hartnett pitched for United States Rubber in Millville, Massachusetts, until American Steel and Wire in Worcester recruited him for 1921. The league's playing rules required Hartnett to be employed by December in order to play in 1922. During those winter months before the season started, his biographer said, Hartnett, hating the long hours, seldom showed up for work. By spring Gabby had left to join a minor-league team, and that same year the big catcher began his long big-league career with the Chicago Cubs.

Carnegie Steel gave evidence of revising its policy on use of pro players. Its welfare director, A.H. Wyman, wrote in three different articles for *Playground* about the company's new emphasis on interdepartmental rather than representative teams. While not excluding pro athletes, said Wyman, the company wanted to eliminate those kept only for athletic skill. In a reaction to wartime overemphasis, Wyman explained, Carnegie's plants had stopped paying professional players extra and used them only to stimulate interest in contests and to coach teams. Carnegie teams also tried to restrict games to after-work hours rather than permitting play on company time, although that was not always possible when competing with outside teams, and to substitute factory letters, like those of schools and colleges, for expensive prizes. Wyman said the former policy of hiring pros just to win games instead of to pour steel had proved "uneconomic," lowering per capita production and making the regular employees resentful. At Bethlehem, Pennsylvania, Carnegie exemplified one of the newest trends in industrial ball when it persuaded citizens to donate $20,000.00 for three new baseball diamonds, after which the company provided matching funds. In his three articles, however, Wyman failed to mention this development.

Auto companies like Willys, Stutz, Studebaker, and White Motor all put teams into city industrial leagues. Entries for the twenties in the *White-Book*, published regularly by the White Motor Company of Cleveland, reveal the close attention paid to "our boys," the representative team. In 1920, after the Whites beat their traditional local rivals, Telling-Belle Vernon Milk Company, 11–3 on Sunday May 16 at League Park before 3,000, a company writer exulted, "It is a source of deep satisfaction to see the increased batting strength of our team over last season's poor showing." The shop organ also exhorted team players to live right and work conscientiously at their regular jobs. Voicing the company line, the writer began by stating that an athlete must pay particular attention to keeping fit, and to do this "a clean life" and "a clear conscience" helped:

> . . . no ball player or athlete can ever give his best to the organization he is working for if he flagrantly disobeys such rules as are considered necessary by the best authorities. This not only applies to diet and habits of life, but also to the industry displayed in our shop work. You can take it from me that the ball player who works steadily in the shop is very apt to play a steady game in the field. Also, he carries less mental handicap. Get me?

The Whites won the Cleveland industrial championship several times, usually alternating with the Tellings. One of the Whites' star players, Frank Delehanty, formerly with the Yankees and other pro teams, had played with both the Whites and the Tellings, representing each in the years it won the city championship. Other ex-professionals on the White Motors team included Wilburt Schardt, who had pitched for Brooklyn, and Willis Cole, one-time outfielder for the Chicago White Sox. After the 1920 season the *White-Book*'s sports writer, Jack Lickert, thanked the company management and officials "for their wholehearted co-operation and assistance in making this a successful baseball season." The following spring three members of the 1920 champions signed with the minor-league St. Paul team of the American Association.

That year, probably because of the depression of 1921–1923, the White Motor Company failed to make its annual appropriation in support of a team to compete in the city league. Only departmental clubs would be furnished with equipment, the company organ stated. Then Director of Recreation S.J. Wettrich announced that the firm's second team, the White Colts, would be allowed to re-enter the city league in a lower class than the "big team," as the Colts had once done in the teens. But baseball results proved disappointing for the next couple of seasons. Then in 1923 the Colts, playing industrial league games at Gordon Park, Woodland Hills, and Brookside Park, against teams like the May Company Department Store and the Disabled War Vets, made a better record. After a rainstorm unfortunately caught them during a game and shrank their uniforms embarrassingly, the players complained. Declared team manager Sellers in a few well-chosen words:

> None of them boys ain't going into the championship series looking like a skinned cat. . . . none of the boys dasts to stoop over to pick up a ball. . . . And our caps—Settin' like a pill on our cocos!

In 1924 Director Wettrich announced that the Whites would again enter a team in the top echelon of the city league, the AAA level, a decision "received with enthusiasm throughout the factory." When the Whites won the season opener against the Rosenblum Clothing Store at Dunn Field (then the park of the local big-league club, the Indians), "nearly all of White Motors was there, including the White Band with its two new Sousaphones." The next day the Cleveland *Plain Dealer* noted that the Rosenblums called in Rube Marquard, famous National League pitcher still on the Boston team, to relieve in a late inning, but the Whites prevailed regardless. That year the Cleveland industrial league drew big crowds, according to the house organ, partly because the Indians "were losers." (They came in sixth that year.) As for the Whites, they lost the city championship to the Grennan Cake Company.

The two big Akron, Ohio, rubber manufacturers, Firestone and Goodyear, sponsored representative teams as well as interdepartmental leagues in the twenties. Sharp rivalry prevailed between the two companies, according to a Goodyear company representative in a letter to this author in 1963, and each rubber company's varsity team included some ex-minor leaguers. The Firestone recreation director confessed in 1924 that in the past "We did shady things" like importing stars and giving them easy and temporary jobs, out of excessive rivalry, but, he said, imposition of eligibility rules had changed that. Every year Firestone tried to induce a major-league club to play an exhibition game with its team. In the Firestone athletic director's 1922 request to the Cincinnati Reds, he assured owner Garry Herrmann that Firestone did not harbor ineligible players or those not in good standing in Organized Baseball. Another rubber company, United States Rubber in New England, had a team at each of its six Massachusetts and Rhode Island plants.

"Baseball is the coal miner's hobby," declared Julius Solter, a former miner who played in the big leagues in the thirties. Jimmy "Rip" Collins, also in the majors in the thirties, played ball on the same mining team as his father from 1920 through 1922. While Jimmy's father worked for the machine shop of the Nanty Glo Mine of Johnstown, Pennsylvania, and played first base for its ball team, Jimmy, at first the fourteen-year-old mascot, soon broke in as a regular. At Nanty Glo only the coal miners played on the club, which had its own park. Red Ruffing, who became an outstanding major league pitcher, and his father also played for the same mining team, the Reliance

Coal Company of Nokomis, Illinois, where the senior Ruffing managed the club that Red pitched for. Dick Bartell, the year before he became a major-league shortstop, secured a white-collar job at a mine in Butte, Montana, where he played with a crack mining league team. At about the same time Earl Averill also played for a Montana team in the Copper league. When Averill reported for work each morning at Anaconda Copper Company, the manager handed him the morning newspaper, gave him a chair, and told him to read! In contrast, Beans Reardon, assured of a soft job umpiring at a mine in Bisbee, Arizona, soon found himself stripped to the waist digging ore with pick and shovel in an underground "slope" in the company of "big rats," so he returned to California and eventually umpired in the majors.

Other heavy industries like brass, oil, lumber, and paper promoted baseball teams. In New Orleans a lumberman named Harry Williams formed a company whose fifteen-year-old catcher and former batboy was Mel Ott, who in 1926 became a New York Giant outfielder. In Houston the Sinclair Refining Company, with George A. Watkins, a big-league outfielder of the thirties, won the championship for 1924 in the local Oil League. Ralph "Red" Kress, later an American League infielder, found that when he joined Standard Oil of California as a clerk and played with the team, it contained many ex-professionals. The management of three Maine paper companies, St. Croix at Woodland, Penobscot at Old Town, and Eastern at both Lincoln and South Brewer, all attested that baseball there had helped foster good relations with labor.

One owner used a novel idea to keep his workers contented. F. Percy Collingwood, a wire manufacturer in Attleboro, Massachusetts, was startled when during the company's busiest season a worker asked for a day off to listen to the World's Series on the radio. Instead of granting the request Collingwood hooked up his own radio set at his home next door to the plant to a speaker in the factory so that everyone could hear the games. When he found the speaker interfered with work, he installed headphones. The results, Collingwood said, were astonishing, so he made the installation permanent. The men were "enthusiastic," worked fast, never showed up late, stopped watching the clock, and worked silently. Collingwood's company thus got the full value of every working minute, and the men, accepting night work as well "without a murmur," sometimes got so interested in their radio programs that they kept at their tasks without taking legitimate breaks.

Railroad employees formed local baseball leagues and published sports news in their company periodicals. In Chicago the ten-team Railroad League represented the general offices of local transportation companies. New York Central in Yonkers ran twilight league games. The Illinois Central and the Louisville & Nashville featured the news of their baseball teams in their house organs. Detroit's Street Railways League selected an all-star team in 1923 to travel to Cleveland, where it defeated the pick of Cleveland's carmen.

Like industries, the railroads hired ex-professional players. The Pullman Company team included ex-Federal League players after the Feds failed at the end of the 1915 season.

Employees could also play ball at electric companies like the Westchester Lighting Company near New York City. Thomas A. Edison, at age seventy-four, pitched five balls at a 1921 game between his company's Lab staff and the Disk Record Department. Joyner White, with Georgia Power & Light of Atlanta, Pepper Martin with Oklahoma Gas & Electric, and Leo Durocher at an electric company in Springfield, Massachusetts, all obtained employment because of their ball playing skills, soon to be used in the big leagues.

General Electric in Lynn, Massachusetts, and Schenectady, New York, developed plant loyalty through baseball, according to articles in *Playground* and *Baseball Magazine*. G.E. considered welfarism a "cold business proposition." Early in the decade the company prided itself on supporting mass participation in baseball instead of backing only a representative team; nevertheless, by the end of the decade both plants sponsored official company teams. At the Lynn plant local officials even experimented with night ball, installing hundreds of high-powered bulbs for the purpose. Soon after, the local New England League professional club played an official game under lights.

The new aircraft industry, as well as the telephone and telegraph companies, sponsored baseball. At Boeing, J.E. Schaefer, who played on the company's first team, in 1928, and shortly became Boeing's vice-president and general manager, was instrumental in the company's continued sponsorship of teams for years thereafter. In 1946 Schaefer said Boeing justified the expense of supporting baseball as "good public relations and an element of good will within the community."

B.J. Pittman, who in the 1920s played for Employers Casualty Insurance, in Dallas, Texas, in 1986 remembered many colorful details of local baseball competition on Saturdays and some Sundays against teams like Southwestern Bell Telephone, Baldwin Piano, Lone Star Gas Company, and the Post Office. Company employees at the games, he said, "acted like school students, yelling and encouraging the players." Most team members were bona fide employees, including the president, Austin Allen, who played right field, but the company did recruit men because they could play ball, some of them not even hired to work for Casualty. According to the insurance company's publication, *Brickbats and Bouquets*, the company team won the 1927 city league championship with the help of B.J. Pittman of the public relations department, whose batting average of .444 was one of the highest in the city.

Some Employers Casualty Insurance stars reached the majors, especially Pinkey Higgins, later with the Boston Red Sox and other clubs, and Dan Davenport, who went to the Chicago White Sox. The company paid for all uniforms and equipment, Pittman recalled, and players practiced after work, playing Saturdays in the city league before several hundred fans on grounds assigned by the city park department.

The year 1929 was Employers Casualty's biggest year. Its team won the all-city championship in Dallas as well as the championship of West Texas. Then it almost took the state championship in an exciting series against a team from Houston, which won the first game 4–1. Employers Casualty won the second 7–0. The third game was called on account of darkness at the end of the sixth with Houston leading 6–5 and therefore becoming champions. Employers Casualty protested, but to no avail.

Another insurance company also developed a strong nine: Lincoln Life Insurance in Fort Wayne, Indiana. The Lincoln Lifers even played big-league teams, losing every time but thrilling the local populace with views of pros like the New York Giants, the Cincinnati Reds, and the Philadelphia Phillies. When Babe Ruth appeared for a few innings one May, 35,000 Fort Wayne fans came to watch.

Bankers leagues still operated in New York, Boston, and Houston. In the latter city Gus Mancuso, employed to discover "rubber checks," helped the First National Bank win twelve straight games. Mancuso later transferred his talents to the big league, becoming an excellent defensive catcher for the New York Giants. Smaller companies handling light industry, such as Corona Typewriter of Groton, New York, the Stromberg Carlson factory at Rochester, New York, and Carter Ink of Cambridge, Massachusetts all played in industrial leagues, although they could hardly develop baseball as elaborately as the giant industrial firms. Jewelry manufacturers like the Ruggles Company of Cleveland and food preparers like the Rivoli Meat Market in Oakland, California, and even funeral parlors such as Geraghty Undertakers in St. Louis produced teams. Firemen, policemen, and politicians continued playing. The annual Congressmen's game, Republicans versus Democrats, took place in Washington, and by 1926 the politicians wore uniforms. Fraternal orders—Elks, Odd Fellows, Rotary, Kiwanis, and Masons—which proliferated in the 1920s, formed teams all over the country.

Baseball Magazine presented a photograph of what it believed to be the most learned ball club in the world: members of the faculty of Carleton College in Northfield, Minnesota. All Phi Beta Kappans and Ph.D.s, they appeared in motley uniforms but serious-looking and ready to play. The team competed against the college seniors in a fund-raising scheme in 1923. As the text of a later display at the college described the game, "Brawn triumphed over brain, with the seniors winning 5 to 1."

Industrial baseball enthusiasts organized their teams into various kinds of leagues. Since in big cities the quality of play varied greatly, teams at the same level of ability frequently clustered together. Thus some city leagues, like Cleveland's, placed teams in three levels according to calibre of play, each team selecting its own level. Chicago in 1924, on the other hand, divided its 24 industrial teams into four groups, the winners of which played each other at the end of the season. In Paterson, New Jersey, leagues formed according to the type of work: eight teams in a silk-dyeing league, eight in a silk-manufacturing league, and ten in general manufacturing. Another separate league of six teams comprised clerks, trolleymen, firemen, newsmen, and local government officials. In smaller cities and towns like Amherst, Massachusetts, West Chester, Pennsylvania, Connersville, Indiana, and Waukegan, Illinois, one or two leagues could be enough to handle all industrial and business teams. In areas with many small communities, teams often joined in an intertown association, as did those of the Southern California Night Baseball Association, which originated in the town of Corona. In New Orleans, although many large commercial houses applied for the 1923 league, organizers chose only four—United Fruit Company, Illinois Central Railroad, Standard Oil, and the Dock Board—so that the league would be representative of the large corporations of the city.

In keeping with the typical American organizational pattern, industrial leagues in 1921 formed an Association of Industrial Athletic Associations, or AIAA, to insure uniformity in eligibility and scheduling. Within a year the AIAA spread from Akron, Ohio, into five states, staged an intercity baseball series, and published its own monthly magazine, *Industrial Athletics*. Despite the organization's name, it focussed on baseball.

The momentum of the big industrial athletic programs held until about 1928, with one exceptional period, the brief recession of 1921–23, when, as W. Irving Clark disclosed in *Industrial Management*, "workers who had proudly won silk shirts and patent leather shoes at great inter-factory athletic events now wandered from factory to factory seeking non-existent jobs." Conversely, baseball could also be enlisted to lighten the effects of the recession, as in Bridgeport, Connecticut, where the long siege of unemployment became serious. The town's Recreation Commission therefore instituted a "Leisure League" for unemployed players, and their "brilliant play" drew large crowds of fans as well as managers of industrial league teams, who scouted the games in search of outstanding players. "Leisure League" players vanished one by one as they obtained jobs, but while it lasted, declared *Recreation Magazine*, the league "did wonders toward maintaining morale."

By about 1925 problems caused by the use of professional players began to hurt huge industrial programs. According to an industrial Y representative in Bayonne, New Jersey, nonplaying employees or those on interdepartmental teams of bona fide employees increasingly resented the overvaluing of professionals hired for the company team, who sometimes practiced on company time. In 1926 a Department of Labor Survey revealed that thirty-eight companies had actually given up baseball, half of them citing professionalism as the reason. The tendency to hire players solely for baseball ability meant they often made unsatisfactory workers, as the authors of the survey pointed out.

Inevitably, strong industrial teams came into close contact with Organized Baseball. Entire teams were even known to switch over to a minor league in Organized Baseball—a clear indication of industrial ball's quality. In 1923 the team of the American Chain and Cable Company in New York transferred to the Class B New York-Pennsylvania League, where it finished among the top three for five years in succession. Organized Baseball also tried to recruit individual players from industrial league teams. When in 1920 a team in the Southern League signed two players who had agreed to play for the Castle Cords of New Castle, Pennsylvania, the industrial club, according to the New York *Times*, sued the Organized Baseball league.

More typical was the reverse practice, in which Organized Baseball's players moved to industrial leagues. Early in the decade of the twenties, several minor-league players jumped their contracts or ignored the reserve clause in their contracts and joined strong industrial teams in Pennsylvania, Michigan, and Idaho, because with industry they were apt to achieve a more stable work life, a longer-lasting, often lifetime, job, and higher pay than with Organized Baseball's minor-league teams. John Farrell, Secretary of the minors, warned contract jumpers to return by June 1 or be barred for five years, reserve clause violators for three. In the resulting negotiations the industrial teams agreed not to sign any more players directly from Organized Baseball. But in 1921 in Maryland, the Baltimore Dry Docks bought the releases of four minor-league players from their former clubs so that the Dry Docks could retain their good standing with Organized Baseball and be allowed to play exhibition games with Organized Baseball's minor league teams, something they would otherwise have been prohibited from doing. The National Board of the minor leagues subsequently gave the Dry Docks a clean bill of health, said *Sporting News*, yet ruled that the four players could never be reinstated into Organized Baseball.

Similar disputes between industrial teams and Organized Baseball throughout the era made several leagues "outlaws" from the O.B. point of view. A member of one such league, the Flakes, represented Kellogg's Corn Flakes of Battle Creek, Michigan, which in 1926 harbored ex-major leaguers and other good players, all well-paid.

During the years before the great depression, business tycoons used so-called welfare capitalism as a facade to mask their steady acquisition of the bulk of the nation's natural resources and wealth. The savings they had effected in their supposed efficiencies were not distributed to consumers, nor were the wages they paid commensurate with their profits. By 1929 when the economic collapse came, the national wealth, as shown by Professor Fred Shannon, amounted to about 365 billion dollars, or a per capita average of $3,000.00, which, if uniformly distributed would have provided economic comfort for every American. Instead, billions were tied up in the personal fortunes and estates of multimillionaires while most families had less than the $2,000.00 required for decent living. They could not even purchase the goods they produced. Cuts in production early in the depression meant many workers were laid off, worked a shorter week, worked at lower wages, or a combination of these. By 1933 a quarter of the work force had joined the army of the unemployed.

Conversely, hours of leisure increased to an estimated seventy a week, and commentators intensified their advice to workers to use their free time "responsibly," "constructively," "properly," and "profitably." The latter word applied better to business, since the business world had already expanded the "leisure industry," putting spending on passive recreation ahead of that for active.

As the depression spread ever wider, some industrialists curtailed or withdrew recreation programs. But by 1935 industrial recreation appeared to have stabilized. Most of the companies studied in a National Recovery Act survey that year reported that their firms still offered company recreation activities. In Akron the city's director of recreation declared that the depression "had very little effect upon industrial recreation as a whole throughout this country" and that although some companies cut back, in others shorter hours meant an increase in programs.

Government, especially municipal government, helped run and finance industrial athletics in these hard times. Although the trend to city responsibility for recreation had begun earlier, in the thirties many more companies located in cities found that they could link or merge their programs with official municipal recreation, where "muny" authorities would provide parks and playgrounds for the workers, schedule games and tournaments, and furnish supervision and officials. In short, socialism for the establishment proved acceptable in the depression.

Industrialists could also collect fees of from one to six dollars in dues from all employees, or contributions from those who participated in sports, or apply to recreation the profits from company stores, cafeterias, and vending machines. Reportedly, the most popular financing plan was joint sponsorship, combining employee fees with budget appropriations.

Company recreation programs might, however, embroil industrialists in trouble with the federal government. The Wagner Act, passed in 1935, plugged a loophole in the National Industrial Recovery Act that, while making it illegal to force employees to join company unions, had permitted them to "encourage" such unions. The National Labor Relations Board found that some companies operated recreational clubs in a way that made such clubs devices for discussing grievances with management. The Board ruled that such clubs were company-sponsored unions and thus illegal. The N.L.R.B., according to Stuart Brandes, said "good sportsmanship" demanded that employers eliminate from their recreation programs any attempts to interfere with collective bargaining. As a result, some industries retreated from recreation and adopted a hands-off policy, waiting for spontaneous requests from workers.

Increased time for recreation called for increased attention to it. The topic of industrial recreation attracted seventy representatives of industry to a meeting held at the time of the annual Playground Association convention in 1931. In Chicago in 1939 representatives of 800 businesses attended a conference held under the auspices of Northwestern University to discuss the best application of industrial recreation. Not only did people from Owens-Illinois, General Electric, Western Electric, and Illinois Bell telephone attend but also representatives from the International Ladies Garment Workers Union and the Amalgamated Clothing Workers Union. These last two encouraged sponsorship of team games among their membership, and at least from 1937 onwards so did the United Auto Workers and the Congress of Industrial Organizations (C.I.O.), destined to become the most powerful industrial union. Many of the unions that belonged to the Jewish Labor Committee sponsored baseball, soccer, and basketball in the thirties for their members, reporting results in *Justice*, the Committee's weekly newspaper.

The Communists, too, developed athletic programs, the party's Labor Sports Union shifting its earlier emphasis on soccer and gymnastics to American sports like baseball. In the fall of 1933 *Young Worker* began reporting big-league baseball just as the daily newspapers did, and from 1936 on the *Daily Worker* did the same. The Young Communist League and the International Workers Order, the party's fraternal and insurance society, also organized sports leagues, according to writer Mark Naison. Communist-sponsored baseball leagues played extensively in Cleveland, which the *Daily Worker* called "the labor sport center of America," as well as in Chicago and Milwaukee, during 1937, as the paper's accounts reveal. Throughout the period 1937 through 1939 the *Daily Worker* continued reporting trade union baseball teams and leagues, many of them in New York City, but the paper's writer may not have been completely familiar with baseball, for part of the time he seemed unable to differentiate between baseball and softball and sometimes referred to the same games, leagues, and championships by either name alternately.

In southern textile mills in the thirties, the owners still ran the recreation programs. William P. Jacobs, public relations director for South Carolina cotton manufacturers, explained in 1932 that the mill owners supported recreation for "their villages" because they knew it to be a good "investment." They hired athletic directors, built parks and playgrounds, and constructed community buildings. Jacobs stated that the fifty-nine mills he surveyed had invested almost a million and a half dollars in recreation equipment and services. He acknowledged that the employees worked "long hours" but believed that the large numbers participating in recreation "disproved" the notion that their work deprived them of "pleasures."

Everett T. Jones, long-time editor of *Textiles Review*, recalling in 1984 the details of textile ball in North Carolina's Gaston County, wrote warmly of the mill owners' support of baseball. Companies like Textiles-Incorporated, Burlington Mills, Firestone Textiles, U.S. Rubber Textiles, A.M. Smyre Manufacturing Company, and Stowe Mills had at least by the twenties begun sponsoring baseball, Jones related, by furnishing some financial aid to teams that employees formed, with other townspeople often on the teams as well. "Gradually," Jones wrote in a letter to this author, "most companies realized the value of good public relations and . . . happier employees" and gave "generous financial support" to company teams as well as to other community teams. Players, he said, got free meals when on the road, and owners paid them as if they had been at work. What Jones, like Jacobs, neglected to mention in this rosy picture was the low wages that in Gastonia finally inspired desperate workers to seek help from a union, but after a few months' bitter struggle the owners were able to suppress it, and conditions remained as before. As a teenager in the thirties, for instance, Kirby Higbe, later a big-league pitcher, played ball in that same area with mill teams in Anderson and in Laurens, South Carolina. At Anderson he got nothing extra for pitching Saturdays and Sundays, and in the mill he worked 53 hours a week at ten cents an hour. Before the NRA established a standard textile salary, Southern mill workers averaged more than 62 hours a week for $4.54; afterwards, they were supposed to work 40 hours for $12.00—a figure still more than five dollars below the national average for all workers. But writer Wilbur J. Cash knew of cotton and hosiery mills breaking the law, paying only $3.00 a week and requiring 55 hours of work.

Southern textile teams produced many players who reached the majors, including Dave Barbee, Jake Early, and Howard Moss. Southpaw Max Lanier, later with the St. Louis National League club, pitched for Bossong Mills of Asheboro, North Carolina, winning sixteen straight for the mill team in 1936, two years before he entered the majors. The mills of Gastonia, North Carolina, produced John "Buddy" Lewis, eventually a first-rate infielder of the Washington Club.

Oil teams proliferated in the thirties as well. Important oil names that showed up in various reports of ball games included Phillips, American, Sunoco, Cities Service, Esso, Shell, Champlin, and Halliburton. The latter two companies produced clubs that achieved national notice. The Champlins of Enid, Oklahoma, also developed at least six players who made the majors, although some, as a company representative explained in 1978, were on the way down rather than the reverse.

At Halliburton Company—then the Halliburton Oil Well Cementing Company of Duncan, Oklahoma—employees played ball in the late twenties, the company organ, the *Cementer*, reported. In the thirties owner Erle P. Halliburton hired a minor leaguer, Lefty Johns, to form a team as "an advertising and good-will venture," a former ball player and employee, Mike Pruitt, noted in a letter to this author in 1977. Johns hired a group of experienced players, some with major-league experience. All were full-time employees, but when they went on the road other employees did their work for them. The players got an hourly wage comparable to that of semiskilled workers at Halliburton, figured on a forty-hour basis, plus a bonus of $25.00 a month during the season to cover time spent on long bus rides and playing weekend games. In addition, the men divided among themselves all prize money won in tournaments. The company paid road expenses and furnished bus and driver along with equipment and uniforms. The Halliburton Cementers played from three to five games a week, and, like earlier pampered players, they had the afternoon off to practice, or to rest before a night game. Because all the major oil companies fielded teams, Pruitt said, the Cementers spent weeks on extended trips to the oil fields of Texas, Oklahoma, Kansas, and Louisiana, playing industrial teams as well as semipros and participating in, and winning, national tournaments. The team did not disband until the onset of World War II.

Pruitt explained later that many good players among the Cementers rejected contracts with Organized Baseball's minor leagues because during the depression years the minors, if they did not collapse altogether, offered only "starvation wages," and their players needed off-season jobs, so they preferred playing industrial ball with a solid company like Halliburton with the security it offered "unless their talent was so great there was a good chance of their making the major leagues."

In the minor leagues in the thirties many players made only $60.00 or $70.00 a month. "You didn't get enough money to keep shoes on you as a league player," said Skip Crouch, a member of the independent Sioux Falls Canaries. Good industrial players agreed. One, a steel puddler named Olly Carnegie, when playing with his company team at Hays, near McKeesport, Pennsylvania, always refused offers of minor-league scouts. He had a family and made a decent living working in the local mill and playing for the mill team. Then the steel mills began feeling the depression, so instead of working double shifts the men went on short schedules, and some were let go. Olly, too, got laid off, so he took the next Organized Baseball offer he received, one from the New York-Pennsylvania league. He was thus literally forced into the minor leagues, where he became a standout slugger in the International, a high minor.

An example of highly developed baseball among miners in the 1930s, unearthed by George Wiley and Dale Landon from the files of a newspaper, the Indiana *Evening Gazette*, shows the close connection industrial ball could have with daily life in coal towns. A group of Western Pennsylvania coal communities, some of them company towns but all in Indiana County, Pennsylvania, formed a league called the R & P League, after the Rochester and Pennsylvania Coal Company. Team membership in the league varied, and in 1933 union quarrels forced cancellation of the entire season, but usually eight or ten communities, most of them coal towns, entered teams in the league.

While the R & P Coal Company had charge of the league, mine super-intendents ran the teams, frequently traveling considerable distances to find promising players and offering them jobs "above ground." Often, players did not even perform their easy jobs, although they got paid for the full week's work, and on game day the mine superintendent dismissed them early, telling each player at around 11:00 A.M., "Get your bucket." In the worst of the depression the mines reduced employees to a three-day week—except for the ball players. Many of the coal town players had tried the minors but with growing families had given up professional ball for higher pay and job security with coal companies, where they could work after their playing days ended.

Each town in Indiana county had its own well-kept ball park, where attendance averaged around 600 or 800, although for an important game a crowd of 1,000 appeared. When a coal town team left for an away game, the town often emptied behind it, the people packing the streetcars and the few autos available, or just walking, arriving to yell encouragement to their team or heckle the opposition. Ladies of the home team furnished supper for both teams after the games. The end-of-season championship series called for a celebration and gifts of cash to each player.

Problems of the R & P league are revealed in the league's imposition in 1934 of a thirty-day rule to prevent hiring a player just before a game and fines for teams not showing up for a game or walking off the field during one. The league's arbitration board might not support an umpire's decision and at least once even reversed its own decision.

The R & P Coal Company assessed each miner fifty cents per pay period to cover the cost of baseball, but when the union gained enough strength it disputed this levy, and after the 1934 season the company had no direct control of the league. Instead, each coal mining town organized its own team, and the league elected to membership some nonmining firms, such as sporting goods companies. When in the late thirties the union removed the ball players' special privileges, the league faltered and in 1939 gave up.

By contrast with these coal town players, newspaper typographers in the thirties carried on their own baseball league annually, each year's tournament in a different city, right up to World War II. The typographers' 1934 cham-pionship series at Yankee Stadium attracted interested fans from as far away as St. Louis. Teams from eleven cities took part in the 1937 tournament at Baltimore. The 1940 affair at Cincinnati included a program of receptions, parties, dancing, and sightseeing.

Railroads in the thirties laid off men by the hundreds of thousands as some great systems passed into receivership. A study of railroad employees' rec-reation revealed that thirty-eight percent had none at all because their fam-ilies believed trips and outings were no longer possible, and they could not even invite friends over because of inability to offer them any food. One family solved its recreation problem, after a fashion, by attending free ball games played within walking distance. Railroad men, however, did play ball when they could. The Pennsylvania road carried on an annual "system championship," which the Fort Wayne, Indiana, railroad team won in two consecutive years. At least two other lines, Grand Trunk Railroad and the Salt Lake City, Denver, & Rio Grand Western Railroad, carried teams that competed nationally against semipros. And the railroad Y still operated, although with fewer branches, only 117 by 1939 as against 196 in 1930. The railroad Y did prevail upon some systems to continue employing "physical directors."

The automobile industry continued in the thirties as a dynamic factor in American business. Ford Motors and Chrysler-DeSoto put teams in the top level, Class A group, of the Detroit Baseball Federation, and both Ford and Buick entered clubs in national (semipro) competition. Buick, Chevrolet, and Chrysler-DeSoto all had local teams playing around Detroit. In Cleveland the White Motor Company team took its eleventh championship in the city's Class A category against Otis Steel company, winning 8–4 in a game at Gordon Park. General Motors, through its Fisher Body Division, promoted baseball generally by backing the preparation of an American League film, "Take Me Out to the Ball Game."

In Jackson, Michigan, a manufacturing company called Reynold's Springs hired Ed Hamman, age nineteen, a former player for the Kellogg Corn Flake team, O.B. outlaws, and the independent House of David team. Hamman had heard that Reynold's Springs hired players to work two days a week for the company and play ball three days. As Hamman's biographer, Bill Heward, tells it, at Reynold's Springs Hamman led the Jackson city league in hitting, then started a rumor that he was about to be signed by the Chicago Cubs, which persuaded the company to name him "efficiency expert" at $5,000.00 a year. The factory manager told Hamman that if he went to night school and studied the efficiency business he would have a lifetime job with the company. Hamman studied until the depression hit the company and 4,000 of the 5,000 employees were fired, along with the manager who had hired Hamman. The new manager, who began firing veteran employees and replacing them with his fraternal lodge brothers, did offer Hamman a three-day-a-week job on the assembly line, but Hamman refused, returned to baseball, and became an entrepreneur, organizing and managing independent professional teams like the Indianapolis Clowns and touring the country with them. But Reynold's Springs, his former employer, survived the depression. In 1935 its baseball team led the Jackson Class A Twilight league and played other good nonleague teams in the area.

The Remington Rand Company of Elmira, New York, took on many players of the Elmira club of Organized Baseball's New York-Pennsylvania League in 1936, employing them in the plant. *Sporting News* declared that Remington Rand always had its "welcome mat" out for "diamond dandies."

At Endicott Johnson Shoe Company, with many New York state locations, the sports program reached its greatest development early in the decade.

In Johnson City, the company park was such a good one that the local team of the New York-Pennsylvania League played its games there. In 1933 the park acquired lights for night ball. Ten thousand E-J workers, more than half the work force, paid a quarter a year dues for sports. William Inglis, owner George S. Johnson's biographer, claimed that Johnson, unlike many employers, who used a pro team for advertising, preferred all employees to play, for their health and happiness. But the E-J company also supported six top baseball teams that charged a dime admission and competed in what amounted to a semipro league of interplant baseball with a championship series. The winning and losing team members in the final game each got $15.00 from Johnson, and he gave all other league players, along with officials, $10.00 each. "We have found," said Johnson, "that our workers not only enjoy their games but are more efficient because they play." Sports "refreshes a worker and enables him to do more."

In the aircraft industry Boeing continued its sponsorship of baseball teams in the thirties, and Lockheed began doing the same. Lockheed's first baseball team formed in 1934, played on Sundays, and passed the hat to cover expenses. From the activities of the baseball team grew the Lockheed Employee Recreation Club.

In all this industrial play, white-collar players and small business participants should not be overlooked. Bankers, grocers, bakers, newsmen, lodge members, comedians, sports announcers, candymakers, and funeral homes played baseball around the country. In Washington, scores of federal departmental teams organized themselves into leagues, whose winners held an annual tournament. Steamship builders and trolley car makers as well as tailors and cereal makers fielded teams. And Sporting News noticed that young fellows who attended baseball schools arrived in uniforms bearing names like Sampson Bros. Tavern, Huckleberry Watson, Meconi Wine, Royster's Fertilizer, and Alderman D.R. Crowe Boosters.

Games of the New York City Municipal League included not only the police versus the firemen but also Mayor Fiorello LaGuardia's office staff versus City Hall reporters. In 1935 LaGuardia wanted an all-municipal New York nine of police and firemen to compete with those of other cities to promote good will among muny employees. William W. Cohen, who handled arrangements for visiting Chicago employees, asked LaGuardia if his secretary would provide cars for the guests, saying, "I hope they will be cars that are not too dilapidated, as some of our City cars are pretty run down looking vehicles." Proceeds of intercity games covered expenses, and Ed Barrow, business manager of the New York Yankees, lent Yankee Stadium for a game. The intercity series continued each year, and by 1939 it was contributing its proceeds to charity.

A policeman's game in Michigan had somewhat different results. When the Lansing Police Department nine played against the prisoners' team at Michigan State Prison, a writer for the prison paper wrote afterwards, "Last

Sunday the convicts administered a good beating to the cops and made them like it."

By the thirties many city governments like those in Chicago and Cleveland were taking over industrial baseball leagues. Newark's Ironbound Industrial League merged with other local leagues in 1938 to form the Newark Industrial Recreation Association, supervised and equipped by the city's recreation department. In Brooklyn, New York, the Parade Grounds Twilight Industrial League included Martinson's Coffee, Brooklyn Edison, and Brooklyn Gas, playing two evenings a week. One summer I umpired on the bases for that twilight league. Brooklyn Edison dominated the league. After a game in which I called out a Brooklyn Edison runner on a close play at first base, I was fired.

FOR LOVE AND MONEY

Professionalism in baseball has been debated ever since the era of the 1860's, when some amateur teams made the transition into professionalism, to the accompaniment of considerable strain, subterfuge, and criticism.* Although this transition resulted by the 1870s in the formation of admittedly professional teams and leagues, other teams continued as amateurs or as quasi-amateurs. Many such teams became known as semipros, although semi-amateurs might have been a more accurate term.

Most semipro players possess the essential characteristic of the amateur in that they play primarily for love of the game (the word *amateur* stems from the Latin *ama*, (to love). Yet they often make money from their play as well, although not depending upon such income for their livelihood. Semipro teams of several different types formed before the turn of the century: those playing only for the results of a bet against the other team, or a wager and a baseball; those who passed the hat to cover expenses; and those who secured an interested party, perhaps a fan or a local business, or a group of fans in a town or neighborhood, to pay the pitcher and catcher, or to hire a ringer for an important game. Players were generally called semipros if they hired themselves out to play weekend games for a few dollars. Semipros who bordered on being professionals were the industrial players who, as described earlier, took full-time jobs in plants in order to play, often for extra pay, a few times a week or on weekends as representatives of the company. Some town teams, too, were semipros, hired by the town to represent it.

Independent teams, some of them "stay-at-homes" and some traveling teams—a few of them both—were usually fully professional, since baseball was their living, but newspapers commonly called them semipros, to differentiate them from teams in Organized Baseball—as they also did the professional black teams, in order to denigrate them.

To many who upheld amateurism as an ideal the introduction of money

*See *Baseball: The Early Years*, pp. 47–58.

258

into amateur play was a "taint," a "perversion of the play spirit," even a "curse," as Theodore Roosevelt insisted in an 1890 issue of *North American Review*. The association of amateurism with "purity" and "good sportsmanship" stems primarily from two sources, the modern myth enveloping the ancient Olympic Games of Greece and the British upperclass tradition of the nineteenth century.

Many have come to believe that the ancient Greeks conducted the original Olympics simply to exhibit physical prowess, but in actuality all Greek athletes competed to win and accepted gifts and money in addition to olive wreaths. As recent books and articles de-mythologizing the Olympics have revealed, such competitions were serious adult activities entered for victory and its rewards. The British tradition influencing American ideas of amateurism consisted mainly of a desire to keep sports competition narrowed to the privileged, those who could afford expensive sports like polo, thereby keeping out the working classes, who lacked the means to participate in such activities. Democratic ideas early eroded the possibility of maintaining such a clear-cut class division in America. Yet some disapproval of accepting money for sport performance remained. Nevertheless, semipros in America eventually became as numerous as acorns in a stand of oak trees.

Already most adult "amateurs" who played ball frequently had before the turn of the century become to some degree semipros. The New York area swarmed with semipros from the 1870s on. The Brooklyn Athletics, a semipro nine, in 1872 included sixteen-year-old Tommy Bond, later a big-league pitcher. Sixty-four years afterwards Bond still cherished the memory of playing with the Brooklyn Athletics as they defeated a bankers' team, the Nassaus, a squad of full-grown men. Bond's goal in life at the time was to join the Brooklyn Atlantics, a professional team in the National Association, and when he made that team in 1874 he celebrated by winning his first game against the Lord Baltimores, a strong semipro team.

A popular Brooklyn team of the 1890s was the Alerts, who charged ten cents admission to the bleachers. Those who could not pay watched from a roped-off area. The manager solicited contributions by passing a cigar box. The Brooklyn *Eagle* reported games of the Alert club, and one of its players, Emil "Heinie" Batch, made the Brooklyn club of Organized Baseball in 1904.

In upstate New York John H. Farrell ran a semipro team in Auburn and persuaded James Wadsworth, a wealthy farmer in Geneseo sixty-five miles away, to bring a team of college men to Auburn by Pullman. "We always trimmed those fellows 3 out of 4," Farrell bragged years after. Wadsworth later became a United States senator, but Farrell remained with baseball, eventually becoming head of Organized Baseball's minor leagues.

As shown earlier, in small towns prominent citizens who liked baseball and wanted to enhance their town's reputation might contribute enough money to strengthen their teams by hiring a few of the best players of the vicinity. Four of the players on a semipro team in Honesdale, Pennsylvania, got salaries in season, from $15.00 to $20.00 a week in 1898 and 1899, and their pitcher, Christy Mathewson, later a big-leaguer, received $25.00. This Honesdale team played the towns of Port Jervis, Goshen, and Chester in the Orange County League.

Partly-paid teams were not confined to the East. Actually, a pure amateur team became about as difficult to find as a living statesman. Houston, Texas, for example, formed a semipro league in 1884 with Galveston, Waco, Fort Worth, Dallas, and San Antonio. Each club in the league played a fifteen-game season and paid a few of its players, usually the battery.

Another type of semipro team, the independent, belonged to no league but paid its players and charged admission. Independent teams, generally called semipro, should strictly speaking be classified as professional. An example, Akron, Ohio, in 1879–1881, supported a salaried team and provided grounds with seats for 800. Akron not only played Ohio city and town teams, it competed against big-league teams like Cleveland, Cincinnati, and Boston, usually losing to such teams but at least beating Louisville twice.

A third kind of semipro, the traveling team, should also be classified as professional. Like independents, traveling teams commonly discharged their players in the winter, unless they were touring the South, so team members often made their living at baseball only part of the year. Independent and traveling teams often signed their players to one-year contracts only rarely containing a clause reserving the player for the following season, as was the custom in Organized Baseball, so semipro players (unless they were on industrial teams) had to make new arrangements at the beginning of every season.

By 1900 the semipro had gained recognition in baseball as a particular breed. Some semipro clubs became known as "heavy"—clubs charging admission and paying at least some players. Others, regarded as "light," passed the hat, played for a bet with the other team, or paid none or only one or two of their players.

Despite general recognition of the status of semipros, disapproval of the financial aspect of baseball play persisted in some quarters. A writer discussing "Christian Character" in the YMCA Jubilee of 1901 thought the semipro team merited only "condemnation" because it stimulated rivalry that made winning seem "all-important." Yet Sporting News drove home only the obvious in 1907 when it said that amateurs remained as scarce as hen's teeth. Even "dubs"—adults playing for fun in silly clothes—were depicted in Collier's as taking up a collection. In 1913 an editorial in Sporting News rationalized the prevalence of the semipro by claiming that "baseball teaches the same principles of decent living and discipline whether it be played for pay or pleasure alone." Thus even semipro ball, like boys' baseball and industrial ball, was touted by its enthusiasts as contributing the growth of "character."

Apologists for semipro baseball as a character builder may not have known about the phenomenon of the "baseball bums," men who throughout their adult lives played ball because they knew nothing else or at any rate wanted to do nothing else. Both the Parade Grounds in Brooklyn and the Golden Gate Park in San Francisco had "Park Bums" in the 1900s.

In the early twentieth century semipros began forming large associations to advance their interests. In 1906, as reported in the New York *Times*, sixty such teams from the New York area met in New York City to lobby for better playing facilities. That same year about a hundred clubs in New York and New Jersey formed the Intercity Association. Some of these teams considered themselves amateurs and others semipro, and the association, too large and unwieldy and with a membership too varied, found it hard to discipline its clubs, but the group did work for the elimination of the law against Sunday ball and published a constitution and guidebook. Booking semipro games also became a new business in New York. Nat Strong, owner of a Brooklyn semipro team, soon got control of the business, but in 1913 Dave Driscoll's Baseball Bureau, in the Singer Building in Manhattan, not only operated three clubs, it also advertised, "High class attractions furnished at short notice."

Albany, too, organized a league, the Amateur and Semi-Professional Baseball Managers Protective Association, to regulate schedules, settle disputes, abolish contract-jumping and rowdyism, and maintain the standing of semipro ball. Other upstate New York towns formed the Hudson River (semipro) League in 1903, with the help of the aforementioned John H. Farrell, at that time president of the New York State (Organized Baseball) League, and William A. McCabe, Poughkeepsie's police chief and a former professional player. Ossining, Newburgh, Hudson, Saugerties, Kingston, and Poughkeepsie joined. A Peekskill team, at first reluctant to join because playing five or six games a week in the Hudson River League would require that players quit their jobs, finally entered the league anyway because playing as an independent team had proved financially unsuccessful. Dissatisfaction with umpires, player rowdyism, and bad weather plagued the league, but it survived into the season of 1907.

Spalding's 1907 guide reported that Philadelphia had more semipro leagues in and around the city than ever before. An example of the various grades of semipro in big cities like Philadelphia is the experience of Jimmy Dykes, later a prominent American League infielder, who in 1913 lived in the village of Preston near Philadelphia and played on a semipro team called the Penn Street Boys Club, which his father had helped form. When the players showed up for a game with the Victrix Club of Philadelphia before 4,000 and the opposing manager saw that Dykes and his teammates were teenagers, Victrix tried to cancel, but the senior Dykes offered $50.00 to Victrix if they won, nothing if they lost. Victrix accepted, and the teenagers beat them. When the boys next defeated the strong Irish-Roman Benevolent

Association of Ardmore, Jimmy Dykes jumped to that team for fifty cents a game plus a dime carfare, then moved up once more to the Garrett Hill team for a dollar a game.

In some areas semipro players, when they were fully grown adults, could command much more pay than Dykes did as a teenager. Garland Buckeye, when he pitched for the Cleveland professional club in the mid-twenties, claimed that before he entered the big leagues in 1918 he received, in addition to his regular semipro contract, $50.00 or $75.00 a game in the Midwest from farmers who won money betting on him. "A good player can make anywhere from $2,000 to $4,000 a year in semipro ball," Buckeye asserted.

Cleveland's development into a leading center for amateur-semipro ball began about the same time as New York's with the formation of the City Baseball League, an association of semipro leagues. By 1907 the association included twelve baseball leagues, and in 1910 the local sports writers and the owner of the Cleveland professional team, the Indians, gave it backing. The association's adult "amateur" games attracted thousands of fans. In 1914 the Telling semipro team, an industrial team referred to earlier, won the city's so-called amateur championship. In 1915, when the White Auto Company, likewise a semipro team, won it, the Whites' house organ, *The Albatross*, declared, "Thoughts of the world's series and submarine warfare become topics of small consequence when someone mentions the race for the Sixth City's amateur title."

Semipros in Cincinnati, Ohio, must have made money, for one club could afford to rent the local big-league park in 1909 and give the Cincinnati Reds twenty percent of the profit from their game. Another local club, the Shamrocks, using an appropriately green letterhead, advertised itself as "Highest Salaried and Best Known Semi-Pro Club in Cincinnati, Playing the Highest Class Independents and League Clubs."

Chicago residents could choose from among hundreds of semipro games played at one time, *Sporting News* reported in 1905, dozens of them on enclosed grounds. In 1908 the Chicago semipros, like the New York and Cleveland teams, joined the amateurs in an association. In the early part of the century the Chicago City League featured black teams along with its other "heavy" semipro teams like the Logan Squares, the Gunthers, and Anson's Colts, headed by the veteran major leaguer Adrian "Cap" Anson. But in 1910 black teams were barred from the league, as noted in the *Chicago Defender*, although one local black club, the Chicago Giants, secured permission to remain. The other black organizations had to be satisfied with playing strong white independents. Then in 1916 Rube Foster, the premier black club manager, with "pull" from a Republican politician, got his team, the American Giants, considered for entry into the Chicago City League, but the league members objected that they would have no chance against professionals like Foster's team and shrank from accepting, so Foster withdrew his club. After the league's season, however, his team did play and defeat the league's champions, the White Magnets.

Midwestern semipro players might hire themselves out to teams in the Trolley League, operating out of St. Louis and playing in Missouri and Illinois. Trolley League teams paid a small sum of money to young fellows who wanted to play ball and soon developed many pros, including Art Fletcher, later a scrappy shortstop for McGraw's New York Giants and Philadelphia Phillies manager, who played weekends in the Trolley League for fun, the love of the game, and extra spending money. Scout Charley Barrett came from the Trolley League, too, where he played with Pete Reiser's father, a pitcher for its St. Louis team. The younger Reiser later starred with the Brooklyn Dodgers. Muddy Ruel, soon to be an American League catcher, and Ray Schmandt, afterwards a National League first baseman, both played Sundays in the teens for a St. Louis semipro club called the Wabadas, where they earned only enough to buy uniforms and equipment. The Trolley League's president, C.M. Hanaway, believed that Organized Baseball should recognize semipro organizations like his and give them membership in Organized Baseball through a special classification, a status that would protect them from player-stealing. He wrote Garry Herrmann, chairman of Organized Baseball's National Commission, to this effect, pointing out that the Amateur Athletic Union governed amateurs and asserting that Organized Baseball should extend its fiat beyond the minors to the semipros. He added that "anyone who is halfway honest" knows that there are, "strictly speaking," no "'Simon Pure,' Amateur Ball Tossers in this country." Hanaway was then and still remains correct.

Even small towns developed semipro teams—places like Lake Ariel, Shamokin, Avoca, and Exeter, in Pennsylvania—where a good player might make a few dollars a week. In Hamtown, Bucky Harris, later a player-manager of the Washington Senators, made two dollars a game at age fifteen in the Suburban League. Danny Taylor, afterward a National League outfielder, earned $3.50 a game at age seventeen playing for West Newton, Pennsylvania. Local merchants of Brinswade, North Dakota, hired a few players in 1915 out of the seven or eight thousand dollars they collected toward forming a good team. The hired members included Bill Drake, a black professional, but most of the players were unpaid local talent. Good ball players could get $5.00 a game with the Portsmouth Navies in Portsmouth, Ohio, as did Al Bridwell, later shortstop of the New York Giants. Branch Rickey, however, claimed he earned $25.00 with the same team and saved it for college. General and President Dwight D. Eisenhower played center field for a Kansas State League (semipro) team in 1910, just before entering West Point, but he used the name "Wilson," perhaps to protect his eligibility for college. Semipro leagues were often temporary organizations. In Arizona a semipro named Lee Grantham played in the 1900s with the Firecracker League, so-called because it started with high hopes in spring but usually "blew up" by the Fourth of July.

Playing for a semipro team might require traveling. A semipro named Ed Morley of Brimfield, Indiana, received $25.00 plus his round-trip railroad fare to travel to Toledo, Dayton, Fort Wayne, and South Bend to pitch. As teenagers Casey Stengel and Claude Hendrix received a dollar a day plus room and meals while touring out West with a traveling team called the Kansas City Red Sox. A more famous traveling team of the teens was the All-Nations. It toured the West and played against top black teams as well as local town teams. The All-Nations and its descendents—there were at least three of the same name—exploited in their publicity the differing ethnic origins of team members, which included Indians, blacks, Latins, and once a Japanese. One such team included a female member.

Some clubs operated as nontraveling independents. The New Haven, Connecticut, Colonials of 1915–1917, headed by George Weiss, later general manager of the New York Yankees, began in a city league, but after the team won the city championship Weiss decided to try for something bigger and scheduled games with O.B. professionals like Brooklyn, the Chicago White Sox, and the Boston Red Sox.

One of the strongest and best-known independent clubs of the era was the Brooklyn Bushwicks, playing at Dexter Park in Woodhaven, Long Island, from about 1910 onwards into the 1950s. Owner Max Rosner, a cigar manufacturer and baseball entrepreneur beginning at least 1902, hired Joe Judge, later a star Washington first baseman, at five dollars a game when Judge was sixteen. Rosner's team, then called the Cypress Hills Club, played Sunday ball despite a local law against charging admission on the Sabbath. To circumvent it Rosner sold pencils, programs, and cushions for grandstand seats at a quarter each, bleacher seats for a dime. Every Monday for fifteen years he was brought to court, where the magistrate, a Bushwicks fan, suspended sentence to the end of the season, when the court levied a small fine. Rosner worked to remove the Sunday ban, and Jimmy Walker, then a state senator, finally got the law removed on the state level in 1917. In 1916 Rosner agreed to lend the hard-pressed Brooklyn Dodgers money in exchange for playing an exhibition game with his team. The Dodgers lost 3–2. Brooklyn owner Charlie Ebbets, furious, begged for a return game, but Rosner denied them. In 1918 Rosner enjoyed one of his best years in baseball and, realizing that his cigar factory had become secondary in importance, sold it.

Clashes between strong semipro clubs and Organized Baseball appeared inevitable. As Sporting News pointed out in 1916, the so-called amateurs were Organized Baseball's competition and might even harbor deserters from the pro leagues. Although independents were an irritant to Organized Baseball, Sporting News advised they be respected, since they had moral and legal rights, but it explained that the independents' one-year contracts left their players open to Organized Baseball's recruiting. Independents also challenged what O.B. clubs claimed as their territorial rights. They might, for instance, lure into their parks Organized Baseball clubs that, according to its territorial rules, had no business there. Once Joe Roesink, owner of a semipro park in Detroit, invited National League clubs to elude Sunday bans on play in their cities by staging their Sunday games in his park. To this Frank Navin, owner of O.B.'s Detroit club, strenuously objected. He wrote American League President Ban Johnson asking him to protest this intrusion of his territory to Tom Lynch, president of the National League, adding that, "As we are all in organized ball, I can see no reason why they [the National League] should not try to protect me in this matter."

The potential drawing power of a semipro club becomes clearly apparent in the protracted and intricate dispute of the Ridgewood club with the Brooklyn National League club. Ridgewood Park stood at the juncture of Queens and Brooklyn, within territory claimed by the Brooklyn club. In 1905 the Ridgewood club requested protection from the National Commission, which the governing body of Organized Baseball felt inclined to grant, provided the Ridgewood club agreed not to play whenever the Brooklyn club had a home game. The Brooklyn club protested vigorously, and Ridgewood failed to commit itself on the matter until the following May, when it refused protection under those conditions. Meanwhile, Charles Ebbets, Brooklyn owner, was persuaded to permit the New York American League club to play at Ridgewood when his own club was away.

Then in the fall of 1908 Nat Strong, who controlled the Ridgewood club and booked games for many independent clubs, used a player on Brooklyn's reserved list, Ernie Lindemann, and had to pay Ebbets $27.00 for the loan of the player. The following fall Ebbets raised his price for renting Lindemann to $300.00! Strong protested this increased fee to Garry Herrmann. Meanwhile, Organized Baseball transferred Lindemann to the New York American League club, so Herrmann could reply blandly to Strong that he would take up the matter with the Yankee club's president, John Farrell. Again in the fall of 1911 Strong tried to use Lindemann in a game, and Organized Baseball warned him to cancel the game. Strong objected to Organized Baseball's interference and protested to Farrell, who after a month replied that there had been some doubt as to Lindemann's eligibility to play in Organized Baseball, but the player had just been declared in good standing—which meant that Strong could not use him.

In June of 1912 the National Commission ruled Ridgewood an "outlaw" because it harbored ineligible players. Organized Baseball warned all O.B. clubs and players to stay away from Ridgewood "under penalty of a severe fine." In a further series of exchanges, all still to be found in Herrmann's correspondence, the Strong-Ebbets contretemps continued. Strong immediately protested once again to Herrmann, charging that the decision against his club resulted from "spite work" by Ebbets, to whom the Ridgewood club had stopped paying "protection." Strong further declared that Ebbets had "willfully lied" to the Commission and interfered in the business of the Ridgewood club. Finally, Strong warned that restrictions on his club violated the Sherman law. *Sporting News*, in reviewing the situation, added that Ebbets wanted a percentage of Strong's gate receipts in exchange for the favor of granting territorial rights to the Ridgewoods!*

Meanwhile, Ebbets picked another bone, this time with his fellow club-owners, over independents. He believed Organized Baseball's players ought to be prohibited from playing on Sundays with independent clubs, and in 1905 he got an O.B. rule passed against the practice. Then in 1911 he himself drew a fine of $50.00 for permitting one of his own players to break the very rule he had proposed.

Another independent club, Johnny Kling's Kansas City team of 1909, also grated on Organized Baseball. This outfit played in the Inter-City Baseball League during Kling's one-year leave of absence from his position as star catcher of the Chicago National League team. The National Commission, despite terming Kling's joining a non–Organized Baseball league "disloyalty and hostility," afterwards permitted him to return to the fold. Kling excused his conduct by explaining that he could not let pass the opportunity to play outside Organized Baseball because he would get as much money for his short-term stint with the Kansas City team as the Chicago club would pay him for the year ($4,500.00). Andrew Hardy of the Topeka Giants, a black club, later corroborated the rich earnings to be had from such play: his club made almost as much in six or seven games against Kling's team as it could earn all summer.

Organized Baseball clubs acted equivocally toward strong independent clubs, resenting their drawing power and yet unable to resist the temptation of making extra money playing exhibition games against them. *Sporting News* had pointed out as early as 1904 that although independents threatened Organized Baseball's monopoly, teams who were members of that monopoly still scheduled games with clubs like the Kendallville Blues of Kendallville, Indiana, or the Hoboken Club of Hoboken, New Jersey, where Sunday games could legally be staged. That year the National Commission had declared Hoboken an outlaw team because it employed players reserved by Organized Baseball and then used those same players in Sunday exhibition games against New York City major-league clubs. In May 1905 the Commission lifted the ban against Hoboken when the club posted a $500.00 guarantee that it would behave in future, but in July the Commission withdrew protection again.

In order to play lucrative games with Organized Baseball, independent

---

*Sunday laws further aggravated Ebbets's problems with Ridgewood. See *Baseball: The Golden Age*, p. 362.

clubs who "harbored outlaws" (that is, employed players no longer in good standing with Organized Baseball) could simply drop the outlaws when they booked major-league exhibitions, as Bob Quinn of the Boston Red Sox explained to Herrmann in 1912. The practice persisted, however. An example of it occurred again in 1916 in Illinois. The secretary of the Moline club of the Three-I League, an Organized Baseball league, accused the Henry, Illinois, club, an independent, of temporarily releasing players raided from O.B. when it played major-league teams, then taking them on again afterwards. The Moline secretary told Herrmann that Henry was a "high-priced outfit" that drew its biggest money from games with big-league clubs.

As early as 1904 the Commission had declared twenty-one clubs outlaw, six of them in Ohio and another six in Pennsylvania. An entire league in California, a fast league known forthrightly as the California Outlaw League, ignored Organized Baseball completely. Its Stockton team featured Mordecai "Three-Fingered" Brown, William Moskiman, and (the later unprincipled) Hal Chase. Its Sacramento club boasted Guy Cooper. Its Alameda team used Duffy Lewis. All of these men later played in major-league baseball.

Another successful independent organization that troubled Organized Baseball sprang up in Chicago: James Callahan's Logan Squares. Callahan had played in Organized Baseball in 1894 with Philadelphia and from 1897–1905 with the Chicago Americans. In November of 1906 *Sporting News* reported that Callahan was out of O.B. and sueing the White Sox for six weeks' salary and a World Series share. Meanwhile, he operated a ten-club semipro "outlaw" league in Chicago centering around his own club, the Logan Squares, which in the fall of 1906 defeated a team of players purporting to be the World Champion White Sox! The Logan Squares were a formidable team. During Ty Cobb's contract squabble with the Detroit club in the winter of 1906–07 he reportedly considered joining Callahan's team, or at least he used such a suggestion as a bargaining chip. In 1907 Callahan's league included players like Mike Donlin, Jake Stahl, Artie Bell, and Moose McCormick, all well-known former big-leaguers.

The Giants wanted Donlin back, so they claimed they had given the player permission to play with the Logan Squares. Donlin and Stahl were fined $100.00 each and reinstated for 1908. That fall the Commission declared ineligible several players on Organized Baseball's Chicago and Washington clubs for playing with clubs in Callahan's league, but their owners wanted them back, too, so the offending players were fined $50.00 and reinstated.

In February of 1909 Organized Baseball appeared to have reached the end of its patience with Callahan and formally made him an outlaw. Charlie Comiskey, owner of the Chicago White Sox, released Callahan, and all other clubs waived on him. Then Callahan told his story in *Baseball Magazine*, advising Organized Baseball that fining its players who competed in his league was no remedy (seventy-eight had just been made ineligible!), and suggesting that O.B. establish a working agreement with his league instead.

Callahan claimed he was doing very well indeed, and that his "classy" club had played both the White Sox and the Cubs before "immense" crowds. On the other hand, a reporter claimed that Callahan drank himself out of Organized Baseball and had formed his semipro team only after no big-league manager would believe he had taken the pledge.

That fall Donlin wired Herrmann asking if he could play again with Callahan, whose team was to compete against the Chicago Cubs, Donlin claiming that the Cubs had the permission of owner Charlie Murphy and manager Frank Chance. Ban Johnson did not object, but Tom Lynch, National League president, did, because Donlin was on the ineligible list again. Murphy then declared that his players would not be permitted to compete against Donlin.

Despite all the recriminations of the past, both Donlin and Callahan himself won reinstatement into Organized Baseball in 1911. Callahan had "performed such miracles" with his "semipro" team that O.B. had to take him back, commented one reporter. Callahan made what *Sporting News* called a "great comeback." Not only did the ex-outlaw play with Chicago through part of 1913, he afterwards became a big-league manager.

Strong independent teams like the Ridgewoods and Callahan's Logan Squares termed themselves semipros, and the newspapers and Organized Baseball officials so styled them, but they were undoubtedly genuine professional teams, wielding much more power, and better positioned to fend off croaking complaints of O.B. owners, than those who fielded only a partly-paid team or could pay players only a dollar a game. If nothing else, their wrangles with Organized Baseball attested to the power and widespread presence of baseball outside O.B.

To further reinforce themselves, independent clubs of various kinds tried early to inject order and heighten public interest by organizing on a regional and even national basis. State and regional groups had formed as far back as the 1860s, but in 1903 independent clubs attempted to organize nationally, establishing a six-state National Association of Independent Base Ball Clubs, but the attempt did not result in a permanent organization. Another try made by E.C. Seaton in 1914, the National Amateur Baseball Association of America, lasted only a few years. Despite the use of the word *amateur* in its title, Seaton's association permitted men who made a living at something other than baseball to pick up three or five dollars for Saturday play.

While Seaton's group struggled to extend its sway, another and much more permanent national alliance took shape: the National Baseball Federation, known as the NBF. It became the first successful and lasting effort at a national semipro organization and in 1915 operated the first national semipro championship. Although Seaton's group and the NBF coexisted into 1916 as "warring camps," as *Sporting News* described them, by 1917 Seaton's group must have given up, for from then on the public prints concentrated on NBF activities.

The NBF came into being in Cleveland after a successful city championship there suggested to Clayton Townes, later a Cleveland mayor, that a national championship might prove just as successful. Townes recommended the inauguration of an intercity series. In 1915 the new NBF held in Cleveland its first national tournament among teams located mostly in a dozen midwestern cities. The White Autos, a Cleveland industrial semipro team, after winning the city championship, triumphed over the various other city winners, and when in the semifinal round the Omaha Luxers came to Cleveland for one game, attendance at Brookside Park soared to 100,000. The White Autos won, earning the right to travel to San Francisco to meet the winners of the Pacific region, the Tacoma, Washington, team, in the final series, which the Whites won, taking the second and third games 8–0 and 15–5, for the national crown.

Dominated as it was by industrial semipros, the NBF operated on a solid and stable base. For many years it conducted national championships, although its Cleveland teams won often. Standard Parts of Cleveland, Telling Ice Cream of Cleveland, and White Motors of Cleveland (again) won in 1918 through 1920. The NBF also by 1917 reportedly enjoyed cooperation from major and minor leagues in the matter of exclusive possession of its players.

During World War I NBF games, concentrated as they were in industrial communities, gained popularity with war workers. Before the 1919 season the NBF, anticipating severe post-war schedule cutbacks on the part of Organized Baseball, planned a greatly expanded schedule of its own to take up the slack, but the precaution proved unnecessary.

After World War I semipros played throughout the country. Boston became a focal point for semipro play. The Boston *Globe* even printed free solicitations for games from amateur and semipro clubs in the area. Requests for games came from company teams, so-called athletic clubs, neighborhood nines, and town teams. Daylight Saving Time, introduced during World War I and later left to local option, stimulated twilight games, and they became the rage in Massachusetts. Many towns around Boston formed semipro twilight leagues, in which some players received salaries. Boston law forbade paid entertainment on Sundays, but the blue laws were interpreted loosely enough so that semipro ball, instead of being classified as entertainment, was adjudged "participative" and so could be played any day of the week. The law also banned charging admission, but teams passed the hat for "voluntary contributions" to cover travel expenses, and occasional complaints about these collections were ignored. Crowds in towns like Revere, Cambridge, Lexington, Dorchester, and Milton ranged from 2,000 on weekdays to 10,000 on Sundays.

North of Boston at Newburyport, players formed a twilight league. To help offset the skimpy collections at their Cashman Park playing field, George Jacques extended credit until after the season for equipment they purchased at his sporting goods store. Newburyport twilight games faced competition from nearby Seabrook, New Hampshire, whose semipro club on some evenings attracted 2,000 or 3,000 fans. Twilight ball proved popular in New Jersey as well, where towns along the Lackawanna Railroad formed a semipro Lackawanna League.

Individual players responded to the good postwar market for semipro players. One named Art Rooney, after signing with the Boston Red Sox for $250.00 a month, left when he found he could make twice that by barnstorming with semipro teams through Pennsylvania, Ohio, and West Virginia, where farmers, millers, and coal miners, making money on bets, might give an outstanding pitcher as much as $100.00 a game.

As before, the Midwest in the twenties remained a hotbed of semipro ball and a center for semipro games at the national level. Cleveland semipros, like those of Detroit, ran successful "amateur" leagues that contained many semipros. A printer, Henry Zander, later remembered watching with his friends the White Autos and the Telling Company team play Sundays at Brookside Park, a great natural bowl, where as many as 50,000 or 60,000 spectators sat on the hilly area surrounding the field and admired the exploits of players whose names were familiar to everyone.

By 1925 the Cleveland Association included at least 2,000 players, arranged according to class, with more than 300 Sunday teams alone. Joe Vosmik, eventually a big leaguer with the Cleveland Indians, came from this league, where he pitched for Ruggles Jewelry and afterward advanced to a higher class with Rotbart Jewelers.

In Chicago the Logan Squares still played other "heavy" semipros. At Juneau, Wisconsin, Al Simmons, afterward a big leaguer of high merit, received six dollars for his first game in the Lake Shore League and twelve for his second because of a timely homer, but when he held out for twenty for a third game he was refused and left the team.

Farther west, if a semipro team's name was not Indians, it was likely to be Cowboys. The Sioux City, Iowa, Cowboys, built themselves into a strong team after Rex Stucker took them over when he obtained work in the local stockyards in 1923. Another Cowboy team was the Dickinson Cowboys of Dickinson, North Dakota, member of a semipro league along with Bismarck of the same state, Moorehead and Miles City of Montana, and Aberdeen in South Dakota. A Dickinson player, Solomon Otto, recalled the enthusiasm of the league's fans, stimulated by the consumption of homemade beer during this prohibition era. Fans sipped the beer from dippers lowered into quart fruit jars, and the elixir spurred both betting and fist fights.

Players in this western league comprised mostly young local businessmen, but managers hired most catchers from minor league teams and most pitchers from traveling teams, including black teams like the Kansas City Monarchs. Traveling black teams also received a welcome in upper Midwestern parks. Dickinson, North Dakota, fans, mostly Germans, hollered heartening words to batters in their native tongue, like "Heinrich, if you get to first base, I'll meet you there with some beer!"

The team of Little Falls, Minnesota, in the Northwestern League, hired John Donaldson, a black professional player, in 1926. When he left, the team engaged Webster McDonald, another black, who stayed for four years, 1927–1930, lured there by the pay, which he claimed amounted to $750.00 a month—even better than he could get in the black leagues. McDonald, Delaware-born and accustomed to dealing with whites, when asked by newsmen how he felt as the only black man on the team, replied that he simply demanded respect. As McDonald told John Holway, the only place he had trouble was in Plentywood, Montana, where the twenty-man Little Falls team once arrived after midnight at a hotel and the clerk said McDonald could not stay. The club manager refused to let the rest of the players register if McDonald could not, so they scattered in groups to stop in private homes and the Y.

All this activity on the part of western independent teams inspired the formation of a new semipro tournament introduced in the West in the 1920s, the Denver *Post* Tournament, supported by the local newspaper. The tournament, like that of the National Baseball Federation in Cleveland, emerged from a highly successful city semipro tournament. Semipro teams representing towns and businesses from Kansas, Oklahoma, Utah, New Mexico, Nebraska, and Montana as well as Colorado entered teams in the Denver *Post* Tournament.

The Denver *Post* Tournament was an invitational tournament. Its rules called for a ten-day summer competition among ten teams selected by the newspaper's sports department on the basis of their past records. Each club could employ up to ten semipros who had not played on Organized Baseball teams that year or the previous one, and it had to post a $200.00 guarantee, refunded after elimination or awarded to the tournament's winner. The tournament champion won $400.00. The four runners-up received less, in graded amounts, but local businesses also contributed special prizes for players' individual feats.

The Cheyenne Indians won the 1923 Denver *Post* Tournament. One of its players, John Pickett, exemplified the reasons many good players chose semipro ball. Pickett had received a trial with the American League's White Sox, who liked what they saw and wanted to send him to the minor-league American Association for seasoning, but Pickett decided to join the Cheyenne Indians instead because as a recent university graduate and aspiring attorney he could, as an Indians player, both play ball and practice law.

While independent western teams tried for a place in the Denver *Post* Tournament, others formed semipro leagues. Such leagues in the southwest included Houston's city league, which in 1924 had a melange of clubs, including church and business representatives. Gus Mancuso at age seventeen organized a club in 1924 at Magnolia Park, a suburb of Houston, and went from house to house to solicit funds for uniforms. He collected $35.00, and a Houston man contributed an additional $80.00. Mancuso's team en-

tered the intermediate class of the city league. That year, when the season
ended in a tie between the two top teams, the First Methodist Church and
the Sinclair Oil Company, the Methodists borrowed Mancuso to catch for
them, while at the same time the oil company had George Watkins. Sinclair
won two out of three to take the championship. Both Mancuso and Watkins
eventually made the big leagues.

Semipro teams and leagues formed in the Far West, too. Curt Davis, later
a National League pitcher, played for the strong Veronica, Oregon, team in
the Lower Columbia League of the Northwest, while to the south many
semipro teams functioned in and around Hollywood, California. Most communities from Ventura and Bakersfield in the north to San Diego in the
south to San Bernardino and Riverside in the east supported semipro teams.
In San Francisco a teenager named Joe DiMaggio played for a semipro team
backed by an olive oil dealer, and his brother Vince, already employed,
played semipro ball Sundays for two dollars a game.

While western semipros contended in the Denver *Post* Tournament, midwestern teams of the twenties continued to take part in the annual championships of the National Baseball Federation, although in this era some
teams from as far west as Dallas and Fort Worth also entered NBF competition, as did those as far north as Toronto. Some eastern teams representing Philadelphia, Brooklyn, and Providence, and more southerly ones
from Baltimore, Washington, and Memphis likewise broke into the tournament. But midwestern teams dominated both the membership and the
championship of the Federation. Cleveland and Detroit teams each won
three times, and Cincinnati teams became the champions in five successive
years. While a few critics like Frederick Rand Rogers in his book, *The
Amateur Spirit*, railed against "those amateur athletic organizations" who
deal amateurism "its most serious blow when they organize the city or state
or nation or world for championships" for "selfish glory," teams flocked to
the national semipro organizations to try their mettle and display their prowess—and win prizes.

By this time the NBF, aping Organized Baseball, had divided its many
entrants into classes according to skill: Class A (Amateur) for those who had
never played professionally, AA (Industrial) for those who had not played
major-league or Class AA ball before June of the previous season, and AAA
(Semipro) for those who might be receiving some pay, although not earning
their livelihood, from playing ball. Class AAA entries put up a guarantee of
$100.00, Class AA $50.00, and Class A nothing. The NBF took fifteen percent
of the gross gate receipts.

The NBF also became a service organization. During May of 1923 a series
of articles written by J.G. Gourley, secretary of the Federation, appeared
in syndicated form in the 643 newspapers served by the Newspaper Enterprise Association, one of the NBF's backers. In the articles Gourley, who
was also secretary of the Cleveland Recreation Council, explained how to

organize and run a baseball association, how to handle player contracts, how to use umpire Billy Evans's *Knotty Problems in Baseball* as a text in meetings with umpires, and how to insist upon "sportsmanship" and "discipline." The NBF also held semi-annual meetings featuring talks on recreation problems and league promotion.

Rules, directions, and advice naturally did not eliminate problems and protests in the NBF. For at least a year Cleveland's White Motors nursed anger over two decisions made in the 1920 championship, which they lost. Twice in the same tournament the Whites disputed decisions made against them. The first took place in the last game of a three-game series played in Detroit between White Motors and Paige Motors of Detroit, when the Whites resented the "miserable decisions on the part of two Detroit umpires," claiming that "Even some of the Detroit fans and baseball officials were indignant." In addition, Paige Motors had, in one of their games, used Allen Conkwright, a utility pitcher for the Detroit professional team, under the name Doreman, and the Whites' house organ commented bitterly, "A group of sportsmen who would stoop to such an underhand method of winning a series is beneath contempt." The Whites forwarded a "vigorous protest" to the central body, which agreed with White Motor and awarded its club the series. After the settlement of that dispute, the Whites became embroiled again, this time with the team of Johnstown, Pennsylvania, after each of the two clubs had won one game from the other by the score of 2–0. The Whites did not want to play the third game of the series at Johnstown, where the NBF had scheduled it, and their manager, William Schardt, asserted that the rules required that the third game be played in a neutral park. But the NBF overruled the Whites, and they dropped the final game 5–3, thus losing the championship.

Despite protests like those of White Motors, the National Baseball Federation remained a strong organization in the twenties. Support for the NBF came from municipal authorities as well as newspapers. A convention photo of NBF backers published in *Baseball Magazine*, along with representatives of the Baltimore *Sun*, Cleveland *News*, Cleveland *Plain Dealer*, and Pittsburgh *Press*, shows men from the Detroit Recreation Commission, a Pittsburgh sheriff, and a Cincinnati judge as NBF officials. Part of the NBF's success may also have stemmed from its decision not to ruffle Organized Baseball's feathers. Its central body, for example, ruled, after the Black Sox Scandal of 1919, that any NBF team booking a game with members of the Black Sox would be made ineligible and barred from playing others in its local league. Accordingly, when the manager of the Lincoln Lifes of Fort Wayne, Indiana, NBF members, wrote to the Cincinnati Reds to schedule a game, he listed the names of all his players, certified that all were in good standing with Organized Baseball, and named other reputable teams his club had played.

The NBF's generally good relations with Organized Baseball did not mean that semipros all respected O.B.'s fiat. There were still "outlaws" in the twenties—in fact, whole leagues of them. Eddie Dyer, who later played for and managed the St. Louis Cardinals, performed in the Midwest League, an outlaw league in Wyoming, which participants claimed was as good as any minor league. The teams of the Midwest League played 120 games a year, and some had oil company backing.

A colorful independent outlaw touring team of the twenties was Scobey's Touring Pros, a team whose story Gary Lucht unearthed for *Montana, The Magazine of Western History*. Scobey, Montana, a railhead of the Great Northern Railroad and an important wheat-shipping town, had a lot of money in this era. Rivalry between Scobey and Plentywood, on the railroad line forty miles to the east, included baseball rivalry, which quickened when Scobey heard that Plentywood had engaged the noted black pitcher, John Donaldson, in 1925. Scobey businessmen decided to make their team completely salaried. Subscribing $3,015.00 and searching for players with pro experience, among others they came up with Swede Risberg and Happy Felsch, two players who had been ejected from Organized Baseball as participants in the Black Sox scandal, paying them each $600.00 and expenses, with much of the money remaining in Scobey because of their taste for drinking and women. Some nights they and some of the other players drank "moonshine" until morning. Discipline was loose. It was said that most team members developed permanent rings over their noses from drinking home-made brew out of quart fruit jars. Arguments commonly marked games. Fans derided Felsch and Risberg unmercifully. After one oral exchange at a game between Felsch and a fan in Moose Jaw, Saskatchewan, two Canadian Mounted Policemen ejected the fan, but Felsch spotted him after the game and hit him, as did another Scobey player. When local Canadians heard about that, the Scobey team had to leave town.

A player on the Scobey team recalled later that Donaldson's opponents hollered insults to him about his color, "but it didn't bother him in the least." When Donaldson pitched against Felsch, the two exchanged remarks denigrating each other's abilities. Games between Scobey and Plentywood guaranteed sellouts, and in one, Scobey netted $1,200.00. The club's monthly expenses totaled $4,300.00, which local businessmen, who bet heavily on games, covered.

Scobey's Touring Pros barnstormed not only north into Canada but as far east as Minnesota, playing on prairies pitted with gopher holes. Autos circling the field provided the only outfield fence. Risberg stayed with Scobey only for 1925, and the team won 30 and lost three; Felsch continued into 1926, when Scobey won 24 and lost 13. After a still poorer season in 1927, backers lost interest, and Scobey no longer possessed a winning team.

The House of David team from Benton Harbor, Michigan, probably constituted the best-known traveling team of the era. The team originated from a religious colony, which required, among other things, that the men keep their hair and beards uncut, so when the colony men played ball they presented a curious spectacle. The players worked up their skill against local teams, especially the semipro Benton Harbor Speed Boys, and by 1920 the House of David possessed a baseball park seating 3,500. The curious came to see the colony when they visited Benton Harbor, then a popular weekend resort because of mineral springs. The House of David colony soon built a hotel to accommodate visitors and furnished entertainment—bands, lectures, restaurants, and baseball. By 1920 the team had added noncolony players. When Ray Doan, then running an Iowa semipro team, booked a game with the House of David, he realized its possibilities as a gate attraction and convinced its manager to begin barnstorming throughout the country.

During those years the eccentric-looking House of David players proved a major semipro attraction. At Shibe Park in Philadelphia they played the black Bacharach Giants before 22,000. While the team traveled, back in Benton Harbor other House of David nines played for visitors. Despite the involvement of its leader in a lurid sex scandal and resulting factional fights, the colony continued, although split in two, each with a baseball team named the House of David.

In 1926 Ed Hamman joined the House of David team. He had been making $60.00 a month in an Organized Baseball minor league, but the sect offered him $200.00, so he grew a beard. Also with the team for part of that season was Grover Cleveland Alexander, the great major-league pitcher, who Hamman said pitched well when the rest of the team could keep him sober. As Hamman's biographer states, one day in 1927, when the team was in Boston, Hamman and two other players walked to the Common. In those days feeling ran high against Bolsheviks, whom the public believed all wore beards. Boston police arrested the three bearded men, and although a magistrate dismissed them as soon as he learned their identity, Hamman used the arrest to publicize the team, with the result that one headline read, "House of David Ballplayers Arrested as Bolsheviks!"

18

TOURNAMENTS, TROPHIES, AND CASH

The term *amateur* as used for the way even youngsters played is a euphemism, as illustrated by one of the teams I organized, taught, and managed
in Brooklyn, in 1936. To form this team I added to seven members of my
former Creston team the best of four from a group that had broken up, and
from another team I selected a pitcher of potential who, after a year of
tutelage and my recommendation, got into Organized Baseball. On their
suits, which I designed, members of the new team fortuitously, as it turned
out, wore a large *C*, and I entered these reorganized Crestons in the Brooklyn
Amateur League—the first and only time I ever placed a team in a league—
which played Saturdays on the Parade Grounds in strictly amateur fashion:
no bets, no prizes, no guarantees, no admission, no pay. In fact, each player
had to contribute ten dollars toward uniforms; I made up the balance myself.

As league members the Crestons played such older opponents as the
Gerritsens, the Hilltops, and the Elmores. According to my ten-year practice, I gathered the club members weekly for skull practice in the off-season
and field practice during the season. Like all my teams, players on the
Crestons observed strict rules and suffered fines for failing to follow signs
relayed from me on the bench to my third base coach, major-league style
("take," steal, hit-and-run).

On Sundays we expected to play other Parade Grounds teams as usual
for team wagers, but before the season started we learned of a New York
booking agent, Everett Millett, who could get road games with semipro
teams for a guarantee. Millett accepted us, dubbed us the Camden Minor
Leaguers, and got us Sunday games for a guarantee to us usually of $25.00
against semipro teams in Manhattan, Long Island, New Jersey, and Dutchess
County, New York—"heavier" teams with members generally well into their
twenties who would sneer, "A bunch of high school kids!" when they saw
the youth of their opponents. They changed their minds when they observed
the way my players handled themselves in pregame practice, for as a former
Brooklyn batboy who had also been invited to big-league training camps I
knew how a pro team should look and act. Opponents respected us even

more for our play. Against these heavy teams we were never badly beaten, and sometimes we won! The players loved to play ball, and I wanted them to get experience against tough opponents. Besides, even if we lost, we had the guarantee.

Meanwhile, playing every Saturday as the Crestons, the youngest team in the Brooklyn Amateur League—average age seventeen and three months—my players won the league championship, and I sent their photograph to the Brooklyn *Eagle*, which published it.

The Brooklyn Amateur League was just one of the many leagues available to amateurs and semipros in the New York area. The New York City Baseball Federation and the New York Municipal League conducted play in the five boroughs. The Queens Alliance, where Phil Rizzuto's team played in 1933 for $10.00 and a ball, operated in the borough of Queens. The New York State Suburban League ran a series of championships in various sections of the state. And the Empire State Baseball Federation planned intercity tournaments for amateur, semipro, and industrial players.

In 1934 the New York City Baseball Federation sponsored an occasion of special interest in conjunction with the Community Council and the Sports Foundation, with proceeds going to amateur ball. First the Federation presented a seven-inning preliminary game in which the team of one department store, Saks and Company, defeated another, Bergdorf Goodman. Then in the main event the Negro All-Stars defeated the White All-Stars 11–0. The whites' team included leading players from "heavy" semipro teams like the Farmers, but they were routed by such skilled blacks as Terris McGuffey, pitcher, and Buck Leonard, outfielder.

Like my Camden Minor Leaguers, many teams in the New York area still played independently. The Bay Parkways, with Buddy Hassett and Hank Greenberg, later members of the "bigs," were well-known independents, as were the Farmers. Both clubs included players with minor-league experience.

In Cleveland in the thirties a new organization, the Cleveland Baseball Federation, succeeded the original Amateur Baseball Association there and installed elaborate requirements "to guard against irregularities," as Leyton E. Carter of the Cleveland Foundation put it, including investigating participants' "family status" and taking photographs and even fingerprints! This prevented, as Carter said, "the substitution during important contests of more able players for less accomplished ones." The Federation, a strictly amateur organization, outlawed all payments of salaries and bonuses. In return it furnished free baseballs and umpires to the lowest two of its six classes, financing this with entrance fees, forfeit fees, and protest fees, as well as with two games per season for which admission was charged, Opening Day and Amateur Day. The Federation had only 90 diamonds available for use, 31 of them miles from the city center—not enough, it admitted, and most of the municipal fields were in "wretched" condition. Nevertheless, in 1935 all of 1,191 teams entered and played before an estimated 375,000 fans, with several single crowds as large as 15,000. Free and cheap entertainment was highly valued in the depression. Al Milnar, George Uhle, and Ray Mack all began their baseball careers in the Cleveland organization, Milnar progressing from lowly Class D, with a team sponsored by his father's candy company, to a Class A team, the Quaker Sugars, in 1932, and by the next year he was a pro.

Chicago in the thirties continued to display a wide variety of amateur and semipro teams. The Logan Squares played in a league that produced professionals like John Rigney, Bob Kennedy, and Nick Etten. The Chicago Amateur Federation cup for best player in 1933 was won not by an amateur but by a semipro, a pitcher who won 20 of his 21 games in the Chicago City League and signed later with Louisville. Some of the so-called amateur clubs in the Chicago Federation charged admission; others played in public parks, where charges were prohibited. When clubs played on private fields, they often asked voluntary contributions, but many "heavy" clubs covered expenses by selling programs with paid advertising.

The Southwestern Illinois Intercity Baseball League, too, contained both amateurs and semipros. Each club in the league could establish its own scale of admission fees. Most players were young fellows just out of high school, but some had already played minor-league ball. All of them had to sign contracts.

Detroit's Baseball Federation, like Cleveland's, established several levels of play. Some Class A teams were industrial, like Eaton Manufacturing, Reynold's Springs, and a Ford dealer. The leading team of the AAA grade in 1934 was Skrzycki Pies. But such divisions were artificial, because Reynold's Springs of Class A defeated Skrzycki Pies of Class AAA in 1934, and the Springs were in turn beaten by Michigan State Prison's second-level team, called Chief Montroy's Terrors. The Federation was suburban as well as municipal, because ex-major-league stars, including Johnny Mokan, played in Dearborn as part of the Federation.

A new league that started in Kansas City, Missouri, in 1927, grew into something larger in the thirties. Sponsored by American League President Ban Johnson and conceived of as recreation for teenagers, it soon allowed young men of 21 to play. In 1933 this Ban Johnson League formed an eight-club circuit with teams from Kansas towns, and as more entered, it became four six-team divisions. By 1936 it had grown to 50 teams with two leagues in Missouri, four in Kansas, four in Oklahoma, and two in Texas. Players of the Ban Johnson League signed contracts, and clubs charged a dime or a quarter admission. Managers received pay. This league gave baseball starts to pro players Morton Cooper, a pitcher, and his brother Walker, a catcher, as well as to Ad Brennan, who managed them in the league.

Senator Eugene McCarthy as a young man played semipro ball Sundays for Watkins in the eight-team Great Soo League of Minnesota. Rules of this league required players to live permanently within five miles of the city limits, not just be hired temporarily by a creamery. Only the pitcher got paid—$25.00. If he weakened, an outfielder or infielder had to switch places with him. There were no fences, McCarthy recalled later. Where drying haystacks dotted the field, the players had to run around the stacks. Teams could not afford to lose baseballs, so they hired children to retrieve them from fans and cornfields at ten cents each. Quarrels with visiting teams over a home umpire's decisions marked the games until the Northeast Umpires Association came into the area with regular paid arbiters.

Another semipro league in the upper midwest became interracial when it recruited players from the professional Negro Leagues. At different times, and sometimes at the same time, several star players like the renowned Satchel Paige played there. The towns of Minot and Moorehead, Minnesota, included a few black players of their own who resided locally, but the other towns—Aberdeen, South Dakota, Miles City, Montana, and Jamestown, Bismarck, and Dickinson, North Dakota—fielded all-white teams until Bismarck began hiring black professionals. The mayor of Bismarck, Neil Churchill, owner of an auto agency, became the prime mover in hiring these stars. Early in 1933 Bismarck recruited two blacks, Red Haley and Quincy Trouppe, and a little later the ubiquitous Satchel Paige arrived, accepting $400.00 a month and the use of a car. Apparently, he earned it: he won twelve out of thirteen. Jamestown also hired three blacks. In 1935 no fewer than six black professionals—Alex Radcliffe, Paige, Trouppe, Haley, Barney Morris, and Hilton Smith—played on the Bismarck team, along with five whites. That year Bismarck won about a hundred games and lost only one or two, and Bismarck's mixed team would shortly come to national attention.

Besides independents, the West in the thirties featured organized groups of semipros. San Francisco's forty-seven clubs were graded from AA down to A, B, and C. Six more listed as AA played in a Golden Gate Valley League. In addition, three winter leagues played in San Francisco.

The number of Southern semipros kept pace with those of the West. The South boasted regional leagues like the Mid-South Baseball Association as well as the Dixie Amateur League, in which the team of Eufala, Alabama, tried to hire the former professional Joe Jackson but was overruled because of Jackson's part in the Black Sox scandal of 1919. In Alabama, said the Federal Writers Program, there are "semipro teams in nearly every town." An outlaw league in South Carolina called the Carolina League, made up of small cities like Lenoir and Kannapolis, called itself semipro, although it had hired Art Shires and a number of other ex-professionals.

Despite all this highly organized league play, some teams like the Bushwicks never joined leagues at all. In the thirties the Bushwicks were going strong, and many major leaguers played with the team after their careers ended. The Bushwicks extended their season well into October in order to play World Series champions and all-star teams. They also made money playing the top black teams of the era. Webster McDonald, a Negro Leaguer whose team played the Bushwicks, said nearly every member of that team either had been a major leaguer or soon became one. The Bushwicks drew so well that players could make as much as $150.00 a game. In 1930 the Bushwicks installed light towers and began playing night ball at Dexter Park, but they lost their first night game to the Springfield nine of Long Island City, 5–2. Teams like the Bushwicks booked games through Nat Strong until he died in 1935. In Chicago, A.M. Saperstein monopolized the booking of games for independent teams.

Touring teams proved attractions in the thirties. Outfielder Harry Heilman, three-time American League batting champion, ended his career after 1932, and when the depression ruined his insurance business he organized a semipro club that toured small Michigan cities. A famous traveling team of the thirties, the Clowns, first called the Canadian Clowns, was organized and run by Syd Pollack and Ed Hamman. The latter traveled with the team, clowning and playing. Players slept in tents and ate together. Hamman split the gate sixty percent for himself and forty for the players. "Everyone made some money," Hamman claimed later, and many towns saw their first night ball under the system of portable lights Hamman devised and carried along.

The House of David team became so popular in the thirties that imitators formed clubs using the same name, some team members donning fake beards. The House itself fielded more than one team. Many of its players were by the thirties hired from outside the sect, and some of these grew beards or wore fake ones—except for Babe Didrickson, the versatile female athlete, who joined the team for a time. Like the Clowns, the House carried a portable lighting system on the road.

Despite the popularity of some individual independent and traveling teams like the Bushwicks, the Clowns, and the House of David, the thirties became the era of short-term tournaments: city, state, regional, national, and even international. Arizona, Nevada, Utah, and New Mexico also ran statewide tournaments in the decade. Semipro clubs took part in city tournaments in Council Bluffs, Sioux City, Cherokee, and Waterloo, Iowa, as well as in more well-known meets. Any clubs that would certify that none of their players were outlawed professionals could attend the Central Missouri Semi-Pro Baseball Tournament in Columbia in September of 1935. In Texas an out-of-state club, the aforementioned Halliburton Cementers of Duncan, Oklahoma, won a semipro tournament held by the Houston *Post*. In fact, the Cementers took the championship two years in succession, winning one prize of $2,700.00. A spring competition was planned for "fast clubs" in Missouri, Indiana, Ohio, and Kentucky as part of the Mid-West Semi-Pro Tourney in Terre Haute, Indiana.

During the thirties the National Baseball Federation, formed back in the teens, continued its annual tournaments, usually holding them in Cleveland, Dayton, or Youngstown, Ohio. Teams qualified for the national finals in the

NBF by winning the championship of a member association, usually one from a large metropolitan area east of the Rockies. Scouts for Organized Baseball found tournaments like the NBF's a fruitful place to recruit young players. Following the 1931 tournament in Cleveland many pro scouts sought Steve Sundra, eventually signed by the Cleveland Indians, and Detroit snared four others for its minor-league farm teams. Soon so many of the NBF's standout players received tryouts for professional leagues that the Federation changed a rule in order to permit amateurs to resume their amateur status after such tryouts.

By the thirties baseball tournaments had become part of the business establishment. Business and civic groups of Cleveland used the 1936 NBF tournament as part of the Great Lakes Exposition, which celebrated the city's centennial. The 1937 tournament opened in Dayton with a parade of the city's civic organizations followed by members of each participating team. Business and town team names continued to dominate the membership of the NBF; religious groups had by 1934 faded out.

In 1937 the team of Ernest, of Indiana County, Pennsylvania, in the Rochester and Pennsylvania League (described in a chapter on industrial ball) qualified for the finals in the National Baseball Federation. Ernest players, having beaten local Plumville for the right to represent the county, thrilled at the chance to play in the national tournament in Dayton. During the season team members, burdened, like so many players, with superstitions, refused to have their pictures taken before crucial games, and during the tournament in Dayton in later innings of a game they "shuffled the bats all over the place," perhaps, like big leaguers, to draw any possible hits out of them. They also tried to keep a reporter off the bus taking them to the deciding game of the championship series because they thought him a jinx. In the tournament the Ernest team won over a tough Akron, Ohio, club, but the precautions they took to ensure good fortune failed to keep them from being eliminated in the third round by Birmingham, Alabama.

Some problems developed in the thirties between and NBF and Organized Baseball, probably because of heavy recruiting in NBF member associations by O.B. scouts. William T. Duggan, NBF president, threatened to resign in 1937 because of the failure of Organized Baseball and sporting goods manufacturers to "cooperate" with him. In 1938 the NBF asked Organized Baseball to cease signing amateurs after July 1 without the permission of officials in its city or regional organizations, but nothing came of that.

Another important national-level organization formed in the thirties: the American Baseball Congress, started in 1935 in part by some dissatisfied members of the NBF. The American Baseball Congress limited eligibility to teams whose members got no pay for playing. It claimed that it admitted no semipro clubs, although it is hard to understand how the players of the 1935 champions, the Bubba Hills Tavern of Houston, or the runner-up, Kibler Clothes of Springfield, Ohio, who were surely paid by their companies to play ball as well as work, would not be considered semipros. Nevertheless, the ABC tried to emphasize amateurism.

Like NBF players, ABC members had to be age seventeen or older, but not all players were teenagers. One of the best players in the 1935 ABC tournament was the catcher of the Mowbridge, South Dakota, team, bald and "no spring chicken," as *Sporting News* described him, and in 1935 a forty-three-year-old pitcher from Lynn, Massachusetts, emerged the hero of the final ABC game.

The American Baseball Congress soon became more comprehensive than the NBF, by 1937 taking in thirty state and city associations, including the NBF itself! State and municipal organizations of various types held local tournaments to select representatives for national competitions in the ABC. They included groups like the Municipal Baseball Association of the United States as well as those representing particular cities, like the Chicago Baseball Federation, and state affiliates like the Association of South Dakota Baseball Leagues. Even one ethnic-religious organization joined: Jednota, the Slovak-Catholic Alliance. By 1937 the ABC was sponsoring 350 qualifying tournaments around the nation involving 25,000 teams.

The ABC succeeded largely because of heavy backing by sporting goods houses through their trade group, the Athletic Institute. The founder and president of the ABC, C.O. Brown, in fact served as the field director of the Institute. Institute members included such well-known sporting goods houses as Spalding's, Hillerich & Bradsby, Wilson-Western, and Goldsmith.

The ABC also obtained cooperation from Organized Baseball. In 1937 it announced the appointment of an advisory council whose members it had selected "in appreciation for help in developing the [ABC] organization." Members included Taylor Spink of the *Sporting News*, George Trautman of Organized Baseball's minor leagues, and Major John L. Griffith of the National Amateur Athletic Federation.

The amateur ideal professed by the American Baseball Congress meant that it could not welcome into membership independent semipros who often bordered on professionalism. Western semipros, attracted by the large financial awards of the Denver *Post* Tournament, tried instead to become one of the few clubs invited to participate in that meet. The Denver tournament still required a guarantee of $100.00, to be returned after elimination, but the top five finishers divided gate receipts after expenses—forty percent to the champions. Even the bottom five received $50.00 for each game won.

None other than the House of David won the 1934 Denver *Post* Tournament, behind the inimitable black professional pitcher, Satchel Paige. That year, 1934, the black Kansas City Monarchs entered the tournament— the first time an all-black club became eligible, according to the Pittsburgh *Courier*, who called the change "the most significant announcement in a decade, insofar as Negro baseball is concerned." But the Monarchs lost the championship to the House of David when, in the deciding game, Paige pitched that team to a 2–1 victory over the Monarchs and won for the House the prize money of about $7,500.00.

In 1935 the United Fuel Company team won the Denver tournament, but in 1936 an all-black team, led by Paige, the Negro All-Stars, the only black team in the tournament, won the prize. It included the professional players Cool Papa Bell, Josh Gibson, and Buck Leonard. The tournament packed the park for twelve days at its capacity of 6,500 people. In one game, when Bell slid into third, as he arose he found the third baseman swinging at him. Bell hit him, and an all-out fight was narrowly averted. A white team from Minnesota that included Alex "Double-Duty" Radcliffe, a black pitcher, also participated in that tournament. Radcliffe won his first six games for his team.

In 1937 even Rogers Hornsby, just fired as manager of the St. Louis Browns, participated in the Denver *Post* Tournament. Hornsby accepted an offer from the Denver Bay Refiners to take part in the tournament with them. He hit a home run in his club's first game, helping defeat a Wyoming team 25–0. In the same tournament Grover Cleveland Alexander, the ex–National League pitcher, helped the Springfield, Illinois, team earn $2,000.00. However, the Negro All-Stars, with Satchel Paige, won again. This time the Denver *Post* identified Paige's team as the Ciudad Trujillo Team because the club had just returned from a triumphant playing tour in the Dominican Republic. Whatever its name, the Negro All-Stars won the prize of $5,179.15. The Halliburton Cementers, a runner-up, brought home $3,560.67. In 1941 the traveling team called the Clowns won the tournament.

In 1935 an entirely new national semipro association formed in Wichita, Kansas. Unlike the American Baseball Congress, it welcomed outright semi-pros. As with other national groups, the association in Wichita grew out of a successful local tournament. In 1933 Wichita had played host to sixteen Kansas teams in a semipro tournament levying a team entry fee of $10.00 and offering a first prize of $400.00. At that time the backers charged forty cents for admission, and 5,000 people paid it to attend. By 1934 this Kansas state tournament had attracted 63 teams to Wichita, and prizes totaled $6,100.00, the state champs earning $2,074.00. About 35,000 attended.

The Wichita tournament went national in 1935. Ray Dumont, the founder of the resulting association, told this author in 1963 that his organization was "founded to create more interest in non-professional ball," but the annual guides from the beginning have strongly played up the attractions of finishing in the money in the national tournament, which was open to players of any age not on a professional club's active or ineligible list. The early name of Dumont's organization reveals its leaning: the National Semipro Baseball Congress. The word *semipro* was shortly dropped, but the idea stuck.

The National Baseball Congress, or NBC, saw itself as the semipro coun-terpart of the amateur group, the ABC. Salaried players, or those who shared in a club's gate receipts, were eligible for this new association, while they remained ineligible for the ABC. The difference between the more amateur ABC and the more semipro NBC was underlined in 1937 when the two organizations signed an agreement dividing the turf between them: state associations that joined one of the two groups could not accept a team registered with the other.

At first the NBC, like the Denver *Post* Tournament, selected its own participants, the ones backers thought would attract the most fans. According to an NBC ad in 1935 for its first national tournament in Wichita, the association limited competition to thirty-two invited teams, which would share $16,000.00 in prize money and $4,000.00 in expense money. Tournament ads also made much of the number of major-league scouts in attendance at the national meet, implying that promising players would be recruited by Organized Baseball. An ad in the spring of 1936 said nine scouts had watched the 1935 tournament and signed twelve players.

In 1935 Neil Churchill, mayor of Bismarck, North Dakota, arranged for Bismarck to play at the NBC tournament in Wichita. He wired for hotel reservations for thirty, and they were confirmed, but when the team arrived in Wichita and the hotel owner saw two blacks among them, he refused to honor the reservation. Churchill threatened to sue, but the black player Alex Radcliffe smoothed things over, taking Satchel Paige with him to Mrs. Jones's rooming house, a place he knew. Radcliffe said later, "Heck, we weren't mad." Radcliffe knew that the Wichita hotel would not allow him to bring girls in anyway, he said.

Bismarck won the 1935 NBC tournament with Paige, Radcliffe, and three other black professional players, taking seven consecutive games and earning $7,000.00, or $1,000.00 a game. Paige was the tournament's leading pitcher, winning four games and tallying sixty strikeouts—a record for the NBC. The Halliburton Cementers, a frequent top contender, lost out to Bismarck.

In 1936 the National Baseball Congress changed its policy on selection of tournament participants. No longer would the NBC choose teams to take part; from then on state or regional associations had to hold local elimination competitions to select participants in the national tournament. An extensive NBC advertising campaign that spring in *Sporting News* constantly repeating the necessity for being selected by a local elimination tourney may have stimulated the formation of many such local associations, as it did the Philadelphia Baseball Federation and the state associations of Arizona, Nevada, Utah, and New Mexico. A planned elimination tournament in Alabama, however, failed to take place because of polio precautions in that state. Meanwhile, the NBC enlarged Lawrence Stadium in Wichita, a two-year-old municipally owned field built with the aid of federal funds, so that it would seat 20,000.

Opening day of the 1936 tournament, between the Arkansas Dubbs of Kansas and the Twentieth Century–Fox Studios of Hollywood, attracted 12,000, including eight major-league scouts, all paying admissions ranging from forty cents to $1.10. At the end of the tournament ten teams divided the prize money of $14,617.45, and the Halliburton Cementers of Duncan, Oklahoma, won the championship. Bismarck took part in the NBC tournament again, but without Paige. Black player Hilton Smith did Bismarck's pitching, winning four games and striking out twenty-two. That year Halliburton employees and other residents of Duncan, Oklahoma, found the tournament games exciting even without attending. Fans gathered in Duncan at Harry's Brown Derby or the Duncan Elks Lodge to follow the games inning by inning over Western Union. When the victorious Halliburton club returned, a local newspaper observed, "All office work was suspended for nearly an hour while employees oohed and aahed at the trophy, which stands nearly three feet high and weighs some 40 pounds."

In 1937 the National Baseball Congress established stricter player rules, requiring all participants to sign one-year contracts and to register with the NBC by paying a quarter each for a card proving eligibility. A contract violation meant a two-year suspension from sanctioned tournaments—and by then every state ran such a tournament. The NBC barred outlaws (players signed to or reserved by Organized Baseball) and let former professionals join only after June 15. Only O.B. veterans could use the spitball.

The 1937 Wichita tournament of the NBC was a spectacle with fireworks, bands, spotlights, movie cameramen, radio play-by-play, and pairs of teams performing from early in the day until midnight, thus requiring marathon watching. The Oilers of Enid, Oklahoma, won the $5,000.00 top prize, and another $10,000.00 was distributed among runners-up. The 1937 tournament inspired pro clubs to sign 156 players, 15 or 16 reaching the majors.

Just before the 1937 tournament some daily papers reported that the NBC planned to bar black and mixed teams after that year's competition. Honus Wagner, who had been named "high commissioner" of the NBC, denied the story, saying, "We feel colored players are not only good as players but also good drawing cards." Ray Dumont commented that no official ruling on blacks would be made until a meeting in Chicago in February of 1938, but admitted that "there has been some agitation among the commissioners regarding this feature." And from then on we hear no more of important black and mixed teams taking part in the NBC tournament in Wichita. (Probably, the skillful blacks were winning too many prizes!) In 1938, eighty percent of the teams participating in the tournament came from industrial firms. After a large woollen mill in Maine reportedly spent $5,000.00 to send a team to the meet in Wichita in 1938, the company's president said it was the best money he ever spent because employees listening to play-by-plays were "highly interested" and forgot their troubles.

Organized Baseball, meanwhile, did not sit idly by watching the semipros capture sports headlines. According to O.B. rules of 1932 its major-league clubs could not sign noncollege players outright, but they could sign such players to their farm clubs. In 1936, after a major-league scout broke the rules by signing Bob Feller, a high school player, new legislation in Organized Baseball required majors to "recommend" semipros to minor-league clubs instead of signing them outright. Even this specious ban prohibiting direct signing of semipros by major-league clubs was lifted in 1938.

Despite such irritations, the National Baseball Congress tried to establish closer relations with Organized Baseball. According to *Sporting News*, Ray Dumont wanted Organized Baseball to guarantee that his players would be protected until the semipro season ended, offering in return to end the luring of O.B. players with promised higher salaries that often did not materialize. Dumont also presented Organized Baseball club owners with the chance to stage district semipro tourneys if they desired, and he saw to it that they, along with sporting goods dealers and newspapers, all got copies of the NBC promotional pamphlet, "Prestige, Profits and Publicity." But Organized Baseball did not take the bait.

All this tournament activity in the thirties, with the Denver *Post* Tournament, the American Baseball Congress, and the National Baseball Congress, occurred for several reasons. One was the lure of prizes. For workingmen in the depression, dividing a prize of thousands among only ten or a dozen people looked very good indeed. Even if the tournament offered no money prize, as with the ABC, it tendered trophies, awards, free housing, free meals, some refunds for traveling expenses, and free tournament expenses. Publicity attracted contestants, too, especially businesses. Another reason is that some city and state governments may have seen tournaments as a distraction for unemployed men. This view can be discerned from the state government's backing of the Indiana State Tournament in 1935, which two groups sponsored, the Indiana Recreation Association and the governor's Commissioner of Unemployment Relief. Even the federal government began to appreciate the possibilities of tournaments for the unemployed. South Dakota's CCC camps sent representatives to the 1933 NBC tournament, and in 1938 every CCC camp in the United States competed for the chance to send representatives to the national meet. Federal officials, said *Baseball Magazine*, hoped that sending young CCC players to the tournament might get them jobs with private industries that sponsored teams. Thus participation in baseball tournaments could be a form of New Deal–type aid and support for men who had no other prospects.

Besides successful national tournaments, the thirties marked another milestone in semipro history: successful organization internationally. Some enthusiasts had even prior to the twenties sought to organize amateur-semipro baseball internationally, Richard Klegin in 1913 and old-time baseball player Bill Lange in 1919. Lange had backing from Ban Johnson and others in Organized Baseball, and he actually sailed for Europe to organize England, France, Belgium, and possibly Italy. His attempt may have germinated from the frequent baseball contacts during the World War I between American soldiers and Europeans. But not until the thirties did Americans form a permanent group that conducted the kind of international competitions in semipro baseball that now take place all over the globe.

Fruitful meetings between national groups like the American Baseball Congress and the National Baseball Congress with foreign countries began in the mid-thirties, and through them American amateurs and semipros got a taste of the growing foreign skill at ball playing. After the ABC season of 1936 the president of Mexico City's Baseball League asked C.O. Brown, ABC president, if the ABC champions could come to Mexico to play against one of his teams. The winners were unable to leave their jobs for the trip, so Brown assembled a team of all-star amateurs who traveled there at Mexican expense and lost four games out of five to the Mexican players.

A similar experience awaited the NBC champions of 1938. By then the NBC had expanded to include Puerto Rico, and Ray Dumont arranged for the Bona Allens, winners of the stateside championship, to meet their counterparts in Puerto Rico in a trip paid for by the Puerto Rican Commissioner of the NBC, the Bona Allens to receive 20 percent of the gross if they won, 15 if they lost. The Puerto Rican champions, the Guayama team, defeated them 4 games to 2, winning $5,000.00. Again in 1940 the stateside NBC champs, the Enid Oilers, visited Puerto Rico, this time with different results, winning over Guayama 4 games to 3.

A more permanent international organization of amateurs and semipros resulted from the efforts of Leslie Mann, an ex–major leaguer and graduate of the Springfield, Massachusetts, YMCA college and a former college coach. In the early thirties Mann, supported by Organized Baseball and sporting goods manufacturers, gave talks to high schools, colleges, and playground centers about the way baseball allegedly built health and character. Soon he began planning a national organization to support his efforts, obtaining the assistance of college, newspaper, and Organized Baseball representatives. He allied himself with groups like the National Collegiate Athletic Association, the American Baseball Congress, the American Athletic Union, and the Municipal Baseball Association of America. Although Organized Baseball and the sporting goods manufacturers withdrew financial support in 1932, his group continued and began planning international competition.

In the fall of 1935 Mann accepted an invitation to take an amateur team to Japan to play twenty games. General Mills, manufacturers of Wheaties, underwrote the expenses, and Meiji University in Tokyo acted as host. The Americans won most of their games, and the Japanese declared them World Champions of Amateur Baseball.

A year before the 1935 visit, the Japanese had been accepted as members of the Olympic Association, and when the Olympic Committee selected baseball as a sport to be demonstrated at the 1936 Games, the Japanese challenged the United States to a demonstration game of baseball against them at the Olympics. Leslie Mann's group, by then called the U.S.A. Baseball Congress, accepted the challenge. Mann asked Organized Baseball for $20,000.00 toward expenses, but was refused; O.B. said it would instead vote its usual $20,000.00 to American Legion ball. Nevertheless, Mann went ahead, asking colleges and commissioners of amateur baseball to select their outstanding players.

An ad for Olympic tryouts in *Sporting News* in March of 1936 urged young men to represent their country in the national game, to "Bear the Name of Your Country and Carry Your Flag" on an "Educational Tour" as the "United States Demonstrates Its Greatest Game to the World." The entry fee for each player amounted to $100.00. Olympic trials were held in Baltimore, and eventually twenty-six persons prepared to go. Despite some protests against participation by the United States in an Olympics to be staged in fascist Germany, two teams and a group of umpires and coaches left for Berlin—two teams because at the last minute the Japanese backed out, possibly because of strained relations with the United States.

The Olympic demonstration of baseball in Berlin took place at the end of regular competition on August 12, at night, in a stadium inadequately lighted for play. The American team that had been given the name "World Champions" defeated the one called "Olympics" 6–5 before about 100,000 people. Program notes explained the game, and an announcer gave information during the warmup. The crowd was not always clear on what was happening in the game but applauded good catches and hits. Afterward, Mann lectured in Europe on baseball, and the two American teams played in London before returning. England by then already had its National Baseball Association and its Anglo-American Baseball Association, and the so-called World Champion American team lost to West Ham 5 to 3.

While in Berlin Mann's group approached delegates of twenty-one nations in the first step toward making baseball a universal amateur sport through an international organization that the New York *Times* announced in 1936 as the International Baseball Federation. Frank Matsumoto of Japan and Dinky Dennis, sports editor of the Miami *Herald*, served as executive and assistant secretary, respectively, but Mann remained the power behind the organization. During 1937 John Leslie of Canada wrote Articles of Alliance for the new Federation, working out rules for affiliation, and Mann planned regional finals for its first international championship, held in England in 1938. Five games there between the United States and England resulted in another loss by the Americans, the British winning four out of the five. The English team members were actually mostly Canadians who played in the National Baseball Association, which by British standards was professional and by North American standards semipro. The Americans, collegians, were relatively amateur by comparison. At this time a wealthy British sportsman, John Moores, established a perpetual cup as a trophy for international play.

While Mann was in England for the 1938 championship a group of Federation members met to discuss Olympic possibilities for baseball in 1940, but Mann realized they had little chance, since to become an Olympic sport as opposed to a demonstrated sport, a sport must show at least ten nations banded together, and Mann had only six. The 1940 Olympics were scheduled for Tokyo, and Japan submitted a request to make baseball a part of the program, but Japan finally had to relinquish the Olympics because of "disruptive political conditions," and the Committee awarded the Games to Helsinki, Finland. Owing to the onset of World War II, those Olympic Games never took place.

Meanwhile, Mann had planned his next international championship, in Havana, Cuba, for 1939. Participants were Cuba, Nicaragua, and the United States. Cuba won the trophy. Again in 1940 Mann's Federation held a world amateur series, and this time seven clubs participated: Mexico, Nicaragua, Venezuela, Hawaii, Puerto Rico, Cuba, and the United States. Panama tried to enter, too, but its players could not make it in time for the opening of the tournament. Cuba won again. At one game a crowd of 13,000 demonstrated its disapproval of the umpire's decision by throwing cushions on the field and held up the game for five minutes while they were cleared off. Thus does international competition inspire friendly feeling and sportsmanship among nations.

In 1941 the world amateur championship took place in Puerto Rico, with nine entries. Venezuela won, and the United States finished sixth. *Sporting News* commented, "It is incredible to believe the United States lacks enough capable amateur players to meet on equal terms those of Central and South America." Thus efforts to obtain an international stage for the amateur or semipro version of the American national game resulted in play in which the Americans found themselves almost regularly bested.

19

THE ARMED FORCES ENLIST BASEBALL

From the time of the ancient Greeks to the present, men have perceived a relationship between sports and the military. Galen, the second-century Greek anatomist and physiologist, believed ball play the best of all exercises because it produced "strength and activity and therefore trained all those qualities which are most valuable to the soldier." General Douglas Mac-Arthur made plain his conviction that sports train men for winning wars: "Upon the fields of friendly strife / Are sown the seeds / That, upon other fields, on other days, / Will bear the traits of victory."

The American Legion preached that athletic training developed the same qualities of character needed for the making of a soldier: initiative, aggressiveness, poise, courage, cooperation, unselfishness, willingness to serve, and the ability to carry on when punished. Other commentators saw connections between sports and militarism. Far-left writer Paul Hoch linked sports with national chauvinism. In a not entirely objective editorial *Baseball Magazine* attributed the Italians' disastrous Piave* defeat in World War I to their want of baseball: they were brave soldiers but lacked the athletic spirit needed to strengthen their mental and physical fiber! Some vented more sanguine opinions. To philosopher William James sport could be "the moral equivalent of war." George Orwell called sport "war minus the shooting," and Thorstein Veblen described it as "an attitude of emulative ferocity."

The connection between war and sport may not be as direct as these commentators assumed. Athletes do not necessarily make good soldiers. Sports writer John Tunis believed that sports fail to instill nerve and courage, as warlike but nonathletic races like Germans and Turks demonstrate. At any rate, it is doubtful that sports appreciably increase physical fitness or impart militaristic traits. The main reason the American military employed them was to provide what authorities considered a wholesome recreational outlet and an aid to morale.

---

*Actually, Caporetto was the disaster after which the Italians were in 1917 driven back to the line of the Piave River. And what they really lacked was artillery.

At first the American Army provided no organized recreation at all. During the Revolutionary War, Congress scarcely supplied food, clothing, and pay to the relatively few willing to fight, let alone anything approaching a recreational program. The soldiers were on their own, so they engaged in sports spontaneously rather than as competitive teams, often when they were supposed to be drilling and performing other duties. They played many games that employed a ball, as described by Professor Bonnie Ledbetter, ranging from forms of cricket to snowballing or chasing and trying to stop cannon balls, sometimes at the cost of a crushed foot. General Washington took part in sports when he could and, according to a camp visitor, "throws and catches a ball for whole hours with his aide-de-camp." Possibly the first record of American "baseball" is the game mentioned in the first volume of this series, recorded in the journal of George Ewing, a Revolutionary soldier, who told of playing "base" on April 7, 1778, at Valley Forge.

By the time of the Civil War the rapid spread of the Knickerbocker style of baseball manifested itself in both the Union and Confederate armies, as Bell I. Wiley recorded in his books *Johnny Reb* and *Billy Yank*. Alexander Cartwright, the inventor of "modern" baseball if any single individual can be so credited, helped pave the way for its martial adoption by teaching the game at nearly every Army post where his wagon stopped on a cross-country journey in 1849 en route to Hawaii.

During the Civil War the *Army and Navy Journal* supported sports for the soldiers, and the United States Sanitary Commission, concerned for their health, listed baseball among those that should be "favored amongst the men." Baseball was, by all accounts, the most popular game among both Yanks and Rebs, although players might have to use improvised equipment, such as a bat made from a section of a farmer's fence. They even played baseball in the prison camps. Returning soldiers told their sons about having played ball during the war: B. Chambers of Albuquerque wrote to *Sporting News*, "My father was in the Civil War and I used to listen to him tell how they played baseball behind the lines in those troubled days."

Not that Knickerbocker-style baseball had yet blanketed the country, although Army experience helped extend it. Town ball still survived, especially among the Confederates, and even the old-style Massachusetts game had not disappeared completely, but the soldiers of New York and New England, where the new game first took hold, naturally preferred baseball.

Most of the organized Army teams emerged from regimental units. During the war the New York Independent Battery, for example, played the New York Heavy Artillery at Rappahannock Station. Soldiers from New York and New Jersey joined in a game in Virginia for a hundred-dollar wager, and the 176th Regiment of the New York Volunteers played the 9th Connecticut Regiment In Louisiana. Members of the same unit likewise played each other, as did the 8th and 114th Vermont Regiments.* Baseball playing could

*For more on baseball in the Civil War see *Baseball: The Early Years*, p. 41.

prove more exciting than anticipated. Some soldiers of the 114th New York Regiment, seeking escape from boredom, once in disobedience to orders played ball beyond their picket line when Confederate skirmishers suddenly opened fire, hitting and capturing the center fielder. The survivors of this incident suffered a reprimand, and one of the players, George Putnam, lamented in his memoirs the loss not only of their fielder but also their baseball, which the Rebels made off with.

Sports, baseball included, could be an inducement to join the Army. Officers believed that the athletic associations of National Guard regiments attracted enlistees. Baseball might also play a part when it came to leave military service. M.A. Tappan, a secret service man, recalled in 1912 that near the end of the Civil War some members of the 133rd Regiment of the New York Volunteers, among them former ball players, were in Washington, D.C., for a few days on their way to New York to be mustered out and persuaded Tappan to arrange a baseball game with some members of his ball club, the Nationals. The game, played at Fort Meigs, in Washington, attracted many soldiers and civilians from surrounding forts and the city. Not a few of the players had met in baseball "strife" on Long Island in prewar days, and the game, Tappan said, seemed to some "a repetition of days of yore."

After the Civil War, hordes of settlers—first a trickle, then a stream, and finally a flood—poured into the high plains and mountain regions of the West. To drive out Indians defending their ancient lands and to guard the settlers who had confiscated them, the United States government established military forts and posts throughout the area. The young soldiers assigned to them, "full of vigor, and longing for comradeship and manly exercise," as an 1868 magazine article put it, found in baseball some satisfaction of their desires. But the federal government offered scant encouragement for organized recreation among servicemen in the postwar decades, only rarely furnishing even the simplest equipment and forcing the soldiers, in Professor Jack Foner's words, to rely for sport on their "ingenuity and determination," along with whatever help they could get from interested officers. Depending on location, military post teams contrived to enjoy baseball on makeshift diamonds against nearby town teams, teams of railroad men, or, in the mountain areas, mining camp teams. Most commanders called off drill and fatigue duties on Christmas, New Year's Day, and the Fourth of July, so soldiers generally played ball on holidays. The typical Independence Day celebration, a gala affair that attracted the settlers of the area, included a baseball game.

Soldiers stationed at San Antonio, Texas, for instance, played baseball among themselves in the 1870s, and later in the decade they competed against local civilian amateur teams. In 1870, shortly after its arrival in Corinne, Utah, following a 400-mile march, the 13th Infantry team played the Corinne town team during a "hurricane wind" and dust storm, and lost 62–41. Out in Wyoming Territory, too, soldiers played in the 1870s and

1880s at Fort Laramie and Fort Sanders. When Phoenix and Tombstone, Arizona Territory, teams played a series at the Territorial Fairgrounds, the Phoenix team used players from Fort Apache, in Indian country, and other military bases to stiffen their nine, which won and sent the Tombstone backers home with lighter purses.

Probably the best-known military baseball team in Indian country was the Benteens, a "club" (thus reflecting the peak influence of the civilian athletic club) formed by men of Company H of the Seventh Cavalry, commanded by F.W. Benteen. The commander had proved the courage of his malconvictions by refusing assignment to the Tenth, a black unit, and instead joining the Seventh under George Custer. The soldiers purchased a dozen and a half bats and a dozen baseballs, and, according to their own record, won twelve out of seventeen games with other units. The Benteens beat E Company's picked nine, which used some of the members of the infantry garrison of Fort Randall, Dakota Territory; but the local Yankton *Press and Dakotaian*, quoted by Harry Anderson, said, "Neither club played up to their standard, owing to the high wind." When the Benteens played the First Infantry, based at Fort Randall, and lost in a game featuring plenty of betting, the Yankton paper said afterwards, "It is hoped that these two nines will meet again soon, as a large amount of money will probably change hands in such an event." Fortunately for the Benteens, they were not among the column that Custer detached from the regiment for his foolhardy attack on the Sioux at Little Bighorn, where the Indians annihilated them. In other sectors of the battle, however, several members of the Benteen club did receive wounds, and one was killed.

During the 1880s Army officers began to subscribe to sport as a method of alleviating the spirit-sapping tedium of dreary daily fort routine. One stationed in San Francisco compiled and copyrighted a manual called "Laws of Athletics and General Rules," using profits to promote athletics in the Army. In 1884 the *Army and Navy Journal* recommended athletics for strengthening soldiers. It declared that post commanders should reserve an entire day each week for sports, based on a regular schedule of intercompany games of baseball and other team sports, to be played according to the standard rules, and that they should keep and publish scores.

Practicality underlay such efforts. Not only would a sports day be the "happiest day" of the week for "nine-tenths of the enlisted men and a large portion of the officers," asserted the *Journal*, it would also reduce the rate of desertion. Oliver O. Howard, commanding general in charge of the Division of the Pacific, encouraged games and sports in 1884 because "There is no greater safeguard against breaches of discipline than to create for the men, when not occupied with their duties, means of harmless amusement and recreation." Sports received a further boost when in June 1889, according to Foner, President Benjamin Harrison's order shifted Sunday inspection to Saturday morning, making Saturday afternoon a half-holiday devoted to sports and recreation and limiting Sunday tasks to guard and police duties only.

Baseball remained second to no team sport in popularity at the posts and forts that by this time dotted the vast transMississippi area. The fort companies were close-knit social as well as military units, composed of volunteers, average age twenty-three, mostly from the bottom of the social ladder, and baseball had likely played a part in their recent boyhood, so fort ball games were common. A few examples will serve. The Durango, Colorado, *Herald* of September 1881 reported a game played at Fort Lewis, Colorado, between the Crofton Baseball Club of the fort and a ball club from Durango, making it sound like a throwback to the gentlemanly practices of Knickerbocker days. After the game the Fort Lewis soldiers gave their guests a "splendid supper" followed by a stag dance in the club's hall, and "altogether it was a most enjoyable affair, and the club and their friends from Durango were loud in their praise of the hospitable treatment received at the hands of the soldiers." At Fort Union, New Mexico, in June 1887 it was so hot that the Kramer Club, a combination of members of a cavalry troop and the post team, played only a seven-inning game against a picked team from the 10th Infantry.

In rugged western country, travel for away games, normally rough, could also entail hardship and even danger. In the fall of 1884 when the fort baseball team of San Carlos, Arizona Indian country, defeated a civilian team from the town of Globe and "relieved them of their spare cash," the visitors demanded a return game. So later that fall the Fort Carlos team, headed by Lieutenant Britton Davis, set out by mule train at noon one day for Globe, fifty-five miles away over the Gila Mountain and across the Black River. It was snowing, and ten miles up the mountainside the men camped for the night in snow two feet deep. The snow fell all night and by morning had become a blizzard; to keep from freezing, the men had to walk instead of riding. Then while crossing the Black River their pack mule slipped and fell in, soaking their bedding. When night came upon them a second time the men were nearly "done in," but suddenly the road dropped into a canyon, and two hours later the ball team was out of the snow and could build a bonfire. In Globe, misfortune continued to dog the San Carlos men. They lost the game, and the Globe players "got back their cash with compound interest." Lieutenant Davis refused to accept the blame for the loss, implying that the culprit was the shortstop, Lieutenant Dugan, because "a shortstop who puts his knees together and leaves his feet a foot apart doesn't throw much of a scare into the opposition, and more than his share of batted balls are likely to come his way."

Fort Leavenworth, Kansas, built in the 1820s to protect the Santa Fe trail, had by the 1880s become a training post for officers and an enthusiastic sponsor of baseball. "All the officers of the school," said the *Army and Navy Journal* in July 1884, "are interested in the Club, and Col. Otis, the commandant, grants it all privileges, in the way of passes, etc., desired." That summer the fort's team defeated the Leavenworth Reds of Leavenworth City 12–3 and planned to play such town teams as the Atchison Delmonicos, the Garden City Club of Kansas City, Missouri, the Topekas of Topeka, the Greens of Leavenworth, the Kansas City Reds, and the St. Joes of St. Joseph, Missouri. One game at Atchison, Kansas, against the local Delmonicos, a crack paid team, drew 600 spectators, hundreds of them ladies. The soldiers were beaten 5–3 "by the umpire," who they said was controlled by the Delmonicos, and the *Army and Navy Journal* reported that he "made such outrageous decisions in favor of his own nine that spectators hooted and hissed him and demanded he retire, but he refused." The fort boys planned to play them again in a few weeks, continued the *Journal*, and "you may look for an entirely different result," adding that according to one officer "The Fort Leavenworth Base Ball Club is, without a doubt, the best ball club the Army ever had."

In 1886 Arthur MacArthur assumed an instructional and supervisory post at the officer training school at Fort Leavenworth, and the family, including Douglas, moved there. When the fort nine played the Platte City club, the fort club, by then called the MacArthurs, "did the handsome thing by spreading a fine dinner at the post" and then entertaining them at supper at the Continental Hotel. The fort club also won the game, 13–9. The baseball team of Fort Scully, Dakota Territory, reading subsequently of the MacArthur club's claim to being champions of the Army, disputed it but added, "we are so far apart" that a series of games between us "would be impossible."

By 1890 the land frontier had technically disappeared. The boundaries of the United States, expanded steadily since colonial independence, stretched from the East Coast to the Pacific and from Canada in the North to the Rio Grande in the South when, under the catchy slogan Manifest Destiny (which implied the inevitability of American continental imperialism), the government secured its last vast chunks of territory as a result of a war President Polk baited Mexico into, the Oregon boundary settlement with Great Britain, and the purchase of Alaska from Russia. After land boundaries had been secured and the Indians largely subdued, some had wanted the western military posts consolidated into a few large ones, but for the most part they were left intact.

Baseball not only continued at military posts in the nineties but ripened under officers who recommended more vigorously the inclusion of baseball and athletics generally, as a desirable part of Army training. Writing in the July 1891 issue of the *Journal of the Military Service*, Lieutenant Charles Noyes urged company commanders to encourage athletic sports, declaring that they "would do much for the physical training and contentment of the men" if the commanders "actively encouraged" such games as "foot racing, boxing, rowing when convenient, lawn tennis, base ball and foot ball." Noyes thought any lieutenants who were at all athletic should both direct and take an active part in those sports. Captain John E. Pilcher, an Army surgeon, struck a concordant note in a paper he read in May 1894 before the fourth annual meeting of the Association of Military Surgeons of the United States. Pilcher favored sports for their competitive spirit and added circumspectly, "The morality of the army will be elevated by substituting the healthful sports connected with physical culture for the less reputable amusements in which soldiers are sometimes tempted to indulge." For ten years Pilcher edited the military surgeons' periodical, and in 1897, during the meeting at Columbus, Ohio, at which he was elected to that post, officers read a series of papers on athletics in the Army, Navy, and National Guard.

No officer advocated Army athletics more energetically than Edmund L. "Billy" Butts, who retired a Brigadier General in 1932 after service in both war and peace. Easily the best all-around athlete in the Army Academy's class of 1888, Butts continued after his West Point years to take unslackened interest in sports of every kind, none more so than baseball. He published articles on athletics in the *Journal of the Military Service* and in *Outing*, and a report on athletics he wrote in 1894 was quoted by General Howard and publicized in the *Army and Navy Journal*. Butts believed that athletic training would see the men "at once transferred into hardened veterans, upon whom the safety of the nation could depend." Baseball, he declared, taught team play and "prompt and individual action" together with the "subservience to the united action of the company" needed by a "skirmisher in the field," and he contended that "an able captain of a ball team will make an abler captain in the deadlier game of war." He further represented that at Columbus Barracks, Ohio, one of the three recruiting depots where enlistees got their first taste of Army life before being sent west, the big drop in desertions was "almost wholly due" to the introduction of athletics, in which the men participated eagerly instead of "drinking and gambling."

The Army dispatched Butts, a lieutenant in the mid-nineties, to various other posts to initiate athletics, and he devised a system of physical training set forth in his well-known "Butts Manual" describing how to "branch off" into baseball and other sports, a system adopted by the Army over the period 1893–96.

Interest and official support showed results at posts in all sections of the country, where by the 1890s a typical eight-company post (about 300 people) contained a baseball diamond marked out on the side of the quadrangle nearest the soldiers' barracks. A few random samples will illustrate. In the North, near New York City at Willett's Point, later renamed Fort Totten, Army officers lost to a team from the New York Athletic Club, but the fort men must have been rough players, because "the treatment with which the [N.Y.A.C.] players were met raised a suspicion that the officers were trying to incapacitate them." In a return game the officers were "burning with desire to be revenged," but the athletic club team won again. The Willett's

Point oficers, although aggressive, were evidently rather inept, because in 1892 they played the Company F team of the New York National Guard, who traveled there by steamer, imbibing freely from barrels of George Ehrets beer while on board, and yet the National Guard players were still able to defeat the officers 12–2. Afterward, the Willett's Point officers treated the Guards to a dinner and band concert.

The New York area was a military baseball hub. In 1891 a team called the Atlantics, of Governors' Island, now Fort Jay, "covered themselves with glory," according to the *Army and Navy Journal*. The Fort Niagara, New York, team won over Niagara University and the Dolphins of Niagara Falls in 1892. David's Island, another of the nation's three recruiting depots for embryo Indian fighters, sent its team to "wipe out" the baseball nine at Fort Schuyler, in New York Harbor, but Schuyler won 11–5 with the help of the commandant's son, who bore the improbable name of C. Wickliffe Throckmorton and starred in baseball for Lehigh University. According to the *Army and Navy Journal*, Throckmorton virtually won the game for the fort himself, striking out 23 of 26 men. The commandant's strategem of inserting his own son as a ringer may have reflected his character, for the following year he was court-martialed for financial misdeeds. Found guilty, he was suspended from his rank and command and ordered to forfeit half his pay for five years. Maybe this sentence gave the David's Island team some belated satisfaction.

In the South, John Heydler, later president of the National League, played regularly with the Washington Light Infantry in Washington, D.C. At Fort Thomas, Kentucky, the Cochrans of the Sixth Infantry, after winning five out of seven games in 1891, went so far as to claim the championship of the Army. Soldiers were active members of teams in St. Augustine and Jacksonville, Florida, too: In 1897 two military teams, the Rifles and the Light Infantry, belonged to a city league in Jacksonville. The Rifles liked to celebrate victories by riding their wagons up and down the streets cheering and waving their standard.

In the West, the first nine of Fort Missoula, Montana, lost a "hard game" to the Lone Stars in June 1897 before officers and ladies of the garrison, enlisted men, and some local citizens. At Fort Supply, Indian Territory (now Oklahoma), soldiers celebrated all day and evening on the Fourth of July, 1891, with sports, among which a tug-of-war and a baseball game attracted the most attention. The diary of a soldier named Hartford Clark, stationed at Fort Niobrara in northern Nebraska, mentioned that he played intramural ball from mid-April through August of 1891. When selected for the fort team and issued a uniform, Clark helped achieve the regular victories over the team of young businessmen from nearby Valentine, won before as many as 500 people. In an August game the Valentine players quit in the fifth inning when, despite a battery made up of ringers, they lagged behind the troopers 26–5. The town team of Chadron, which traveled more than a hundred miles to play the fort team on the Fourth of July, was more formidable, and in front of a large crowd it led for the first four innings, but Niobrara rallied and won 13–9.

Ball games have been called for many reasons, but possibly the only one interrupted because of an Indian escape was the one cancelled when the aforementioned Lieutenant Britton Davis, who was umpiring a game between two post teams near Fort Apache, learned that Geronimo, the great Apache leader, had fled from the San Carlos reservation, and Davis had to stop the game, saddle his men, and give chase. Baseball relieved boredom when Troop F Cavalry, marching from Fort Robinson, Nebraska, to Fort Duchesne, Utah, had to wait at Rawlins Stock Yards, Wyoming, for Troop H. They "killed time" playing croquet and baseball. Out in California at Benicia Barracks, an ordnance supply depot, the Post Exchange expended $75.00 for sports apparatus, including a dozen baseball bats and baseballs. In those days military teams could purchase uniforms of various grades for prices ranging from $3.00 to $9.00 each and shoes from $1.00 to $9.50 a pair, according to an ad in 1890 in the *Army and Navy Journal* from Brooklyn's Kiffe sporting goods store.

Official support for athletics, baseball included, came in 1896 in the form of a decision by the Secretary of War and through the command of Major General Nelson A. Miles, who admired athletes and favored physical fitness. Miles authorized the Quartermaster's Department to "transport gymnastic and athletic appliances, purchased with regimental or company funds, for the use of the troops, from the nearest market to the post or station of the troops." Henceforth the Army could legally ship athletic equipment to its posts and troop stations at Army expense.

An Army officer credited athletics with putting soldiers in condition for the 1898 war. Just after the Spanish-American-Cuban war (as it should rightfully be called), Cavalry Lieutenant Edward L. King in a not entirely unbiased statement asserted that on the eve of the war "The regular army [was] universally acknowledged to have been the best army of its size ever gotten together." King thought the "superb" physical condition of the men could be "ascribed to a great extent" to "the universal application of athletics throughout the Army for the physical betterment of the men." By then, "athletics [which included baseball] in the Army was a subject which interested the whole military service." Each post had to give some time and attention to athletics, King added, because development of the men athletically had been made the subject of orders from both department headquarters and Army headquarters. Thus "an equal appreciation of the value of athletics to these professional soldiers existed even in the remote posts on the frontier."

King, who had an illustrious Army career, was a prime example of the way baseball at the United States Military Academy influenced Army baseball. He had played the game during all four of his years at West Point,

1892–96, where baseball had just begun in earnest. The academy had been founded in 1802 and in 1866 was formally placed under the War Department, but before the 1890s, severe restrictions on athletic sports limited the cadets to a few interclass games or to spontaneous and sporadic baseball play "as they fancied."

Probably the academy's first baseball game with outsiders took place on August 2, 1890, against the Merriams of Pennsylvania, composed in part of Pennsylvania University players, a game the *Army and Navy Journal* called an "innovation" and "a welcome departure from the routine and seclusion of cadet life." That year the cadets also reportedly played the Riverton Club of Philadelphia and even took on the strong Atlantics of Governors' Island. The following year the West Pointers defeated the Atlantics and lost to the Manhattan Athletic Club, this time journeying to the club's own grounds in Manhattan. The loss was unsurprising, since the Manhattan Club led in athletics among New York athletic clubs through most of the era 1880–1892, with the New York Athletic Club its only serious rival, as Joe Willis and Richard Wettan have pointed out. A few officers and the cadets themselves covered expenses.

In 1892 objections to West Point athletics intruded the columns of the *Army and Navy Journal* when a graduate predicted that meeting other colleges in athletics would detract from discipline and complained that permitting West Point to appear in the sporting papers was "undignified" and "detrimental to the interest of the academy." But the *Journal* disagreed and even proposed that the cadets of the military and naval academies should meet in sports and in other ways, reinforcing its stand by printing two letters supporting athletics at West Point, one written by Lieutenant E.E. Hardin of the Seventh Infantry, a graduate who had also been on duty at the Point for five years ending only a few days before his letter. Hardin claimed that the Academic Board at the Point believed that, with certain restrictions, athletic sports should be permitted, and that sports participation had not lowered discipline, tone, or scholastic work. The same year a writer in *Harper's Weekly* declared that gray-haired officers watching cadets play baseball and football told him they'd have given a bar off their straps to have had the same training in athletic games while at the Point and thus gain the "dash and verve of the young athlete while sacrificing none of the soldierly qualities."

In the spring of 1892 the cadets played baseball every Saturday afternoon. That year they won their first game, against the military team of Willett's Point, New York—not the most skilled team, as we have seen. They also formed an athletic association, and it solicited memberships, and contributions of from $10.00 to $100.00, from outside the institution. In 1893 the West Pointers doubled the hours spent at baseball practice and won over three out of five opponents, most of them colleges.

In 1894 the Seventh Regiment of the National Guard arrived on the West

Point campus, with 500 of its members, to play the cadet team. Thereafter, a game between the cadets and the regiment became an annual event, and the most thrilling occasion in the life of Malin Gray, later a general and chief of staff, was the no-hit, no-run game he pitched against the regiment in 1897.

By that time if a cadet had no baseball experience before entering the academy, it was almost impossible for him to make the team. Yet the academy was winning only one or two games a year, and in 1896 the athletic association at the Point considered discouraging outside games, believing that the limited time available for practice would prevent the cadets from ever developing a team on the level of other educational institutions. But the cadets still wanted a baseball team, and in 1897, playing six colleges and the Seventh Regiment, they won two.

In the spring of 1898 the West Point team lost five out of seven, and the baseball representative had to appeal for permission to keep baseball going. That fall Stephen Abbot, of whom more later, matriculated. Abbot untiringly promoted baseball at the Point both during and after his years there. The Point added Cornell to the baseball schedule for 1899, and although the cadets lost that game it stimulated interest, and they won four games that spring. Douglas MacArthur entered the academy in the fall with such a passion for baseball that it threatened his academic standing, although he was a weak hitter and barely adequate in right field.

Increased attention to baseball and other sports at West Point coincided with increased interest in athletic training throughout the regular Army. Familiarity with baseball at the Point disposed future officers to promote or at least sympathize with baseball and sports generally after leaving the academy and joining their units. Lieutenant Billy Butts had good reason to believe that graduating officers from the academy who were familiar with athletics had done much to develop athletics in the Army.

In the Navy, by contrast, baseball had little opportunity to take early root and flourish because of the Navy's ancillary position and limited function and the government's niggardly financial support for that branch of the service. From the first the fleet constituted only a coastal force supplemented by privateers preying upon enemy commerce, limited to defense and engaging in occasional single-ship duels. Powerless to fight a fleet action in wartime—except for sending a squadron against the Barbary pirates in 1801—in peacetime the Navy drifted into the doldrums. Its small wooden ships, most of them placed in storage during peace, deprived sailors of the relatively permanent attachments, stability, and space that provided soldiers an opportunity to play baseball.

The same cycle that swung between attention and neglect reminiscent of previous wars prevailed after the Civil War. The Navy failed to capitalize on the huge changes created by the industrial revolution, and while modernizing European powers exploited American wartime innovations, the restored Union allowed its several hundred vessels, some of them the most modern in their class, to deteriorate into rotten wood and rusty iron—"a collection of naval junk," as the *Army and Navy Journal* called it.

At last, jolted by the humiliating knowledge that even Chile in the Pacific War of 1873 had employed three modern warships of European make that outclassed any ships the American Navy possessed, and chagrined to learn that the United States ranked only twelfth among the navies of the world, America began in the eighties to adopt a new naval policy that would in due course redound to the benefit of Navy baseball.

About the same time, another wave of Manifest Destiny swept the country, one more chauvinistic and racist in form than the pre–Civil War kind. This wave stemmed from distortions of Darwinism that inspired assertions of the superiority of teutonic races, institutions, and governments. Claims of superiority led to a conviction that Western nations had a divine commission to spread their civilization among "backward" and "barbarous" peoples—or, as Kipling called them, "lesser breeds without the law." They thus provided a rationale for imperialism and a mission to "enlighten" nonwhite peoples. This duty, simply called "the white man's burden," was a hypocritical rationale for imperialism. (One might say that never were so few so eager to assume the burden of so many.) Two distinguished American historians wrote that the slogan was nowhere more full blown than in the United States. Baseball, at any rate, would accompany America's venture into overseas imperialism.

The new Navy got under weigh in 1883 when Congress authorized construction of three modern steel-hulled light cruisers. From 1883 to 1889 Congress sanctioned some thirty additional vessels and two second-class battleships, one of them the *Maine*. But progress was slow and opposition strong from old-line naval officers, who preferred the pleasant, easier cruising of sailing ships to the 150-degree boiler rooms, filth, coal dust, oil vapors, and noise of the modern steamships, which they derisively called "stinkpots." Another drawback was the difficulty in enlisting enough seamen to man the new ships because of poor pay and the barriers to rising through the ranks.

In 1890, though, Captain Alfred Mahan, especially in his first book, *Influence of Sea Power upon History, 1660–1783*, produced the single most potent stimulant for a big navy. America must "look outward," was the basic message of this avatar of imperialism. Sea power, he pointed out, had raised Great Britain from a second-rate nation to the world's most powerful state. Not only must America build a two-ocean battle fleet, it must acquire the essential adjuncts—bases in the Caribbean and Pacific Islands for coaling and repairs, a merchant marine, and colonies—as European powers were already doing. Nor was Mahan unmindful of the need for the United States to control isthmian territory, should a canal be constructed there, so that the fleets of each ocean could combine quickly.

Nourished by this favorable zeitgeist and with important support particularly of Theodore Roosevelt and his friend Henry Cabot Lodge, Mahan's policy prevailed. Congress authorized three first-class battleships, the *Indiana, Massachusetts*, and *Oregon*, which with the *Iowa* were to form the core of the fleet. The United States had decided to keep a battle fleet afloat even during peacetime, not simply to defend both coasts but to command the approaches and strategic sea lanes to them, as well as to confront a hostile fleet in distant seas, thus providing inadvertently the permanence and stability that development of Navy baseball required.

Fragmentary evidence indicates that as the new Navy slowly took shape, sailors stationed in home ports formed ship ball teams. The men of the U.S.S. *Powhatan* played ball during the 1870s or 1880s in uniforms bearing an ornate *P* on the chest. Officers of the *Pensacola* formed a team about the same time. The baseball team of a similar ship, the *Jamestown*, which in the Civil War had flown the Confederate flag, played the crew of the *Portsmouth* in the 1880s. When the teams of the gunnery ship *Minnesota* played the team of the *New Hampshire* at Newport, Rhode Island, in June 1882, sailors on both sides bet heavily, according to the *Army and Navy Journal*. Baseball was popular in the area around the Norfolk, Virginia, Navy Yard, too, and the Coast Artillery School of Fort Monroe, Virginia, often played sailors whose ships were moored at Norfolk. The sailors, for want of practice, were usually defeated easily, but the team of the *Ossipee* nearly overcame the Artillery School team in June of 1887, playing an "exciting" game before officers, their ladies and friends, and many strangers, the *Army and Navy Journal* reported.

In April 1890, when the U.S.S. *Galena*, a lightly-armed monitor, anchored at Key West, Florida, a picked nine from the ship reportedly played one of the best games ever seen locally against the Havana Base Ball Club of Key West. Both teams had good batterymen, but the sailors won 6–5. Sailors enjoyed watching professional ball, too. Many members of the crew of the *Baltimore* were treated by the city fathers to a baseball game at Oriole Park when the cruiser was anchored offshore near its namesake city in May of 1890.

Support for Navy baseball eventually came from the United States Naval Academy at Annapolis, opened in 1845. Baseball got an early start there under Superintendent David D. Porter (1865–69), when athletics were encouraged by the superintendent and baseball teams were organized, and by the seventies each class had a team. But in the eighties, according to an academy publication, sports were allowed to deteriorate until the administration of William T. Sampson, who later commanded the American naval force at the battle of Santiago in the Spanish War. In 1890, however, alumnus Robert M. Thompson complained of the poor physical condition of the cadets and inspired a resurgence of athletics as well as the formation of a support group, the Naval Academy Auxiliary Athletic Association.

The naval cadets were already playing football against area colleges when the Annapolis baseball team entered intercollegiate competition. In 1890 the cadets played baseball Saturday afternoons against such teams as Georgetown, Gallaudet, and Johns Hopkins, as well as the Pastimes of Baltimore, and managed to win some of these games.

When the University of Virginia ball team wired to cancel an 1890 game at the last moment, the cadets were sorely disappointed. It was a beautiful day, said the Annapolis correspondent of the *Army and Navy Journal*, and "a large crowd were cheated out of a fine game of ball." He concluded, "It's hard to tell what might have happened to one of the Virginias had he shown himself inside the Yard."

The Naval cadets scheduled nine games for 1891 and won a few. Analyzing Annapolis baseball, the *Army and Navy Journal*'s correspondent opined that although the team had good individual players, it showed a lack of practice. "Baseball seems to be the weak point of the academy, and has been for several years," with the baseball record in "sad contrast" to the football. He blamed this weakness on "the large amount of practice necessary to ensure a good baseball team and for which the cadets cannot spare the time."

Before the season of 1892 Yale's famous football and baseball player, Alonzo A. Stagg, treated the cadets to a pep talk, complete with stereopticon pictures, on "The Modern Athlete." Besides playing outsiders, the middies participated in an annual "baseball throwing" contest and a contest of speed in baserunning. The winner of the interclass baseball contest of 1892 got its class recorded on a blue silk banner with gold fringe that was hung in the mess hall. In 1893 the Academy team won six and lost four.

The cadets also occasionally played the officers of the institution. The academy's yearbook, *Lucky Boy*, for 1895 stated that the officers organized their own nine in at least 1893, 1894, and 1895. The ship on which the middies took summer training cruises had a separate baseball team in at least one of those years.

Increase in baseball interest at the academy 1893–1895 is confirmed by the greater number of men going out for baseball each year until in the latter year about twenty-five came out to begin practice. In 1894 the Naval cadets reached a milestone when the Annapolis team beat Yale 4–3. That year the team recorded a six and one winning season. The team had no regular coach, but Professor T.J. Dashiell devoted a lot of his time to coaching the men. In 1895 the team's won-lost record was 3–2.

In the mid-nineties Army and Navy officers discussed the possibility of baseball and football games between the two service academies, an exchange hitherto banned, although football had already been tried. Many officers of both services approved of such interacademy contests, provided they were carried off without interfering with discipline or taking much time from studies. Yet the superintendents of both institutions still opposed them on the ground that such games "disconcert the cadets and obstruct their course of studies." The *Army and Navy Journal* editorialized that one reason given for the ban—that the games caused bad feeling between the academies—was "puerile and unworthy of the two military institutions," and declared that proof lay in the response of the cadet audience when Alonzo Stagg, during his stereopticon presentation, projected on the screen a photo of the West Point eleven that had defeated the Annapolis team, and the audience "burst into uproarious applause." Annapolis had actually played West Point in baseball back in 1868, but that was probably a chance encounter occurring when the midshipmen's training ship stopped at West Point during its summer cruise. Establishment of an annual series between the academies, however, had to wait until the new century opened.

Annapolis baseball in the 1890s proved weak. Its record is blank for the years 1896, 1897, and 1898. There was a game in 1897, however, with the officers. Most cadets stayed away on the day set aside for sailing and boating races, in part to protest against "a system that prescribes the sports they may indulge in." In 1899 the baseball team started playing again, but it broke even in six games.

Besides having a chance to play these more or less opportune games in home ports or as cadets at Annapolis, Navy men could also play baseball abroad. For despite government post–Civil War neglect and well before Mahan's urging to look abroad, America began to cast its gaze across salt water and station some warships in foreign ports. At first these vessels did little more than "show the flag," and their outmoded state made them an embarrassment and their officers the butt of smirking innuendo from foreign counterparts. Nevertheless, the indefinite and comparatively lengthy stays of these ships provided opportunities for their crews to beguile free time with some baseball when shore leave and local conditions permitted.

In 1868 a team from the American frigate *Piscataqua* won a game probably played at Singapore against a team from the British China Squadron. Since crews in those days were multinational, the British could scrape together enough men sufficiently familiar with the American game to form a team, but the lopsided score, 66–28, in a fifteen-inning, five-hour affair indicates that the participants were probably playing some hybridization of folk ball and baseball.

At least as early as the 1870s American ships' teams played baseball in Japan. In 1877 and again in 1879 sailors from the American fleet played the Yokohama Base Ball Club, whose members were not Japanese but foreigners from the Yokohama foreign settlement, and who counted among their number an American diplomat, Henry W. Denison. In 1881 the U.S.S. *Swatara* and *Monocacy* combined to defeat the foreign compound in Yokohama 9–3, despite the efforts of Denison at first base and of Dr. J.C. Hepburn, medical missionary and linguist, at second.

Disturbances in the Far East involving Japan, China, and Korea frequently brought American and other ships to the area to protect extraterritoriality, so by the 1890s sailors from various American vessels regularly played Japanese teams. The battleship *Kentucky*, the cruiser *Detroit*, and the *Yorktown*, which periodically moored off Yokohama, over an eight-year span often contributed players to the Yokohama Athletic Club for its games against the Japanese team called Ichiko (First Higher School), most of them won by the young Japanese players. A stanza from Ichiko's song, quoted by Professor Donald Rodén, commemorates a victory over Yokohama in which the sailors proved unable to help the other foreigners: "The valorous sailors from the *Detroit, Kentucky,* and *Yorktown,*/Whose ferocious batting can imitate a cyclone,/Threw off their helmets, their energies depleted./Behold how pathetically they run away defeated."

As part of an Independence Day celebration in 1897 in Yokohama, a baseball team from the cruiser *Olympia*, soon to be Dewey's flagship at Manila, lost 15–14 to a foreign settlement team of Yacht Club and Athletic Club players combined.

American ships also turned up in other parts of the world. A number of foreign warships lay at Algiers while the French suppressed an insurrection in Algeria in 1883. There a young officer, C.T. Hutchins, arranged a baseball game at the city's race course between sailors of the flagship *Lancaster* and the junior officers of both the *Lancaster* and the corvette *Kearsarge* combined. Flags and banners decorated the grandstand, and the *Lancaster*'s band played. Many Europeans and Arabs, including a number of officials, came to see the game. The sailors beat the officers 12–9, after which the United States Vice-Consul, "with rare presence of mind," as the *Army and Navy Journal* put it, presented "a collation with tonic properties."

During the course of a long cruise in 1881, officers of the *Brooklyn*, a sloop, played a practice game against the ship's apprentices on the grounds of the English Cricket Club at Montevideo, Uruguay, the officers winning. A few days later the players arranged a "match game," ten men to a side, and invited a number of ladies and gentlemen. The officers appeared on the field in blue pants and white shirts, leggings, and caps; the seamen came in blue. Lieutenant William H. Beehler, who umpired, reported later that after two and a half hours of play the apprentices "seemed to be discouraged," and "owing to the lateness of the hour" the game was called at 5:00 P.M., with the score 20–9 in the officers' favor. Beehler noted that he himself had "pluckily received several hot balls on his feet and arms" and had filled the position of umpire "very satisfactorily."

Visits of ships like these with ball players among their crews smacked of imperialism. Imperialism may be regarded as a manifestation of mitosis in that it tends to replicate itself. Acquisition of one territory leads to securing another to protect the first, and so on. Appropriating the Philippines and Guam was to lead to the long-desired annexation of Hawaii and shielded it from increasing fear of inundation and even takeover by the Japanese—the so-called Yellow Peril, as it appeared to loom ever more threateningly after Japan's victory over China in 1895. Taken together, these acquisitions also served to protect American trading concessions in China.

The sequence of imperialistic events began, however, not in the Pacific but in the Western hemisphere, where Cuba became the pivot of America's outward thrust. The United States had had designs on the island since the days of Thomas Jefferson. Among the reasons for American intervention in 1898 were accounts in the yellow press of Spanish atrocities, real and fabricated, perpetrated on the Cubans, which inflamed American public opinion. When the battleship *Maine* blew up in Havana Harbor with a loss of 260 lives, demands for war reached hysterical pitch amidst the cry, "Remember the *Maine!*" The Spanish or Cuban insurgents were blamed, although neither had anything to gain by the deed, and six weeks later a Naval Board investigation found that an internal explosion had caused the ship's destruction.

All but one member of the ship's baseball team died in the *Maine* disaster, as did, presumably, the goat that was kept on board as the team's mascot. *Baseball Magazine* later published a photo of the ill-starred team, its members standing or crouching around their goat, a flag bearing the ship's name draped across its back. Other ships, including the *Richmond* and the *Galena*, had also kept a goat on board as a mascot. But as the Naval Institute *Proceedings* explained, beginning in 1892, when C.M. Chester, president of the Naval Academy's athletic association and Commandant of Midshipmen, sponsored the goat as the Navy mascot, navy men adopted the animal as a good-luck athletic symbol.

The "splendid little war" that followed the *Maine* disaster—and, one might add, a needless one—lasted less than four months, and the United States emerged as a world power with imperial interests beyond its borders. The results of the war had a direct impact on baseball in the former Spanish territories, such as Puerto Rico, Guam, and the Philippines, where the American flag now flew, as well as in Cuba.

Nowhere more sharply than in the Philippines did victory whet America's imperialist appetite. The Filipinos had already been fighting for freedom from Spain, and upon the outbreak of war with that country America declared its intention to free the islands and encouraged Emilio Aguinaldo and the insurgents in their fight. After Dewey's victory at Manila, 18,000 American soldiers occupied the city, dropping off en route an occupation force at Guam. The army of Philippine occupation, then mostly volunteers and upper-middle-class Protestants with above-average education—"Progressives in Uniform," as Professor John Gates called them—opened and conducted schools. Like their fellows at home they sought to instill their charges with "progressive" traits of character, replacing cockfighting, for instance, which was deemed uncivilized, with baseball. Soldiers playing ball among themselves further won natives to the game.

But after defeating Spain, instead of leaving the Philippines to the Filipinos, America reneged on the promised freedom and took possession of the islands as a protectorate. The Filipinos for some perverse reason preferred independence to becoming America's "little brown brothers," so they switched from their war with Spain to one with America during which the Americans employed the same methods, such as the water cure and concentration camps, for which they had so loudly condemned the Spanish.

When the islands were "pacified" in 1900, a commission with William H. Taft as chairman and governor general replaced military government in the Philippines, although the Insurrectos under Emilio Aguinaldo fought on for two more years. Under the Philippine Commission soldiers again often took the lead in promoting baseball. They did this through government schools, for the commission instituted a system of free education, and the American government supplied hundreds of teachers, many of them soldiers discharged from the Army, to serve in native schools during the "pacification." They taught baseball and other American games to children and their elders. According to a 1901 report of the superintendent of public instruction, published by the commission, school superintendents noted that the children were playing baseball and that "it can be made of advantage to the schools." One of them, the superintendent in the island of Masbate off Southern Luzon, stated that when he took charge, baseball was unknown, but after he explained the game the natives "took to it," and by 1902 the island enjoyed regular baseball games, which everyone attended. A teacher of the "wild Moros," quoted in another commission report, said, "I have always found baseball a good way to interest the children in the schools."

In Hawaii the baseball situation differed from the one in the Philippines. American missionaries began arriving there about 1800, and by the time of the Spanish war America had already achieved cultural hegemony in those islands. The missionaries gradually suppressed native games and introduced American ones. In 1840 a local periodical, *The Polynesian*, referred familiarly to "good old bat-and ball." After the turn of the century others recalled that rounders, old-cat, and town ball had been played in the 1840s, and that college boys on the Punahou Campus near Honolulu were playing baseball in the same decade, having learned it from a Boston clergyman. In 1852, according to the Reverend C.P. Goto, a Hawaiian of Japanese extraction, Alexander Cartwright organized and taught the game all over the islands. In April 1860 the *Polynesian* reported two baseball games, one between college and town boys and another between local businessmen. Traditionally, the first "official" game was played on the Fourth of July, 1866, when the Foreigners beat the Natives with the "super pitching of Major Charlie L. Gulick," minister of the interior and doubtless a member of the Gulick missionary family that produced Luther Gulick, the YMCA specialist. Another early game was played by the

Pioneers versus the Pacifics in August 1867 on Punahou Campus. By 1884 there were many reports of baseball being played in the islands by natives as well as whites. In 1898 the Honolulu YMCA leased baseball grounds and in 1902 started a baseball league. The American military was playing in Hawaii by at least 1904.

In Cuba, soldiers probably did not, as some writers have claimed, introduce baseball, although they played it there. Cubans played the game there before the Spanish-American-Cuban war, although its precise origin is murky. It may have been brought to Cuba by students. In 1922 a Cuban sports writer declared that a student named Nemesio Guillo had attended school in New York and then introduced baseball to Cuba in 1857. Manuel Alfonso and F. Valero Martinez, in *Cuba Before the World* (1915) claimed that baseball had been known in Cuba since the 1860s, and a thesis on Latin American baseball by Samuel Regalado dates the first regular game at 1866, when a group of American sailors stationed at Havana invited a few locals to participate in a game.

Another clue to early baseball in Cuba involves Esteban Bellan. In the 1870s he played in the United States for the Troy and Mutual teams in the National Association of Professional Base Ball Players, but he was born in Cuba in 1850 and so likely played there as a boy. In any case, Cubans played baseball long before the war, because, according to Cuban sources Ramon Mendoza, *El Base Ball en Cuba y America* (1908) and Raul Diez Muro, *Historia de Base Ball Profesional de Cuba* (1949), by the 1870s Cubans had their own teams and their own leagues.

After the war the United States repudiated its promise given in the Teller Amendment to the war declaration to "leave the government and control of the Island to its people" and instead made Cuba an American protectorate, allowing the island to become a "republic" but only upon its acceptance of the right of the United States to intervene and also to establish a naval base (Guantanamo) on the island, where servicemen played ball among themselves and soon with Cubans.

Nearby Puerto Rico is another island where the military is often credited with introducing baseball but probably did not. As in Cuba, students returning from the United States are said to have introduced the game. One story related in 1936 by a Puerto Rican enthusiast, Camilo Crosas, has it that a group of students on vacation from college in the States met every afternoon during the summer of 1893 to play baseball at a field on the outskirts of San Juan where a bull ring had once stood. They paid dearly, from four to five dollars, for each baseball and had to fashion bats from the majagua tree, which furnished light, tough wood used for canoe outriggers. One day, as the governor general from Spain was passing the field in his carriage, a baseball landed on his head. The players were rounded up and arrested by the Guardia Civil, but while they were awaiting deposition of their case they were released with a reprimand. Not until the American soldiers and Marines took possession of the island in 1898 did Puerto Rican baseball become somewhat organized.

Altogether, America's venture into overseas imperialism would affect not only the country but also baseball.

20

SOLDIERS AND SAILORS PLAY BALL
AT HOME AND ABROAD

Now that the United States had acquired a far-flung overseas empire and commercial interests reaching from the Caribbean across the wide Pacific Ocean, the Navy had become an established institution with the up-and-down cycles of the previous 125 years behind it. The war with the Spanish had demonstrated the necessity for fleets "in being" to be stationed on both coasts. The impact of these permanent steam-powered fleets on ships' crews quickly became apparent. Short, daily periods of drill and setting-up exercises and a "practical interest in general athletics," as Martin E. Trench, an officer of the battleship *Kearsarge*, put it in *Outing Magazine*, replaced the rigorous exercise that handling sailing ships had once imposed. Preliminary work of young apprentices during their first six to eight months at training stations included the use of spacious grounds for baseball. The ships themselves each supplied complete sets of athletic equipment, including baseballs, and officers encouraged the seamen to use it freely for practice at every opportunity. Ships' teams usually wore "proper" uniforms, purchased with money subscribed by the ship's company, Trench stated in 1902.

Then in 1903 the *Army and Navy Journal* reported that a new government order permitted naval vessels to requisition the Bureau of Equipment for (free) baseballs, bats, fielders' gloves, catchers' mitts, masks, and protectors. Furthermore, when a commander informed his department that his ship had a "well-developed" baseball organization, he would be supplied with ten uniforms consisting of shirts, with the name of the ship on the breast, plus trousers and stockings. Vessels with 600 or more men could also secure a blue-and-gold banner; those with fewer, a red-and-gold one. In addition, the order directed each station's commanding officer to appoint a board for planning competition and awarding trophies.

Athletic competition among ships' crews, according to the general departmental belief, cultivated esprit de corps and made the men happier and more contented in addition to benefiting them physically. Naturally, regular games could be played only when ships were in ports where passable grounds availed. Martin Trench predicted that the men would never excel in shore games, but when they did play, he said, they performed better in baseball than in football because of having had more practice at it, since nearly every sailor had played the game as a boy. Trench also declared that the Navy offered more opportunity for baseball than for football because it could be played all year 'round in the climates where ships cruised; hot climates did not seem to interfere with it. Officers representing each ship in the North Atlantic Squadron even formed a committee with the object of promoting athletics among the men and encouraging sports ashore when conditions permitted. Officers of ships sometimes used baseball to distract sailors. While the men of the U.S.S. *Buffalo*, on a southern cruise, were quarantined because of diphtheria, they had no shore leave for about four months except for a stop in Jamaica, so officers tried to keep up their spirits by holding baseball games and other athletic events "on land and water."

Ships' teams naturally generated intership baseball competition. Keen rivalry developed between the teams of different vessels stationed in home ports, and in summertime matches occurred frequently. As early as 1902 Martin Trench reported seeing ships' teams at Key West playing baseball all summer. The team of the U.S.S. *Virginia* won over the Training Station team at Newport, Rhode Island, in July 1905. It was haying time, but the haymakers had not yet reached the outfield of the ball ground, and the game proceeded despite the difficulties of fielders in the long grass. In Province-town on the Fourth of July that same year the schedule of the day's events called for a ball game beginning at 9:30 A.M. between the new U.S.S. *Maine* and the *Missouri*, followed by other athletic sports. The Naval base at Key West remained the scene of much baseball, as evidenced by the victory of the team of officers of the Fourth Divison Submarine Flotilla over that of the officers of the Second Division Torpedo Flotilla of the Atlantic Fleet, in what by 1916 had become an annual event. During the game the cheering section for the submariners sang an "amusing parody" of "I've Been Floating Down the Old Green River," and afterward all hands gathered at the local Delmonico's for a "sumptuous feast."

Navy yards provided suitable locales for ball playing. Men of the newly organized team on the U.S.S. *Illinois* stationed at the New York Navy Yard claimed boldly in May 1904 that they could "vanquish all teams that may appear against them." Another navy yard, League Island in Philadelphia, was destined to become a lively center of Naval baseball. Sailors there in 1903 while awaiting orders formed baseball teams, made five diamonds on the recreation grounds, and played games, watched by rooters, every fine afternoon. They also formed a league for Saturday play. Lacking uniforms, they tucked their wide pants into their socks or tied them with garters or string.

A game described in *Army and Navy Life* as "exciting and important" took place at League Island in 1907 between wardroom officers of the armored cruisers *Tennessee* and *Washington*. The *Tennessee* won 21–18, helped by Lieutenant Commander Robinson, whose home run hit "traveled like a projectile from a 13-inch gun." That professional managers were not admitted to the grounds for fear they might sign star players indicates that not all Navy players were "humpty dumpties."

In 1910 the baseball team of the battleship *Nebraska*, by defeating the champions of the receiving ship *Hancock* of the New York Navy Yard 10–8 at American League Park, New York City, became champion of all service vessels and received a pennant offered by the Navy Department in Washington. Proceeds went to the Navy relief fund. Two Navy brass bands played, but the crowd, not more than 500, proved disappointing.

Raw talent may turn up anywhere, as any baseball scout knows. Some time before 1914 a poor country boy, Sam Rice, who had joined the Navy discovered that by becoming a capable pitcher he "escaped a good deal of the disagreeable work which falls to the lot of a sailor." He played for the battleship *New Hampshire* in a championship game against the team of the *Louisiana*. When his ship came to New York he pitched and won against Columbia University. On his return to Hampton Roads a minor-league manager offered to buy his release from the Navy if he would join a club in Virginia at $90.00 a month. He decided not to accept, but after being sent to Vera Cruz during the "Mexican trouble" he found that he was "tired of cruising the world" and accepted the Virginia League offer, which had grown to $135.00 a month. From there he went in 1915 to the major-league Washington team, where he became a fine outfielder and hitter, compiling a .322 lifetime batting average. He played in 2,404 games and lasted in the majors for 20 years. "I can't complain of the Navy," he said in 1920. "It gave me my first opportunity to see the world and it made a ball player out of me."

Sailors were affected by the Sabbath issue then prominent. In November 1907 when some Philadelphia clergymen demanded that bluejackets stop playing Sunday ball at League Island, George E. Woodhouse, secretary of the Naval YMCA, upheld the sailors, telling the clergymen that their demand would come with better grace if they had "done their share to protect the sailors ashore." Although he believed in the Sabbath, Woodhouse declared, he would "rather take chances on a game of Sunday baseball that keeps sailors on the island than to take measures that will drive them into the dens to which sailors are usually drawn." Think of the sacrifices these fellows make for us, Woodhouse admonished; "we must take care of them while they are ashore, and no man, minister or layman, need talk to me about shutting off the Sunday games . . . until he shows some real interest in these neglected and often sorely tempted boys."

The following month the *Army and Navy Journal* went to bat for the Sunday ball players. Declaring that the Pennsylvania Sabbath Association expected the bluejackets of the League Island Navy Yard to behave "as primly on Sunday as if they were lads in knee breeches in an old-fashioned

Sunday School," the *Journal* went on to explain that the Sabbath association wanted the Secretary of the Navy to ban Sunday games and Congress to pass a law giving shore-duty sailors half-holidays on Saturdays so that they could play ball then instead of on the Sabbath. About a month later the Secretary of the Navy responded. He said he did not deem it appropriate to restrict the commanding officer in deciding when the men needed recreation. After all, he pointed out, many kinds of "wholesome recreation" cannot be conducted on board ship. He did say, however, that when baseball games were held on Sundays, "the presence of spectators is not regarded as desirable." The *Journal* commented that this ruling excluded many well-behaved fans used to watching good ball games.

The sailors played civilian teams, too, opportunity and time permitting, and did well against landlubbers, according to Martin Trench, because young officers with "expert knowledge" derived from playing on Naval Academy teams coached them. In a May 1907 contest against the Franklins, a professional team, sailors of the Norfolk, Virginia, Navy Yard, although they lost, reportedly made a "good showing." The team of the *New Hampshire* defeated a club called the Orient Baseball Team at the Greenpoint section of Brooklyn, 7–5, in thirteen innings, on Decoration Day of 1908.

Warships began visiting Rockport, Massachusetts, summers beginning in 1906. On that first visit Rockport's team beat those of both the new flagship, the *Maine*, and the battleship *Iowa* in close, low-score games. A photograph in a town history shows sailors, townsmen, and some ball players clinging to the sides of a crowded open Rockport trolley as it moved up Broadway to a 1908 ball game at Webster's Field. In August of that year the U.S.S. *Montgomery* team lost in eleven innings to a team called the Old Colony in Newport News, Virginia, but later won over another shore team, the Rangers. Then the very next month the Yeoman class at Newport News, regarded by *Army and Navy Life* as the best amateur team in the vicinity, defeated the Old Colony, formerly considered the strongest team of the area.

Convalescing, imprisoned, or retired Navy men did not stop playing ball when their circumstances changed. Some fifty ex-bluejackets, their wives and female friends, held a reunion at Cincinnati on the Fourth of July, 1908, at which a baseball game between two teams selected on the grounds featured the day's activities. Baseball players at the Naval Sanatarium at Fort Lyon, Arkansas, belonged to a four-team professional league in the teens, together with the town teams of Lamar, La Junta, and Rocky Ford hard by. The league played a five-month season, charged fifty cents admission, and paid salaries to its players.

At the Portsmouth, New Hampshire Naval Prison, the director, Thomas Mott Osborne, of whom more below in a chapter on prison baseball, sent his director of athletics aboard a battleship anchored in the harbor to arrange a game, but the ship's captain was "cut to the quick" at the suggestion that his men should play with "jailbirds," and such an argument ensued between

Osborne and the captain that Secretary of the Navy Josephus Daniels and Osborne's friend Franklin D. Roosevelt, Assistant Secretary, were called in to restore peace.

When a ship anchored near an Army post, sailors might get to play baseball against soldiers. In 1908 when the *Mayflower* moored off Fort Schuyler, New York, the bluejackets played and beat the soldiers 16–4. But at Fort Adams, Rhode Island, in June of 1913, when the battleship *Wyoming* was in the vicinity of the fort, the soldiers won over the sailors 8–3. Ladies of the garrison served refreshments during the game, and Army officers entertained both players and fans afterward.

As the battle fleet continued to expand between the Spanish war and World War I, so too did baseball at the Naval Academy in Annapolis. Under the aegis of the Navy Athletic Association, the academy fielded varsity baseball teams together with teams in fencing, football, and crew. Membership dues were three dollars. As an incentive for athletics the athletic association offered a prize during the annual "June Week" to the middie who had done the most for athletics at the academy, and his name was engraved on a trophy presented annually. In 1904 the name put on the cup was that of William F. Halsey, Jr., whose father had pitched on the academy's 1873 class team and who during World War II would command the Pacific carrier squadron.

Early on, the academy employed professional coaches, including such major leaguers as Bill Clark, well-known catcher for the Washington American League Club, who coached before the big-league season opened and later became a lawyer, and Dave Fultz, former major-league player who also became a lawyer and head of the Base Ball Players' Fraternity, an early union of professional players.*

The bulk of Annapolis baseball opponents consisted of college teams. The baseball schedule for 1906, for example, included George Washington, Penn State, West Virginia, Columbia, Syracuse, Trinity, Harvard, North Carolina, Georgetown, Bucknell, Washington and Lee, Dickinson, St. John's, Carlisle, Maryland Agricultural, Maryland Athletic Club, and West Point. After all, both military academies were themselves colleges of a sort, and so college athletics exerted considerable influence on them.

In general, at Annapolis the number of scheduled ball games increased each season, from seven in 1900 to twenty-four in 1916. Accounts of games were usually uncritical, but an exception appeared in *Army and Navy Life* in 1906 referring to a game with George Washington when the reporter said it was "loosely played," "uninteresting," and "devoid of features," and another game of which he stated, "Wretched fielding marked the work of the midshipmen." The following year ninety cadets reported for indoor practice, with Fultz in charge, but he soon cut their number to 63. Graduation had "robbed" the squad of the old men, so the team was nearly all new. A cage

*See *Baseball: The Golden Age*, p. 194.

in the gym was divided into two parts, one for the batterymen, the other for batting practice, in preparation for a twenty-game schedule.

Baseball was part of a cruise the middies made along the East Coast in 1908. When they arrived at Solomon's Island, at the tip of the Maryland peninsula, they cleared all available space on the island and converted it into a baseball diamond. Each of the four ships in the squadron—*Olympia, Hartford, Nevada,* and *Arkansas*—sent a representative team ashore, liberty was granted all hands, and the middies spent the afternoon playing ball and sightseeing.

In the 1900s the Annapolis campus came alive with baseball, three games a week being common. Interclass games absorbed nonvarsity students. The class of 1907 won one interclass series with three victories and no defeats. An observer commented, "Class games and intercollegiate games fill the spring season from March 25th to graduation" and praised the diamond at Worden Field as comparable to a major-league park. The Navy Athletic Association spent $5,041.38 on baseball for 1909–10, with 110 men participating. On the eve of America's entry into the Great War, Commander Ralph Earle described athletic life at Annapolis as including well-attended baseball contests with outsiders two or three afternoons a week and inter-battalion games as well. An officer coached and supervised baseball with the assistance of a professional player who, Earle said, "does good work with the team in the two months at his disposal for training and developing the players."

The highlight of each baseball season at Annapolis was the final game, the one with West Point, staged alternately at each academy beginning in 1901 except for 1903, when disagreement over eligibility rules caused cancellation of the traditional game. Annapolis not only won most of its baseball games with West Point, it showed itself superior against other teams; for in its 17 seasons, 1900–1916, Annapolis registered 184 victories, 95 losses, and 6 tied games for an overall average of .659.

In the meantime baseball and, for that matter, athletics, which invariably included baseball, became a fixture of Army life. America, having attained at a stroke world-power status and its attendant responsibilities after its quick victory over Spain, may well have placed greater stress than earlier on Army training, discipline, and esprit de corps. The conviction endured that athletics constituted a nourishing tonic for these objectives, for reasons similar to those given before the Spanish war.

As early as 1902 the *Army and Navy Journal* noticed increased interest in Army athletics. It attributed the increase in part to the detailing of an athletic officer at each post. That year cavalry officer Edward L. King again asserted that a company that excelled in athletics would excel in military duty as well. Instituting athletics instilled increased pride and camaraderie without harming discipline, King said, because the men realized their officers took a personal interest in their welfare. King cited the "marvelous results" obtained with the 11th Cavalry Regiment when officers added athletics to military instruction: recruits changed from being "soft and awkward" into men who were "rugged, hardy, active, and tough as nails." At the end of that year Elihu Root, the Secretary of War, approved a plan proposed by General George M. Randall to encourage interpost athletics by counting the time athletic teams were away from their posts to play other posts not as leave or furlough but as permission to be absent, in the same way men could be absent to hunt. Shortly thereafter Major General Arthur MacArthur, Commander, Department of the Lakes, ordered that each post in his command set aside a day a month for individual and team athletic games, baseball among them. He recommended that every effort be made to give the sports day the air of a holiday, including the use of music.

The aforementioned Lieutenant Edmund L. Butts continued to press hard for athletics as part of a soldier's training. "A successful team of any kind in a regiment arouses pride in officers and men, and increases . . . esprit de corps," Butts claimed, and the duty of all officers was to "develop athletics in its proper sphere in the Army." "A confident baseball player will be a confident soldier," he declared. Athletics "should not be made a fad, but a part of a soldier's training, and should be properly subordinated to the more important and practical duties of a soldier's life." In this view he was echoing Theodore Roosevelt, who in *The Strenuous Life* (1901) wrote that participation by soldiers in "sports and pastimes" was "healthy if indulged in with moderation."

In fact, each company should have its baseball and other sports teams, Captain Adna C. Clarke of the Coast Artillery Corps insisted in *Outing Magazine* in 1908, because a good game not only furnishes exercise for players, it also provides entertainment for others. "If it has no greater effect," he concluded, "it will at least avoid a growl about the supper."

Linking obedience, a military essential, with sports, Harvard physical training instructor George E. Johnson said in 1911 that obedience was not only a characteristic of the good soldier, "it is also the mark of a good football and baseball player." Other military benefits of sport to soldiers, like alertness, initiative, and self-reliance, obtained mention in a glowing 1907 *Army and Navy Journal* editorial on the Army's sports program. The editorial asserted that the Army's program was practical, progressive, carefully regulated by the officers, and characterized by fair play. In other words, early in the century the Army had already converted what used to be spare-time fun into a military requirement.

Military men had by 1915 begun to think about the possibility that the war in Europe would affect America. The Secretary of War, Lindley M. Garrison, replied to *Baseball Magazine*'s query about military use of baseball in recruiting by declaring that in the Army "athletics are always encouraged," and since baseball "is one of the most popular athletic sports throughout the

Army, . . . in securing good clean men for the Army" there is no better place to look than "among baseball players."

One drawback to operation of the athletic program was money. Even Secretary of War Elihu Root, in advocating annual athletic tournaments, did so with the proviso that they be held without government expenditure. In 1903 General Order 16 set up an elaborate system of athletics at all camps, but prizes for the tournaments had to come from Post Exchange profits. Thus instead of financing all aspects of the program the government ordered the plan without supplying the funds to carry it out. Lieutenant General A.R. Chafee, Acting Secretary of War and Chief of Staff in 1905, husbanded the government's money, too, ordering that during 1905 no department could hold division athletic meets that involved expenditures for Army transportation.

Yet a little money judiciously expended, as Lieutenant King remarked, considerably increased the interest and enjoyment of the men. King, then stationed at Fort Myer, Virginia, pointed out that nine men playing baseball would enjoy it—they would travel from 150 to 200 miles to play another post team—but if they had distinctive uniforms, no matter how simple, their interest and that of the spectators would increase. To get money for equipment and travel soldiers usually resorted to their company funds, which were obtained in various ways but mostly from the earnings of the post canteen.

"It is a pity," wrote Second Lieutenant F.B. Terrell of the 19th Infantry in 1910, "that our Government allots no money for the support of its national game (baseball) in the Army." Teams representing Army companies found support from the players themselves, along with some funds from the company, he said, but they should have more, because

> the men take pride in having a good regimental team, so they can go down and trim the town people. A good baseball team is a constant source of amuse-ment to the garrison, as well as an impetus and a reward to those players who have come up through the school of the company team to the "big team."

Terrell recommended that the government allot $500.00 to each regiment for baseball.

Meanwhile, military players found financial support wherever they could. Soldiers solicited money to defray expenses of the Military Baseball League of the Department of the East, a nine-fort league in the New York area, so the fort teams could order uniforms varying from the bright red of the Artillery to the navy blue of the Brooklyn Navy Yard. The league also re-ceived a cash contribution from a blanket group called the Military Athletic League, a benevolent organization that sponsored tournaments to benefit athletics in the Army, Navy, National Guard, and Naval Militia. This covering group also furnished baseball equipment and uniforms to several posts in the New York area.

At Fort Riley, Kansas, both the baseball and the football teams received support from popular subscription. Out in Fort Crook, Nebraska, the post athletic officer, who also managed the baseball team, arranged a "grand ball" for 800 people with proceeds to go to the team.

A popular way of providing outfits for baseball and other sports teams was using the proceeds of the beer canteen. Teams at Fort D.A. Russell, Wyoming, for one, were supported in this way. At one point Congress passed a law discontinuing the sale of beer in Army canteens, so that source dried up. One result was that the men sought stronger drink (whiskey) elsewhere, just as the Association of Military Surgeons had predicted. While it lasted, observed Lieutenant Butts, "the beer canteen was a great friend of the soldier in the matter of all sport."

A lesser obstacle to the progress of Army baseball was civilian objection to Sunday play. Like sailors, soldiers playing baseball came under the scowl of Sabbatarian intolerance. In this jaundiced prohibition baseball had plenty of company. The Methodists, for example, had a blacklist of some five dozen activities ranging from opera to blindman's buff.

The same year the sailors in Philadelphia were being castigated for Sunday play (1907), soldiers at Fort McPherson, Georgia, were criticized by local Baptist and Methodist ministers because their Sunday play attracted many civilian spectators. Local ordinances regarding Sunday play did not affect the federal government, and the fort's commanding officer encouraged Sunday sports in order to keep his men happy and occupied, but according to Professor Steven Riess, the Army did try to mitigate its override of local law by not permitting civilians to play soldiers on Sunday unless they put a couple of soldiers on their teams.

Sabbatarians busied themselves in all parts of the country in those days. In 1908 a group of Kansas City religious zealots went all the way to Washington to protest to the Secretaries of War and the Navy about Sunday ball by soldiers and sailors. Kansas City was only about twenty miles from Fort Leavenworth and about fifty from Fort Riley, where baseball was very popular. But government authorities held their ground, informing the protestors bluntly that "enlisted men have little opportunity for relaxation" and that

> after the usual hours of Sunday worship it will be entirely proper to allow
> them to play baseball on the naval and military reservations where such contests
> do not interfere with other people's observance of the Sabbath.

At Fort Banks and Fort Heath, near Boston, Massachusetts, the Women's Christian Temperance Union complained in 1908 about ball playing on Sunday. Colonel J.D.C. Hoskins, in command of the artillery district of Boston, defended the practice, explaining that the soldiers played behind the officers' quarters, out of sight of the townspeople, and, so far as I can see, their playing does not disturb anybody. There has been Sunday baseball in the Army for forty years. It is a clean sport, and so long as the game is played without disturbance, I shall continue to permit it.

In this stance Hoskins received unequivocal support from President Theodore Roosevelt, who in a letter to the WCTU of Boston favored Sunday ball for soldiers, considered exercise as important for military training on Sundays as well as other days, and saw no reason for discriminating against baseball. These depositions did not stop the complaints, for they cropped up again in 1910, but the Sabbatarian tide was already ebbing even among ministers, who were themselves being influenced by the play movement.

Military baseball teams played a wide variety of opponents. Companies and regiments at the same fort played each other, of course. Soldiers could participate in games in which officers were pitted against enlisted men, fort against fort, and soldiers against sailors or National Guardsmen. But soldiers also played schools, colleges, town teams, athletic clubs, country clubs, semipros, and even big leaguers. After all, baseball was the people's game.

School and college teams were popular adversaries. One time the post team of Fort Logan H. Roots, Arkansas, beat the Arkansas Military Academy team, and the *Army and Navy Journal* claimed the soldiers won because of "determination and grit," but perhaps just being older had something to do with it. In 1908 the Fort Totten (Queens, New York) team played near-by Holy Trinity School with a sergeant umpiring. To stop the argument when one of the umpire's decisions was disputed, the colonel stepped from the sidelines and called "Sergeant!" At once, said *Army and Navy Life*, the umpire became a soldier again and saluted. The colonel said to him, "The umpire's decisions are not disputed on this field." And thereafter, none were.

Fort teams frequently played local town teams. The team of Fort Rodman triumphed over the town of Middleboro, Massachusetts, on Sunday, May 7, 1908, 13–1 before 7,000 fans, but then Rodman had several spectacular players who had played either on town teams, elsewhere in United States, in Cuba, or on a crack Army team in the Philippines. One even expected to go into professional baseball.

In 1913 the Seventh Regiment team of New York followed a victory over West Point by defeating the suburban South Orange Field Club 10–6. At Washington Barracks, Washington, D.C., in 1908, Company C of the Hospital Corps won over the Potomac Athletic Club 3–1. The soldier's pitcher struck out twelve men, despite having just been released from the hospital; afterward *Army and Navy Life* quipped that he should in future be kept in the hospital between games!

Arch-rival of the Fort Leavenworth, Kansas, team was the Kansas City Country Club. Douglas MacArthur, commander of Company K and the fort team's player-manager, played enthusiastically but still could not hit. According to his biographer, William Manchester, MacArthur was not above using questionable tactics. Once he feasted the country club players sumptuously, and they lost the game after gorging themselves. Another time MacArthur introduced two players as recent West Point stars when actually they were Texas professionals he had hired for twenty dollars; the soldiers won again.

Games in which one fort played another were still common. The Fort Columbus team visited Sandy Hook, New Jersey, to play the Fort Hancock team but lost 12–2 as the Hancock players took revenge for having previously bowed in defeat at Governors' Island. Many officers and their families watched that game. Fort Slocum, also in the New York vicinity, played several games in 1908 against another nearby team, the one from Fort Totten in Queens. The visitors arrived by boat and were then serenaded by a military band as the home team escorted them to and from the field.

Forts in the same section also created fort leagues with regular schedules. The teams of Forts Banks, Warren, Revere, and Andrews formed a four-fort league in the Boston area in 1908. Another fort league was organized in Maine in 1908 among Forts Preble, Williams, and McKinley, competing for a cup given by a Portland business firm. In Rhode Island in 1903 Fort Adams, champions of a four-team league, won the Garrettson Cup, offered by the Honorable F.P. Garretson, and were honored by a parade in Newport. In the New York region six forts, the Quartermaster's Corps, and the Brooklyn Navy Yard competed for a championship in 1902.

Perhaps the most popular type of military game was one against major leaguers. The Yankees beat the 22nd Infantry team 15–2 at Texas City, Texas, in March of 1914 before a crowd estimated by the New York *Herald* at nearly 6,000.

Sometimes winners of intercompany tournaments held at one post received a handsome trophy, as did those at Fort Mason, California, in 1903. Perhaps the most extensive of these company tournaments took place at Fort Slocum, a recruit depot, where each of the six recruit companies participated in a forty-six-game schedule. Visiting teams were brought in, too, at the expense of the Post Exchange.

Officers of one regiment might play those of another, as at Camp McCoy, Sparta, Wisconsin, in 1912, where the officers of the 27th Infantry won "by a hair" behind Lieutenant Lanza's "whisker ball," obtained by rubbing the ball vigorously in his beard before each delivery. Rules prohibited use of a "foreign substance," but after all, the beard is hardly a foreign substance!

A considerable variety of ball games could be arranged at the important Fort Monroe base in Virginia. For instance, in the course of one summer the fort team defeated Cornell University, beat the officers of the U.S.S. *Texas* in a game called in the fifth inning, divided two games with the men of the 73rd Company, and shut out the Newport News Athletics of the Peninsula League on Decoration Day. Army officers at the fort also challenged their Naval counterparts in the North Atlantic Squadron, and the

Artillery School there played the Old College Point town team. And as a lark the officers of the Artillery School played each other by dividing themselves into fat men versus thin and married versus single.

An uncommon variety of games was also played at Fort Riley, Kansas. In 1902 the team undertook a so-called southern trip, playing such towns as St. George, Queen City, Emporia, Topeka, Abilene, and Chapman. The following year the team went as far south as Lindsborg, about 150 miles from their post, and put several Kansas colleges on its schedule, while back at the fort, company teams were playing for a silk banner.

In fine, Army men played a multitude of military baseball games all over the country during the period just before the first World War. My research on military installations revealed baseball at 32 forts, 14 of them in the East, 3 in the South, and 15 in the West, although many more forts doubtless enjoyed the game.

The pervasiveness and popularity of baseball between the Spanish War and World War I at Army posts sprinkled throughout the United States owed much to the deepening inroads of the game at West Point, where the basic attitude and approach apropos baseball had changed from one in which authorities regarded games as an amusement of which the outcome mattered little to one in which a "must-win spirit" should be instilled. In a word, as the *Army and Navy Journal* said in 1938, during the 1900s at West Point sports became a major part of cadet life.

Signs of the transformation included withdrawing sole control of teams from the captain and replacing him with professional coaches and instructors, providing a training table, and undertaking longer playing schedules against stronger, more diverse opponents. Moreover, an Army Athletic Association, with two lieutenants covering baseball, assumed control of sports. The association's treasurer reported a total expenditure for 1901 of $11,006.50, leaving a balance of $4,000.52. Cadets contributed $1,632.50, officers at the post $1,510.25, officers not at the post $6,442.58, and civilians $2,034.00. The *Army and Navy Journal* credited the good athletic record of the 1901 season to the consideration given sport by the Army authorities, the excellent spirit of the squads, the able work of the coaches, and "the splendid financial support received from the friends of the Army team all over the world," adding,

> All who knew West Point and the life of a cadet when there was little or no interest taken in athletics here and who see the difference now, would be sure that the money contributed does a great deal of good, and is used for a good purpose.

Such changes brought rapid results. In 1902 West Point won 10 out of 16 ball games against leading colleges, and in 1903 it won 5 out of 10, including "the brightest event of the season," a defeat of Harvard 6–4. Renewal of the annual game with the Naval Academy in 1904, which West Point won 8–2, stimulated interest, and the Army team won 5 and tied 1 out of 9 games versus colleges and the Seventh Regiment. Only 3 games out of 15 were lost in 1906, and not one of them could be termed an overwhelming defeat, thus demonstrating, said Lieutenant Stephen Abbot in *Army and Navy Life,* the great value of a professional coach. Abbot, who had graduated in 1902 and had been called back to West Point to teach in 1904, was in 1908 made baseball representative of the West Point Athletic Council.

About fifty fourth-class men turned out for baseball in 1908, but the academy won only four and tied one game out of sixteen, a reversal attributed to the loss of players by graduation and of six others whose studies were "not up to the mark."

In 1910 at West Point the Army Athletic Association not only assumed responsibility for financing sports, it arranged schedules, purchased equipment, provided coaches, and built an athletic field. That season the West Pointers won 14 ball games, including the game with Annapolis, against 6 losses for a percentage of .700 because of good fielding and hitting and superb baserunning, according to baseball representative Captain C.A. Trott. The baseball team for 1912 scheduled 17 games, mostly against the usual assortment of colleges as well as opponents played previously.

Besides Douglas MacArthur, two more future generals became baseball candidates at West Point in the era before the Great War: Dwight Eisenhower and Omar Bradley, both members of the class of 1915. Coach Sammy Strang, former New York Giants player, told baseball hopeful Eisenhower in the spring of 1912 that he could play if he changed his batting style from chopping and poking at the ball to free-swinging. Ike practiced all year, but a leg injury the following spring prevented him from trying out again, and he never did make the team. Later he lamented, "Not making the baseball team at West Point was one of the greatest disappointments of my life, maybe the greatest."

Omar Bradley did make the team, as a .380-hitting outfielder with an outstanding throwing arm, and he became one of the best players the Point ever had. In 1937 the New York *Times* quoted him as saying that in developing soldiers, team sports cannot be beat: "every member of our baseball team at West Point became a general; this proves the value of team sports for the military."

West Point athletics were an important springhead of baseball in the Army. Edward L. King, then still a lieutenant, said it was easy to trace the results of athletic training at West Point from its recent graduates who had benefited by sports there to the men they commanded afterward. In such commands the young officers "put the athletic spirit into the men" and obtain "astonishing results in a short time." More than that, Lieutenant Butts felt it "incumbent" on recent graduates, "who have had the benefit of games, sports and athletic training denied to older officers," to encourage athletics upon joining their regiments, "coaching baseball and football teams, promoting field days, and thus developing better and cleaner soldiers."

After America's acquisition of an extensive overseas empire, men of both services played more baseball abroad. The Navy also introduced to the actual operation of the warships themselves certain practices commonly associated with baseball and sports generally in the expectation of deriving benefits attributed to them. And oddly enough the officer mainly responsible for these new policies, William Sowden Sims, was not himself a devotee of baseball or even sports.

The fresh relationship between sports and warship operations developed in a roundabout way. Although the Navy had discarded its build-and-neglect cycles, the enamel of quick, decisive victory over a decrepit Spanish fleet concealed serious weaknesses, including atrocious marksmanship—for example, of 9,433 shells fired at Santiago only 122 hit targets. Behind the scenes, however, Sims, Annapolis '80, led a group of Young Turk reformers who sought to overcome the Navy's backwardness. Confronted by insensible and indifferent old-line conservative admirals, Sims wrote directly to Theodore Roosevelt explaining the necessity for change. The president proved well-disposed toward Sims and his ideas, and as a result continuous-aim firing and new ship design won approval. Sims emphasized traits in harmony with those attributed to military baseball: teamwork among ships' crews, especially among the gunners, and intership competition and prizes to winning gunnery crews.

At the same time, military ball spread even farther in the American empire and beyond it, introducing the game to other peoples in other lands. This is not to say, however, that other groups—black professionals, teams from Organized Baseball, and college teams—did not also fertilize baseball abroad.

In Cuba, where the United States retained (and still holds) a base at Guantanamo, by 1905 servicemen were using three baseball fields in its vicinity. When the North Atlantic fleet anchored there a ball game took place at 2:00 P.M. every other weekday, as well as on Saturdays and Sundays. Meanwhile, after "pacification" of the island the Cubans themselves resumed their own baseball play. In 1909, at the time of the inauguration of Cuban President Jose Miguel Gomez, the steam frigate *Mississippi* anchored in Guantanamo Bay, and the ship's team took the opportunity of playing and beating the teams of both the *Tacoma* and the *Maine*. On another occasion, in February 1911, pandemonium reigned during a tight game at the target grounds when $4,000.00 reportedly rode on the outcome; the score was tied several times, but finally the team of the *Idaho* "walloped" the *Virginia* outfit 12–8.

In March 1914 the commander of the Atlantic Torpedo Flotilla at Guantanamo sent what passed for a jocular challenge to the commander and officers of the Battleship Fleet and all other vessels in the bay, inviting them to a game in which only officers of the grades lieutenant and above would take part and the pitchers must be lieutenant commanders or men of higher rank who had not pitched for the previous five years. Certain odd ground rules were also established. Players who made two-base hits would get soft drinks at the expense of the losers, those who got three-base hits would receive a drink "with a stick in it," and those who hit homers could apply for twenty-four hours' "rough liberty in Santiago." Runs scored by a commander, captain, or admiral would count as three, four, and five runs respectively. Whether anyone actually took the commander up on this challenge is doubtful.

After the American military occupied Puerto Rico, military play dominated baseball there. Service teams played each other on the parade grounds at El Morro and at Mayaguez. By 1900 soldiers were playing at Ponce, and baseball equipment could be purchased in local hardware stores. Companies E and G of the 11th Infantry held a series of athletic events in Puerto Rico in 1901, and Company G won the baseball competition. About the same time four teams played a mostly military series in a suburb of San Juan at a field called Puerta de Tierra, but this time they included a few native players. One team was the 59th Marines, another consisted of players from various Army units, a third, called "Red D Line," included several Puerto Rican players, and the fourth represented the Department of the Interior in the insular government.

Meanwhile, in the Philippines, baseball had, with the help of the military, become firmly established. Mark Sullivan said stories were trickling out of the islands "about games between teams clad in uniforms noteworthy for their scantiness" and of threats to umpires "to correct faulty decisions with bolos." Major General J. Franklin Bell, in command at Manila, may have been unaware of the scanty uniforms and the bolo threats, for he said baseball had done more to "civilize" the Filipinos than anything else. A magazine writer reported that when two military teams played, if a ball was hit into the crowd, "it disappeared like a soap bubble." Like Americans, the natives watched and gambled on every play. Some tribal chiefs were said to be taking baseball only on their own terms, believing that they alone should go to bat and that the baserunning should be left to their followers.

By 1908 a Philippine League of American military teams, including the Marines, the Infantry, and the Naval Station, was playing a regular season. Service teams also played Al Reach's touring professionals when they stopped in Manila on their 1908–09 tour. Military teams charged admission to Manila League games, played Sunday afternoons. In a Manila League game February 10, 1910, at Dagupan, where the 12th Infantry beat the 17th Infantry 7–5, $1,000.00 reputedly changed hands. The League also accepted the Standard Oil Company's offer to build a stand seating 300.

Physician Victor Heiser, who was commissioner of public health in the

Philippines and whose autobiographical book, published in 1936, found wide readership in America, related how he was once startled by coming upon a group of yelling Igorots (members of headhunting mountain tribes) playing baseball in a clearing. They paid no attention to him, deeply involved as they were in an intervillage ball game. The catcher was clad only in a g-string and mask. When a batter made a base hit with a man on base, the runner started for second amidst cries of "Slide, you son of a bitch, slide!" The Igorots, said Heiser, had watched the games of the American soldiers at the local hill station and were "letter perfect in their lines."

Two pieces of contemporary fiction, one in *Harper's Weekly* in 1907 and the other in *Army and Navy Life* in 1909, reveal baseball relations between occupying soldiers and Filipinos. In both stories, the Filipinos hoodwink the soldiers into believing they know little about baseball before the soldiers challenge them to a game. After the soldiers have bet everything they can lay their hands on, including their rifles, the Filipinos defeat them and clean up the winnings. Explanations for the natives' ability given in the two stories are similar. In the first story it is later revealed that the Filipino pitcher had learned to play ball when he attended an American college; in the second, an Army lieutenant who had been a Harvard player taught his Filipino Scouts to play, and they had even displayed their skills at the St. Louis Exposition of 1904 before "giving up civilization" and returning to the islands.

In Hawaii, where baseball had long been popular, both natives and whites, as well as the military, continued to play the game after American annexation of the islands as a Territory in 1898. Amateur players among the natives knew the game so well by 1912 that both the Oahu Plantation League and the Maui Athletic Association wrote Garry Herrmann, chairman of Organized Baseball's National Commission, to ask for help in settling disputes. (Herrmann backed away from such decisions.) As for local military units, the Coast Artillery Corps team received frequent mention in the *Army and Navy Journal* and in *Baseball Magazine* for its victories over other military units. In 1916 the C.A.C.'s 91st company won its second championship in the five-team Fort Kamehameha League on Oahu.

When American college players came to Hawaii to play baseball they might meet military teams. Upon the arrival of the Santa Clara, California, college nine in the islands during the 1908–09 college year, sailors of the *Milwaukee* played the college boys. The sailors were supposedly Navy champions, but the college players, according to a 1912 issue of Santa Clara's magazine, *The Redwood*, "rendered the sailor lads helpless."

Nor did the Navy neglect to bring baseball to Samoa, desired by the Americans for its strategic position. The United States first became interested in Samoa when a steamship company owner called President Ulysses S. Grant's attention to the fine harbor of Pago Pago on the Samoan island of Tutuila. Disputes that later developed in Samoa with two other imperial powers were settled in 1899 when the islands were divided, the United States taking over Tutuila with its harbor and some smaller islands, which became known as American Samoa.

Early on, the Navy introduced baseball to the Samoans, who began playing with a castoff ball and a bat made from the stalk of a coconut palm leaf. By 1916 the Samoan native guardsmen, called Fita Fitas, were ready to play the sailors. In September they and a team of civilians formed a league that included two bluejacket teams, one from the naval station and the other from the station ship, the *Fortune*, setting up a thirty-game schedule. Lieutenant R. O'Hagan, deeply involved with the league, said later that its equipment, which had been ordered from San Francisco months before opening day, did not arrive in time, so uniforms for the two native teams had to be improvised. Materials for their uniforms were ordered by cable from Australia, and the families and friends of team members devised uniforms to the Fita Fitas' own design: an undershirt worn with a white lavalava (loin cloth) fastened about the waist, and a white sailor's hat. The Fita Fitas asked that the other teams refrain from wearing spikes because the Polynesians could not wear shoes. "A Samoan needs no shoes," explained O'Hagan; "he grows them—callused coverings on the soles of his feet."

Only one plot of ground, the parade ground between the Fita Fitas' barracks and the bay, was big enough to play on, although the left fielder had to wade into the water to retrieve long hits to his territory. There was no admission charge to the games; fans had paid in advance by donations to the equipment fund for all four teams. On the day of the opener, groups from outlying districts came into Pago Pago. The Palagis (whites) sat on the shaded porch of the Custom House while the others sat or stood under nearby palms along the base lines. A band entertained until the 2:00 P.M. game time, when the governor threw out the first ball. O'Hagan avoids revealing who won that first game, but the sailors must have been good teachers—or the Polynesians good students—because at the end of the season the Fita Fitas stood second in the league, just behind the civilian team, the naval station was third, and the team of the *Fortune* came in last.

The Chinese got a taste of baseball before the turn of the century. In the 1870s and 1880s Chinese patricians began sending young men to study in the United States. William Lyon Phelps recalled later that a group of Chinese students at Yale, who played games wearing their long queues, became good at baseball. Such students when they returned to China may have contributed in a small way to the introduction of baseball there. Others could learn about western sports right in China as early as the 1880s at the Christian universities that westerners established there.

So baseball was not completely alien to China when Navy personnel played a charity game there in 1900 for the families of men on the gunboat *Wheeling* who were accidentally killed or wounded while firing a salute on the German Emperor's birthday. For the game, officers of the *Wheeling*, *Baltimore*, and

Monadnock, anchored off Hong Kong, formed two ball teams, calling them-selves the Apaches and the Sioux. The game was conducted under auspices of a committee that included commanders of the American and British fleets and Sir Henry Black, governor of Hong Kong, and it netted more than $1,500.00, which was added to the $1,000.00 already subscribed by British residents and given to families of the victims.

During the Boxer Rebellion (1900), when an international relief force hurried to relieve the siege of the foreign legations at Peking and Tientsin, British and American forces both entered the sacred Temple of Heaven in Peking (Beijing). As soon as the fighting was over, the British moved to lay out cricket and hockey fields, but they found two teams of the American Army Baseball League ahead of them: the Sixth Cavalry and "Riley's Battery" were already playing baseball among the altars, with hundreds of blue-shirted Americans rooting for the teams.

American ships stationed in the Far East kept baseball alive in the new century. In 1903 and 1904 the Navy operated a ten-ship Asiatic Station Baseball League. The *Kentucky* took the pennant the first year. In the second, the Marines joined the league and put in a team.

Shanghai quickly became a venue for Navy baseball. In 1911 the sailors presented a doubleheader on the local cricket grounds, and they had a large tent erected there for the ladies. All American servicemen in Shanghai got leave and soon took possession of the town, riding around in rickshas that flew little American flags. Bubbling Well Road, the city's most fashionable drive, thronged with people on the way to the game—British, American, and Chinese. Fans got free refreshments; sailors had plenty of beer. In the opener, the *Raleigh* won over the *Elcano* (a ship that was originally a Spanish gunboat, captured at Manila) and in the second game the *New Orleans* beat men from the *Monadnock*.

Four years later in the same city, a team picked from gunboats gave the players of the flagship *Saratoga* a "drubbing" 10–8, and when a second game was scheduled later, excitement ran high because the *Saratoga* wanted vengeance. The flagship band played before the game and between innings, and Admiral A.G. Winterhalter, commander of the Asiatic Fleet, and his staff, all baseball enthusiasts, joined the large crowd of spectators. The *Saratoga* players were said to be "out for blood," and they got it, 6–0.

Meanwhile, a spectacular demonstration of naval power got under weigh in December of 1907. By order of Theodore Roosevelt, sixteen battleships, accompanied by colliers and auxiliaries, set out from Portsmouth on a world cruise of 48,000 miles. The fleet split up in some places and called at South American ports, Australia, Japan, China, and other Asiatic, Near East, and Mediterranean ports. The armada of ships, painted white as a symbol of peaceful intention, was in fact meant as a message to Japanese jingoes that the United States was not intimidated by their bellicosity emanating from Roosevelt's peacemaking between Japan and Russia, which the Japanese deemed deprived them of possible further spoils after their decisive victory over the Russian fleet in 1905, or by their continued smarting over restrictive American immigration policies concerning Japanese citizens and the segregation of Japanese children from California schools, even though Roosevelt had taken steps to appease them. In short, Roosevelt had "spoken softly," and then to disabuse the Japanese of any idea that America had acted out of fear, wielded the "big stick." Despite these tensions, the Japanese, who had invited the White Fleet to visit them, concealed their feelings with smiles and bows of greeting and competed with the sailors in baseball.

On their way around the world the sailors played ball at several other ports. In Brazil, for example, they played against Americans employed by local corporations. In Australia, where cricket was the national game but baseball had been played since at least 1875, sailors played Aussies. In fact, at a series in Sydney, held in August 1908 at the University Oval under the supervision of Lieutenant Weaver of the U.S.S. *Connecticut* and Midshipman Cohen of the *Kansas*, fleet teams beat the Australians three out of four, and the Sydney *Sun* reported that the "sensational" catches and "speedy" throws of players from the American fleet "made our best cricketers, who were present, simply gasp with astonishment."

When the White Fleet reached Japan, the Japanese college students who played the American squadron won most of the games. In China, at the port of Amoy off China's southeast coast, the bluejackets put on a series of exhibition games, and the team of the *Kentucky* took the championship by vanquishing the *Louisiana*. Prince Yah Lang presented a trophy to the champions. In Colombo, Ceylon (Sri Lanka), the sailors held another championship series among themselves, the *Nebraska* winning it by overcoming the *New Jersey* 22–10.

Military players probably did not introduce baseball to Mexico. The Mexicans themselves had regularly organized teams, leagues, and pennant play in the 1890s. But when the Marines occupied Vera Cruz from April to November of 1914, ostensibly to secure an apology for a supposed insult to the American flag but really to oust President Victoriano Huerta, Navy Captain John C. Leonard made the usual ethnocentric declaration: that baseball—which he implied the soldiers were graciously bringing to Mexico—would civilize the country.

Two years later the United States Army intervened in Mexico, this time to run down Pancho Villa, who had been raiding the American border and who led them a long and futile chase. Baseball came along with the Army, brought especially by the Knights of Columbus, which established nine recreation centers for the men, and by the YMCA, which established forty-two of them. At Camp Cotton, on the American side of the border, baseball proved popular among the three Massachusetts Guard regiments stationed there; and at Las Crusces, New Mexico, National Guardsmen who were enthusiastic players but without the funds for equipment got balls, bats, and gloves from the townsfolk, who also played against them, splitting two games.

Perhaps the largest-scale imperialist event of the era in which baseball played a part was the building of the Panama Canal. Following French withdrawal from the project, the United States contrived to take over construction of the canal in 1904 after aiding and abetting a brief, bloodless revolution whereby Panama broke away from Columbia, became a protectorate of the United States, and gave up a strip of land through which the canal would pass. The remarkable engineering job directed by Colonel George Goethals, aided by the success of Colonel William C. Gorgas in wiping out the yellow fever and malaria that infested the area, brought the project to completion by 1914.

Some canal workers were members of military units, and they quickly established baseball in the isthmus. Within a few years baseball gloves could be purchased at the commissary. Three baseball teams played in 1905, independently at first but by 1906 as members of the seven-team Isthmian League, playing from November to June. The league flourished throughout the building of the canal, although often with only four teams, and for a while another league, the Atlantic League, fielded teams, too. During the 1907–08 and 1908–09 seasons the president of the Isthmian League was none other than Colonel Goethals.

"When there is a ball game," said a canal observer in 1908, "people from all along the line flock in." The teams of the Isthmian League, which usually represented stations, functions, or camps, in some years included military units. The Marines stationed at Camp Elliott several times entered teams in the Isthmian League but never finished near the top and sometimes withdrew before the end of a season. In 1909–10 the Marines' team record was five won and twenty-two lost! But the Marines' poor performance may have been caused in part by interruptions stemming from transshipment of units back to the States and also to Nicaragua to assist in "maintaining order" there, as the *Canal Record*, a local news sheet, put it. Baseball was also popular among the Marine companies at Camp Elliott, who formed their own intercompany league. Once a team of Marines lost to civilian players in a game played at the bottom of the canal's biggest excavation, the Culebra Cut, and had to buy the winners a barrel of beer. In October of 1911 the Tenth Regiment, an Army infantry unit, arrived at Camp Otis in the Canal Zone and by December had a team in what was by then called the Canal Zone League, but it had no better luck than the Marines, ending up last with a record of three and twelve.

On the eve of World War I the United States was unquestionably a world power. From twelfth place among world navies, the American fleet competed with Germany for second or third place, behind Great Britain, which had produced the world's most powerful warship, the dreadnaught. America had also completed the Panama Canal, thus giving its ships the long-desired quick transit from one ocean to the other. When America finally entered the Great War, baseball went along with the armed forces.

21

THE ARMED FORCES DRAFT BASEBALL

America entered the war in April, 1917, woefully unprepared to engage in such a formidable undertaking. The Army was pitifully small. The previous year it had been increased, but only to less than a quarter million. Conscription seemed essential, for entrance into the war necessitated mobilization of a vast force of millions. A draft was undertaken with some trepidation, however, in view of memory of the Civil War draft riots. But this time conscription, conducted on a much fairer basis, proceeded without any serious opposition. Even so, poor physical condition caused rejection of about 35 percent of those registered.*

Those considered sufficiently fit and called up in the beginning were hustled to makeshift camps, mostly in the South, to drill and learn the rudiments of soldiering, while simultaneously gangs of workmen hastily threw up barracks for them. At such camps the War Department put heavy emphasis, both at home and later overseas, on physical training and sports as part of the men's preparation.

American military leaders drafted sport, and of course baseball, to perform a particular function in World War I: they used it especially to distract the men from prostitutes and prevent venereal disease. VD had incapacitated many British and French soldiers—an estimated million of the latter by 1917. Secretary of War Newton Baker, already cognizant of the problem of rampant prostitution on the Mexican border as a result of Raymond B. Fosdick's report the previous year, told the president there should be a "comprehensive program" of "wholesome recreation" to occupy the leisure hours of soldiers in the camps. Baker stated that most of the men were of college age, so the experience of the colleges with recreation would "go a long way by analogy to aid us." Americans were issued prophylactics, but the War Department wanted less interest in sex as well as safety. Believing that interest in sex could be reduced by channeling it into sport, the War Department concluded that organized athletics would offer a "wholesome"

*See Chapter 5.

330

recreational alternative to off-duty soldiers both at home and overseas. Secretary Baker later admitted that military athletics "was an attempt to occupy the minds of the soldiers and to keep their bodies busy with wholesome, healthful, and attractive things... to free [the body] from temptations... which come to those who are idle."*

On top of the benefit to the men of avoiding VD, the War Department expected other advantages from its sports and recreation programs. As with business and education leaders, those in the military held that character benefits would accrue from sports. They predicted sports would develop team spirit and confidence and thought aggressiveness and "the fighting instinct" would grow. The YMCA believed sport developed the men physically, too, through increased agility, as well as developing them morally. Moreover, sport was expected to counter boredom and serve as an outlet for surplus energy and nervous tension.

Sport in the service during World War I may have aided in these ways. But it also had some unanticipated benefits: Athletics helped transfer the home environment to camp by offering familiar activities to homesick men placed in strange surroundings. And for men who had never played such games, sports gave them new enjoyment and taught them something they could participate in after the war. The spread of sports and the emphasis on it in the service helped to legitimize and popularize postwar sport, especially in the schools through physical education. A special advantage fell to the Army from those who had thrown baseballs many times in their youth: they proved to be excellent grenade throwers.

To carry out the War Department's extensive recreation policy, in which athletics played a large and vital part, Secretary Baker appointed a Commission on Training Camp Activities that included well-known people like Joseph Lee of the Playground Association; Major Palmer Pierce of the Army, who had been associated with the organization of athletic clubs; and Dr. Joseph Raycroft of Princeton University, a physical education specialist. Raycroft chaired the Army's Athletic Division of the Commission. An experimental two-week course Raycroft developed in 1918 led the War Department to order that physical training include competitive games to develop "the greatest possible efficiency and power in offensive combat." This might have been applicable in earlier wars, but the War Department omitted to explain how competitive games could help the men when they suffered a barrage of artillery fire or went "over the top" in the face of a hail of machine gun bullets.

By February of 1918, thirty-two Army and National Guard camps had athletic programs in action, each under an athletic director. There were never enough trained athletic directors for the camps, however, and some

*Unfortunately, soldiers contracted VD in France anyway and brought it with them to Germany.

had few qualifications and required training on the spot. Others were former professional baseball players like Kid Elberfeld and Ted Breitenstein.

Such an extensive program required equipment. Thousands of baseballs, gloves, chest protectors, catcher's mitts, and bats, as well as paraphernalia for other sports, ordered from companies like Reach and Goldsmith, were sent to home camps and overseas, many of them purchased by welfare organizations acting under the supervision of the Commission. Some were paid for by many small donations, as little as twenty-five cents, and even President Woodrow Wilson contributed his quarter to Clark Griffith's Bat and Ball Fund.*

Stars and Stripes, the official American Expeditionary Force newspaper published in France in 1918–19, reported early in 1918 that the Y had placed an order with various sporting goods houses for $300,000.00 worth of A.E.F. equipment, including 79,680 baseballs, 1,600 dozen bats, thousands of gloves, and 1,200 catchers' masks. James McCurdy, head of the Y's receiving department in France, commented that the main purpose of all the athletic activity there was "to help the Kaiser get a new job." By March the Y had already distributed $69,000.00 worth of equipment in France, according to *Stars and Stripes*, but a serious shortage still existed because equipment worth $30,000.00 had gone down with the torpedoed transport *Oronsa*. A call went out for an enterprising person in France to make bats—"For we've got to have bats." Shortly thereafter, *Stars and Stripes* announced that both the Y and the Knights of Columbus had placed orders with French manufacturers for equipment, but French-made balls fell apart when hit, and as for French bats, the writer could say only that they were "better than none."

Soldiers hungered for news of the professional players, too. The editor of Spalding's guides, John B. Foster, urged readers in 1918 to forward their used copies of the guide to military men abroad in order to satisfy the demand there for them. "It's like getting money from home to read a National League box score and find out who drove in the winning run," rhapsodized Hank Gowdy, major-league catcher then in Europe, to the editor of *Baseball Magazine* in May 1919. The War Department and the YMCA determined to radio the result of the 1917 World Series to "our boys" in Honolulu, Manila, the Canal Zone, Paris, Coblenz, Vladivostok, and Constantinople, whence it would be relayed to smaller points.

Taylor Spink, editor of *Sporting News*, found his circulation falling at the war's start when thousands of fans were inducted, so he got an idea for boosting circulation after hearing Colonel Tillinghast Huston, one of the owners of the New York Yankees, tell of seeing soldiers in France reading the paper and passing copies around. Huston said baseball news seemed to be one of the chief interests of servicemen in Europe. The Postmaster had devised a plan whereby each paper printed a notice telling a civilian reader

*See *Baseball: The Golden Age*, p. 246.

that if he wanted to send his copy to a soldier overseas, all he had to do was put a one-cent stamp on it. Through Ban Johnson, American League president, Spink went further. He got the American League to buy copies of the paper at a cut rate and send them to the American Expeditionary Force at the League's expense. Individual club owners in the league, and Johnson himself, contributed, too, and the added circulation permitted the paper to resume its regular circulation of 75,000 and even gain new postwar readers. Next to *Stars and Stripes*, *Sporting News* became the most popular publication in the A.E.F.

To handle recreation in the training camps the War Department's Commission relied heavily on private agencies like the Knights of Columbus, Jewish Welfare Board, Playground Association, YMCA, YWCA, Salvation Army, and Red Cross. Confusion resulted from rivalry among them and from the zeal of the volunteers, who sometimes duplicated services. Nevertheless, these groups, at the behest of the War Department, set up enormous athletic programs, of which baseball proved to be the most popular summer sport.

In fact, the Jackson, South Carolina, edition of *Trench and Camp* claimed in the spring of 1918 that the Commission, evidently to exploit this interest, had adopted the slogan "Every American soldier a baseball player," and that Raycroft intended to organize a good baseball team in every one of the companies of soldiers training in the States, as well as organizing camp teams and camp leagues. Where travel conditions permitted, intercamp games would also be scheduled, and some trainees would even be able to watch major-leaguers play. The New York *Times* predicted in 1918 that Army camps and Navy bases would have two million baseball players.

Some camps were big enough for twenty diamonds, which the recruits put to full use on Wednesday and Saturday afternoons, practically holidays in camps, and also on Sundays, when whole families from nearby towns commonly visited them. In addition, recruits received daily athletic instruction, typically for a half-hour each morning.

In the East, at Hoboken, New Jersey, an embarkation point for troops headed for Europe, the War Camp Community Service organized a Soldiers' Major Baseball League of eight teams. At Camp Dix, in Wrightstown, New York, major- and minor-league players formed the nucleus of teams, and the former White Sox pitcher, Doc White, coached an aviators' team. At Fort Slocum in New Rochelle, baseball continued as important as before the war. There Al Schacht reported for an induction exam, explaining to the examiner that he was "as deaf as a Cigar Store Indian," but a soldier who had seen Schacht pitch wanted him for the company's team and said he would "fix it up." Schacht's subsequent hearing test amounted to having someone yell "'sixty-two' loud enough to blow out a window." Asked if he heard it, Schacht had to say yes, "and, boffo, I'm in the Army." Schacht, later a big-league pitcher and entertainer, said he pitched all but one of his company team's games at Slocum.

Midwestern camps like Summerall at Scranton, Pennsylvania, had inter-camp baseball play, and military personnel at Cleveland's Nela Park, a General Electric plant where the Chemical Warfare Service worked, entered a team in the city's Twilight League. At Allentown, Pennsylvania, where the Ambulance Corps set up a camp in June 1917, on the Fairgrounds, recruits represented thirty-six colleges and included some college baseball stars. The chairman of the Officer Athletic and Entertainment Committee at Allentown believed that this wealth of college athletic material should be used, so the trainees quickly organized a team, which won most of its games.

But the Army established most camps for recruits in the South, and at these southern camps the soldiers played both summer and winter. During June through September of 1918 in the Southeast, at Camps Jackson and Gordon and Fort Oglethorpe and Parris Island, the Y handled 37,819 baseball games, with 548,980 men playing and 2,253,864 spectators attending. Sixty percent of the trainees at Camp Gordon, Atlanta, played baseball, and every soldier there at least watched his regimental team in action. Leon Cadore, a professional pitcher training at Gordon, claimed he won all the games he pitched for his team. When on a ten-day leave from camp he went to New York and pitched two games for the Brooklyn National League team, one of them a shutout.

Recruits played scrub games daily in the winter of 1917–18 at Camp Johnston, Florida. Then an Inter-Block (company) League opened, and a Boston semipro named Jimmy Kelly ran one team, selecting for his company only men with at least semipro experience. The players at Johnston raised money for equipment with a minstrel show, and they practiced daily. The big event of the season was a game played before a large crowd at Rose Field, South Jacksonville, against Company D of the Motor Supply Train.

YMCA workers at Camp Sheridan, Montgomery, Alabama, decided to invite a pro team to do its spring training there. Since many of the troops came from Ohio, the Y selected the Cincinnati Reds. Montgomery businessmen made a financial offer to Garry Herrmann, Reds' president, who accepted it, and the professionals arrived March 12 and began practicing at a park called the Coliseum. Soldiers came to watch every chance they got, and in the afternoons, when the officers released them from duty, the men crowded the bleachers to cheer and "josh" the pros. The camp's own best ball club, a team from the artillery headed by an ex-professional named Ralph Sharman, practiced at the same field.

Grantland Rice, the sports writer, stationed at Camp Service in Greenville, South Carolina, as athletic director, was told to clear a forest for a baseball field so that an Army baseball game scheduled two weeks hence could be played. The soldiers cleared the forest in time, said Rice, and the game was played.

At Camp Jackson in Columbia, South Carolina, *Trench and Camp* reported enthusiastic play in interbattalion, intercompany, and interregimental leagues. The Y director there offered a prize to the winner of the Inter-Signal League, which played three games a day. Outsiders who played against Camp Jackson baseball teams included the Charleston Navy Yard and Camp Wheeler. Several big-leaguers played in Camp Jackson games, including Rube Benton and Pat Duncan, and players from the Southern, Virginia, Northern, and International leagues took part. Benton pitched about ten games for the Depot Brigade, he said. Many college players, semipros, and at least one industrial league star, Frank Schaller of the Pennsylvania Steel League, participated in baseball at Camp Jackson.

Baseball reigned at southwestern camps, too, like Fort Douglas, Arizona; Camp Pike, Little Rock, Arkansas; and Fort Brown, Texas, where big-league ball players could be found playing. At Camp Cody, near Deming, New Mexico, Army engineers converted an unused fifteen-acre reservoir into an amphitheatre where 20,000 soldiers could watch baseball and football games. At Camp Travis, in San Antonio, Texas, according to the New York *Times*, soldiers averaged twenty-five baseball games a day.

One wartime spring the New York Giants decided to visit several camps in the vicinity of Marlin, Texas, where they trained. In that area more than 100,000 soldiers were preparing for war at various forts and cantonments. At Camp McArthur, near Waco, the Giants played two games against an officers' team of the Aviation Corps, which afterwards recklessly tried to out-drink the baseball writers accompanying the Giants on their tour; "they lost both engagements," recalled reporter Frank Graham. The Giants also played a group of aviators at Kelly Field, near San Antonio, where the airmen had their own twilight league of twelve teams; beat the soldiers at Camp Travis; and moved south to New Orleans, meeting the Cleveland Indians and visiting Camp Shelby at Hattiesburg, Mississippi. About 30,000 men, many of them fellows who had never been fifty miles from home, were quartered in this raw, desolate spot, said Graham. They watched a five-inning game seen only through a haze of sand blown by the wind, but it broke the monotony for them, Graham added.

Camps in the Far West did not neglect baseball. At one, Raycroft boasted, soldiers played simultaneous games on ten baseball diamonds. Fort Sill, Oregon, had thirty-five teams in a league playing twice a week. The War Camp Community Service organized soldiers in San Diego and Des Moines into teams and leagues and secured fields for play.

The commanding officer of Camp Lewis, in Washington state, ordered that company baseball games be played every Wednesday afternoon, and the Division Athletic Board decided to form a picked team from the entire division (about 40,000 men). James Scott, an ex-professional, was selected for the team, but the camp was full of pro players, including Walter "Duster" Mails of Brooklyn, Louis Guisto of the Yankees, and some men from the

Coast League, as well as college and semipro players. The Division team that resulted must have been good, because the Northwestern League invited it to become a member, but the offer was refused "for military reasons."

Players who later became professionals reported favorably on the start in baseball that the Army gave them. Said Curt Walker, who served for sixteen months before joining the Yankees and then the Reds, the Army had many good players, and some of the games were "thrillers." Walker thought his Army experience "invaluable" because it gave him a chance to play frequently.

But modern armies are not made overnight. It took many months before United States' manpower and illimitable economic strength could be harnessed. Not until June 1917 did the first American contingent arrive in France and parade through Paris streets, primarily to lift Allied morale. Britain and France provided the first American troops, and for a time others that followed, with materiel, and it was a year before American soldiers reached France in numbers sufficient to affect the Western front. At that, not a single American tank and only a few airplanes appeared in France during the war. Meanwhile, the American Navy became involved with convoy duty.

Unlike the Army, the powerful American Navy, with its two-ocean Battle Fleet and additional big ships under construction, seemed well-prepared should war come. But new technology in the form of the German *untersee-boot* changed the character of sea warfare. When war began both Great Britain and Germany violated what America had long regarded as its neutral freedom of the seas. The British, with the world's most powerful fleet, blockaded Germany, and the Germans countered with their submarines as the only way of blockading Britain. But the submarine depended on stealth and surprise. For it to surface and inspect a merchant vessel or give passengers time to take to the lifeboats exposed the submarine to destruction. Soon the Germans embarked upon what was called unrestricted submarine warfare, which involved not only ships and cargoes but also lives, including American lives.

After modification of this policy during a fragile agreement with the United States, the German government announced its intention to resume unrestricted submarine warfare, a decision that was the proximate—though not the only—cause of America' declaration of war, since the United States was already committed to the Allies. Officers of the German High Command felt confident they could win the war before American power could be brought to bear. And they nearly did.

A few days prior to declaration of war, the American government sent William Sims, the previously mentioned reformer of the American Navy, to confer with British naval chiefs. Sims was shocked to learn from Admiral John Jellicoe, commander of the British Grand Fleet, that Germany's submarine blockade had left Britain with only a few weeks' supply of food, and unless something was done about the German submarine menace, he expected Allied surrender by November. In this crisis, and in the face of strong opposition from some British admirals (and the American high command), Lloyd George, exercising his authority as prime minister, and supported by young British admirals and of course Sims, introduced, as the solution to Britain's plight, the convoy system to supplant the single-ship escorts for vessels steaming to British ports.

Sims fully backed the convoy strategy and called upon the United States to send, as soon as possible, small, fast ships—destroyers and submarine chasers—many of which the United States quickly supplied. Along with a chain of heavier, stronger mines laid across strategic areas of the English Channel, new listening devices, and a few airplanes, the convoy system succeeded in subduing the submarine menace, most subs destroyed by the British Navy. In time the loss of ships dropped from twenty-five percent to one percent, and the morale of German submarine crews drained steadily away. The United States and Britain built merchant ships faster than the Germans could build submarines. And the navies performed their convoy duty with outstanding success. As a result, the Americans ferried across the ocean, mostly in British bottoms, supplies and, all told, some two million American soldiers without loss of a single soldier by enemy action. Sims himself was made Commander of United States Naval Forces Operating in European Waters, and from his London headquarters he supervised their activity in Europe and would soon find himself responsible as well for a formal baseball occasion in London.

For through all this, the Navy managed to fit in baseball. Former major-league and college players in abundance were scattered throughout the fifteen naval stations, and every station had its athletic director and its ball teams, all under the general direction of Walter Camp, former Yale coach, as the Navy's General Commissioner of Athletics.

By the time Camp took over in midsummer of 1918, the plan to place a hundred thousand men in the naval stations was well along. In many cases incomplete quarters made the young men restless, discomfited, and homesick. As Lawrence Perry pointed out in his 1918 book, *Our Navy in the War*, Camp's provision for such homelike amenities as YMCA buildings with libraries and writing desks helped recruits adjust to conditions. Nothing helped more than athletics. As one Navy man pointed out, "Athletics are an important part of the life of a sailor." Camp's directors introduced seasonal sports comparable to those each man would have enjoyed as a civilian: football in fall, boxing in winter, swimming, rowing, and baseball in spring and summer. His directors—one for each of the Naval Districts, such as Boston, Newport, League Island, Cape May, Philadelphia, Charleston, Great Lakes, Puget Sound, and Pensacola—all had years of sports experience and set up massive sports programs.

Baseball, said Perry, "furnished the greatest solace" for the sailors. Major and minor leaguers scattered abundantly through the stations strengthened teams. In addition to watching individual stars and district teams, the men played in their own leagues.

Jack Barry of the Red Sox joined the Navy at the end of 1917 and then ran the ball club in the Charlestown Naval Base near Boston, which featured other professionals including other Red Sox and Braves players, men from the Brooklyn, Pittsburgh, and Athletics teams, and some semipro and college players. In 1918 the team competed for the championship of the First Naval District and the $100.00 trophy that went with it. Clark Griffith, then manager of the big-league club in Washington, had given the Boston Navy Yard ten dozen baseballs. The Yard's own publication, *The Salvo*, reported in June that on Decoration Day the team, under Barry's leadership, had defeated the Battleship Fleet team 3–2 in 14 innings, a pitcher's battle between Johnson of the *Alabama* and Ernie Shore, formerly a Boston American League pitcher. In the game Del Gainor of the Red Sox played first base for the Yard team and Rabbit Maranville, infielder of the Boston National League club, covered third.

In Newport, Rhode Island, where "Toots" Schulz, an ex-Philadelphia National League player, ran the team, the War Recreation secretary acquired the use of a 125-acre property called Coddington Park, with a local organization to underwrite expenses, and the Navy laid out diamonds and other athletic facilities and built a road to town. Sailors also played ball at Hampton Roads and Norfolk, Virginia, where Davy Robertson, a National League pro whose home was Norfolk, headed Navy baseball.

Easily the most important naval base was the one at the Great Lakes. Prior to the war it ranked athletically only on a par with some of the smaller midwestern colleges. The war changed all that, as described in Francis Buzzell's 1919 account of the Great Lakes Training Station. Overnight the base expanded from a few hundred men to many thousands, including some of the best athletes in the country, and Constitution Field developed into a great athletic field. Commander John B. Kaufman, athletic director of the base, made games and sports part of the men's training, in the conviction that athletics developed the "fight instinct." An assistant company commander there thought athletics "an important part of the life of a sailor" and stated that athletic teams' trips helped recruitment by "attracting young men of virile type to the Navy."

Kaufman set up two kinds of athletic teams at Great Lakes: representative teams, consisting of the best athletes in a given sport, which would play other training camps and athletic organizations; and regimental teams, in which every man would play, as part of the slogan "sports for all." Every conceivable sport had its active players at Great Lakes during 1917 and 1918.

Felix Chouinard, former White Sox player, was chosen to select the Naval Station's 1917 baseball team, but when the call went out for candidates Chouinard was astounded to be faced with 921 aspirants! After he finally selected a team, it made only a fair record, possibly because only five of the thirteen on the team survived the depletion caused by the shipping of men overseas. The regimental teams were affected by the same problem. No regular interregimental league could function, since players picked for a unit team one day might be on their way to sea the next. Nevertheless, sailors played numerous regimental games at the base during 1917. Charles Weegh-man, Chicago Cubs president, said in a *Baseball Magazine* article that he watched scores of young athletes at the Naval Station play 150 games one Sunday from early morning until mess call at night. Impressed, Weeghman arranged to lend the station three Cubs players, Jimmy Sheckard, Jimmy Archer, and Vic Saier, as coaches, and he also sent them enough baseball equipment "to keep them going for some time," as he remarked.

The year 1918 proved to be the best one for Great Lakes baseball, both for its base team and for the regimental system. The representative team, again handled by Chouinard, included seven former big leaguers and two more obtained later. On the Fourth of July the Great Lakes team became champions of the Navy by defeating the Atlantic Fleet team at Yorktown, Virginia, 2–0. It then beat the fleet team three more times, twice at Great Lakes and once at National League Park in Chicago. Further, it defeated the team of the Fifth Naval District, which boasted the services of outfielder William "Baby Doll" Jacobson of the St. Louis Browns as pitcher.

The regimental system at Great Lakes also registered success that year. At mid-season the twenty regimental teams, each outfitted in a distinctive uniform, organized themselves into two leagues called National and American and played a schedule terminating in a five-game series for the championship, won by the Seventh Regiment.

Although Annapolis and West Point discontinued interservice academy games for 1917 and 1918, the Army and the Marines played each other at American League Park in Washington, D.C., and President Wilson, himself a fan, threw out the first ball.

For some Navy men, Navy ball stood out as the highlight of their service. "Those ball games [at the Naval Airplane base in Miami in 1918] were the only exciting things I experienced during the war," declared George Watkins, later a St. Louis pro outfielder. Even in France in 1918 the Naval Airmen found time to organize teams and play ball. *Stars and Stripes* reported games abroad of the "Flying Bluejackets" against an Army team, a team of Canadians, and a nine from a Naval Dirigible Station.

Sailors kept their ship teams, too. A photo in the Navy's Washington file shows the team of the *New Hampshire* in 1918, its members wearing baseball caps, sweat shirts, pants, and dark socks with one wide white stripe; their baseball gear lies on deck in front of them, and gun turrets loom behind. The *Pennsylvania* team, pictured on board ship, also got to play on land in their uniforms bearing the ship's name. Even submarine chasers found a chance to organize a baseball league among other such craft in the fleet.

Once some of the men from Sub Chaser No. 100 got leave to watch one of their league games on shore. The rest of the men found themselves fleet-bound, but the sub chaser's wireless man, Don Damond of Rochester, in-geniously rigged a radio-telephone relay atop a warehouse and gave the men back on board a play-by-play description of the game.

Meanwhile, the Army, too, had of course brought baseball abroad. In fact, soon after the American Expeditionary Force went overseas, Raymond Fosdick joined General John Pershing's staff as civilian advisor for morale, and he organized for the troops abroad a recreation program with heavy emphasis on athletics. Joseph Raycroft, chairman of the Army's Athletic Division, had fourteen physical educators commissioned as captains in the Army and sent overseas as athletic directors with the A.E.F.

To develop more athletic directors for the A.E.F., the Army established a two-week course during which two full days were devoted to baseball instruc-tion, one of them spent in playing the game itself. By March of 1918 the Y had 86 trained directors abroad with the A.E.F. In fact, the Y carried much of the responsibility for athletics with the American Army abroad. James H. Mc-Curdy directed the Y's efforts for the Training Camp Commission, with the help of James Naismith of basketball fame and George Meylan, another phys-ical training man. Before the war was over the Y had established 1,300 recre-ation centers in Europe. It laid out 77 baseball diamonds at St. Nazaire, at the mouth of the Loire, a disembarkation point for American troops.

The Knights of Columbus, a Roman Catholic laymen's association, became another heavy contributor to wartime athletics. John Evers, a National League veteran of fifteen years of baseball, spent six months in France organizing a staff of athletic specialists that traveled all over the country coaching and distributing equipment.

By June of 1918 an average of 200 baseball games were being played every day in the A.E.F. Each issue of *Stars and Stripes*, carefully omitting the exact names and locations of units, reported many games, referring especially to engineer, hospital, and motor transport teams. Entire leagues played ball in France in 1918, one at a big hospital base and another at A.E.F. head-quarters, for example. In fact, said *Stars and Stripes*, baseball was "the favorite outdoor sport of the A.E.F."

Soldiers supposedly had baseball on their minds even in the trenches, if we are to believe *Stars and Stripes*. Early that year the newspaper published a photo of a helmeted lefthanded soldier about to pitch a hand grenade over the trench barrier, along with a poem—itself eloquent of the indelible in-fluence of the game on young Americans—using baseball as a metaphor for trench warfare, presumably to hearten the doughboys:

> He's tossed the horsehide far away to plug the hand grenade;
> What matter if on muddy grounds this game of war is played?
> He'll last through extra innings and he'll hit as well as pitch;
> His smoking Texas Leaguers'll make the Fritzies seek the ditch!

He's just about to groove it toward a ducking Fritzy's bean.
His cross-fire is the puzzlingest that ever yet was seen.
His spitter is a deadly thing; his little inshoot curve
Will graze some Heinie's heaving ribs and make him lose his nerve.

Up in the air he never goes; he always cuts the plate,
No matter if the bleachers rise and start "The Hymn of Hate";
And pacifistic coaching never once has got his goat—
Just watch him heave across the top the latest Yankee note!

The Boches claim the Umpire is a-sidin' with their nine,
But we are not the boobs to fall for such a phoney line;
We know the game is fair and square, decisions on the level;
The only boost the Kaiser gets is from his pal, the Devil!

The series now is opened, and the band begins to play,
The batteries are warming up; the crowd shouts, "Hip-Hurray!"
The catcher is a-wingin' 'em to second, third and first,
And if a Heinie tries to steal, he's sure to get the worst.

So watch the southpaw twirler in his uniform O.D.
Retire to the players' bench the boches—one, two, three!
He'll never walk a bloomin' one, nor let 'em hit it out—
Just watch him make 'em fan the air and put the Hun to rout!

Some claimed that, with so many pros in the ranks, "you could see better baseball games and prize fights in France than back home." A YMCA director asserted that "more than one wounded doughboy, when they brought him from No Man's Land into the triage, still carried his cherished baseball glove in his hip pocket."

In August of 1917 the Y offered to establish recreation facilities at the areas set aside for troops to spend their leave. The first such area, called the Savoy Leave Area, included the town of Aix-le-Bains, which soldiers had christened "Aches and Pains" as part of their resentment at not being allowed to spend their leave in Paris. One of the Savoy Leave Area's organizers was the wife of Teddy Roosevelt, Jr. She and others leased parts of eleven farms for an athletic field so the soldiers could play baseball and other games, and soon the soldiers began to enjoy their leave. In June of 1918 *Stars and Stripes* published an ad for Aix-les-Bains soliciting soldiers who were looking for a place to spend their "Military Vacation": "Come and play at Aix-les-Bains. . . . You can enjoy yourself at any of the usual out-of-door sports at a popular resort. . . . " An Ambulance Corp major, Paul Chaudron, spent his fall leave there and wrote later that the week passed "all too quickly" and seemed "more like a dream," filled as it was with entertainment, including baseball games. In contrast with Mrs. Roosevelt, her husband, Teddy Jr., in command of the first Battalion at Demange-aux-Eaux, found no means of recreation for his troops. He thought he would find a sports store like Abercrombie and Fitch at Bar-le-Duc, but when he failed he wired his wife, then at the Paris Y, for a complete baseball outfit, as well as a dozen soccer balls, six basketballs, fifes and drums, ten pounds of pipe tobacco, a dozen barrels of soft drinks, and a phonograph. In response she made friends with the man in charge of supplies in her Paris office and, said T.R., Jr., "got the first baseball outfit to reach France."

About the same time, the commander of the 41st Depot Division at Saint-Aignan, below Touraine, did better than T.R., Jr. He not only set up a baseball league, he even got the French Mint to make the medals and trophies for it, and morale in his division was reportedly "fabulous."

By fall of 1917 the Y and the Paris edition of the New York *Herald* together offered a cup to the champion of a Paris baseball league in which teams from the U.S. Regulars, the American Ambulance, the U.S. Field Service corps, the Day Off Group, and the Canadian Regiments competed. In the spring of 1918 eighteen clubs attended a meeting to form the Paris League for the year. Ten games were played on April 22, before the regular season even opened. Paris clubs played league games Sundays at the fifty-acre athletic field at Colombes, a Paris suburb, where at least ten A.E.F. games could be played simultaneously and where a grandstand seating 25,000 catered to spectators. Parisians also saw ball-tossing and ball games inside Paris proper. Once gendarmes found it necessary to restrain an admiring crowd when four privates started four-cornered catch in the Tuilleries. Another curious crowd gawked in the Bois de Boulogne when Army, Red Cross, and YMCA units laid out two diamonds there and played five-inning games.

In the summer of 1918 George C. Marshall, later World War II chief of staff, was stationed at American Headquarters at Cantigny, in Picardy, when the division staff, noting that the long evenings did not end till after 9:00 P.M., started daily baseball games after dinner. Marshall found that "These little interludes had a surprisingly good effect on morale." General Robert L. Bullard always watched the games, despite the increasing difficulty of drawing officers away in time for Bullard's daily 9:30 P.M. staff conference. Marshall and others even drew their French associates into the games, but most of them proved unable to hit the ball or to get a good start in running toward first if they did manage to hit it. The Count de Tortigny, an ex-general and aristocrat still in residence at the Chateau in Cantigny, often watched the games in puzzlement over "the complete sacrifice of dignity by the players and the freedom of comment by the soldiers."

Professional ball players were still joining the Expeditionary Force. When Bill Lange, a pro of the 1890s, went to France to direct baseball there for the Y he took along $40,000.00 worth of equipment bought with Griffith's Bat and Ball Fund. Other pros from the Browns, the Cubs, the Eastern League, the Coast League, and the Nebraska League got themselves photographed playing in their leisure hours at Blois, a general reassignment center for officers. Colonel Huston, co-owner of the Yankees, serving with the 16th Engineers, saw the young men of his regiment playing ball every evening. Grover Cleveland Alexander reported from the 342nd Field Artillery, 89th Division, that his company team had three major leaguers and good college or semipro men at every other position. His team practiced whenever possible and had beaten five good clubs, Alex pitching four out of the five games.

Not all baseball stars maintained popularity among soldiers. *Stars and Stripes*, in praising Hank Gowdy, revealed resentment of some big-leaguers' tactics in avoiding military service: Gowdy, said the writer, was "Our Kind" because:

> To keep from having to join the Army he didn't scuttle into an easy job with a shipyard ball team, as many big leaguers did when called through the draft. He didn't protest that baseball was an essential war industry. He didn't suddenly remember that a whole flock of relatives was dependent upon him for support. He didn't say he'd wait until the season was over and then come in.

Further, in mid-year of 1918 *Stars and Stripes* decided to discontinue all baseball news until the war was won. The writer recognized the value of sport in developing stamina and team play but declared that sport as entertainment was passé and that headlines like "Star Players Dive for Shipyards or Farm to Escape 'Work or fight' Order" and "Cobb Is Thinking of Enlisting This Fall" hardly helped morale of men at the front. After the end of the 1918 major-league season there was a move to send the pennant winners to France to play exhibition games for the soldiers. The plan fell through, perhaps providentially, for at that time servicemen in France had heard too many stories about professional players who sought refuge from induction in shipyard leagues and other "safe havens" and were in no mood to welcome the teams.

Most ball games were played well behind the lines, but one in March of 1918, according to *Stars and Stripes*, was played within range of German guns with German aviators overhead and German shells falling nearby. Said the writer, instead of suffering the traditional hurled pop bottles and seat cushions, the players endured shrapnel splinters. The game, however, lasted only an hour and forty minutes.

In the spring of 1918 when Elwood Brown came to France as a Y athletic director, he found that little had been done for troops at or near the front, and he decided to get equipment spread more widely. Driving a Ford full of baseball equipment, Brown entered the area where Major General James Harbord's 5th and 6th Marines were holding Belleau Wood during the fierce battle of Chateau-Thierry. Harbord let Brown move up to the front "just as far as you've got the guts to go." Soon Brown came upon a division of 10,000 men on the line and 15,000 more concealed in the woods with gas masks and in steel helmets, none of whom had anything to do but keep under cover. Understandably, Brown said later, they were "getting into a blue funk." The Division Commander assented to Brown's offer to help, and

Brown's distribution of athletic material was greeted with "muffled yells of joy." When Brown approached a gun battery and offered a baseball, a sergeant was astounded: "Well for the love of God, just lend us a look at her." The ball was passed around, and in a moment half the men were playing one-old-cat until a scowling captain emerged and asked who started the game. When the sergeant explained, the captain directed the men to play behind the gun, where it was safer: "Take it over there back of the trees— and I guess I'll come into this game myself."

The Chemical Warfare Service attracted several major-league professionals, including Ty Cobb, Christy Matthewson, and Branch Rickey. The Army put Cobb and others in charge of training hard cases and rejects from other groups, theorizing that such men would listen to well-known baseball figures. But in a training accident in Cobb's group eight men died and Matty got a dose of gas. Cobb, who had also inhaled a little gas, was whisked home on the *Leviathon* (formerly the German ship *Vaterland*) on December 16, 1918, according to the New York *Times*.

Prisoners in German camps benefited from Y athletic supplies. A Swiss national, Dr. A.C. Harte of Bern, agreed to receive a half-carload of athletic gear from the Y for reshipment to soldiers imprisoned in Germany. The Y secretary in charge of prison work, who was permitted to visit Rastatt prison camp, was agreeably surprised on arrival to hear the shouting and rooting of enthusiastic fans at a prison ball game. Such games, he said, went on throughout the day at Rastatt, where 2,600 Americans and many men of other nationalities were imprisoned. The camp paper, *The Barbed Wireless*, published "spasmodically" by the "American Overseas Publishing Company, Incarcerated," thanked the Y for its generosity in furnishing games, books, and baseball equipment.

England glimpsed wartime baseball as early as 1916 when American citizens serving under the British flag played in a London League against Canadians. The "London Americans" also had a team in the 1917 London League. American servicemen stationed in various smaller British cities played, too. Ernie Koob, formerly with the St. Louis Browns and in 1918 with the 380th Aero Squadron at Selfridge Aviation Field, reported the local attitude toward athletes as friendly, especially to those representing Selfridge Field against outside competition.

That year, in London, four American and four Canadian teams competed in what was called the Anglo-American Baseball League, financed in part by du Pont and other industries. One of the American teams represented the Navy and the others the Army and Air Service. A percentage of League gate receipts went to war charities.

Admiral Sims threw out the first ball at an Army-Navy game in London, which Army won, 7–6, before 5,000 on May 18. Navy then beat Army on Decoration Day. But the biggest London Army-Navy game of 1918 took place on the Fourth of July before 40,000 spectators, including important personages like Winston Churchill and various "royals," including King George and Queen Mary. Before the game the prospective presence of the sovereigns caused some consternation among the diplomats, since protocol failed to dictate the procedure to be followed when royalty attended a baseball game. Nobody knew who should meet the King and Queen and escort them to their box! Wires went back and forth between London and Washington. Finally, in the absence of the Ambassador, Admiral Sims was settled upon as the person to represent the United States. He met the Queen at the gate and escorted her across the field on his arm, all the while explaining to the King that he would be expected to throw out the first ball! Presumably, the King performed adequately. Navy won the game and received congratulations from Navy Secretary Josephus Daniels, and afterward Sims introduced the team captains to the King. Thus did Admiral Sims help not only to assist in the rescue of Britain from the submarine menace but also to reintroduce American baseball into Britain.

THE ARMED FORCES AFTER WORLD WAR I

The signing of the armistice left about 1,800,000 men longing to return home. Manifestly, they could not all be transported back to the States at once, so to keep the troops occupied while they awaited passage home, General Pershing resorted to an intensive program of military instruction, drill, and busywork. As a result the men became bored, disgruntled and embittered to the point that in some parts of France mutiny broke out.

To ease the situation, Pershing substituted a program of athletics and amusements, a change of policy that had a palliative impact. As *Stars and Stripes* stated in June of 1919, after the armistice baseball and other sports "proved a boon to the Yanks," diverting the soldiers' minds at a time when "the call of home was strong." Baseball, said the reporter, scored its greatest triumphs in the Army of Occupation and at the base ports abroad, where the men were permanently stationed and had time to practice.

The athletic program began in January of 1919 when Army Headquarters at Chaumont, France, issued General Order 241 instituting a series of A.E.F. championships in athletics, especially baseball but also football, basketball, track and field, boxing, and wrestling. Divisions received orders to hold contests in these sports that would lead to finalists competing for A.E.F. championships.

As part of the athletic championships *Stars and Stripes* announced the launching of "the world's greatest baseball league" of 1,900 teams in France competing for the championship of the First Army, an event scheduled for May, and the Army rushed wagonloads of baseball equipment to headquarters for distribution.

Representatives of the Bordeaux region's three main leagues announced that Bordeaux sought the championships, but the Nevers League, comprising the ports of embarkation like Le Mans and St. Nazaire, and a league on the Riviera, as well as teams of soldiers studying at the University of Beaune, all participated eagerly. The Blackhawks, representing the 86th or Blackhawk Division stationed at the Le Mans embarkation center, won the championship. The 11th Regiment of Marines, however, became service champions

346

of the United States. Every member of the Marine team had professional experience. Its major leaguers included Paul Cobb (Ty's brother) of the Washington team and Mike Cantwell of the Yankees.

Meanwhile, some soldiers in France still played for sheer pleasure rather than a championship. Officers and men studying at the French universities of Aix-Marseilles visited the island of Corsica, bringing along enough baseball equipment for two teams. Players who got seasick on the trip to the island formed one team and those who stayed well the other. They staged a game in the town square of Ajaccio, birthplace of Napoleon, as the populace stood about, said *Stars and Stripes*, "with mouths agape at this weird performance." The seasick athletes won 11–9 and claimed the championship of Corsica and islands of the Meditteranean!

When the Army occupied Germany and based itself at Coblenz, at the confluence of the Rhine and Moselle Rivers, baseball needed no passport to move there from France. Company A of the 314th Engineers, 89th Division, for example, found plenty of time for athletics, including baseball. To aid the occupiers, four truckloads of athletic equipment, including 10,456 baseballs, bumped along snowy and muddy roads to Coblenz in February of 1919, a shipment "long and prayerfully awaited by doughboy athletes there," said *Stars and Stripes*. A Coblenz League soon numbered ten baseball teams. By April of 1919 the city of Coblenz had been "persuaded" to contribute 40,000 marks toward the expense of completing the Third Army's athletic field on Insel Oberwerth, an island in the Rhine where the Army planned an athletic carnival in April. Meanwhile, detachments in the Coblenz area engaged in feeding Russian prisoners also tried to teach them baseball.

The Coblenz post also established a school for umpires that trained many arbiters for Army baseball. The Knights of Columbus conducted the school, but Bill Coughlin, former Detroit infielder who had become a K. of C. athletic secretary, conceived the idea for it. Coughlin taught the umpire volunteers at the school and went through the rule book with them. In addition, athletic supervisors learned at this school that in order to defuse a heated dispute in a servicemen's game, if it became so acrimonious as to endanger the umpire physically, the umpire should have the band strike up "The Star Spangled Banner," thus forcing everyone to stand at attention. Then, said a K. of C. representative, "rocks held ready to avenge an unpopular decision" would fall from "reverent hands."

Once the Army needed an umpire for an important game and flew in a specialist. Tommy O'Mara, a Nebraska League umpire in charge of athletics at Colombey-les-Belles, received a telegram from Trier, Germany: "Important ball game here today. Suggest you get in touch with aerodrome and come. This credential will be sufficient to allow air force to give you machine and pilot." To O'Mara this message offered the opportunity of a lifetime. He fitted himself up with the goggles, leather cap, and heavy coat needed in the open planes then in use (parachutes were not yet standard equipment) and was soon airborne over the battlegrounds of France. In seventy-five minutes the pilot landed amidst 25,000 cheering soldiers, who welcomed O'Mara on the ball grounds. After the game O'Mara "had some chow" and then flew back again.

Soldiers of the occupying army brought baseball to unexpected parts of Germany. When two infantry brigade teams laid out a diamond on the tennis courts of Kalmuthof in Remagen, where the ex–crown prince and his royal suite used to disport themselves, servants, the only Germans left there, looked askance at the way hobnailed boots tore up the carefully pressed earth. But the game the infantrymen played there in March of 1919 merely opened the Kalmuthof season. Baseball leagues soon sprang up all over the occupied area. A Lutzel League, a Rhine League, and a Moselle League all played during the occupation under a regular "American Forces in Germany" schedule. Another league operating in northern Europe included seven clubs representing soldiers stationed at Antwerp, Brussels, Rotterdam, and the Hague, along with sailors plying between Rotterdam, Hamburg, and Danzig.

The most grandiose athletic event of the world War I era was a postwar spectacle called the Inter-Allied Games but often billed as the Military Olympics. Elwood Brown of the YMCA proposed it in October of 1918, and after the signing of the armistice in November the Y renewed its suggestion. The organizers gave many reasons for staging the athletic exhibition—to strengthen international understanding, to display the athletic ability of the troops, to popularize sport—but the most compelling reason was to divert the interest of men waiting impatiently to be sent home. The Army still kept troops at replacement and embarkation ports drilling in the mornings, but afternoons and evenings, athletics took over. A huge athletic meet would continue to turn the men's attention to one of their biggest interests and pacify them until they could be shipped out.

Accordingly, General Pershing wrote twenty-nine allied nations in January of 1919 inviting them to send participants to an athletic meet in May or June. Eighteen nations accepted. Athletes from defeated nations were not welcome. Neither were the Russians, for fear of Bolshevik infection. Thus only those nations with which the Americans already had good relations got invitations.

Meanwhile, the American Army prepared to put on a good show. To strengthen its athletic position the Army went so far as to ship back to France several athletes who had already gone home and also to bring in a number of athletes who had never gone overseas during the period of the United States' involvement in the war. Besides using these ringers, the Army also spent a lot of money building Pershing Stadium, constructed by Army engineers at a cost of anywhere from $80,000.00 to $250,000.00 (estimates differ) and afterward presented to France as a gift. The Army created an Olympic village for 1,500 athletes, most of them American servicemen, offering entertainment, medical supplies, and that American staple, free ice cream. The Y furnished equipment and coaches, and the K. of C. contributed money.

The games took place between June 22 and July 6, 1919, at Pershing Stadium in Joinville and also at Colombes Stadium and other sites. Free admission attracted a daily attendance of about 20,000. Hand-grenade throwing was one of the events, and some contestants threw as they would hurl a baseball from the outfield to the infield.

Baseball was of course an event of the Military Olympics. Two military teams, an American and a Canadian, played a four-game series, the American team, the Blackhawks, winner of the A.E.F. tournament, taking three out of four. And after beating the Canadians the Le Mans team toured Germany, playing three more games.

The Military Olympics made no discernible imprint either on international relations or on the traditional Olympic Games, although one observer thought Franco-American relations improved temporarily. The Inter-Allied Games may be seen as one aspect of American missionary zeal in trying to teach baseball and other athletic sports to other nations. American soldiers' many wartime attempts to teach British Tommies, French *poilus*, and soldiers of other nations to play baseball had little effect, but that never seemed to discourage the effort. Those who believe they have the answer to the world's problems never tire of communicating it to others. The British, of course, as a missionary in Siam explained, were years ahead of the Americans in teaching the play ideal to the world.

The sports experience of the doughboys in baseball during the war carried over into the twenties, both in the military and in the public sector. Broad recognition of the importance of athletics permeated American life. As shown earlier in this book, public concern over the poor physical condition of draftees contributed to the widening approval for athletics as an aid to physical fitness. Athletics may also have helped fill the gap left by the sudden loss of a national purpose with the end of the war. At least, Professor R. Tait McKenzie of the University of Pennsylvania could declare in 1922 that "Athletic activity is the best substitute for war, and every virile nation must have one or the other." Athletics and nationalism could thus be knitted together, as they were by General Douglas MacArthur, who in a report to President Calvin Coolidge propounded the catch phrase, "Athletic America," which, said the general, "arouses national pride and kindles anew the national spirit. . . . Nothing has been more characteristic of the genius of the American people than is their talent for athletics. . . ."

The Army recodified its athletic policy in mid-1921, establishing post and station games quadrenially, area games biennially, and departmental games annually. Individual soldiers could participate in local civilian competitions, too. The War Department undertook to fund all Army athletic events. The Army also reiterated its support for Sunday baseball and even for charging admission to Sunday games where local laws did not forbid it. Soldiers who competed in sports had to be amateurs, but the Army defined amateurism rather loosely: men who accepted prizes authorized by commanders would not be excluded as professionals. And near the end of the decade the secretary-treasurer of the Amateur Athletic Union told the War Department that to enter a civilian meet a soldier-athlete need not certify himself as an amateur. It would be enough if his commanding officer certified him as such.

Another war carryover was the retention of Citizens Military Training Camps, where members of the National Guard performed their annual two-week service. To dramatize the link between athletics and the National Guard, the Army used Babe Ruth, the country's most famous professional baseball player, in a well-publicized annual re-enlistment ceremony during which he autographed bats and balls as prizes for the champion baseball teams of the fifty-one camps.

Those National Guard camps were baseball hotbeds. At Camp Devens, in Ayer, Massachusetts, for example, Major General Alfred Foote planned an elaborate athletic center featuring a baseball diamond and other sports facilities, which he hoped to have ready for the annual two-week encampment of the 26th Division of the Guard in 1929. Meanwhile, other units of the Massachusetts National Guard played ball on their own Parade Grounds. According to the Ayer *Divisional Review*, the team of the 101st Medical Regiment, an ambulance company (referred to as "the pill-rollers") won all the ice cream and cake its members could eat (doubtless an aid to fitness!) and "strutted like peacocks" in their new uniforms after defeating the 181st Regiment 13–2.

After the war the regular Army not only picked up where it had left off in sports, it intensified and elaborated upon them, especially baseball. Eastern camps like those at Governors' Island and Fort Slocum, New York, and Camp Meade, Amherst, Massachusetts, manifested undiminished baseball interest, with teams playing in camp leagues, divisional competitions, and interfort leagues, as well as against nearby industrial teams.

As in World War I, southern forts and camps offered much baseball in the twenties. Fort Benning, Georgia, is a good example. There the Infantry School team played a schedule that included Georgia colleges, and by mid-June of 1923 it had won 14, lost 8, and tied 2, for a percentage of .636. In 1924 the Infantry School at Fort Benning planned to "go all out for championships in everything," soliciting support outside the Army for a new recreation center. Colonel A.W. Bjornstad, one of those behind the plan, used athletic opportunities at Benning and the men's "magnificent appearance" on parade to attract enlistments, with the result that the Infantry, according to the *Army and Navy Journal*, had a waiting list of nearly 200. That same year Fort Benning's Chief of Infantry established a two-year athletic training course covering theoretical, administrative, and practical work in baseball and other sports. The stated purpose of the course was to keep men and officers fit as well as to enable officers to conduct all kinds of games "so as to interest their men." In 1926 the Fort Benning Infantry School's nine undertook a heavy schedule that included intercamp play, college teams, and marines, as well as exhibitions against the Columbus, Ohio, American Association team and the Washington Senators, champions of the American League the previous year. The team played its games in one of only two federal stadiums in the country, Doughboy Memorial Stadium.

Professional players likewise lent their skills to the Army. The commanding officer of Third Corps Area, headquartered in Washington, D.C., in 1923 announced the appointment of Buck Herzog, former major-league infielder, as head baseball coach. Third Corps Area's policy sought to encourage every man to participate in baseball, and each post, camp, and station in the Corps was exhorted to organize as many teams and leagues as possible, with the best players permitted to try out for the Corps team, which Herzog coached personally.

In the Midwest, Fort Snelling, near Minneapolis-St. Paul, emphasized baseball. The post ran a championship series, and Snelling's representative team played college, industrial, and Navy teams. Out in California the 30th Infantry team made a name for itself with a good record against amateur, semipro, and Navy clubs.

In the Southwest, Fort Sam Houston, Texas, accentuated the national game. One match between the 12th and 15th Field Artillery attracted a record crowd and heavy betting. A promoter offered $500.00 if the teams would play that game in town instead of at the fort, but they refused, and so many spectators then came to the fort that their cars completely surrounded the field. Fort Sam Houston is credited with being the place where Jerome "Dizzy" Dean, the star pitcher, got his baseball start in 1929, under Sergeant Jimmy Brought of Company C, who said he had to put Dean under arrest three times for walking away from Army chores to play ball. After Dean became a pro, the Army quickly took credit for his success, printing a promotional piece about the pitcher as an example of the slogan, "The Army Builds Men."

If so, the Army also kept building such men abroad as well, especially in places where baseball was long established, as in Schofield Barracks, Hawaii. There interregimental and interfort baseball reigned. When the University of California team came to Honolulu in 1926, however, it beat the Schofield Barracks team. Even during war maneuvers in Hawaii, units took time out to play ball. One afternoon in 1929 the "Call to Arms" sounded while a team from the 35th infantry was playing one from Ewa. So the soldier-players grabbed their rifles and packs, boarded a narrow-gauge train used for hauling sugar cane, and soon "rushed to repel a [pretend] enemy on the west coast of the island." *The Army and Navy Journal* commented, "Even in the midst of battle, soldiers must have their athletics."

In the Philippines, several military leagues, including intercompany leagues, played. One of the best teams of 1922, the 43rd Infantry team, all Filipino soldiers, tied a civilian team for third place in the Philippines Baseball League. In China, American regulars on duty in Tientsin with the 15th infantry spearheaded baseball there. Once incensed Chinese fans disputing an umpire's decision threatened to attack him, and a cordon of doughboys had to escort him from the field. The 15th Infantry also won the baseball championship at the 5th Far Eastern Games, an international competition, held in Shanghai in June of 1921.

Closer to home, in Puerto Rico, an Army team representing the 65th Infantry, all Puerto Ricans, traveled to Governors' Island, New York, to take part in a series for the championship of the Second Army Corps Area, of which Puerto Rico was a member.

If the Army supported sports wholeheartedly in the 1920s, the Navy kept pace with it. Secretary of the Navy Josephus Daniels averred, "In the navy we encourage . . . athletics [because] a keen interest in baseball and in other wholesome sports is one of the things that will help keep up the morale of the navy." Besides touting its "wholesomeness" and morale-building qualities, the Navy, like the Army, tied athletics to nationalism. The Navy, said Major John L. Griffith, vice-president of the National Amateur Athletic Federation, in *The Athletic Journal*, "attempts to indoctrinate its men" with the idea that "true Americanism" in athletic competition is "characterized by clean sportsmanship" and "friendliness." The Navy also belonged as a unit to the National Amateur Athletic Federation. Its policy toward enlisted men's athletics, according to the *Army and Navy Journal*, was to promote sports among as many participants as possible, so the naval commanders advocated intramural contests among ship and station teams rather than establishing a superteam or teams of just a few contestants. In practice, however, the Navy promoted both kinds of competition.

Besides promoting ship teams, like that of the U.S.S. *Langley* and the U.S.S. *Colorado*, through the athletic officer appointed by every ship's commander, the Navy also used athletics at all its training stations as part of recruit training. At the Philadelphia Navy Yard thirty teams competed in 1922, including the teams that played a doubleheader every afternoon on the single first-class diamond in the Yard. Nine ships and the Receiving Station were represented in the league.

The Portsmouth, New Hampshire, Naval Prison became an unexpectedly active spot for baseball. There Thomas Mott Osborne had organized a league representing ships and other groups, including one called the Outlaws. They played not only each other but also outside teams, inviting them to come and compete with the reassuring words, "You will find a bunch of young fellows, confined for violation of rules, but everyone a gentleman, and you will be given a good welcome if you care to take on our team, which we believe is the rightful championship team of the Portsmouth Navy Yard."

The prison newspaper declared that baseball helped the men stay contented and happy and that recreation periods helped keep them fit. A 1929 visitor charged with evaluating the recreation program at the naval prison for the National Prison Association thought that the men had ample recreation space, adding that privileged men could play games Saturday, Sunday, and holiday afternoons. The rest received outdoor recreation at noon and after supper, financed by laundry profits. Baseball, said the visitor, was "the chief sport."

Abroad, sailors managed to play ball in a surprising number of countries. Naval play in Hawaii continued; the Pearl Harbor submariners became 1928 baseball champions of the Hawaii League. In Haiti in 1923 a Naval Detachment team competed in a league composed mostly of service teams. Sailors from a flotilla of destroyers at Calcutta, India, in 1924 challenged and won over a group of resident Yankees 3-2. When a cruiser visited Riga, Latvia, in 1929, some local Americans on hand "naturally" arranged a baseball game between two Navy teams, said *Baseball Magazine*, and the Latvians turned out in crowds to find out what the word "baseball" on the billboards meant. Teams from both the *Utah* and the *Leviathon* took the opportunity of playing Anglo-American teams in London when their ships visited England. Sailors from the *Detroit* played against those from its accompanying destroyers on a visit to Tunis in 1927. In Holland in 1923, sailors from the *Pittsburgh* won a game from a group of Dutch players. The New York *Times* credited the battleship *Nevada* with reviving desultory baseball in Brazil when the ship visited on the occasion of the Brazil Centenary Exhibition (1922). The Navy also continued playing against Samoans at Tutuilla. And even on board ship sailors could practice: on the *Delaware* the crew strung nets from the superstructure down to the guard rail to keep from losing balls overboard while the pitchers, catchers, and batters practiced.

Ships' teams not only played these occasional pickup games, they took part in fleet and even interfleet championship series. For in the twenties the Navy established competition at the highest levels. The prediction of Secretary of the Navy Daniels that "now that the fleet has been divided . . . the competition will be between Atlantic and Pacific fleets" came true.

But first each fleet had to establish its own baseball champion. Atlantic Fleet games often took place at the American base in Guantanamo, Cuba. In 1921 Rear Admiral Henry B. Wilson, commander in chief, announced a schedule of a dozen games to decide the winners of the various divisions of the Atlantic Fleet so that the championship could be contested for and he could bestow the trophy on the winner. The same sort of program was arranged for 1922.

The Pacific Fleet held a similar championship series. In 1921 the *Charleston* won it. And when the Atlantic Fleet under Admiral Wilson and the Pacific Fleet under Admiral Hugh L. Rodman took part in joint exercises, how could they resist playing a series to see which fleet's top team was better? The interfleet games took place off Panama in February 1921, and when the Atlantic beat the Pacific fleet champions 12–3 in the deciding game, the *Army and Navy Journal* opined, "The scene at the baseball game in enthusiasm was equal to that at a world's series and in sportsmanship was without an equal."

One Navy pitcher, Bill Posedel, became a pro because of his exploits in a Pacific Fleet championship series. Posedel joined the Navy in 1926. First stationed on the *Colorado*, he transferred to the aircraft carrier *Saratoga* and received a watch from the crew for pitching the carrier into the championship of the B Division of the Pacific Coast Fleet, beating a team from its sister ship, the *Lexington*, in the deciding game of the series. The *Saratoga* sailors, recalled Posedel later, "wagered everything they could beg and borrow to get it down on our club. If I had lost, they'd probably have thrown me overboard." Posedel's feat attracted the attention of the Pacific Coast League, and its Portland Club signed him before the Navy had even discharged him. Posedel eventually made the big leagues.

The champion team of the United States Battle Fleet, after winning the Fleet title in 1925, engaged Navy teams and Air Squadron teams in baseball. The star pitcher of the Battle Fleet for four years, Marvin Moudy of the U.S.S. *California*, like Posedel became a pro. He joined the San Francisco team of the Pacific Coast League when he left the Navy, and on the occasion of his first professional game his former shipmates came to see him pitch. Before the game the flagship's band marched around the diamond, followed by the ship's crew, and then the Chief Signalman presented Moudy with a gold watch and gold baseball from the crew.

The Battle Fleet also took on the Scouting Fleet in baseball. Once the New York *Times* described an interfleet game with a naval metaphor: "The Battle Fleet today buried the Scout Fleet under a salvo of twenty-two hits and won the final of the interfleet baseball championship with a score of 18 to 2."

The Marines, too, resorted to baseball in the twenties, using it for recruiting and for morale-building. Clyde Metcalfe in his *History of the Marine Corps* asserted that after World War I, when the attraction of war, serving the flag, and wearing a uniform began proving insufficient lures in recruiting, the Marines hit upon sports as one inducement for joining that branch of the service. Before the war, athletics in the Marines had been haphazard. Afterward, declared Major General John A. Lejeune, "We found that nothing like these games had been devised to keep our boys going. We needed them." He believed that games maintained morale and esprit "when there were those who feared a let-down." Athletics, Lejeune said, were now compulsory in the Marines. So the Marines planned, for all Marine training centers, representative baseball teams bearing such names as "Quantico Marines" and "San Diego Marines." And like the Navy the Marines joined the National Amateur Athletic Federation. In 1926 Marine Headquarters announced its new policy: "Every Man An Athlete."

At Quantico these plans took effect quickly. One year the Quantico baseball team won 39 of 43 games, and the Marines started building their own stadium, even quarrying their own rock. This stadium would become, like the Army stadium at Fort Benning, one of the only two federal stadiums in the country. The Quantico team averaged a game a day against colleges in the spring of 1926. The Marine Barracks team of Parris Island, South Carolina, coveting the Service Championship of the Southeast in 1924, challenged all service teams "within reasonable distance" in order to determine the champion.

Marine teams likewise played abroad, against locals or other service teams. News filtered back to the States in sporting papers, sporting magazines, and the *Army and Navy Journal* of Marine teams playing in Puerto Rico, Haiti, Santo Domingo, Nicaragua, and China. The Coast Guard, too, formed teams and played American Army and even Royal Canadian Navy baseballers. All these far-flung ball games of the armed services dispelled any lingering doubt of America's global economic and imperial interests.

Interservice play at various levels took place in the States and even abroad. A few leagues at home, like the District of Columbia League, included teams from all services, but baseball play among teams of the different branches of the service was likelier in spots like China, the Canal Zone, Hawaii, Haiti, and the Philippines. In 1921 the 15th United States Infantry, stationed at Tientsin, China, claimed "the championship of the Orient" after its baseball team beat the 4th Philippine Infantry team, holders of the championship of the Philippine Islands. The Filipinos had just whipped the Marines in a three-game series in Peking before the Infantry defeated them. A baseball league in Haiti combined service teams from the Marines, Aviators, the Navy, and the Army with resident Americans who, said the *Army and Navy Journal* in 1923, "despite their handicap of bulk and other infirmities of old age . . . are full of pep and determination."

In the twenties the three main branches of the service, Army, Navy, and Marines, each decided to develop a superteam in baseball, one that would represent the entire branch. With the establishment of these champion teams, interservice play took on more drama, since the "honor" of an entire branch of the service depended on the outcome of a contest. In 1926 during the Sesquicentennial Celebration in Philadelphia the Navy and Marine superteams met to decide the service championship. Marine James Levey, among others, was ordered to report to Philadelphia to play on his service superteam; and after the Marine team won the championship, Levey continued to play in Quantico until the St. Louis Browns, with the aid of some United States Senators, pried him away from the Marines. He lasted four years as a big leaguer.

Underpinning all this service baseball were larger athletic programs within the service academies. When Brigadier General Douglas MacArthur took over as superintendent of West Point in 1919 he made intramural sport a required part of physical training, in the belief that athletics developed fitness as well as skill. Every man was to be grounded in the fundamentals of all leading sports. MacArthur considered that every cadet should be able to play some form of sport, even if only a few could play on the varsity level. To provide time for this athletic mandate, he reduced the prewar schedule of gymnastics and calisthenics.

MacArthur turned the academy's sports program over to the Director of Athletics, Captain Matthew B. Ridgeway, West Point '17, later a World War II and Korean War general and also postwar commander of NATO (North Atlantic Treaty Organization) forces in Europe. The Point requested congressmen to recommend gifted athletes for the Academy. Like the Marines in this era, the academy adopted the slogan, "Every Man an Athlete." Grantland Rice, New York *Tribune* sports writer, thought the new requirements at the academy meant cadets would develop finer coordination and "broader vision," and later as officers they would be brought closer to their men because they could lead them in every sport.

At first MacArthur appointed West Point's chaplain, Clayton E. "Buck" Wheat, as baseball coach. Wheat had impressed the superintendent by working out with the team. When the coach recommended breaking the hundred-year-old ban on Sunday ball, MacArthur consented, and Sunday afternoon at the Point became a time for intramural athletics. Requirements for earning the athletic letter were stiffened. And MacArthur tried, although unsuccessfully, to get Congress to let him build an elaborate 50,000-seat stadium.

The New York Giants developed a special relationship with West Point. Former Giants became baseball coaches, Hans Lobert in 1925 and Henry "Moose" McCormick in 1927. MacArthur also invited the Giant team to play an exhibition game at the academy in 1922; Casey Stengel starred in the game, scoring two runs and amusing the cadets with his antics. The Giants returned annually. Although the cadets could hardly hope to win against big leaguers, they did undertake a heavy schedule of college baseball opponents.

One result of the heavy emphasis on sports at West Point was the emergence of some outstanding baseball players. Connie Mack, owner and manager of the Philadelphia Athletics, signed Walter French, an ex-academy player, who played for six years with the Athletics. John McGraw, manager of the Giants, wanted Russell Reeder, an academy player who hit .413 in a spring training tryout with the Giants, but Reeder could not bring himself to resign his commission and stayed with the military. He was wounded in World War II and became a writer.

The Naval Academy at Annapolis similarly developed intramural athletics in the twenties and, like West Point, also supported varsity teams in the major sports, including baseball, where Charles "Chief" Bender, former pitching star of the Athletics, coached the team. The Annapolis varsity baseball team enjoyed a successful decade: during the twenties in almost every year the team won more games than it lost. In this period the Naval Academy improved in its annual baseball games against West Point, beating the cadets six times during the decade. The middies had less success abroad, for in 1923, on a cruise to the Canal Zone, Annapolis cadets played against local residents and college men but lost several games.

At least one Annapolis player became a major leaguer, although only briefly: Nemo Gaines, a pitcher who, on graduation in 1921 got special military leave to pitch four games for the Washington Senators, then returned to resume his Navy career.

The Depression of the 1930s made a difference in service baseball. During the drab decade, while baseball continued in the Army, Navy, and Marines, we hear no more of superteams and their exploits. The Marines forthrightly announced the abolition of their all-star team on account of the "excessive financial burden" it entailed. (In six years it had won 135 games and lost 27.) All services continued intramural games; fort teams played other forts and outsiders; Army units held intercamp tournaments within their respective Areas; and fleets held championship series. Nevertheless, compared with the service baseball of the twenties the action in the thirties seems somewhat muted.

The Citizens Military Training Camps, where National Guardsmen trained, still operated in the depression, and the Army continued to use athletics as an aid to recruiting Guardsmen. Outstanding athletes at these camps received prizes of baseballs and bats from Babe Ruth and Lou Gehrig. And the YMCA promoted military athletics at home and abroad, the Army and Navy Ys creating the United States Athletic Fraternity to honor all-around athletes. By 1940, Army and Navy Ys were operating forty-five centers in the States, the Canal Zone, Hawaii, the Philippines, and China.

Aside from the fifty-three centers for the Civilian Conservation Corps (CCC), where young civilian men helped servicemen build training fields and athletic fields and played baseball themselves, another military portal for athletics opened in the 1930s: the Army Recreational Camps, set up late in the decade in Texas, Maryland, California, Georgia, and Washington State.

In the 1930s the regular Army kept up intramural baseball tournaments and varsity games with outsiders and with other Army units at such posts as Mitchel Field, near Hempstead, New York; Camp Upton, New York; and Fort Adams, Rhode Island. The Fort Niagara, New York, team entered a local league in 1930 and came out on top. At Fort Monmouth, New Jersey, too, the fort team played in a local league, becoming champions of the first half-season of 1931 and winning the league championship in 1933. As league members the Monmouth team competed against the strong semipro and industrial teams of the area. Major O.K. Sadtler, a West Point pitcher who had refused a big-league contract on graduation, coached the Monmouth team, and when he left for Washington, D.C., the team, in appreciation of his help, gave him a silver tray and cocktail set, which he no doubt used to good advantage in the capital.

Fort Benning continued its baseball tradition in the thirties with a strong intramural program (the winning team got a trophy) as well as a varsity that included among its opponents colleges, semipros, and even the professional Atlanta Crackers. At the end of the decade the regimental commander of the 29th Infantry at the fort, addressing its 2,400 officers and men on parade, praised the unit for holding the current garrison championship in baseball and basketball.

The various Army forts, depots, and medical units stationed around Washington, D.C., that made up Third Corps Area banded into their own baseball league in 1930 and 1931, but in 1932 so many units and posts joined that the Area had to be divided into four groups, a few units per group, in order to operate an elimination series for the Area championship. In 1934 Fort Meade won the Third Corps Area championship and received a plaque. Each team member got a sweater. One of the many officers viewing the presentation was Captain Yasuto Nakayama of the Japanese Army. Fort Meade participated not only in Third Corps Area league games but in contests against athletic clubs, the Quantico Marines, a Navy ship, a brewing company, the Baltimore Police, the Baltimore Fire Department, and the Federal Bureau of Investigation. The team of Fort Belvoir, Virginia, won the 1936 Third Corps Area championship, taking the final game against Fort Hoyle.

At another Fort Meade, the one in South Dakota, the Headquarters Troop played nearby town teams. Fort Snelling, Minnesota, played a six-game series against Fort Lincoln, North Dakota, and the team hoped to arrange games with other northwestern forts "if funds are available." At Fort Sill, Oklahoma, the Eighteenth Field Artillery took the championship of the Field Artillery School league after winning four straight games.

A highly organized athletic setup at Fort Sam Houston, Texas, home of the Second Division, included intramural and varsity ball, the latter played in a lighted park seating 4,500 named Christy Mathewson Field. Strong Army post teams on the West Coast, like those at Fort MacArthur and at the Presidio, played the "fast" amateur and semipro clubs of the area. At Fort Lewis, Washington, by the end of the decade, when the worst of the depression ended, new athletic facilities, including two baseball diamonds with bleachers, were under construction.

Soldiers could still play league-style baseball abroad in the thirties in countries where military ball had a long history. In the Philippines, teams in the annual tournament were segregated into two divisions according to national origin: the American Division, for Stateside citizens, and the Scout

Division, for the Filipino Scouts, who had been inducted into their own separate units. In Panama, posts and forts competed in an Army League. The Albrook Field team, champion of the Panama Canal Zone League in 1941, flew to San Salvador as guests of the host government to play the national teams of El Salvador and Mexico in the First Decennial International Sports contest there. Later that year the Nicaraguan Baseball Club, a member of the Central American League, returned the visit to Albrook Field and lost a three-game series to Albrook.

Navy baseball went forward, to a degree, during the depression, under the supervision of ship and base athletic officers. Even the Naval Prison at Portsmouth, New Hampshire, where baseball continued as the chief sport, had its athletic officer.

In 1936 the Naval Training Station at Portsmouth, Virginia, ran afoul of the International League, an important minor league in Organized Baseball. The Station's baseball club had planned to play the Albany, New York, International League Club, which was coming to town to entertain the naval trainees, but the Norfolk, Virginia, International League Club protested, on the ground that in the Portsmouth area it held territorial rights. According to league rules, no other International League Club could play there. William Bramham, president of the league, felt he had no choice but to deny permission for the game, whereupon Lieutenant J.W. Dillinder of the Navy responded, as reported in *Sporting News*, "We are not pleased and are quite surprised at the belligerent attitude taken by the Norfolk Club in this instance."

The Navy lost again in the case of Howard Mills. When Mills joined the Navy and the aircraft carrier *Lexington* at San Diego, he found that members of the baseball team worked less and received more shore leave and days off than others, so he made the team in early 1933 and won fourteen games that season pitching for it, including a no-hitter against the *Vestal* that brought the *Lexington* the Navy championship. Fans voted Mills an automobile, although he had just signed up for two more years in the Navy. Then the St. Louis Browns of the American League approached Mills about joining their team. The *Lexington*'s commander took exception to the recruitment of Mills, but with the aid of senators and congressmen, Mills squirmed out of his Naval re-enlistment and joined the Browns, where he pitched for several years.

Naval baseball in these years connects with American naval presence abroad, for reports in the New York *Times* and *Sporting News* tell of Navy teams playing in Managua, Nicaragua, in 1933, and in Cuba and San Salvador in 1936.

The Marines, despite discontinuing their All-Marine baseball team, could still offer strong college teams as opponents for trainees at Quantico. Abroad, the team of the Marines' Fourth Regiment, with many outstanding athletes, after being stationed in Shanghai for four years, embarked on the Steamship

Shanghai Maru of the Nippon Yusen Kaishen Line for a "Goodwill Baseball Tour of Japan," where in 26 days it won 10 out of 14 games against Japanese college and civilian teams.

Airmen stationed at Scott Field, Illinois, and at Kelly Field, Texas, participated only in intersquadron tournaments, although those at Langley Field, Virginia, played some games against Army teams.

Interservice play did not fall completely by the wayside during the depression. In 1931 the 30th Infantry claimed the service baseball championship of California when it won five games in five days against three ships of the Battle Fleet—including the *Tennessee*, that year's fleet champion—then at anchor, and also beat the teams of Fort McDowell, Fort Scott, March Field, and the Mare Island Marines. Interservice games seemed especially common abroad, where the different branches were stationed in close proximity. Hawaii's ship, submarine, and infantry units all played each other, and in 1931 the Pearl Harbor Submariners, Squadron 4, defeated the 21st Infantry of Schofield Barracks to take the service championship of the Hawaiian islands. On Guam, where servicemen's games had long been played in the Plaza at Agaña, ground was broken for a new eleven-acre athletic field, expected to be one of the best in the Orient.

In Panama, with twelve or fourteen thousand soldiers and sailors on hand, the Army and Navy units combined in an eight-club league. During a visit of Ford Frick, National League president, in 1935, the servicemen pulled off a dramatic stunt: Frick threw out the first ball at the season opener February 22 between Army and Colon on the Atlantic side of the isthmus, then boarded a Navy plane, flew to the Pacific side, and similarly opened the game there between Navy and Balboa. The 15th Infantry, still stationed in Tientsin, played in the North China League and defeated civilians, American sailors, and the Japanese there.

At the two major service academies, during the depression the cadets and midshipmen did not have to give up either intramural or varsity ball. At West Point General William R. Smith, then superintendent, reiterated the Point's commitment to athletics: "We have discovered that the best junior officers are of the athletic type." Through the intramural system, Smith said, cadets continued to be trained to handle all major sports; baseball, still coached by Moose McCormick, was one of them. "Athletics for every cadet" remained the West Point slogan, Smith declared. Under the athletic rules the varsity ball team could play two away games in a season, and its opponents included strong college teams like Harvard, Amherst, Pittsburgh, Brown, Colgate, Columbia, Williams, Penn, Springfield, and Fordham.

The decade began unpropitiously at West Point with an investigation of the Army Athletic Association by the War Department, which had seen Dr. Howard T. Savage's Carnegie Report criticizing recruiting practices at the academy. Major General Hugh A. Drum, the Army's Inspector General, investigated those practices, and he claimed that he established "beyond doubt" that "there is no professionalism or commercialism associated with athletics at the Academy." An examination of vouchers, he said, showed no payment of extra compensation to athletes, no evidence of stealing or grafting by scouts, and only limited recruiting. Drum added that Savage had found no evidence of athletic subsidies at the Marine Academy, either. The Inspector General further noted that although Savage found recruiting at the Point, it was so limited that the academy should not be compared with the colleges and universities he, Savage, had named as offenders. Drum pointed out that West Point rules prohibited athletes deficient in their studies from playing with athletic teams. He also quoted Savage's praise for the intramural athletic program at the academy: "Few colleges or universities can give to their students the experience of games which the United States Military Academy requires of its fourth-class men." Thus the matter of preference for athletes at West Point was resolved, at least to the War Department's satisfaction.

Both class teams and a varsity team continued at Annapolis, the varsity coached by Ernest "Kid" Mohler, who had had a brief stay in the big leagues in 1894. Even the plebes (freshmen) had a former professional, one with limited big-league experience, as coach. Class teams played local businesses, like banks in Baltimore, as well as semipros and even the Washington, D.C., Police Department. The varsity's record for the decade, however, despite the team's pro coaching, was only fair: in most years the team lost more games than it won. Middies on a practice cruise to Europe also lost a game played against the London Americans.

Interacademy baseball broke off suddenly in 1929. The depression did not cause the break. New eligibility rules instituted at the Naval Academy gave rise to it. Annapolis decided to follow the large colleges and universities that had limited athletes' eligibility in football to three years, and West Point, believing the Navy's adoption of the new rule to be misguided idealism cloaking a desire for parity with West Point in football, broke off all athletic relations. The eligibility rule had been designed to prevent athletes from moving from college to college, and since athletes could enter the service academies only by congressional appointment and by passing competitive exams, the three-year rule, according to the New York *Sun* sports writer George Trevor, was hardly appropriate for the academies and saddled them with unnecessary restrictions. Athletic relations resumed in 1933, and after that the Naval Academy won the interacademy baseball games slightly more often than did the Army Academy.

The decade in service academy baseball ended on an ironic note in 1939 when the Army, celebrating General Abner Doubleday's supposed invention of baseball at Cooperstown, New York, in 1839, while on leave from West Point, named its academy baseball park Doubleday Field. Actually, Doubleday, a plebe in 1839, could not have been in Cooperstown that summer unless he had gone AWOL. If those who accepted the story of Doubleday's feat, touted by a Commission appointed by Organized Baseball, had bothered to check with the Point, they would have learned that like all plebes Doubleday got no leave at all in 1839 and had to stay at the Point all summer. His first leave came in the summer of 1840. But this conflict of fact with myth may not even have bothered those who wanted to believe that an American general had invented the game instead of the reality—namely, that it grew from a child's pastime and was codified in basically its present form in large part at New York City by Alexander Cartwright and his team, the Knickerbockers, in the 1840s.* Baseball as played by servicemen remains an important part of its history, but its invention by Doubleday is mythology rather than fact.

*See "How Baseball Began," *New-York Historical Society Quarterly*, Vol. XL No. 4 (October, 1956), pp. 369–385; and *Baseball: The Early Years*, pp. 4–12.

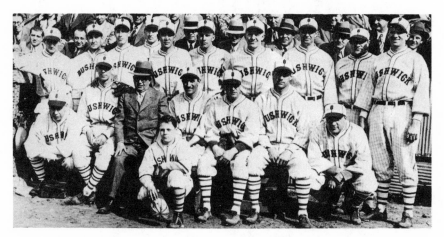

23. Bushwick Baseball Club, a top semipro team in Brooklyn, New York, about 1930. The man in a business suit is owner Max Rosner. *The Cooperstown Hall of Fame and Museum Library, Cooperstown, New York.*

24. The House of David baseball team of Benton Harbor, Michigan, a famous independent touring team, about the 1900s. *The Cooperstown Hall of Fame and Museum Library, Cooperstown, New York.*

25. The scene at Brookside Stadium, Cleveland, Ohio, as 100,000 people watched the White Autos defeat the Omaha Luxers 11–6 for the National Baseball Federation Championship in 1915. *From* The Albatross, *house organ of the White Motor Company, Cleveland, Ohio, October 1915.*

26. The Union baseball team of the Annapolis Class of 1873. The pitcher holding the ball at upper left is William F. Halsey, father of Fleet Admiral W. F. Halsey, Jr. *Courtesy of the Naval Academy Archives.*

27. The baseball team of the West Point class of 1901. Cadet Douglas MacArthur is at far right in the second row. *Courtesy of the United States Military Academy Archives.*

28. Ship's baseball club of the U.S.S. *Powhatan* during the 1870s or 1880s. *United States Department of the Navy.*

29. Soldiers of the American Expeditionary Forces playing baseball somewhere in France during World War I. *From the National Archives.*

30. Mutual Welfare League baseball team of Sing Sing Prison, Ossining, New York, May 1923. *Ossining Historical Society.*

31. Inmates playing baseball in the federal prison at Atlanta, Georgia. Undated. *Federal Bureau of Prisons.*

32. Mount Holyoke College baseball team of 1883, South Hadley, Massachusetts. *Mount Holyoke College Library/Archives.*

33. The catcher tags the runner out at Wellesley College, Wellesley, Massachusetts, in the 1920s. *Courtesy of Wellesley College Archives.*

34. Batter and catcher in a Wellesley College baseball game, Wellesley, Massachusetts, 1922. *Courtesy of Wellesley College Archives.*

35. Women's touring team of 1890 and 1891, managed by W.S. Franklin. *The Cooperstown Hall of Fame and Museum Library, Cooperstown, New York.*

36. Moses Fleetwood ("Fleet") Walker, catcher, the first known black man in major-league baseball (1884). *Ralph E. LinWeber, Baseball Research Bureau.*

37. Varsity baseball team of Howard University, Washington, D.C., 1915. *Moorland-Spingarn Research Center, Howard University, Washington, D.C.*

38. The Commonwealth Giants, employees of a steamship company, the Fall River Line, in Massachusetts about 1910. The team included Lorenzo Dow Turner, later a University of Chicago linguist. *Courtesy of Mrs. Lois Turner.*

delegates were opposed to it and they would advise me to withdraw my application, as they thought it were better for us to withdraw, than to have it on record that we were black balled. This your delegate declined to do, and waited for the Com. to report, which they shortly did and reported favorably on all the credentials presented to them save that of the Pythian which they purposely left out of their general report. On their report being read a resolution was hastily passed and Mr. Ellis quickly springing to his feet moved that the Com. be discharged. Your delegate was . . .

39. Copy of part of the beautifully written manuscript, December 18, 1867, by R.S. Bun, delegate of the Pythian Baseball Club of Philadelphia to the state amateur convention, reporting the association's unwillingness to accept his black club into membership. *Courtesy of the Historical Society of Pennsylvania, Philadelphia.*

40. "The World's Brainiest Baseball Nine," so-called, all Ph.D.s and all Phi Beta Kappans—the Carleton College faculty baseball club, Northfield, Minnesota. Donald J. Cowling, the college president, is fourth from right, in the striped uniform. Photo by Harvey Stork. *Courtesy of the Carleton College Archives.*

41. Leroy "Satchel" Paige, superlative black pitcher on the professional Kansas City Monarchs during the segregated era when Organized Baseball and newsmen denigrated black teams as "semipros." *Courtesy of the National Baseball Hall of Fame and Museum, Cooperstown, New York.*

23

BASEBALL'S PROGENY

Potent though it was, baseball's widespread public appeal, presented in the preceding chapters and to be further elucidated in succeeding ones, cannot be completely appreciated without grasping the eager acceptance of the game's lusty offspring, eventually to be known collectively as softball.

In effect, baseball became the mother of invention, for the inability to satisfy the well-nigh insatiable demand for regulation baseball because of lack of space in the congested urban areas, combined with the want of baseball equipment in recreation centers, YMCAs, schools, colleges, and Turnvereins, inspired invention of a facsimile of the national game suitable for playing in limited space, indoor or out, even all year 'round. Sources differ on its origin, but most agree that in 1887 at the Chicago Boat Club George W. Hancock, a reporter for the Chicago Board of Trade, first hit upon a way to play "baseball" in winter by using a style of play soon called indoor ball.

The structure of the game as it developed differed from standard baseball in some fundamental ways. The pitcher delivered the ball from a shorter distance, using a windup and underhand release with speed that could, however, be comparable to that in baseball, but even when struck, the large, soft ball first used could not be batted far. The distance between bases was also shorter. To compensate, a runner had to keep one foot on his base and take no lead off it until the pitcher released the ball. Altogether, the game favored the defense. Despite these obvious differences indoor ball unmistakably revealed its lineage from the parent game, baseball.

Apart from requiring less space and permitting indoor as well as outdoor play, the new game offered other advantages over standard baseball. It involved relatively little expense to play: as little as a bat and ball sufficed for informal games. It took less skill to enjoy, entailed less chance of injury, and more easily accommodated the participation of young and old of both sexes. As a rule, play was faster and games took less time to complete.

Indoor ball caught on quickly. At first it was merely a fad in Chicago social clubs. Then the military in Chicago, New York, and Brooklyn found the game well-suited to their armories in winter. Military units played indoor ball on the roof of the 13th Regimental Armory in Brooklyn as early as 1890. Military authorities encouraged the game, believing it strengthened esprit de corps. Brooklyn regiments took the lead in forming a winter indoor ball league as part of their athletic program. The number of Manhattan and Brooklyn regimental teams soon grew to the point of necessitating organization of the league into two sections, Manhattan regiments in one, Brooklyn in the other. They played from three to six games Saturday nights up to mid-March, followed by a championship series in April between the leading teams of each section. The companies of some regiments also formed indoor ball teams and played intramurally. Those of Brooklyn's 23rd Regiment, for example (where my uncle was an officer), played among themselves five nights a week in winter.

Before long Hancock and his group realized that indoor ball could be brought outdoors. Early in the 1890s children played it on city playgrounds, particularly Chicago's, and public schools found it a desirable game for their less-than-spacious schoolyards. Hull-House Settlement also welcomed the game on its 100-foot parcel of land, where a policeman detailed by the city usually umpired.

By the turn of the century indoor ball had established outposts in all parts of the country. News of softball leagues came especially from cities. In November of 1900 the New York *Times* reported the existence of a National Indoor Association, looking after leagues in six cities—Baltimore; Washington; Concord, New Hampshire; Savannah, Georgia; and Middletown and Syracuse, New York—and in sixteen states from Maine to Oregon. Minneapolis organized its first league in 1900; Lewis Rober of the Fire Department put it together. According to *Sporting News*, indoor ball was the "big interest" in Syracuse in 1903, and a few years later a league started in St. Louis. By 1909 other large metropolitan areas were promoting the game. Even Dick Merriwell played it: *Tip Top Weekly* ran a story in 1906 entitled "Dick Merriwell's Satisfaction; or Hot Work at Indoor Baseball."

Indoor ball, converted into "playground ball" around 1907 by E.B. De Groot, Director of Chicago's South Park Playgrounds, kept pace with the advance of the playground movement. Recreation people looking for a competitive game that could be played outdoors in limited space with inexpensive equipment modified indoor ball by lengthening its baselines and pitching distances, incorporating a few baseball rules, and baptizing the result playground ball or recreation ball. The game not only created interest among boys, it presented a greater opportunity for girls and women to play a form of baseball.

At the outset, female physical training instructors approved of the new game, among them such important figures as Gertrude Dudley, director of the physical education department at the University of Chicago, and Frances Kellor, director of the research department of the Women's Municipal

League in New York City. They were co-authors of *Athletic Games in the Education of Women*, published in 1909, in which they expressed the view that although regulation baseball contained the greatest educational possibilities, it presented problems for women: the hard ball, the heavy bat, the long throws, and the complex rules. Indoor ball, on the other hand, with its soft ball, short, lightweight bat, mask but no gloves, straight-arm pitching, and light exercise offered less danger of injury and more chances for teamwork than basketball, declared the authors, while retaining the fun and value of baseball. Dudley and Kellor also credited the new game with strengthening moral, physical, and motor qualities and offering opportunities to correct poor posture.

About the same time, the Playground Association affirmed its commitment to playground ball by publishing a handbook of rules similar to those later called softball except that if a base runner ran counterclockwise, succeeding runners had to follow suit! In a 1910 *Playground* article Helen McKinstry, director of physical training at the Springfield, Massachusetts, high school, recommended indoor ball as an ideal team game "for the weakest as well as the strongest girls." Another article in a Playground Association pamphlet pointed out that the game could be played by girls on a smaller diamond. The PSAL handbook for 1913, too, listed the game among those girls could play.

The game won favor in girls' schools. An "official" indoor ball guide for 1917–18 told how one high school divided girls into two indoor ball teams from their second year on, but for girls' play the guide recommended eliminating sliding, blocking, and tripping! In San Diego high schools in the teens, girls took part in an annual county indoor ball tournament. Even Mayor Anton Cermak of Chicago stressed the importance of teaching the game to girls because "the way to teach physical culture [to girls] is by having them play something they enjoy." By the end of the decade observers noted major growth of the new game among girls and women.

Amidst its nationwide urban spread in the teens, the indoor ball vogue still remained strongest in Chicago, where many institutions—high schools, YMCAs, even semipro and professional clubs—took it up. Street boys, with their usual resourcefulness, modified indoor ball so as to play it in Chicago's thickly populated areas, where trolley cars clanged behind players' backs and line drives whizzed under the nostrils of horses. At the other extreme, professionalism became rife in Cook County's indoor ball. Calling for regulation, Herbert W. Gates of Boston's Congregational Education Society said loyalty to an indoor ball team had come to depend on material inducements, and amateurs and professionals played on the same team, some on more than one. In a Chicago Sunday school athletic league, organizers often induced star players to leave one school to play with another. Within a year, however, the National Amateur Athletic Federation imposed strict rules in Chicago and ostensibly cleared up the abuses. But professionalism spread.

Elsewhere, a mix of sponsors also tossed their caps for the new game. In New York City the public schools sponsored it. Spalding's PSAL handbook for 1911–12 reported that ten teams participated in a school tournament of indoor ball and that many more would have done so had they been able to find diamonds to play on. The deciding game for the championship took place at the 71st Regiment Armory, and the winning team, P.S. 83, whose photo the handbook published, featured five players with Italian names.

At Benton Harbor, Michigan, men showed their interest at a night school where a physical training class began playing indoor ball. When in the winter of 1918–19 the class grew to 49, the group divided into four teams, each playing a five-inning game twice a week. The season ended with a banquet given by the two teams with the lowest season standing. The following winter enrollment in the course jumped to 82 men aged 21 to 56, including executives, professionals, merchants, salesmen, factory supervisors, ministers, bankers, clerks, and engineers. They formed six teams and played a 45-game schedule. From time to time during the season they altered the personnel of teams in order to even up the competition, because the ability of the participants ranged from those who had played professional and semipro baseball to those who had to be told to run after hitting a fair ball!

Business and industrial establishments awakened to the game as an instrument for enhancing public relations and employee good will and loyalty. *Spalding's Illustrated Catalog* (1900) went so far as to claim that "every large commercial house has its team." General Electric's Nela Park plant in Cleveland built a softball field in 1917 and reduced the size of its baseball field so that employees could play two games of indoor ball simultaneously on it. In addition, a women's twilight league played at Nela Park. Occasionally, female workers also played a game preliminary to the regular Saturday afternoon game of the men's "varsity." According to Hollis Townsend's history of Nela Park, the women's team was outstanding and competed with the best of other such teams in the Cleveland area.

During the Great War the military became a fertile environment for the game. At Camp Jackson, South Carolina, the soldiers' newspaper, *Trench and Camp*, stated in the summer of 1918 that "King baseball has been partly dethroned by playground ball." Soldiers played the new game all over the camp, perhaps because of a shortage of baseball gloves and baseballs at Camp Jackson. Playground ball also held advantages over baseball in military camps in that it could be played on almost any company street and nearly everyone could play it. Besides, the game eliminated the danger of beanballs and split fingers. The *Army and Navy Journal* said in 1918 that the War Department furnished servicemen with 3,500 playground ball bats and 10,500 balls, half as many as the bats and balls it provided for regular baseball. In the A.E.F., for a while indoor ball overtook baseball in popularity. In the fall of 1918 the YMCA reported more than 90,000 servicemen playing the new game while only about 68,000 played regulation baseball. Then in

1919 the figures changed: nearly 940,000 for regular baseball against some 723,000 for indoor. Prison camps received indoor ball equipment, too, with the Y contributing equipment for both indoor and regular ball to prisoners of the Germans in Ukrainerlager, Rastatt, and Baden.

In the twenties the popularity of modified baseball reached its crescendo throughout the land in crowded urban playgrounds as well as remote country schools and among adults and children alike. This expansion owed much to a widening variety of sponsorship. The game became the most popular field sport of Chicago street gangs, as welfare agencies used it to deal with such boys. In West Chicago's park system, nearly every playground had a twilight league of young workingmen playing an organized schedule of "kitten ball" (another name for the game) between 6:30 and 9:00 P.M. all summer before audiences of as many as 3,000 per game. Public-spirited citizens contributed prizes for the winners. Later in the decade the Chicago *Evening American* started a citywide tournament among 400 teams of men, women, and boys.

In Florida, "diamond ball," as it was called in St. Petersburg, began as recreation for businessmen. Later in the twenties a civic league operated. Night games, begun in St. Petersburg in 1928, stimulated much public interest. People also played the game at Winter Haven and Miami Beach.

Business and industrial firms continued to respond to the softball siren in the twenties. The United States Labor Bureau reported that 122 Cleveland businesses sponsored several forms of indoor ball played outdoors. Minneapolis ran city kitten ball leagues open to teams of employees from commercial firms on payment of a five-dollar entrance fee per team and an umpire's fee of a dollar a game. In Pontiac, Michigan, when the director of recreation learned that two teams from a city foundry desired to play indoor ball in the local armory but could not afford the twenty-dollar fee and that other teams wanted to join them, he persuaded the armory authorities to reduce the charge to two dollars an evening, two evenings a week. The workers' teams organized an industrial league, each depositing ten dollars to cover deficits or penalties. In Gallatin, Missouri, in 1925 the town found that an admission charge of a nickel covered all expenses of night games for men and women both. The United States Department of Labor reported in 1926 that although baseball remained the favorite game in industry, softball was popular, too. Two years later in an article entitled "Responsibilities of Industry for Recreation," *Playground* gently reminded employers that playground ball was a sport that appealed to older men.

Indeed it did. As regular softball developed into a fast-pitch game with numerous strikeouts and few runs, and middle-aged and older adults became unable to cope with it, they contrived their own version of the game: slowpitch softball, which required that the pitch be delivered underhand in an arc. Consequently, the balance of the game shifted to the offense, thus resulting in fewer strikeouts and higher scores. In Florida around 1928, for instance, players founded the Three-Quarter Century Softball League, the name originating from the fact that they set the minimum age for membership at seventy-five.

Female industrial workers found greater opportunity opening to them to enjoy softball in the twenties. At Western Electric Company women employees acquired the use of an indoor ball diamond at one of Chicago's settlement houses in 1923. In Cleveland, Joseph & Feiss Company and the Cleveland Hardware Company provided indoor ball for women employees during the noon hour. Some companies began furnishing uniforms and equipment and paying their team's entrance fee in a municipal league, as they did with baseball. The Industrial Federation of New Haven, Connecticut, in combination with business firms and the YMCA and YWCA, sponsored indoor ball, as well as other sports, for both sexes. During the twenties even the American Athletic Union sponsored a women's softball team along with other sports teams.

In the twenties, girls and young women played variants of softball under municipal sponsorship, too. Playground directors at Washington Park in Chicago tried to stir the interest of girls under twelve by teaching them "leadup games" like relays, batting, pitching, throwing, long ball, and captain ball. Playground girls in Oakland, California, used a soft ball and played by regular baseball rules, but, rejoiced their director, the city furnished no finals or championship for them. In Paterson, New Jersey young women over 18, many of them employed, played indoor ball at an armory under the sponsorship of the Board of Recreation. In Minneapolis girls under 16 played in a diamond ball league conducted by the municipal association; women from 18 to 55 had 47 teams, 27 commercial and 20 city, and the assistant director announced that diamond ball had proved "an outstanding success." In Florida some softball for women took place on district and state as well as local levels.

While women and girls played on, a cadre of physical training people gave only qualified acquiescence. Gladys Palmer, assistant physical education professor at Ohio State and member of the subcommittee on baseball for the influential National Committee on Women's Athletics in the American Physical Education Association, asserted that the "intricate technique" of baseball was "too difficult for the average girl to master"; to obtain its educational benefits, therefore, sponsors must alter baseball's rules "to fit the peculiar needs and abilities of girls and women." She elaborated in her book, *Baseball for Girls and Women* (1929), listing separate rules for indoor and outdoor versions of the women's modified game. Illustrations in Palmer's book reveal the desired costume: short-sleeved white blouse with black tie, black bloomers, white belt, black stockings, and ankle-high tennis shoes.

Others also thought girls could play indoor ball, though not regular baseball. Dudley Sargent conceded that girls could play games like baseball, but only if they were "regulated to the use of girls." Henry Curtis, director of hygiene and physical education for the state of Missouri, thought playground ball, with its smaller diamond, enabled girls to throw across it as they could not in regular baseball, and found that girls who learned to play the new game in grades four and five performed nearly as well as boys. Jesse Feiring Williams of Columbia's physical training department, after surveying 36 physical education directors, found indoor ball rated fourth on a list of 13 sports they deemed suitable for girls, and they gave it a 7.5 rating on a scale of 10.

Ethel Perrin, associate director of the American Child Health Association, differed. She expressed the sensible view that girls should have the same sports opportunities as boys and pointed out that on many playgrounds, while directors gave the most space to boys practicing for some big event, they forced girls to play baseball in the gym.

The military, meanwhile, did not neglect softball in the twenties. Leagues of California National Guardsmen played playground ball, and soldiers at Fort Snelling, near Minneapolis-St. Paul, played kitten ball on company teams. The game meanwhile seeped into prisons, too. Inmates of the Columbus, Ohio, State Penitentiary played softball daily, and the *Handbook of American Prisons* listed a women's reformatory team in Iowa as having intramural softball competition among its cottage teams.

Nevertheless, problems, the usual companions of success, accompanied the march of softball. The dissimilar supporters in different environments with different needs and purposes inevitably imposed their varied imprints on the new game. In addition to playground ball and recreation ball, standard baseball sired still more mutants, until the modified game acquired enough names to suit a Prince of Wales: kitten ball, mush ball, diamond ball, indoor-outdoor ball, and one especially for girls in which they used an open hand as the bat. In the end, all these names were finally identified under the rubric of softball, which gradually emerged as the standard form. The term *softball*, first suggested in 1926 by Walter Hakanson, a Denver YMCA director, as a collective name for modified baseball, would not become generally accepted until the mid-thirties. At that time even the Playground Association's organ dropped the term *recreation ball* in its favor. Paradoxically, the game eventually described by the term *softball* would be played with a hard ball!

Furthermore, a mishmash of playing rules as baffling as an income tax form worsened the confusion, particularly for those arranging competition, increasingly afoot on the intercity, interstate, and interregional levels. Pitching distances in the different forms of the game varied from twelve to forty-five feet. The size of fields differed, and even the number of players per team varied according to locale. Availability of a dozen balls of different size and resiliance and bats of varied length and weight added to the disarray.

Accordingly, the Playground Association tried in 1923 and again in 1927 to standardize the rules and inject a semblance of uniformity into the hodge-podge. In 1926 the American Physical Education Association adopted a simplified set of rules for women. These limited efforts proved increasingly futile, however, made so not only by the geographic expansion of the game but by the entrance of new sponsors other than recreation and physical education people, with their own goals and practices. The spread of the game carried it beyond the purview of its early custodians and, in short, outgrew them.

During the 1930s the American scene pullulated with softball. Various sources cite conflicting numbers of players, teams, leagues, games, and spectators, but without exception they indicate an unbroken increase. In particular, those figures reported annually to the Playground Association rose steadily throughout the decade. In 1935 the Association estimated that about nine million participated in the game, and in 1937 the figure jumped to twelve million.

Some samples will illustrate the ubiquity of softball and the variety of auspices under which it was played in the thirties. Chicago, its birthplace, continued as a softball mecca. The city's 1937 recreation survey estimated that 2,500 teams played 4,800 games watched by more than a million spectators, and it named softball the most popular game after bowling. Most Chicago teams played on playgrounds or vacant lots and depended on passing the hat to raise money, but outstanding league teams played in floodlit parks and charged from fifteen to thirty-five cents admission. Industrial softball outstripped baseball in Chicago companies; 264 of them reported nearly 1,000 teams. A single Chicago company supported almost a hundred softball clubs, one of them an outstanding team of nonemployees assembled for advertising purposes. Annual championship games in Chicago drew as many as 30,000 people and realized $7,000.00 in gate receipts, which went to charity. In 1939 another survey of Chicago parks showed that softball had become the favorite game of delinquent boys! And oldsters formed a league with the clever name "Cripple A League."

Softball figured prominently in Cleveland, where in 1937 organizers inaugurated night games on three softball diamonds funded by the Cleveland Baseball Federation, the Cleveland Foundation, the Municipal Softball Association, and a public-spirited citizen. The city furnished technical assistance. In that city the White Motor Company sponsored an indoor team as well as a baseball team in 1935, and the Hollenden Hotel Garage's indoor ball team finished its 1938 season undefeated in its league.

To promote sports in Dayton, Ohio, the National Cash Register Company in 1934 developed a forty-five-acre tract that included both baseball and softball diamonds. In Massillon, Ohio, future major-league outfielder Tommy Henrich played on a drug company softball team in his last two years of high school.

Farther west, early in the thirties about a thousand teams played softball in Wisconsin under the aegis of municipal recreation departments in Racine, Kenosha, Milwaukee, Oshkosh, Sheboygan, and Two Rivers. One of the

Milwaukee players was Ken Keltner, not yet started on his way to major-league success. State championship games among Wisconsin teams played over the Labor Day weekend concluded the muny softball season.

But the game had long since spread from its midwestern hub. In New York state the Westchester County Recreation Commission's annual report of 1938 boasted that no county-sponsored sport took the "spectacular leap" into popularity that softball did. All the factories of the Endicott Johnson Shoe Company around New York State featured women's softball teams, the workers donning "smart uniforms," an observer noted, and showing the ability to "wallop the ball with all the ardor of college boys." The Recreation Commission of one New Jersey town attributed the 600 percent rise in recreation for industrial employees to the formation of softball teams that increased in two years from five to thirty-two.

Greenwich, Connecticut, with 38,000 inhabitants, reportedly had more softball teams than any other city in the state and more teams in proportion to its population than any city in the country. Its softball association ran eight leagues composed of 82 teams and 930 men. In neighboring Massachusetts the General Electric plant in Lynn alone had fifty softball teams.

Such was the lure of softball in Fairmont, West Virginia, population 25,000, that by the end of the decade 56 organized teams in 16 leagues played on all available athletic fields and even vacant lots. Its eight-team city league proved the fastest, followed by the six-team Rocking Chair League, and the rest in descending order included a six-team Lame Duck League and eight teams of boys aged twelve. Older men played in the Father Time League. Salt Lake City reserved two parks for softball, scheduling four games per evening and staging its first state championship series among 29 teams in 1936, while Arkansas sponsored its first softball tournament in 1935.

The salubrious West Coast climate provided a receptive venue for softball. At Fresno, California, young and old played the game year 'round as well as under lights. Schoolboys and businessmen played, and the grownups vied in a city championship at season's end. At Oakland, softball and badminton became the most prominent adult games. Stimulated by the opening of three lighted diamonds in 1936, softball attracted 4,000 Oakland players the following year. The city scheduled four games each night during the summer before an average crowd of 2,500 per game. All of Oakland's neighboring cities had softball leagues, too, bringing the total of teams in Alameda County to nearly 500.

At Los Angeles in June of 1939 softball players made history when the city's softball association, sponsored by the Playground Department and the city, staged its first annual softball "jamboree" in the Colosseum to celebrate having grown from 325 teams to 1,628 in five years. Between 6:00 and 10:00 P.M., sixty softball teams limited to an hour each squeezed in thirty games on six diamonds laid out on the field. The enormous sports spectacle was viewed by 25,000.

In Seattle more than 5,000 youngsters and adults on 325 teams participated in softball leagues of the city's park department during the summer of 1930. There softball ranked above other team games, and by 1939, 420 organized teams were using Seattle's softball fields.

In addition to industries and city recreation agencies, a host of other backers and their proteges attest to the swift spread of the softball contagion in the thirties, among them schools, colleges, churches, suburban communities, stock exchange employees, country clubs, village organizations, labor unions, the military, the Veterans of Foreign Wars, and, of which more below, women. Most companies in Gaston County, North Carolina, between the wars financed numerous softball as well as baseball programs, although softball did not prevent the violent labor-management disputes in the cotton mills of Gastonia, the county seat. In Seattle at least 140 independent teams including longshoremen, women, De Molays, and Boy Scouts utilized the softball fields. Ethnic teams also appeared. The Italo-American National Union operated three softball diamonds in Chicago on which four leagues of 120 teams played. The Czechoslovak Society of America, another ethnic fraternal society, set up softball teams in Chicago and Cleveland for women and men.

Leftist unions ran softball teams in the thirties. According to the *Daily Worker*, union teams sponsored by the New York Trade Union Athletic Association played every weekend throughout the 1937 season, fighting for a championship finally won by the Fur Dyers Union, Local 88. The following year the newspaper claimed that Yankee stars Joe DiMaggio and Lou Gehrig had endorsed the International Workers' Order's tournament that would decide the New York City softball championship, in which teams from Ys, settlements, clubs, and other organizations would compete with about 40 I.W.O. teams. That same year, the *Worker* commented on the difficulty high school girls had in trying to find softball diamonds in the New York area, because the system usually served boys first.

One group received help from an unusual source. When Joe Louis, famed heavyweight boxer, visited Detroit, his home town, in 1935, he was distressed to find many of his boyhood friends jobless. He bought them a bus and uniforms, christened them the Brown Bomber Softball Team, after his sports sobriquet, and gave them money to start touring the country. He promised to help them draw fans by playing with them when he could, and in fact after he became heavyweight champion in 1937 he spent the first few weeks of July touring the Midwest with them.

Softball also progressed in prisons, notably at the Michigan State Prison where, according to the prison newspaper, a softball team of "colored boys" called the Kats, whose pitcher, named White, was their all-around star, played against white teams from the Central Office and the Vocational School. The *Handbook of Juvenile Institutions* for 1938 and 1940, reporting on private, state, and federal institutions for youth, said intramural softball existed side by side with baseball and other sports in several of them. Reformatories for women furnished softball in the thirties for inmates in at least three institutions, those in Delaware, Kansas, and Minnesota.

Such was the ardor for standard baseball that it also produced, in addition to softball, some rather bizarre offspring. In the winter of 1867–1868 some enthusiasts, to use a polite term, played baseball on ice skates. In 1908 an article in a Playground Association publication explained how to use baseball diamonds in winter by playing "Snow Baseball," a combination of baseball, tag, and prisoner's base with snowballs substituting for baseballs. At Greenfield, Massachusetts, in the 1920s residents reportedly played baseball on snowshoes at carnival time, and *Baseball Magazine* printed an illustration showing a player being tagged out while sliding into a snowy base.

The maze of softball rules and diversity of equipment, further exascerbated by the variety of sponsors that accompanied the nationwide spread of the game, made ever more essential the need to inject into it some order and rationality, particularly as the idea for staging national tournaments developed. In addition, the prevalence of gambling and exploitation of players in some areas caused concern. To extricate themselves from the tangle of rules, representatives of prominent organizations and agencies involved with softball met in Chicago in 1932 and formed a joint rules committee charged with standardizing the rules of the game. To prevent domination of the committee by promoters, physical training instructors, or recreation executives, they confined its membership to representatives of six national agencies: the Amateur Softball Association, the National Industrial Recreation Association, the YMCA, the association of the physical training instructors, and the girls' and women's division of the latter—a lineup that in itself bespoke the far-reaching extent of the game and its following. This committee managed to chop through the hampering thicket of regulations and in 1934 finally agreed on a standard body of rules, although minor regional differences remained. In time the Amateur Softball Association emerged as the most powerful overall agency of control and received recognition by the AAU, although a National Softball Association also retained some prominence. Thereafter, tournaments flourished.

Separate rules for women developed, since rarely did women and men play softball against each other except informally. In addition to tournaments, women also enjoyed the game on all levels, ranging from the local municipal playground type and industrial teams all the way to semipro softball. Women physical training leaders reacted sourly to these trends. Bent on maintaining their influence and control, they sought to regulate in detail women's and girls' softball on the playgrounds, in schools, and on the industrial teams and leagues that used city grounds, as well as to prevent commercialism by having trained people—that is, instructors like themselves—in charge.

To these ends Ethel Bowers in *Recreation for Girls and Women* (1934), with the zealotry of a cultist, advocated that girl softball players be classified for play according to age, height, or weight, or a combination thereof, and that only senior high girls or working women should play the game with a bat. Others should use an inflated ball and hit it with their hands. In her opposition to professionalized and commercialized industrial ball Bowers unrealistically laid it down that working women should not play for the benefit of advertisers and spectators, and if they did, trained women in charge should determine the costumes worn and the publicity permitted.

Bowers cited several examples of the proper way, in her opinion, to conduct playground softball. She related, for example, that in Galveston, Texas, when a "play leader" invited groups of girls from public and parochial high schools, the Girl Scouts, the Girls' Reserve, the Camp Fire Girls, and others to form teams and enter a league, women leaders of the groups acted as their coaches, and to avoid commercial exploitation they gave out only simple individual awards of felt letters and a small loving cup.

Meanwhile, the stream of girls' and women's softball continued to flow, not all of it through channels favored by Bowers. Around 1930 in the East, where participants often played twilight ball, said one writer, playground instructors dominated the game, yet the girls rejected the special ball as "sissy" and played with a regular men's ball. In the West, night games prevailed, frequently run by males who were former baseball players. In many cities like Cincinnati, Seattle, and Knoxville, Tennessee, girls and women generally played municipal ball under the overall supervision of the city park department.

Some women players, however, came under the sway of promoters. The Sugar Products Company of St. Louis extracted publicity by conducting a contest and awarding the Dizzy Dean prize, a trip to the 1935 World Series, to the winner, Mildred Clobes. This mild form of exploitation paled compared with the promotion of Slapsie Maxie Rosenbloom's Curvacious Cuties, the Balian Ice Cream Beauties, the Bank of America Bankerettes, and the Columbia Pictures Starlettes, female teams promoted by a California entrepreneur named Marty Fiedler. These teams reputedly played a faster game than the men did. Toward the end of the decade businesses in California, led by Phil Wrigley, owner of the Chicago Cubs, sponsored thousands of women's teams there. Tournaments, too, featured highly skilled teams of young women. In fact in 1935, only a year after the Bowers book appeared, one tournament included 40 men's teams and 16 women's teams from 33 states playing before 160,000 spectators.

On balance, the course of female softball fell considerably short of what Bowers envisaged, so much so that Mabel Lee, another physical training leader, felt impelled in 1937 to retrace the ground covered by Bowers five years before. In *Conduct of Physical Education* Lee again emphasized that trained women physical directors should run women's sports, a point she returned to several times. Declaring that every high school should offer girls the socializing values of team play, she specified that only "modified baseball"

belonged in girls' programs, formulated, of course, by "women authorities."
Lee, like Bowers, wanted girls classified according to nicely-graded formulas.
She produced a table consigning girls to four groups according to the size
of diamond and ball they should use.

Bowers, Lee, and other instructors, with their stifling over-organization
and regimentation, sound like precursors of Little League Baseball, with its
consequent loss of youngsters' freedom to sort themselves out, play ball in
their own way, settle their own quarrels, and learn to socialize naturally,
unhampered by adults, as they once did on the sandlots.

Lee also decried the bad manners, rowdyism, inappropriate costumes,
and emotional strain that pervaded so many games:

> If sporting goods houses and industrial and business firms persist in using this
> game for the exploitation of girls, as they have been doing for the past few
> summers in all parts of the country, the game will fall into disrepute.

Instead, it prospered.

The steady rise and spread of softball that lifted it to the number one
game played by ordinary Americans derived from several advantages in
addition to those previously mentioned. One was the adoption of standard
rules, which conferred the coherence necessary for organizing and conducting intercity, statewide, interregional, and national tournaments. Second, softball helped cast a gleam of light on a dark decade. Many members
of the army of unemployed with much time on their hands and little money
in their pockets found in softball an inexpensive outlet for recreation and a
brief respite from care, so much so that in some quarters softball became
known as America's depression game.

The softball medal also had its obverse side. Male fans scoffed at the
game's "effeminacy," and on their part some women baseball players sneered
at the game as "sissy." Organized Baseball's moguls, at first laudatory of
softball, began to regard it with jaundiced eye as it threatened to outrank
baseball, although they might have found solace had they possessed the wit
and grace to regard it as a worthy child of standard baseball. Phil Wrigley
in effect did this by sponsoring women's teams, perhaps on the theory that
if you can't eliminate them, use them.

In 1935 an inmate of the Michigan State Prison wrote a scathingly sarcastic
poem about softball redolent of an attitude widely subscribed to at the time:

> Muggsy McGraw looked out from his coffin,
> Dead men, you know, don't speak very often,
> "Who started Soft Ball, this country to soften?"
> Muggsy sighed and he yelled,
> He fought and rebelled:
> Why this is a girl's game invented for missies,
> What are we coming to—a nation of sissies?

What kind of game is this that they're playing?
Do I see the third base coacher crocheting?
Gone are the spike shoes, each foot sports a sandal.
They're swinging a bat thin as a candle.
Bad Bill McDuff plays with Bessie and Tillie,
His first name's too tough, so they changed it to Willie.

Oh, it may be the berries,
But when tough guys turn fairies,
Oh Lord. Pull the lid again,
Let me be hid again,
Bury me head again,
Let me be dead again.

Nothing however, not even sarcasm, prevented the steady growth of the game. One scholar estimated that by 1940 there were 300,000 organized softball clubs. In June of that year the Playground Association claimed that seventeen and a quarter million people played softball, and the following year it asserted that more played softball than baseball, basketball, and football *combined*. Even allowing generously for exaggeration, the figures remained impressive.

On the eve of America's entry into World War II softball had not only established itself firmly in the United States but had already gained footholds in several foreign countries—a portend of the future, when the game would spread to more than fifty countries and its rules would be printed in a dozen languages. Baseball's offshoot rivaled the parent game in popularity, although not necessarily in quality.

PART THREE

THE HOUSE OF BASEBALL:
THE BASEMENT

FROM TRADITIONAL PATHS TO BASE PATHS

Of the two races that fared worst in the United States, the blacks and the Indians, the Indians came off better as far as baseball was concerned. Unlike the blacks who, except for a short space, were barred from the House of Baseball until after World War II, the Indians at least had access to its basement, from which they could aspire to its upper story. For Organized Baseball accepted Indians and rejected blacks. Prejudice toward blacks was racial, but toward Indians it was mainly cultural.

The main conduit for baseball among Indians became the federal government's Indian schools. As part of its campaign to obliterate Indian culture, the government eventually established boarding schools at which the directors pressed baseball upon the pupils, thus inadvertently aiding some of them to get a chance in Organized Baseball.

Before whites tendered this baseball experience to them, however, the Indians suffered as much if not greater oppression than did the blacks. Whereas the whites wanted little but toil from the Negroes, from the Indians they wanted their vast, rich domain. And from the beginning the white invaders commonly regarded Indians as heathen savages, a view that made it easy for them to stamp out Indian culture entirely and substitute mainstream ways of life, including the playing of baseball.

Although some early settlers behaved decently toward the natives, the two dissimilar societies soon clashed. As white settlements became more firmly established and steadily reinforced by land-greedy newcomers, Indians fought fiercely for their way of life. General Philip Sheridan described the situation succinctly: "We took away their country and their means of support, broke up their mode of living, their habits of life, introduced disease and decay among them, and it was for this and against this that they made war. Could anyone expect less?" Their prime weakness, their failure to unite, did them in. As Indian resistance slackened and finally broke at Wounded Knee, the victors began to assimilate survivors through cultural imperialism. Their chief instrument became the school.

After 1870, when the federal government assumed prime responsibility for Indian education, the government boarding school operated as the chief agency for eradicating Indian culture and instilling American ways. By 1900 the government operated 113 boarding schools, 88 on reservations and 25 off them. The growing influence of the boarding school coincided with the early flowering of baseball as the national game. Participation in it, or at least appreciation of it, had become the badge of an American, so it is unsurprising that school administrators used baseball as one of the tools to accomplish their goal of deracination.

Most boarding schools assumed more the aspect of reformatories than they did schools. Residents had often been removed from their families by force and taken as far away as possible for three years without leave, the better to cut their ties with Indian life and to discourage running away. They also served as hostages to ensure the peaceful behavior of Indian adults. Their curriculum was primarily vocational, that is, industrial training and farming for males, and home economics for females, designed to channel them into low-level jobs and to train them to handle the work in their own schools, such as laundering and furnace tending.

On arrival at such schools students received white men's haircuts and restrictive clothing. Instead of having their Indian names translated into English, they were given American names, so that Standing Bears, Spotted Eagles, and Yellow Birds became Luthers, Johns, and Maggies. Teachers forbade them to speak Indian languages. They mixed children of different tribes in the dormitories to prevent their speaking anything but English to each other. Rarely did a teacher learn an Indian language, so instruction depended on sign language. The government did not relax policies on haircuts or languages until 1929. Schools suppressed Indian religion and punished lapses harshly. Children sickened from poor and unaccustomed diet, lack of fresh air, tuberculosis, apathy, and homesickness. Some fled and "returned to the blanket," as it was called. Yet others of these woebegone youths survived and even succeeded in the white world as teachers, preachers, physicians, writers, government employees, politicians, and, as we shall see, professional ball players.

The first major government boarding school, and the best-known, was Carlisle, founded in 1879 almost accidentally as a spinoff from an Indian school connected with Hampton Institute, an industrial school in Virginia established for blacks by a Civil War veteran, Samuel C. Armstrong. Another veteran, Captain Richard H. Pratt, recalling the intelligence of the Cherokee scouts he used in the Army, noticed the quick response to good treatment shown by Indian prisoners he supervised at a Florida fort. Armstrong permitted Pratt to settle some Indians at Hampton, but in 1879 he left Hampton to open Carlisle in Pennsylvania at a stockaded Army barracks. By the end of Carlisle's first year it housed nearly 200 students from fifteen tribes, most of them teenagers. Eventually the school served a thousand students, and the usual three-year residence period was extended to five. The federal government appropriated $67,500.00 for Carlisle in 1881 plus an additional $150,000.00 for other government Indian schools.

Pratt, energetic, persistent, single-minded, and a strict and consistent disciplinarian, believed that the Indians' future lay in assimilation and that vocational education offered the best path to it. As the Indian publication *Wassaja* put it much later, Pratt's idea was to "kill the Indian and save the man." At Carlisle he set great store by his widely-copied outing system, which provided students with experience living and working during summer vacations with families in white communities, and provided those families with cheap, docile workers.

Carlisle stressed sports. Early on, football and baseball became what Pratt called a "great motivation force" in school life. Pratt encouraged students to form class or shop teams, and the best players from those teams played on a varsity. The opportunity to get away from school for games in town, especially at nearby Dickinson College, stimulated effort among all students, and distant games provided an added incentive for the varsity.

Carlisle soon produced some exceptional baseball and football players, since young Indians, "seeing their chances for physical development," as Pratt put it, "proved quite as ambitious to seize their opportunities as our own youth." At first Pratt had some trepidation about introducing football. His reason reveals not only attitudes toward Indians but also an understanding of the relative violence of football as compared with baseball. When asked by Dr. Charles A. Eastman, a prominent Indian, why he did not introduce football, Pratt replied, "Why, if I did that, half the press of the country would attack me for developing the original war instincts and savagery of the Indian! The public would be afraid to come to games." Eastman retorted that this was exactly why he wanted Pratt to introduce the game: It would prove that the Indian was a gentleman and a sport, would do nothing unfair or underhanded, would play the game according to the rules, and would not even swear—at least, not in public. As things turned out, according to Eastman, the Indians always played a clean game and lost few matches.

Because many Carlisle students were of college age, its football and baseball teams gradually entered into competition with college teams and eventually gained national athletic fame. In 1897 Pratt reported to the Commissioner of Indian Affairs that "of late" the Indians had shown "decided capacity" at sports, its ball teams holding their own with leading universities. He believed that "helpful association" with students of other institutions was invaluable for the Indians. Carlisle encouraged sports, he declared, because the Indians' experience on the athletic field aided them greatly in coping with "the broader and keener contentions of life they are to engage in later."

The following year Glenn "Pop" Warner came to Carlisle, on the recommendation of Walter Camp, as athletic director and coach of baseball, football, track, and boxing. Warner, like Camp, believed firmly in the character-building qualities of athletics.

Although Carlisle became better-known for football, Pratt wrote that baseball also showed "high results" in games with the best of the nearby educational and YMCA teams, and a number of Carlisle baseball players went into professional baseball, foremost among them Charles Albert "Chief" Bender, of whom more below.

An awards ceremony held in the school auditorium in February 1910 underlined the importance of sports at Carlisle. The school band played, and forty-five athletes received letters. The school paper, *The Red Man*, reported talks given by speakers at the ceremony praising the benefits of sports and explaining the attitude students should take toward them. The school superintendent, for example, called athletic training "a great educating and developing factor" and "good backing for any mental or industrial training." The head of Mercersburg Academy, Dr. William M. Irvine, expanded further on the list of alleged benefits: "Boys, the physical basis of our country depends upon athletics," which teach "the abilities of mind and spirit" and "how to work." They help to reach "boys that are lazy," and they instruct athletes in "self-control, purity, democracy, and obedience." Glen Warner took the opportunity to disabuse the boys of any misconceptions they might have, telling them that in playing for the school they should not feel they were doing the school and the athletic department a great service. They should instead realize that they were being favored by being allowed to participate and obtain the same advantages other boys enjoyed in other schools and colleges.

Very likely, the admonitory tone of these speeches reflected in part the summer baseball problem that, as we have seen, troubled so many colleges at the time. At any rate, that same year the superintendent terminated varsity baseball. The reason for this "advanced stand" in athletic policy, *The Red Man* explained, was that lengthy summer schedules with other colleges and prominent outside teams directed undue attention to some Carlisle players and subjected them to overtures by "the larger league clubs" to play professional baseball during the summer. One player thus tempted was Jim Thorpe, whose celebrated case is discussed below. The school paper went on to announce that Carlisle was belatedly substituting lacrosse, an Indian game, that year in order to overcome "the professional tendency which attends an extensive playing schedule." Students would continue to play intramural baseball, but the school arranged no schedule with outside teams. It is ironic that by discouraging the development of professional-level players Carlisle was defeating its own purpose by penalizing the Indians for moving toward assimilation.

Possibly inspired by the apparent success of Carlisle, Meville Wilkinson, another Army man, established a boarding school for Indians, Chemawa Indian School, in Oregon in 1880. To fill his school, Wilkinson scoured the Pacific Northwest for Indian children. The average Chemawa student was a teenager, but residents ranged from as young as one year to above forty.

As with Carlisle students, they received English names and never heard their native tongues spoken. A five-year curriculum was established. In the 1880s Chemawa earned a very poor reputation among the Spokane Indians. Mortality at the school was high: of nineteen transported there during a three-year period, eleven died. In fact, so many Indian children died at Chemawa in its early years that the Spokanes had a saying, "To go to Chemawa is to die."

Student life at Chemawa soon became invigorated by a substantial program of extraclass activities. The 1902 report of Chemawa's superintendent, T.W. Potter, to the Commissioner of Indian Affairs setting forth his view of education and describing the program at Chemawa reflected the progressive outlook of the times: "A school without entertainment and amusement," he wrote, "would soon be looked upon as a prison and fail in accomplishing the desired results." Consequently, Potter said, he had endeavored to supplement work and study with a "sufficient amount of healthy and innocent amusement" to keep pupils "contented, happy and in proper spirits." Among the chief means of reaching his goal, Potter listed seven, with baseball first.

As early as the 1890s Chemawa's record in baseball lent credence to Potter's remarks. The school's athletic records show that in 1896 its team defeated the Monograms, considered one of the best independent teams in the Northwest, 22–12, at Gladstone Park, Oregon City. The following year the Chemawa club won over the Orions, a team of soldiers, at Vancouver, and in 1899 beat McMinnville College on its home grounds.

One of Chemawa's outstanding players was Reuben Sanders, who entered in 1894 and graduated in 1900. Sanders is also a member of the Indian Hall of Fame. Judging by a story told about him, Sanders quickly learned white ways. After Chemawa lost badly to Mount Angel College, which had a reputedly unhittable pitcher, the Indians invited the Angels to a return game at Chemawa and, with Sanders' help, contrived a way to beat them. Their pitcher never found out why he did not do so well his second time against Chemawa: Sanders had moved the pitcher's slab back just enough to throw him off his stride.

A member of the Chemawa class of 1900, Charles Larsen, enrolled in 1893 at age ten and later worked at the school. Larsen served at least a year as manager of the baseball team and prepared a manuscript about the history of the school's sports that provides much information about Chemawa baseball.

By the turn of the century baseball at Chemawa had come into full bloom. The varsity marked its 1900 season by defeating all teams in the valley to win a large silver cup presented by the Willamette Valley Baseball Association. Chemawa's ball club put on another noteworthy performance in 1902 when it emerged from five games—two each against Willamette University and Oregon State and one with Portland Academy—with three victories, one over each opponent.

The high point of enjoyment for Chemawa students was the invitation proffered them each year, beginning 1897, to attend the two-week Willamette Valley Chautauqua at Gladstone Park. At this July gathering the Indians camped out with several thousand other students. Chemawa's band furnished the music. In six baseball tournaments at the Chautauqua, Chemawa's team proved its mettle by earning three silver cups. Perhaps more important, as Superintendent Potter indicated, Indian attendance at these affairs "helped combat race prejudice."

The recognized abilities of two Chemawa players offer another clue to the caliber of its baseball. A pitcher, Sam Morris, earned $200.00 a month during the summer of 1903 pitching for the Portland Browns. He and another Chemawa player, Joseph Teabo, reportedly traveled to St. Louis to play in the interscholastic baseball games staged there in connection with the combined St. Louis Exhibition and 1904 Olympics, the first that exhibited baseball. Eligibility rules set up by James E. Sullivan and Luther Gulick of the PSAL apparently did not prevent Morris from participating or else were ignored.

Chemawa suffered no dearth of ball players. At times the school fielded a second team, the junior varsity, and in some seasons even three nines. The Chemawa varsity could also draw from a sturdy underpinning of intramural teams that, apart from enhancing student life and lifting morale, served as feeders for the varsity. In 1902 a game between two such teams, the Literaries and the Industrials, the men of brain, as Larsen put it, lost to those of muscle and had to treat the victors to strawberries and cream. Two years later the Hole-in-the-Wall team defeated the All-Stars, and in 1905 teams from A and B companies of Chemawa's cadet battalions met to decide the intramural championship. In 1908 the school operated a four-club intramural league with teams named White Sox, Portland, Boston, and Ohio.

One year a Chemawa club traveled to a place named Slick Rock to play a team called the North Stars. The ball field had just been prepared the morning of the game, and the spot chosen was level but rough. Six-foot ferns had to be cut down and the stumps left standing. There was no backstop. Before the game Chemawa's pitcher, Graham, caught two live rabbits on the field. Then as he prepared to deliver a pitch to the batter, the third baseman and shortstop began a race with a third rabbit frightened out of the ferns by the spectators. Graham threw the ball at it and, said Larsen, would have hit it if its tail had been longer! Chemawa won the game, but the whole episode, from improvised field to comic relief, shows that manicured diamonds, stands, and fences, however desirable, were unessential in those vanished days. Playing baseball was all that mattered.

Another Chemawa trip ended unpleasantly. The thirty-five man squad and the school band made a 300-mile journey by steamer to California to attend the Humboldt County Fair at Eureka and play several ball games. On the return trip everybody became seasick.

Vocational students in Chemawa's tailor shop did their bit for the ball team in 1911 by producing "up-to-date" uniforms—gray with white trim and the letter *C*, surrounded by a diamond, on the left sleeve—cut on a pattern made from a Spalding suit. The school used money that otherwise would have been spent for made-to-order uniforms to purchase more bats, balls, shoes, and other baseball gear. That year Chemawa fielded two teams to play fifteen games against local schools, colleges, the Oregon State Penitentiary, the Idaho Indians, and the Grand Ronde Indians. To its growing collection Chemawa added another trophy, this one presented by Chapter 36 of the United Artisans of Rickreall, a nearby town, after Chemawa prevailed in baseball at the Artisans' annual picnic.

Before the 1914 season even started, Chemawa held an athletic banquet. Coaches, players, and a Salem high school teacher gave speeches on such topics as "Early Training for the Team." Amidst a display of banners, pennants, and trophies, the company enjoyed a chicken dinner with all the trimmings.

Team photographs in *Woki-Ksuya-Pi*, the Chemawa school annual, demonstrated that baseball continued during the 1920s, and in 1928 a 24-man squad coached by R.G. Downie went undefeated, playing some of the school's old area opponents. Even in the precarious thirties the Chemawa baseball tradition remained alive, as shown by the school annuals for that era. In fact, a 30-man team played during the 1930 season. The following year the school added another trophy to its collection, this one from the sporting goods firm, the Rawlings Manufacturing Company, for winning the championship of Marion County. Chemawa's annual reported in 1939 that "The Indians took the scalps of Dallas, Oregon City, and other outstanding teams."

The government opened another Indian boarding school in 1884 in Haskell, Nebraska, and in 1890 its name became Haskell Institute. Haskell began with an agricultural and manual labor curriculum for grades one through five. It started with fourteen students but by January 1885 had 280. Baseball figured early on in Haskell's program, and in 1899 a contemporary writer reported that "the Indian students are enthusiasts on the subject of base ball. They have a well-trained nine which has won more games than any other nine in Kansas. In this they take much pride." A year later the school laid out an athletic playground, Haskell Field.

The exploits of Haskell football received much national publicity in the early 1900s, but in piecing together fragmentary evidence, it becomes clear that baseball also counted at Haskell. In 1903 the baseball department of Fort Reilly's athletic association reported that the many requests for playing dates included one from the Haskell Indians. *The Indian Leader*, a Haskell school publication, announced in April 1905 that the varsity now had new canvas baseball suits. The same publication printed a Haskell sports song sung to the tune of "Marching Through Georgia." A passage from the chorus goes like this:

> All the palefaces seem afraid
> they'll lose their hair
> While we go plunging to vict'ry.

—a phrase as redolent of sportsmanship as the one in Brooklyn's Erasmus Hall High School's so-called pep song in the 1920s: "We're out for gore, we're out for gore!"

Haskell athletes showed their ability on other sports occasions. When a stadium, reputedly the first lighted one in the Midwest, opened at Haskell in 1926, Jim Thorpe, who had spent two years at Haskell beginning at age eleven, and John Levi (Charging Buffalo), another outstanding Haskell athlete, returned to give a football exhibition. Levi had a baseball tryout with the New York Yankees at their training camp in 1925 and later became football coach at Haskell. When in 1928 Haskell's unit of the National Guard put on an athletic competition as part of an exhibition at Lawrence, Kansas, *The Southern Workman*, Hampton Institute's house organ, said that the twenty-nine different tribes of full-blooded Indians represented in it "clearly displayed" their "traditional prowess."

Baseball became a staple in a good many Indian schools. To the students it offered a measure of relief from the dull round of daily routine and injected a bit of cheer into their cramped, dreary lives. To school administrators it possessed many virtues, not the least of them inexpensiveness and, like the popular band instruments, the capacity to be taught by imitation.

A catalogue of schools that enlisted baseball would include a number of such relatively well-known establishments as Chilocco in Oklahoma, founded in 1884, whose uniformed baseball teams played match games with teams not only in neighboring Kansas, Oklahoma, and Indian Territory but sometimes those at a distance. Chilocco also participated at the St. Louis World's Fair in an exhibit demonstrating how such schools "reclaim the Indian boys and girls from the semi-barbarous state," as the *World's Fair Bulletin* put it.

Kickapoo boys played baseball, too. In his 1897 report to the Bureau of Indian Affairs Superintendent Wilson of the Kickapoo School, Netawaka, Kansas, boasted that the "successful career of the Kickapoo nine in defeating all the crack clubs of this section of Kansas speaks well for their industry and sobriety."

In California an Indian boarding school named Sherman Institute possessed a campus that a visitor, Gertrude Golden, called "beautiful beyond description"; a baseball diamond was part of it. The same year of her visit, 1905, *Sporting Life* reported on a Sherman game that the reporter believed was the first instance of two different non-white races playing baseball. In that game, in Fiesta Park, Los Angeles, Sherman played Tokyo's Waseda University team, and

> the Orientals . . . had it over the Aborigines during all stages of the game, with the exception of the sixth inning, when the Sherman braves with a whoop broke from the reservation and went tearing madly about until six of them had scored. . . .

The final score was Waseda 12, Sherman Institute 7.

Students, mostly Sioux, at the Indian school at Rapid City, South Dakota, took part in sports, too. The school's prospectus for 1910, a sort of catalogue displaying the benefits of attending, said the Rapid City school was fortunate in having an athletic field unequalled in that part of the state and that baseball, football, and basketball frequently took place there. Gertrude Golden, a faculty member there for a couple of years, in her book *Red Moon* described the older boys at Rapid City as "independent and remote," asserting that the only activity that could "win them body and soul" was athletics. They excelled in basketball and football and took great satisfaction in beating the white students of Houghton Mining College and other schools, but for some reason they were less attracted to baseball.

When the Indians of the Fort McDowell Reservation, about 40 miles from Phoenix, Arizona, planned a Fourth of July celebration at Flagstaff, they invited some other tribes, the program to feature baseball and other sports, according to the newspaper of an Indian school in Phoenix, *Native American*. Afterwards the paper reported that it had been a great day. McDowell played a practice baseball game in the forenoon, and in the final event of the day McDowell defeated another Indian team 11–3. Participants in the celebration included the band and baseball team of the Indian school at Phoenix, where the boys took a lively interest in baseball—as do all normal boys, reported the *Native American*—and the school nine took part in contests with other area clubs. In 1910 the "dusky sons of the desert," as the paper called the Phoenix school team, "wiped up" the cavalry team of Fort Wingate 4–0 —a victory that must have given them particular pleasure.

Indian school superintendents often mentioned their institutions' baseball teams in their reports to Washington. L.M. Compton, superintendent of the school at Tomah, Wisconsin, reported to the Commissioner of Indian Affairs in 1902 that "the usual baseball and football games have been kept up," and the superintendent of a similar school in Chamberlain, South Dakota, in his 1907 report, declared, "I encourage all sensible, healthful sports. As a result we had the best baseball team in this locality last year, if not the best amateur team in the state."

Mission schools contributed to the cultural assault on the Indians. They were the oldest educational institutions for Indians, and in the 1880s the federal government aided them financially. Not until 1917 did federal funding of religious schools for Indians end. Mission schools closely resembled government schools except that they emphasized religion and conducted less broadly-gauged sports programs. Nevertheless, baseball was not entirely absent from such institutions. Missionaries at St. John's, an Oklahoma boarding school of several hundred students in Pima County, maintained a large playground for athletic contests, including baseball and football. *The Sentinel*, published annually by the Bureau of Catholic Missions, commented in 1910 that Osage boys at St. John's school were not only experts with bow and arrow but also "good ball players."

Another mission boarding school that encouraged baseball among Indians was a school within a school. Hampton Institute, the Virginia industrial school for freed slaves, continued to accept Indians even after Captain Pratt left with his band to start Carlisle, and it did so until 1912. The federal government paid the school $150.00 for each Indian enrolled. Although tuberculosis kept their death rate high, at least in the early years, by the 1890s Hampton housed about ninety Indians from a number of different tribes, as well as some 400 blacks, according to *Southern Workman*, the school's publication.

Hampton's head, General Armstrong, saw Indians as "grown up children," claiming that whites were a "thousand years ahead of them." At Hampton he instituted a policy of segregation, separating the Indians from the blacks— themselves, ironically, the most discriminated-against in the society at large. According to Elaine Goodale, later the wife of the Indian physician Charles Eastman, Armstrong justified his separation policy on the ground that the Indians spoke no English, used no chairs or stairs, wore unconventional clothing, behaved differently, and practiced different customs. As a result of his policy Indians found themselves separated not only in dormitories, classrooms, and dining rooms but also in baseball teams. Not until later years, as better-prepared Indians entered Hampton, did bonds of segregation generally loosen.

Baseball proved popular among the Indians at Hampton. Those who did not return to their reservations during summer often played ball instead. Hampton fielded two Indian teams in 1892, the First Nine and the Pony Nine. The former once played a white team, the Roselands, on the grounds of the nearby National Soldiers Home. The Roselands, according to the *Southern Workman*, had secured the strongest battery in the county, and the game was a "hot one." Although the umpiring "was decidedly in favor of the white boys," said the *Workman*, the Indians won 13–0. A month later a picked team of Hampton Indians played two seven-inning games against a group of officers who were on campus to give military training to these descendants of their former enemies. The officers won both by close scores, but in one game the Indian battery, pitcher Longtail and catcher A. Metoxen, both "made splendid home runs."

The following year, 1893, the Hampton Indian boys, feeling the need for new baseball uniforms, decided to earn the money for them instead of taking up a collection among teachers. By selling homemade Easter cards and some other objects they realized $22.00 for their new suits.

During the nineties at Hampton, reported the *Workman*, the Indians carried on baseball "vigorously," and in 1899 from the 135 Indians then in the student body, two teams were formed: the Western, mostly Sioux, and the Iroquois Star, mainly from tribes of the Six Nations. These teams played each other every Monday afternoon. The Indian girls attended and cheered the good plays. Hampton made no effort, according to the *Workman* in 1906, to develop athletic championships among the Indians, because "The champion athlete's reputation would serve a young man little in his efforts to teach the older Indians the new life."

Various government reports of life at Indian institutions made some severe criticisms of them, but the most devastating was the Meriam Report, prepared by a staff headed by Professor Lewis Meriam of the University of Chicago and issued in 1928. Among other things, it revealed the poor diet, overcrowded dormitories, support by the labor of very young children, poorly-prepared teachers, regimentation, and serious health hazards that prevailed at such schools. It pointed out that the outing system, originally of sound purpose, had degenerated into a method of obtaining cheap contract labor. The Meriam Report also criticized the schools' recreation. Government boarding schools, it said, usually included athletic teams in their programs, but instead of providing play space and time for all pupils, most schools, particularly the larger ones, stressed "first-team," specialist athletics. Only "star" athletes or those "approaching stardom" had a chance to participate, thus leaving the student majority mere spectators, passively watching the select few.

The report cited Haskell Institute as a prime example of a school that harbored "athletes of the most dubious kind." While the Haskell administration had "cleaned up the worst part of the situation," it had apparently continued to feel the need for "recruiting" for its teams. The Report also questioned the presence of Haskell's elaborate stadium, especially in view of the distressing need for other educational features. It was a pity, added the report, that at a time when colleges and schools everywhere were cleaning up athletics, the national government should openly countenance outdated practices. Haskell and other Indian schools should eliminate abuses and adopt standards of eligibility used by nonIndian schools.

The Meriam staff also examined recreation on the reservations, where the government had pursued a repressive policy because of some undesirable side effects, such as gambling and neglect of animals and crops, that accompanied traditional forms of recreation. The Report pointed out that Indians clung to traditional celebrations, which usually included a ball game, and instead of trying to stamp out such practices, the government should use existing recreational activities as a starting point, supplementing them with those borrowed from whites. The Report urged avoidance of the kind of athletics leading to commercialization, but hedged by adding that athletic games should be "cultivated" for the excellent "character effects" to be derived from them.

The Meriam Report's suggestion that Indian games be revived was not entirely new. When anthropologist Clark Wissler toured boarding schools at the turn of the century he noticed that children often lacked spirit even at play. On inquiry he learned that they would not play games unless forced to. When Wissler asked if Indian games had been tried he was met with a "blank look" and told that government rules specified the games to be used with the children.

The superintendent he was talking to must have been referring to the publications of the Bureau of Indian Affairs, several of which encouraged outdoor play, including the standard team games of whites. They made no mention of Indian games. The Office of Indian Affairs even published some books, like one that came out in 1911, explaining the educational value of play and games as quickeners of perception, strengtheners of motor power, and a way to bring Indian children "from their conservative hiding places to master the essentials of our civilization." A 1915 publication described games suitable for Indian students, including baseball and town ball, recommending that institutions provide baseball diamonds. And a 1919 book by the assistant supervisor of Indian schools gave a paean to athletics as a force developing such characteristics as loyalty, alertness, judgement, justice, and fair play.

As well-known as Indian games were, none of these government directives suggested using them. After all, Indian women had been observed playing a form of soccer as early as 1613. George Catlin, who studied Indians in the 1830s, painted Choctaws in a rough game of lacrosse, and a Frederick Behman painting shows Indian women playing shinny, an ancestor of hockey. Ball play seems to be associated with Indian legends and religion, as publications noted as early as 1887. Indian children of the nineteenth century played one game that involved tossing around leather balls stuffed with animal hair.

The classic study of Indian games is Stewart Culin's *Games of the North American Indian* (1902), in which Culin presented a long list of Indian ball games, including shinny, double ball, ball race, football, hand-and-foot ball, tossed ball, and hot ball. In most such games the ball never touched the hand, since that was against the rules. Games of racket, shinny, and double ball, he said, were widespread. Most of the balls used in these games were covered with buckskin and stuffed with deer hair.

The Creek Indians, as described by Angie Debo in *The Road to Disappearance*, had their own ball games and by the 1800s a code that regulated them. One rule provided that an unintentional killing in a game was not murder. Under another, a Creek town using ineligible players in a ball game stood liable to a fifty-dollar fine. The Dakota and Zuñi people had tip cat, a game similar to that played for generations by white boys in city streets.

Ball games were important in Indian life. Indians esteemed successful athletes. Usually grave and thoughtful in serious matters, in sports they were ebullient and sometimes rough. As many as 300 young men in two teams might take part in a wild game of shinny. Equally violent was lacrosse, which included pushing, pulling, butting, and biting. Bloodshed and broken bones were common, and betting was reckless. Prizes, in the case of the Arapaho, could include valuable beaded robes. Spectators made heavy private bets, too. Some tribes even staked their hunting grounds. Beyond all else, as the head of the Smithsonian Institute explained in a report to the government, the Indian games were an integral part of their culture, connected intimately with religious beliefs and practices.

Such games were not impervious to the influence of baseball, and the Indians' experience with them probably contributed to their receptivity to baseball. While the Navajos were imprisoned at Bosque Redondo (Round Grove) in New Mexico, according to Culin, they saw whites playing baseball and, despite tribal traditions, incorporated some of its elements into their own ball games.

In addition to government and mission schools, other organizations that used baseball touched the lives of Indians. The YMCA began work among them in the 1880s, and by 1886 ten Y branches with more than 150 Indian members operated under the supervision of the Sioux physician Charles Eastman. The Y did not, however, bring with it enough baseball to suit some Indians. An Indian publication, *The Word Carrier*, before the turn of the century urged the Y to organize more sport, saying Indians needed something to brighten their lives. "It is a great pity," the paper went on, "that the YMCA among the Indians runs so strictly to piety and long prayer meetings and so little to baseball, football, and track athletics."

The Department of Agriculture's farm clubs for children sponsored baseball, too. These clubs were similar to the 4-H clubs, aiming to train boys for country life, develop cooperation, dignify farming, and spread scientific farming practices. The children formed what were designated as Pig Clubs, Sugar Beet Clubs, Potato Clubs, and so forth. Two Pig Clubs from different parts of Nebraska played each other at baseball before a large crowd in 1925, reported a publication called *Indian Boys' and Girls' Club News*.

Opportunities to play on town teams opened to Indians early on. In Oregon a player named Soosap (Suisap), son of a Klickitat father and a Clackamas mother, was considered one of the best in the Northwest. He also belonged to a Clackamas County team that won the state baseball championship in 1879.

In Texas in 1914 a town with a rich baseball tradition, Eagle Lake, hired an Oklahoma Indian spitball pitcher, Roy Chouteau. The season began well, and the "chief," as most Indian players used to be called, attracted big crowds, especially when a gambler-controlled team from Moulton came into town for a three-game series. The visitors took two games and the chief as well, having offered him more money to play for Moulton. Unhappy at his new town, Chouteau then declared his intention to rejoin the Eagle Lake team when it came to Moulton for a series. The enraged Moulton manager, Robbins, got Chouteau into a bar argument and shot him dead. Although Robbins was arrested and indicted, the case never came to trial. As Mary Lou and Austin LeCompte wrote about this omission, "Apparently no one demanded justice for a 'Drunk Indian.'"

When the great depression of the thirties struck and the chronic poverty of the Indians worsened, the New Deal included them in its reform and relief measures, especially through the Indian Allottment Act, which halted the abuses by which Indians lost their land. The New Deal also provided direct aid to Indian youth through the Civilian Conservation Corps. Some 85,000 Indians of many ages entered separate CCC camps established for Indians between 1933 and 1942, their work administered and supervised by the Office of Indian Affairs. Professor Donald Parman in his study of Indians in the CCC showed that camp leaders used a full program of sports as their best weapon against misbehavior. Every camp of any duration, said Parman, sponsored baseball and basketball teams, and the Indians played schedules against other CCC teams, including those from white camps, as well as local teams. Frequent news of these contests in a publication called *Indians at Work* provides additional evidence of interest in sports.

Indians also formed their own baseball teams. All-Indian and mostly-Indian semipro teams, like the Wild West shows of Buffalo Bill Cody, capitalized on the stereotype of the Indian as a picturesque, colorful curiosity. One traveling baseball "circus," as it was sometimes called, toured the West during 1897 through 1908. Its white owner-manager, Guy Green, published two books about his team, and one of them, *Fun and Frolic with an Indian Ball Team*, portrays what Green thought was their ridiculous and humorous side.

The team Green poked fun at is probably the Nebraska Indians. One fan who watched them play in Bemidji, Minnesota, in 1904, where he played center field for the local team, reported that the Indians traveled in a private railway car that sidetracked in towns where they stopped to play. They enclosed the Bemidji field with a canvas fence supported by tall poles on which they hung lights, powered by the local electric system, for a night game. They also won the game by a large score.

A team of Chippewas from Northern Wisconsin toured Iowa in 1908, lighting their field for night play with old-fashioned gas torches hung on iron rods.

In the twenties the Passamaquoddy tribe fielded a baseball team on its reservation near Eastport, Maine, that often played nearby town teams and had its own fine diamond. Visiting white teams could not understand the tribal team's verbal signals. A large delegation of fans from their village always showed up to cheer them on. Nevertheless, they took the further precaution of using a native umpire and scorer!

Some Indian, or part-Indian, players became full-fledged professionals, many reaching the major leagues of Organized Baseball. At least 29 appeared on major-league teams of the era before World War II. Of these, 16 may be considered solid big-league players, three of them stars: Albert Bender, Zack Wheat, and Bobby Doerr. An additional 13 played briefly in the majors, and others had tryouts. *Baseball Magazine* asserted in 1916 that many smaller leagues had Indian players as well.

Despite the prevalence of Indians in Organized Baseball, Indian stereotyping did not disappear. As late as 1921 when David Puckee, an Indian, applied for a job as an umpire, the Boston *Globe* printed this reply from W.G. Bramham, president of the Piedmont League:

> Big Indian got job. Come one, bring tomahawk, big and sharpee. Lots fight— Heap war dances by Sept. 12. Heap scalps in belt if poor Indian not in happy hunting grounds. Won't need tepee. Umpire no sleep. Bring medicine doctor instead. If married, bring squaw, make good living selling paint.

Probably the first Indian in the majors was outfielder Louis Sockalexis, a Penobscot from Maine with uncommon natural ability, and his feats reputedly inspired Gilbert Patten, another Maine man, to create Frank Merriwell. The Cleveland Spiders, who signed him in 1897, reputedly renamed themselves Indians in his honor.

Two Indians made the Baseball Hall of Fame, Charles Bender and Zachary Wheat. Bender, son of a Chippewa mother and a German-American father, was sent east at age eight to a mission boarding school in Philadelphia where the superintendent permitted baseball in an organized way only on holidays, as part of the outing system. Bender did not see his home again until age thirteen, when, distressed by the deterioration of life on the reservation, he ran away to Carlisle. He played fifteen seasons in the majors and pitched in five World Series.

Zack Wheat played for eighteen of his nineteen big-league years in Brooklyn, where he was the most popular Brooklyn player ever. Bobby Doerr may well belong in the Hall of Fame with Bender and Wheat. Most of his career extended beyond the era covered in this book, but he was one of the finest second basemen in the game. Among other established major leaguers, were two catchers, "Nig" Clarke and John Meyers. Clarke, a Wyandotte, caught for nine seasons. Meyers was a Cahuilla Mission Indian from California who learned of special provisions for Indians at Dartmouth while he was playing at a semipro ball tournament in Albuquerque. Dartmouth accepted him, but he could not play ball there because of having been a semipro, and he left after his freshman year.

Meyers and Bender expressed different views regarding prejudice toward Indians in Organized Baseball. While Bender was pitching for the Athletics a newspaper quoted him as saying he had found no traces of prejudice toward him, although a couple of years later he hinted otherwise on a Carlisle questionnaire. Meyers is recorded by Professor Stephen Thompson as saying after his career that in baseball he was treated like a foreigner, and an inferior foreigner at that.

Three Indian pitchers had substantial careers: Thornton Lee, Johnny Whitehead, and Elon Hogsett, a Cherokee. Three Indian infielders became fixtures on big-league clubs: Arvel Odell Hale, Johnny Hodapp, and Rudy York. Among good Indian outfielders one must list the Johnson brothers, Bob and Roy, along with Ben Johnson. The Johnsons' mother was a Cherokee. John "Pepper" Martin, outfielder and third baseman, was one of the most colorful players of the decade.

Other Indians had brief careers in the majors. Of these, nine were pitchers: Jim Bluejacket, a Cherokee-Shawnee; Louis Bruce, Iroquois or Mohawk; Lee Daney, Haskell graduate; George Johnson, a Winnebago; Louis LeRoy, Algonquin and Iroquois or Seneca, from Carlisle; Billy Phyle, a Minnesota Sioux; Moses Yellowhorse, a Pawnee; and Euel Moore and Ben Tincup, Cherokees. Deserving mention are the catcher Mack Wheat, Zack's brother; shortstop Michael Balenti, a Cheyenne, and outfielder Frank Jude, identified variously as Iroquois, Algonquin, or Chippewa.

Perhaps the best-known Indian was Jim Thorpe (Wa-Tho-Huck, or Bright Path), who may have been the most versatile and gifted of all American athletes. Born in Oklahoma, part Potawatamie, part Sac and Fox, Thorpe, after attending the local day school, spent two years at Haskell. In 1904 he enrolled at Carlisle, where he starred at football. At the 1912 Olympics he became the first ever to win the pentathlon and decathlon in the same year. The following year a newspaperman revealed that while a Carlisle student, Thorpe had played summer baseball for money in 1909 and 1910 in North Carolina and thus was not a "pure amateur." The American Athletic Union revoked his amateur status and deprived him of all his medals and trophies, seeing to it that his runners-up received them. The Olympic Committee eliminated his name from the records on the ground that accepting money for playing ball those summers made him a professional athlete and so ineligible for Olympic competition.

Thorpe readily admitted that he had received money for his summer ball play. The amount paid him has been estimated at about $25.00 or $30.00 a week. In those days, as has been shown, college athletes usually played summer ball for pay, protecting their amateur status with assumed names, but Thorpe had not thought to use another name. He said later that he had not considered his summer ball job as making him a pro, that it was "just another job that provided a means to exist." In recent years evidence has been found that Thorpe's summer ball playing may merely have been an assignment as part of Carlisle's regular outing system, a job arranged by Coach Glen Warner. But when the Indian's Olympic awards were withdrawn, Warner failed to defend and support him.

Thorpe played outfield for six years with three major-league teams. He had trouble hitting the curve ball, and he also had a drinking problem. In the early thirties Thorpe lent his name and ball playing skill to a traveling Indian baseball team, the Indian All-Stars, formed by Ben Harjo, a Haskell graduate. Harjo's team received a $500.00 grant from the Indian Bureau to get it started, but in 1933 the team went broke and could not pay Thorpe and the other players. Through the governor of Oklahoma Thorpe finally got Harjo's wife to pay him $500.00 of the $1,465, he claimed, as documented in a dissertation by Michael E. Welsh.

Thorpe died in 1953, and over the years since then his family and many supporters tried to obtain his reinstatement in the Olympics and the restoration of his Olympic awards, but not until the 1970s did they make any progress. Finally, in 1982, the International Olympic Committee agreed to restore his medals, although only replicas were presented to his descendants.

In 1904, the year Thorpe entered Carlisle, the St. Louis World's Fair sponsored "Anthropology Days" in which aborigines from various parts of the world and some American Indians competed among themselves in a series of events that included kicking a baseball for distance and throwing it for accuracy. The result, pontificated James Sullivan, the PSAL panjandrum, "proved" that the average "savage" did not equal the average white man in strength. The success of Indians in Organized Baseball, together with Thorpe's capture of just about everything in the 1912 Olympics except the torch itself, should demolish such a notion.

25

BASEBALL BREAKS INTO PRISON

The Indians shared the House of Baseball's basement with a group of a different stripe. Its members, having run afoul of the authorities, had been confined to prisons or reformatories. When the institutions in which they were imprisoned provided opportunities for inmates to form prison baseball teams or watch such teams play, as well as to follow the major-league pennant races, the ready response of so many not only revealed their previous familiarity with the game but also showed that their interest and skill had by no means died. On their part, prison authorities soon claimed that baseball served as a broad mainsail that helped carry health, morale, and discipline to their incarcerated charges.

Prison policy reached this more enlightened stage only after traversing at snail's speed a long, arduous route, prodded along by such eighteenth-century European critics as Beccaria, Voltaire, and Montesquieu, and by such nineteenth-century writers as Charles Dickens and especially Jeremy Bentham, who anticipated most elements of later prison sociology when he complained of "the state of forced idleness to which prisoners are reduced. ... Want of exercise enervates and enfeebles their faculties, and deprives their organs of suppleness and elasticity. ... "

In America, authorities gradually transformed prisons from holding pens for prisoners awaiting trial and corporal chastisement into places of punishment by confinement. William Penn and the Quakers laid the foundation for this transition into what became the first of two main prison systems of early nineteenth-century America, the Pennsylvania or "separate and silent" system, under which prisoners worked separately in cells, exercised in private yards, and could not communicate with each other, the purpose being to induce introspection and penitence.

The other plan, known as the Auburn system, established at Auburn, New York, in the early 1800s, also imposed silence, but inmates, with eyes downcast and with respectful demeanor, worked together silently in prison shops during the day and returned to solitary confinement at night. The Auburn congregate plan, as it was called, won out because of its lower cost.

396

So long as these astringent conditions prevailed, baseball had no possibility of breaching adult prison walls.

In the meantime, baseball did make its way into a related branch of the prison system, the young men's reformatory. Its penetration resulted from a growing conviction that young adults, especially first offenders, should not be thrown into penitentiaries with hardened criminals. Instead, an institution intermediate between reform schools for juveniles and prisons for adults should be provided. This idea traced from the French penologist Charles Lucas to a group that in America became known as the child savers and from there to prison reformers after the Civil War, finally coming to fruition in the 1870s. Effective rehabilitation of those committed to such institutions called for a more flexible program, reformers argued. Many inmates suffered from undernourishment, sickness, and poor posture. To deal with these problems the reformatories gradually developed a varied program of clubs, entertainments, exercises, military drill, and games, especially baseball—all efforts toward inculcating self-respect and health.

By the early nineties the young men's reformatory had established a foothold in the American penal system, with seven institutions in as many states. The fugleman for the reformatory system was Zebulon R. Brockway, who had worked his way up through several institutions to the post of superintendent of the new Detroit House of Correction, where he conducted several successful experiments. At the first Congress of the National Prison Association in 1870, Brockway, a gifted speaker, called for what were then revolutionary steps, at least in America—dormitories, libraries, and indeterminate sentences—calculated to protect society by "prevention of crime and reformation of criminals," although not with "sickly sentimentalism." Criminals were either to be cured or kept restrained in order to safeguard society.

In 1876 Brockway accepted the superintendency of the New York State Reformatory at Elmira, New York, a post he would hold for twenty-five years. Elmira, which had opened only six years before, was the first state reformatory for males over fifteen and would become the bellwether for others. Given a free hand to pursue his ideas, Brockway initiated a parole system and a method of marking through which prisoners could earn credits toward achieving parole. He demanded strenuous labor but supplemented it with a prison school. To balance the work program Brockway instituted activities like calisthenics and military drill. By 1890 Elmira also had what a writer on prisons called a "creative recreation" program with a glee club, a new gym, and playing fields.

Brockway was hardly a coddler. When the state later brought charges against him for maltreating prisoners, he admitted that he had, upon occasion, spanked them, slapped them, and given them bloody noses, but denied he had ever beaten them, kicked them, or knocked them down! The

Prison Reform Association backed Brockway's methods, and the governor's investigating commission dismissed the charges.

It remained, however, for the Concord, Massachusetts, Reformatory, which opened in 1884 under the superintendency of Gardiner Tufts, to introduce organized sports. Tufts adopted the grading system and other Elmira features, but his most notable veer from the past was the formation of clubs, including baseball, football, and wrestling organizations. Participation in these sports took place on Saturday afternoons, and on special occasions neighboring town teams often came to play the reformatory teams.

The Concord Reformatory's in-house publication, *Our Paper*, reflected the inmates' interest in baseball. It printed scores of reformatory games— for example, the Stars beating the Waxed Ends (apparently, moustachioed players) 20–19 in an intramural game—as well as news of major-league and college clubs. In 1885 the institution recognized the 110th anniversary of the Battle of Bunker Hill, according to *Our Paper*, by the granting of yard privileges that included opportunities to play baseball and football. The paper also announced that the Fourth of July would be celebrated with a day off for track and field contests and ball games, with two cash prizes to be offered for each event. Bunker Hill Day continued throughout the period to be recognized with baseball games.

In 1890 the Concord paper reported the victory of "Our Boys" over a ball team from nearby Lincoln on the reformatory grounds, and allowed that

> Much praise is due the boys for the manner in which they handled both the ball and the willow. The game abounded in sharp plays, and Capt. Convery particularly distinguished himself. . . . Take it all round, Our Boys are a hard team to beat on their [own] ground, and outside clubs are beginning to realize it.

The newspaper also reprinted articles from other publications, for example a piece from the children's periodical *St. Nicholas Magazine* called "How to Throw a Base Ball."

Reformatory leaders soon attributed beneficial properties to such baseball activities. In his 1888 annual report, Superintendent Tufts of Concord explained to the state commissioners of prisons his baseball program and its advantages to the inmates. He set aside part of each Saturday, he said, for outdoor recreation in the yard, which was ample for 800 men, where they played baseball and other games. Several times during the summer, baseball clubs from neighboring towns also

> come within the walls to try conclusions with Reformatory clubs. On Holidays the schedule of games rivals in number and kind that of a Caledonian club on its great days. No trouble has ever arisen in the yards at any recreation time, not even a rude commotion. The men return from the enjoyments and sports invigorated in body and improved in spirit. . . .

Following Concord's example, Brockway in 1895 introduced organized sports at Elmira. A few other reformatories had already begun to allow freedom of the yard on special occasions, but none, not even Concord, according to an authority on the subject, Blake McKelvey, developed sports to the extent Brockway did at Elmira in his efforts to foster self-control and team spirit.

The number of reformatories climbed steadily. By 1910, according to the Federal Bureau of the Census, they had increased to at least twenty. Clearly, the reformatory supplied a needed adjunct to the penal system. Its flexible age limits, permitting commitment of those up to thirty and sometimes older; its varied program, embracing schools and workshops, farms and military drills, bands and newspapers; its indeterminate sentences, measured by marking systems—all set it apart from the traditional adult prison, as did its lexicon, containing words like *rehabilitation, resocialization*, and *integration*, which reflected the growing impact of psychology, psychiatry, and psychoanalysis, and which indicated an emphasis away from coercive restraints to controlled persuasion, an environment in which baseball could play a part.

As the annual reports and other in-house publications of various reformatories reveal, the innovative baseball and other programs of Brockway's Elmira and Tuft's Concord proved infectious. At the Washington State Reformatory, which opened in 1907 at Monroe, inmates played baseball Saturday afternoons and, according to an observer, "invariably" the game "greatly improved their tempers" as well as their sense of humor.

The Anamosa, Iowa, reformatory operated a four-team baseball league as early as 1914. The warden himself acted as league president, his deputy as vice president, and Number 6137 as secretary. To distinguish the teams, the administration had colored stripes sewn on their trouser seams. Strict rules prevailed, according to the reformatory newspaper, against "unruly players" and "unbecoming conduct." That same year an Anamosa inmate, Robert J. McCombs, Number 7199, a former Cincinnati resident, wrote Garry Herrmann, president of the Reds, asking him for some baseballs because "Occasionally some player with more enthusiasm than brains knocks the ball over the wall, in which case it is lost forever to us."

At the Illinois State Reformatory at Pontiac, inmates were taken out in relays between 7:00 A.M. and 5:00 P.M. daily, each group being allotted an hour to play baseball. On Saturday afternoon the authorities granted a full holiday for baseball games between inmates and outside teams. Superintendent Charles H. Johnson of the Connecticut Reformatory at Cheshire, in his 1916 official report, mentioned that the reformatory baseball team opened the season equipped with a complete baseball outfit, and that the boys out on a road gang were also fitted out with everything, except for uniforms. Profits from candy, tobacco, and confections sold to inmates at Cheshire covered expenses.

Heed given to recreation and open-air exercise in other reformatories, as reported by those like Michigan's Ionia Reformatory, leaves the inference that they, too, included baseball in their programs. Superintendent David C. Peyton of the Jeffersonville, Indiana, Reformatory in his annual report of 1913 and subsequent years asserted that every fair-minded person with intelligence to understand the conditions that pertained in "an institution like this" readily recognized the large part played by recreation, and he had therefore set aside every Saturday afternoon for relaxation in some form of amusement or "sport"—a term that usually covered baseball.

As for Elmira, Brockway's superintendency lost standing in 1900 after Governor Theodore Roosevelt's shakeup of Elmira's Board of Managers, the subject of frequent scandal. The forced resignation of several Elmira prison officers, including Brockway's brother, followed. Brockway's methods again came under fire, although the new board made no charges against him. Shorn of power and realizing the board wanted to get rid of him, Brockway finally resigned.

After Brockway, Elmira's program remained essentially the same, however. The seed of organized sport sown by Brockway germinated. Every August when the reformatory's school closed, baseball took over. That month the place resembled a combination of military camp and baseball camp with a reformatory attached. A five-team league recruited from the military trainees and the office force "battled valiantly each afternoon for the honor of receiving the institutional pennant," as the reformatory's annual report had it.

Appropriations for amusements at Elmira also increased. They rose from $193.29 in 1903 to $352.89 by 1906. And the reformatory management decided that the ball field, which at first stood on the parade ground within the reformatory's enclosure, needed improvement. Determining upon a "larger and more conveniently shaped" plot, directors chose a four-acre tract adjacent to the institution and enclosed it on three sides by a twelve-foot-high fence. One of the enclosure walls made the fourth side. The diamond, "an excellent surface for the players to work with," was by 1916 made of sifted clay, compactly rolled. The management even installed a scoreboard and provided benches on one side of the field for the inmates, all of whom were admitted to the games.

At the Elmira reformatory, as in schools and colleges, interest soon centered on a varsity team. In the summer of 1916 the more experienced reformatory players organized a varsity or "big teams," and it enjoyed a successful season, winning ten out of seventeen games played against the strongest teams of the area. The 1917 report of the board of managers stated that the reformatory's inmates "are ardent fans, take keen interest, root hard for the 'Big' team in its weekly games with outside teams," and, apparently not intending to condemn with faint praise, added that "The spirit of sportsmanship which is displayed would do credit to any assemblage in the country." At the same time, well-sustained interest in the intramural baseball schedule continued, he said, and the general morale of the inmates stood high "because of the opportunity to discharge harmlessly a superabundance of animal spirits. . . . Baseball of itself," the report concluded, "is now an institution at the reformatory."

By the early twenties the reformatory had become an integral part of the American penal system. Reformatories numbered at least 38 in 1923, as the Federal Bureau of the Census reported, and baseball continued to play an important role in the efforts of their directors to rehabilitate the occupants.

Meanwhile, the grim adult penitentiaries had begun to modify their harsh discipline and loosen their severe restraints. The silent system, always difficult to enforce, fell into desuetude. Other stigmata of prison life—prison stripes, short haircuts, and the lockstep—disappeared almost entirely. Some prisons even introduced the indeterminate sentence and a marking system.

At the same time, counterparts of the playground movement, the settlement house, the athletic clubs, and other insignia of the progressive movement appeared in prisons. Most important for baseball, "freedom of the yard" on national holidays, already granted in a few states by the 1880s, had by the early 1900s spread to others and even expanded to an hour or two daily. This privilege of outdoor assembly led to the introduction of various forms of recreation, culminating in the adoption of organized sports, baseball foremost among them. Some penitentiaries went so far as to build baseball fields and provide seats for spectators.

It took a while for penitentiary officials to admit baseball. The prison at Joliet, Illinois, moved in that direction on the Fourth of July, 1875, when the warden permitted freedom of the yard for a couple of hours, at which time the prisoners talked, laughed, sang, and engaged in athletic sports. A May 1904 issue of *The Mentor*, organ of the State Prison at Charlestown, Massachusetts, claimed that since 1889 "on every fair Saturday and holiday between April and October" two baseball teams chosen by the inmates had played a game. By 1904 baseball had become a fixture at Charlestown. According to a claim in *Baseball Magazine* in 1920, baseball in the Washington State Penitentiary at Walla Walla dated from 1896 or 1897.

Not until the second decade of the twentieth century, however, did baseball secure a substantial lodging in adult penitentiaries. By then a number of conditions had made prison authorities more receptive to baseball. Most important of these was the example of reformatory baseball like Elmira's, which, McKelvey rightly states, would "prove the most popular of the reformatory's contributions to prison discipline, . . . although few institutions were able to derive other than entertainment value from it." Prison officials could keep abreast of reformatory programs because the periodic issues of the *Handbook of American Prisons* included reports on the reformatories, too. Sometimes an official moving from a reformatory that had baseball to one without it carried the baseball gospel to his new post. In addition, the growing protest of businessmen and workers against the competition of prison-made goods in the open market, and subsequent legal restrictions on prison shops, inadvertently aided prison baseball, because as a result prisoners' work declined, and their free time had somehow to be filled. Wardens, casting about for a solution, turned to such activities as military drill and baseball. Lastly, the salubrious social climate of the progressive era made itself felt on both prisons and reformatories.

A sprinkle of samples will serve to illustrate. In 1907 baseball teams representing various occupations and categories at Massachusetts State Prison played each other: Weavers versus Lasters, Lifers versus Harness Shop, Carpenter Shop versus Kitchen, Band versus Trunk Shop. The prison paper, *The Mentor*, reported in the fall of 1907 games between the Colored Men, also referred to as the Smokes, and the Lifers. Neither had all the other lumps in the famous pot melted. The paper reported a game between the Children of Israel and the Sons of Italy, but their second encounter was simply called "Jews versus Wops." At the opening game of the 1910 season on April 2, the prison band played the traditional piece, "Take Me Out to the Ball Game."

Players experienced some "rough stuff" when the Oregon State prison team at Salem split a doubleheader with the Chemawa Indian team in 1910. Arguments occurred during the first game, but after Warden Curtis changed the umpire to Number 6145 on appeal from the Indians, things apparently went smoothly. The prison paper, *Lend a Hand*, tried to make amends:

> We wish to thank the boys from the government school who so kindly journeyed to the local diamond to amuse us and help to drive the cob-webs from our brains. You are all a high class bunch of ball players, and your tactics are of the highest order. We wish to apologize for any mistreatment that was handed you through ignorance of a few who don't and can't understand.

The strictest prisons were often slowest to change. Take California's Folsom and San Quentin, both maximum-security prisons: the former did not abolish corporal punishment until 1912. The latter by the early 1900s merely allowed its thousand or more inmates to mill around in the vast prison yard at stipulated intervals, calling it recreation. San Quentin prisoners had to wear stripes until 1912, so a photo that appeared in a prison history showing the San Quentin prison baseball team wearing stripes indicates that some baseball relieved the scene before that date. At Folsom, baseball apparently fared better, the prison team playing outsiders in the same era. Folsom beat the Christian Brothers College of Sacramento in 1913, and in 1917 a convict boasted in a letter to *Baseball Magazine* that the prison team had beaten the best semipros in the area and ranked with the fastest teams in the state.

Not until the end of the first decade of the century was the lockstep abolished and the silent system relaxed at Kansas State Penitentiary in Lansing, where, according to Lester Johnson, a prisoner, cruelties and deplorable living conditions made it one of the most feared and hated prisons in the country. In 1910 Warden J.K. Codding expanded the little commissary and spent its profits on baseball equipment for use of the prisoners when granted freedom of the yard. Codding justified his reforms with the statement, quoted in *The Annals of the American Academy of Political and Social Science*:

> A half hour's relaxation at noon at which [time] the men play ball, pitch horseshoes and indulge in athletic games is as much a part of the regular programme of the institution as is the day's labor or the regular meals.

Another year passed before baseball and open-air concerts were introduced to relax prisoners at the federal penitentiary in Atlanta. With approval of the Department of Justice, the national game, said the New York *Times* in 1911, "will be played between two teams picked from the prisoners, and spectators will be only those who have had good marks during the year."

Another tough and tardy convert, the Federal Penitentiary at Leavenworth, Kansas, achieved "wonderful changes" in 1915 in the behavior of prisoners, according to the *Times*, "through the magic of baseball." Three convict teams provided the means for the magic. Heretofore, from twenty to fifty men wore striped uniforms as the penalty for infraction of any rule, but after notification that rulebreakers would in addition lose their baseball passes, the chronic troublemakers behaved so well that, to the amazement of prison officials, for the first time in the prison's history not one man wore stripes.

At the State Prison in Carson City, Nevada, the cry "Kill the Umpire" became reality. The victim was Patrick Casey, a convicted murderer condemned to die. Asked for his last wish by the warden, Casey, a lifelong baseball fan, said he had always wanted to umpire a baseball game. The warden arranged a match between two convict teams, and Casey umpired it. The next day he was executed.

A couple of events unusual at the time marked baseball at the Columbus, Ohio, State Penitentiary. First, twenty-odd prisoners let out of the penitentiary on their honor in 1914 chose one of their group to write Garry Herrmann asking for a few old bats, balls, and gloves so they could play baseball. Then, after the state decided to abolish shops and contract labor, the warden had a baseball diamond laid out in order to give the men better recreation, in the belief that "fair and manly sport" was one of the greatest "lifters of lost humanity," and that "when a man gets so low he won't play or watch baseball, he's lost indeed." The warden even allowed the home team, which included three black players, to play an away game against the Standard Oil Company team, one of the fastest teams in Columbus, at Neil Park, home of the Columbus professional club, and permitted prison trustees to announce the game beforehand by selling copies of the prison paper on Columbus streets. The team traveled to the ball park in a state-owned truck, and the prison band went along, but the team lost its game despite the fact that its squad contained five robbers, two gunmen, one burglar, two second-story men, one forger, one assaulter, a horse thief, and one man imprisoned for failure to provide for his family.

Baseball took precedence over chapel at the McAlester, Oklahoma, Penitentiary, and nobody drew the color line. Sunday evenings, weather permitting, white and black prisoners associated freely in the yard playing baseball, cards, and checkers. On one such evening in 1914 some fifty inmates were attending chapel in the dining room, where services were held, while others played baseball just outside, the dust from their play drifting through the windows and the hollering and jeering of the fans sounding through the room. Three different times the ball hit the building, but in contrast to what would then happen in the outside world, as prison officer Robert Park remarked, no one complained about the disturbance to public worship.

Baseball became incorporated into the unwritten by-laws at the Stillwater, Minnesota, State Penitentiary with the appointment of Charles S. Reed as warden in October of 1914. Although inmates had played one or two games before his arrival, Reed encouraged the baseball spirit supposedly "inherent in every man." He put up a huge scoreboard at the front of the dining hall, where everyone could see it. Each day before the noon meal he had the scores of all major-league and double-A minor league games posted. The men received permission to converse at table every other day, and comments on the deeds of Cobb, Speaker, Johnson, and other stars filled the air. In an even more radical move, Reed continued the pay of Stillwater men working in the prison industries when the shops shut down for ball games. Although this policy cost the prison an estimated $1,200.00 per game, or from $5,000.00 to $6,000.00 a month, Reed believed the money well forfeited. "We try not to forget," he said, "that the purpose of the institution is not to make goods and revenue for the state, but to . . . make better men of the inmates, while at the same time protecting society." Inmates at Stillwater fielded both a first and a second team, and the prison's weekly newspaper published accounts of games, played every Saturday afternoon and on holidays and attended by all inmates except those deprived of the privilege for misconduct. High walls and buildings bound the field, and balls hit over them were lost. Although four iron lamp posts stood in the outfield, no accidents ever occurred. An outsider, usually a Stillwater citizen, umpired games. All costs of uniforms and equipment came from a quarter admission fee charged visitors.

Paradoxically, two of the most antiquated penitentiaries, New York state's Auburn and Sing Sing, became the locus of a progressive experiment on the part of Thomas Mott Osborne that contributed heavily to prison baseball.

Osborne became interested in prison reform as early as 1904, and as a result of his association with the George Junior Republic* he conceived the idea of introducing to adult prisons the Republic's principles of individual responsibility and self-government, a plan in which baseball came to have a starring role. In 1913 Osborne chaired New York state's commission for prison reform and was in a position to act. He chose Auburn Penitentiary, in his home town, for his experiment and, with the permission of Warden Charles F. Rattigan, entered the prison as a convict to study convict life first-hand. For a week Osborne followed Auburn's regular routine, and once in the basket shop, when he won the confidence of a convict named Jack Murphy, he broached the idea of unsupervised recreation, asking if Murphy thought it would work. Murphy assured Osborne that the men could be trusted, but said that to avoid stool pigeons they should be allowed to elect their own officers.

Osborne's official report and recommendations following his experience created a sensation. State superintendent John D. Riley approved of his work, but the New York *Times* remarked tartly that Osborne could have learned more from books.

More important, at Osborne's suggestion State Superintendent of Prisons John B. Riley and Warden Rattigan granted the convicts permission to organize a Mutual Welfare League, through which to exercise a degree of self-government, including a large measure of control over prison recreation in general and baseball in particular. This plan would serve as a stimulus to prison ball, a benefit to discipline, and an instrument of control, since a privilege granted could be withdrawn as punishment.

The Auburn men elected a forty-nine-man Board of League Delegates, and at a ceremony in the prison in January of 1914, 350 convicts pledged to observe good conduct, aid in maintaining discipline, improve themselves, and cooperate in their own reformation. The most radical outcome was Rattigan's acquiescence to the prisoners' request for an outdoor field day on Memorial Day.

For several weeks before the field day at Auburn an athletic committee of prisoners busied itself preparing the program. On the appointed day, May 31, the sun shone brightly, and after an early dinner, prison officers opened the cells and all 1,400 convicts marched into the prison yard—a spectacle that sent chills through the guards. According to Osborne's account, the convicts seemed dazed at first but soon began to greet and jostle each other good-naturedly and to take part in the activities. The program alternated band music, singing, and dancing with athletic contests. Everyone, wrote Osborne, "was wildly interested in the sports; and I was constantly reminded of some good-natured intercollegiate rivalry." The South Wing, victor in the athletic contests, received a banner. After this unprecedented afternoon of outdoor recreation, the men marched back to their cells in perfect order.

*See above, Chapter 7.

Auburn authorities further loosened the traces when, hoping to prevent an epidemic of scarletina from spreading, they permitted an hour of daily exercise and recreation in the open. When they withdrew the privilege after the epidemic ended, the prisoners petitioned for its restoration and got it. Another and better field day took place on the Fourth of July, 1914. Orlando F. Lewis, secretary of the New York Prison Association, called it a significant day in prison annals. The 1,400 inmates, said Lewis, "ran off their own sports" and "practically ran themselves through their appointed 'delegates' and were very orderly."

No doubt the "sports" at Auburn in 1914 included ball playing. The following year they definitely did. Billy Sunday, the former Chicago White Sox outfielder turned evangelist, visited Auburn on one of his soul-saving tours and posed with its Mutual Welfare League baseball team, which *Baseball Magazine* called "a rattling good nine," and told the "ball tossers" several stories.

A state prison inspector visiting Auburn in 1915 found that to the convicts with whom he talked, the Mutual Welfare League was one of the prison's most attractive features, and the league's recreation period impressed them most. Without doubt, he reported, the spirit of the prisoners at Auburn had improved. No longer "sullen and bitter" toward the administration, many seemed to take an interest in the affairs of the prison. A 1920 report on the Mutual Welfare League in the state prison survey pointed out that it provided such athletic diversion as baseball, handball, and field sport. It commented ominously, however, on the "bad" condition of the building, declaring the cells at Auburn "worse than those of Sing Sing."

The other old New York penitentiary, Sing Sing at Ossining, dated from 1825. In the eighties and nineties its annual reports confirmed the need for the new reformatories: prisoners, many of them teenagers, some as young as thirteen, had been forced to double up because of overcrowding and lived under "morally debasing" conditions.

Interest in sports, however, was not absent. In 1899 Sing Sing's prison newspaper, *Star of Hope*, contained news of National League and New York State League baseball players and club standings. Newspaper offices of prisons, Sing Sing among them, and of reformatories soon exchanged papers and printed news of each other's doings. This exchange of information no doubt helped the baseball virus to spread among them, although not all prisoners benefited immediately. Sing Sing's paper quipped in 1901, "As for outdoor games, Grade C men had any amount of . . . races when unloading flour. Grade B men amused themselves in the athletic sport of shoveling coal."

Baseball made its debut at Sing Sing under Warden McCormick only in mid-July of 1914, by which time McCormick certainly knew of Osborne's well-publicized experiment and the two field days at Auburn. In preparation, McCormick ordered wash lines torn down, trees rooted out, and a baseball diamond installed. Some of his friends raised $150.00 for equipment. On the day of the first games the warden was absent, leaving the keepers aghast at the sight of the entire population (1,510), except for 45 sick and 18 condemned, congregated in the south yard after the noon meal.

When the warden's secretary, Watson, threw out the first ball, a great shout went up, and the prisoners cheered McCormick in absentia. Nearly all the men wanted to play, so Watson used fungo hitting to select teams. By 2:00 P.M. he had reduced the candidates only as low as sixty-four, so instead of the two teams planned he formed six. Captains then took over, and the prisoners conducted the games themselves, each team to play three innings, umpired by a keeper. All proceeded smoothly except for some friction over pitchers. Half the sixty-four wanted to pitch! Fortunately, perhaps, no close decision occurred, although the prisoners overlooked a good many apparent outs in order to increase their time on the diamond.

In one of the games at Sing Sing that day, a player who hit a home run (inside the park) celebrated with a handspring and was cheered loudly for his showmanship. A ball hit over the wall was retrieved by a trustee. During the games a Jewish chaplain arrived to hold services, and "only four men preferred services to baseball," he remarked, "But it was all right. This baseball game is a great drawing card." After ten minutes he let the faithful go back outside and enjoy themselves. When playing time ended, a bugle sounded and the men walked into the mess hall, picked up bread and tea, and returned to their cells.

Thereafter, McCormick allowed four hours on Saturday afternoons for talking, running, and playing games at Sing Sing. In addition, a baseball game took place every Sunday, with all inmates allowed to attend. McCormick's objective, said the New York *Times*, was to establish discipline and

> to prevent unrest, riots, and incendiary fires. His rule was simply: Be good boys. If you are good you can hammer away at the baseball every night after work and all Saturday afternoon during the season.

He gave them leave to play and yell, but they had to observe the rules or get sent to their cells while others were "having the time of their lives." In other words, the prisoners, knowing the carrot offered could be withheld, would be more tractable.

On Sunday August 2, the warden of Sing Sing loosened the reins still further by allowing prisoners out of their cells nearly all day, with their own monitors watching over their recreation. McCormick then announced that this practice would continue the rest of the summer and that output of prison shops at Sing Sing had increased thirty-three percent as a result of the first Sunday freedom.

McCormick did not go as far at Sing Sing as had Osborne at Auburn in relaxing strictures on prisoners. He granted less leeway, permitting only a modicum of self-government, marching inmates into the yard under prison officers and surrounding baseball players and spectators with a cordon of guards. But before 1914 had ended, McCormick had been removed after a commission reported he had shown favoritism to a prisoner who was a former banker. In December Thomas Mott Osborne succeeded him as warden.

Osborne, in his book *Society and Prisons*, and Rudolph Chamberlain, his biographer, neither of them disinterested commentators, were highly critical of the conditions Osborne inherited from McCormick, perhaps in an effort to make Osborne's contribution seem greater. According to Chamberlain, Osborne inherited a prison marked by lockstep rules, shaven crowns, zebra clothing, and cruelty in an atmosphere of corruption and filth. Sing Sing did have something called a Golden Rule Brotherhood, wrote Chamberlain, but, in an attempt to bribe men to be good, it granted privileges before the men earned them. Osborne saw in the plethora of guards a lack of complete trust, causing prisoners to abuse what trust there was.

At Sing Sing Osborne intended to complete the plan he had begun to put into operation at Auburn. According to the New York Prison Association's report, he envisaged a system of self-government, removal of unnecessary restrictions, and all the liberty consistent with good order. Under the Mutual Welfare League, which Osborne introduced to Sing Sing, the prisoners chose fifty delegates who supervised the mess hall and recreation, athletics included. He also allowed outdoor recreation weekdays from 4:00 to 5:00 P.M. and all afternoon Sundays and holidays.

Baseball flourished at Sing Sing in 1915 under Mutual Welfare League auspices. The New York American League club helped out with old uniforms and gloves. An internal prisoners' league played intraprison games, and on Sunday afternoons the Mutual Welfare League team, the varsity, played such outside clubs as the Holy Rosary Lyceum from New York City. Such was the enthusiasm at these Sunday games that the noise made by prisoner spectators disturbed residents in the village of Ossining, and the town trustees wrote Osborne asking him to terminate Sabbath games. The town received no formal reply, but officials of the Mutual Welfare League did go among the audience at Sunday baseball games cautioning against noisy rooting, and apparently that appeased the locals.

Two special occasions highlighted the Sing Sing baseball season of 1915. The peripatetic Billy Sunday treated a thousand convicts on May 15 to a sermon, as usual enlivening it with autobiographical passages from his major-league career. In June actor DeWolf Hopper and musician Irving Berlin arrived from New York City with a large party from the Lambs Club and attended a ball game that the prison team lost to the Tarrytown All-Stars. The Lambs also entertained the prisoners in the chapel and, as they were about to leave, a chorus of requests arose for Hopper to recite his famous monologue, "Casey at the Bat." Hopper complied. Another prominent figure, Jimmy Cagney, the "bad guy" of many movies, played on a team that visited Sing Sing in the late teens and heard from the stands the greetings of many New Yorkers from his old upper East Side neighborhood.

Osborne credited the improved physical well-being of the men at Sing Sing not only to "the cessation of the use of drugs and liquors," which, he said, had pervaded the prison before he took charge, but "by reason of the exercise the recreation hours afford—in summer swimming, baseball, handball, and bowling."

Nevertheless, Osborne's system started a nationwide controversy almost from the time he introduced it at Sing Sing. Critics charged he was undermining the intent of the courts and society to deter crime by punishing criminals. Sing Sing's future famous warden, Lewis Lawes, who had some fish of his own to fry, later called Osborne's Mutual Welfare League worthwhile but badly administered: prison self-government overlapped with the warden's responsibility, and the warden became an advisor rather than a leader and ruler, so abuses crept in. By July Osborne's former supporter, Superintendent Riley, had turned against him, disapproving of his "pink tea" methods, and undermined him by transferring seventy-nine Sing Sing inmates to Auburn prison despite Osborne's prior promise that the men themselves could decide who would be sent.

In December, following an investigation, the Westchester Grand Jury handed down two indictments against Osborne, one for perjury, the other for mismanagement. Osborne denounced the action as a "foul conspiracy" by politicians and disgruntled inmates. His biographer called it a frameup. Frustrated, Osborne was forced to ask for leave pending the outcome of the trial. Dr. George W. Kirchwey, dean of Columbia Law School, who replaced Osborne, adhered closely to his policy. Judging by a description in *Atlantic Monthly* at the time, Sing Sing, except for the walls and bars of steel, might have passed for a country club: "Ball games, tennis matches and other athletic sports, a swimming pool, moving-picture shows, lectures, and other entertainments have been provided for the recreation of the prisoners."

In 1916, under Kirchwey, baseball became the centerpiece of this congeries of recreational activities at Sing Sing. Besides the varsity—the "renowned" Mutual Welfare League team, as the prison paper termed it—men played on such regular shop teams as those for printers, wagonmakers, shoemakers, and foundrymen. M.W.L. regulars played shop teams as a preseason tuneup. During one such game, all the balls were fouled into the Hudson River, a disappointment that called attention to the need for a screen on the wall behind the backstop. The regular varsity season opened Sunday, April 15, and continued through October, with games against outside teams on Saturdays and Sundays. Holidays were special: a doubleheader on Decoration Day and four games on the long Fourth of July weekend. The prison team won all four, one of them against the Garrison Athletic Association, a group of friends of State Representative Hamilton Fish, who was, said the prison paper, a staunch supporter of the prisoners' welfare. Fish himself played first base, and the prison lent his team a player, who was derided as a "traitor" because of his good performance for the visitors. The prison paper, at fifty cents and then a dollar for a season subscription, reported extensively on the Sing Sing varsity games, and the New York *Times, World,* and *American* frequently mentioned them.

There was no want of opponents for the Sing Sing varsity, either as to number or type, willing to come not only from Ossining but from such New York areas as Jamaica, Manhattan, Brooklyn, Staten Island, Haverstraw, Palisades, Bay Ridge, and Chappaqua. The plenitude of visiting teams bespoke the right of baseball to the title of The People's Game. They included so-called athletic clubs—Crescent, Chapel, Highland, Oakwood, Pleasantwood, and Tottenville; religious organizations—Sacred Heart, Ascension, and St. James Working Boys; business groups—Hudson Motor Company, Underwood Typewriter Company, Yonkers *Herald,* Charles Williams Stores, New York Stock Exchange, Astor Trust Company, U.S. Tire Company, Music Publishing Company, and Metropolitan Life Insurance Company; government groups—county clerks, Municipal Light, and Mazeppa Engine Company; and finally a YMCA Club, the Washington Heights Y.

The scene at these Mutual Welfare League games in Sing Sing differed little from that at college games. The prison band played. The spectators rooted enthusiastically, although, as in other prisons, some perversely rooted and bet against the home team. The official bootblack of the prison officials, a convict called Nickel Dick (shoeshines cost five cents in those days) provided amusing byplay before games. Humorous incidents also occurred. Once the umpire called a prison player out on a close play. "Robber!" shouted the player. The umpire walked over and whispered, "Don't get personal; this is only a friendly game." Sometimes a contingent of rooters accompanied a visiting team. The Stock Exchange team of bankers and clerks brought more than a hundred, including twenty-five or thirty women, and they sat in reserved seats while gray-capped convicts packed the bleachers and hundreds of others watched from the barred windows of the mess hall.

After a game at Sing Sing in June, the manager of the Palisades Baseball Club marveled that none of the Sing Sing players acted "in a way that would make you think they were convicts." He saw only three guards, and the prisoners seemed to "run the whole thing themselves, with the system and courtesy of college students." All wore M.W.L. buttons, but otherwise none of the 1,500 inmates "looked or acted any different from a similar body at the Polo Grounds." Osborne, he said, "has worked wonders. The men have pride."

Prison officials were often ardent baseball fans. Sing Sing's Principal Keeper Dorner rarely missed a game, and his son Freddie served as the team's mascot, a role that no doubt broadened the boy's education as much as my three summers as batboy at Ebbets Field did mine. Deputy Warden Spencer Miller sacrificed much personal time to be the team's manager. On occasion he even became a ringer of sorts, donning a uniform and playing second base, "turning the tide of battle with his versatile fielding and heavy batting." Miller also appeared at the Tenth Annual Recreation Congress in October, 1916, to make a plea for the preventive work of the recreation movement.

The Sing Sing prison paper, *M.W.L. Bulletin*, commented in a November, 1916, issue that the Mutual Welfare League team had enjoyed one of its best seasons, winning 38, losing 14, and tieing one. The batting and fielding averages it published, the writer asserted, showed the players on a par with outside professionals. The prison paper also extended the "heartiest thanks" and "deep and heartfelt appreciation" of M.W.L. players and fans to all the outside opponents for their "sacrifice of time, convenience and money that it cost them to journey here." Whether they won or not, the prisoners trusted that the pleasure the visitors had was "the equal, if not the superior, of that gladness, hope and sunshine that they brought into the lives of the men behind the walls of the grim, old Sing Sing Prison."

As for Osborne, the case against him was dismissed in July. Said the New York *World*, his "persecution" had been attributed less to his reforming methods than to "his assertive independence of the prison ring that so long controlled prison management." When Osborne returned as warden of Sing Sing he was welcomed by a parade that included the band, a series of floats, and the baseball team. At a ceremony attended by prominent people and punctuated by the usual speeches, the prisoners awarded "honorary degrees" to Osborne and to Acting Warden Kirchwey, who resigned.

Three months after his triumphant return Osborne himself resigned. In his letter of resignation he accused Governor Charles S. Whitman of acquiescing in the "shameful attacks" on him and for breaking every promise made to him. According to the New York *Times*, the direct cause of Osborne's quitting was the new state superintendent's order restricting lifers and men serving long sentences to the prison walls, thus preventing them from participating in recreation.

The wardens who served brief terms at Sing Sing before the appointment of Lewis Lawes in 1920 carried on the essentials of the Osborne system, although opinions of that system remain mixed. Harry Elmer Barnes in his *Society in Transition* (1939) maintained that Osborne realized "active discipline" in prison must be put in the hands of convicts "if they are to obey the law once they are out of sight of guards and the arsenal." Dr. Kirchwey believed that whether the Mutual Welfare league worked for good or evil depended on the warden and whether he could get the men's cooperation.

The New York Prison Survey of 1920, however, criticized the passivity of recreation at Sing Sing. Prisoners should do things for themselves rather than having others do them, said the survey, and while passive entertainments like movies and baseball were perhaps "necessary," the real success of the program depended on getting prisoners to provide their own recreation. "Out of the grandstand and into the game" should be the slogan for a prison recreation leader, asserted the survey.

Of course, the prisons merely reflected the trend in the rest of the society toward spectatoritis, and, as in the rest of society, the perceptive observation of the survey would become more applicable as the next two decades of prison baseball unfolded.

26

MOSTLY HOME GAMES

In the 1920s and 1930s baseball ripened into a full-fledged feature of prison life, reaching the full season of its maturity. During that span no prison surpassed Sing Sing either in emphasis on baseball or in the prominence of its warden, Lewis Lawes. He came to Sing Sing seasoned by long familiarity with prison work. Born in Elmira in 1883 within a mile of the reformatory, where his father worked as a guard, he followed in the latter's footsteps, becoming a guard at Clinton Prison in Dannemora. After service in the Army, there followed a succession of prison jobs. Dismayed at the repression in the first of these, Auburn, where he was a guard, he secured a position at Elmira Reformatory and rose to chief guard.

In 1915 Lawes received an appointment as overseer of the New York City Reformatory at Hart's Island. Arriving in the midst of unrest following a revolt among the inmates, he established firm but humane discipline, and after extracting a promise from their leader and his followers to behave like men, released them from the "cooler." Lawes permitted the malcontents to "play games, read, and otherwise enjoy themselves" under the supervision of uniformed officers instead of "twiddling their fingers in the dormitories," as he expressed it.

Once at Hart's Island during a Sunday afternoon ball game, a number of the inmates dropped to the ground. Investigation disclosed that the drug room had been burglarized and almost ninety young men poisoned. Fortunately, the large doses acted as an emetic and so probably saved their lives.

Lawes soon gained consent to establish a new reformatory at New Hampton, in upstate New York, and supervised the five hundred young men transported there to help build it. As a result of his work at Hampton, Governor Alfred E. Smith offered him the wardenship of Sing Sing, where he assumed control on New Year's Day of 1920 at age 37.

Lawes gradually transformed Sing Sing after the discordant Osborne administration until it became possibly the most progressive prison in the country. He continued Osborne's Mutual Welfare League, but with modifications that placed him firmly in control. Although refined and expanded, the essentials of the recreation program he inherited became the basis for his own. A Mutual Welfare League committee under the supervision of prison officers took charge of the athletic program. Another committee interviewed each new arrival to ascertain what the committee could do for him, what job he liked, and whether he was interested in baseball and wanted to join a team or the baseball committee. Funds for equipment came out of profits from the commissary, the annual M.W.L. show, and the twenty-five-cent admission charge to visitors. A large recreation field, including a full-sized, "splendidly-graded" baseball diamond and bleachers, constructed in an area cleared of some old buildings ruined by incendiary fires, provided the means of implementing the athletic program.

The Sing Sing prison varsity, still called the M.W.L. team, quickly became known as one of the best prison teams, winning ninety-five percent of its games in 1920. The team played as usual on Saturday and Sunday afternoons and on holidays against strong semipro teams from New York, New Jersey, and Connecticut. Inviting one type of visiting team, however, drew criticism from a judge in 1922: "The idea of having baseball games at Sing Sing and bringing in a high school team to play with crooks . . . ! That's the way to encourage crime."

Intramural baseball continued to play a vigorous part in Sing Sing baseball under Lawes. In 1921, for example, a nine-team league composed of the shoe shop, brush shop, knit works, and other shop teams played each other, the winning team to receive a huge cup donated by Sir Thomas Lipton in commemoration of his 1920 visit to the prison, and each winning player to receive fifty dollars, to be sent to his relatives at home. These shop teams served as farms for the varsity. They played each other after supper before grandstands filled with convicts yelling and shouting encouragement to their favorite players.

Visits by the New York Yankees, Giants, and other major-league teams highlighted M.W.L. seasons in the twenties. In 1929 the coming of the Yankees, with Babe Ruth in the lineup, caused Sing Sing inmates to be "choked with joy" and "intoxicated with delight," according to a description of the event in *Baseball Magazine*. After lunch at the home of Warden Lawes, the major-league players' tour of the premises evoked many sallies from them, for instance: "These fellows aren't badly off, all home games and they don't have to worry about base hits." Autograph seekers swamped Ruth. During a game with the M.W.L. team he hit three balls over the prison wall, and, each time, the prison infielders shook hands with him as he circled the bases, and the plate umpire patted him on the back. At Sing Sing, added the writer describing the scene, "they don't hoot and hiss the umpire or hurl bottles at him—they haven't any."

Further elaboration and refinement marked the recreation program at Sing Sing in the twenties and thirties. An athletic director, Gerald Curtin, now headed the program. A fine new gym, contributed by Warner Brothers after they made a film at Sing Sing, improved the facilities. The M.W.L. team played a regular schedule of games with outside teams, seventy of them in 1936, and all the prisoners except those in hospital, solitary confinement, or the death house turned out to watch. Lawes also admitted the public to these games. He granted further latitude by allowing some games outside the prison. In one of them in 1936, for example, Sing Sing defeated the New York Athletic Club at Travers Island. On the Fourth of July, always an important holiday at Sing Sing, athletic events included a doubleheader, and the inmates enjoyed a chicken dinner. The administration also granted, to those who had participated in baseball, a special Labor Day meal at picnic tables on the lawn.

"It is impossible to overestimate what baseball means to these men," said Director Curtin. "It is their chief link with the outside world and their main interest here." Similarly, the warden's secretary commented, "You'd be surprised at the interest these men have in baseball. Why, even the inmates in the Death House asked the warden's permission to listen to the broadcast of the World Series games. This privilege was granted them." A newspaper story going the rounds told of a young man discharged from Sing Sing who held up a policeman at pistol point. His explanation for the holdup was "I want to go back to Sing Sing. Down here I'm just a bum, but up there I was on the ball team."

Two outsiders umpired the varsity games. The prisoners christened one Dillinger; the other, whose name was Jesse Collyer, they called Jesse James. Collyer, who once umpired in Organized Baseball, liked to stroll about the prison stopping to talk with the men and answering questions about Ty Cobb or Joe DiMaggio. He was also an informer. "I had good rapport with the inmates," he said in an interview much later, "and could get anything out of them." So when the warden wanted to know who stole something or why someone was dead, Collyer got the job of finding out.

Two ball-playing Sing Sing inmates, Richard Whitney and Alabama Pitts, earned much publicity in the thirties. Yet other than their place of public residence and their ball-playing on its grounds, they had nothing in common. A broad chasm separated them in background, social class, and scope of their crimes. Whitney was the epitome of privilege: graduate of Groton and Harvard, member of numerous exclusive clubs, and staunch advocate of so-called free enterprise, especially as it pertained to the freedom of the New York Stock Exchange, over which he presided when arrested, to govern itself unhampered by government regulation.

Pitts, a country boy, had made his way on his own from North Carolina to Mississippi after his father and stepfather died. At age fifteen he entered the Navy. Receiving an honorable discharge after serving three years, he found himself in New York City, alone and broke. Unable to find work in the deepening depression, he turned to robbery. After several small "stickups" he was arrested for holding up a drugstore and taking $76.00 from the cash register. He was nineteen when the court convicted him of second-degree robbery and sentenced him to from eight to sixteen years in Sing Sing, with three years off for good behavior.

Whitney, as befit his status, stole on a far greater scale. When the stock market crashed, at first he borrowed heavily to shore up his holdings. Then, as the market continued to plunge, he grew increasingly desperate to the point of using as collateral some securities of which he was merely a trustee. In March of 1938 his whole rickety edifice finally collapsed, leaving him owing about four million dollars. Tried and convicted of embezzlement, he was sent up the river.

As prisoner No. 94835 Whitney received an assignment to teach in the prison school. He had captained the baseball team at Groton, and although there is no record in the *Harvard H Book* of his having won a letter in baseball at Harvard, as is often claimed, he did play intramural ball at Sing Sing as first baseman for the prison school. When his mentor, the Reverend Mr. Endicott Peabody, headmaster of Groton, visited Whitney and asked if he could do anything for him, Whitney replied, "Yes, I need a lefthanded first baseman's mitt!" Apparently, Whitney played very well for a man of fifty. Guards commenting on his performance in a June game said he made two hits in three times at bat, fielded well, and ran the bases professionally. (There is no evidence that he stole any of them.) Considered a model prisoner, Whitney received parole at the earliest possible date, August of 1941.

Unlike Whitney's crime, which deservedly received copious publicity at the outset, that of Pitts went unnoticed until his ball-playing at Sing Sing brought him to the attention of the metropolitan dailies. During the five years he played on the M.W.L. baseball team, word of his skill gradually spread to the outside by members of visiting teams and the efforts of Sing Sing's press agent. One move almost certain to attract the press was to book a game with the Port Jervis, New York, police team. Efforts of the "cops" to catch Pitts on the bases were called "pitiful and funny," and the New York papers made the most of the story. The wire services also used it.

No sooner was Pitts released from Sing Sing in June of 1935 when Joe Cambria, scout for the Washington Senators and owner of their Class AA Albany International League farm team, signed him. Almost as quickly, Judge William Bramham, president of the minors' National Association, refused to let Pitts contract with Albany or with any other minor league club, on the grounds that as president he was "expected to safeguard the interests of baseball" and that Pitts would be a "detriment" to the minors. Although Bramham did not mention it then, according to *Sporting News* he had also consulted Commissioner Landis before handing down his decision.

Perhaps, as seems likely, the thought of Pitts cavorting on Organized Baseball's diamonds rekindled in the minds of Bramham and Landis memories of the Black Sox scandal of 1919. Most certainly, neither they nor the minor league Executive Committee, chaired by Warren Giles (which, un-surprisingly, fell into line with the decision), anticipated the Niagara of protest that broke upon them from all quarters.

Warden Lawes in a New York *Times* feature article said that keeping Pitts out of Organized Baseball would inspire a feeling of "What's the use?" in the minds of prisoners. Pitts received hundreds of letters and telegrams of support, one from the victim of the holdup that sent him to prison! His backers planned a pardon appeal to Governor Herbert Lehman, and Pitts himself decided to petition Landis. Hard-bitten Johnny Evers, known as "the crab" in his playing days and presently the Albany club's manager, threatened to quit baseball if the decision were allowed to stand, and he reportedly declared melodramatically, "as tears streamed down his face un-ashamedly," that "This decision tramples on sentiment and stabs fair play to the heart."

The press rallied to Pitts. Feature writers produced "Jean Valjean" stories of protest against the decision. Newspapers syndicated Pitts's life story in serial form. The New York *Times* called the decision "unfortunate" and Bramham almost certainly wrong in thinking the public would resent Pitts's hiring. The *Times* echoed Lawes in declaring that a ban on Pitts would confirm the belief of many prisoners that an ex-convict "hasn't got a chance" and might just as well resume a life of crime. Influential figures, including editor William Allen White and lawyer Charles Evans Hughes, Jr., also spoke out. Clarence Darrow needed only one word to describe Bramham's decision: "Rotten."

The prime target of protests and appeals was Landis. As the deluge of letters, telegrams, and phone calls swelled, he began staying away from his office. The "last straw" was reputedly an advance copy, shown him by a reporter, of a blistering editorial scheduled for publication the following Sunday in the bearer's paper unless Landis ruled in favor of Pitts. "No one could resist this tide," Landis told Bramham afterward.

Landis gave way. "Never one to pass up a chance to grab the publicity limelight," as sports writer M.A. Bealle wrote later, Landis ordered all pertinent records brought to him, called Cambria and Pitts before him, and ruled that Pitts could play, but only in regular games, so that his "notoriety" could not be exploited in exhibition games. Landis wrapped his decision in face-saving verbiage, at once attempting to justify the original edicts of the minor-league officials and varnishing his reversal of them. Landis avoided portraying Pitts as wronged, omitted any comment on the scarcity of jobs, and, in sentiments still current, asserted that Pitts's crime was typical of the "moral disorder" of "modern youth" seeking "easy money" and "thrills." He approved of a distinction American Association executives had made, he said, between employing an ex-convict in a business capacity and hiring one as a player, coach, manager, or umpire. In the latter case, "character qualifi-cations" must apply, because the hiring affected other clubs and baseball generally. (Presumably, owners and front-office people need not meet such a standard.) Finally, Landis claimed that the situation had changed. "Reputable people" had pronounced Pitts completely reformed. To deny him admission to baseball would therefore have a "destructive effect" (on rehabilitation of convicts).

Pitts said he was "more than grateful" to Landis and would do his best. The decision met with applause throughout the country: "generous and sensible" (New York *Times*); "the best break for baseball since Ruth came along" (Dan Parker, New York *Mirror*); "It gives Pitts a chance and it stops an ugly undercurrent that was rising against baseball" (Jimmy Powers, New York *Daily News*); "I am very glad the boy will get a chance" (Joe Cronin, Red Sox playing manager); "a fine, humanitarian decision" (Clarence Darrow).

The decision also jogged some people's memories of Benny Kauff, acquitted in a court on a charge of car theft but barred by Landis anyway because he thought Kauff unfit to associate with other National League players. Some called for reinstatement of Jimmy O'Connell, "a boy who has committed no crime," banned by Landis a decade earlier for an alleged attempt to "fix" a game.* At least one person urged lifting the ban on the Black Sox. Others, however, saw no parallel between the cases. And no notice was taken of Piggy Sands, probably a better baseball player than Pitts, who, according to Robert Boyle of *Sports Illustrated*, averaged .440 in batting in twelve seasons at Sing Sing and could play any position. Piggy Sands was a black man.

Pitts signed for $200.00 a month and made his debut with the Albany Senators on June 25, 1935, getting two hits. His mother attended, and the fans acclaimed him. Although Pitts averaged only .233 in forty-five games that year, Albany signed him again for 1936 at a pay increase. Thereafter, however, he steadily descended the minor-league ladder, finishing up in Organized Baseball in Class D, its lowest league. He died at age thirty of stab wounds received in a roadside tavern altercation.

At Sing Sing Lawes, said the New York *Times*, "stretched humanitarianism to the breaking point." At the same time he maintained control. In his promotion of baseball and other games, Lawes encouraged even those with long sentences to play on the various teams, because, he said, the experience gave prisoners something to do and discuss. Former convict R. Benton attributed the absence of riots in Sing Sing to the "unswerving fairness" of Lawes, who administered deserved punishment as promptly as an earned privilege, and to the good food, comfortable quarters, and recreation he provided. Benton continued,

> When a man gets up from a decent meal and, conscious that he has kept to the rules of the prison and so earned his privilege, can go to a pleasant game

*See *Baseball: The Golden Age*, pp. 378–81 and 374–75.

of baseball, football, basketball, or boche [bocce] ball in the yard, he is not in a frame of mind to grumble or to listen to others who are. A prospective prison riot is not of much interest to anyone if it is apt to interrupt a good game!

He might have added that another reason Lawes experienced less difficulty maintaining order than some wardens was that he could, in effect, hand-pick his clients, sending long-termers to Auburn and Dannemora. At any rate, when those prisons erupted in riot, Sing Sing remained quiescent.

Although less well-known than Sing Sing, the Michigan State Penitentiary at Jackson yielded the baseball palm to no prison. Measured by winning teams, facilities provided, and interest within and outside the prison, Michigan State Prison's baseball program was outstanding, so much so that it invited criticism from those who valued intramural ball played by the many over varsity games with outside teams played by the few.

Recreation took root early in Michigan State. A former inmate, Charles L. Clark, even claimed that in the summer of 1894 the penitentiary introduced the "humane treatment and mild self-government" that Osborne later made famous at Sing Sing. Twice weekly, Clark wrote, prisoners enjoyed recreation in the yard, and if any "hoodlum" started a fight he never did again because he would be "properly slugged by others" as an example. Warden Otis Fuller of nearby Ionia Reformatory stated in his 1909–1910 report that in recreation his reformatory served as a model for Michigan State, which adopted Ionia's successful experiment of a half-day in the yard in good weather each holiday and three-quarters of an hour each work day.

In any case, according to Michigan State's own reports, by 1914 baseball was a fixture at the penitentiary, with regular Saturday afternoon games during the summer months. In 1923 *Playground* reported that the prison's first team played outside clubs on Sunday afternoons, and in addition its lesser teams played each other and those of the prison's annexes.

Baseball at Michigan State reached its meridian in the 1930s. It constituted the principal piece in the penitentiary's comprehensive recreation repertory. By that time the establishment actually consisted of two prisons, the Old Prison on the outskirts of Jackson, known as the O.P., and the New Prison, not completed until mid-decade, located about three miles north of town and called the N.P. The varsity team of each prison played the other as well as a mixture of outside opponents, occasionally on the latter's own grounds. Sometimes the two prison varsity teams joined forces, the pick of their players uniting against the cream of an industrial league's talent, for example. Each prison also fielded a second varsity team.

Inmates at Michigan State were allowed an hour weekdays as well as all Saturday afternoons, Sundays, and holidays for recreation. A physical director headed the overall program, and another official managed the baseball portion of it, with a third acting as field manager, who selected and organized the players. Funds for recreation came largely from inmate contributions and tickets. It cost thirty-five cents to see a game. As of September 1931, the O.P.'s recreation fund amounted to $2,751.61. The N.P.'s fund totaled $7,829.14, more than six thousand of it contributed by the inmates, but after expenditures for movie and stage equipment the account showed a deficit of $2,764.95. In June the N.P. installed its baseball players in a new clubhouse back of the laundry, with the boxers.

A strong supporting arm of the Michigan State penitentiary's recreation program was the prison paper, *School News*. It gave ample coverage to baseball, and much of what follows is based on its files in the penitentiary archives. Although it concentrated on the two prisons' first varsity teams and details of their games, in addition it devoted space to the second teams and to intramural games.

School News also reported intelligently on varsity team affairs in general. Nor did it shy away from criticisms. Subsequent to a defeat by Pleasant Lake in May 1932 the paper admonished, "Warming the bench with some of the best players we have is not going to win ball games." In 1933, referring to the N.P. team's performance, the *School News* reporter complained of the number of errors, from five to twelve per game, or a total of sixty-one since the beginning of the season. "With five thousand men to choose from," said the reporter, the prison should have a winning team.

Later, after a 10–2 defeat, *School News* waxed philosophical. "There is a saying that chastisement is good for the soul, and if that saying is true, then surely the M.S.P. baseball club was reduced to a state of true humility by the thorough trouncing they took at the hands of the Pleasant Lake outfit last Saturday." In 1934 following the loss of a doubleheader to two industrial teams, the paper castigated the prison team for its "ragged play." The pitching was good, but again the men made too many errors—fourteen in two games. The club had "nine players outfitted in nice looking uniforms, but they haven't got a ball team." They should "go through some stiff fielding sessions and stop shirking their work." Some of their hitters were "just as good, if not better than any group of Triple A hitters in the country but they made themselves ridiculous" swinging at bad balls. They ran bases "like a blind rabbit in a rain." Bats and gloves should be donated to "the Old Men's Home."

Some Michigan State players took this sort of fault-finding amiss. They "don't like it when we criticize their ball playing or boxing and regard it more or less as a personal matter," said the *School News* reporter, but they should not, because he was "more than ready to give credit wherever possible . . . but we will always . . . report the figures and ball games as they are." The N.P. team, in fact, drew praise that season of 1933: "The team seems to have developed a real team spirit instead of individual playing and there is real harmony among players."

The prison press also sprinkled its copy with humor, at times somewhat heavy-handed. The reporter claimed overhearing in the O.P. dugout, "That batter can't hit hisself in the face!" After the O.P. team defeated the Sunoco

Cardinals in 1933, the visitors, said the *School News*, although they had *SOC* on their uniforms, "their socks were few and far between" and judging by the score" (9–0, prison) perhaps it stood for "sure-out club." The manager of the champion prison Vocational team, according to the prison paper, claimed that he had a pitcher with an unbeatable change of pace: "he can throw a ball through a wire fence" or "throw one so slow you can walk with the ball while it is in the air and write your name on it." A lopsided loss in 1934 to Detroit's Friendship Lodge moved the reporter to wonder how the visitors had the fortitude to use the word "friendship . . . when they come into this poor defenseless territory and attack our unsuspecting hurlers with the unwarranted savagery they displayed."

The Michigan State Penitentiary house organ remained sensible of the difficult task of a prison team's manager. Such a man "must have the happy faculty to combine discipline and praise skillfully. . . . Prison ball players are more temperamental than opera stars and handling them is a much more tedious job." The paper took cognizance of the interest of players in the major leagues, too. It printed National and American League schedules for the first week of the 1931 season as well as a "dope sheet" on the teams prepared by an imprisoned "demon baseball statistician." It even reported with shock the deaths of American League president Ban Johnson and of his successor Ernest S. Barnard. The progress of the nearby Detroit Tigers received coverage, as did important big-league games, and the World Series always commanded attention. One year the paper offered a prize for the correct guess on the outcome of the Series. In 1931 its reporter noted that the administration had installed a new loudspeaker in the prison bleachers for broadcasting big-league games and music during yard privilege time. Once it reported the admiring view of an opposing pitcher. Batted from the box early in a game won by the O.P. 15–8, he commented, "They ain't human, they hit everything."

As far as baseball was concerned, the system at Michigan State functioned smoothly, considering the number and character of the residents. Spring and baseball were synonymous at the penitentiary. To the average person, said the prison paper at the beginning of the 1931 season, it was spring, "but to us behind the walls it is 'Baseball Time.' " In 1933 around two hundred prisoners tried out for the varsity, but only about four players were thought good enough to displace veterans of the previous year, despite the fact that some claimed semipro or minor-league experience and one even a tryout with a big-league club. Administrators eventually found it necessary to organize tryouts: in 1935, those desiring a trial had to write a note to the director of education describing where and how long ago they had played. Besides a first and second team, the director planned a third team for that year, the O.P. having been closed and the talent consolidated. In response to the request for written applications, the director received eighty-five letters.

At the 1931 opener the band played on an elevated stand, and about 3,800 men attended. Said the paper, "The only reason that the crowd was held to that amount was, there was no more." Special sports celebrations marked holidays. On Memorial Day that year the morning began with a field meet with cash prizes for winners, and after dinner the varsity played a baseball game with Toledo University.

The profusion and variety of outside teams that played Michigan State provides striking testimonial to the ubiquity of baseball in pre–World War II America. They represented industries, towns, police, firemen, lodges, colleges, labor unions, ethnic groups, and service clubs. A few examples will suffice. In 1932 the Michigan State College Spartans from Lansing beat a combined O.P.-N.P. team, and Abe Ellowitz, Spartan first baseman and football star, hit the longest homer ever hit at Michigan State Penitentiary: 472 feet 6 inches. The college's own newspaper said the homer "caused the crowd of 4500 spectators to gasp for breath." In 1931 the Capital City Cops (the Lansing Police) played Michigan State Penitentiary, and the prison paper commented, "Quite a spectacle that—a bunch of coppers playing a team of convicts."

Many industrial teams visited, for example the Indestructo Trunks of Indiana and the United States Wire Company. A frequent opponent was the team of the American Oil Company, whose manager, Paul Callahan, was one of the most popular men to come to the prison with a ball team and showed the inmates many favors—for instance, he always brought a box of candy for the home players. As might be expected in Michigan, many of the visiting industrial teams had connections with the auto industry. Blackhurst Chevrolet of Midland and Chrysler Jefferson Motor Corporation of Detroit both brought their teams in the thirties. The manager of the Chrysler team was the foreman of the paint department in Chrysler's Jefferson plant, and over a span of eight years he brought teams into the prison five different times, always leaving undefeated.

Other visiting clubs represented government, religion, political, and union groups. The New Prison defeated the Lansing Fire Department and the Knights of Columbus of Kalamazoo. A union team, the Federation of Labor of Pontiac, lost to the N.P., but the Northwest Democratic Club of Detroit shut them out 13–0 in 1933. Once in 1932 the O.P.'s second team beat the Dawn Donuts of Jackson, a team of "shy and bashful" lads under seventeen who had never played inside a prison before. One of the stars of that game was the son of a Michigan Penitentiary guard.

Some clubs came from out of state to play the prison team, but most of them hailed from such area towns as Flint, Hartford, Ypsilanti, Lansing, Grosse Point, Stockbridge, Ann Arbor, Pontiac, Dearborn, Detroit, Kalamazoo, and of course Jackson. At least one came from Canada: in 1932 the British American Brewers journeyed from Walkerton, Ontario, only to lose to the prison 22–2. In 1935 the consolidated prison team's manager, a prison officer named George Ashenbaugh, wrote to all teams who had beaten the prison inviting them to try it again. For a visiting team to bring fans along was not unusual. In 1932, for instance, when Blackhurst Chevrolet came to play the N.P., the auto team brought quite a few along, including the owner and publisher of the Midland *Times*.

Inmates commonly bet on the games. Often the convicts rooted for and bet on the outside team, and at times this perversity reached extremes, as when in 1934 they booed a fine performance of their own pitcher. The convict pitcher struck out thirteen in a game with Chrysler-DeSoto, and yet some fans, said the reporter in the prison paper, had the "gall" to boo that performance "because they had two packs of Stud wagered on the game. That booing turned the stomach of every good sport in the place. . . . Even the Chrysler boys couldn't fathom it and said so after the game." My own experience, when I accompanied a club that was to play the prison team at Rikers Island, New York, bears out this habit of rooting for the opposition: as the convicts filed lockstep past our players into the prison park, some muttered, prison-style, out of the sides of the mouths (talking was forbidden), "We hope you guys win" and other encouragement.

On the other hand, convicts could also be thoughtful and generous toward their fellow inmates. Tickets for games with outsiders at Michigan State had to be purchased, and in 1932 the prison paper commented,

> It is a most commendable spirit which actuates the men of the institution who can afford it, to give of their personal funds so those less fortunate can enjoy an afternoon watching one of the foremost teams in Michigan in action against our own Prison Team.

Once before a Sunday game in 1932, the O.P. versus Paw Paw, the team presented gifts to Swede La Crosse, a pitcher who was going home. He received a suitcase, a baseball kit bag, and other equipment useful for a traveling ball player. The presenter said "the boys" really appreciated Swede's helping the O.P. win most of its games thus far. Overwhelmed, Swede said he regretted leaving so many good friends, thanked the boys heartily for their wonderful gifts, assured them the presents would be his most cherished possessions, and wished them all early release. He then pitched a first-class game and hit a triple with his new bat. The O.P. won 18–3.

A chance to see major leaguers play always provided a special treat. The thriller of the Michigan State Penitentiary's 1931 season came the time Benny Frey, who hailed from a nearby town and played with the Cincinnati Reds, pitched for an allstar (O.P.-N.P.) team against another big leaguer, Guy Bush of the Chicago Cubs, pitching for Stockbridge, the Central Michigan champion. About a thousand outsiders and more than three thousand inmates attended. The convict team gave Frey good support, and he himself retired eleven on strikes. He "looked like a whole big league pitching staff to us," said the prison paper. Bush "seemed to get as much kick out of pitching for our entertainment as the boys in here got out of watching him pitch. He was continually grinning while on the mound and apparently was having a fine time." Before the game the prison paper cautioned readers that a crowd from downtown would be at the game, "so let's be careful what we say, for there will doubtless be numerous ladies present."

For prisoners, an opportunity to play outside the prison walls offered even greater refreshment. In 1932 the N.P. team played Ionia Reformatory as part of a home-and-home series, but the Reformatory won both games. In 1934 the prison varsity traveled all the way to Manitou Beach at Devil's Lake, where they defeated the American Oils and "inhaled some free air" before a good crowd that rooted for Jackson. The prison reporter remarked, "They have some swell scenery over at Manitou Beach and the water is very fine indeed, yes, sir, very fine indeed."

From time to time the Jackson prison paper cited individual players and listed their records. One such player, Napoleon Mitchell, was also the "colored heavyweight champion" of the prison in 1935, but he retired from the ring until the close of the baseball season. The prison reporter called Mitchell a "sweet prospect" for any semipro baseball team in the country. Another black team member, a pitcher identified only as Giles, in a 1933 game foiled an attempted squeeze play in a novel way: according to the prison reporter he prevented the batter from bunting the pitch by rolling the ball to his catcher, who tagged the runner coming home!

Michigan State prison teams maintained consistently good records. In 1933 they won 28 and lost 6 games. The 1935 team won 13 straight before losing to an allstar team of players from Jackson Twilight League clubs, but the year before, the prison paper had already announced that reporters throughout the country rated the Jackson penitentiary team the third best in the country, with only Sing Sing and San Quentin ranking higher. How the experts managed to deduce the relative ability of those teams remained "a little beyond my comprehension," the reporter remarked, since there was no way to compare the teams or to schedule competition among them.

San Quentin's rise to a level of baseball prominence comparable to Sing Sing's and Michigan State's dated from the appointment as warden in 1913 of James A. Johnson, former chief of Folsom Penitentiary. Johnson supplied a fresh impulse, revivifying and refurbishing the prison's recreation program with baseball as its kernel. Johnson began by holding, in 1914, an athletic field day conducted by the Olympic Club of San Francisco, of which he was a member. To promote the event he founded *Wall City News*, a one-page sporting sheet.

San Quentin officials soon announced the abolition of torture and the substitution of baseball for straitjackets. According to an ex-convict writing in 1928, the skepticism with which inmates greeted these measures dissipated when the administration issued privilege cards entitling each man to watch all baseball games and other entertainments unless he breached discipline.

In the main, San Quentin's baseball operation paralleled that of other prisons like Sing Sing and Michigan State. It ran two leagues of four teams each, the so-called minor league, which played Saturdays, and a major league playing Sundays. A varsity, called the All-Stars, chosen from the best players, dealt with outsiders, and in one four-year period the varsity lost only about five games to the strongest teams in the San Francisco area. Another team comprised the men serving life sentences, and one of them, sent to "the hole" (solitary confinement) for three weeks after stabbing a Mexican in a race riot, reportedly said when he emerged, "I thought out some swell plays to beat those guys next Sunday."

Most advantageous for baseball at San Quentin was the mild California climate, which permitted an eight-month season and brought an unusual number of professional ball players and teams to the prison because of the popularity of winter ball on the West Coast in the twenties and thirties.

Inmates at San Quentin kept individual and team records, and a monthly magazine printed accounts of games. As usual, inmates bet, generally tobacco, on the games—in violation of the rules, but, as Warden Johnson said in his book, *Prison Life Is Different*, "a little official blindness is a virtue." Some San Quentin prisoners, in order to insure their wagers, tried unsuccessfully to bribe an umpire or player.

At the close of each San Quentin baseball season Johnson gave the players what he called a "night-time feed" with "a few extras," an event that the prison paper inflated into "The Grand Annual Baseball Banquet." About half the prison population, the warden recalled, jockeyed to get invited to the affair by trying to convince him they had participated in baseball as player, umpire, scorer, groundkeeper, bat-carrier, or ball retriever. After the meal the warden presented the pennant to the champions and spoke on the banal themes of baseball's similarity to "the game of life," the necessity for cooperation, the importance of teamwork, and the value of sacrifice, all concluded with a tribute to such supposed exemplars of clean living as Ty Cobb.

By the 1930s San Quentin boasted one of the strongest teams in the West, aided in the early part of the decade by ex–big leaguer Jerome Downs, who took charge of baseball. Downs had played in 241 big-league games with Detroit, Brooklyn, and the Chicago Cubs and was serving an indeterminate sentence for robbing a jewelry store. So important was baseball in the thirties at San Quentin that the prison published a sports bulletin to replace *Wall City News* and to supplement the monthly magazine. Jammed bleachers testified to the popularity of baseball, and as well to the rise in the prison's population to about 6,000, according to then Warden James D. Holohan, from about 3,400 in the twenties.

Congestion sharpened awareness of the ameliorative aspect of prison baseball, and if the previously-mentioned San Quentin alumnus is to be believed, baseball did alleviate the frets and frictions of confinement at that prison. The ball players themselves, he said, were the best-behaved prisoners there. As for the rest, if it were not for baseball, San Quentin "would be a much tougher place." Baseball gave the prisoners something to think about, the former inmate explained. On the first three days of the week they discussed the previous Sunday's games, and on the following three days they busied themselves trying to pick winners for the coming Sunday. The dreary winter months were harder to "do" than all eight summer months put together, especially the monotonous Sundays sans baseball, relieved only by new arrivals claiming connection with some minor league, most of whom proved "dubs" come spring. Consequently, the former inmate pointed out, the fights and serious outbursts generally occurred in winter. Warden Johnson in effect endorsed the view that baseball, "the favorite form of recreation here," lifted spirits at San Quentin. It "furnishes the players," he told *Baseball Magazine* editor F.C. Lane, "with healthy exercise and the fans with a clean sport which they enjoy."

By the thirties, baseball at San Quentin had become mostly a spectator sport. A successor warden, Court Smith, acknowledged that more men needed to take part in athletics. The problem of space persisted, however. After visiting San Quentin in 1940 a representative of the National Prison Association pointed out that the two baseball leagues reached only "a fraction of the population" and declared that the administration should furnish all inmates with "daily, directed recreation."

At Folsom, California's other state penitentiary, baseball had by 1921 become the chief form of recreation, the state Prison Board reported. The 1929 National Prison Association handbook seconded this estimate, disclosing that funds for the recreation program came from interest on the prisoners' own money. In the thirties Folsom baseball maintained its popularity: "In this city of 3,000 [Folsom] two thirds of the population eat, sleep, drink, think, and talk nothing but baseball during the season," wrote Jack Montgomery in *Baseball Magazine*. Except when a visiting team came, the teams played in four-team leagues leading up to league playoffs—the most hotly-contested games—at the end of every season. Two special matches watched by everyone were annual games of the old-timers against the youngsters and the lifers against the varsity. "The players put heart and soul into every play," said Montgomery, "and men of 50 and 60 get right in there and root with the youngsters."

The reputation of Folsom's varsity baseball team was such that games with it had to be booked a year in advance, and outside teams traveled as much as fifty miles to play the prison. Each year, too, the Sacramento Solons of the Pacific Coast League played a game at Folsom before their season opened. Jimmy "Putt-Putt" Wright, a Folsom varsity player, demonstrated the height of prisoner devotion to baseball. After serving a six-year term he was to be released on the morning of a game with the Sacramento Sacs.

Knowing that the prison team was riddled with injuries, Wright volunteered to stay on and play. Folsom lost, but Wright got two hits.

Many prisoners felt indebted to baseball. An inmate of a California prison published a letter in the institution's bulletin written in the vein of a modern pop psychologist, expressing appreciation to prison officials for recognizing the benefits of sports and for realizing that "the human mind must have something to occupy it . . . or else it will create something to supply the lack," and at times that produced "undesirable results." The opportunity of "relieving our minds and exercising our bodies" through sports meant that many men, when their time was up, would go out of prison determined to be better citizens, he claimed, when otherwise

> our minds would perhaps be filled with the leaven of I.W.W.ism, Radicalism, and Redism—soured on society and the world in general. God save us from such! Three cheers for our baseball game played by the inmates ball league for 1920.

A poem of appreciation for prison baseball by a former inmate of the Ohio Penitentiary at Columbus, C.J. Doyle, doubtless reflected the sentiments of many prisoners:

> Taps for Sports
> The field of sports is desolate,
>   The baseball season's o'er;
> The goodly fun—'neath shining sun
>   Has lost its gay allure.
>
> A gallant sight it was to see.
>   Those men of pale-like hue,
> A-romping 'round—on sunlit ground
>   And gaining life anew.
>
> The distance from the cell house block
>   To baseball field is short,
> But worlds of space—between the place
>   Of ghost-like things and sport.
>
> The lines of gray will march again
>   Beneath the winter skies,
> With sprucer step—renewed with pep
>   As when the spirits rise.
>   • • •
> It was such a little thing,
>   To add such health and vim;
> A noble thing—a soulful thing.
>   We thank you! Warden Jim.

27

OTHER BREEDS WITHOUT THE LAW

In a variety of other institutions that introduced baseball before World War I, most of them less well-known than those already discussed, the game survived and in some gained strength in the decades between the wars.

In two such prisons, Walla Walla and Salem on the West Coast, baseball thrived. At the former, in Washington state, a varsity team played outside semipros Sunday afternoons, and each year it engaged Whitman College in a three-game series. Baseball also prospered as the principal sport in the Salem, Oregon, state penitentiary, where on holidays the first team played outside teams, among them their perennial opponents, the Chemawa Indians. Both Walla Walla and Salem maintained well-kept fields, the latter's situated in a separate section of the enclosure and used only for baseball.

The Kansas state penitentiary at Lansing underwent a decided transformation since early in the century, when it was identified nationally with the water cure. Encouraged by the authorities, inmates formed baseball and football teams to occupy their time. On Saturdays the institution's two leading baseball teams played each other or outsiders, among them some of the best semipros of Kansas City, Topeka, and towns in the vicinity. They also played home-and-home games with the federal penitentiary at Leavenworth and the disciplinary barracks at Fort Leavenworth. The prison band played at Saturday home games. Two successive wardens, W.H. Mackey in 1928 and Kirch Prather in 1932, in their respective reports, named baseball the principal sport of the Lansing penitentiary and praised it highly as a morale-builder. The National Prison Association, however, voiced its not unusual reservation, that the objective of the Lansing prison's recreation program seemed limited to "preserving contentment." Reflecting the popular concern in the thirties over the so-called problem of leisure, it added that the prison administration should instead be furthering rehabilitation by creating leisure-time interests.

The baseball program of the federal prison in Leavenworth, like that of similar institutions, consisted of games with outsiders played by the varsity and an intramural league of shop teams administered by a committee of inmates but subject to approval by a deputy warden. The large recreation yard at Leavenworth, already inadequate in 1928, reported the Prison Association's handbook, would probably be taken over for additional buildings because of overcrowding, in which case fenced recreation grounds outside the prison should be provided. Nevertheless, late in the thirties the wardens of the main prison and its annex reported a full baseball program still in operation.

Baseball became the chief sport at the Columbus, Ohio, state penitentiary where, in addition to daily games played by an intramural league, the prison's first team played not merely outside teams on Saturdays and holidays but also in an outside league. The prison paper, *Ohio Pen News*, covered these games and as well discussed professional ball and other professional sports. At the end of the thirties the forty-piece prison band opened all athletic contests. The Ohio penitentiary's best black players performed on the Colored All-Star team, which played the White All-Stars, but outsiders faced a mixed team, named Henderson's Hurricanes, after the warden, Frank D. Henderson, a former Army general who believed that sports took men's minds off troubles and made rehabilitation easier. In 1941 *Life Magazine* applauded the Ohio penitentiary program as one of the most comprehensive in prison sports.

The federal penitentiary in Atlanta continued its variegated recreational system, including baseball, funded by interests on prisoners' funds and money found in their cells and confiscated, as well as by the sale of old paper.

Some prisons stagnated, however. Nevada's state penitentiary at Carson City had no industry, so the inmates, in the yard all day, passed the time with informal baseball and handball, the predominant games. For want of sufficient room at the McAlester, Oklahoma, prison, baseball remained laggard. At Charlestown, Massachusetts, the state prison needed more recreation space. Baseball, Charlestown's only organized sport, was limited to games between prison teams scheduled by the deputy warden and to the posting of big-league team scores on bulletin boards throughout the building. Nevertheless, the warden declared baseball helpful in "maintaining order" and important in aiding prisoners to become "useful members of society." On the other hand, the state prison at Stillwater, Minnesota, although it had sufficient space, limited baseball, the only sport, to little more than a weekly game with outside teams.

Two Illinois prisons at Joliet presented a glaring internal contrast. The New Prison there provided ample space and operated a full baseball program of Saturday and Sunday afternoon games, probably with outside teams, and an intramural league of cell block teams playing each other. Joliet's Old Prison, a vestige of the pre-reform era, because of insufficient space permitted what passed for recreation only on the Fourth of July. This situation caused the National Prison Association to declare of Joliet's O.P. in 1929 that no other prison of the United States practiced "the repression that until a few decades ago characterized most prisons." A few years later, however, the superintendent of Illinois prisons, Frank D. Whipp, avoiding a specific reference to Joliet's O.P., claimed baseball at Joliet helped keep order, announcing that it would continue to be the major intramural sport at all Illinois prisons and that inmates preferred it to football. By decade's end the Joliet varsity reportedly played, and sometimes beat, an all-star team of major and minor leaguers managed by Ray Schalk, outstanding catcher of the Chicago White Sox.

Ironically, Auburn, the scene of Thomas Mott Osborne's first experiment with self-government embodied in the Mutual Welfare League, erupted in spectacular riots in July and December of 1929. The brunt of the blame for the riots fell on the M.W.L. and therefore on baseball as an adjunct to it. The outbreak revived the classic and still unresolved issue over the function of prisons and the treatment of prisoners: whether prisons should punish or rehabilitate, whether they should treat prisoners repressively or humanely. "The men in this institution," Warden Sullivan asserted, "have been coddled too much," and shortly thereafter a recommendation resulting from Governor Franklin D. Roosevelt's investigation called for the abolition of the Mutual Welfare League on the ground that it contributed to demoralization of discipline.

Not everyone agreed. The National Society for Penal Information denounced the ruling as hasty and ill-founded. Osborne's biographer, Rudolph Chamberlain, attributed the riots to overcrowding, not enough work to occupy everyone, bad food, bad sanitation, and the indifference of prison authorities to problems. After a personal investigation Professor Harry Elmer Barnes concluded that holding the M.W.L. responsible for the riots was "nonsense." The League did not work well, he said, because unlike Osborne the current warden failed to participate in its operation. Osborne's weakness, Barnes added, lay in his failure to distinguish between those who could be reformed and those who could not, and in any case a return to a repressive system would not work.

Baseball at Auburn had continued in the twenties despite a shortage of equipment and inadequate space, which the administration relieved somewhat by cutting down part of an avenue of trees. After the riots of 1929, when the M.W.L. ended, baseball went along with it. But by 1933 Warden Joseph H. Brophy reported to the National Prison Association that restoration of stability in the institution had permitted resumption of some recreation. Like dried-up vegetation after a monsoon, baseball at Auburn revived rapidly, assisted by the removal of a stockade fence that opened a large yard in which it could be played. Twelve baseball teams, each under its own elected captain, played intramural games under the Brophy regime, and a first nine played visitors in games arranged by the prison chaplain and conducted, without interference, by the inmates and their captain.

Prison baseball became well established nationally in the post-World War I decades. Prisons not only allowed baseball, declared *Playground Magazine* in 1923, they encouraged it. New York State made recreation part of its prison requirements in the late twenties, and a United States Department of Justice pamphlet stated about the same time that baseball had become "traditional" in American prisons. In the mid-thirties the *Encyclopedia of Social Sciences* called recreation in prisons "vital," saying only short-termers got little exercise. At the close of the twenty-year span following the war, a survey of 127 prisons by Norman Stone, director of the Riker's Island prison, named baseball as the most popular prison sport.

This author's own examination of records of about 50 prisons in addition to those already discussed reveal that at least 44 had baseball at some point during the twenties and thirties, and that 25 of them specifically named baseball as their leading sport or one of their main sports. These figures, together with the general statements complementing them, evidence the proliferation and popularity of baseball in the American prison system between the wars.

Describing the conduct of baseball in these fifty additional prisons would be largely to repeat the practices already set forth, but the data collected does offer some new tidbits. No prison official advocated baseball more staunchly than the deputy warden of Western State Prison at Bellefonte, Pennsylvania. In response to a *Sporting News* query, he wrote that baseball offered the prisoners an outlet for their "excess vitality," a sort of "safety valve." It taught cooperation to many "who have played the lone wolf" by showing them that laying down an occasional bunt would help the other fellow without hurting their batting averages. Teams at Western State, he went on, had the best equipment, and the entire prison population enjoyed both intramural and outside games. Never was there a case of disorder or a complaint from visiting teams; to the contrary, the prison received more requests for games than could possibly be accommodated, although visitors' only compensation was a free meal after the game (lodging was neither requested nor offered).

At the opposite extreme lay prisons hampered by serious problems of space in which baseball somehow survived. In the state penitentiaries of Bismarck, South Dakota, and Nashville, Tennessee, for example, tiny yards precluded regulation-size diamonds. In Maine's state prison at Thomaston players had to resort to a partly-filled quarry for games—"not ideal for baseball," as the National Prison Association's observer reported in 1935. Likewise, at Concord, New Hampshire, the prison's narrow yard included a fire plug between second and third base. So small was the recreation yard at the federal penitentiary at Alcatraz that a portion of the wall behind first base had to be padded to absorb the shock to players overrunning the bag.

Imprisoned baseball fans greatly enjoyed baseball's trade paper, *Sporting News*. The so-called restoration director of Western State Penitentiary in

Bellefonte, Pennsylvania, said the 900 men at his institution had access to it and that reading it took a great load off the prisoners' minds and gave them "good, clean, informative" reading. In the Trenton, New Jersey, prison twenty-five or thirty men read each copy of the paper. Such avid fans were some of the men there that they claimed willingness to do three months' extra time to see a Yankee-Tiger game.

Evidence that inmates paid close attention to professional ball as well as to their own games was the $100.00 first prize won in 1932 by Dannemora inmate number 30605 for the best letter to *Sporting News* in its all-star player selection contest. No wonder: his infield was composed of Gehrig, Frisch, Cronin, and Traynor; he chose Simmons, Averill, and Ruth for his outfield; and for his battery he named Grove, Earnshaw, and Cochrane. All except Earnshaw became members of the Hall of Fame.

In parts of the deep South where the prison system was apt to comprise a group of camps or plantations, each unit often had its ball team. In the Louisiana and Mississippi systems, for instance, teams of the various units played each other. Prison officials in Louisiana even formed their own team and played against the convict teams.

Once in Newark, Delaware, a jailer got so involved with baseball he forgot his responsibilities, with the result that a reverse jail break occurred. The New York Yankees were coming to Newark for an exhibition game, and factories and schools closed so that all the townsfolk could attend. The sheriff even told the jailer, Albert Lyons, to take his seventeen prisoners with him to the game. There the home team actually beat the Yankees, and Lyons, caught up in the celebration that followed, forgot all about his charges. The prisoners, like lost sheep without their shepherd, failing to find Lyons, returned to the jail for supper, only to find it locked and the irresistible odors of steak and coffee wafting out. They tried the window, but it too was locked. The cook finally opened the kitchen door, and they rushed into the dining room. That the French magazine *Revue de Paris* reprinted the story illustrates the absurdity of the incident as well as the propensity of humans to prefer food and shelter over freedom.

When a team of high-school-age players I accompanied to advise the manager played at the Riker's Island, New York, prison, we had a memorable experience. First we were told that every spring the prison team's excellent black catcher got himself arrested on a minor charge so that he could play on the prison team, and also that the names of the umpires were Hook and Steal! Then in the game that day, with our team leading 2–1 in late innings and a Riker's runner on first, the prison pitcher lashed a long, hard drive along the right field foul line. One runner scored easily and the hitter surely would have, putting Riker's ahead, but the umpire, running down the foul line for a close look, finally called the ball foul. Prisoners in the packed grandstand groaned and shouted in protest, and the situation became a bit uncomfortable, but two mounted guards rode forward and restored calm. After the crowd settled down, a prisoner stood up, cupped his hands to his mouth, and in a bullhorn voice shouted, "That's the trouble with this place, too many crooks!" Everyone, including the guards, laughed. The tension was broken, we held our lead, and we won the game.

As the adult penitentiaries groped toward more enlightened practices, the task of young men's reformatories grew more difficult because of their changed population. According to a New York state prison survey of 1920, private organizations, the spawn of the progressive era, like the Boy Scouts, Big Brothers, and Boys' Brigades, were catering to youths who committed minor offenses, thus siphoning off mild cases of criminality readily amenable to reform and hitherto handled by the reformatories, which were then left heavily populated with serious offenders.

If so, this change in the population of the young men's reformatories did not appreciably affect baseball there. An examination of records from three dozen of these institutions in 24 states, those reformatories already mentioned and others—including a few that, strictly speaking, were not reformatories but similar minimum security institutions—showed that all 36 employed baseball in the twenties and thirties. In 25 of them, baseball was either the principal sport or one of the principal sports.

Elmira, New York, for instance, remained a bastion of reformatory baseball, despite a shortage of money for proper equipment. The inmates supplemented state funds for athletic supplies with money they contributed to an athletic fund. In 1927 their funds amounted to $317.81, of which they spent $19.50 for a dozen bats and $209.76 for eighteen uniforms and six extra caps. Besides an intramural league of departmental teams playing a regular schedule, the Elmira reformatory team not only competed in the twelve-team Elmira city league but also won silver championship cups offered in 1921 and 1922 by the Chamber of Commerce and by Community Service respectively. We can only speculate on the reaction of the presumably law-abiding members of the league teams when the convicts beat them out for the prize! In addition, the reformatory varsity played local industrial, athletic club, and church teams, as well as the Elmira high school varsity. A rather touching comment in the inmate paper pleaded the importance of these ball games to the reformatory inmates. Recalling that three times in 1926 outside teams had forfeited games by failing to show up, the paper remarked,

> Of course, we don't blame these fellows for not wanting to come to prison, but, as they are privileged to come and go as they choose, we are sure they would not disappoint if they knew how much these games mean to us. It is through these things which, to the uninitiated seem trifles, but to us mean so much, that many of us are brought to look at life in a different way and are spurred to greater efforts to become men in every sense of the word.

Voicing his faith in the restorative powers of the game, Elmira's head said that any boy who came to him early enough and with a willingness to enter cheerfully into the system of games could be saved or cured, and that no boy who refused to join in should be freed because he would surely return to "dangerous pursuits."

Elmira instituted an even broader recreational program in the 1930s under a trained director. The reformatory not only encouraged but required inmates to take part. Baseball, still one of the principal sports, included both intramural and varsity games. Inmates who showed exceptional ability in the former were promoted to the latter, which played outstanding high school, church, and industrial teams on Saturday afternoons and holidays before the entire reformatory population.

Another baseball outpost was the Chicago House of Correction. Its monthly paper, with a circulation of several thousand copies internally and to other institutions, in 1922 asked all inmates who could play ball and wanted a place on a proposed varsity team to send in their names and state their experience. Some two hundred responded. After tryouts, managers picked first and second teams, which then played high school and semipro teams each Saturday and with permission of the state authorities planned to play other institutions, including the team then being organized at Joliet prison. *Playground Magazine* reported that House of Correction inmates allowed to see the games paid better attention to their work, improved their conduct, and evinced greater satisfaction and contentment than others.

Some reformatories showed signs in the late thirties of heeding the repeated urgings of the National Prison Association to shift emphasis from varsity to intramural baseball, among them the Concord, Massachusetts, and the Hutchinson, Kansas, reformatories. Concord instituted an organized system of recreational activities with the object of getting participation of as many as possible, thereby reducing "harmful use of leisure." The reformatory at Hutchinson emphasized intramural baseball and other sports in order for everyone to get a chance to participate. The superintendent there believed that it was "an established fact that athletics tend toward building up healthy bodies and minds" and that young men who took an active part made their sentences more bearable because they had less time to brood. Interest on the inmates' money and seventy-five percent of the profits from the canteen financed the Hutchinson program, reported the welfare committee's treasurer, thus making it unnecessary to ask taxpayers to pay for inmate amusement.

Even a few prisons began to fall in line in favor of intramurals. The National Prison Association lauded Iowa State Prison and the recently-opened Lewisburg, Pennsylvania, penitentiary for stressing participation. Nevertheless, the association complained that too many prisons still limited sports to the "varsity system," which left most inmates "in the grandstand as spectators of entertainment by the relatively few," whereas the true measure of a sports program remained the number who participate.

In the 1930s the federal government itself maintained two reformatories and several camps similar to them. One of the federal reformatories, at Chillicothe, Ohio, conducted an extensive program for young first offenders who were "immature, irresponsible" products of underprivileged backgrounds, as the superintendent reported. His program for them included organized intramural athletics, in which ninety percent of the men participated. Baseball was the major sport at Chillicothe. A league of dormitory and cell house teams in which 150 young men played was divided into four sections, and the four winners played each other for a trophy awarded by the Supervisor of Education. School and shop teams also played on weekends. Inmates repaired their own baseball equipment in the reformatory's shop. Chillicothe required few stands, the superintendent declared, first because most of the men participated, but also because no visitors could watch the few games played with outside teams. Since many of the young men who were inmates came from mountain districts, the superintendent said, and had no experience with "modern means of spending leisure time," at first he found it difficult to get them interested in the program, but once they finally took part they often developed a "different frame of mind," and many continued athletics after their release.

Chillicothe soon became overcrowded, so another federal reformatory opened near El Remo, Oklahoma. Its extensive athletic program, which featured baseball, differed somewhat from Chillicothe's in that its team played more games with outside teams, and only ten percent of the inmates played on the various teams, according to the superintendent's report, although a large number watched.

The several camps operated by the government in the thirties functioned primarily for men under thirty but included some who would otherwise go to federal prisons or were transferred from them as a reward for good behavior. Each provided education, recreation, and library services, and inmates performed hard work like building, clearing, moving, and salvaging. The federal reformatory camp at Petersburg, Virginia, emphasized athletics organized along Osbornian lines. An athletic council of elected representatives from each dormitory met with a civilian athletic officer to plan the activities. Often as many as 400 out of the 500 residents attended baseball games in the evenings after work between inmate teams and on Saturdays and Sundays with outside civilian teams.

Not to be overlooked in a discussion of institutional baseball were small, hardly visible groups of occupants on the ground floor in the House of Baseball who were akin to those in the penitentiaries and reformatories only in that they were confined, as were the mentally disturbed, or restricted, as were the blind. Not until near the close of the nineteenth century did the work of Dorothea Dix come to fruition and were the insane transferred from poorhouses and penal institutions to hospitals. In these institutions as early as the 1880s baseball came to be used as therapy.

The Maine Insane Asylum reportedly organized a baseball team in 1888. The medical superintendent of the Middletown, New York, State Hospital for the Insane emphasized in his 1890 annual report the remedial qualities of baseball, boasting that for two seasons his institution had operated an organized and fully equipped baseball club of "acknowledged skill and reputation" trained by an amateur player. This club had won twenty-one of twenty-five games played against noted teams. All institutionalized older groups, according to F.H. Nibecker, superintendent of an institution at Glen Mills, Pennsylvania, should have "baseball diamonds and all the essentials of regulation baseball" with a director to "enforce the ethics of sport." Nibecker made his remarks at the Playground Association meeting of 1909, where other speakers also cited baseball as one of the therapeutic agencies used at two institutions for epileptics, one in New Jersey and one in Indiana, as well as by the Danvers State Hospital in Massachusetts.

Two state hospitals for the insane in New York state used baseball in 1913. At one, teams of patients from the north and south wings of the institution competed for baseball supremacy. About this time two similar institutions in Washington state also provided opportunities for ball playing. At a hospital for the insane in Illinois, baseball was the chief activity for many patients, and at one in Rhode Island baseball provided physical stimulus and an energy outlet, according to articles in *Playground*, and it also developed sportsmanship and wholesome interests. Official recognition of the therapeutic value of play for neuropsychiatric patients was recognized, said *Playground*, by the authorization of the Veterans Bureau for construction of a six-acre recreation field, with a baseball diamond and football field, at a Veterans Hospital in the Bronx.

Institutions for "mental defectives," too, employed sport. As early as 1914 inmates at the Washington State Institution for Feeble Minded played "exciting games of baseball," and at the Napanoch, New York, Institution for Defective Delinquents in 1929 the sports equipment included baseball implements paid for partly by contributions from visitors.

In 1933 the United States Department of Justice opened a hospital at Springfield, Missouri, for treatment of federal prisoners with mental disease and chronic ailments like tuberculosis. Patients played baseball in the inner court, and prison camp inmates played it in the outer court, where their nine also engaged outside teams Saturday afternoons when games could be arranged.

Baseball has for a long time been used successfully with blind people. In 1939 *Playground* reported the San Francisco recreation department as using a baseball game that depended on sound, originated by R.V. Chandler of the Home for Adult Blind in Oakland. Several teams in San Francisco used it. The technique was similar to that used with blind children, as described earlier in this book. The only sighted person on the team was the pitcher, who did not bat or field. He rolled the ball to batters, who used a hockey stick. The ball contained "jinglers," and buzzers sounded to alert fielders when it was hit into their territory. Much later, Cornell University engineering students improved the game as beep-ball, which used a ball that beeped continuously once a pin was pulled from it.

The host of virtues attributed to prison and reformatory baseball gave the game the aspect of a panacea. These benefits may be thought of as a continuum, starting with claims that the game simply counteracted idleness among inmates. The next point on the continuum is the opinion that baseball diverted prisoners' attention from the undesirable to the acceptable and therefore actually improved prisoners' behavior and so tightened prison discipline. Beyond these, others credited baseball with making inmates into better persons. Thus baseball received praise for improving the mental and physical health of inmates and teaching them cooperation, teamwork, sportsmanship, and so-called constructive use of leisure—in brief, to shape character. Finally, some contended that playing baseball actually prevented crime by deterring those likely to commit it.

No doubt baseball (and other activities) influenced the outward behavior of prisoners. Idleness was a potent cause of disquiet, especially where civilian business interests compelled curtailment of prison-made products. By capitalizing on the inmates' interest in baseball, wardens reduced idleness and so dampened unrest. Furthermore, the privilege of baseball, either playing or watching, could be a disciplinary weapon for the warden, since he who giveth could also take away. It is likewise reasonable to believe that baseball helped to better the mental and physical condition of the players and, to some degree, the watchers.

Whether baseball had properties capable of altering the character and personality of prisoners remained questionable. To skeptics among the public, especially taxpayers and politicians, whatever baseball's impact on personality, it seemed inapplicable to convicts. Cognizant of the need to convince doubters who maintained that inmates were being coddled in country club settings, the wardens in their reports expounded on the presumed power of baseball to transform and rehabilitate prisoners. In these views they received outside support from the National Prison Association, recreation people, and boosters of baseball like *Sporting News* and especially *Baseball Magazine*, which gladly published the self-serving statements of wardens together with its own praises for prison baseball. Most of all, prison officials could count on general support or at least acquiescence in a society in which the cult of baseball was already firmly implanted and on the way toward superseding Marx's opiate.

Indeed, if the claims for baseball as an agency of rehabilitation were valid, prison conditions, like overcrowding and dissatisfaction with the sports program, presented enormous obstacles to demonstrating it. James V. Bennett, director of the Federal Bureau of Prisons, said in 1938 that even the federal prisons were chronically crowded, by as much as fifty or sometimes a hundred percent. In addition, a 1940 study of a supposedly typical prison found paradoxically that the baseball program, instead of solving problems, created some—gambling and contention, for example. The description of baseball at this prison varied considerably from the picture received from studying wardens' reports and articles in popular periodicals. At this typical prison, most of the incarcerated men at games were spectators and did not even like the prison team. They thought its members were stoolpigeons and, knowing the guards out of loyalty wanted the convict team to win, rooted for the visiting team. Some of the older men who were never fans disliked the baseball program, complaining of the hard benches and the restriction of movement that watching compelled. Sophisticated inmates bet on the games, but as the season wore on interest faded and bickering flourished.

Nevertheless, the National Prison Association continued its support for sports. In the 1940s it asserted that recreation was not "a luxurious privilege. It is a vital necessity," and recommended that a trained director be employed to develop esprit de corps by organizing and conducting athletics. The association also issued three pages of standards for prison recreation.

Belief in baseball's curative power has suffered further erosion in the years since the thirties. It is still debated, for example, whether power-sharing, of the Osborne type, with prisoners leads to any improvement in discipline or any lessening of prison violence. And Max Kaplan, an author of books on leisure, pointed out in 1960 that although it is possible that learning can be transferred, the "notion that skills, attitudes, or virtues are automatically transferred from one activity [like baseball] to another" has been abandoned—"Actually, one can be a first-rate 'sport' on the playground and a scoundrel away from it." A prison official in Indiana, Mike Misenheimer, asserted in 1970 that

> baseball has very little rehabilitating value in spite of such terms as "team play," "responsibility," and "discipline." What it does is give some degree of badly needed emotional release, burn up energy that might otherwise be used destructively, and provide both the fan and the player with hours of simple pleasure. But it has damn little to do with transforming a criminal into a law-abiding citizen.

Perhaps an unrecognized benefit of sports is the wry humor they sometimes seem to inspire even in prisons, as in the popular prison song "Eleven More Months and Ten More Days," by Arthur Fields and Fred Hall, recorded in 1929 by Columbia. It contained this stanza:

> Now, we play baseball once a week
> And you should see the score.
> Ev'ry player steals a base—

They've stolen things before.
There's lots of folks would like to come
And see us when we play,
But they've built a wall around the place
To keep the crowd away!

PART FOUR

THE HOUSE OF BASEBALL:
THE ANNEX

28

WHO EVER HEARD OF A GIRLS' BASEBALL CLUB?

From their annex adjacent to the House of Baseball, women exerted relatively modest influence. Their presence in the House emerged from the women's movement in nineteenth-century America, and their entry was difficult because, as Professor Gerda Lerner has stated, "By indoctrination, training, and practical experience women [had] learned to accept and internalize the beliefs which would keep them 'adjusted' to living in a subordinate status in a patriarchal world."

Limits on women's participation in sport stemmed from the tangle of prejudice and stereotype that had long enmeshed them. One limit was the stereotype of the delicate, sickly, passive female, with its fashionable diseases, worsened by harmful and even brutal treatments for "female complaints" inflicted on women by male physicians. Another restraint was the obsessive belief of society in women's primary goals as marriage and motherhood. A third inhibiting idea, that women should behave in a "genteel" manner, placed them on a pedestal where, loaded down with some thirty pounds of unfunctional clothing, they found about as much freedom to maneuver as the footbound women of old China. Feminist Carrie Chapman Catt once recalled those days when women were thought incapable of throwing a ball. She blamed their clothing for keeping them from engaging in athletics. Such limitations affected middle- and lower-class women who, as "ladies," had been part of the American scene since Colonial days. The new slant, Lerner has noted, was the lady as a cult.

Before "ladies" could participate in physical activities more strenuous than serving tea, they had to dispel the conventions that restricted them, and from early in the nineteenth century some tackled this formidable task. By mid-century women had coalesced from isolated fringe groups into a broad-gauged movement signalled by the Seneca Falls Women's Rights Convention of 1848.

The connecting principle coursing through this movement was action, a theme that would help lead to women's participation in baseball. As the heroine in Charlotte Brontë's *Jane Eyre* said,

It is vain to say human beings ought to be satisfied with tranquility: they must have action. . . . It is narrowminded . . . to say that [women] ought to confine themselves to making puddings and knitting stockings, to playing on the piano and embroidering bags. . . .

The process of dissipating the superstition against exercise and, by extension, sports, for women began in the 1820s and 1830s with calls for calisthenics, gymnastics, and games by such leaders as Sarah Josepha Hale, who as editor of *American Ladies Magazine* published articles favoring exercise, and later as editor of *Godey's Lady's Book* she printed the recommendation of a Glasgow physician recommending that girls be given as much freedom as boys and be allowed to run, leap, throw a ball, and play battledore as they pleased. The *Journal of Health* urged riding without a corset. *The Casket* printed woodcuts illustrating calisthenics for women, and the *The Mirror* urged athletic exercises. Amelia Bloomer's *The Lily* advocated ball-throwing, and in the same publication Elizabeth Cady Stanton asserted that women might be strong physically "if the girl were allowed all the freedom of the boy in roaming, swimming, climbing, and playing hoop and ball." But as late as 1862 an *Atlantic Monthly* article declared girls must be kept from "over-exerting" because athletic girls could make themselves into invalids.

Early on, some men backed women on the score of exercise and games. William Russell, who started the *American Journal of Education* in 1826, advocated riding and walking, and some male physicians gave attention to physical training for women. John Warren, for example, in 1846 declared girls should play ball with both hands. Walt Whitman looked forward in *Leaves of Grass* to "hardy" women and added, "I say a girl fit for these states must be free, capable, dauntless, just the same as a boy."

Simultaneous with these representations, educational institutions began to spring up that would become a conduit for putting them into practice and a steppingstone to women's baseball. Founders of the female seminary, a type of secondary school and the first such institution, recognized the value of exercise for women. Emma Willard at Troy, New York, Mary Lyon at Mount Holyoke, Massachusetts, and Catharine Beecher, who ran several schools, used such activities ad walking, riding, dancing, and light gymnastics to improve the health of women. Beecher in particular committed herself to physical training in schools and wrote two influential books on the subject.

In brief, as Professor Roberta Park has shown, before the Civil War some rejected the argument that woman's physiology rendered her inferior and spoke up for calisthenics, games, exercises, less-confining clothing, active recreation, and more physical activities.

Girls and women were not raised in a vacuum with respect to baseball. Even in the colonial era they knew of such related games as barn ball and stool ball, and in the late eighteenth century they saw boys and young men on village greens engaged in various versions of baseball. English milkmaids had long played stool ball, an early ancestor of baseball, and women probably played it in America. (It is ironic that the game of baseball, so closely associated with men as to become a male preserve, should have a partly feminine origin.) Some so-called tomboys must have given other ball games a try. And some women had from the 1840s onward been familiar with the more modern style of baseball as played by the New York Knickerbockers and their contemporaries, having attended these games and enjoyed social evenings afterward.* Women at the 1858 All-Star series between New York and Brooklyn were even seen making small wagers on the game.

The Civil War slowed the women's movement, and after the war it lost much of its cohesion. Exclusion from the thirteenth and fourteenth amendments providing black males with civil rights dealt women a painful setback. Moreover, women were often their own worst enemies. For example, Meg admonished her sister Jo, the tomboy of *Little Women*,

> You are old enough to leave off boyish tricks, and behave better, Josephine.
> It didn't matter so much when you were a little girl, but now you are so tall,
> and turn up your hair, you should remember that you are a young lady.

Far more popular even than Louisa May Alcott's book was Augusta Evans Wilson's *St. Elmo* (1867), a virulent denunciation of suffragettes as "crazy fanatics" and "embittered old maids."

Women's rights advocates nevertheless persisted, and in the 1870s and 1880s education for females moved beyond the seminaries into an era of women's college foundings, a development that led quickly to women's college baseball.

Ironically, women's participation in college sport grew out of assumptions of their delicacy. Skeptics, especially physicians, warned that women's physical weakness unfitted them to withstand the stress and strain of college study and would damage their health. E. H. Clarke, a retired Harvard professor of medicine, in his book *Sex in Education* (1873), used "research" based on seven Vassar students to conclude that American methods of education contributed to female weakness and that the regimen of male colleges would make it worse. Clarke's book went through seventeen printings and brought agreement from G. Stanley Hall, the panjandrum of psychology, ridicule from Michigan State students, refutation notably in a book of similar title by Julia Ward Howe and others, and testimony contradicting it from alumni of a number of colleges, including Vassar, during the 1870s and 1880s.

Such caveats as Clarke's boomeranged: if young women were too weak to bear the rigors of college study, answered supporters of women's physical activity, all the more reason to make them fit by providing gymnasiums, appointing instructors, and requiring calisthenics and gymnastics. Led by those in the East, college after college for women began to do just that. Sports in women's colleges often developed directly out of their physical training.

*See *Baseball: The Early Years*, pp. 18, 21, 29, 31, 38, 40–42.

Coincident with this trend was the work of Dudley Sargent of Harvard and Amy Morris Homans, a physical training teacher. Sargent opened a gym for women in 1881 in Cambridge, where beginning with six students he trained women to teach gymnastics. So great was the interest that by 1891 the project had evolved into the Sargent School for Physical Education, a major source of gym teachers for colleges. Sargent also supplied gym apparatus.

Homans, financed by Boston philanthropist Mary Hemenway, founded her own gym school in Boston in 1889 and, as Professor Betty Spears put it, became a "one-woman placement bureau," placing her graduates in colleges and YWCAs all over the country, including the prestigious colleges of the East. Among her students were Senda Berenson, director of physical education at Smith 1892–1911, who brought basketball there, and Ethel Perrin, another prominent advocate of women's sports, who became supervisor of physical training in the Detroit public schools. Homans's goal of creating a cadre of trained teachers fit in with women's pressure for adoption of gymnastics in public schools, and according to writer Shelley Armitage by the 1890s most American schools had gyms and sports programs for women.

Like most innovations, the introduction of physical training programs encountered opposition, for example from outraged parents of Newcomb College students in New Orleans. Even physical training instructors disagreed over policy. In search of order, like so many groups of the period, they had organized in the 1880s, and at their 1894 convention they argued over the use of heavy apparatus by women. Sargent supported it but Luther Gulick deplored it. Dr. Eliza Mosher argued that it should be started in childhood so that most women and girls could then engage in it with ease.

Proper Victorians also clucked in dismay over the costumes required for exercise. A French visitor to the United States in 1894 remarked upon the Bryn Mawr girls she saw exercising in an unconventional costume consisting of loose Turkish trousers, shirtwaist, leather belt, black silk stockings, and heel-less shoes. Other colleges used similar outfits. Sargent told a story of a shocked young woman from the Midwest who headed a group of visitors to his school: gazing at the gym costumes of the East, she exclaimed, "Well, this is a hell of a joint!" turned on her heels, and fled by the nearest door. Sargent also said southern girls, unwilling to let men see them in unmaidenly bloomers, wore skirts until they found that in the course of the exercises they were expected to perform, skirts revealed more than bloomers. Gym suits at Mount Holyoke caused dismay, too, as a poem in the 1899 college annual shows:

> Who is this shrinking maiden
> With horror she is mute
> A modest little freshman
> Beholds her first gym suit.

As with college men, however, sports had greater appeal for college women than did the dull drill of calisthenics and gymnastics, and physical training directors began a search for an indoor game suited to the confines of a gym. They devised and tried various games, including an ancestor of softball played with short distances between bases, underhand pitching, a broomstick or similar implement for bat, and a projectile that could be hit only a short way, such as a boxing glove wrapped in twine. They finally solved their indoor game problem with the overwhelming success of basketball, probably invented in 1891 at the behest of Luther Gulick by James Naismith of the YMCA Training School at Springfield, Massachusetts, although the claim has recently been disputed.

By the time basketball became popular indoors, outdoor sports had already sprouted on women's college campuses. Leading the way as a rule were relatively tame lawn sports: croquet, archery, and tennis in its pat-ball stage. These sports promised to keep upper- and middle-class parents mollified. Baseball, however, became the first active team sport for college women. It began as early as the 1860s with students sometimes playing scrub and interclass games. Gaps that appear in women's college baseball records do not necessarily mean that students did not play baseball in those intervals: some college authorities out of deference to parents may have banned the game officially for a time while letting it be known on campus that they would look the other way if students continued to indulge discreetly.

Vassar, for instance, chartered in 1861 and opened in 1865, from the outset boldly grasped the nettle of physical education and sports. It made provision for a gym and a riding school in its original plan and stated openly in its prospectus that sports and games would be offered along with calisthenics, instructing students to bring suitable outdoor clothing.

Frances Wood, who came to Vassar in 1867 as a substitute teacher and became the college librarian, wrote in her book *Early Vassar* (1909), "It was a wonderful thing when Vassar opened for a girl to have the chance to go to college" and recalled that from the first, Vassar provided baseball and croquet clubs, horseback riding, and even a bowling alley. Moreover, the initial issue of *The Vassariana* (1865–66), the first Vassar student magazine, reported two baseball clubs on campus in the spring of 1866, the Laurel Base Ball Club with twelve members, including four officers, and the Abenakis Base Ball Club with eleven members, three of them officers.

Frances Wood also remembered that "it took a good deal" (of courage) to organize such activities "in the face of popular opinion at the time," a comment that may account for the fact that baseball fails to appear in Vassar's chronological list of important college events until 1875, when the list states that three baseball clubs, the Sure-pops, the Daisy-Clippers, and the Royals formed. A freshman that year, Sophia Richardson, in fact claimed much later that seven or eight baseball clubs formed "suddenly" in 1875, at the suggestion, she thought, of the college physician, a Dr. Webster. The public, said Richardson, disapproved, but the students continued to play in their "retired grounds. . . . protected from observation . . . by sheltering trees. . . . " One day a student fell while running the bases and injured her leg, and the baseball players feared the accident meant the end of their games. Webster, however, remarked that if the student had hurt herself while dancing, the public "would not condemn dancing to extinction." A few days later a Vassar student did fall while dancing and broke her leg. So the baseball teams continued playing "with the feeling somewhat lightened that we were enjoying delightful but contraband pleasure." Although interest in baseball at Vassar waned (Richardson thought disapproving mothers exerted pressure against it) and incoming classes did not form teams, her own class continued to support two clubs until its senior year, 1878–79, and indeed the Vassar archives contain an 1876 photo of "The Resolutes," in long skirts and regular baseball caps, but it is mislabeled "The First [team]."

Smith College, founded in 1871, began with gymnastics conducted by a former pupil of Dio Lewis, who himself in an 1871 book, *Our Girls*, approved of baseball clubs formed by young women. Where regular exercises were prescribed, sports were not far behind, and a document in the Smith College archives reveals that Smith students soon organized baseball teams spontaneously. Minnie Stephens, an 1883 graduate, wrote later describing with the flavor of an old-time movie serial how baseball began at Smith in 1878. Feeling a need for some "lively games," Minnie gathered a few friends and organized a baseball club. They had no place to play except the front lawn of Hubbard House, which although "not ideal . . . did very well for beginners." One summer evening, their plans yet incomplete, Minnie and another student while taking a long walk wandered into a Northampton neighborhood "more or less foreign and different," where they chanced upon a baseball bat lying on the ground—"a special providence," since "We would need a bat and there it was!" No one was around, so Minnie picked it up and "proudly carried it over [her] shoulder." On they went, Minnie "making occasional gyrations with the club" when suddenly an "awful yell smote the air. We looked behind us" and to "our amazement and horror" saw about "two dozen dirty little boys running after us as fast as they could, shouting 'Gimme my bat. Gimme that bat. . . . !!' What could we do? The number of pursuers was increasing rapidly and we were facing trouble if not tragedy." So Minnie flung the bat as far as she could toward the boys and "we ran for our lives. If anyone had seen us," she wrote, "we would have been chosen for the Olympic games. . . . " After they escaped, she said, they decided that thereafter they would "get their balls and bats in the accustomed manner."

After the Smith girls organized a second baseball team in order to have competition, they staged what Minnie Stephens called "a wonderful match, never equalled in the history of athletics for intelligent gentlewomen," in which one "vicious batter" drove a ball "into the belt line of an opponent" and, had it not been for "the rigid steel corset clasp worn in those days, she would have been knocked out completely." When the game resumed, the second nine, all "more intelligent since they all wore glasses, which was then a sure test of brain power," tried again, "only to have their glasses knocked off." The result was "hysterics," and the game was over "for the time being."

Smith College authorities then declared baseball "too violent" and pointed out the danger of breaking windows in Hubbard House. The girls were "politely ordered to give it all up," although according to Stephens "the fire of the base ball club still smouldered." She was right, as confirmed by a story in the Boston *Herald* of May 1892 in which the reporter described a game between Smith freshmen and sophomores. Judging it "great ball," he thought the freshman pitcher, Laura Woodberry, who wore glasses and a long braid, "pitched a good game," especially in the second inning, when her "good curves" made the sophomores "bat the air." (After graduating, Woodberry became a physician.) Her catcher, Margaret Long, used a mask and glove. (Long, daughter of the ex-governor John Davis Long, eventually became a social worker.) The sophomore catcher, however, used neither mask nor glove, and the sophomore pitcher had an "amazingly swift delivery." Nevertheless, the freshmen made some "terrific drives away out under the apple trees," including home runs with bases full by Woodberry and Long. The reporter could not resist quoting an exchange he heard from the field when the freshman center fielder caught the ball with her clothing: The umpire called, "A muff," but the fielder responded, "No, my skirt, Mary." Two outs retired the side, and "with the dinner hour near," the three-inning game "adjourned" 29–9 in favor of the freshmen.

In the spring of 1898 and 1899 Smith's Dickinson House baseball team, called the White Squadron, and teams from other residences played inter-house ball games. Student Rachel Studley's team, as she described in a letter written years later, practiced with a regular hard ball that had been used in an Amherst-Williams game. Team members elected their pitcher and catcher, and a "wonderful umpire" enforced the rules. Smith furnished no ball field, so the teams usually payed between Dickinson and Hubbard houses. Once someone asked President Laurenus Clark Seelye (1873–1910) if he did not think it "very unladylike" for the students to be playing baseball "just like men." President Seelye asked the inquirer if he had ever watched the women play, and the man said no. "Then," the president replied, "You wouldn't say they played like men." Anyway, Studley wrote, "He didn't stop us."

Conventional attitudes at Smith remained strong, however. At the turn of the century, wrote Minnie Stephens (actually it was 1904), her husband, Frank Gates Allen, gave an athletic field to the college, but the president and trustees reportedly considered the "obvious and natural name," Smith College Athletic Field, objectionable because it contained the word "athletic" and so was "inconsistent with the aims of an institution for higher education of gentlewomen." They called it Allen Field instead.

At Mount Holyoke, officially chartered as a college in 1893, students played baseball at least as early as the 1880s. In view of the long tradition of physical exercise dating from Mount Holyoke's seminary days under Mary Lyon, which began with required walks and proceeded through calisthenics and gymnastics to boating and tennis, probably informal baseball games took place early. Strengthening this assumption is the first archival clue, a photograph of the 1884 baseball team, believed to be the college's first formal team, showing nine young women uniformed in long striped dresses, blouses with crisscrossed strings like those of the men of the era, and caps lettered *MHC*. Such an organized, uniformed team must have been the outcome of prior baseball experience on campus rather than of sudden impulse.

This supposition is fortified by an 1887 article in the Lowell, Massachusetts, *Daily Courier* praising the college's program of sports for young women and mentioning daily walking, boating, tennis, and skating, according to the season. Although the writeup omitted mention of baseball, in such an environment it seems likely that students continued to play it if only on an informal basis.

In 1891, according to Mount Holyoke records, baseball instituted by student clubs became the college's first organized team sport. *The Mount Holyoke* described the baseball scene on campus that spring:

> Out first base ball club, organized during the spring term, has flavored the average conversation with "strikes," "innings," "home runs," etc. The diamond is in the quadrangle, and with the slopes above fitted out for spectators the Greeks would have thought it an ideal theater. Already the members have gone through most of the experiences naturally connected with the game, though disabling the umpire is a pleasure in store for the future.

A further comment in the Mount Holyoke periodical reveals the presence of baseball at other women's colleges in the area: "The [baseball] organization was completed so late that they will not play in the intercollegiate league this year but doubtless next season they will compete on equal terms with the nines of other colleges." In the mid-nineties, Mount Holyoke students also formed and operated an athletic association, holding field days on which students took part in the popular "baseball throw'" contest.

Wellesley's founder, Henry Fowle Durant, realized that success of the college depended on healthy students, so Wellesley, like Vassar, emphasized physical training and sports from its beginning in 1875. As with Mount Holyoke, although baseball received no mention in Wellesley's archives until later, students doubtless played it informally early on. By the mid-nineties the college boasted baseball as part of a full-blown program of outdoor "educational and recreational sports" carried on at the campus's three-acre Playstead under the supervision of an athletic association supplemental to but not governed by the physical education department. Each student decided on the amount of play to take part in. These "pleasure players" received no instruction or regular practice but took part in "social sports" and played as studies permitted. The sport clubs included baseball clubs, although rowing usually had the largest membership, as might be expected in view of the lake in the center of the campus.

Bryn Mawr, opened in 1885, soon felt the impact of the remarkable M. Carey Thomas, who, after serving as dean, took over as president in 1894 and lasted until 1922. Dr. Thomas, a Cornell graduate and holder of a University of Zurich Ph.D., deplored the low academic level of faculties and students at some private women's colleges. She changed the character of Bryn Mawr from its original concern with moral discipline to emphasis on academic excellence, and she saw fit to provide a full complement of sports along with physical training. Bryn Mawr featured outdoor sports in the 1880s, and its athletic association reported in 1892 that students played baseball out of doors. At a field day that year the eight events included "throwing a baseball," and the winning toss measured 137 feet one inch.

By the 1890s team sport was an accepted part of college experience for women. Mills College in California, founded as a seminary in 1865, became a college twenty years later; in the 1870s young Mills women exercised by taking long trips into the hills, but soon baseball, the first outdoor team sport at Mills, became popular, along with quoits and croquet.

While college women underwent their sports baptism, all manner of opportunities, some involving sports, opened to women outside academia. The prime source of these opportunities lay in the industrial and technological revolution that reached full flood in the late nineteenth century. Jobs for women increased in number and variety, and by 1900 the number of women wage workers had climbed to five million, twice that of 1880. For some of these women the drudgery of sweatshop and mill at low wages would be relieved by playing ball on a company team.

For educated middle- and upper-class women, opportunities opened in callings that filled a social need, such as nursing, clerical and library work, and teaching. Social work, a theatre of action especially suited to educated women, gave them an opportunity to help reform social conditions, including working for playgrounds for children.

The path of emancipation remained steep, however. The magazine debut of the more active "New Woman" and the new ideal of feminine beauty expressed in the less-passive Gibson Girl of the 1890s did not completely undermine the Victorian ideal of womanhood. But women were experiencing a growing sense of self, as Professor Carl Degler put it, and creating a climate of opinion in which sports like baseball could grow. They disputed the latest notion put forward in medical circles: that leisured women were subject to a complaint called neurasthenia, caused by preoccupation with their inability to follow men's way of life. In rebuttal to this theory Dr. Mary Taylor Bissell declared that physical exertion provided woman as well as men with "endurance, activity, and energy, presence of mind, and dexterity." Dr. Clelia

Mosher amassed data proving that inadequate exercise and the weight of women's clothing, not "neurasthenia," caused many of their health problems. Others confuted the theory by example: author Harriet Beecher Stowe walked from five to seven miles a day at age seventy-five; reformer Charlotte Perkins Gilman did calisthenics and ran a mile daily.

The embryonic liberal trend reflected itself in the growing number of magazines that published serious articles on women's exercise and health, including *Munsey's, Scribners, Saturday Review, North American Review, The Nation, Science,* and *Business Women's Journal.* The safety bicycle, introduced in the mid-eighties, played an immediate role in making women's outdoor activity and less cumbersome clothing more acceptable. Frances Willard of the Women's Christian Temperance Union, who learned to ride a bike at age fifty-three, exulted in her book, *A Wheel Within a Wheel* (1895),

> The old fables, myths, and follies associated with the idea of women's incompetence to handle bat and oar, bridle and rein, and at last the crossbar of the bicycle are passing into contempt in the presence of the nimbleness, abilities, and skill [of women].

By then an estimated 30,000 women owned and rode bicycles.

Women began to enter the sports arena as never before. Frances Willard, in another book, *How to Win* (1886), urged girls to make "exercise in the open air" a daily habit and to "cultivate athletic sports." *Ladies Home Journal* suggested that "earnest girls" who wanted to "gain physically" band together and form an athletic club, as had a group in a New England manufacturing town, and obtain equipment for tennis, quoits, badminton, beanbag, and ball games. Such clubs still amounted to little, however, and at first working girls and immigrant women had only slight access to sports participation. On the whole, progressives gave little attention to the need of working women for exercise, although a few working women's clubs with exercise classes did open. Working women were thought to be inherently healthy, too tired from work to exercise, and at any rate more in need of "uplift." Sargent's school did offer setting-up exercises for working girls two evenings a week, and the YWCA began to feature physical education at many of its branches and to consider constructing gyms. Not until the turn of the century, however, did the Playground Association recognize the need of all women for recreation.

On the other hand, upper- and middle-class women's clubs proliferated, and some incorporated physical culture into their programs. A few organized for physical activities only. The Outing Club of Concord, New Hampshire, for example, formed in 1895 for "the promotion of outdoor exercise and healthful pleasure for women," favored bicycling and snowshoeing according to the season. The Dover, New Hampshire, women's club included among its seven units a Physical Culture Department. And Charlotte Perkins Gilman participated actively in a women's gym in Providence, Rhode Island.

The Chicago Women's Athletic Club, founded in the 1890s, served wives of industrialists seeking beauty through physical culture and offered a pool, gymnastics, and some basketball. The program of the Staten Island Ladies Athletic Club also included games. Even men's athletic clubs opened their doors slightly to women: the Brooklyn Athletic Club built tennis courts for them, and the New York Athletic Club condescended to allow them in the clubhouse twice a year. The Berkeley Athletic Club of New York, however, established a separate Ladies Athletic Club, reputedly first-class in every way. Noticing the trend, *Women's Home Companion* commented that the progress of women in business required them to have "a higher physical development." These clubs no doubt increased awareness of athletics among other women, but they carried on their athletic activities largely in private. About the only sports women could freely engage in publicly without "insinuations of rompishness" were croquet, archery, and to some extent lawn tennis and golf. Bicycling, for women, was more a gymnastic exercise than a sport. Mores of the times continued to make public participation in more strenuous sports like baseball exceptional.

Even as spectators at sporting events women were not always welcomed. Boston banned them from boxing matches in the 1880s, although some bluebloods were smuggled in by husbands or escorts, and the independent Boston society woman Mrs. Jack Gardner sponsored a bout herself for an exclusive audience from her own circle. In baseball, however, club backers not only received but sought female fans. After the Civil War baseball club owners, appreciating the financial and, so they thought, refining value of women's presence, went out of their way to secure their patronage by offering inducements like Ladies Days (free admission if accompanied by a man), special facilities in the ball parks, and, in some cases, even a ban on beer sales in the stands out of deference to their wishes.*

Such inducements to watch men's games helped stimulate women's interest in baseball between 1860 and 1890. In fact Mrs. Barney Dreyfuss, wife of the owner of the Louisville Club, remembered that before the turn of the century, for local women to visit the Louisville ball park was "something of a fad." Women also rooted as vociferously as the men. A New York press report claimed that at one game in the Polo Grounds, among those who stood on the seats and screamed were housewives, mothers, well-to-do women and girls, working girls (identified by their rough hands), and "sporting women." At another Ladies Day game women reportedly rioted when the umpire put a home-team player out of the game. Sports writer Fred Lieb once described the "Ladies Auxiliary" of the Philadelphia Athletics

*See *Baseball: The Early Years*, passim.

of the 1880s as having some members with "slightly tainted" reputations. They called themselves the "Big Bosom 'A' Gals." Without disparaging by faint praise, therefore, it may be said that the female fans equalled the male in intelligence and deportment.

Women connected with baseball more directly, too. As early as 1868 a woman reported a baseball game for a Cincinnati newspaper between the Muffins and the Biscuits. Another woman, Mrs. Elisha Green Williams, using her maiden name, secretly served as official scorer for the home games of the Chicago White Stockings from 1882 through 1891. At games Mrs. Williams usually sat between the wives of two players, but they remained unaware of her purpose, and neither her son, who mailed the scores, nor the league secretary, who received them, knew the scorer was a woman; only club president A.G. Spalding did. In the late eighties the wife of Detroit catcher Charlie Bennett made a significant contribution to baseball: worried over his safety, she designed, with his help, a chest protector that created as great a sensation when he used it as did Roger Bresnahan's shin guards.

Some spirited young women did not remain on the fringes of baseball. Like college students, they wanted to play the game themselves, but, unlike the collegians playing in campus seclusion, they had to brave public disapproval if not derision. "Who ever heard of a girls' baseball club?" asked William Blaikie in *The Tribune Book of Open-Air Sports* in 1886.

Those noncollege women who ventured to play baseball in public, like the poor and unsung, often left only faint traces of their passage. A few women's teams are said to have existed as early as the late sixties. One team that is documented is a group of high school girls that played in Los Angeles in 1874, and a reporter for the *Record* described what he considered a typical game: The pitcher wound up like a windlass, using either hand (it did not matter which), then let go when she got up good velocity, the ball careening through the air with a "charming uncertainty of direction," sometimes lighting·on the head of a spectator or passing through a schoolhouse window or going "plunk into the extended apron" of the catcher, who received it with "a little feminine squeal" that was "perfectly killing" to a "susceptible young gentleman observer."

The first Washington, D.C., women's game reputedly took place in 1879, and the players, wearing dresses, gave what was described as a poor exhibition of baseball. Besides, their hair kept falling down. In July of the same year female nines from New York and Philadelphia played in Boston before 1,600 people, some of whom attended just to jeer and make "shocking remarks" (and so reconfirm their conviction that baseball was a man's game). A month later the same clubs played in Cincinnati, and according to the *Enquirer* the women, most of them "quite young," were passably good looking and well developed and endured a lot of "kidding and razzing" from male spectators. In 1883, according to an 1884 guidebook, two "artistically dressed" teams of "ladies of color" (black women) from Philadelphia and

Chester, Pennsylvania, played baseball. The one from Chester, called the Dolly Vardens, sported red and white calico dresses "of remarkable shortness" with caps to march. (The original Dolly was an attractive character in Dickens's *Barnaby Rudge*.)

The same year the Dolly Vardens played, two other itinerant women's teams—sixteen females supplemented by two lads—called the Blondes and Brunettes or Reds and Blues, played ball in several large cities. Members had been selected from a hundred applicants, and variety actresses and ballet girls had been barred. Three, however, had been on the stage, and one, Daisy Muir, had played Eva in "Uncle Tom's Cabin." Although some were working girls or schoolgirls, most were reputedly normal school or "Sunday school" graduates who, the *Times* explained, yearned to emulate Yale, Harvard, and Princeton students by "traveling wholly on their muscle." The newspaper quoted one player as saying that the women had joined partly for the fun of it and partly to see the country.

The Blondes and Brunettes wore white bathing-style dresses with knee-length skirts trimmed in blue, one team wearing red stockings and the other blue, except that the captain of the Reds wore a full suit of her color and her opposite number wore a "lovely outfit" of cerulean blue, with a little hat flaunting a blue ribbon. All wore belts around their "little waists," along with "jaunty white cloth hats" and regulation baseball shoes, although one player "luxuriated in sixteen-button gaiters" that reached above her ankles and, the *Times* reporter observed, must have taken half an hour to fasten.

After ten days' practice the Blondes and Brunettes began their exhibitions in Philadelphia on August 18, 1883, before five hundred spectators. Unfortunately, their play fell far below the level of their appearance. From the start it became apparent that the regulation diamond was too large for their throwing, the novelty of which moved spectators to "uncontrollable laughter." Their fielding also left much to be desired: if the ball was well directed and came at a soft curve, they caught it well enough, but if not, their courage failed and they got out of the way without delay.

In another game, in New York at the grounds of the Manhattan Athletic Club in September, 1,600 fans "laughed themselves hungry and thirsty" watching the "sad and sorrowful" play of the Blondes and Brunettes. Only four players had by then become expert—"for girls," said the *Times* in its sardonic account—while the rest found that their determination to hang onto anything that came from the bat diminished as the number of their bruises increased. When fielders failed to stop the ball in any other way, they sat down on it, to the applause of the spectators. Soon the players looked weary and were "evidently sighing for the end of the season." After five innings the umpire called the game.

The Blondes and Brunettes did not quit, however. To compensate for their playing weakness they adjusted the structure of the game by shortening the distance between bases and using a yarn ball. Twice they joined forces, pitting sixteen women against five men of the Allegheny and Delaware clubs, with the men further handicapped by having to field and throw lefthanded and bat one-handed. By late fall their financially precarious expedition had come to grief. In December they reached Chicago where, after a benefit given for them brought only $35.00, they waited to get home by means of charity.

In New Orleans several women's nines competed during the last quarter of the century. One team at the fair grounds in 1879 refused to take the field until each member got ten dollars. The New Orleans *Picayune* said members were home talent, describing them as clad in knee-length white dresses trimmed in blue and red and ranging in age from childhood to middle age but "none of them beautiful." A Bloomer Girls team (a name used by a number of women's teams) that came to the southern city near the close of the century received more attention from the *Picayune* for its playing. The reporter thought that "for women they played well, their handling of the ball, of course, being in that style that is characteristic of the feminine sex— a side and hip throw."

Visiting women's teams were not always welcome. A nomadic team of "buxom beauties" run by Harry H. Freeman played hard but poorly on several visits to New Orleans in the 1890s, according to Professor Dale Somers. Reports implied strongly that Freeman recruited the young women as prostitutes, and after a number of complainants accused him of "inducing young girls to leave home and parents to join his troupe of base ball players," he was arraigned in May of 1886 as a "dangerous and suspicious character."

One Sunday in 1890 police arrested a team of women playing ball against a team of boys in Danville, Illinois, before 2,000 people, on charges of violating the Sabbath. The women pleaded guilty. Fines and costs levied the following day totalled a hundred dollars, paid by their manager, W.S. Franklin, after which they left by train for Covington, Kentucky. (The Danville boys were arrested and fined the same day.) Franklin's team also posed charmingly in 1891 for their photograph wearing striped knee-length dresses and black stockings.

A civic uprising of sorts threatened Freeport, Long Island, when a rumor spread that a gaggle of bloomerettes planned to invade the community to play a game. The women of the town rallied in righteous wrath and let their husbands know that attendance at the game would constitute grounds for divorce. The town elders cravenly applauded the wives' stand, and, as Robert Smith reported in his *Social History of the Bicycle*, the anti-bloomer forces seem to have won. A genuine uprising occurred in March of 1893 at a game in Cuba between the American Female Baseball Club and a team of "young men of good class." Their poor play caused the audience to feel cheated and to demand a refund of their money. A riot followed. The Cuban players gallantly fought to protect their young opponents, some of whom nearly passed out with fright. The women players took refuge in a house that soon came under attack, but the police finally broke up the riot.

A miscellany of other women's teams received brief press notice in the eighties. Young women employed in a Philadelphia shoe factory organized a baseball club; in Huntsville, Alabama, a Miss Walker and eight other "young ladies" reportedly defeated a male nine; in Rockport, Massachusetts, a coed game took place in 1890 between the Priscilla and Granite lodges; and the Brooklyn *Eagle* reported a girls' team challenging young men in Ohio in 1891 and another girls' club playing baseball at Shelter Island, New York, in 1899. Doubtless many more such amateur or impromptu games took place around the country unnoted in print.

Some individual players also received mention in the nineteenth century for their baseball skill: a twelve-year-old in Pottsville, Pennsylvania, who reportedly could "pitch a base-ball with as much skill, dexterity, and accuracy as the average amateur pitcher," and "three comely young women" in Scranton who could "sting the first baseman's hands from home plate, knock a ball beyond the diamond, or throw it through a six-inch hole at a distance of 10 feet."

Probably the best female player of the period was Lizzie Stroud, who played under the name Lizzie Arlington. Ed Barrow, later general manager of the Yankees, claimed he brought her into professional ball in the late 1890s when he was president of the Atlantic League. Details of her brief stay in professional ball remained virtually unknown until Al Kermisch, a baseball enthusiast, ferreted them out.

Arlington came from the Pennsylvania coal region, where she began playing ball with her father and brothers. A promoter named William J. Connor, after watching her play, engaged her for $100.00 a week in the hope of making money on her as a gate attraction. She made her debut in 1898 pitching for the reserve team of the Philadelphia Nationals. Thereafter, she pitched and played infield against various professional teams. She also did well playing for the New York Athletic Club.

On July 5, 1899, Arlington appeared briefly for Reading, Pennsylvania, in a regulation minor-league game against Allentown. More than a thousand fans, including 200 women, attended, mostly, according to the Reading *Eagle*, to see what she looked like and what she wore. They were not disappointed. Lizzie entered the grounds in a "stylish carriage drawn by two white horses" and, responding to applause by lifting her cap, revealed hair done in the latest fashion. She wore black stockings and a gray uniform with knee-length skirt. During the pre-game practice she played second base like a professional, "even down to expectorating on her hands and wiping them on her uniform."

With Reading leading 5–0 in the ninth inning, the manager sent Arlington in to pitch, and after filling the bases with two out, she succeeded in retiring the side as the crowd shouted, "Good for Lizzie!" The verdict of the *Eagle*'s sports writer was that she might do all right among amateurs but lacked control and the strength to get much speed on the ball. However, "for a woman, she is a success." A writer for the Hartford *Courant*, anticipating her coming to play for the locals against Newark, commented, "It is said that she plays ball just like a man and talks ball like a man and if it was not for her bloomers she would be taken for a man on the diamond, having none of the peculiarities of women ball players." But authorities cancelled her appearance in Hartford, reportedly because the home team management wanted to take no chances on losing the game, and thereafter her name disappeared from the sports pages.

Apart from Lizzie Arlington and a handful of other female players, women's baseball in the nineteenth century caricatured the game, but for young women with a yen for adventure, women's baseball teams presented a novel opportunity, provided they had the courage to disregard the stuffed-shirt and starched-blouse guardians of propriety and endure the derision of male spectators and the gibes of the press. In so doing they constituted one segment, however minor, of the women's movement and did their bit to weaken prejudice against them.

29

MORE DIAMONDS FOR COLLEGE WOMEN

"**T**oday there is not a girls' [college] that does not include in its curriculum a course in gymnastics and encourage or insist upon some sort of outdoor exercise," said *Munsey's Magazine* in 1901. The writer might also have remarked on the trend toward sports instruction in such institutions, for even physical training instructors, notably Oberlin's Delphine Hanna, Wellesley's Lucille Eaton Hill, and the University of Chicago's Gertrude Dudley, as well as reformer and social worker Frances Kellor, plumped for sports.

The clinching example of women students' propensity to favor sport over gym and calisthenics was basketball. Its rise to the premier team sport of college women dates from the innovative work in the 1890s of two products of Amy Homans's Boston School of Gymnastics: Senda Berenson and Clara Baer. The former introduced a modified version of the game to Smith students in 1891–92. About the same time, Clara Baer assumed directorship of the new physical education department at recently-founded Newcomb College in New Orleans, where announcement of the department had, as described by Professor Dale Somers, drawn many letters of protest from parents and physicians on the ground that gym exercise would make young women coarse and unfeminine as well as on health grounds. Baer had also to teach gymnastics to many who regarded exercise as unladylike and to overcome the Victorian modesty concerning gym costumes. After opposition to physical education quietened, Baer began to teach basketball, only to elicit another volley of protests concerning its danger, whereupon she changed the rules to make it a little less strenuous and named her version basquette, eventually publishing five books of rules on the women's game and on the value of regular exercise for female students.

Basketball's rapid spread strengthened the desire of physical training instructors to meet and organize, and in 1899 several met to discuss basketball rules. More important, disciples of Amy Homans around the country began to organize to establish their autonomy apart from men as college physical education teachers and to effectuate a policy in which all women students would participate in some form of physical activity to the end of producing healthy, vigorous graduates. Homans led the way, and the first professional organization emerged from an invitation she issued in 1909 to meet at Wellesley. Eventually, women instructors joined the male national organization and gradually changed attitudes toward them from condescension to respect for the special character of women's college sports. The culmination of their action was the appointment in 1917 by the president of the American Physical Education Association of a committee on women's athletics to set rules and standards for women's sports.

Basketball's mounting popularity also intensified demands for intercollegiate play. The game had already reached the West Coast, where under the leadership of Clelia Mosher, Professor of Personal Hygiene at Stanford, women of the universities of Stanford and California played what was possibly the first intercollegiate basketball contest. But Mosher was an exception. Other women instructors, reflecting Homans's teaching and Dewey's philosophy emphasizing the social goals of education, overwhelmingly opposed intercollegiate competition. They concerned themselves more with benefiting the health and education of the entire student body through intramurals and interclass games than with the interests of the few skilled athletes. Senda Berenson wanted to confine all of women's sport to intramurals. Elizabeth Burchenal, prominent PSAL leader, in a 1919 article opposed interscholastic competition and favored only "sports for sport's sake." Lucille Hill of Wellesley maintained that "competitive" sports developed "manly strength" and "unwomanly qualities." Two male deities of recreation, Luther Gulick and Dudley Sargent, held that the strenuous training required by competition would injure women mentally and physically. Many women instructors even regarded sports as of limited benefit compared with gym exercises in all-around physical development of certain aspects of women's physiques. Most revealing, women instructors accepted the charter given their rules committee at the 1917 conference that it keep in view the "limitations, abilities, and needs of the sex."

As a result, colleges by and large rejected intercollegiate competition for women. As recorded in Ellen Gerber's comprehensive 1975 article, a 1909 survey reported that most women's colleges in the East and many coeducational institutions played no outside games at all, although in the Midwest and far West intercollegiate competition was more common. Another survey in 1916 revealed that only 14, or 21 percent, of 66 colleges responding to the query had any form of intercollegiate sports.

Intercollegiate or not, the rising tide of basketball lifted other women's college sports, including baseball, with it. In 1910 a study of more than twenty colleges showed sports, not gymnastics, central to their physical education programs. In partial fulfillment of physical education requirements, colleges gradually permitted women students to choose from a generous menu of sports like basketball, tennis, hockey, swimming, golf, volleyball, soccer, cricket, track, riding, and even baseball, depending on the college.

Observing in 1909 that famous girls' colleges offered baseball, actress Caroline Carter, known for her physical exertion on stage, noted the game's benefits: it combined exercise and amusement, she said, and the girl who played baseball would have a good figure. From their college baseball teams, she thought, women learned the "blessed privilege of self-assertion, of individual confidence," and the "hothouse girl" had become a thing of the past.

If the vaunted American national game of baseball possessed all these attributes, why did basketball outstrip it in popularity among college women? Here are some of the reasons. Apart from requiring relatively little space and being impervious to weather conditions, women's-style basketball could be picked up easily without prior experience. All but the "klutzes" could readily learn to bounce the large ball and toss it to a teammate or at the basket. Besides, in basketball all players on both sides remained constantly in the game. Action was continuous, and yet there was little chance of injury and less of serious injury.

Baseball, on the other hand, cannot be learned anytime, or quickly. To achieve even a semblance of skill in throwing, fielding, and hitting a small ball with a stick, one must begin at an early age. Furthermore, only one full team is on the field at a time; what is the instructor to do with those waiting their turn? Then again, if the pitcher cannot throw accurately enough for the batters to swing at the ball, or if the pitcher has good control and the batters cannot connect reasonably often, the other players, inactive, become bored. Moreover, the small, hard ball used in the game increases the chance of injury. Nevertheless, some college women continued to play baseball in the new century.

At Mount Holyoke, administration and faculty continued the college tradition of encouraging physical exercise and sports. In 1904 President Mary E. Woolley remarked on "one of the most important changes in American life, the increased attention paid to physical exercise out of doors," and between 1895 and 1900 outdoor sports multiplied at the college. Nonetheless, a writer in the student magazine complained of "lack of interest" in the college athletic association because many felt they had no special athletic ability. The writer called for more "general participation" simply "for the sake of playing, for the pure fun of playing."

In the teams at Mount Holyoke, while sports seemed to be the only activity that generated class spirit, the problem of lack of general participation persisted because of the monopolization of sports by the few excellent athletes. To remedy the situation the college required freshmen to go out for a sport; upperclass women could do so voluntarily. As an incentive, Mount Holyoke awarded numerals and letters. To prevent the best athletes from dominating all sports and to encourage more women to try out for teams, athletic leaders restricted the number of sports a student could take part in. As a result, twice as many won numerals.

During World War I, although the administration curtailed sport programs somewhat to allow students to volunteer for farm work, by 1919 sophomores as well as freshmen at Mount Holyoke had to choose a sport. *The Alumni Quarterly* allowed that the enthusiasm shown for sports promised greater enjoyment of athletics by the college as a whole.

As at a majority of women's colleges, at Mount Holyoke a student athletic association chose a student "head" for each sport. A faculty member, usually a physical training instructor, acted as advisor to the association, and other faculty members helped the "heads" run the various sports. Field days also became common, as a substitute for intercollegiate competition. Mount Holyoke held them in the fall, when competition peaked; students played off all interclass sports finals, including baseball finals, in the fall. Indoor sports finals took place in the spring.

At Mount Holyoke various sports, including baseball, went in and out of vogue in the 1900s. According to the student handbook for 1901–02, each residential house fielded its own baseball team that year, and students played games between the different houses. Alumni questionnaires and archival notes also show that the women played baseball off and on in the teens. A 1918 Mount Holyoke handbook, for example, listed baseball as the outdoor spring sport. Although there were no regular class teams, house teams played, and everyone had a chance to try for the college team, which played a game each spring with the faculty. Baseball also appeared on the 1919 list from which sophomores and freshmen had to choose a sport. The student head of baseball acquainted incoming freshmen with the baseball arrangement at Mount Holyoke:

> Baseball is our all-the-year sport. Outdoor baseball begins in the spring and ends in the fall when the class teams play off games for the championship on Field Day. Indoor baseball is played during the winter term, and at the end of the season there are interclass games for the championship.
>
> Since there are no class games in the spring a tournament is arranged in which each house enters a team in the race for the championship. Best of all, a picked team of students plays a faculty team, which always ensures plenty of fun and excitement. And so . . . we are looking forward to [seeing] you play on some of these teams and [making] it lively for the upperclassmen.

At Wellesley, sports remained informal in the first years of the new century, and Lucille Hill, director of physical training, propounded "Health and Beauty" as the ideals and "Moderation" as the motto. But the appointment of Amy Homans as director imparted a fresh impulse to sports. That year baseball became part of the physical training program. By 1911 Wellesley was offering instruction in baseball, and the game could also count toward fulfilling the physical education requirement. As physical training became more deeply entrenched in 1916, when Wellesley required two years of it, so too did baseball: freshmen could choose from eight sports, including baseball, the choice subject to the approval of the resident physician. The athletic department graded student players for skill, effort, and carriage. The following year, 1917, a makeshift baseball diamond appeared.

A Wellesley department chart revealing the number of students engaged in the various accredited sports for the six-week season in the period 1917–20 shows that in comparison with others, baseball, with fewer than 20 engaging in it each year, remained a minor sport. Students did not lack equipment. The department inventory listed an ample supply of mitts, masks, bats (indoor and outdoor), and balls for a full season. A 1919 letter of Roxana Vivian, Director of the Hygiene Department, reported outdoor sports being carried off successfully and that in baseball, among other sports, "a reasonable and cordial spirit has been maintained."

In 1913 the Wellesley college annual, *The Legenda*, began printing baseball pictures, sometimes of entire teams, other times of only a few student players, with names of each. Costumes remained Victorian. Although the kilt with union underwear had supposedly replaced the gym suit in 1905, photos show students still playing baseball outdoors in the old-style long bloomers as late as 1917. By 1919 Wellesley baseball, or the uniform, was apparently sufficiently interesting to the public for *Baseball Magazine* to print a photo of a batter in long Turkish trousers and a catcher in shorter ones, with the caption, "Baseball has its place on the calendar of sports for women at Wellesley College."

At Smith, Senda Berenson revitalized physical education and by 1901 had expanded it to include baseball and other sports. In 1906 a senior student, Gertrude Cooper, prepared a little booklet with the following declaration on the cover: "Base-Ball Saturday at 4 p.m. Hockey Field Everybody Wanted Be on time." Her booklet contained a collection of caricatures poking fun at specific Smith girls as they played baseball in long dresses and rolled-up sleeves: dodging a thrown ball, slipping and falling while trying to catch a ball, throwing a ball from a sitting position, poised at bat looking "wrathfully contemptuous" at a pitch, holding up a corner of a skirt while running, and examining an injured finger but remaining "intrepid" behind the bat—all with clever caption.

The enthusiasm of Smith freshman Margaret Townsend for baseball inspired her to write home in April of 1908:

> Please ask Morgan if he has a baseball mitt he can send. We are practicing all the time now, and trying curves, and playing with a real baseball. Sometimes I can throw an in-curve. Marjorie Browning spent the afternoon over here yesterday and we played baseball and diabolo [a game played with two sticks with cords attached, and a spool] until we were weary, and then we went in the tank.

Smith archives show that students continued playing baseball in the teens. A photo labeled "Haven House baseball team" indicates that house teams still played. A 1916 photo even shows Marion LeRoy Burton, Smith's president, dressed in a baseball uniform! Smith students also attended men's baseball games, probably Amherst's. In 1917 Smith baseball was organized and prominent enough to warrant a student head. And there is no evidence in this era of any Smith players trying to acquire baseball equipment not belonging to them!

Vassar prescribed physical education three times weekly, and, by 1910 at least, tennis courts and an athletic field were available. Class teams in baseball played each other regularly, but although they practiced hard, few were rated good at the game. A student explained that the teams played only among themselves, never with other colleges, because "intercollegiate sports are not encouraged here."

Vassar also held an annual spring field day, and the one of May 1911 was particularly noteworthy because that day Dorothy Smith, an eighteen-year-old freshman, reportedly broke two long-standing women's collegiate records, the running high jump and the baseball throw for distance. Her record throw measured 204 feet 5 inches. The reward for breaking two college records in one day was the coveted V on her sweater.

When the New York *Herald* learned of Miss Smith's feat at Vassar, it dispatched a reporter to the campus. He learned that on the day she set her records the students had gone "wild with joy" because her accomplishment raised Vassar's already high standing in college sports. The freshman's throwing record in particular "amazed" the reporter because, reflecting popular belief, he thought that "girls do not throw a baseball further than the average boy without some sort of training. . . . Girls are popularly believed not to know how even to hold a baseball. And as for throwing it straight and true, it isn't expected of them." More astonishing to the reporter was Miss Smith's claim that she had no special training and did not even have brothers to teach her, but "I have always played ball with boys ever since I can remember." The reporter described her as "tall and slim and lithe" and "the modern type of girl athlete . . . not marred by overdeveloped muscles, but so well trained that every bit of her strength counts." He believed that her accomplishments showed that "the tomboy still exists" but that "the modern variety has all the charm of the sweet young girl, to which are added a strength and a knowledge of sports [of] which her alma mater has reason to be proud."

At Simmons College, founded in Boston in 1899, students played baseball "in one form or another" early on, but according to the college archivist college publications unaccountably omit mention of it until 1914. That year *Microcosm*, the college yearbook, reported that the athletic association wanted to emphasize baseball more than ever before because the women felt the need for some activity to take the place of basketball, which concluded early in March, and baseball could best serve the purpose. To that end, managers chosen from each class organized class teams at Simmons. Training began indoors, but as soon as the weather and the condition of the regular diamond permitted, outdoor practice commenced with "great enthusiasm." In 1915 the only game reported was one in November, seniors outscoring juniors 6–4. Simmons also held an annual track day, which routinely included the baseball throw competition. The record in 1916 was 163 feet.

Radcliffe, having experienced a lengthy and frustrating period of gestation as "the Harvard annex," belatedly joined its sister colleges when it was finally chartered under its present name in 1894. Nevertheless, an athletic association and a director of the gymnasium sponsored sports as early as 1902. The 1906–07 report of the gym director, Elizabeth Wright, although expressing pleasure at the interest of the 236 students who used the gym voluntarily, already hinted at a desire for a more formal organization, including accreditation of physical training as a college course:

> Though it is desirable that interest in physical education should be based less upon competition and more upon an intelligent understanding of the fundamental importance of the work, it is encouraging to feel that the students recognize the value of systematic training for whatever reason.

Step by step, Wright brought gym and sports closer and finally married them into a single course. To persuade Radcliffe students to participate more systematically, the department made outdoor sports part of the gym course in 1910. Gym and "outdoor exercise" were considered a unit, with sports replacing gymnastic exercises in the fall and spring terms. An "unusually satisfactory" year resulted, Wright reported, and "many students to whom it would not have occurred to join the Athletic Association were thus induced to take out-door exercise."

Although annual reports of the department head at Radcliffe named field hockey, swimming, and interclass basketball as the most popular sports in the first half-decade of the new century, students also played baseball. During the teens participants in Radcliffe baseball numbered about the same as those at Wellesley. In the college year 1910–11, baseball attracted 29 of the 233 registrants for sport, only three more than those who settled for walking, but for the first time in an annual report it had received mention as a spring sport.

Wright's report for the following year, 1911–12, listed 70 Radcliffe students out for fall sports, 29 of them for baseball; only 15 selected baseball in the spring, however. Still, the director remained optimistic. The new plan "worked well," she reported. "The attendance was good and the sports thoroughly enjoyed." The next year she tried a new tack to encourage sports: all students using the gym had also to select some outdoor sport, and of the 253 who used it, 27 chose baseball.

Again in 1914–15 Radcliffe stiffened physical education requirements. This time the course consisted of a choice of either ten weeks of outdoor sports or five of sports and five of swimming, plus nineteen of gym. Again baseball held its ground, at least as a spring activity. Although baseball apparently ceased as a fall choice, it was the first event on the program when the athletic association entertained the college at its October field day, the Crazy-nuts playing the Diffy-batters, with Charlotte Bruner, class of 1916, umpiring. The minutes of the association reported that the Diffy-batters won and praised the spirit of both teams as "excellent."

The next year, 1916, baseball remained alive at Radcliffe when of 170 sport selectees, 12 kept the faith by choosing it. That fall the department further tightened requirements. Beginning with incoming freshmen, all students had to take physical education. Radcliffe had come abreast of its sister colleges.

Barnard, opened as an undergraduate college in 1889, endured frustrating relations with Columbia University similar to those of Radcliffe with Harvard. Columbia balked at admitting women until 1898, when it condescended to grant adjunct status to Barnard. In time, Barnard gained the right to recruit its own faculty. Eventually, Columbia would accept women undergraduates, but Barnard remained a separate women's college.

Already in 1899 Dean Emily Putnam noted that Barnard students, as elsewhere, found gymnastics less attractive than athletics. The gift of a valuable piece of land for use as a campus gave Barnard sports a major lift and stimulated students to organize an impromptu sports event that started its annual sports Field Day tradition. Construction of a new gymnasium building soon afterward removed another obstacle to Barnard sports development.

By the early 1900s Barnard afforded a lively sports program that included baseball. An old photograph in the college archives shows a baseball game in progress on the Barnard campus before World War I, with the players attired in middies and knee-length Turkish pants. Spectators standing around the edge of the field wear long dresses.

By 1913 an athletic association, in place at Barnard for some time, inaugurated a point system for the same reason others had done: to prevent athletic students from participating in too many sports at once. Apparently, participation in sports did not jeopardize classroom work, for according to a writer in *Good Housekeeping*, the women athletes at Barnard, unlike their male counterparts, did as well as the nonathletic students.

This judgement applied equally if not more so to Bryn Mawr, where in accordance with President Carey Thomas's proclaimed intention, the college maintained a robust sports program that, far from detracting from its rigorous academic regimen, complemented it. Under physical education director Constance Applebee, recalled former student and professor Cornelia Meigs, in the early 1900s the college "reeked with athletics." No sport went untried, including water polo, and the zest for field sports was such that Applebee would have a dozen teams practicing at a time.

Bryn Mawr stipulated that each student exercise a minimum of four hours a week, and, to satisfy this requirement, many participated in such sports as hockey, lacrosse, and track. Although Bryn Mawr records of this period do not specifically mention baseball, some students presumably played it, especially since the athletic association reported the playing of indoor ball beginning with 1903 and continuing during the teens.

In the South, where all levels of education lagged, prewar female seminaries, academies, and institutes lingered on as contributors to the cult of the lady. In that section of the country the "southern belle" was part of its mythology. In fostering this ideal such institutions as Nashville Female Academy and Alabama Female Institute limited young women's physical activities to jumping rope, playing battledore, and perhaps engaging in some light gymnastics. Students disinclined toward such strenuous activities could substitute walking.

In contrast with the routine followed at southern female academies, Miss Porter's School at Farmington, Connecticut, seeking to prepare privileged young women for a useful social role, encouraged athletic activity beyond walking and calisthenics. In winter students skated and sledded. Rowing and tennis came in. And as early as 1867 Miss Porter yielded to student requests and permitted them to play baseball, provided the field was not visible from the road! A graduate, Grace Aspinwall, recalled later that she "had the honor" of being selected pitcher on the 1867 baseball team at Miss Porter's School. Another former student, Kate Stevens, remembered that the girls named the club Tunxis, after an Indian tribe. The club, said Stevens, "played, or tried to play, a few games," but after it received a challenge from the Trinity College team at Hartford, parents sent "rather peremptory letters" that put a stop to baseball at Miss Farmington's—but not before the girls had their photo taken in white shirtwaists, dark ties, and dark skirts, hair severely piled on top, and with solemn expressions on most faces. Baseball revived later at Miss Farmington's, because the school archives also contain a picture of the grinning team of 1889 wearing long skirts and smart bonnets, two members holding a bat each.

Although students at Nashville Female Academy had nothing like Miss Farmington's baseball, in the post-bellum South a few institutions that gradually achieved respectable academic status brought in gymnasiums and physical education courses. Mary Baldwin, in Staunton, Virginia, installed a gym and pool. Goucher, influenced by nearby Johns Hopkins, established physical education in 1889, its first year.

Agnes Scott College, founded in 1889 at Decatur, Georgia, by 1905 boasted a fine gym building and pool. Agnes Scott required gymnastics, and its program even included athletics, which in 1910 for the first time included baseball. Teams in baseball and other sports were managed by the athletic association, with coaching by the physical director. A college photo shows the 1911–12 baseball team on the field in ankle-length white skirts; a man in dark clothes is evidently umpiring an intramural game before a few on-lookers. That year's catalog said, "Baseball, with Mr. Johnson as coach, is an innovation at Agnes Scott, but the girls have entered this new field of athletics with their usual zest."

Another institution of high intellectual standards, Randolph-Macon Women's College, opened in 1891 at Lynchburg, Virginia, from the outset made physical education part of its curriculum, and sports followed within a few years. In 1902 the yearbook, *Helianthus*, reported that students played baseball, "a rather new development here," and "There are two teams whose playing surpasses anything ever known in the athletic world." The college catalogue boasted in 1910 that Randolph-Macon encouraged students to participate in all outdoor sports:

> Interclass games are held annually, and also competition in field sports, because an opportunity to show skill and represent a class in athletic games, as elsewhere, is of social and moral value.

While baseball developed in private women's colleges even in the South, it lagged in coed institutions. Although the Morrill Act of 1862 fueled remarkable growth of higher education, it failed to mention women specifically, and for the most part such institutions admitted them with all deliberate slowness, often only after women lobbied legislatures and in at least one case, at Cornell, resorted to legal action. Even so, by 1900, except in the South female students equalled or even outnumbered males in a dozen state universities, where their sheer number reignited debate over the proper place of women. Psychologist G. Stanley Hall and others shifted the weight of the opposition to women's education to the reason that women's presence represented a distracting influence on male students—especially when women outstripped males academically!

Prestigious private men's colleges interposed even more formidable barriers, as with Harvard and Columbia. Randolph-Macon Women's College was established as a separate institution only after the men's college of the same name refused women admission because, as a faculty representative asserted, educating women at the university would "draw them away from the home," and

> under the arcades they would be certain to grow boisterous, familiar, and bold in manner, and perhaps even rudely aggressive, under the influence of an ambitious rivalry with the male collegians.

Even after gaining grudging admission to some institutions females encountered further difficulties, like being shunted into segregated classes or watered-down courses, or placed in separate buildings or different campuses, or even by temporary exclusion altogether. On the other hand, at the University of Chicago the presence of the graduate school and a sizable number of women on the faculty provided a mature atmosphere relatively favorable to women, at least during the school's first ten years. Nevertheless, males ran almost everything at Chicago, as Professor Mary Kelley stated in *Woman's Being, Woman's Place.*

Women's physical training and sports did not escape the glare of disfavor and discrimination at coed institutions. Female gym instructors, feeling constrained to appear "ladylike" and diffident about asserting themselves, even though famishing for space and materials kept apart and appeared at meetings only to coax equipment for their students. Coed institutions also expected women students to support the male sports teams and in at least one case, the University of Illinois, required them to do so. They usually had to sit in separate sections of the stands. At Berkeley they could not even use the same yells to cheer the team on. Whether male students should watch women play could also be an issue. And women's baseball play could be prohibited. Once in 1904, according to researcher Rich Tourageau, when some University of Pennsylvania coeds joined in a student ball game and one produced "pandemonium" by knocking out a two-base hit, the faculty prohibited women from playing on campus.

By the time coed schools got around seriously to providing sports for women, basketball had become the most popular women's team sport. Yet baseball, though a latecomer in coed institutions, proved a hardy perennial, as verified by a sampling of records of more than two dozen coed institutions for all regions of the country.

Iowa, which led the way among state universities in adopting coeducation, only to abolish it briefly and then restore it, is a good example of the boost basketball gave to other sports for women. In 1895, according to Janice Beran, women organized a baseball club, playing in long skirts. They also wrote a constitution for their club. By 1905, according to Mary Crawford's contemporary book on college women, basketball had become the chief interest of University of Iowa women outside their regular work, even though they had found it necessary to hold a bazaar to raise money to enclose the basketball court in the school's small gym. College publications gradually gave sports and recreation more space, and by 1907 the physical education department had added baseball, along with hockey, to its program. Indoor baseball soon followed.

At the University of Chicago the earliest known baseball for women dates from 1902, when a first and second team played four games against each other. A photo in the 1902 yearbook, *Cap and Gown*, reveals them outfitted in dark skirts and light turtleneck sweaters bearing a large *C* and smaller *BB*, accompanied in the picture by a woman in dark mufti, probably the coach. Later the women's athletic association, founded in 1904, promoted baseball and other sports and sponsored both interclass and intercollegiate sports contests.

After a painfully slow evolution beginning in the early eighties, a broad-gauged program of women's physical training and sports emerged at the

University of Wisconsin, undergirded by the opening in 1910 of Lathrop
Hall, a well-equipped building for gym and sports. One writer asserts that
Wisconsin introduced baseball in 1906 as part of instruction. In any case,
according to the college archivist, between 1910 and 1935 baseball reached
the height of its popularity as part of the physical education program. An
active women's athletic association stimulated sports and according to
Blanche Trilling, director of physical education, probably represented the
biggest factor in encouraging physical development there.

Beginning with 1911, the first year such figures were recorded at Wisconsin, and continuing throughout the teens, yearly participants in baseball
and softball combined ranged from a low of 60 to a high of 119. Figures for
indoor ball, played in winter, leaped from 46 in its first year of 1915 to a
peak of 175. Wisconsin, to get as many women as possible interested in
sports, followed the practice of other colleges in limiting female students to
one sport each, so that those "not as strong" in a sport could still compete.
As in many other institutions, a student "head" of each sport assisted the
faculty instructor, helped pick the teams, aroused enthusiasm, and saw that
participants obeyed training rules. A system of awards, letters, and sweaters
based on the number of points accumulated added incentive, and in 1913
Wisconsin adopted a special award, the Senior W, given not only for points
but on the broader basis of "womanliness and service to athletics at Wisconsin." In 1915 an annual field day program replaced the May fetes, winding
up all women's outdoor contests in baseball and a few other sports. At these
field days Wisconsin had neither entrance fees nor grandstand, and spectators wandered about the grounds as their interests dictated.

Oberlin pioneered coeducation in the late 1830s, although it confined
women to a "Ladies Course." It introduced calisthenics as early as 1847,
and in 1858 a recreation ground for the use of "young ladies" appeared, but,
as Robert Fletcher's *History of Oberlin College* remarked, "what use it was
put to is hard to imagine." By 1873 Oberlin had added a gym. After Lucy
Stone, Oberlin's first female student, worked her way through and had to
take a separate course, eighty years slipped by before women's baseball
made its debut on campus in 1917. "The [belated] introduction of the national
game was met with much enthusiasm," averred the college annual. The
women of all four classes fielded teams that year, as did the Conservatory
(the music institute). Some of the women who had worked out at home
under the supervision of young brothers proved to be good players. Other
"stars" developed, and students played regular games. Scores ran high at
the beginning of the season, the annual noted, but increased practice brought
improvement. The 1919 annual declared that "the 1919 [class] team lost no
games at all."

Not until 1890 did the University of Indiana appoint its first director of
women's gymnastics. Fifteen more years elapsed before the school acquired
Dunn Meadow, adjacent to the student building, for sports. At that time

another leap forward occurred when knee-length black bloomers replaced the former ankle-length pants. Finally, Indiana introduced baseball for women in the 1912–13 academic year and offered it as an "activity course" in the physical education department. The same year, mounting interest in athletics led to the organization of an athletic association, with eligibility for membership based on a point system. Although the program included only baseball, basketball, and hockey, Indiana's women students became so enthusiastic for sports that by the year's end nearly a hundred had joined.

Ohio State University, founded in 1870, was equally slow to encourage physical training for its women students, and not until 1896 did the administration hire a female director of physical training. According to the university archivist, a 1915 photo of women playing baseball as part of the physical education program marked the first official appearance of the game on campus. The women in the picture wore the ubiquitous long, dark Turkish trousers. A similar 1919 baseball photo shows that by then the pants had been raised to the knee.

Cornell became the first major Eastern educational institution to accept women, beginning in 1875, but presumably it accepted only those who did not violate President White's assurance to "friends" of Cornell that "no flippant and worthless boarding school misses" would be admitted. Baseball for women at Cornell sprouted by 1916, as indicated by a senior who, in the 1917 classbook, listed membership on the women's baseball team during her junior and senior years at the university. No seniors listed it in the previous year's classbook, so the archivist concludes that the 1916 team must have comprised only juniors and underclasswomen. After that, the classes of 1917 through 1920 all had baseball teams, as shown in the second edition of Charles Young's photographic study of the university.

At the University of Missouri, after an apparently indifferent start, the women's athletic organization reorganized in 1912 on a stronger footing, armed with measures like compulsory membership for students desiring to participate in sports, a system of awards for those who made class teams, and sponsorship of social events. As a result, reported the student annual, *Savitar*, membership jumped above 100 in 1913–14 and exceeded 200 in 1914–15. Baseball, adopted as the spring sport for women at Missouri only a few years before the athletic association's reorganization, by 1915 ranked as one of the university's major sports for women. The 1915 *Savitar* boasted that Missouri women played "regular baseball," and "the outfit used was the same as that used by any boys' team."

Savitar explained that baseball, until recently considered a boys' game, had within the previous few years become a fairly widespread sport for girls. In many places the general sentiment of the community disapproved of young ladies' participation in the game, said the writer, but owing to the interest women showed and to the fact that "no dreadful thing resulted from their playing baseball," the game was "fast becoming a popular girl's game."

Savitar pointed out that baseball required the cooperation of team members, and "as girls especially need training of this sort," baseball was "welcomed in the field of girls' sports as one of the best games to be had." Continuing to laud the game, the 1916 issue of the annual declared, "Missouri may boast of truer sportsmanship, cooperation, and enthusiasm in athletics from its girls by reason of baseball." The panegyric concluded with a perceptive observation:

> That the great American national pastime should find a place in the hearts of American girls is only natural, particularly among the girls of the Middle West where the social whirl and strict aristocratic conventionality are less noticeable.

Savitar's writer also proved at ease with contemporary sports writers' lingo:

> Baseball has been played by the University women for several years and is each year getting more popular. Playing on a regular diamond, with a girl pitcher, a girl receiving, and a girl in the center, left and right gardens, it's almost big league style. "Whew! I'm stiff!" This is the correct salutation for the girl diamond stars. At least that is the usual greeting when lady artists come out for their first workout on the diamond. After the preliminaries the season opens up in full swing and the series is on. The slab artist goes through the necessary contortions, the stick swinger hits madly at the elusive horsehide, and, meeting it, goes scrambling to the initial sack.

Women's athletics at Missouri continued viable through the end of the decade. Association membership in 1918 numbered about 250, and, said *Savitar* that year, baseball, "although usually considered a man's game, is also very popular among the girls."

Unlike the sources of baseball information at universities like Missouri, those for some institutions, such as the University of Cincinnati, fail to distinguish clearly between baseball and indoor baseball, often played out-doors, and they even use the terms interchangeably. Such is the case with the University of California at Berkeley, where the first known mention of the game occurred when the *Daily Californian* of October 18, 1911, reported that the Sports and Pastimes Club had decided to introduce it "provided enough women are interested," practice to take place on the basketball court, located outdoors. Enough were: thirty signed up, and the club set practice times. In March 1915 practice sessions were again announced in the paper and efforts made to secure games with Mills College, so students at Berkeley probably played at least sporadically in the intervening years, and there is evidence of continued interest for the rest of the decade. The summer session also offered a baseball course for future playground workers. In the fall of 1915 the casts of Berkeley's music and drama productions, after the manner of Hollywood movie actors, played baseball against each other. Two group snapshots picture the teams, the drama players wearing sashes bearing the name of their production.

Construction of a women's gym building in 1915 permitted women's indoor baseball for the first time at the University of Cincinnati, where, according to the archivist, the university considered baseball a spring quarter indoor game. By 1915 class teams each had a class manager, all under a general manager, in turn responsible to the women's athletic director. These teams played for a varsity championship.

The first annual field day at Cincinnati, May 1919, included the baseball throw and senior-sophomore and junior-freshman baseball games. Hermina Hoppe, winner of the baseball throw, "caused the horsehide projectile to travel 136 feet," reported the *University News*. During one of the ball games a rabbit appeared on the field and refused to leave, interrupting the game, but "Dr. Morrison, who was on the job as usual, soon had Mr. Bunny hitting it for the East bleachers." That June when eighteen University of Cincinnati women won numerals for baseball, the school paper claimed that "America's leading game has found great favor with the girls, and it now constitutes one of their leading sports."

Although sources relative to sports at such colleges and universities as Tufts, Brown, Minnesota, Washington, Utah, and Boston (University) made no specific reference to women's baseball, they provided some gymnastics or sports or both, and women students at these institutions may well have played the game at least informally on their own. But some colleges proved reluctant to provide sports and physical education facilities to women. Coeds at the Universities of Michigan and Utah had to fight for gyms. At the former institution they descended on the state legislature to lobby for a gym, but when the bill came up it lost by one vote, and not until 1895 did they get a gym, through philanthropy. At Utah, even though the women's athletic program actually preceded the men's by some years, the women got little support. They, too, lobbied the legislature but won only partial use of the school's gym. The men then requested, and got, a new and larger one, leaving the women in possession of the old gym.

The relatively late germination and slow maturation of women's baseball in coeducational colleges compared with that in women's private colleges may stem from more than the primacy of women's college basketball at the time. Among the advantages of basketball vis-à-vis baseball as a women's team sport already mentioned, two were particularly applicable in coed schools: its adaptability to indoor play in the relative privacy of the gym and its simplicity as compared with baseball, which made it less embarrassing for beginners to play—attributes of special importance in coed institutions, where female players risked ridicule and heckling from male students. The secluded campuses of private women's colleges permitted students much more leeway to "let themselves go." Shielded from the jibes and derision of male students and outsiders, students at women's colleges could essay baseball early on and establish it before basketball had entered the picture, or even before women's team sports amounted to much in coed institutions.

Support for such a hypothesis concerning the bearing of different environments on baseball's development comes from the somewhat different academic atmosphere in the two types of institutions. In the private women's colleges toward the latter part of the century, some students had become dissatisfied with education for ornament supplemented by giggly fudge parties and leading to conventional, sheltered futures. Having in mind the need to realize more return on the expense of their education and more fulfilling lives afterwards, they took to discussing the possibilities of careers in such fields as law, medicine, social services, and even politics. Some began working even as students, as Professor Lynn Gordon has shown, in such organizations as the College Settlement League, the Consumers' League, the College Equal Suffrage League, and the Intercollegiate Socialist Society. Led by Bryn Mawr, Wellesley, and Mount Holyoke, the private women's colleges had begun to grow out of the seminary stage into genuine academic institutions.

The different academic setting of the coed institutions offered little opportunity and less encouragement for young women to question the sex roles instilled in them during their early upbringing. As a result, fewer of them had the wish or the will at college to raise their sights and entertain more ambitious goals than those in keeping with their pre-college rearing. Nor were they encouraged to do so. Benjamin Wheeler, president of Berkeley, made plain what was expected of them:

> You are not like men and you must recognize the fact. . . . You may have the same studies as the men, but you put them to different use. You are not here with the ambition to be school teachers or old maids; but you are here for the preparation of marriage and motherhood. This education should tend to make you more serviceable as wives and mothers.

Given this combination of restraints, it is unsurprising that many coeds were slower to assert themselves than students in women's colleges. They tended to avoid studies that would prepare them for professions. Some coeds dared, however, to hazard baseball, and as a result women's college baseball as a whole acquired a greater amplitude by 1920.

30

WOMEN TOUCH ALL THE BASES

In the pre–World War I years of the twentieth century women's passivity continued to fade. Changes in women's status made slow headway in the face of tenacious prejudices and practices, but old attitudes steadily lost force and credence.

The plainest sign of women's growing self-determination was the enlarging scale on which they participated in the burgeoning, swirling economic life outside the home. From about 20 percent of the work force in 1900, by 1910 the percentage of women working had risen above 25. After 1910 women also became increasingly prominent in white collar jobs. A 1913 report revealed widening opportunities for them in schools, businesses, hospitals, publishing firms, libraries, department stores, and government service.

Another instrument closely associated with the workplace, the struggle for unionization, helped loosen further the traditional traces on women, and under the leadership of such redoubtable women as Mother Jones, Susan B. Anthony, Florence Kelley, Rose Schneiderman, and Emma Goldman, they carried on in the face of formidable opposition. By the twentieth century they had established the first union of their own of any strength, the International Ladies Garment Workers Union.

Greater participation of women in sports also played a part in breaking down restrictions on them, but advance along the sports route continued to meet with obstacles. Like Tannhäuser badgered on his march by the imps, women had to contend with tirelessly iterated arguments against their liberation tailored to hinder their pursuit of sports.

A fundamental contention raised even in the 1900s was that athletics, like suffrage, would destroy women's femininity by teaching them male traits. Psychologist Richard Krafft-Ebing linked their participation in athletics to lesbianism and declared that preference for playing boys' games was the first symptom of perversion. In young adult fiction, the gentle heroines, rather than displaying sports ability, at most dabbled in intramural athletics, and in any case their futures lay in marriage. Baron Pierre de Coubertin, founder of the modern Olympics, believed the games should be the province of males only, and James E. Sullivan, a power in the Amateur Athletic Union, opposed public competition for women. As late as 1914 many still condemned the growing adoption of bloomers by women playground instructors, and one New York City inspector expressed shock that such "unnecessary" and "unladylike" garments should be worn outside a gym in the sight of men.

Some gave women's sports tepid support hedged with reservations. Thomas Wood, a physical education professor at Columbia, quoted in a 1910 article, thought athletics had only good effects on women, if practiced within reason. Standards should differ for women, he said, and rarely should women train under a male coach. Dudley Sargent's support for women's sport in a 1912 article in the *Ladies Home Journal* was so larded with equivocation and contradiction as to leave readers baffled.

Nevertheless, the volume of opinion favorable to women's sports rose, strengthened no little by the women's own defiance of opposition. As early as 1901 *Munsey's Magazine* termed women's entrance into sports second in importance only to their improvement in legal status and said that both those gains were more important than winning the latchkey and the ballot. A 1903 article in *Outing* declared "nonsense" the belief that athletics made women coarse and their muscles knotty. Richard Duffy in a 1910 *Good Housekeeping* article made the same point: proper sport, he thought does not "coarsen [a woman's] fiber" or "blow the charm from her womanhood. It keeps her an active social unit in school and college, and impresses on her the great principle of fair play. . . . " Articles in other journals like *Harper's Bazaar* supported sports for women as beneficial to their health. Winifred Buck's 1917 book, *The American Girl*, said sports aided strength, mental work, social life, mental attitude, and character development.

Some academic figures, like historian Frederic Paxson, backed sports for women. Gertrude Dudley of the University of Chicago thought athletics might be helpful to women's later social and professional success. John Dewey contradicted Krafft-Ebing and lent powerful support to the cause:

> The idea that certain games and occupations are for boys and others for girls is a purely artificial one that has developed as a reflection of the conditions existing in adult life.

A speaker at a world conference of women physicians in 1919 made the most novel contribution of all: parents, instead of giving dolls to their baby girls, should instead give them bats and balls.

The scroll of supporters for sport included other prominent women leaders as well as public and private organizations. Athletic Crystal Eastman, labor lawyer and pioneer in the fight for industrial safety, promoted women's sports, shocking local society by riding a horse astride and wearing a man's bathing suit for swimming (without skirt or stockings). But as much as anything, women's sports waxed because many working girls, as Professors Mary

Leigh and Therese Bonin have rightly noted, proved willing to face public disapproval and ridicule to assert themselves in the sports arena.

As for baseball, women and girls to some degree penetrated practically all facets of the game in the years before American entry into the Great War. By 1909 they were sufficiently noticeable as spectators to be accorded two lines in the famous song, "Take Me Out to the Ball Game":

> Katie Casey was baseball mad
> Had the fever and had it bad.

Collier's announced in 1911, "Baseball for girls is growing in favor season by season." Spalding's 1913 guide claimed that twenty percent more women attended games than ten years previously. Many were faithful fans. *Sporting News* reported in 1911 that Emma Sargent of Malden, Massachusetts, had attended all Boston American and National League games since 1904. In Cincinnati, after a fan named Casey Jones received a silver cup for being the most ardent Reds fan, a twelve-year-old boy wrote clubowner Garry Herrmann in 1915 that "my mother beat Mr. Jones to the home plate there" because she had attended from 150 to 160 of the Reds games for the previous seven or eight years. She even told him and his brother that she would rather see them become Reds players than "presadent" of the United States, because a ball player had to display "very good habits," while "many times a politician [and Herrmann was one] is the opposite."

Another fan of the Reds, Estelle Allison, wrote a poem she wanted the National League to adopt and told Herrmann she was a "Ball Doll Fan-ie," adding, "That's also the name of the poem." In New York, every afternoon she could get away, Stella Hammerstein, actress daughter of Oscar, was at the Giants' ball grounds. "Do I like baseball?" she laughed. "That is just the same as asking an American if he likes pie." Interest in baseball among the students of Girls' High School in Brooklyn in 1913 was so great that Principal William Felter could capitalize on it each day in mathematics class by having the students figure out the batting average of Casey Stengel, Brooklyn outfielder. And, according to a 1919 issue of the New York *Times,* women rooters "now yell and shout at the players with just as much frankness as the men."

But female fans remained subjects of condescension and irresistible butts of jibes. A 1909 poem about the "Female Fan" published in *Baseball Magazine* had her standing on a neighbor's feet yelling for the wrong team until she was hoarse and not knowing a ball from a bat; "She shrieks and she squeals at base hits and steals" but "takes the next morning's paper to see which team has won."

Some writers pictured women spectators as merely bored. One *Baseball Magazine* writer described the trials of young women "dragged by some amiable though misguided cavalier" to a "boresome game" or of a wife with a husband tied to the sports pages, "silent or cryptically ebullient." A few

writers delineated them as informed and interested. A female character in
Lefty o' the Blue Stockings, a boys' book by Burt Standish, revealed the
requirement for winning a male's good opinion: Although of "daintily feminine appearance" the girl

> talked mainly of baseball, tennis, motoring, and kindred subjects, in a way
> which showed she was more than familiar with her ground.... She was like
> a good pal, a chum to whom one could talk almost as one talked to another
> man ... a good sport in the best sense of the word.

A constructive though still condescending approach to the problem of
women's need for more sports background was a 1901 instructional manual
by J. Parmly Paret, *The Woman's Book of Sport*, which explained baseball
so that women could become knowledgeable spectators at men's sports and
thus enjoy them more. His emphasis on watching accorded with his assertion
in an article a year previously that baseball, football, and rowing had proven
"too severe for the feminine physique."

The widely held view of women as moral guardians still permeated baseball. In contrast with other reports of women as yelling at games, a 1909
issue of *Sporting News* claimed that women represented a restraining influence on the loud element of the other sex who, through partisanship or
rowdyism, were "apt to go beyond bounds in word and deeds." Judge Thomas
F. Graham, a minor-league president, apparently forgetting that somebody
had to prepare the dinner, went so far as to say in 1910 that "if women
attended games with their husbands there'd be fewer divorces."

With the announcement that two women would serve on the grand jury
investigating the 1919 Black Sox scandal came a *Sporting News* editorial
mixing praise and patronization. Referring to women's supposed special
moral qualifications, the editorial suggested that the appointment of two
women would provide them with a chance to show they were worthy of "the
new sexual equality," and although they were members of "the deadlier sex"
and had a tendency to "lie about their age," the paper expressed confidence
that the higher ideals of women fans would be of great assistance in cleaning
up the game.

It remained for A.G. Spalding, the leading promoter of baseball in its
early years, to produce the ultimate sugar-and-spice picture of the female
fan. In what decades later would be labeled a sexist description of women's
relationship to the game, Spalding pronounced his dictum: A woman "may
take part in the grandstand, with applause for the brilliant play, with waving
kerchief to the hero ... loyal partisan of the home team, with smiles of
derision for the umpire when he gives us the worst of it.... But neither our
wives, our sisters, our daughters, nor our sweethearts, may play Base Ball
on the field.... Base Ball is too strenuous for womankind."

At bottom, what counted most with owners of professional ball clubs was
the clink of women's gate money (and that of their male escorts) dropping

into cash boxes. To perpetuate that pleasant sound, owners continued to cater to female patrons, and by 1912 most of them had made some special arrangements and accommodations inside their parks for women.* As for whether women should vote, an Organized Baseball club owner could be either for or against it, whichever was convenient. The New York Giants once sold the local suffrage group many seats at a cut rate and permitted the women to resell them at or above regular prices, in effect contributing the difference, about $3,000.00, to the cause of suffrage. The Cincinnati Reds, who made a similar arrangement with a local anti-suffrage group, did the same, thereby helping those opposed to suffrage make more than $500.00.**

Spalding's disapproval notwithstanding, women continued to play baseball. Women's semiprofessional teams, many itinerant, became more numerous, better organized and managed, improved in skill, and more financially remunerative. Many exhibited the same flair for showmanship as the traveling male clubs. And reporters often wrote straight stories about their games, without condescension and heavy humor.

One team, called the Chicago Stars, with J. Bolson as manager and Maude Nelson as pitcher, planned its 1902 season: after opening in Tampa, Florida, the players intended to work their way North, traveling with their own canvas fence and a portable grandstand seating 4,000. "They bill their games," added the report, "like a circus." The following year, 1903, the Cincinnati *Enquirer* announced that a women's club known as the St. Louis Stars, managed by Al P. Giblis, which had organized and trained in Cincinnati, would play the Interurbans at Columbus, Ohio, and that the Stars expected a large number of local rooters to accompany them to Columbus.

That year, according to the recollections of Harold Keith, an Oklahoma player, the Boston Bloomer Girls, on tour carrying their own canvas fence, poles, and gas arc lights, brought night ball to Oklahoma Territory. In his account Keith explained that the big white, soft ball they used was quite easy to see at night. The women won over the local town team Keith played with, possibly, he guessed, because they were accustomed to the ball and the lights. The home team tried to "slip in" a light fungo bat "to deal with that ball," but "the girls were on to us. They threw it out."

A number of women's and mixed teams played in the Boston area. The Boston *Herald* announced in 1903 that the Hickey and Clover clubs, each made up of five women and four men living in the vicinity of Jamaica Plain, would play each other at Forest Hills. The *Herald* also pointed out that the Hickey team had been playing all season against both women's and men's clubs, and the report credited most of the Hickeys' victories to the fine work of the battery, Elizabeth Conry, pitcher, and Mary Rowe, catcher. Miss

*See *Baseball: The Early Years*, pp. 328–9.
**See *Baseball: The Golden Age*, p. 62.

Conry, said the *Herald*, had no equal among any of the female players around Boston, and few men could "twirl a faster ball or furnish a better assortment of curves." The women on the Hickey team, added the paper, played the most important positions; the men were mostly in the outfield. (So much for A.G. Spalding.) The account listed the names of both team members; most were Irish. The column concluded with a solicitation: Rose Duffy, manager of the Hickeys, wanted to hear from any team of women and men to arrange games. Such ads and other brief newspaper references indicate the existence of more women's teams than those that left definite traces.

The designation "Bloomer Girls" was as popular for women's teams as "Giants" for men's. A flyer, circa 1913, described "The Original Bloomer Girls" as "Refined and Moral, Bring the Ladies, Indorsed by Public Press and Pulpit, only Female Club Recognized by League and Reputable Managers," implying that many such teams fell short of being custodians of morals, or that local pecksniffs required reassurance about the character of the players. The circular mentioned having three male players and announced that the six females included a "lady twirler who takes her turn every 3rd day." With a nice mix of modern and old-fashioned terminology the ad said that the team featured "Norine McAlvaney, 1st Base Woman," and "Elsie McDonald, Star of all Lady Infielders." For use of the Cincinnati Reds' ball park to play "some popular lodge team" the club's owner, L.J. Galbreath, offered Garry Herrmann a choice of the first $250.00 taken at the gate or twenty-five percent of the total receipts.

The manager of another Bloomer Girl team sought Garry Herrmann's help in booking games. Christ Kunkel of Cincinnati wrote him in December 1913 to introduce the Texas Bloomer Girls, a mixed team of seven women and four men, including one male and two female pitchers. The team also carried a one-armed center fielder. "I guess you heard of this boy," Kunkel wrote; "he was the feature of a game last season when we defeated the Weedmans 7 to 2 and beat the strong Madison, Ohio, and Richmond, Indiana, teams." (So Pete Gray, outfielder for the St. Louis Americans during World War II, was not the first one-armed ball player ever.) Kunkel went on,

> If you want to make some money, this is one of the best ways to make it, you get the games for us, we would like to play everyday ball, you can make about three hundred dollars clear money yourself every week if you get the games and I know you can get the games.

Women's teams also attracted attention they did not desire. In New York City at Lenox Oval on a Sunday in 1913 the police, much to the displeasure of the 1,500 spectators, stopped a Female Giants game in the seventh inning claiming that one of the players had been selling programs to the crowd when her team was at bat. The Giants played in white middy blouses, blue skirts with bloomers, and white shoes. Another Lenox Oval game, mentioned in June 1915 in the New York *Age*, which reported games of black clubs and sometimes mentioned others, stated that the New York Bloomer Girls had defeated the Clinton freshmen at the Oval on Memorial Day, when the battery for the Bloomer Girls consisted of a Miss Demerest and Joe Wall. Wall, incidentally, had caught and played outfield in fourteen games for the New York and Brooklyn Clubs, and in the twenties and thirties he was still hanging around the Prospect Park Parade Grounds, hitting fungoes to any who wished to shag them.

Established major leaguers, such as Johnny Warhop, Smokey Joe Wood, and Rogers Hornsby did not disdain to play on women's teams early in their baseball careers. After Wood beat a Bloomer Girl team while pitching for his home town in 1906, the manager asked Wood to join them. That Bloomer Girl team already included four men in wigs, but Wood, then about sixteen, did not have to wear one because of his "baby face." He made $20.00 playing with the team for the last three weeks of the season, and, as he told Lawrence Ritter, "the crowds turned out and had a lot of fun." Warhop was playing on a railroad team in West Virginia in the early 1900s when a touring Bloomer Girls team persuaded him to take off with them.

A women's team carrying some male players appeared in fiction, too. In a 1919 story Charles E. Van Loan included a Baltimore Bloomer Girls team with men dressed as women for pitcher and catcher. The rest were "tough dames" good at heckling as well as playing, except for one pretty player, who turned out to be a boy impersonating a female.

Women's baseball offers another illustration of the mutual support that various women's groups were capable of. Suffragettes sponsored a small number of women's baseball games in the mid–1910s. A game between a women's team and a men's team preceded a regular Federal League game at Newark in June 1914, and in between, suffragettes lectured and distributed literature among some 2,000 spectators, many of whom were also suffragettes.

Some individual female players also performed creditably on men's teams, judging from their self-descriptions. A woman named M.E. Phelan of Cincinnati sent a letter of application and a photo to the manager of the Flora Baseball Club stating, "I have played with a number of lady ball clubs and am considered the equal of the average country player." Saying she played center field, Phelan went on, "Besides, a lady in your club would prove an attraction and would justify your team paying the salary I would ask—$60 per month and expenses. . . . Please let me know at once, as I have other engagements pending." Her photo, however, showed her not in uniform but in fur piece and a big black hat! A couple of years later Margaret Ongford placed an advertisement in the Cincinnati *Enquirer* announcing she had "a few open dates" and would pitch exhibition games with any "well-supported" baseball team.

Elizabeth M. Larrabee won recognition in New England and Canada as a first baseman around 1920. On one of her biggest days she played first base in an exhibition game for the American League All-Stars against the Boston Red Sox. The Providence *Journal* described her as a slender girl who fielded professionally, had a quick and accurate arm, and was an excellent batter. She first drew fans as a novelty but later attracted them as an expert player. Ed Carr, manager of the All-Stars of Boston, featured her picture on his letterhead and said later, "She was worth every cent I was paying her. She swells the attendance, but most important, she produces the goods."

By all accounts, no woman baseball player of the era surpassed Alta Weiss, who was reared in Ragersville, a central Ohio hamlet. Alta was a "tomboy" from the first, sturdy and athletic. She preferred farm work to housework and liked "sock ball" (possibly *Schlagball* anglicized) and one-o'-cat. Her father said that even as a child Alta never threw objects with the pushing motion "characteristic of a girl." At age fourteen she had already earned a county-wide reputation as a pitcher on boys' teams, using an assortment of pitches including a spitball, for which she chewed gum in order to assure saliva. Her father, a combination of physician and farmer, encouraged her to develop her considerable athletic talent. Alta played on the local two-year high school team and was also a good pianist and violinist.

In 1907 when Alta was seventeen, Dr. Weiss sent her and her two sisters to Vermilion, a Lake Erie resort, for a summer vacation. There Alta asked a couple of boys if they would like to play catch. They were amused until she put on a mitt and began throwing. The mayor of Vermilion, an ardent baseball fan, after watching her play, urged Charles Heidloff, manager of the Vermilion Independents, a semipro team, to sign Alta. When Heidloff refused to even consider her, the mayor arranged a game between two local men's sandlot clubs with Alta pitching for one of them. She pitched a shutout, striking out fifteen. Then Heidloff signed her, and the rest of the summer she pitched, and usually won, games against teams from nearby towns. One post-game writeup in a Cleveland newspaper reported that Alta, wearing a gym suit with a long skirt, looked somewhat frail and delicate rather than masculine, but the muscles of her forearm were like steel. She had good control, and her fast ball went over the plate "like a rifle shot."

The high point of that 1907 season for Alta came in the fall when, in response to popular demand, Manager Heidloff booked a game with Vacha's All-Stars, a fast semipro Cleveland team, to be played in the major-league park in Cleveland. So much interest did the "phenomenon," as the Cleveland *Press* called Alta, arouse that special excursion trains ran from Vermilion, Lorain, and other points to accommodate the crowd. At the park she reputedly became the darling of the fans. She won the game 7–6 and again received favorable press notices. The Cleveland *Leader* said her arms looked muscular and her legs were built for speed and strength, but she was graceful and pretty. The *Leader* reporter advised her to shed the cumbersome skirt she wore and put on bloomers instead, in order to give her limbs freedom. She would field her position at least twice as well, and be able to run bases creditably. She looks ridiculous now, out there with that dress on. . . .

Realizing he had a star on his hands, that winter Alta's father built a private gym in Ragersville so Alta could work out. He also founded the Weiss Ball Park, complete with diamond and grandstand, where the Ragersville team, which he managed, practiced and played. When Alta graduated from high school in 1908, the school board switched the commencement date in order not to conflict with one of her pitching engagements.

The following summer Alta's father purchased a half-interest in a Vermilion semipro team and changed its name to the Weiss All-Stars. A picture of the squad, managed by Heidloff, shows the men in white uniforms and Alta in black (she had finally shed the skirt). Alta's sisters Nita and Irma alternated traveling with her to rub her sore arm. The Weiss All-Stars played four or five games a week with northern Ohio clubs as well as some in three other states, and performed at annual picnics, county fairs, and other summer celebrations—one of the many proofs of baseball's remarkable pervasiveness and grip throughout America. Handbills and window posters announced Alta's coming in advance. Many of them included testimonials, one, for example, by the sports editor of the *Plain Dealer* lauding her as "very effective against some of the best semiprofessionals in Cleveland."

At one point the Cleveland papers began a half-serious campaign to secure Alta a chance with the Cleveland American League team, nicknamed the Naps for their manager, Napoleon Lajoie. "If the Nap Pitchers Can't Win Regularly, Why Not Sign Alta Weiss to Help?" ran one eight-column banner headline. Lajoie admitted, "She looked to me to have as much as many men pitchers, but I hardly think I will release Addie Joss or Heinie Berger [two of his regular pitchers] to make a place for her."

Alta proved to be more than a fine baseball player. She figuratively pitched her way through college, since her baseball earnings helped defray expenses at Wooster Academy, Wooster College, and the medical college at Columbus, Ohio, from which she received a degree in medicine in May 1914, the only female in her class. Alta wanted to continue on to Harvard that fall to prepare for teaching college physical education, but at her father's insistence she began practicing medicine with him in Ragersville. Thereafter she occasionally played ball with a Vermilion team called the Pirates before settling in Norwalk, Ohio, in 1925, where she married and for twenty years practiced medicine.

A handful of other women seeped into different baseball-related work in the 1900s. Ina Eloise Young, sports editor of a Trinidad, Colorado, daily, received national publicity when she covered the 1908 World Series. Two years later a Pittsburgh paper sent one of its women reporters to cover the Pirates during spring training, but the editor published her stories on the society page instead of the sports page.

Another woman, Amanda Clement, deserves mention in any account of the tough-fibered pioneer women of the American frontier. In 1905 the manager of a local semipro team in Hudson, South Dakota, Amanda's home town, needed an umpire and persuaded her mother to let the seventeen-year-old girl umpire a game. By that time Amanda had not only played first base on the Hudson team when it was short of players but had already gained quite a baseball reputation as one who had studied the rules and knew how to interpret them. The location of Amanda's home across the street from a local sandlot probably hastened her initiation into baseball.

According to clippings from unidentified South Dakota newspapers collected by Will Talsey, a local sports writer, so well did Amanda perform in her debut as umpire that she received further assignments that year, including handling crucial town team matches between Hudson and its old rival, the team of the nearby county seat of Canton—games played before large crowds of partisan fans and ones she ran without receiving complaints. Her reputation spread, and she herself became a gate attraction. Posters billed her as "The Only Lady Umpire." Before long she could expect, according to a South Dakota paper, fees ranging from $15.00 to $25.00 a game and could average 50 or 60 umpiring stints a season in the Dakotas, Minnesota, Iowa, and Nebraska—a record that not only speaks well for her ability but further substantiates the popularity of baseball even in then-remote towns of the American West. Amanda refused to umpire on Sundays, and for away games she lodged with ministers.

No mushy-slushy character was she. The "Lady in Blue," as some called Amanda, made an impressive figure: a pretty woman five feet ten inches tall in full-length blue skirt, dark necktie, and white blouse with UMPS stenciled on it, her hair tucked under her cap and extra baseballs in her waistband or under her blouse. She stationed herself behind the pitcher instead of the catcher, as all single umpires soon did, and as I did myself. Once she umpired a seventeen-inning tie game in 100-degree heat.

Above all, Amanda Clement controlled the game. A Boston journalist quoted in 1982 by Sharon Roan in *Sports Illustrated* called her a "heartless arbitrator." She demanded respect and threw out those who did not give it, although that seldom happened, for what rugged countryman could afford to browbeat in public a tall, competent, comely woman? To the contrary, one journalist claimed she refused more than sixty offers of marriage from players. (She never married.)

Even more remarkable was Clement's versatility. She earned enough money to attend Yankton College in South Dakota and then, at age twenty-seven, the University of Nebraska, where she also played basketball but, according to university records, did not return for her senior year. *Sports Illustrated* said that while in college she reputedly won tennis championships and set official world records in the shot put, sprints, and hurdles, and in 1912 threw a baseball 275 feet—another record. During World War I she taught ballet to the Wyoming University football team and later refereed high school basketball.

Although Amanda continued to umpire occasionally, after a six-year career her interests shifted to coaching youngsters' baseball teams, organizing men's and women's baseball teams in midwestern colleges and Ys, and serving as director of physical education at Wyoming and other colleges. As if all this were not enough, she also worked as a newspaperwoman, police matron, city assessor, and justice of the peace. Eventually, she became a social worker.

Arresting though it was, the reality of a woman capable of successfully umpiring men's ball games pales before that of another's gaining entree, though not on her own, to that most exclusive of groups, the sixteen-man body (as it was then) of major-league owners. On the death first of her father, Frank DeHaas Robison (1905) and then of her uncle, Stanley Robison (1911), owners of the St. Louis Cardinals, club ownership fell to Helene Robison Britton, a thirty-two-year-old socialite and suffragette, and the wife of a printer, Schuyler Britton. Although at various times she appointed men, including her husband, as club president, she made the decisions. She was also the first woman to attend the National League's annual meetings, where she was received with ill-concealed disfavor as the "matron magnate."

During Mrs. Britton's first year of tenure with the Cardinals, the team improved, rising from seventh to fifth place in the league standings and turning a neat profit. Braced by this advance, Mrs. Britton hastily, and, as it turned out, unwisely, rewarded her playing manager, Roger Bresnahan, the veteran catcher, with a lucrative five-year contract. In 1912 the team dropped to sixth place, and a smoldering disagreement between Britton and her manager climaxed in his dismissal and a lawsuit.* Henceforward, her affairs went downhill. By the end of 1914 club ownership began to pall, and she contemplated selling. The other owners, however, tried to force her hand, bruiting it about that her departure would be good for the game. News of the difficulties circulated widely; it almost certainly inspired Burt Standish to have Lefty Locke, a fictional character in *Lefty o' the Blue Stockings*, say,

> Women may vote, hold office, and go to war if they want to, but baseball is one thing they'd better keep their noses out of. No team ever did well with a female monkeying with it.

Stung by such disparagements, Britton stiffened and fought back. The ball club improved under the new manager, Miller Huggins, but marital troubles ending in divorce added to her distress, and she finally sold the club.**

---

*See *Baseball: The Golden Age*, pp. 136, 412–13. Also see Bill Borst's article in *The Baseball Research Journal*, January 1977, pp. 25–30.

**Mrs. Harry Hempstead came into possession of the New York Giants in 1912 on the death of her father, John T. Brush, but she put the club in the hands of her husband, who was president 1912–18.

In 1917 *Baseball Magazine* interviewed Helene Britton and published some revealing statements about her baseball background and the growing popularity of the game among women. In the interview Mrs. Britton pointed out that, growing up in a baseball atmosphere (her father and uncles constantly talked baseball), she had always loved the game. As a girl she had played baseball, too. Her father insisted that she learn to keep score, and "he didn't have to use any coercion. I was only too eager to do so once I had mastered the details of the game." Keeping score, Britton said, "is a fascinating pastime." She was pleased that "women are taking an increasing interest in the sport" and that "the game is played in a somewhat modified form in hundreds of girls' camps and elsewhere by young ladies all over the United States."

Mrs. Britton was right. Women's interest in baseball was such that some businesses began to find advantage in exploiting it. In 1913 *Woman's Home Companion* offered drawings and directions for mothers to show their sons how to build a batting strength tester. In 1911 a movie company filmed a comedy called "Baseball and Bloomers," in which a girls' seminary challenged a men's college in baseball.

More significantly, women industrial workers had begun to play baseball much more widely than earlier. The 1918 Cleveland Recreation Survey revealed that forty-four percent of Cleveland's women employees played it in their spare time. Some factories had already found it in their interest to promote women's sports. An article in *Industrial Management* in 1917 described an unnamed factory where women played baseball on the company's playground at the regular noonday break as well as on the company's field day. "Over there," a company representative pointed out to the writer of the article, "are some new girls who would feel strange if it were not for the 'old girls' who are asking them if they wish to play a game of ball which the manager is umpiring."

Ida Tarbell, famed for her Standard Oil Company exposé, wrote favorably of the women's athletics on her visit to a midwestern factory called Clothcraft, owned by Joseph & Feiss:

> I doubt if there is an athletic field in the United States which has as much use to the square inch as the girls at the Clothcraft shop in Cleveland give to a bit of enclosed land at the side of the factory. It is not larger than a city lot, but it teems with excitement during noon hours and after the shop closes at four-thirty. Mr. Feiss will tell you, in explanation of the time he and his associates give to encouraging the use of this bit of land, "I can't afford to have people working in my shop who don't have fresh air and fun."

Maude Miner, secretary of the New York Probation Association, by inference favored such factory sports. She thought lack of healthy recreation was one cause of prostitution in that working girls in search of entertainment frequented dance halls, where they might meet prostitutes or male procurers. At any rate, sports for working women were soon to increase.

Working-class women were not the only ones to play baseball. Upperclass women did, too, although as a rule they used sports as an instrument of conspicuous consumption and a means of demonstrating their exclusivity, so an inexpensive game like baseball would seldom do. But the exception again proved the rule. A 1901 article, "Sports That Make Women Beautiful," cited by Stephanie Twin, said "Ball playing is too spectacularly masculine for the average women's taste, but since it gives the shoulders such splendid beautifying opportunities" some "ultra smart" women engaged in it in private. Perhaps, but a more likely reason was that they had played baseball in college, liked the game, and continued to enjoy it afterward. Some upperclass women may also have been emboldened to have a go at baseball (though more may have been dissuaded!) by the likes of Eleanora Sears, who broke out of her Boston Brahmin background and as a teenager played hockey, tennis, and football, and even boxed. She also rode a horse astride, set a record in walking, and supported sporting organizations. Five different accounts credit her with playing baseball as well.

Any one or combination of these reasons doubtless swayed the young guests, including two Bowdoin undergraduates, at the Hotel Kearsarge, New Hampshire, in 1903 to form mixed baseball teams and play an "exciting" game. The young women played in white gowns and, as a lark, the young men wore girls' clothing.

Informal baseball games at social occasions might often place women and men on the same teams. Marian Lawrence, daughter of the head of the Harvard Theological School, attended the school's annual picnic in 1911 and captained one of the teams in the baseball game played after lunch, taking "my usual post at first base," where she "made several runs by stealing bases." During the game "Prof. Nash cheated horribly and bullied the umpire. . . . Prof. Drown was a first-class catcher and coach [but his] elderly sister, who I think may never have seen a ball game before, was something to remember at bat. . . . It was great fun."

At a more formal occasion, society "buds" in Philadelphia organized two teams headed by Rachel Biddle Wood and Marion Wood, daughters of the multimillionaire ironmonger, Howard Wood. They played the game in private, if the small army of socialite friends looking on are not counted, at Dolobran, summer home of shipbuilder Clement A. Griscom. An article in a 1908 issue of *Baseball Magazine* described the scene: hundreds of guests seated on camp stools and rustic benches scattered on the lawn watched the women play in shortened skirts. After the game, tea was served. "Secure in their social position," declared the writer, "they could afford to show the natural American love for the game of baseball."

Another group of wealthy young women, members of the Society Country Club at Belfield, in the exclusive Germantown section of Philadelphia, organized a club in 1911 and played regularly in long-skirted dresses with *B* on the front. *Collier's* declared that this "social baseball club" had "opened the season with vigor and effect" and published a picture of their catcher in a long skirt.

In Brookline, Massachusetts, Katherine Sergeant, a New England blueblood, played baseball on the large lawn of her home and became a Red Sox fan. Grown up, she married a Clevelander. In 1916 Red Sox player Tris Speaker was traded to the Indians, and in 1917 Katherine, as a young mother, often wheeled her baby carriage past League Park, listening to the roars of pleasure from within and feeling less lonely to think that perhaps Speaker had just done something special. "Tris Speaker and I were traded to Cleveland in the same year," she would say. In the baby carriage lay Roger Angell, who grew up to write baseball books.

Besides penetrating the realm of privileged women, baseball gained entry into the world of those removed from society altogether. At first incarcerated women were part of the general prison population and confined in large rooms or small cells. Owing to increased numbers in the mid–nineteenth century, authorities relocated them in separate buildings in or near men's prisons, where they languished as a much-neglected minority, often without a matron and part of a world in which rules dominated, order and obedience reigned, and the silent system prevailed. Prison authorities concerned themselves mainly with keeping inmates busy, mostly at machines. Lack of facilities limited programs at first to some instruction for illiterates, a modicum of gardening, and domestic or vocational work. In any case, badly underpaid officers at best showed only perfunctory interest in rehabilitation. Want of space restricted recreation to a half-hour's exercise in the yard.

Improvement of conditions for incarcerated women traces from the establishment of women's reformatories as an alternative means of female imprisonment beginning in the late 1860s, the major impulse behind them emanating from women reformers. Stressing training and rehabilitation as they did, reformatories soon played a major role in the women's prison system. They commonly consisted of a group of cottages bordering a quadrangle. Women's reformatories were not intended for hardened criminals; such women were considered social threats and sent to prisons. In keeping with their purpose of inducing conformity to middle-class standards of propriety, reformatories envisaged a generous fare of learning, moral training, and encouragement of femininity, sexual restraint, genteel demeanor, and domesticity, as well as recreation, including sports.

Jessie D. Hodder at the Massachusetts Reformatory for Women in Sherborn, Massachusetts, opened in 1877, and Katherine B. Davis at the New York State Reformatory for Women in Bedford, New York, opened in 1901, introduced comprehensive programs that included ample provision for outdoor recreation. These two women were perhaps the most effective reformatory administrators of the era, but they were exceptions. Skimpy finances and scarcity of instructors caused most reformatory programs to fall short of the ideal. At Sherborn, for example, the amount spent for "Games, &

C[etera]" in 1879 amounted to only $20.39. To handle recreation Davis at Bedford had to rely on summer volunteers from the Seven Sisters colleges. The Bedford reformatory was so overcrowded by 1913 that women slept in the gym and in the corridors.

Under such stinted conditions baseball did well to gain a precarious foothold, much less prosper. A 1909 book entitled *Athletic Games in the Education of Women* mentioned only two unnamed reformatories that used baseball. One maintained a baseball field for competitive games between groups of cottages. The other reformatory had two baseball clubs, two basketball teams, and a tennis club, which competed frequently for prizes. The writer reporting the club activities claimed that the inmates looked forward to games because such pastimes absorbed "all their time and energies." In addition, the games, while not requiring coercion, helped maintain discipline "a hundred fold."

Other reformatories for girls and young women found sponsorship of baseball advantageous. A speaker on "Play in Institutions" at the Playground Association convention in 1909 described her two months' stay a few years earlier at a girls' "industrial school," also unnamed, where she saw ten "nines" learning to play baseball. Many of the participants had "sordid backgrounds," she said, but

> On the baseball field their passion for activity was satisfied and they forgot for a time to be vain and foolish and self-conscious. They fell in the dust, they scratched their faces and tumbled their hair, and one girl lost a tooth in the heat of the conflict. But they struggled on with good courage, and forgot utterly that they did not look pretty at all.

A 1910 article on "training schools" for delinquent girls reported that nearly half the fifty-seven institutions possessed athletic fields, so they probably included baseball in their programs. At the Chicago Home for Girls, for example, the recreation director, a young woman graduate of the University of Wisconsin, had formed an athletic team "for membership in which the girls strive hard" and in which they develop "initiative." The writer of the article, Arthur B. Reeves, thought recreation should be a part of the program at every "progressive" training school in order to form the girls' character, to "teach them to be good losers and to take responsibility for their own actions."

A study of girls in Cleveland reformatories and reform schools as part of the Cleveland Recreation Survey of 1918 indicates that, given the opportunity, many more would have played baseball if they could. The survey reported that forty percent of the inmates claimed baseball as one of their spare-time interests.

Women's prisons occasionally permitted baseball. At the Oklahoma State penitentiary at McAlister, which confined twenty-eight young women in 1914, a prison officer reported, and even photographed, two teams of them, both "white and colored," wearing long white dresses and playing a Sunday baseball game on the lawn.

The experience of another institution furnishes further evidence of the claimed benefits of baseball for incarcerated women. In a report to the American Prison Association in 1912 Mrs. Charlotte Jones, a trustee of a women's prison in Indianapolis, strongly supported the game in women's prisons. "At first thought," she said, "baseball does not seem an appropriate game for women to play." Some of her inmates did not know how to play it and needed to learn, but soon baseball was "a popular and beneficial pastime at our institution." Every Wednesday afternoon in summer and fall, as a reward after the city work in the laundry was finished, "a game of baseball is entered into with eagerness and zest," the "white girls against the colored." The enthusiasm not only of the players but also of the spectators, including prison officers, became vigorous, noisy, and contagious. Amusement, Jones concluded, improved the prisoners' general health, and they worked better and more cheerfully because of it.

Any benefits from baseball were sparsely distributed, however. Only about half the women and girls in institutions were receiving what seemed to be a fair attempt at recreation, according to a 1912 study of 49 replies received to a query of 82 women's penal institutions representing more than 5,000 inmates. A Mrs. J.K. Codding, reporting on this study before the American Prison Association, revealed that only six of the responding institutions offered participation in basketball and baseball, two had calisthenics, and ten had croquet and tennis. Codding declared that wise recreation should include healthy sports, where give-and-take was prominent and "an unfair act" condemned by associates. "Athletic training is splendid for this purpose," she declared; it builds physical fibre and trains the brain to act and the body to obey. Tired bodies from outdoor play and work, Codding remarked, also meant better sleep.

Meanwhile, with the progress of schoolgirl athletics and the gradual opening of PSAL branches for girls, the issue of interscholastic competition arose in the public schools, as the issue of intercollegiate contests had arisen in women's colleges. In both instances female physical training teachers and coaches generally opposed them. Elizabeth Burchenal, a prominent member of the Playground Association, who in 1905 launched the Girls' Branch of the PSAL in New York City, emphasized promotion of folk dances and refused from the first to sponsor interscholastic contests for girls.

Some differed, however. Beulah Kennard, a speaker at the 1908 meeting of the Playground Association, declared that games many girls played, like Farmer in the Dell, had a "sickly sentimental tone," and girls needed other games in order to develop the idea of team spirit, in which they were deficient. Nevertheless, the Playground Association's committee on athletics for girls at its 1908 congress stated that interplayground competition was as

unnecessary and undesirable as interscholastic, and further, that competition
with boys opened "possibilities of danger."

The question of the kind of activities that should be available to girls
became pressing enough for the Playground Association to hold a session on
girls' play in institutions at its 1909 meeting. There Mrs. Charles F. Weller
of Pittsburgh staunchly defended active games:

> . . . let us not make our girls care only for things that suggest grace and beauty
> and charm; let us let them play sometimes with the wild abandon that drive
> away self-consciousness and with a force that will strengthen their womanhood.

Organized games, she said, develop honor, fidelity, and consideration for
others; if it is true that women are sometimes short-sighted and narrowminded, then girls need training in play. "Let us lay aside the 'women for
the hearthstone and men for war' theory. . . . Let us not talk about the lack
of traditions favorable to sports for girls." Mrs. Frank Roessing agreed that
athletics were desirable for girls, and since the right kind of play should
consist of "games of all varieties," a suitable athletic field costume should
be devised for them. But the general sense of the session seemed to be that
lively games for girls remained of doubtful benefit and that girls liked dancing best.

The place of girls' athletics stayed unsettled not only in the Playground
Association but also in the public schools, where their status varied markedly
from one school to the other. According to a 1902 article in *Outing*, private
schools and exclusive finishing schools everywhere had begun introducing
athletics, claiming moral as well as physical advantages. Through games the
rich girl reputedly became less snobbish and more aware of her body and
the necessity not to abuse it, and it dawned on her that money and position
meant nothing on the playing field; she learned to get her emotions in hand
and was taught accurate observation and patience as well as the principle
that good work eventually brought rewards. Moreover, there were physical
benefits: athletes developed ease of carriage different from that taught ar-
tificially for the drawing room. By 1909 an estimated eighty percent of private
schools for women had provision for outdoor sports.

Although public schools adopted athletics less eagerly, by 1918 baseball
had made appreciable gains among schoolgirls, judging from the results of
a Cleveland recreation survey. Those who reported baseball as one of their
spare-time activities included 17 percent of Cleveland public elementary
schoolgirls, 53 percent of private school girls, 67 percent of public high
school girls, and 72 percent of private high school girls.

Some Playground Association members and others continued from time
to time to speak out for athletics for girls. George Johnson favored "modified
baseball" (probably playground ball) for girls: "Physically and socially there
could hardly be a better game for girls from 10 to 12 years of age . . . , and

if begun at that age, it continues as desirable when they are older." Joseph Lee in 1915 urged lively games for girls eleven to fourteen "lest they suffer from premature young ladyhood." He even favored baseball playing between preteen boys and girls, pointing out that at this age some girls could still beat boys in baseball, and with equal training many could come close enough in skill to that of the average boy to make competition interesting. "Baseball is a good game for girls," he went on. "They are said to lack the boy's throwing instinct, but it requires a professional to know the difference; certainly some girls can throw farther than most boys."

Some so-called tomboys of the 1900s played baseball so well as to excite public notice and admiration. Glenda Collett, the champion women's golfer of the twenties, as a youngster played third base on her brother's team because she could make the long throw better than any of the boys. While growing up in a small Pennsylvania town, Carrie Mayer always played ball with the boys. Then when Carrie was seventeen and attending Normal School at Kutztown early in the century she drew the attention of *Sporting News* as a pitcher who could "give a ball more twists and curves" than her baker father could to a pretzel.

About the same time, Margery Bell, an excellent high school athlete and daughter of Frank Bell, a well-known amateur pitcher in the Northwest in the 1880s, won a bet with her father that she could equal the best women's record for throwing a baseball. She threw it 204 feet 4 inches, said to be a new women's record. In Massachusetts three sisters of Gabby Hartnett, star catcher of the Chicago Cubs, played on a top women's team in Millville, a textile town. The best of the three, Anna, called Charlie, could throw better than most men. So good was she that one day in 1920 a family friend brought her to Braves Field, where she performed by warming up Jess Barnes, then on the New York Giants' pitching staff.

Another skilled player was Coralie Beale, discovered by Charles "Red" Dooin, well-known catcher who had played with the Philadelphia Nationals. Coralie had been playing for five years with her brothers and friends (and striking them out) and reportedly displayed "a throwing arm of which any man could be proud" when Dooin saw her on the back lots of Philadelphia and was so impressed that he arranged for her to pitch a game against the strong Belfield Country Club team, mentioned above, in 1911.

Probably the youngest female player that came to public attention was Sunshine Bessie, age six, of Lynn, Massachusetts, who had her own baseball uniform and reportedly played better than most boys of her age. Another youngster, Beatrice Gould, who was to become editor of the *Ladies Home Journal*, played ball before 1920 as a child in Iowa City. "My younger brother, Roger," she said, "allowed me to play baseball with his team, thus fostering a lifelong passion for that most dramatic game, each player chewing, hawking, spitting, artful as any ballet dancer, at every turn alone with his skill, alone against his fate." (Or her fate.)

Girls were not entirely incapable of teamwork or wanting in courage, as the stereotype of the time would have them. Mayme Dwyer's vivid and straightforward recollection of girls' high school baseball experience in Manito, Illinois, demonstrates this fact. When in 1914 a group of the boys in the school wanted to play tennis, the school constructed "a fine court" for them. Some of the girls then got together and wondered, "What is there for us?" They consulted a teacher, who suggested they form a baseball team.

Not all the girls wanted to play; a few were "deathly afraid" of the ball, but Dwyer, who had played sandlot ball with neighborhood children, wanted to try it. But where? The school grounds afforded only a large piece of land mostly overgrown with two-foot-high prickly pear. Nevertheless, "we grubbed it all out," said Mayme in a 1985 interview, despite "fingers full of prickles."

The Manito girls formed two eight-member teams and played every day after school and sometimes at noon or even before school opened. Their physical training teacher occasionally let them play during their weekly class session, but she refused the girls any help or supervision because, she said, their play was only "a flash in the pan" and they would "get over it." So the girls played on their own, without even an umpire. As a result, some of their games got rough and were interrupted by arguments.

Nor did they receive encouragement from the other high school teachers, most of whom thought their playing baseball was "terrible" and repeatedly asked, "Are you sure your parents want you to play?" The teachers also seemed "quite vindictive," Dwyer recalled. If the girls reached their classroom from the ball field a few seconds after the late bell, they received a demerit, but if the boys who played tennis did, they went unpunished.

The school board, which did not object to the Manito girls' playing, supplied two balls and two bats and told the girls those were all they would get. Dwyer's parents did not seem to mind, either, but her mother and some of the others thought the girls should play in bloomers. Her father, however, refused to permit her to wear "short pants" in public. The school administration would not allow the girls to wear their gym suits outdoors, and the baseball players did not know where they could get bloomers even if they could afford them, so they played in their "regular clothes"—dresses that reached about midway between knees and ankles.

Originally, the Manito players wanted to call themselves the Bloomer Girls, but unable to get bloomers and having begun playing as juniors, they decided on "Jolly Juniors" instead.

While the Jolly Juniors were playing ball, boys sometimes came and sat on the slope behind the playing area. Soon they began hollering at and harrassing the players, so the girls devised a plan to stop this annoyance. They piled some of the grubbed-up prickly pear onto the slope, so if the boys wanted to watch they had to stand. One day Dwyer, who usually caught for one of the teams, turned her head when someone on the other team hollered at her and was hit in the mouth by the pitched ball. Her mouth swelled "quite a bit," but she shrugged it off, until her upper teeth turned black! After many unsuccessful visits to a dentist, she finally had the teeth removed.

Apparently, some of the Manito boys contradicted their stereotype, too. One day a "handsome" new boy came to town and enrolled in the school. He did not want to play tennis, but he accepted Dwyer's invitation to play baseball with the girls. Each team wanted him on its side, so the girls decided he had to play with both, and they let him play any position he chose. Usually, he decided to pitch. Dwyer recalled, "We had a glorious time" until the boys who did not play tennis discovered what was happening. When they did, they insisted that if the new boy could play ball with the girls, they could, too. They invaded the play and tried to take over. The girls struck back by "accidentally" hitting the boys with the ball, especially the leaders. When one of the boys got hit in the ear and tattled, the principal came down to watch the game, but the invaders did not show up that day. In consequence, however, the principal ruled that either all the boys could play or none could, so the new boy's participation ended.

The Jolly Juniors continued to play baseball until their graduation in 1915, beginning in March, when it was still very cold, on through spring, and again in the fall. In the afterlight, Mayme Dwyer (now Mrs. Seelye and the mother of a college president), believes that "We tried hard and stuck with it largely because so many were against us."

31

GOLDILOCKS IS BENCHED

The impression of the twenties as a decade of substantial female liberation derives in part from the fact that the shower of publicity on the decade's sports titans descended on female champions as well as on male, for instance Glenna Collett (golf), Helen Wills (tennis), and Gertrude Ederle (swimming). Sports clothing for women became more practical and fashionable, and so many popular magazines published articles on "women as athletes" that in 1922 the *Reader's Guide to Periodical Literature* added the term as a new category.

The big change in manners and morals exemplified by the flapper was real, as Professor Barbara Deckard has pointed out, but otherwise the evidence of genuine independence is essentially superficial. Women's suffrage, for example, fulfilled neither opponents' misgivings nor radical suffragettes' expectations. It failed to appreciably affect women's attitudes, and it did not diminish assumptions that women would continue in traditional roles.

Equally frail is the notion that the unprecedented surge of women into sports during the twenties evidences genuine liberation. But it did contribute greater enjoyment to the lives of women and girls and may well have relaxed the strictures on their behavior and improved their sense of well-being more than did the flapper culture.

Inspiration and assistance came from many sources. Individual stars endorsed sports for women and girls. Helen Wills assured women that sports participation in no way lessened femininity. Glenna Collett told them, "The tomboy ideal is far more healthful than that of the poor little Goldilocks of the seventies and eighties, who was forbidden vigorous activities lest she tear her clothes." Grantland Rice noted that in some competitions, backstroke swimming for example, women were "not outclassed by the best of men." Amateur sportswomen supplied leadership for females in schools, churches, and social institutions.

The new summit reached by female sports participation also became broader-based. Women of all classes enlarged their repertoire with a greater variety of both individual and team games from baseball and basketball to swimming, tennis, golf, bowling, and even rougher pursuits like bob-sledding.

Industrial and business sponsorship of sports, reflecting industrial capitalism's zenith, waxed in the twenties. Sports teams for men and women representing banks, insurance companies, sporting goods companies, chambers of commerce, and large corporations played intramurally or as members of leagues backed by local municipal departments.

Some companies undertook elaborate programs that included women, and, although descriptions of them did not always mention baseball for women specifically, it was in all likelihood available in most such programs. General Electric of Schenectady, New York, maintained six camps and vacation clubs, and between the camp tents were fields for athletics where women employees from branches in nine cities could play while vacationing for less than a dollar a day. Another unnamed company laid out two twelve-acre playing fields, one for each sex, and set aside an additional seventy-acre field for general use. At Ludlow Manufacturing in Massachusetts, where 1,400 women represented about forty percent of the total membership of the company's athletic and recreation association, the company provided two baseball diamonds for women. In the same city the American Woollen Company's house organ published in 1920 a photo of grinning Susie McCarron, pitcher for No. 6 Twisting Room, leaving the diamond after a hard-fought twelve-inning game. Susie wore a standard baseball suit but set her cap at a rakish angle.

The Cleveland Recreation Survey of 1920 revealed that women employees of the Kaynee Company played baseball at noon as part of the program of the firm's athletic club of sixty women. The National Carbon Company in Cleveland also endorsed baseball clubs for its women employees, and both the Perfection Spring Department of the Standard Parts Company and the Nela Park branch of General Electric sponsored baseball for women after work.

Women played baseball at the second annual field day of the Rumford Printing Company in Concord, New Hampshire, where "Ball games proved the most entertaining feature of the morning program," said *Playground*, especially a contest between teams of young women which, according to the newspaper report the following day "showed some promising material." The city recreation department of Oakland, California, which lent a hand to local industries, aided women's baseball, and by 1921 Oakland working women's teams played ball during the noon hour. In Wilmington, Delaware, the 1923 *Bulletin* of the Joseph Bancroft & Sons Company stated that besides the existing men's interdepartmental baseball league, a women's league had been organized.

The white suits with knickers worn by women employees at the Calumet Baking Powder Company in Chicago seemed particularly adapted for baseball, which they played during noon hour. Seeing them play at least a half-dozen baseball games one noontime, John J. Glenn, secretary of the Illinois Manufacturers' Association said,

> Those girls were pitching curves, catching hot ones and sliding to bases with all the joyous abandon of youth. . . . Anyone who gives the matter any thought must appreciate that those girls went back to their work after the noon hour in a more satisfied frame of mind and in better physical condition than if they had merely sat around on benches and talked on the usual subjects which are popular among girls of that age.

Industrial sports as operated in New Haven shows the way business and private agencies could cooperate to offer sport for women. There the YMCA and YWCA joined local businesses in an Industrial Federation to operate leagues in six sports. In New York the powerful International Ladies Garment Workers Union, known for its comprehensive recreation programs, advertised the sports program of its Pennsylvania vacation center in its periodical, *Justice*.

Tragedy could also strike during baseball play. Katherine Reinert, supervisor of sewing machine operators at Richman Brothers Clothing Manufacturers in Cleveland, where men and women played baseball during lunch hour, recalled that during a game in 1926 a woman player fell, seriously injured, never stopped bleeding, and died. "The accident didn't end the baseball games, however," Reinert remembered.

Informal industrial play for women became usual. The 1926 bulletin of the United States Bureau of Labor Statistics found that although regularly organized baseball teams of women workers were not common, large numbers of women played ball during lunchtime and after working hours. Interest varied depending on degree of skill, but often spectators averaged several hundred, and where there was a grandstand or stadium, several thousand might watch an important game. In one case a company even furnished the women's uniforms and equipment and paid teams' entrance fee to the local municipal league.

At the Chicago gum company owned by William Wrigley, Jr., Physician L. Grace Sitzer, manager of the Medical and Welfare Departments, explained why the company sponsored baseball for the women employees. "Baseball and other sports at the company are considered health activities," she wrote in 1929. Such activities, Sitzer went on, helped reduce absenteeism. Baseball, together with the wide variety of other recreational projects, was not a matter of company charity. "It costs money to train girls and men—and the fewer we are obliged to break in the better. We believe that the work done by our welfare department has a great part in keeping down our labor turnover rate." Keen competition prevailed in Wrigley baseball, and departments showed great interest in the standing of their teams. Baseball playoffs took place at the summer outing, and winners earned prizes.

Some companies hung back, however. Of 51 replies to questionnaires sent to 101 factories in 23 states in 1922, about half reported furnishing only bare necessities like rest rooms and lunch rooms, and only two provided baseball for women employees. The following year another survey, conducted by Ruth Stone, director of the Women's Service Department of Western Electric's Hawthorne Works in Chicago, found that of 35 industrial firms in the city, only five offered athletic facilities and playgrounds for women. But at Western Electric itself, the company's Hawthorne Club, already ten years old in 1923 and called by sports writer Hugh Fullerton the largest athletic association in the world, had 28,000 members. The Hawthorne plant's ten-acre athletic field included a baseball diamond as early as 1921, when only a small group of women showed interest in athletics, but efforts to attract them soon produced results until two years later fourteen sports availed, including a form of modified baseball.

Much about the organization and administration of women's industrial baseball and sports in general repelled some women, especially female leaders of physical training, for the usual reasons: absence of the play tradition, insufficient recognition of women's limitations, lack of safeguards to their physical and moral well-being, and failure to avoid their exploitation through highly competitive contests.

The reformers had little success. Mabel Lee of the American Physical Education Association admitted that they failed to break the grip of the American Athletic Union on industry-sponsored ball. The AAU paid little attention to their urgings, as demonstrated by sporadic remonstrances throughout the decade, such as the rather fatuous 1928 suggestion by Helen Coops of the University of Cincinnati that industrial players compete for the sake of play alone, as in the school and college "play day."*

In the girls' world, Goldilocks remained much in evidence in the twenties. The elementary school kept boys and girls separated as much as possible. On the street, the playground of city youngsters, the twain seldom met: boys played boys' games with boys, and girls played theirs with girls.

Nevertheless, a sprinkle of evidence indicates progress in girls' baseball in the twenties. By then more than thirty states required physical training in public school, and this requirement led to the organization of state high school athletic leagues, thus creating an environment receptive to girls' as well as boys' participation in sports. At a Paterson, New Jersey, high school, for example, a 1925 field day included girls' baseball, and the New York *Times* published action photos of individual girls playing in knee-length skirts, short-sleeved blouses, knee sox, and what appeared to be tennis shoes. One photo showed Minnie Bursten catching a ball over her head, another pictured Jennie de Marco at bat with Dot Firth catching, and a third showed Emma Yates sliding home in a cloud of dust! Early in the twenties the Keene, New Hampshire, high school added girls' baseball to its sports pro-

*See below, Chapter 32.

gram as a minor sport. A group of sports-minded women teachers in rural Illinois initiated for their students a girls' baseball league representing four country schools. At Mary Institute, St. Louis, an exclusive girls' school, a young woman who later became the wife of Joe Medwick, star of the 1930s St. Louis Cardinals, played baseball and other sports.

Teaching baseball "leadup skills" became usual in schools. A high school physical education text for girls prepared by the University of Michigan physical training department (1928) recommended teaching baseball skills that supposedly could be practiced in a gymnasium: bunting, throwing at a target, batting flies, fielding grounders, running bases, and performing defensive tactics like making double plays. Teaching girls how to throw a baseball and holding throwing contests were fairly common. Frederick J. Reilly, writing in a 1921 issue of *Playground*, claimed that every schoolgirl, not merely a select few, was learning to throw a baseball. The Illinois High School Athletic Association established a set of requirements for baseball skills: girls were to throw a league outdoor ball 140 feet and throw a 12-inch indoor ball 130 feet. The New York *Times* published in 1925 a photo of a Miss Gilliland, winner of the baseball-throwing contest at the Savage School with a mark of 188 feet. Elinor Churchill of the Robinson Female Academy, Exeter, New Hampshire, after surpassing this mark with a 234-foot throw, found her picture in *Collier's*.

A 1928 issue of *Ladies' Home Journal* mentioned an Alice Beeckman who, like Margaret Gisolo, played well enough to win a place on her otherwise all-boy high school team. The team lost its opening game of the season, but Beeckman not only played errorless ball in the field, she made a three-base hit, although she was left on third because none of her teammates could drive her home. Nevertheless, some editorial writers viewed with dismay her presence on a boys' team.

Interscholastic ball for girls came under criticism in the twenties. According to Emmet Rice and Mabel Lee, one reason for organizing the first state league of the Girls' High School Athletic Association was to counter "undesirable" programs of interscholastic athletics by promoting sports for the many rather than the highly skilled few. A corps of influential physical training Cassandras, among them Florence Somers, assistant state supervisor of physical training in Massachusetts; Elizabeth Quinlan, physical training director at Boston Teachers' College; and Willystone Goodsell, an education professor at Columbia Teachers' College, continued in books and articles to hammer away against sports, including baseball, that furnished high-level competition. To guide school heads, the women's division of NAAF published in 1925 a circular setting forth its arguments, which particularly emphasized putting women in control of girls' sports.

A less restrictive position came from Janet Walker, supervisor of girls' athletics for Philadelphia's board of education. She emphasized the need to establish "the joy that comes from the contact in the game and competition."

This approach, she thought, might improve on the adolescent girl "obsessed with the powder puff." While recognizing differences between boys and girls in physical abilities, Walker asserted that girls were improving steadily in jumping, running, and throwing.

In a carefully thought out, well-balanced argument made in 1929, Jessie Hewitt, teacher at the Ethel Walker School in Simsbury, Connecticut, expressed clear-cut opposition to the majority opinion. She declared flatly that in girls' schools athletics should be both compulsory and competitive. Competition, she held, resulted in the "best playing," and "if you excel, you have not only fun, but also the enduring joy of knowing that, ranked with your peers, you are good." Hewitt advocated a program of daily games, with baseball one of the spring activities. At her own school, said Hewitt, such a regimen improved the girls' "vigor, vitality, and energy," including that of the "delicate." Athletics were therefore even more important for girls than for boys. While conceding that competition should be limited to contests among local schools and recognizing possible "evils" in competition—excitement, noise, fatigue, and expense—Hewitt believed that benefits to the girls compensated: broadening one's view, adjusting to new conditions, learning to be a good guest or hostess, seeing and overcoming flaws in one's character, and learning to do better than one thinks one can when necessary.

More trenchant even than Hewitt's argument was that of William S. Packer, a member of the Winchester, Massachusetts, Park Board, who in 1926 delivered a broadside against a "diluted intra-mural system" which, he said, "cannot be expected to fill the bill" because this is a "hard world" and "no place for soft girls. . . . The rearing of women of sufficient fiber," he declared, "requires a certain severity," and when a girl learns "to bear her part in team play and competition against strangers, she has a fair prospect of picking her way wisely through life." Taking aim at the physical training women, he continued:

> The movement now on foot to restrict and abolish, or denature sport for girls, is part of the enslavement from which women have suffered through the ages. It cannot finally succeed, although it may gain sufficient vogue . . . to cheat a generation of girls of the contact with the world which is their right.

Packer's remark about a "hard world" soon proved all too true. The leaden impact of the great depression afflicted women at least as much as men. Not only were women dismissed from jobs, but employers, unions, and government pressured them to quit to make openings for men and refused to hire married women for the same reason. Even the WPA, organized in 1935, gave men preference in employment, and feminist hopes for economic equality raised in the past disappeared like the smoke from the idle factories.

Some women, whether as players, fans, or ancillary workers, found in baseball something of a buffer against the worries and travails of hard times, a relief from the spirit-draining enforced leisure of unemployment. For girls as well as boys, the WPA's construction of playground and other recreational facilities provided added opportunities to play ball. Response to these opportunities doubtless contributed to greater public tolerance of female participation in sports. A review of studies by a physiologist in 1932 concluding that women's sports participation had no effects on menstruation, pregnancy, childbirth, or the condition of the uterus may have contributed to public lenity.

Sponsorship of girls' baseball in the thirties came from many quarters, public and private. By the late thirties at least eight states had set up girls' high school athletic leagues that included baseball, and some sponsored state tournaments. A wide variety of sports, baseball among them, opened to junior and senior classes at Horace Mann High School for Girls in New York City. A girl starred on the Webster, Massachusetts, high school team in 1936; another pitched for the high school in Mercedes, Texas.

In country schools it was not uncommon for girls to fill gaps on the baseball team when it suffered a shortage of boys big enough to play. Girls growing up in rural areas sometimes played baseball in cow pastures with boys, as writer Jeane Westin did in Oklahoma. In the thirties, girls' and senior women's baseball teams participated in playground divisions of some city park departments as well, such as Seattle's.

Girls attending summer camps wanted change and freedom to do new things, declared Porter Sargent, writer of camp guides, and baseball was a good camp game for them, especially since they did not get as much chance to play during the year as boys did. Camp Ar-e-wa, in Fredericksburg, Pennsylvania, offered girls 8 to 18 baseball, among other activities. In the hills of Keene, New Hampshire, at a camp for girls 6 to 14 called Trails End, baseball was one of a half-dozen activities emphasized. At an international camp for girls in Norway in 1931 an American counselor taught baseball in a mixture of languages, and when mastered the game proved the most popular among the "land sports." Baseball terms, however, were never rendered quite accurately: foreign girls "beat" the ball with the "stick," basemen became "fieldermen," and an inning became a "play."

Industrial and business firms continued to sponsor women's teams in the thirties—to "exploit girls," as Mabel Lee would have it in her book, *Conduct of Physical Education*. There appeared to be a trend away from independent teams, however. Perhaps they were made impractical by the depression and by outworn novelty and made redundant by greater opportunities to play under public and private sponsorship. Nevertheless, an independent all-women's team occasionally received press notice. The New York *Times* reported, for example, that the Philadelphia Bobbies, a team of venturesome teenagers, somehow found themselves stranded in Japan without funds after a tour there, and that a wealthy East Indian merchant paid their passage home aboard the *Empress of Russia*. The Caruso All-Stars of New York, captained by a well-known player, Josie Caruso, defeated the Pennsylvania

Coal Miners Baseball Club at the Polo Grounds 4–2 in 1930 in an experimental night game during which poor visibility from only 13,000 watts caused
the crowd of 3,000 to dwindle to 1,000 before the game ended. Professors
George Wiley and Dale Landon cited another traveling girls' team that
played a club belonging to a league of company towns in the mining district
of Indiana County, Pennsylvania, in the 1930s.

A number of individual female players were, however, sufficiently skilled
or brash to qualify for exploitation as drawing cards by male promoters and
also to earn some notoriety and money through baseball. In 1931 *Baseball
Magazine* reported that Mae Arbaugh, known professionally as Carrie Nation, had reputedly played 4,600 ball games over a three-year period. Thus
she surpassed Ty Cobb's record before Pete Rose did, and in far less time!
About then, the New York *Times* mentioned Vada Corbus, a female pitcher,
as having signed with Joplin, Missouri, of the Western Association, a league
in Organized Baseball. The Joplin *Globe* pictured her in a Joplin uniform
with a caption announcing that she was expected to work in part of the Joplin
Miners' opening game April 30. Nothing came of this, however, probably
because the advance publicity alerted National Association officials, who
quashed any plan of the Joplin Club to use her in a game.

Another woman, Frances "Sonny" Dunlap, actually managed to get into
an Organized Baseball game. She appeared in the lineup of the Fayetteville
Bears of the Class D Arkansas-Missouri League on September 7, the next-
to-last day of the 1936 season, when her team won 5–1 over the Cassville
Blues, the first-half champions of the league, at the Fayetteville Fairgrounds.
The next day the local newspaper reported that Dunlap "gave a swell exhibit
of herself" at third base during pregame infield practice but that during the
game she went hitless, although in each of her three times at bat she connected with the pitch. She had no chances in right field. Dunlap may have
been the first woman to play an entire game in Organized Baseball, apparently because league officials had not been alerted by advance publicity in
time to prevent it.

Kitty Burke, a nightclub singer, was permitted to come to bat in a 1935
major-league game, St. Louis at Cincinnati. Various accounts that appeared
later have embellished the story, but *Sporting News* reporting at the time
explained that the game had taken on a carnival tone, the park having been
oversold because of interest in night ball as a novelty, and thousands of
standees crowded the field within ten feet of home plate. During the game
Burke carried on a shouting match with Joe Medwick, Cardinal outfielder
and one of the best hitters ever, claiming she could hit better than he could.
In a late inning she grabbed Babe Herman's bat from him and stepped up
to hit. Neither Umpire-in-Chief Bill Stewart nor Commissioner Landis, both
of whom were spectators, attempted to interfere, so Paul Dean, the St.
Louis pitcher, tossed a ball underhand to Burke, who dribbled it toward
the mound and started running to first. Dean fielded the ball and threw
her out.

In contrast to Burke, Jackie Mitchell (Virne Beatrice Mitchell), the subject of another publicity stunt, was a real ball player, reputed to have been pitching curves since she was six years old. Mitchell had played for her prep school team as well as in a women's baseball league. Joe Engel, owner-president of the Chattanooga Lookouts of the Southern League and a baseball showman par excellence, conceived her brief appearance against major-league players. She was still in her teens when he first saw her and made her a star of his Engelettes, a women's road team, then signed her for the Lookouts for the season of 1931. According to the New York *Times*, the Memphis Chicks tried to get her, in exchange for two players, but Engel refused. That spring the Yankees, barnstorming north from their Florida training camp, played an exhibition game against the Lookouts before 4,000 fans, and when Babe Ruth came to bat, Engel sent Mitchell in to pitch. She struck out both Ruth and Gehrig, and some later writers claimed the two batters fanned on purpose, although in 1984 Mitchell denied it and said, "I was pitching real good. . . . " When she walked the next hitter, Tony Lazzeri, Engel took her out, satisfied with the publicity he had obtained. Judge Landis disallowed her contract with the Lookouts because, said sports writer Cy Yoakam in 1987, he felt that the world of baseball would be too hard for a girl. By July Mitchell had left to join the House of David team, and in the next several seasons she played ball for several small cities before leaving the game.

The best female ball player ever, and possibly the best all-'round athlete of all (only Jim Thorpe rivals her) was Mildred "Babe" Didrickson. She came from an athletic Texas family and as a child played baseball on the Beaumont sandlots. She hit so many homers that her friends gave her Ruth's nickname, which lasted throughout her life. She also played on the girls' baseball team (as well as on every other girls' sports team) of Beaumont High School.

When she was still a teenager a Dallas insurance team recruited Didrickson for its basketball team and gave her an office job. At the same time she starred in a local women's softball league. From there she went on to break national records in sport, especially golf, and in international competition, where she won the baseball throw for three years in a row, qualifying for the Olympics in several sports and winning gold medals.

When the insurance company basketball season ended, Didrickson toured with the House of David team as its only female, pitching the first inning of each game to draw crowds. With the House she played against top black teams like the Pittsburgh Crawfords and the Kansas City Monarchs. Babe could hit but was reputedly not much of a pitcher. Newt Allen, a member of the Monarchs then, later said opposing players tried to "make her look good," although another black player, Bill Holland, said, "She was a good athlete."

Babe also pitched briefly in a few major-league exhibition games for the Cardinals, Athletics, and Indians. In a game against the Cardinals, with bases loaded she pitched her "high hard one" to Jimmy Foxx who, she admitted ruefully later, "knocked it into the next county." Her favorite baseball position was shortstop, because, as she said, she liked to "scoop 'em up." She numbered baseball people like Ruth, Medwick, and Leo Durocher among her best friends.

Babe Didrickson became the center of the haggard controversy over whether women in sports lacked femininity. Because her appearance did not conform to the current ideal of feminine beauty, and because she excelled in sports not generally considered women's, some condemned her as a "muscle moll." Yet she maintained that she had always liked traditional women's activities like cooking, sewing, and decorating, loved "all the pretty things," and had dates and boyfriends from the time she took the Dallas job. She also had what was evidently a successful marriage to George Zaharias, a professional wrestler. More important, she did much to promote the acceptance of women in highly competitive sport, and many qualified to judge believe she fulfilled her childhood dream: "My goal was to be the greatest athlete that ever lived."

In the thirties A.G. Spalding and Company encouraged and at the same time attested to the growth of women's baseball. An article, "Baseball for the Elementary School Girl," in its 1937 guide to women's ball, reminded the teacher that she should drill girls in baseball technique, teach them the sidearm method of throwing, and demonstrate the correct batting position, remembering that girls do not step up to bat "naturally, the way boys do." (That is not necessarily so, of course.) In a foreword to another guide, Organized Baseball's commissioner, in a burst of broadmindedness, declared that baseball should "adapt itself admirably" to play by women, and "I hope to see baseball played as widely by young women in the years to come as it is by young men today."

The deeply prejudiced never surrender, however, and opponents of baseball for females were no exception in the thirties. Often an irate mother, according to Spalding's 1937 baseball guide for girls, demanded to know why her "little Mary" had to play ball, did not think the game would help her Mary become a perfect lady, and did not want Mary to be a tomboy. The guide explained that good health required outdoor play and that baseball developed critical thinking, good physical health, and a spirit of comradeship desirable to social relations.

Others expressed either grudging tolerance or outright opposition to ball playing by girls. Mary J. Breen, author of a book on mixed play, disapproved of rivalry and competition between the sexes. She believed that groups of adolescent girls and boys should play together only those games that depended little on physical endurance and involved no "personal contact." Others warned of physiological differences: Donald Laird, a Ph.D. and Sci.D., asserted in *Scientific American* that "In socking the baseball out into center field . . . the men can bat it about twice as far as women." Stephan K. Westmann, a Berlin-trained M.D. and holder of a German silver medal for gymnastics and sports, recommended that women throw light objects as an admirable way of developing skill but cautioned that to avoid "one sided development . . . both arms should be used equally." Westmann failed to make clear whether "one-sidedness" was acceptable for men.

Nonscientists expressed their own versions of femininity. Frederick R. Rogers, a physical training leader, in 1930 opposed baseball playing by girls because it developed muscles, scowling faces, and the competitive spirit. Paul Gallico, a well-known sports writer of the time, qualifies for a post-humous award as a male chauvinist with his "Women in Sports Should Look Beautiful" article in a 1936 *Reader's Digest.* In only eight out of twenty-five sports did women meet Gallico's standard, and he liked some of the eight only because of the grace and "cute costumes" associated with them. Ball games were out; they were too strenuous, Gallico declared, and they made women sweat. That same year the women of the National Screw and Manufacturing Company of Cleveland won the national amateur women's softball championship, even though winning probably involved some sweating—or perhaps perspiring.

One place where women did not have to be fussy about looking pretty while playing baseball was in the reformatories and prisons. And, ironically, incarcerated women had more freedom in playing the game than those outside the walls. Unlike the disapproval of intense competition encountered by those who played ball outside, not only permission but encouragement awaited those who played it inside.

Women's reformatories of the late twenties were dreary places at best. Most of them offered only token programs of rehabilitation because of lack of funds, petty rules, overcrowding, and sometimes mistreatment by underpaid, overworked matrons. In such squalid environments baseball cheered and helped divert residents. Teams at the Ohio State Reformatory played ball daily between 12:00 N. and 1:00 P.M. during the twenties. Young women not on a team gathered on the lawn to watch and root from the sidelines. Twice annually, exhibition games took place. The administration at Ohio State used proceeds from the quarter admission charge, a total of $60.00 on Labor Day of 1922, to purchase baseball equipment. In Bedford, New York, in the twenties the State Reformatory offered baseball and other games under a trained physical director. At the Minnesota State Reformatory, baseball, supervised by the staff and using supplies furnished by the state, ranked as one of the principal sports.

According to Nicole Rafter's 1982 book on incarcerated women, by the 1930s the women's reformatory movement was on the wane. Nevertheless, as the National Prison Association reported, baseball continued at some of them. At Skowhegan, Maine, baseball was the chief sport, and at Clinton Farms, New Jersey, inmates could play ball and other sports at any time outside working hours. Each residential cottage at the Rockwell City, Iowa, Women's Reformatory used the recreation field in turn for softball and other sports. At Bedford, New York, in the institution then called the Bedford Hills State Farm, the administration still encouraged baseball in the thirties, and the game continued to be welcomed enthusiastically. A "commendable competitive spirit" had developed among the cottages, the Prison Association investigator reported, and it had cut discipline problems an estimated seventy-five percent.

By 1935 the optimism of the Progressive period had subsided, and with the deepening depression, states became unwilling to finance expensive separate institutions for petty offenders. As administrations gradually replaced such inmates with serious offenders, women's reformatories began to resemble prisons. In a number of states the two types of institutions merged during the thirties and operated with little provision for education and training.

Few women's prisons of the thirties had space for recreation. The Federal Industrial Institution for Women at Alderson, West Virginia, was an exception. According to the report of its superintendent in 1930, baseball teams gave 200 inmates a chance to "develop a sense of play, clean sport, and the necessity for teamwork," an aid to those considered "extreme individualists." The superintendent's report for 1934–35 stated that the recent increase in population at Alderson had eliminated the necessity for evening work in the fields and so released a "great amount of energy" for baseball games. The inmates organized six teams out of a population of 469, and there was "scarcely an evening when either a practice or match game is not in progress." The next annual report recorded baseball as even more popular than in the previous year.

In 1931 New York State designated the Albion State Training School as its institution for "defective delinquent females," and it transferred normal inmates to Bedford. Most of the remaining 373 women had been incarcerated for crimes against "public order," many of them for some type of what was then considered "sexual misconduct" not regarded as criminal in men. By 1937–39 their median age was twenty-five. Numbers of them were physically below par and lacked initiative and interest. Authorities enrolled most of them in a physical training program that included baseball and other competitive games.

Most important, in the twenties and thirties women penetrated virtually all categories of Organized Baseball other than the playing field itself, and even there, as we have seen, a few appeared occasionally. Their attachment to baseball was most conspicuous as fans, but they had become more enthusiastic and increasingly knowledgeable ones. Club owners continued to cater to them even in the minor leagues. In the thirties, reputedly, few ball parks equalled the accommodations for women at the Louisville park, with its new ladies' lounge containing mirrored powder rooms of ten units, five wash basins, and hot water, attended, as one might guess in the South, by an "old-fashioned" black maid "appropriately costumed"!

Professional clubs in both major- and minor-league cities and towns, realizing the value of creating future fans, set up knothole gangs to encourage not only boys but girls to interest themselves in baseball. About 3,100 girls attended one St. Louis game through its Knothole Club in 1936. In Memphis girls as well as boys from nine to fifteen could see games free on Wednesdays and Saturdays.

Ladies Days, by now a fixed practice, sometimes backfired. At a St. Louis game in the fall of 1922 with the Browns, who nearly won the pennant, playing their last series against the Yankees, who did win it, some 35,500 women, fighting to enter the ball park, broke down one of the gates and lost tempers, shoes, and "a lot of other things," remembered Margaret Murphy, Browns' assistant treasurer. So many mobbed into Chicago's park for a Brooklyn-Cubs series in 1930 there was not enough room for paying fans, so the owner limited them to 15,000 tickets, to be obtained in advance, at downtown outlets. This requirement failed to stem the flood. Two years later so many women poured out during a Cubs winning streak in August that the club made them appear in person on Tuesday to secure free tickets for Friday. This scheme still failed to solve the problem, so the management decided to require women to apply on Monday for the coming Friday by enclosing stamped, self-addressed envelopes, the first 20,000 applications to get tickets. At the peak of a close pennant race, nine mail bags totalling 35,000 requests arrived.

After a Ladies Day game in Philadelphia two rabid women fans approached Umpire Charlie Moran accusing him of favoring the visiting St. Louis Cardinals. One hit him over the head with a closed umbrella, and the other tried to kick him. He escaped by running away. Female attacks on an umpire had occurred before that, at least in fiction. In "Baseball Betty," a 1924 story by sports writer W.O. McGeehan, the heroine's criticisms of the umpire's decisions began to influence his work. But when the crowd grew hostile because of his erratic judgments, she befriended him, and ultimately she married him.

The female baseball bug could cause domestic difficulties, too. In one extreme instance a Chicago judge fined the husband of Mrs. Ann Pilger $100.00 and put him on probation for blacking both her eyes after she went to a ball game against his wishes and returned home so angry (evidently over her team's defeat) that she refused to cook his dinner.

Some female zealots followed their home teams around the circuit. Those "crazy about" players, then called "Baseball Daisies," sent "mash notes" to players, who on their part boldly eyed the stands for possible conquests or became Peeping Toms by using holes they cut in the back of dugouts, then sending notes to the women via ushers.

In the thirties girls and women won prizes in various baseball contests, such as for identifying players in pictures. Alma Burhop of Hot Springs, Arkansas, won several, and after receiving letters from surprised fans she

denied having brothers or getting any help. *Sporting News* thought a "remarkable number" of women entered a contest to choose the most popular
baseball broadcaster. In 1935 a married woman from Ohio won first prize
in a baseball crossword puzzle contest, and in 1939 three women, one of
them a schoolteacher (none from a major-league city) won the top three
prizes in a *Sporting News* baseball puzzle contest. By 1940 the puzzles were
themselves being written by a woman, Mrs. Francis Briggs of Provincetown,
Rhode Island, who became interested in baseball at an early age, married
a former minor-league player, and then began constructing the puzzles.
Another woman, Dr. Anne E. Gray, an optometrist from Selma, Alabama,
became executive secretary of the Hot Stove League, a national fan club.
As a child she had been forbidden to get into boys' games, and finding the
girls' games "sissy stuff" and umpiring too dangerous, settled for being
a fan.

Other women knew enough baseball to get into sports broadcasting. On
Clark Griffith's recommendation, the General Mills Company hired Helen
Dettweiler, 23, to join its baseball announcers and to handle roving assignments. Dettweiler had played baseball from early childhood and had become
an all-around athlete in baseball, golf, tennis, basketball, and swimming.
Radio Station WMCA employed Alice Brewer as sports commentator on her
own women's program, covering all major sports five days a week on an
equal footing with male announcers except for the play-by-play. Mrs. Leslie
Scarsella, wife of a Cincinnati Reds first baseman in the 1930s, handled the
play-by-play broadcast of a 1939 Reds game and demonstrated that she knew
not only baseball but the game's slang as well.

A behind-the-scenes figure in the history of the famous Spink publications
was Marie Taylor Spink, wife of *Sporting News* owner Charles C. Spink and
mother of the next owner, J.G. Taylor Spink. At first Marie did bookkeeping
and clipped articles from other papers. With the birth of her children she
dropped her active role at the paper, but by entertaining prominent baseball
figures in the Spink home she became well-known in baseball circles. After
her children reached adulthood she returned to part-time work at the *Sporting News* as vice president and treasurer of the company and until 1941,
according to her obituary, "exercised a greater influence on baseball than
any other woman in the history of the game." Her son Taylor married Blanch
Keene, who accompanied him to baseball gatherings, developed a wide
acquaintance among baseball people, and smoothed over difficulties arising
from Taylor's disputes with officials over policies he deemed unworthy of
the game.

Regardless of their deepening interest in and increasing knowledge of
baseball, women fans could still find themselves subject to condescension
and targets of lame humor. An article in *Baseball Magazine* entitled "Ladies'
Day" represented them in 1929 as concentrating on the players' looks during
the game, or saying that the baseball would "make a dandy ball for darning

socks." The New York *Times* claimed in 1935 that a woman fan approached Babe Ruth while he was lunching and said, "I hope you make a lot of touchdowns this year." A 1936 article in *The Delineator* adjured women to impress their families and male friends by learning about baseball, thus avoiding their fathers' and brothers' disdain and preventing boyfriends from spending the afternoon at a ball park instead of with them.

A bevy of capable women belied these tenacious stereotypes by penetrating various operational and administrative facets of baseball. Mrs. Lucille Thomas may have been the first woman to buy a club in Organized Baseball. Most women owners of the past had inherited clubs from relatives, but Mrs. Thomas made the investment on her own. Before doing so she had already run a string of movie houses in Missouri and Kansas and had operated a chain of drugstores in Tulsa. After men had failed to bring a Western League franchise to Tulsa, Mrs. Thomas succeeded by purchasing the Wichita club and moving it to Tulsa in 1930. Buying the team was not "a whim," she said; "I wouldn't have bought it unless I expected to make some money." Relatives predicted she would "lose," Thomas went on, "but I'll show 'em." She hired an experienced manager, adding that she did not intend "hanging around the dugout or office and messing things up."

In 1935 Mrs. E. B. Branconier ventured into minor-league club ownership in the midst of the depression by purchasing the Omaha Packers of the Western League. Undaunted by its loss of $6,000.00 the previous season, she determined to try with a new team.

Other women became club owners through inheritance, as some had in the past. Ownership of the Cleveland American League club fell to Mrs. James Dunn on the death of her husband in the 1920s, but she took no active part in running the club, leaving operations to Ernest Barnard, who was named president. In 1928 another woman with the same last name, Mrs. Jack Dunn, widow of the late owner of the Baltimore Orioles, took over the Baltimore club. In 1936 she also assumed its presidency, on the death of incumbent Charles H. Knapp. *Sporting News* declared of her, "There is hardly a woman in baseball who knows so much about the sport." By 1939 Mrs. Dunn headed two ball clubs, having just become president and major stockholder of the Dover Orioles of the International League.

Florence Killilea in 1929 inherited the American Association Milwaukee Club from her father, Henry J. Although she took a keen interest in the club's affairs and traveled with it, she apparently played no active role in managing it. The first female National League owner since 1911, when Mrs. Helene Britton had been in charge of the St. Louis Cardinals, Mrs. Florence Wolf Dreyfuss in 1932 inherited the Pittsburgh Pirates as part of her husband's estate. Although elected chairman of the board of directors, she turned the presidency over to her son-in-law, Bill Benswanger. In 1932 Mrs. William Wrigley, Jr., was elected to membership of the Chicago Cubs' executive board, taking the place of her husband on his death. In Chicago, after a one-year trusteeship held by a bank, Mrs. J. Louis Comiskey took over the White Sox from her husband and the former owner, his father, Charles Comiskey.

Unlike other female club administrators, who had been forced into the game by circumstances, Mrs. Gerry Nugent, wife of the Philadelphia Nationals' president, was chosen on her own account. She began as secretary to the former owner, William F. Baker, then became treasurer and then assistant club secretary before being named vice-president. While her husband attended to player contracts, trades, and public relations, she suggested changes in club management and tried to make the game more attractive to women.

A husband-and-wife team, Bob Seeds and his wife, operated the Amarillo Club of the West Texas-New Mexico League. Mrs. Seeds acted as vice president and business manager while he played outfield for the New York Giants. Mrs. Seeds kept on the job every day and into the night despite having two small daughters. Of course, *Sporting News* pointed out, she had a maid. Mrs. Seeds averred,

> There's no good reason why a woman cannot run a ball club as well as a man. . . . In fact there are apt to be things that we on the feminine side can see in connection with a team, that the male of the species might overlook. Certainly, the woman belongs—just as much as she does in other sports.

Other couples in Organized Baseball included Tony Rego and his wife, of Big Springs, in the same league as Amarillo, and Buck Marrow and his wife, of Tarboro, North Carolina, in the Coastal Plain League. In fact, *Sporting News* listed ten such couples operating in Organized Baseball and remarked that females administering clubs were not new, but partnerships of married couples were.

Other women held important posts in the front offices of Organized Baseball clubs in the thirties. Margaret Donohue served as executive secretary of the Chicago Cubs. Jeanette E. Parkinson of the Albany Club was the only woman club secretary in the International League. The Louisville team employed the Knebelkamp twins, Florence and Lillian, sisters of the club president. Florence, a lawyer and accountant, began as temporary traveling secretary in 1933 and in 1935 became permanent road secretary. Sports writer Lee Allen said hotel managers often embarrassed Florence by scheduling her with male roommates. Lillian Knebelkamp worked as office secretary. For twenty-three years Margaret Murphy served as assistant treasurer of the St. Louis Browns while her sister Mary was secretary to President Sam Breadon of the Cardinals in the same city. Mrs. Helen Snow was statistician for the Western Association, and Mrs. Ora Bohart acted as co-statistician for the Arkansas-Missouri League, although she did most of the work herself, and after two years of serving with her newspaperman husband she became official statistician on her own. Emma Dreskill acted as official scorer for a minor-league club. The American Association appointed Florence Walden, a Columbus newspaperwoman, director of a new department of women's activities; she obtained speakers for clubs and planned special events for them.

Two scouts, Roy Largent and his wife, both worked for the Chicago White Sox in the late 1930s. They took scouting trips together and discovered some players who later became outstanding major leaguers. Mrs. Largent signed Carl Reynolds, who then played for twelve years in the majors, after her husband had failed to do so, and she recommended Luke Appling, who became a well-known Chicago White Sox shortstop, to Harry Grabiner, the club secretary.

By the eve of World War II, women interested in sport were disregarding the tides of adverse public opinion and, in the words of the once-popular song, were following their "secret hearts" and pursuing baseball in all its aspects.

32

INTRAMURAL VS. INTERCOLLEGIATE
BALL FOR WOMEN

While women in the world at large explored baseball's possibilities for them, others attending college found it a different place from what it had been in the prewar decades. Curriculums were changing, and the comprehensive liberal arts education offered earlier suffered dilution by the introduction of courses like "Husband and Wife," "Motherhood," "Family as an Economic Unit," and "Home Economics." The students themselves differed from their predecessors of the progressive era, taking less interest in social problems and displaying more acceptance of what Sheila Rothman has termed the view of woman as a romantic companion of man.

Similar attitudes affected women's sports on campus. Out of fear of undermining the home and making women less attractive to men, female physical training faculty promoted what they called femininity—a reactionary objective, as Professor Twin has remarked. Through their various organizations, these female instructors secured the control over women's college sport they had long sought. Achievement of female faculty autonomy culminated in the formation early in the twenties of the Women's Division of the National Amateur Athletic Federation, headed by Lou Hoover, wife of Herbert Hoover. This umbrella organization for women's sports established standards and policies under its motto, "A game for every girl and every girl in a game," or "Sports for all," stressing the social rather than the individual value of sports. As Professor Ellen Gerber observed, the idea stemmed from the current theme "Education for all," which in turn originated in John Dewey's doctrine promoting the needs of the majority rather than those of the few. In sports, this doctrine meant that the few very talented would receive little or no attention in favor of giving everyone, including the untalented, a chance to play. Few thought of doing both.

A NAAF pamphlet set forth the organization's policy on intercollegiate competition for women: unswerving opposition. Competition, said NAAF, only produced experts instead of encouraging participation of students generally. NAAF therefore supported intramurals, emphasized sportsmanship, sought to protect athletes from exploitation for the enjoyment of spectators, and recommended medical exams as a prerequisite for participation. Lastly, NAAF insisted that trained women be in charge.

Much could be said for the NAAF position. Women instructors had before them the spectacle of male intercollegiate athletics fraught with abuses, soon to be pointed up by the Carnegie Report of 1929. And it may well be that organizers of tournaments, especially in basketball, exploited women. Henry S. Curtis maintained that spectators subjected female players to discourtesy or insults. Advertisers, too, seized on the image of women athletes in revealing attire in order to sell their products. The problem of chaperonage and the cost of transportation presented other obstacles.

Even so, women physical training faculty, by persisting in their unrelenting antagonism to competition, spurned its benefits, thereby slighting excellence in sport and opportunity for skilled athletes. Like a mother insisting on an unvaried and restrictive diet of pabulum and spinach in order to keep junk food away from her children, these instructors swung to the extreme. By insisting on a special kind of sports for women, as Twin noted, they isolated female athletics, made their status more precarious, agreed that sports were fundamentally male, and fed the public's perception of female athletes as masculine.

Not all agreed with the physical training leaders. Those instructors and women students not under their close control often voted in favor of competitive sports. Wellesley students, for instance, as the American Physical Education Association reported in 1924, voted 237 to 33 for intercollegiate contests, and students at several colleges in the region would have been glad to compete with Wellesley. Even Mabel Lee, adamantine opponent of intercollegiate competition, acknowledged that it had some advantages. Ethel Perrin, another noted physical education writer, even agreed that "any amount of time, money, equipment, and service" could be spent on the top team if the same amount of attention were given the unskilled—a situation that would not be approached until after the passage of a civil rights amendment, Title IX, in 1972.

All the same, the upper echelon of instructors prevailed. A number of surveys told the story. One made in 1922 of 50 colleges revealed that only 11 had intercollegiate competition, and even this did not approach varsity competition in the modern sense. A 1923 survey cited by Gerber showed that 60 percent of women physical educators thought intercollegiate sport was harmful, especially physically, to women.

So the bulk of college women had to settle for intramurals and insipid "play days" foisted on them in lieu of genuine competition. On the play day, women from different colleges met, not to compete against each other as college teams but arbitrarily mingled on two teams, Red and Blue, that played each other. Eleanor Metheny, then a student but later a physical education instructor, took part in "play days" and recalled, "the better players felt frustrated by the lack of meaningful team play. . . . [and] these play days did little to satisfy our desire for all-out competition with worthy and honored opponents."

A sampling of women's and coed colleges provides an inkling as to the extent to which they carried out their narrow policy, or failed to carry it out, in baseball.

The framework of Mount Holyoke's prewar athletic program remained in place after the war, when the college offered six sports under the overall supervision of the athletic association, which sought to give every student a chance to participate in some sport. Students heads still directed each sport, and the student paper, *Llamarada*, and the *Alumni Quarterly* agreed that the popularity of sports had never been higher. Furthermore, most students eschewed "refined archery and ladylike volleyball" in favor of the "more rousing pursuits" of baseball, hockey, track, and soccer.

Class teams in baseball competed yearly at Mount Holyoke. One season, for example, the class of 1925 captured the interclass championship for the second time, clinching it 12–6 in what the student reporter called an "exciting game." In 1923 the students also planned dormitory teams in baseball. Faculty-student games highlighted the spring baseball seasons. For one of them, in May 1923, the Springfield *Republican* reported that the team formed by students included two "star" pitchers to counter two on the faculty nine, organized by a faculty member. In 1925 *Llamarada*, declaring that for "real sportsmanship look to the baseball team," reported that the faculty team, "showing good fighting spirit," defeated the students by a "margin of 1 or 2 runs."

Softball also bulked large at Mount Holyoke, as a fall sport. As it had done a decade earlier, the college handbook still explained to incoming students that "In winter we play indoor baseball and when spring comes we go to our outdoor field. So . . . come to college prepared to play the game and make your class team. You'll like it." The Mount Holyoke annual field day, held in May, included baseball. The college also espoused a play day, inviting some Connecticut College and Smith students to participate. It turned out to be more like a social affair, and the Mount Holyoke *News* said it raised the question whether play day would really take the place of intercollegiate rivalry, because some students skillful at sports were "bored" and disliked the "bungling play" and "confused though amusing mass of games."

Radcliffe's slow progress in adopting baseball and sports generally received an important nudge when President L.B.R. Briggs in a report for 1920–23 recognized that "Most young people enter eagerly into athletic sports," obtaining "new bodily vigor, that freshness which comes from complete forgetfulness of daily worries and responsibilities, and is thus literally recreative," whereas exercise becomes more of a chore. Perhaps the president was simply acknowledging the popularity of spring sports on campus, baseball one of them. Of 154 Radcliffe students participating in sports in the spring of 1920, 23 chose baseball. The following year only 2 out of 147 elected baseball, but in the spring of 1923 the director of physical education announced that baseball was for the first time introduced as an "organized sport" at Radcliffe and showed "promise of having come to stay." Increased enrollment the following year reflected in the larger number that turned out for sports, 394, of which 39 came out for baseball.

The 1928–29 school year brought a pronounced change in Radcliffe's limited interscholastic play. Up to then, varsity matches had to be played within twenty-five miles of Cambridge, thus restricting competition mostly to nearby normal schools. That year the dean lifted the ban, and varsity teams could play those at Brown, Wheaton, Simmons, and Jackson (the women's college then associated with Tufts). Varsity baseball, although not specifically mentioned in the twenties, may well have been played then; it certainly was later.

At Wellesley in the twenties, baseball remained among the sports offered in both spring and fall and rated "medium" as compared with other sports rated "light" or "strenuous," according to Department Chairman Ruth Elliott's report of 1928–29. In winter students played indoor ball; 116 came out for baseball and basketball in winter of 1927. Almost every year the annual class yearbook, *Legenda*, published a baseball team picture labeled "Varsity," an ambiguous term some colleges employed that did not necessarily indicate intercollegiate play and might refer only to the class champions or an aggregation of the best players, so whether Wellesley played intercollegiate baseball in the twenties remains unclear.

A collection of baseball pictures in the Wellesley college archives reveals the evolution of costumes during the decade, the Turkish pants gradually becoming shorter and finally evolving into bloomers extending just below the knee, and the white middie blouses replacing the former serge ones. A.G. Spalding and Company furnished team uniforms.

To solve an athletic financial problem in 1928, Wellesley held a fund drive that raised $54,470.00, Chairman Elliott reported, and the college centralized all student athletic funds with the treasurer of the athletic association. That year Wellesley also arranged for a play day, inviting students from other New England colleges, including Radcliffe and Mount Holyoke, to play games together. "Some girls threw baseballs at the archery targets to test their accuracy," stated *Playground*, and the students "learned many new games and played old ones."

"A Foul Tip! Baseball on the new Allen Field is a popular sport at Smith" reads the caption on a 1920s baseball photo in the Smith College archives. In it a student in gym shoes is swinging at a pitch, the catcher in action back of the plate, and seven others are sitting or standing in the background, most wearing knee-length bloomers, black stockings, and white blouses with dark jerseys over them. Class teams at Smith played each other regularly in the twenties, as other pictures in the Smith archives bear out. Some show a coach or instructors giving tips on play.

Field days, on which the Smith faculty usually played baseball against students, were held annually. An undated but probably 1929 newspaper release promised added interest in that year's faculty-student ball game with the announcement that Jack Chesbro, former major-league pitching star, was on campus visiting a student and would pitch in the game. To assure impartiality, he planned to pitch alternate innings for each team!

Athletics continued to thrive at Barnard in the 1920s under an active athletic association and the vigorous administration of Agnes Wayman, another leading physical training instructor. Barnard historian Marian C. White rated baseball second only to basketball in student interest during this period. Not only did interclass ball games continue to thrive, but Barnard sports teams often played alumnae and Teachers' College teams and even went to Bryn Mawr for varsity baseball games. Team costumes improved during the twenties, reflecting the increasingly liberal trend of the decade. A 1927 picture reveals the Barnard baseball team in trimmer outfits: more snug middies without the usual ties, less-baggy bloomers worn above, not below, the knee, and knee-length socks instead of long black stockings.

Students at Simmons still played baseball, although the college's publications continued to slight sport. The Boston *Sunday Post*, however, reported a baseball game between the men faculty and the students in May 1925 on the college's athletic field. Because of the large number of applicants for the student team organized for that game, tryouts had to be held. The faculty players, named the Amazons, made spectacles of themselves by dressing in female costumes: one as a ballet girl, others as farmerettes, Boston debutantes, sunbonneted babies, and schoolgirls.

In the South, interclass baseball at Agnes Scott College gained stature in the twenties to the point where *Agonistic*, the student paper, wrote of a "traditional enmity" in baseball between freshman and sophomore classes. The student baseball manager planned to keep a record of the runs scored by each player during the season. The paper, reporting a senior-freshman game in 1926, called the 42–16 score "appalling," saying that the seniors "seemed to have done their very best to establish a world record in scoring."

The Goucher College annual, *Donnybrook Fair*, listed a baseball team for the first time in 1920, but according to the college archivist baseball had appeared at Goucher prior to that, although the 1920 season proved more satisfactory than previous ones because that year the college had not attempted to combine baseball with field day. Interclass baseball teams at Goucher played both outdoors, on a Maryland Avenue field, and indoors. Seasons closed with a final game for the college championship, followed by a game between the champions and the faculty, which historians of the college called "one of the most satisfying of sports events to the students looking on"—apparently, the faculty usually lost! Alumnae maintain, however, that teams in 1920 really played softball, not baseball, a claim confirmed by emeritus professor of physical training Josephine Fiske, cited by the archivist. Fiske explained that at first Goucher students played regular baseball, but on account of a small field surrounded by buildings, they brought in the larger softball, reduced the size of the diamond, and adopted women's rules.

Sports at Goucher received no academic credit in the 1919–20 school year, and baseball, like other sports, had to be "arranged" with the athletic association and supervised by the physical training department. The following year, however, the catalog for the first time listed baseball (really, softball) as a class offering for the required gymnasium credit.

Goucher students hailed ball players injured during play as "heroines of the diamond," according to the college paper in April of 1923, and little groups of admirers clustered around them. The paper described lines formed outside the medical office made up of baseball "injured" seeking excuses from gym for a day. Some filed out wearing bandages of adhesive tape, but most were enjoined only to wiggle their injured fingers or other "injured members" as much as possible, to the great annoyance of their instructors, who did not understand the reason for their peculiar actions. "Ye baseball season has arrived at last!" the account concluded.

"The great American pastime has come to Randolph-Macon to stay," declared the *Sun Dial* at the college in May 1927. "Baseball has at last gained a footing as an inter-class sport." That year's college catalog substantiated the writer's assertion, listing baseball as one of the sports offered in both the spring and fall quarters, when the college required students to elect a sport. During the winter term students had to choose three hours of work from among a variety of activities that included one hour of baseball.

Class baseball teams played each other at Randolph-Macon for the chance to take part in a championship game, played on field day in May. In 1927 the *Sun Dial* said, with some exaggeration, that "if the Yanks or Senators could see the senior team [in action], they would turn green with envy." That season the vaunted seniors defeated the sophomores for the championship in a close game. *Helianthus*, the Randolph-Macon yearbook, declared that all who witnessed the games that year thought them "most exciting." A posed photograph shows the champion senior team in light gym suits with colored arm bands.

The next spring Randolph-Macon students played off the preliminary class games "with quite a lot of snap and enjoyment in spite of many weak places in the teams," according to the yearbook, and in the championship games played the afternoon before May Day the sophomores "quite outplayed the seniors and won . . . with an easy margin." The yearbook also displayed four photos: the four class teams, all of which included not only a captain but also a manager.

The following year, 1929, the *Sun Dial*, under the heading "Athletic News," published the Randolph-Macon interclass baseball schedule. In a long column it also reported on games: the juniors' batting order was much stronger than the frosh had surmised, and although their fielding was not poor, before they could "put three men down" the juniors had scored three runs.

Women in some coed institutions, too, registered baseball advances in the 1920s, among them the University of Cincinnati, which consolidated its prewar gains in women's baseball, as indicated by documents supplied by the archivist. Women organized a "C" club in 1921 and planned to confer the letter on those accumulating points from baseball (indoor) and other sports. They also continued to hold an annual field day, which included a baseball-throwing contest.

After the Miller Jewelry Company donated a silver loving cup in 1923, interest in intersorority baseball mounted at the University of Cincinnati, and some women skipped lunch in order to practice. A team winning the sorority championship three seasons in succession could keep the cup. Several prominent members of the college's male varsity, showing unwonted interest, volunteered to coach these teams, but the women disdained all such offers. By that year women's play at the University of Cincinnati, in addition to intersorority baseball, included interclass and independent teams. They all played, however, by "Spalding's Indoor Rules," so the games, although labeled baseball, must be considered softball.

A writer for the *University News*, the University of Cincinnati's newspaper, reported in 1923 that while there was no surprise at the sudden appearance of ten new baseball teams on campus formed by the sororities to participate in a Panhellenic tournament, he did "gasp with astonishment" upon discovering that female members of "our austere faculty" had organized a regular team and arranged a five-game schedule. The faculty team, not having chosen a "definite" uniform, came out for its first game in "a unique array of knickers, bloomers, middies, dresses, pleated skirts, and sweaters." The writer also revealed the farcical character of the event: one player acted as cheerleader for her side "in true spinster fashion," accompanied by the proverbial "old maid's cat" and "clasping a bag of peppermints"; another served as waterboy, "running from one team to another with the desired H_2O; a third declared in writing that she "would not play on the team for $20,000" and instead consented to be publicity manager. Making their participation into slapstick demonstrated that these women accepted the conformist view of female ball playing as fantasy.

In 1924 the umpire opened the University of Cincinnati's women's baseball season with a blast on his saxophone, but there is no evidence of a repetition of this singular ceremony in succeeding years.

Regular outdoor baseball began at the University of Cincinnati two years later, and the *University News* reported that at the deciding game for the championship "the enthusiastic gallery included loyal rooters from both so-rorities, representatives of practically all the other Girls' Greek letter or-ganizations, and interested men students." The final score was 46–38, but the reporter, putting the best face on it, stated that "because of the excellent playing of both teams" the outcome was "a close thing"! The paper went on to say, "The reception of intersorority baseball since its inception this spring has been such as to encourage most warmly the continuation of this sport and possibly even the extension of intersorority activities into other fields of sport." The teams of 1928 adopted "League of Nations" identities, using such names as Amazons, Spartans, Tartars, Trojans, and Vikings. The solid position attained by women's baseball at the University of Cincinnati by the end of the decade is demonstrated by the twenty-one game schedule adopted in 1929.

Another outstanding coed institution, Ohio State University, expanded its women's sports program markedly in the twenties under the leadership of Gladys Palmer, an instructor prominent in interscholastic sports and in women's organizations as well as in the national physical education and athletic associations. She would serve at OSU for thirty-six years beginning in 1922.

In 1923 at Ohio State women took the field in a variety of sports, includ-ing baseball, during the spring season. Any individual student or campus women's organization (dormitory or rooming house, religious or professional organization, or independent organization) could form a team and compete for the intramural baseball championship for an entry fee of $2.00. Trophies were awarded to the winner of each group and to the intramural champion. Class teams participated in a separate interclass tournament.

Thenceforward, women's sports steadily became more firmly implanted at OSU. In 1928 students could choose from twelve sports, one of them baseball, each with a student head. OSU even introduced motion pictures to acquaint incoming students with the various sports, baseball included, that the university offered, with the aim of giving every girl an opportunity to acquire skill in one sport not only for reasons of health but for "making social contacts" and "enjoying leisure."

In 1929 the intramurals office at OSU published the rules for groups of teams playing in a spring round-robin baseball tournament: street clothes were banned, certain gym costumes had to be worn, no more than half the players on a team could be gym majors or minors, and, to avoid outside ringers, only university students were eligible. Teams played by the rules of indoor baseball. They formed four leagues of five each, some representing sororities, others independent organizations. A similar league of eleven teams, each with 12 members, played intramural ball.

The promising baseball beginning made at the University of Wisconsin in the teens proved hardy. Every year in the twenties Wisconsin women took part in baseball, the highest figure, 128, turning out in 1924. Indoor baseball attracted even more, reaching the highest number, 402, in 1925. Among photos still extant, one for 1928 shows a Wisconsin game in progress, a woman at bat in blouse, light jerkin, black stockings, and bloomers that end just above the knee, and a masked catcher with a glove.

Women students at Wisconsin in 1929 could satisfy their physical education requirement by participating in sports, one of them softball. That season the physical education division staged a baseball tournament as well. Outdoor baseball was also played at Camp Randall, a few blocks away from Lathrop Hall.

In the twenties the University of Indiana showed some signs of progress in baseball, too. The physical training department had by 1927 replaced formal gymnastics with sports, including baseball for women. Instructors also offered courses for physical training majors in how to teach baseball and other sports. In addition, the athletic association set up an intramural program geared to participation by women less highly skilled in sports.

But these programs were exceptional illustrations of women's baseball in coed institutions. Many others realized only flimsy gains or even regressed. The University of California at Berkeley reportedly discontinued women's baseball, such as it was, in 1920 because of a field "too small to accommodate both basketball and baseball." But in 1923 the student newspaper announced that although no students had signed up for baseball, for want of space on the playing field, impromptu games could take place when the field was not in use by other teams. The University of Southern California at Los Angeles for a time had a women's baseball team, captained by an all-around athlete, Lillian Copeland. In 1926 women at Stanford University, the University of California, and Mills, a women's college, began holding an annual triangular sports day to replace interclass and intercollegiate athletics. Mills, too, had interclass baseball, as well as sports days, in the twenties.

At Boston University interest in the Girls Athletic Association, which had diminished, revived in 1921–26. Its name was changed to Women's Athletic Association and more sports, including baseball, were added.

In the 1930s, women physical education instructors further stiffened their opposition to intercollegiate competition, widening the divergence between women's and men's college sports, particularly by utilizing a strengthened NAAF to impose their policies. Some men supported them. Frederick R. Rogers, he of the player-management idea described earlier, thought competition "women's greatest enemy because it caused them to lose their womanliness." The physician-gymnast Stephan K. Westmann chimed in: "Competitive sports are alien to the characteristics of the female constitution and are useless as well as harmful in relation to the primary task of women's life, maternity." In consequence, genuine intercollegiate competition—that is, varsities against each other—for women remained virtually nonexistent, with extramural sport restricted largely to play days, telegraphic meets (comparing scores by telegraph or telephone), and the ultimate absurdity, sports days in which girls could represent their own schools, but in order to suppress the competitive urge, sponsors did not even announce scores.

Yet in the course of the decade women's baseball held its own and even gained strength in those coed institutions and universities in which the game had taken root in the twenties. The University of Cincinnati, for one, in 1937 constructed a new ball field for women, and two years later it introduced a so-called "hobby period" in which women could either play baseball on their own or engage in "home-run contests." Throughout the period, according to the University of Cincinnati archivist, two conflicting opinions pervaded the campus: athletes could engage in competitive sports and still be feminine, and yet women's sports had to occupy a position subservient to men's.

Under Gladys Palmer's forward-looking supervision, of which more later, Ohio State solidified its robust sports program for coeds, who had access to all athletic facilities, among the best in the country, including the baseball diamonds. In 1930 the university annual, *Makio*, even listed a women's baseball coach. Team sports became more popular at OSU, among them baseball played in the spring and indoor ball tournaments carried on in winter.

The University of Wisconsin, always keen to keep abreast of changing attitudes toward sports, as director of physical training Blanche Trilling claimed, reorganized the athletic association in 1930 on the basis of clubs, which sponsored the various intramural sports. Mixed teams of men and women actually played together at Wisconsin in intramural baseball, tennis, golf, and volleyball. Playing five-inning games under "Official Women's Rules," the baseball teams fielded four men and five women. A man caught, and male and female pitchers alternated. These games were initiated mostly by university church centers and sororities, and the number of participating groups increased steadily.

Outdoor sports facilities improved little at the University of Indiana. According to Edna F. Munro, chairman of the physical education department, Dunn Meadow, resodded in the 1930s, continued to serve as athletic field. Although convenient for students, the Meadow unfortunately lay adjacent to the public thoroughfare of Seventh Street and at times provided humorous or embarrassing handicaps to play. "Frolicking dogs" attracted to the field chased and recovered balls, resisted releasing them, and disrupted class activity. Also obstructing learning were boyfriends and other passers-by who loitered on Seventh Street, distracting and sometimes flustering the women by making remarks disparaging their unskilled efforts.

Other coed institutions colleges evinced interest in baseball in the thirties. In a survey of twenty-one Eastern schools published in a spring issue of the New York *Tribune*, a copy of which is in the Mount Holyoke archives, Janet Owen mentioned Adelphi, Pennsylvania State, Cornell, and New York University as awakening to baseball. Adelphi students, after the college moved from Brooklyn to a seventy-acre campus in Garden City, Long Island, could enjoy new advantages, such as a baseball diamond. Sport for women at Adelphi took place in the form of mass participation: interclass competition and play days. Adelphi abolished varsity competition entirely.

With the exception of rifle shooting, Penn State sponsored no intercollegiate competition for women, either. Baseball, however, was one of the two choices available to satisfy a spring sport requirement.

Cornell included baseball as one of the spring sports in the thirties, on the theory, according to Professor C.V.P. Young, that sports inculcated attitudes of team play, fair play, and group cooperation. A later monograph on women at Cornell by Charlotte Conable, however, revealed the lesser importance placed on women's sports by calling attention to the *Cornellian's* one page reporting them compared with seventy-two pages devoted to men's sports.

Although New York University maintained a full intercollegiate sports schedule in the 1930s, it did not list baseball among its intercollegiate sports for women, but students played indoor ball in interclass and intersorority tournaments. The physical director commented dryly, "If it were not for college athletics, hanging on the [subway] straps would be the only exercise our girls would get."

At the University of Maryland, baseball first entered the college curriculum for women in 1931, although the women's athletic association had been sponsoring it for at least a year. During the thirties baseball was a popular sport on campus, and students could earn college credit by playing it.

The size of the school did not necessarily govern the extent or caliber of the sports program. Even Keene State College, a small New Hampshire teachers institution, formed an athletic association to encourage physical activity, and its twenty-four sports for women included baseball. In accordance with the slogan, "A sport for every girl, and every girl in a sport," as the college annual, the *Kronicle*, of 1934, announced, the association sponsored sport days in spring and fall during which "red and white" teams competed in baseball and other games.

The late start and relatively tardy development of women's baseball in the male-dominated public coed colleges contrasted with the steady growth of the game in the older, established, more secure and independent women's institutions. Increasing numbers of applicants and their growing diversity in the thirties, however, impelled both types of schools to discriminate against so-called ethnic minorities, especially in the women's colleges determined to maintain the ASP character of their student bodies. It did not occur to them that students coming from privileged ethnocentric backgrounds might derive educational benefit from association with a more heterogeneous group. Had colleges recruited such students, they might even have acquired a few good ball players! After all, coed colleges welcomed any males if they could play football.

Radcliffe made impressive strides in athletics in the thirties. Baseball, together with a half-dozen other sports ranging from hockey and tennis to lacrosse and basketball, became firmly rooted, and in line with the trend in women's colleges, Radcliffe no longer required a gym class, which was supplanted by individual sports. Team sports, however, remained popular, according to Miriam Arrowsmith, then director of physical training. The athletic association ran sports through committees, one of them for baseball. The game continued to be played at Radcliffe on a less formal basis as well. An Outing Club, formed as part of the athletic association, sponsored a variety of outdoor activities that occasionally included baseball. A photo in the Radcliffe archives labeled "Outing Club 1930s" reveals, against a background of trees, a batter swinging, a catcher flinching a bit as the pitch approaches, seven others sitting on the ground, and all wearing knickers and long socks.

At the other end of the athletic spectrum was the Radcliffe varsity, for Radcliffe took part in intercollegiate baseball. The athletic association's report of its 1939 spring meeting stated that "the teams were moderately successful, none disgracing the R.A.A.," but made sure to conform to the current views of sport by adding that they were "always outstanding in their love of games for the sake of games, never placing a desire to win above a desire to play well." Radcliffe's opponents in these intercollegiate contests were Jackson, Pembroke, and Wheaton colleges. Minutes of meetings in 1940 and a scrapbook of clippings from the college paper and the New York *Times* showed that the baseball varsity practiced an hour every afternoon from 5:00 to 6:00 o'clock. That year the baseball team, "clicking in fine style," won over Wheaton 25–5, making many hits and one home run.

In 1936 Radcliffe's athletic association met with those of Jackson, Pembroke, and Wheaton to compare methods of administering and financing sports. The minutes of the meeting reveal the modest amounts allocated for women's sports by these colleges. Radcliffe's association reported that it realized $175.00 from fees for use of gym equipment; that paid for transportation, teas, and half the suppers. Pembroke's association was wealthier, gaining $400.00 from sports fees and earning the rest itself. Wheaton did nearly as well, collecting $400.00 from fees and raising the balance with an annual vaudeville show. Jackson did best, earning $1,000.00 by means of fees—all it needed.

At Mount Holyoke in the thirties baseball and indoor ball were included in the spring and fall sports seasons with emphasis on "good fun for all." Baseball games starred on field days and sport days. A father-daughter game highlighted commencement; the fathers usually won, but "Of course," said the college annual in 1932, "they are guests of the college and the hostesses are concerned for their happiness!" Competition at interclass, interdorm, and student-faculty games was often keen. In this era the college annually selected an All-Holyoke Baseball squad—not a varsity, just a naming of the best players of the year, who won the college letter. Some students, like Ruth Green, attended Harvard and Yale baseball games, too, and kept programs and admissions badges in their "memory books."

Baseball at Wellesley started the decade as part of a sound film, "Feminine Fitness," showing actual instruction in sports, photographed by the well-known sports writer Grantland Rice and circulated by the Pathé Company. It was "good publicity for the college," wrote Director Ruth Elliott in her 1929–30 report. Like Mount Holyoke, Wellesley had no intercollegiate competition, but it usually recognized a "first team" and a "varsity." The "first team" was probably the winner of the annual tournament among class teams, while the "varsity" doubtless represented the year's best individual players. More important, during the thirties Wellesley students played baseball every year, either on a required basis or voluntarily, and "many a time was the air rent with sharp cracks of bat connecting horsehide, thuds of balls nestling into padded mitts," said the college annual in 1939. Elliott reported that in 1931–32, 83 students participated in baseball, the high seasonal point of the decade; the annual number of participants averaged about 44, although figures given in Elliott's reports omit informal and extracurricular play, which Wellesley encouraged. The annual faculty-student game was a tradition at Wellesley, and the college yearbook rejoiced that the "wonder team of '39" had snapped the faculty's three-year winning streak by trouncing them 16–14.

Smith College continued to encourage sports in the thirties with a broad offering of more than twenty, including baseball, under an elective system. Baseball was further enhanced by the formal opening of New Field and its baseball diamond supplementing Allen Field. Archival photos of the thirties show Smith games in progress with students wearing bloomers and white blouses. Smith had no intercollegiate sport, but the traditional faculty-student game, which, as at Wellesley, always aroused enthusiasm, marked the high point of the baseball season. The student team found its annual faculty game particularly gratifying in 1938 when it defeated the professors 14–13.

Intramural baseball continued as one of six most popular sports at Barnard. There it was also one of the group of sports, according to Owens in her New York *Tribune* survey, in which a minimum standard of performance had to be attained.

Other colleges ventured into baseball in the thirties. New Jersey College for Women held no intercollegiate contests, but it wanted students to develop sports skill because of a belief in the high correlation between skill and enjoyment. It offered intramural competition in baseball and other sports with interclass, alumnae-student, and faculty-student games.

Skidmore required students to attain a knowledge of one individual and one team sport from among a considerable number available in the 1930s. Team sports, especially baseball and hockey, were particularly popular at

Skidmore. Vassar, too, sponsored intramural baseball among its variety of sports offerings. The college provided abundant coaching and created the impression among students that less-expert players had an opportunity to take part.

A number of colleges, Wells and Sarah Lawrence, for example, reported offering sports in the thirties without mentioning baseball in particular. At Wells the authorities offered only intramural sports, believing intercollegiate competition would "ruin the college spirit . . . of friendly rivalry, of good will."

In the South, despite the 1920 baseball casualties, Goucher students still engaged in baseball in the following decade. Agnes Scott College, according to a 1932 monograph on southern women's colleges by Elizabeth Young, required participation in sports, so baseball doubtless continued there. At Hollins in Virginia, baseball was a popular sport in the thirties. Other colleges that sponsored sports may have included baseball: Newcomb, Wesleyan (Macon, Georgia), Judson (Alabama), and Salem (West Virginia).

At North Carolina College for Women, the administration required sports for the development of poise, endurance, leadership, and character, but a story told by the physical education director in the thirties revealed a possible additional purpose: keeping a husband. Some years before, an anxious mother had written the college asking that daughter Mary not be required to wear gym shoes because they might make her feet big and so interfere with matrimonial prospects. "Today," said the physical education direction, the "Marys and their mothers" know that the "clinging vine" might be successful in acquiring a husband but "the girl who keeps him is the one who can swing a wicked tennis racket and lead the stunts at a swimming party."

Probably no women's college in the South surpassed Randolph-Macon in the extent of its baseball program and the enthusiasm for it during the thirties. Although without intercollegiate play, the college officially designated baseball a major sport in 1930, and the "growing interest in the sport was both the cause and result of this change," asseverated the college annual, *Helianthus*.

Randolph-Macon required all juniors to elect a sport from a list that included baseball. In addition, throughout the decade four class baseball teams competed in a spring tournament that lasted a couple of weeks, culminating in a championship game as part of an annual May Day festival. One year sophomores showed so much interest they formed two teams.

Students and faculty at Randolph-Macon apparently took these class-team games quite seriously. A Miss Harrison, evidently a faculty member who coached them, drilled "complex plays" into the players' heads. Players wore bloomers of the color of the class they represented, dotting the field at various intervals, said the school paper, the *Sun Dial*, with green, red, tan, and blue. Winners of the class-team tournament usually received *R-M* armbands and sometimes a cup. Large, enthusiastic audiences attended. In 1938 the *Sun Dial* commented, "Judging from the exuberant crowds that turn out for each baseball game . . . , this institution is really baseball-minded."

Ardent reportage in breezy style frequently marked the *Sun Dial's* coverage of baseball in the thirties: left fielder Fannie Terry "dragged in flies like pouring apples in a basket," Lib Loy's pitches should have a speedometer attached to show they were as fast as Dizzy Dean's, fielder Sweet always stopped the ball "even if she has to lie down to do it," and "Slug" Sommerville was "really dynamite" on the ball field.

The person who ran the college infirmary at Randolph-Macon evinced less enthusiasm. Players who went there for help were met with sour remarks about baseball's being "the most unladylike and rowdy game," concluding with "young ladies are supposed to sit around and look pretty. I want you to stop this game." Evidently, students paid little attention to such grousing. Some expressed mild concern at the championship game of 1936, however, because shortstop McKee, who hit two homers in a single inning and brought in four runs in quick succession, was also the May Queen, and "The sight of the May Queen and two of her attendants in imminent danger of bumps and bruises was rather nerve-racking." Apparently, however, Queen McKee remained both unconcerned and unmarred.

As in so many women's colleges, the attractions of gym at Randolph-Macon paled as compared with sports. A student letter to the editor of the paper commented that most students didn't think they gained much from marching around the gym or "vainly trying to pull ourselves hand over hand up the ropes." On the other hand, "Very few of us object to learning how to hit a ball correctly," and "there would be very few tears wept if the whole present idea of winter gym were done away with. . . . "

Randolph-Macon students elected an All-Star baseball team at the end of each championship season. Although class teams sat for photos in what looked like gym attire, members of the All-Stars posed in dresses, usually with the college letters on the front. In 1939 after the regular championship season, an extra post-season game took place between the All-Star team and the Reserve Team, a sort of second All-Star squad.

Randolph-Macon further underscored its support of sports in the thirties by creating an honorary sports society, the Blazer Club. To qualify for election candidates had to have been members of three different teams, one of them the All-Star, and to have demonstrated good sportsmanship and interest in sport for sport's sake. In 1939, to encourage baseball players to develop more skill, the college made some changes in the style of play, injecting some softball rules, such as allowing both underhand and overhand pitching.

Sporadic faculty-student baseball games at Randolph-Macon occasioned much joshing of faculty players in student publications. Once, for example,

Helianthus declared that "the 'Old Ladies' [which often included men] were crippled in the first two games and did not recuperate all season."

Throughout the years between the wars, an undercurrent of opinion favoring interscholastic competition flowed among some students and faculty on college campuses. A serious move in support of intercollegiate sport materialized toward the end of the decade. The catalyst was Gladys W. Palmer of Ohio State University, who in 1938 called boldly for "excellence of play," "admiration of excellence for its own sake," and provision for competition to "maximize expertness." In 1941 she ventured a further step, circulating to college directors and teachers of physical education a three-page "open letter" arguing cogently for competition and pointing out that current policy limiting it had caused college teachers to abdicate their responsibility to the highly skilled students, control of whom fell to outside agencies, which ran sports efficiently but whose main purpose was to "establish championships" rather than to "consider the health of the entrants."

Palmer and her OSU colleagues believed that competition had a contribution to make to women's education and that college teachers should be supervising a suitable program for the highly skilled. She suggested the formation of a Women's National Collegiate Athletic Association to direct intercollegiate sports for women, and further, as an experiment, she went so far as to invite college women and their teachers to an intercollegiate golf tournament on the OSU campus June 30–July 3, 1941.

Palmer carefully cloaked her radical proposals in the usual conservative dogma, avowing that intercollegiate competition would be "properly organized and directed," promising that no practices violating the standards of the Physical Education Association would be countenanced in her new organization, and assuring that no exploitation, paid admissions, or overemphasis on record-keeping would be tolerated. Thirty-eight modestly dressed students took part in her well-controlled golf tournament.

But, as so frequently happens, Palmer's was a voice crying in the wilderness. The leaders of the women's section of the Physical Education Association rejected her proposals out of hand and demonstrated the sportsmanship they so zealously preached by sending Palmer and her staff to coventry. Palmer's hopes for intercollegiate competition would not be fulfilled for decades.

PART FIVE

THE HOUSE OF BASEBALL:
THE OUTBUILDING

33

THE BEGINNINGS OF BLACK BASEBALL

King Solomon himself would have been baffled by the question of whether Indians or blacks have suffered the worst of any group in American history. Far from the least of the blacks' suffering arose from the maltreatment by Organized Baseball of black baseball players and leagues, recorded in accounts by Robert Peterson in his pioneer study, *Only the Ball Was White*, and in other praiseworthy books by John Holway, William Rogosin, Janet Bruce, and Rob Ruck.

Some writers and former black professional players have understandably, and doubtless correctly, been at pains to prove that during Organized Baseball's decades of segregation many blacks were sufficiently qualified to merit admission. They have done so by citing numerous examples of individual black baseball skill, as well as instances of success in playing and defeating major leaguers in exhibition games. Such evidence, impressive though it be, is inconclusive, sometimes to the point of "protesting too much."

More valid evidence is available that long before the color line disappeared blacks unquestionably possessed the ability to play in Organized Baseball. Because this book is about ball playing outside O.B., discussion of the professional Negro Leagues is omitted, but to make the point of black ball playing ability an exception must be made. So before discussing black playing outside Organized Baseball, two types of evidence is presented proving without cavil that, from the first, blacks qualified for the white majors.

For the first piece of evidence one need only note the performance of black players in the major leagues once they gained admission in the 1940s. Here a few samples will suffice to show that blacks not only belonged in the major leagues but were often outstanding players once they got in. Major-league records from a publication of the Society for American Baseball Research reveal that in the quarter-century since Jackie Robinson's debut in the majors, no fewer than twenty-five black players won the annual Most Valuable Player Award in their leagues. Three of them won it twice, and one, Roy Campanella, won it three times. Four black pitchers (one of them, Bob Gibson, twice) won the Cy Young Memorial Award for pitching. Frank

Robinson in 1966 won the (American League) triple batting crown (for most home runs, most runs batted in, and highest batting average), and Lou Brock broke the lifetime record for stolen bases. A perusal of the record books will reveal many other topflight black players.

The second piece of evidence takes us to the beginning of both the amateur and professional baseball spectrum in the late nineteenth century, when black players, including the first one (not Jackie Robinson) to break the major league color ban, performed capably on white teams, albeit often with grudging acceptance, until gradually forced out by the barrier of segregation, both amateur and professional, higher and more effective than the Berlin Wall.

The outbuilding behind the House of Baseball where black ball players were once relegated is gone, but during the many years it stood it made a mockery of the frequent assertion and widely held belief that organized professional baseball was a democratic game open to any man provided only that he possessed sufficient talent.

Organized Baseball's exclusionist policy was hardly exceptional. Even after Emancipation—which, compared with that of European countries, including so-called backward Russia, came late in the day and required a civil war to accomplish—the black man remained what Daniel Boorstin called the indelible immigrant as racism became routine and pervasive, poisoning every neighborhood and institution, sports included.

In baseball as in other spheres, Afro-Americans, excluded from Organized Baseball and allowed only tenuous contact with some of its white players and teams during its off-season, established their own baseball world, forming amateur teams, developing skilled players, exhibiting a colorful style of play, and eventually even organizing functional professional leagues, all largely unnoticed or ignored by white fans and press.

Some years ago one-time baseball commissioner Ford Frick attempted to explain away the long absence of black players from the lineups of Organized Baseball. "Colored people," Frick said in a fatuous taped interview, "did not have a chance to play" during slavery, "and so were late in developing proficiency. It was more than fifty years after the introduction of baseball before colored people in the Untied Stated had a chance to play it. Consequently, it was another fifty years before they arrived at the stage where they were important in the organized baseball picture." Wrong on all counts.

Actually, blacks did play ball about as early as whites and organized the games along roughly parallel lines, though more slowly and less successfully because of the greater difficulties that confronted them.

Among other things, Frick was unaware of or chose to ignore the many blacks who in slavery days were not slaves. In fact, some blacks, like numerous whites, had come to the colonies as indentured servants, legally free after fulfilling their contracts. In the North slavery had been virtually eliminated by 1820, and at the time of the Civil War some 240,000 free Negroes lived north of the Mason-Dixon line. Jim Crow and the vagaries of the omnipresent James Crow, his more slick, sophisticated cousin, severely restricted their lives, but despite prejudice and hampering conditions, employment opportunities lay open to free Negroes in service jobs as well as in skilled work. An 1856 count, for example, listed 1,144 of Philadelphia's free Negroes working in thirteen different skilled trades.

More important for the development of black baseball, a cadre of entrepreneurs, editors, publishers, musicians, teachers, and physicians formed the nucleus of an urban, though ghettoized, black middle class that eventually provided much of the leadership for black progress, including baseball progress, through most of American history. By the outbreak of the Civil War, for instance, blacks in New York City held a quarter of a million dollars in savings banks and an equal sum in real estate. Philadelphia's 25,000 blacks, who comprised the largest black population of any Northern city and constituted the leadership of Northern blacks, probably owned even more property than those of New York. These comparatively affluent blacks entertained others with music and refreshment in well-furnished apartments. As Benjamin Brawley observed, in a day when many of his people had not yet learned to get beyond showiness in dress these blacks were temperate and self-restrained, lived within their income, and retired at a reasonable hour.

In the face of rife discrimination, the nascent black bourgeoisie perforce established separate institutions, such as churches, publications, fraternal groups like the Knights of Pythias, and benevolent associations. Its members also formed baseball organizations. Although there is little concrete evidence, it is reasonable to assume that even before the Civil War, as Knickerbocker-style baseball gained in popularity among whites, Northern blacks also began to take it up. There is also reason to believe that several member teams of the National Association of Amateur Base Ball Players were uneasy enough about the presence of black teams to include anti-black clauses in their organizational charters. A game reportedly took place in the fall of 1860 between teams in Brooklyn called the Unknown Club and the Colored Union Club, the latter's name chosen to distinguish it from the white Union Club. Another such game was reported by the Brooklyn *Eagle* in 1862 between the Unknowns and the Monitors of Brooklyn. So at least in the North, blacks organized some formal baseball clubs before the Civil War.

After Union victory in the bloodiest war of the nineteenth century, as droves of Southern blacks migrated North for economic reasons and to escape the terrorism perpetrated on them by so-called Regulators to prevent them from exercising their newly won freedom, discriminatory attitudes and practices hardened. Although millions of northern whites disapproved of slavery, they also shrank from the idea of equality for blacks. Alarmed at the influx of these "strange hordes," whom they regarded as threats to society, northern whites strove to contain them by keeping them out of white neighborhoods, relegating them to unsanitary housing at high rents, and offering them only the most menial, lowest-paying jobs. Despite these heavy odds blacks North and South managed to forward their own institutions, including baseball.

During the baseball fever of the post-Civil War years the relatively low cost of playing ball placed the game within reach of blacks as it did whites. For many the love of baseball became the ruling passion of their lives, the enjoyment of it their greatest treasure. Such was their attachment to the game that writers have attributed motives peculiar to blacks to explain it. It may well be that, as black author E. B. Henderson suggested, "nothing meant so much in the lives of an impoverished people after a day or week of toil as the scene and setting of a country-side baseball game." And as with immigrants there is also warrant for the claim of writer William E. Bohn that baseball catered to the desire of blacks to belong, because baseball was not only a game but an important part of American life, and to be "out of it" meant being "only a fractional American."

Black amateur ball teams of the period were "in it." Apart from skin color and financial means they were hardly distinguishable from the white.* The comments of the Brooklyn *Daily Union* in 1867, quoted by Peterson, furnish a clue to the character of black amateur ball. The Brooklyn Uniques and Monitors and the Philadelphia Excelsiors, said the *Union*, were "reasonable colored people, well-to-do . . . and include many first-class players," adding that it trusted that none of the "white trash" that disgraced white clubs by "bawling for them" would be allowed to mar the pleasure of "these social gatherings."**

The likeness of the black amateur clubs to the white comes through in the papers of the Pythian Base Ball Club of Philadelphia, 1867 to 1870, a collection that I was the first to examine (1962), squirreled away in the archives of the Historical Society of Pennsylvania. In beautiful handwriting they reveal a form of organization, code of conduct, and set of social practices so similar that with some justification the Pythians may be called the Knick-erbockers of black amateur baseball.

The first necessity for such a group was a meeting place. The Pythians rented a room or rooms in the Banneker Institute, at 718 Lombard Street, the street on which the rich black family of James Forten lived at number 92. The institute was named for the black astronomer and most noted black of the eighteenth century, Benjamin Banneker. In addition to covering rent and janitorial services, the club paid for plastering, papering, and white-washing the premises. Members paid a dollar a year dues and had to abide by the rules of the Institute adopted in March of 1867. "Spirituous liquors" and all card playing, gambling, and betting on games were strictly prohibited. Furthermore, "for unbecoming language or conduct tending to bring either

---

*Early white clubs are discussed in *Baseball: The Early Years*, pp. 15–17, 20–21.
**The account did, however, say that a subsequent game between the Unions and Excelsiors was marred by arguments and "pretty rough" Philadelphia fans.

association [the club or the institute] into disrepute" a member could be fined, suspended, or expelled.

Pythians and other black amateur clubs, like the white, were social as well as baseball clubs, whose members appeared as interested in wielding knives and forks as in swinging bats. After a game the home club customarily wined and dined the visiting team, though less sumptuously than their more affluent white counterparts. One collation the Pythians served the visiting Mutual Club of Washington, D.C., consisted of cheese, ham, tongue, pickles, rolls, bread, butter, and ice cream, complemented by wine and "segars." Dishes and cutlery were rented, and the club even paid visitors' "Car Fares." The bill for the occasion, including "porterage" and the janitorial services of a Mrs. Furman, came to a modest $58.16 on the reception committee's carefully itemized account. On another occasion the Pythians spent $30.03 to entertain the Monrovia Club of Harrisburg, Pennsylvania, after a game.

Female friends of the players might assist with postgame entertainment. J.C. White, secretary of the Pythians, referred to women in a letter to Charles E. Douglass, then corresponding secretary of the Alert Club of Washington, D.C., about plans for a game in Philadelphia in 1867: "This will allow the ladies, whose consideration for our Club is so manifest, to proceed with any arrangements for the 30th which the kindness of their hearts may have suggested." The Pythians also occasionally permitted members to invite "distinguished, meritorious or worthy strangers sojourning in the city" to socialize with them.

The Pythians made some contact with whites. Researcher Jerry Malloy's excellent article about the early black players mentions a game against a white team, the City Items, whom the Pythians beat in 1869. The Pythian manuscript collection shows that just before the visit of the Washington Alerts, a Pythian wrote their captain, "There are considerable interest and no little anxiety among the white Fraternity concerning the game." He did not elaborate, but perhaps the reason was that the Pythians had obtained the use of the grounds of the famous white Athletics, with "all its conveniences (the best in the city)," along with the services as umpire of E. Hicks Hayhurst, prominent member of the Athletics.

In 1869 at least one game between black clubs was played on the new grounds of the (white) Nationals in Washington, too. So by the sixties a precedent had been established in black baseball for the use of white parks and white umpires, practices that were to become common. By the eighties major-league clubs would be renting their parks to important black teams in such cities as Baltimore, Cleveland, and St. Louis. White-owned businesses benefited from the blacks' purchase of equipment as well. The Pythians, for example, purchased their baseballs from the well-known local sporting goods dealer, A.J. Reach. Ten uniforms, presumably also from Reach, cost them $60.43. Thus insofar as their prejudices permitted, teams in Organized Baseball, like other white businesses, quickly discovered blacks as consumers—"a new and highly lucrative" view of Negroes, as LeRoi Jones, black writer, put it: "an unexpected addition to the strange portrait of the Negro the white American carried around in his head."

Black teams undertook long trips for games, just as whites did. In response to a challenge from the Mutuals, the Pythians traveled to Washington in 1869 to play not only the Mutuals and the Alerts but also Howard College and the team of the Ashmun Institute, soon to be Lincoln University. The cost of this rather ambitious schedule came to $149.60. Another stable black team of Philadelphia, the Excelsiors, set out in another direction and played the Unions and Monitors of Brooklyn and another black team in Williamsburgh, which was then a part of Long Island. It is certain that West Chester, Pennsylvania, had at least one black club, because one challenged the Pythians in 1867. This club apparently was a strong one, for in preparation to meet "the West Chester boys" at least one member of the Pythians was ready to cut a couple of amateur corners to make the Pythians "heavier" by enlisting two players from the neighboring Excelsiors. Wrote Octavius Catto of the Pythians, "With proper precaution and advances—Clark and Wilson could be obtained to play on our nine—as corresponding members—without touching or in any way affecting their membership in the Excelsior Club." He concluded with an enigmatic sentence: "It had best be done immediately—and especially in view of the probability of our meeting our white brethren."

Some scattered information provides a clue to the position of black players in the community. Charles E. Douglass of the Washington Alerts, after three years with the Freedmen's Bureau, secured a clerkship in the Treasury Department. His father, Frederick Douglass, an escaped slave and abolitionist who became the most distinguished black of his generation, as a freedman had the satisfaction of watching Charles, his youngest son, play ball in the nation's capital. A member of the Mutuals, George D. Johnson, was evidently an employee of the Freedmen's Bureau. Jerome Johnson of the Alerts was probably also a government employee, having written to the Pythians on the stationery of a government bureau, possibly the Freedmen's Bureau, to say he could not attend a social affair because of "Official Business."

Two members of the Pythians are of particular interest. William Still, a coal dealer and local black political and civil rights leader (he was clerk of the local antislavery society), published two books, one a collection of materials on the Underground Railway, in which he was an active participant, and the other commemorating the struggle of Philadelphia blacks for the right to ride city streetcars, a right they finally won in 1866. In 1869 Still repudiated his Pythian membership, refusing to pay two dollars back dues for 1868 and 1869 on the ground that "Our kin in the South famishing for knowledge, have claims so great and pressing that I feel bound to give of my means in this direction to the extent of my abilities, in preference to giving for frivolous amusements." Pythian Secretary J.C. White dismissed this explanation, replying tartly that "neither the acquisition or disposition of your means is a matter of interest to us as an organization" and telling Still to pay up.

The other interesting, and tragic, Pythian was Octavius V. Catto, a respected black teacher and the principal of the Institute for Colored Youth, established by Quakers at 716 Lombard Street to teach useful trades and principles of farming to blacks. Catto was a founder and the captain of the Pythian team. He was also an officer on the staff of General Wagner, a commander of a local black brigade. On October 10, 1871, Catto received orders to join his unit armed for duty at the scene of a riot that had erupted when blacks tried to vote. Before doing so Catto reputedly bought a gun but no ammunition. One Frank Kelly, apparently a white, passed Catto on the Street en route to the scene and shot him at least twice. Catto died of his wounds. His murder aroused great sympathy and indignation, and protest meetings were held. After a ten-day trial finally held six years later, Kelly was pronounced not guilty.

Afro-Americans' enthusiasm for the game, their successful organization and operation of their own amateur clubs, the white-collar status and considerable education of their membership, their adoption of strict codes of behavior, their enterprise in undertaking trips to distant cities to play games and enjoy civilized social intercourse afterward, all proved to no avail when the Pythians attempted in 1867 to break the barrier of segregation.

It is commonly known that for many decades Organized Baseball had an unwritten rule against admitting black players. It is clear that as far back as December 1867 the National Association of Amateur Base Ball Players (then made up only of northern clubs) barred black players and clubs from their ranks with a mealymouthed statement worthy of James Crow in his best form.* New evidence since uncovered in the papers of the Pythians reveals that even before the imposition of this "national" ban the application of blacks for admission was refused by a state amateur association. This step was taken in October of 1867. So two months before the National Association's ban, Pennsylvania's association of amateur baseball players, in an action belying a stock white declaration that once the Negro proved himself acceptance would follow, deflected the Pythians' application for membership, again with all the finesse and hypocrisy for which James Crow became infamous. The sorry tale is revealed in the straightforward, detailed report of the Pythian delegate to the convention, R.S. Bun.

Bun's report begins on the morning of October 16 when the Pennsylvania association convened in the Harrisburg courthouse and immediately appointed a committee on credentials. While the committee prepared its report the other delegates clustered in small groups to discuss what action should

*Baseball: The Early Years, p. 42.

be taken regarding the admission of the Pythians' delegate. Presently the convention secretary, a Mr. Domer, told Bun that a canvas of the delegates revealed that a majority opposed seating him, and Domer advised Bun to withdraw his application, because, as Bun reported, "it was better for us [the Pythians] to withdraw than to have it on record that we were black balled." Bun declined, preferring to wait for the credentials committee's report.

The committee then reported favorably on all credentials except that of the Pythians, which they purposely admitted doing. Next a resolution, evidently to accept their report, was "hastily passed," and a Mr. Ellis, "quickly springing to his feet," moved that the committee be discharged. Bun was about to object when Mr. Rogers of the Chester Club pointed out that the committee had not reported on the Pythians, a "colored" organization from Philadelphia—something they were bound to do in order that the delegates "might take such action on it as they should deem fit."

When the Pythians' application was read aloud separately, Ellis moved that it be tabled, and two-thirds of the convention concurred. But another Rogers, of the Batchelor Club of Philadelphia, and Hayhurst of the Athletics intervened and asked that the matter be deferred until the evening session, which a larger number of delegates would probably attend. It was unfair, they said, that the few (about twenty) present should take the responsibility of rejecting a delegate when perhaps "a greater portion of those present in the evening would be in favor of his acceptance." The convention agreed and turned to other business.

After adjournment of this first session, members of the convention gathered around Bun and, while "all expressed sympathy for our club," only about five declared willingness to vote for its admission. The others told him openly that they would "in justice to the opinion of the clubs they represented be compelled, against their personal feelings, to vote against our [the Pythians'] admission," and most of the delegates, including Domer and Hayhurst, again tried to get Bun to withdraw his application. Again he refused, but this time he telegraphed home for instructions, which were to "fight if there was a chance." Hayhurst, Rogers, and others invited Bun to accompany them to a local baseball match that afternoon. He accepted.

When the evening session convened Bun found only about the same number of delegates present as in the morning, so "as there seemed no chance of anything but being black balled" Bun withdrew the Pythians' application. Bun said that all the delegates "seemed disposed to show their sympathy and respect for our club by showing every possible courtesy and kindness," and Secretary Domer even gave him a pass home over the Philadelphia Central Railroad.

Neither the Pennsylvania Association's kid-glove rebuff of the Pythians nor the National Association's quarantine of all black players and clubs two months later stayed the increase and spread of black amateur teams in the

North. In Buffalo, for example, where in August 1869 the Fearless Club of Utica beat the local Invincibles, the game was billed as for the colored championship of New York State. The Buffalo *Express* reported that women of all colors attended the game. In May 1871 two black clubs, the Auroras of Chelsea and the Resolutes of Boston, played in Massachusetts what the New York *Clipper* reported as "an excellent game." The Lord Hannibals and the Orientals, members of a so-called Colored League, played each other in 1874 in Newington Park, Baltimore. Two other black clubs, the West End Club of Long Branch and the Crescent Nine of Princeton, played at the Polo Grounds in the fall of 1883, and the New York *Times* reported that the West End men, unlike those from Princeton, had mastered the catching of "sky-scrapers" and felt at home picking up "hot liners."

As northern black baseball increased in growth and popularity, varying degrees of professionalism crept in, as it had done in white baseball. A well-known professional team was formed at this time from waiters at a hotel—a type of business that employed many blacks North and South. In 1885 Frank Thompson, headwaiter at the Argyle Hotel of Babylon, Long Island, organized a team from among fellow waiters, and later in the year he named it the Cuban Giants. The word *Cuban* was sometimes used by players as a counter to racial prejudice and by the white press to avoid mention of blacks, while *Giants* would be adopted by many black teams because of the popularity of Organized Baseball's New York Giants. To add credence to their disguise the Cuban Giants allegedly communicated with each other in a gibberish of their own intended to be taken for Spanish. Plausibility was added to the Cuban caper by the fact that baseball had taken hold in Cuba by the 1860s.*

The Cuban Giants were not, however, the first black professional team, as they have traditionally been regarded ever since Sol White, the black pioneer chronicler of early Negro baseball, who played briefly for the Cuban Giants early in his career, said they were. At least three years before the Cuban Giants formed, a black professional club, probably the Orions, was playing in Philadelphia. Another professional team was the Black Stockings of St. Louis, who, according to the Cleveland *Leader* of May 1883, enjoyed the pick of the best colored players in the country. When the Black Stockings came to Cleveland that year to play the local Blue Stockings, the game was sufficiently important to be played in League Park and to receive full coverage in the *Leader*. That year the Black Stockings also defeated the Akrons, a strong white team.

The Cuban Giants did, however, quickly become the outstanding independent black team in the East after taking three players from the Philadelphia Orions. According to Sol White, the Giants were backed by Walter Cook, a Trenton, New Jersey, "capitalist," apparently a white, and managed

*See above, Chapter 19.

by a black man, S.K. Govern. The players were paid weekly, outfielders $12.00, infielders $15.00, and batterymen $18.00, or from $48.00 to $72.00 a month—better pay than for most jobs open to blacks then.

By the mid-eighties the Cuban Giants were playing other leading black clubs like the New York Gothams, their big rivals in the metropolitan area, as well as crack white teams in Philadelphia and leading college teams. They even tackled some of Organized Baseball's minor- and major-league clubs. In 1885 they defeated Bridgeport, champions of the minor Eastern League, but lost to the major-league New York Mets and Philly Athletics. Sol White said the Cuban Giants "closed the season of 1886 with a great record made against National League and leading college teams." On a long western trip in 1887, according to Peterson, they again played major-league clubs, this time in Cincinnati and Indianapolis, as well as minor-league clubs. The Indianapolis *Freeman* even claimed that in 1888 the major-league St. Louis, Chicago, and Detroit clubs, "unable to bear the odium of being beaten by colored men, refused to accept their challenge." In any case, there seems no doubt of either the skill of the Cuban Giants or the vigor of black baseball generally during the Gilded Age.

In 1887 a group of prominent black clubs, all but Louisville based in cities of the Northeast quadrant, undertook to form a league, meeting in March 1887 at the Douglass Institute in Baltimore, according to Leroy Graham's book on black Baltimore. Members listed by Sol White were the Resolutes of Boston, Pythians of Philadelphia (possibly the descendants of the original club), Lord Baltimores of Baltimore, Capital Citys of Washington, Keystones of Pittsburgh, Fall Citys of Louisville, and Gorhams of New York. The Cincinnati Browns and a club called the New York Cubans (not the Cuban Giants) were apparently also members. The Cuban Giants did not join; as the most prominent black club and best crowd attraction, they evidently believed they could do better financially as independents.

The league's modest schedule called for each team to play two games in each of the other's cities, visiting teams to receive a small guarantee or the privilege of choosing half the gate receipts. The Resolutes journeyed to Louisville for two games, the Gorhams went to Pittsburgh, and the Washington and Baltimore clubs met. Gate receipts were disappointing, however. The clubs lacked financial backing sufficient to carry on, and the league collapsed in a week.

The league's failure did not necessarily mean the demise of its members. The Capitals broke up, but the New York and Pittsburgh entries in particular continued to distinguish themselves against white as well as black teams, and all derived some satisfaction from the knowledge that their short-lived league helped demonstrate that black players of ability abounded.

A tournament held in New York in 1888 attested further to the vigor of early black baseball. Besides the Cuban Giants, entrants cited by Sol White were the Keystones of Pittsburgh, the Gorhams of New York, and the Red Stockings of Norfolk, Virginia. The Cuban Giants won the prize, a silver ball donated by one of the team's owners. After watching the tournament a *Sporting News* correspondent (quoted by Peterson) wrote, "There are players among these colored men that equal any white players on the ballfield. If you don't think so, go and see the Cuban Giants play. This club, with the strongest players on the field, would play a favorable game against such clubs as the [National League] New York or Chicagos."

Although the failed league of 1887 was the first Negro league patterned after the white majors' plan of limiting membership to clubs in leading cities, it was not the first effort to form a professional Negro league, as Sol White thought it was. A Jacksonville, Florida, group had already attempted one. For despite the disorders of Civil War and its aftermath, black baseball was unfolding in the South.

Among Southern blacks as well as whites, the seeds of baseball were planted before the Civil War. Bondage failed to expunge either the urge or the opportunity of blacks to play ball any more than it did their impulse to resist slavery. They participated in a variety of sports, such as boxing, boating, fishing, hunting, cockfights, and horse racing. They also became familiar with various forms of ball play early on. Already in 1797 the Commissioners of Fayetteville, North Carolina, directed town constables to give fifteen lashes to "negroes . . . that may be seen playing ball" on the Sabbath.

Slaves seldom determine their personal affairs, much less those of mankind, so ball-playing Negro slaves may reasonably be regarded as having little direct impact on the history of black baseball. But the seed had been planted. And even in the antebellum South, not all Negroes were slaves. By 1860 the region contained approximately a quarter million free Negroes. They lived untrammeled by strict Jim Crow regulations simply because in slavery days whites saw little need for such rules. To be sure, free Southern Negroes endured various constraints and indignities, and they were always at risk of kidnap or arrest as suspected fugitives and of re-enslavement. Nevertheless, they made substantial gains on many fronts and, like their brothers in the North, established stable middle-class communities, founding their own schools and newspapers as well as benevolent societies and churches, which were centers of social activity, sponsoring suppers, picnics, fairs, and, as we shall see, baseball teams.

These developments were especially conspicuous in the New Orleans area, where by the Civil War free Negroes constituted a fourth of the population. As Professor Ira Berlin has explained, a shortage of white women as well as the spread of French and Spanish cultural patterns, with their more tolerant racial attitudes, led to considerable miscegenation and to offspring often acknowledged by their white fathers as free Negroes. Consequently, no Southern city had as active and as educated a population of free Negroes as

New Orleans. Many set up as self-employed shopkeepers and artisans. Some even entered professions. Local laws and military service gave them a measure of equality. A few became wealthy and, alas, even owned slaves.

Under such relatively tolerable circumstances, black baseball in New Orleans thrived and continued to prosper during and well after the Civil War. In the 1860s and 1870s the black employees of exclusive social clubs organized baseball teams named the Boston and the Pickwick after the clubs of their white employers. Other black teams were occasionally mentioned in the New Orleans *Picayune*, as Professor Dale Somers found. By 1875, according to Professor John Blassingame, no fewer than thirteen black clubs were playing in the city, and in the fall of that year they formed a city-wide league and even staged a state championship game.

Black clubs of Louisiana and Georgia soon developed ties with those in Florida, where Negro baseball had also made progress, helped perhaps by a congenial environment. French and Spanish cultural patterns predominated in Florida and Gulf ports where, for reasons similar to those in New Orleans, many free Negroes worked at skilled trades and some enjoyed privileges denied other free blacks. By the early eighties, as shown in Bess Beatty's research, black baseball in Jacksonville was well-organized and in 1883 its most prominent club, the Athletic Baseball Team, accepted an invitation to a tournament in Savannah, Georgia, in September. Two years later another local team, the Roman Cities, had improved sufficiently to share leadership with the Athletics among Jacksonville's black teams and to travel to Georgia to play the Savannah Broads. In June the following season, 1886, a series of games began for the Negro championship of Florida. The Florida *Times-Union*, quoted by Beatty, predicted colored play would "eclipse anything of the kind ever witnessed in Jacksonville," but then, in keeping with the usual spotty coverage of Negro ball by the white press, neglected to report the results.

White press coverage of black baseball in Florida fluctuated with the fortunes of white baseball: when the latter throve, the Negroes drew a blank; when white ball fell off, the Negroes received attention. Thus in the last seasons of the decade a press gap occurred for the blacks until August 1890 when a local paper complained that baseball among whites was dead for the rest of the season but "the colored population has enjoyed baseball all summer and their champion team, the Roman Cities, have wiped the earth with each and every aggregation of players they have tackled."

Indeed, the Roman Cities had reached their peak form. On June 8, 1890, appearing in yellow uniforms described as "after the color of a canvassed ham," they defeated the strong Chathams of Savannah for their first victory of the season. Great excitement arose when the Chathams arrived in Jacksonville in August for the three-game series with the Roman Cities. More than a thousand fans, many of them white, attended the third game—the largest crowd ever to witness a game in the city during the Gilded Age. A local paper described the game, which ended in a 5–5 tie, as "a first class exhibition of scientific baseball. . . . The white spectators all pronounced it a very pretty game and the colored onlookers were simply frantic over a good play." White fans, however, were often fair-weather followers. Like the white press they showed interest in Negro ball in inverse proportion to the success of the white teams. The saying "turn about is fair play" did not apply, however. Blacks could see white games only from a segregated bleacher section.

Black teams continued to dominate Jacksonville baseball in 1891. In May the Savannah Chathams, backed by 200 fans who divided their attention between baseball and barbecue, took on the Roman Cities in Jacksonville once more. Some 500 demonstrative fanatics crowded onto the field and along the fences, cheering wildly and betting heavily throughout. With the score tied 14 all, the Chathams refused to continue because of rain, so the Roman Cities were awarded the game 9–0. In another series later that season between the same two teams, however, the best the Roman Cities could do was to tie one of the three games. When this setback was followed by a loss to the Tampa Never Fears, the Roman Cities began to decline.

Meanwhile, New Orleans continued as a center for Southern black ball during the eighties. By this time such clubs as the Dumonts, Orleans, Aetnas, Fischers, Unions, Cohens, and Pinchbacks almost certainly were professionals of varying degree. All played frequently, often featuring brass bands at their games and attracting as many as a thousand spectators. The better clubs among them arranged matches to decide the Negro championship. Black teams from cities all over the South came to New Orleans to play, and New Orleans teams traveled to Mobile and Natchez for games. The Pinchback Club, named for P.B.S. Pinchback, the Negro who had served briefly as acting governor of Louisiana in 1875, was reputedly one of the best in the state and even toured the North. In 1887 the Pinchbacks defeated a white team in a game of which the Negro paper *Pelican* said, "the playing of the colored club was far above the average . . . and elicited hearty and generous applause from the large crowd . . . which was about evenly divided between white and colored."

Like the white amateurs in the twilight era before professional leagues, many prominent black teams operating in southern cities during the 1880s were moving away from amateurism. How far each had strayed from it— whether by placing individual and team bets on their games, accepting financial aid from sponsors, sharing gate receipts, or paying fixed fees per game to players—is impossible to gauge precisely. Judged by their skill, their willingness to travel considerable distances, and the large crowds they attracted, one must assume that by this time at least the leading black teams of the South had left pure amateur ranks. Further evidence of their professionalism came in 1886 with the formation by a group of black promoters in Jacksonville, Florida, of the Southern League of Colored Baseballists. For the account of this league, which was probably the first attempt to organize a professional Negro league, we are indebted largely to researcher William Plott.

The story begins in March 1886 when newspapers carried an invitation to captains of all "colored" clubs in Georgia, Florida, South Carolina, Alabama, and Tennessee who had a "fair record" to enter the league by writing the manager of the Jacksonville, Florida, club. The following month an organizational plan was announced, providing for a board of twelve directors "representing a capital of nearly $100,000." Clubs must have "good backers," pay a five-dollar entrance fee, and purchase a $1.50 annual subscription to the *Southern Leader* of Jacksonville, the official organ of the league. They were also to furnish a statement of available board and lodging for visiting teams and a guarantee sufficient to cover such expenses, as well as carfare. Umpires must be acceptable to both teams; no "cooked and dried" ones would do. Clubs were to be suspended "for repeated disorderly conduct, cursing, fighting, drunkenness etc."

After the league missed its May 10 opening day, a meeting was held in Jacksonville on the twenty-second to prepare a modest schedule of games to start June 7 and end August 25. The New York *Official Base Ball Record* of May 31 stated that the first game would take place in St. Augustine, following which a series of games would be played at New Orleans, Memphis, Savannah, Charleston, and Jacksonville. During the season the papers mentioned various teams as members. According to Plott the league listed ten at the outset: the Eclipses and Eurekas of Memphis, the Georgia Champions of Atlanta, the Broads and Lafayettes of Savannah, the Fultons of Charleston, the Athletics, Macedonias, and Florida Clippers of Jacksonville, and the Unions of New Orleans. Later in the season the names Jerseys of Savannah, Roman Cities of Jacksonville, and Montgomery (Alabama) Blues appeared in the newspapers, too. Most if not all these clubs had white fans as well as blacks. The Eclipses and Eurekas of Memphis were both crack teams; in 1886 the Memphis *Appeal* hailed both as champion colored clubs of the South. Of the first game between the Eclipse team and the Unions of New Orleans that year the *Picayune*, quoted by Plott, said, "Judging from the first game the colored clubs will furnish good sport and the teams can play ball. The Eclipse boys all fielded well and threw the ball like the best professionals."

The Fultons of Charleston, who were evidently short-term members, played in uniforms flashy enough to rival modern major-league teams: dark blue shirts, light blue pants, white belts, and white caps trimmed in red. They also used a Peck & Snyder red ball—evidence that experiments with colored baseballs in the majors many years later were not as innovative as thought at the time. Unfortunately, the ability of the Fultons did not measure up to the splendor of their attire.

After playing relatively few games the Southern League of Colored Baseballists fell apart. It would not be the last league to do so. Apart from the probability that it was the first attempt to establish a black professional league of more than local, city-wide dimension, the effort in itself speaks for the growing strength of Negro ball in the area. Indeed, its failure may be attributed at least in part to over-ambition in admitting too many teams and attempting to organize on a regional basis rather than arranging a tight schedule among a limited number of teams, as the white pro leagues, and later the black ones, learned to do.

Such progress as black baseball made in the South during the immediate postwar decades took place in an increasingly inhospitable and even barbarous environment for blacks generally. Although they were better off than under slavery, their hope for "forty acres and a mule" proved largely phantom while their relegation to peonage through the pernicious crop-lien system and their expulsion from many skilled trades were guarantees only too real of the Negroes' future as the mudsill of the southern economy, itself severely straitened.

Moreover, for various reasons, mainly economic, northern interest in the welfare of southern blacks flagged. Compromise resulted: pledges of full and equal protection of all rights of black as well as white citizens were given by supposedly honorable Southerners like South Carolinian Wade Hampton, who in his campaign brochure proclaimed "Free Men! Free Ballots!! Free Schools!!!" but when in 1877 the last Federal soldiers left, the pledges became as worthless as Confederate money. Then in 1883 the Supreme Court declared unconstitutional important provisions of the Civil Rights Act of 1875 calculated to guarantee to blacks equal accommodations in public conveyances, inns, and places of amusement—a bitter blend that was to affect all of black baseball.

Negro ball in the South soon felt the effects of such strictures. Interracial teams and games were gradually banned and the fans segregated. Even the Gulf Coast imposed Jim Crow laws. In Florida, according to Beatty, invitations to baseball tournaments around the state often specifically excluded blacks, leaving them with no recourse but to hold tournaments of their own. Professor Somers says that relatively liberal New Orleans also felt the pressure for segregation: in July 1885 two white teams protested a proposed black-white game there and threatened to boycott white players who crossed the color line. That same month the *Picayune* warned that any white clubs that played Negro teams would have to "brave considerable opposition on the part of the other [white] clubs." Thus threatened, the city's white teams restricted themselves to lily-white competition. In the late eighties the professional white New Orleans Pelicans of Organized Baseball's minor Southern League did play black teams, and the local "champion white club," the Ben Theards, played a few games with the Pinchbacks, the "colored champions," before crowds of both colors. But these games were exceptions, and by 1890 interracial baseball in New Orleans had ceased.

Meanwhile, black baseball in the North was taking a different turn.

34

IF HE HAD A WHITE FACE

While black ball players in the South were passing under the yoke of segregation, in the North, where the lot of Afro-Americans was only marginally better, some black professionals were gaining admission to Organized Baseball. During the period 1883–1898, fifty-five of them, according to an indispensible register laboriously compiled by Merl F. Kleinknecht and colleagues, gained entrance to some twenty of Organized Baseball's leagues. Limited and short-lived though this essay at integration proved, it is nevertheless memorable not only on its own account but because failure to continue and nourish the experiment provides an uncomfortable reminder that discrimination exacts a price not only of the victims but of the society that practices it. In Organized Baseball alone, the delay of integration carried an immeasurable cost: more than a half-century of injustice to black players and deprivation of fans, white as well as black, to say nothing of loss of profits to club owners.

This early venture in integration took two forms. In one, individual black players were truly integrated. White teams employed them because of their skill and perhaps their drawing power as curiosities as well. In the other, all-Negro teams were occasionally admitted to white leagues. This arm's length—or, we may say, bat's length—quasi-integration doubtless reflected a prevailing attitude that playing against blacks was more tolerable than playing with them.

Such collective entrance happened to three full black teams, and during only four seasons. The Cuban Giants were admitted to the Middle States League in 1889 as the entry for Trenton, New Jersey, although according to the Harrisburg *Morning Patriot,* cited by researcher Ocania Chalk, there was much complaint about their admission, especially after they proved their superior strength. In mid-season the New York Gorhams also joined the Middle States League as a replacement for the white Philadelphia Giants. The following year the Cubans played for York, Pennsylvania, in the same league, which had been renamed the Eastern Interstate. Then in 1891 the

Cubans played their third and last season in Organized Ball, representing Ansonia in the Connecticut League.

Seven years passed before another all-black team entered a minor league. In 1898 a white man formed a team of young, inexperienced blacks and entered it in the Iron and Oil League to represent Celeron, a western New York resort town. Outclassed, the team made a miserable showing and dropped out of the league early. During the interval, however, the 1895 Adrian team in the Michigan State League became a partly black team when, to bolster itself in a close pennant race toward the end of the season, it enlisted five or six players from the Page Fence Giants, a skilled black club backed by white men apparently connected with the local fence company, manufacturers of metal chain link fences for playgrounds and other purposes.

Blacks playing as individuals in Organized Baseball's leagues were thinly distributed. Their number in a given year never exceeded the 1887 high of about ten. The length of service of black players, either singly or as members of black teams, ranged from one season to eight, although most played only a few years. In four out of the sixteen years 1883–1898, no known blacks were employed, and in four others only one participated.

Of the fifty-five known blacks who got into Organized Baseball, two reached the major leagues. As I was the first to record in a previous volume— and it bears repeating—Moses Fleetwood Walker, not Jackie Robinson, was the first known black admitted to the majors.* He caught for Toledo of the American Association, then a major league, in 1884. Fleet's younger brother Welday or Weldy joined him later that year as an outfielder. But whereas Fleet, who played in forty-odd games, at least secured a cup of coffee in the majors, brother Weldy, having played in just five, got only a whiff of its aroma.

Fleet Walker's background was exceptional for a professional ball player in those days. He was born in 1857 in Mount Pleasant, Ohio, but his family soon moved to Steubenville. Although some have claimed Fleet's father was a physician, the 1870 census of the First Ward listed him as a minister. After a year in the preparatory school at Oberlin College, a school that Oberlin, like many other colleges, operated in those days, Fleet in 1879 entered the college proper, which since 1835 had offered equal educational opportunity to blacks.

Walker was no semiliterate athlete posing as a student and coasting along on bogus courses. His college record shows that he studied the standard curriculum of the time, including courses in science, rhetoric, logic, philosophy, and ancient and modern languages, and he proved to be a somewhat better than average student. He also caught for Oberlin's first intercollegiate team in 1881. On summer vacations he played semipro ball; one summer

*See *Baseball: The Early Years*, p. 334.

he took a job with the White Sewing Machine Company of Cleveland, or at least with its ball team.

After three years at Oberlin Walker left to study law at the University of Michigan. It was rumored, however, that Michigan was interested mostly in his baseball talents. Records of the university's athletic department show he won letters in 1882 and 1883, and he is listed in Michigan's all-time athletic record book. In keeping with the loose character of college ball a century ago, Walker returned to Oberlin in 1882 at commencement time to catch for his former school. He did not take a degree from either institution.

In 1883 Walker joined Toledo of the Northwestern League. Then, when the club entered the major-league American Association in 1884, Walker went along with it. He batted only .251 but usually did good work behind the plate, although at times he had trouble throwing out men stealing. The hometown Toledo *Blade* praised Walker, and several times its reporter wrote that his hands and those of the second-string catcher were so sore that neither man should be playing. Although the claim in the Louisville *Courier-Journal* of May 3 that Walker was "something of a wonder" may have been exaggerated, there was no doubting the Cincinnati *Enquirer*'s statement that with Tony Mullane, the colorful Cork Irishman, pitching and Fleet Walker catching, the Toledo battery was a sure gate attraction, even though Mullane was said to dislike pitching to a black and to ignore his signs.

Brother Weldy had followed Fleet to Oberlin's preparatory school for the years 1881 and 1882, playing right field on the college team those years. A photo of the 1881 team shows the Walkers as the only black members. Weldy left Oberlin in 1884 and, as mentioned, joined Fleet briefly on the Toledo team, after which he played two years on minor-league teams. Toledo released Fleet near the end of the season, after which he played five more seasons in the minors.

That only two of the known fifty-five blacks who managed to play in Organized Baseball did so on a major-league team does not, of course, prove that none of the others qualified. Bigotry is blind to competence. Even in the case of the Walker brothers chance may well have been responsible for their admission. It does not diminish them to point out that if Fleet had not been with the Toledo team when it joined the American Association, he may never have been given the opportunity to play in the majors, and Weldy's chance to follow him would doubtless have been lost as well. No one can be certain that others among the fifty-three blacks who were never called would have merited being chosen. Baseball history is sprinkled with outstanding minor leaguers who failed in the majors. Assuredly, however, some of the blacks who played in Organized Baseball's minor leagues were prime major-league prospects who deserved a chance to prove themselves, especially men like George Stovey, Bud Fowler, Sol White, and Frank Grant.

Stovey, a lefthander, was the first of a lengthy line of outstanding black pitchers that would eventually extend down to Bob Gibson. He played six seasons, 1886–1891, in Organized Baseball's minor leagues. He had two fine years in the Eastern League, with Jersey City (1886) and with Newark (1887). In the latter year he won 33 games and lost 14, a percentage better than .700, and he also played the outfield. Fleet Walker was his catcher there, and together they formed the first black battery in Organized Baseball.

John W. "Bud" Fowler was reputedly the first black professional, having been paid to play for a white team in New Castle, Pennsylvania, as early as 1872. Sports writer Lee Allen discovered that he had been born John Jackson, at none other than Cooperstown, New York, presumably the son of an itinerate hops-picker. If so, he certainly took after his father, traveling about in the next twenty-five years from New York to Colorado playing for various teams, including at least a dozen white ones. Fowler's peregrinations included eight stopovers in Organized Baseball, one with a black club and seven with white. Whenever he was out of a job he formed barnstorming teams. One of them, the All-American Black Tourists, which he organized in 1899, according to Peterson traveled in their own railroad car and before each game paraded the streets in full-dress suits.

In a testament to Fowler's ability, twice in 1885 *Sporting Life* sounded the big *if* that would become only too familiar to black ball players down through the decades of proscription: Fowler was a "crack colored player" and "one of the best general players in the country, and if he had a white face would be playing with the best of them." Later the paper remarked, "The poor fellow's skin is against him. With his splendid abilities he would long ago have been on some good club had his color been white instead of black."

Sol White, already mentioned as author of a *History of Colored Baseball* (1907), logged forty years in baseball. Five were in the minors, two with white teams and three with the Cuban Giants and Gorhams. He broke into Organized Baseball in 1887 at nineteen with Wheeling, West Virginia, of the Ohio League (the league's name is in some dispute), where he played third base and, he wrote later, found a congenial atmosphere. Local papers of league cities reported that White was an agile fielder adept at cutting off line drives and that he batted .381 for the season. Nevertheless, Wheeling did not re-sign him, apparently out of deference to prejudiced fans, although, according to Professor Gordon B. McKinney, when he returned the following April playing with the black Pittsburgh Keystones in an exhibition game against Wheeling, White received an ovation as he came to bat.

White returned to Organized Baseball for three straight seasons, 1889–1891, with the aforementioned black clubs. He made his second appearance on a white team in 1895 with Fort Wayne of the Western Interstate League, but it broke up in mid-season, and he returned to all-black clubs. Thereafter, White revealed exceptional versatility as player-manager and organizer, often in combination, with at least fifteen black teams, among them various kinds of Giants: the Cuban, Genuine Cuban, Cuban X, Columbia, Lincoln, Quaker, and Page Fence, the latter being the team organized by Bud Fowler. Probably his longest tenure was with the Philadelphia Giants, a crack team he organized with others in 1902, but in 1910 he left and formed his own club, which failed because of booking troubles with the important agent Nat Strong, and the following year he returned to managing.

Finally, there was Frank Grant, probably the best black player of the period. His six seasons in Organized Baseball date from 1886 with Meriden, Connecticut, of the Eastern League and Buffalo, an International Association team he joined in July after the Meriden club disbanded. Grant proved himself quickly with his new club. He led the team in hitting and distinguished himself in the field. Grant could play more than one position, but at his primary post, second base, he soon became known as the Black Dunlap, after the National League star Fred Dunlap.

The following year Grant did even better. According to Joseph M. Overfield, the authority on Buffalo baseball, reports from Baltimore, Washington, Boston, and Pittsburgh, where Buffalo played a series of pre-season games, described him as "a sensation," and the Boston *Globe* noted that he was attracting "a large attendance of gentlemen of his color, and not a few dusky dames." In the regular season he again led Buffalo in batting with a .340 average that included 49 extra-base hits, 11 of them home runs. He also led the team in stolen bases with 40. In the morning game of a Memorial Day doubleheader against Toronto, he accomplished the rare feat of "hitting for the cycle": making a single, double, triple, and homer. The Buffalo *Express*, describing him as a "Spaniard," said he was the club's most popular player.

Grant left Buffalo to become captain of the Cuban Giants in 1889, when they represented Trenton in the Middle States League, but in 1890 he got into trouble by signing with both the Cuban Giants and Harrisburg in the same league with a new name, the Eastern Interstate. When the issue went to court the judge awarded him to the white club. The Harrisburg *Morning Patriot* of May 6, 1890, quoted by Kleinknecht, reported the eagerness of the fans to see "the most famous colored ball player in the business. . . . When he appeared on the field a great shout went up from the immense crowd to receive him, in recognition of which he politely raised his cap." His club's shift to the Atlantic Association that year made no difference in Grant's batting; he hit over .300 in both leagues. Grant's last appearance in white baseball was again with a black club, the Cuban Giants, representing Ansonia in the Connecticut State League. When the league broke up in midsummer Grant and the Giants had to fend for themselves.

From the first, black players on white teams, major and minor, were subjected to harassment and hazard, within and without Organized Baseball, on the field and off it. They often contended with indignities like those Jackie Robinson would experience more than a half-century later, such as hostility of teammates, verbal abuse and threats from opponents and fans, and discrimination by hotel managers. Referring to the "marked degree" of racial prejudice in Organized Baseball, *Sporting News* in the spring of 1889 allowed that any black member of a white professional team "has a rocky road to travel."

White players sometimes refused to sit with blacks for team photographs, for instance. Frank Grant's popularity in Buffalo didnot extend to his white teammates, and although they acknowledged his skill they reputedly did not believe "colored men" should play with whites and declined to sit with him for a team picture. Bob Higgins, pitcher-outfielder for the Syracuse Stars of the International League, suffered similar humiliation. According to *Sporting News* Higgins showed much promise on the mound and was also a fine fielder, strong batter, and fast runner. No matter; Dug Crothers, a fellow pitcher, refused to sit next to Higgins for the club photo, not only for reasons of race but reportedly because he feared Higgins was replacing him as the team's number one pitcher—as well he might, for Higgins won 25 games that season. The newly-appointed team manager, believing the former manager had allowed the player too much leeway and it was time to rein him in, fined Crothers fifty dollars (which he never paid) and suspended him for a month, One version had it that Crothers attacked his manager physically when ordered to join the team for the picture. In either case, Crothers was penalized not for racist conduct but for insubordination.

Opposing players tried to intimidate blacks and even put them out of action. Beanballs and spikes-high slides were part of baseball, but black batters and infielders became prime targets for such tactics. Grant and Fowler, for example, adopted protective shinguards to shield their legs from slashing spikes.

Players on opposing teams might simply refuse to play against blacks. Fleet Walker met with this problem early on, while playing for the White Sewing Machine Company team. In Louisville he was forced to sit in the stands because a player on the Louisville Eclipses refused to play against him. He may have received some balm from the Louisville *Commercial*'s comment that Louisville was the first of all league cities to ban Walker, and that he was well-educated and"probably more intelligent than 16 out of 18 players." Refusal to play, as we shall see, was to become more serious later when an entire team balked at playing a club with a black in its lineup.

Abusive and at times violent fans have likewise been a baseball perennial, but black players offered unruly spectators conspicuous and safe prey. Three years after the Louisville incident Walker as a major-leaguer was again humiliated in the same city, this time by spectators who, said the Toledo *Blade*, "hissed" and "insulted" him "because he was colored." Apparently, the abuse affected his playing, for the *Blade* said Walker was one of the most reliable men on the club, and his poor playing "in a City where the Color line is closely drawn as it is in Louisville . . . should not be counted against him."

The newspaper also criticized the Louisville management for permitting "such outrageous performances to occur on the grounds." After the game a crowd followed the Walker brothers in the streets, hooting and pelting them with sticks and stones. Toledo fans, with whom Walker was popular, did not forget the episode, and several weeks afterward, when Louisville visited Toledo, the team was roundly booed. Later that season the Toledo manager received a letter from six Richmond, Virginia, fans warning that seventy-five "determined men" had sworn to mob Walker if he appeared in uniform in an exhibition game in their town, but by then he was no longer with the club.

In some ways Afro-Americans found Northern Jim Crow practices more burdensome than Southern legalized segregation, because at least under the latter they knew only too well where they stood, while under the former they could not always be certain. Outside the South, for example, black players were never sure of admission to hotels. Sol White, citing acceptance of the Cuban Giants by the McClure House in Wheeling, West Virginia, claimed that black clubs were accommodated by some of the best hotels. Yet when Frank Grant was playing for Harrisburg in 1890 he was barred from the club's hotel in Wilmington, Delaware. His white teammates, to their credit, left and went to another hotel, but even at this one he was told to eat with the colored help or get his meals elsewhere. He accepted this indignity. A little-known black player, James Randolph Jackson, pitcher for the Live Oak Club of Herkimer, New York, deserves all the more recognition for his courage in having the proprietor of the Central Hotel at Richmond Springs, New York, arraigned in 1879 before a United States Commissioner for the same treatment that Grant endured.

Sol White called 1887 a banner year for blacks in white baseball, and the fact that it was the year of their peak number on white teams in Organized Baseball supported his view. But it was also an ominous year. Speaking to a reporter after his career was over, Ed Williamson, star shortstop of the Chicago White Stockings in the 1880s, recalled the "deep-seated objection" of most white players to Afro-Americans. "No," Williamson concluded, "ball players do not burn with a desire to have colored men on the team." This attitude became more evident in 1887. The sheer success of the blacks, such as it was, in entering white ball doubtless increased antagonism toward them.

As a high minor employing seven out of all the blacks on white clubs in Organized Baseball that year, the International League furnished the most targets for racists. The incidents concerning team photos and the previously-mentioned attitudes of Buffalo players toward Grant showed the growing resentment toward black players in the league.

These sentiments were complemented by the antics of Adrian C. "Cap" Anson, player-manager of the National League's Chicago White Stockings. Anson, an outstanding baseball figure,* was also a vehemently outspoken

*Baseball: The Early Years, passim.

and active opponent of black admission to Organized Baseball. His autobiography revealed his attitude toward blacks in his reference to Clarence Duval, whom the White Sox used as singer, dancer, and clown on their world tour of 1888–1889, as the "chocolate-covered coon" and the "no-account nigger."

Of more import, except perhaps to Duval, was Anson's conduct on the playing field. In that pivotal year for black players, 1887, Anson declined to play an exhibition game with the International League's Newark team if George Stovey pitched against his White Stockings as scheduled. (In view of Stovey's skill, Anson may have been moved by more than racist reasons.) Anson had employed the same tactic against Fleet Walker four years before, refusing to play an exhibition game with Toledo if Walker played. On that occasion Toledo had not planned to use Fleet, who had a sore hand, but decided to call Anson's bluff: either Walker plays, or no game. Sources differ as to details of the incident, but Anson, apparently putting gate receipts before prejudices, caved in and went through with that game. In 1887, however, when Anson objected to Stovey, the climate had become more favorable to discrimination: opposition to black players was stiffening, especially in the International League. Anson's attempt to keep Stovey out of the Newark game succeeded. According to Robert Peterson, Stovey complained of sickness and did not play, and a year later *Sporting Life* declared that his "complaint" had been involuntary; the real reason was Anson's refusal to field his team if Stovey worked. At any rate, Anson won his point that time.

Anson's bigotry was equaled only by his persistance in promoting it. One source claims that at this time he went to the winter meetings of the major and minor leagues to lobby for a rule banning blacks (although their unwritten ones were to prove quite sufficient and more politic). In fact, Sol White asserted that had it not been for Anson's objections, the New York Giants would have purchased Stovey's contract from Newark in 1887. Even after Anson's major-league career ended he still nursed his animosity toward blacks and indeed narrowed his horizons and broadened his compass, so to speak. The Chicago *Defender*, a leading black newspaper, charged in 1922 that Anson had not only waged a one-man campaign against mixed teams and against white ones that played blacks, but also made it his business to urge every player he ever met to refuse to play with any team that included a Negro, Chinese, Japanese, or Indian, or to take the field against one that did. In those days, the *Defender* claimed, teams were composed of "ignorant men, 75% of whom could neither read nor write," so Anson found it easy to "sow his seeds of prejudice." The same paper also reported that Anson absolutely refused to allow his Chicago semipro team, Anson's Colts, to play such local black teams as the Columbia Giants or the Union Giants.

Anson need not have fretted himself over the possibility of integration in Organized Baseball. The pitifully small chance of it in the major leagues in the person of Fleet Walker died swiftly; in the minors the relatively brighter hope merely took a bit longer to expire.

As the 1887 season progressed, discontent over the presence of black players grew in the International League. In June *Sporting News* said their introduction was "causing trouble." According to the New York *Clipper* and the other leading sporting papers, at a secret league meeting on July 14 at the Geneseo House in Buffalo several representatives reported that many of the best white players were anxious to leave on account of the "colored element." Dissatisfaction was such that, as Joseph M. Overfield has written, a motion to bar Negroes completely might have passed had not the Buffalo representatives opposed it, possibly out of enlightened self-interest in retaining their star, Frank Grant. As it was, the league's board, in an apparent holding action, directed the secretary to approve no further contracts with black players. At a winter meeting the league's clubs reached a compromise whereby each club was permitted to retain no more than two black players, with the understanding that henceforth none would be signed. In other words, an immediate quota system combined with an eventual color line by attrition was agreed upon. The number of black players in the league immediately dropped from seven in 1887 to three in 1888, Grant with Buffalo and Bob Higgins and Fleet Walker with Syracuse.

Similar action was taken in the Ohio State League. Three of the ten known blacks in Organized Baseball in 1887 played on Ohio State League clubs: Sol White in Wheeling, Weldy Walker in Akron, and Dick Johnson, a hard-hitting catcher-outfielder, in Zanesville. The league decided that these were three too many. At a special meeting in February of 1888 the league rescinded a rule that had allowed blacks to be hired. Zanesville had already signed Johnson for 1888, but the league refused to ratify his contract, claiming that he was "vicious and quarrelsome." Zanesville protested and threatened to withdraw from the league unless Johnson was permitted to play. The league must have relented on Johnson, because he did start as regular catcher for the club in 1888, but he bore the pressure of being the only black left in the league that year. In one incident, cited by Professor McKinney, during a game against Wheeling he was fined for shouting a protest from the bench over the umpire's decision, although white players who virtually assaulted the umpire either escaped penalty or were fined no heavier than was Johnson.

Weldy Walker, incensed at the new ban on blacks and the league's partiality in exempting Johnson from it, sent to league president McDermit a trenchant letter of protest that deserves a place in the literature of black dissent. In the pertinent passages he stated that the ban was "a disgrace to the present age" and "casts derision at the laws of Ohio—the voice of the people which say all men are equal. . . . There should be some broader cause—lack of ability, behavior, and intelligence—to bar a player, rather than his color," he wrote, and he called on the league to reconsider its action in its next meeting.

It was Anson who was primarily responsible for Organized Baseball's drawing of the color line, Sol White believed. White attributed to Anson all the "venom" of Pitchfork Ben Tillman and James K. Vardaman, two early twentieth-century Southern demagogues who sullied the United States Senate with their anti-Negro diatribes. White's ire, though understandable, exaggerates Anson's role, because despite his force and influence as the player-manager of the Chicago White Stockings, who dominated the National League during the 1880s, Cap could not have carried the players with him had not most of them been of the same mind as he. Confirmation of this is the great player revolt of 1890, in which the big-league players overwhelmingly joined the Brotherhood League and left Anson almost in isolation on the side of the club owners.*

However ample was Anson's share of responsibility for drawing the horsehide curtain on blacks, he was only the point man for those in baseball who wanted to keep blacks out. In their aversion to the Negro player they, in turn, were in accord with practically all white Americans, who by the mid-eighties were convinced of the Negro's proper place: he was, in the words of Robert Wiebe, regarded as a curse, a barbarian, or a clown, manipulated by employers and politicians North and South and told by the Supreme Court to find his own level.

Nor were such views confined to the untutored. Since nearly all contemporary biologists, physicians, and molders of public opinion were certain that blacks were inferior beings, well-educated Northerners could hardly believe otherwise. Northern magazines of quality repeatedly made blacks the butt of crude jokes. *Harper's Weekly*, for example, printed derogatory illustrations of black ball players, such as one showing a batter being hit in the face with a ball, another depicting players lolling about lazily and grotesquely, and a third picturing a black umpire smoking a cigar. Other derisive caricatures would appear over the years. The *Official Baseball Record* in the mid-eighties consistently referred to a Negro as a coon, and an 1892 issue of *Sporting News* published what passed for a joke in which a judge says that Negroes would make good ball players; why? Because they were "so good at catching fowls." In sum, the black was in a no-win situation: he was condemned as shiftless, stupid, and generally of no account, but if he tried to improve himself he was judged "uppity."

The steps to bar black players taken by Organized Baseball were part and parcel of the nationwide segregation steadily enveloping the Negro with python embrace. Long prevalent in the North, legal segregation soon spread over the South even in areas where race separation had been relatively casual and, as we have seen, had remained so even in the early days of freedom. As the New South emerged, however, strict barriers gradually arose until the black's place was sharply defined everywhere, even to sidewalks and cemeteries. The Supreme Court furthered this constriction of

*See *Baseball: The Early Years*, Chapter 19.

Negro rights with decisions that somehow nullified or curtailed them, notably with the separate-but-equal doctrine in Plessy v. Ferguson (1896), which, by permitting separate public accommodations provided they were of equal quality, opened the way for separate but in practice grossly unequal public accommodations, including those for education and recreation, the establishment of which also were to have a bearing upon black baseball. Furthermore, most Northerners supported the Court and the hands-off policy of the other branches of the federal government.

Organized Baseball was not the only sport to gradually eliminate the semblance of integration it had permitted. As black athletes became prominent, the race issue became manifest in other sports. Black jockeys, long dominant in horse racing, were being ousted from the better clubs. White boxers refused to fight black ones. The discussion of the race question among members of the League of American Wheelmen is especially instructive. In reply to the Louisiana division's 1892 protest, reported by Professor Somers, against forcing "obnoxious company upon Southern Wheelmen" by admitting black cyclists, the league's chairman replied that while it would be "most unwise" for black members to be accepted in the South, it would be "unfair" for us to ban the Negro here, "where he is not so obnoxious and does not rub up against us as frequently as he does in the South," but if it came to a choice between accepting Negroes or Southern whites, the league would favor the latter; "We, all of us, both north and south, have a feeling of antipathy towards the colored brother. . . ."

The following spring the wheelmen's league, which had a total of six black members, all from northern states, debated the question at its national convention and, according to the New York *World*, decided not to refuse admission to blacks. It made this decision, however, in the face of much opposition: *Sporting Life* reported that when Chief Consul Luscomb of New York declared, "We believe in the exclusion of the negro. Don't let us be afraid to say so!" his remark was greeted with "tremendous uproar and shouts, yells, foot-stamping and hand-clapping. . . . " *Sporting Life* added perceptively that it should be kept in mind that the league was merely reflecting the society at large. Anti-Negro delegates continued to press their point at a convention in 1894, when they fell only a few votes short of the two-thirds necessary to ban blacks, but, according to Somers, successfully inserted *white* into the membership section of the constitution, thus accomplishing the original intention.

That segregation grew steadily more widespread and that Organized Baseball was not the only sport moving toward banning black players completely does not, of course, excuse O.B.'s policy, particularly in view of its constant boast of being democratic.

In addition to its dislike for blacks and its measures to keep them out, Organized Baseball reflected society in a third way: the employment of violence against them, except that the violence (spiking and beaning) was less harsh. To maintain the myth of white supremacy and to keep the black in his assigned place, segregation, both by law and by custom, depended ultimately upon violence. Consequently, there were, throughout the nation, frequent race riots that, according to historian John Hope Franklin, were as vicious and almost as prevalent in the North as in the South. No fewer than 2,500 blacks were lynched by rope and faggot in the fifteen years following 1885, not all of them in the South, and of those in the South not all of them by "rednecks." The 1890s were peak years for lynchings: in the worst year, 1892, they climbed to four a week. To be sure, the abuses and violent actions in Organized Baseball, already described, against black players because they were Negroes did not approach in extent or ferocity the horrors inflicted upon blacks outside the game, for whom the Gay Nineties were about as cheerful as for the crew of a torpedoed ship.

Nevertheless, for black players on white teams the 1890s were locust years. In 1891 an issue of the Jacksonville, Florida, *Evening Telegram* reported with satisfaction that the practice around the country of hiring Negroes to play on white teams was practically stamped out. A few blacks managed to hold on as members of isolated white town teams; for example, Billy Miller in Port Jervis, New Jersey, according to local history writer Keith Sutton; a black battery in Dubuque, Iowa, described by the Reach Guide as "the Watermelon Battery"; and in California, Jack Nutting playing for Etna, Jim Booker for Redding, and two half-black, half-Indian men playing for Yreka, all according to the Siskiyou, California, Historical Society. As for blacks in prominent leagues, in 1896 *Sporting News* quoted an "old timer" as saying that the prejudice against black players was so effective that no league manager would dream of signing the fastest colored player that ever lived.

In Organized Baseball during the period 1891 through 1898, four white teams employed only three known blacks, two of them for not more than a season. The third one, Bert Jones, a lefthander known as the Yellow Kid after a comic strip character, pitched for Atchison in the Kansas State League in 1897 and briefly in 1898. That year the Atchison *Globe*, in a story found by Kleinknecht, reported that a new pitcher on trial with the club refused to play in a game with the Yellow Kid and would "have nothing to do with a Cuban." Whether forced to depart or moved to do so out of expediency, Jones left the team, the last known black of his era to play in Organized Baseball. With his passing, the guttering torch of hope that Organized Baseball would accept blacks flickered and died. Nearly a half century would pass before it was relighted.

But by their skill in these distant, long-vanished baseball seasons blacks dispelled beyond dispute the claim that they lacked the ability to play in Organized Baseball. Let it not ever again be said that they failed to measure up to Organized Baseball's level of performance.

These two chapters have laid out the two main pieces of evidence proving blacks' ability: first, their skill demonstrated in the white majors after 1946, and second, the history of their successful play in white leagues of Organized Baseball back in the nineteenth century.

35

NOT FROM DRAGON'S TEETH

Organized Baseball's completion of its horsehide barrier against them did not stop blacks. They went on to develop skilled players, form professional teams, and finally establish stable, organized leagues, patterned largely after those of the whites and composed of players many of whom, as I have demonstrated, were sufficiently skilled to play in the white leagues had they been given the opportunity.

But where did all these competent players come from? Assuredly, they did not spring magically readymade from dragon's teeth, like the soldiers of Greek mythology. Baseball begins with boys, black as well as white. The game itself is colorblind and of itself makes no distinction between white boys and black. This truism applied even in America's slavery days. The testimony of former slaves interviewed in the 1930s by agents of the Works Progress Administration is replete with evidence that among slave children and young people, ball playing and marbles were the favorite games.

Among them, Douglas Paris, born to slaves in Florida, recalled that as a small boy he spent his time shooting marbles, playing ball, racing, and wrestling with the other boys. Addie Vinson, ex-slave on Ike Vinson's place in Georgia, said he didn't remember what "gals" played, but "boys played ball all day long" if they were allowed to.

Slaves also included ball playing among their activities on festive occasions. John F. Van Hook, former slave on a North Carolina plantation, remembered cornhusking parties, after which the workers had a feast, then played ball and engaged in other amusements. Frederick Douglass, who admitted in his biography that as a slave boy his "plays and sports" took him from the corn and tobacco fields, said that in the 1830s between Christmas and New Year most slaves "engaged in such sports and merriments as playing ball. . . ."

The ball games played by slaves ranged from the oldest and simplest to the contemporary and complex, from once-over and cat to town ball and baseball. Several slaves, including women, recalled playing once-over in the 1840s and 1850s in Mississippi and Kentucky: groups on either side of a

559

house attempted to catch a ball thrown over the house, and if a person caught it he or she would run around to the other side and hit someone with the ball, then start over. There is evidence of similar games having been played in northern states and even Canada. Former slaves in North Carolina also mentioned playing cat, long popular with white children. One in Florida told of playing a game called "home ball."

The ball used in these simple games was usually homemade. "The kids nowadays" (1937), said Hannah Davidson of Kentucky, "can go right to the store and buy a ball to play with. We'd have to make a ball out of yarn and put a sock around it for a cover." Anderson Furr, one-time Kentucky slave, and William McWhorter of Georgia both said slave boys improvised balls out of rags. An ex-slave in West Virginia, Nan Stewart, told of playing yarn ball, probably so named because of the kind of ball used. White boys who sometimes joined in were welcomed if for no other reason than their ability to provide a store-bought ball. Former Arkansas slave Ed Allen used to play with white boys and "All had a good time. We never had to buy a ball or a bat. Always had 'em. The white boys bought them."

Older black boys and young men played both town ball and the "new game," baseball. Tom Singleton and fellow slaves on a Georgia plantation played; so did Henry Baker, a former slave born in 1855, who said that when his friends played town ball, if a runner was hit with the ball he was out. The ball, he said, was made out of rags. White boys played with them and even came from other plantations to play. According to James Avirett, blacks on the tidewater North Carolina plantation where he was born and reared would sometimes display such dexterity in throwing or batting "as can be found on the modern baseball ground."

Baseball, too, was played on the plantation. Joe Barnes, once a Texas plantation slave, said that as a tiny child he played marbles and ran rabbits and rode a stick horse, but when he got bigger he and his friends played a ball game "sort of like baseball." William McWhorter of Georgia remembered that when he was "a chap" his most frequent games were baseball, softball, and marbles. Willis Williams, who spent the first nine years of his life as a slave on a Florida plantation, recalled playing baseball there. James Henry Stith, born in 1868 to a former slave in Georgia, stated, "There were boys playing baseball when I was born. There were boys much older than I was already playing when I was old enough to notice, so I think they must have known about [baseball] in slave times."

After slavery was officially abolished, the next institution through which baseball became available was education. The work of northern missionaries who went south just after the war was somewhat handicapped by their lack of rapport with blacks and their failure to encourage black autonomy. And in the retrenchment after federal troops were withdrawn in 1877, public education, especially that for blacks, was hit hardest, and black schools in some states virtually disappeared. Yet such a desire for education did blacks evince that by that date about 600,000 southern blacks were attending schools of various kinds, many set up through black churches, and they reduced their illiteracy from an estimated 95 percent in 1865 to 44.5 percent in 1900 and thereafter made even greater progress. Despite conditions, southern black schools produced black teachers, and W.E.B. DuBois, Harvard Ph.D. and professor at Atlanta University, in a teachers' conference at Hampton Institute in the summer of 1897 recommended athletic sports for primary school youngsters, urging the teachers to "make them play and play hard and joyously" at running, throwing, and jumping.

In a few pockets in black schools, baseball could be developed. James Weldon Johnson, later a poet and statesman, played baseball and marbles in the 1880s while attending Stanton School, Jacksonville, Florida, where his mother taught. In Washington, D.C., black schools had no physical instruction and no school playgrounds until the 1880s, but some black boys played baseball in the capital. Just before the turn of the century E.B. Henderson, later one of the giants of black physical training, was a student at the M Street School, which later became Dunbar High School, then considered the best black high school in the country. It was located about five blocks from the White House. M Street School had its own baseball team, for which Henderson pitched. The boys played in the streets (there were no cars then) and in the grounds of the Washington Monument, between the Ellipse and the Tidal Basin.

Black colleges, many of them colleges in name only, developed baseball in the nineteenth century. During Reconstruction the Freedmen's Bureau founded or helped found most of the best-known black colleges, including Howard, Fisk, Talladega, and Atlanta University. Blacks gradually took over the leadership and instruction in such colleges, which became separate little worlds. These institutions developed their own recreation, to avoid the humiliation students might face in town. By the 1890s about 800 blacks were attending colleges, mostly the all-black ones.

Hampton and Tuskegee became two of the best-known such institutions, and soon after opening, both introduced baseball. Hampton Institute, in Virginia, was founded primarily to train black teachers, although in the nineteenth century and well into the twentieth the quality of education obtainable there was not on the college level. But whatever the students learned they afterwards taught all over the South. Hampton's first baseball team appeared in the 1880s, and by the 1890s, the *Southern Workman* reported, separate black and Indian nines played. On August 18, 1894, a black team called the Invincibles, which may have been the first nine, lost to the Second Nine 10–3.

Tuskegee, founded in 1881 by Booker T. Washington after he graduated from Hampton, became the largest and most famous black educational institution of his day. Washington's Atlanta Compromise speech of 1895 obligated blacks to acquiesce in partial disenfranchisement and segregation in exchange for low-level jobs. But the speech probably did lessen the terrible effects of lynchings, which in 1892 reached a high of 162 in the South alone. The ever-present threat of lynching, which was accompanied by sadistic torture, began to fall off in the 1900s.

At Tuskegee, Washington emphasized "industrial education," but the school also developed teachers and farmers, and many similar institutions emulated its curriculum. Baseball was Tuskegee's first sport, played for a time by class teams and by faculty members as well. According to college records, in 1892 another Washington, J.B., organized the college's first team, which that year made only a fair showing, playing all its games on campus. The following year, however, the team traveled to Georgia and Florida playing town teams, city teams, and school and college teams. One of its outstanding players, probably as a prep school student, was William Clarence Matthews, who was learning to be a tailor but would later enter Harvard.

The Freedmen's Bureau helped create Howard University in the District of Columbia, and when the Pythian team traveled to Washington in 1869 it played against a Howard aggregation. By the 1890s Howard possessed a large athletic field for baseball and other sports and had established an athletic council to regulate sports: the two major ones, baseball and football, and lesser ones as well. In 1894 James Francis Gregory, who later played at Amherst and Yale, took part in at least one game for Howard.

Atlanta became a center for black colleges and consequently for black baseball. Benjamin Brawley's history of Morehouse College, then called Atlanta Baptist, claims that baseball represented the only sport known at Morehouse in the 1890s but that the college could point to "an unusually successful baseball team." The students themselves controlled athletics at the college, and they engaged in at least one of the same questionable practices as the white colleges: they allowed nonstudents as well as students to play on the teams.

One of Morehouse's chief Atlanta opponents was Clark University, where William "Sug" Cornelius, later a pro, played ball. A third Atlanta college was Morris Brown, where C.I. Taylor, later a baseball promoter, studied and may have played. Atlanta University added another local college to Morehouse baseball opponents. There the previously-mentioned James Weldon Johnson played on the baseball team. Students at Atlanta University played baseball as early as the 1880s. By the nineties, students practiced on fall afternoons and played games on Saturdays. Johnson recalled later that female as well as male students and "crowds of townspeople" attended those Saturday games. As on the Morehouse campus, the Atlanta University baseball season closed with a big game on Thanksgiving.

James Weldon Johnson was also a fan of big-league teams, and once his eagerness to see a game got him into trouble. In the fall of 1887 (at age sixteen) he learned from the newspapers that the St. Louis Browns were coming to play in Atlanta. "I became feverish with desire to see them play," he wrote. "I especially wanted to see Arlie Latham, the famous third baseman of the Browns." So Johnson risked the displeasure of "Professor Francis" and asked for a half-day off from classes for himself and his two roommates to see the game. Francis was at first astounded by the request but ended by granting it. The next day Francis revealed that he knew that at the game the three students had violated their pledge not to smoke. Francis had either been at the game himself or had an informer there. Johnson fails to reveal his punishment, but at least he escaped expulsion. Later he became an attorney, secretary of the NAACP, and a well-known writer as well as Untied States consul for two South American countries.

In 1896 Morehouse formed a league with Atlanta University, Clark University, and Morris Brown College. The Morehouse college paper, *The Advance*, exulted in the league: "The interest shown by every one speaks well for the standing of our schools in the city." The sewing department of Spelman Seminary made new baseball suits for the Morehouse team. The league's schedule called for a series of six games for each institution, three at home and three away, with a pennant for the winner. Morehouse took four of the six games scheduled and so won the first pennant.

Outside Atlanta, students played baseball at other black colleges in the nineteenth century. At Florida Agricultural & Mechanical College in Tallahassee, which opened in 1887, baseball became "widely known," according to the college history, and the game most frequently played on campus. The school hired no coaches. A & M teachers volunteered to supervise athletic contests. Students also played ball in Mississippi at Rust College and at Tougaloo. At the latter institution the Thanksgiving Day exercises included a ball game. At Highland Park College, Des Moines, Iowa, J.L. Wilkinson, later an owner of a Negro League team, pitched for three years on the college team.

But even at "white" colleges black baseball players could take part in baseball games in the nineteenth century. James Francis Gregory, a good hitter, played for Amherst College and performed well against Trinity, Harvard, and Dartmouth. College records show that he played for four years, three of them as Baseball Director, and he captained the team his senior year. Gregory's brother, Eugene, pitched for Harvard between 1894 and 1897.

J. Francis Gregory wrote later that while he was playing at Amherst his relations with players on other campuses were "invariably comradely," and that spectators, too, were friendly, but that he experienced hotel trouble. The team manager had to insist that he and Captain Gregory follow the usual custom and occupy the same bed, despite pointed hints of disapproval by the proprietors. Gregory went on to study theology at Yale and became captain of the Divinity School team. He believed that the college player might be the one to blaze the way for the Negro back into Organized Baseball. In a way, he was right, but it took a lot longer than he probably thought it would!

Another good Amherst athlete was William Tecumseh Sherman Jackson, a black man who graduated with a bachelor's degree in 1892 and a master's in 1896. At Amherst he won letters in baseball, football, and track. Later, as a teacher at M Street School in Washington, he aided the development of sports there, encouraging intramural competition. At Dartmouth Julius P. Haynes, later a dentist, played baseball for the 1887 Dartmouth Medical College team, according to the Dartmouth archivist.

Oberlin, as already mentioned, had Fleet Walker in 1878–1880 and Fleet's younger brother, Weldy, in the preparatory department. But Professor Eugene Murdock, biographer of Ban Johnson, has revealed that about 1880 Oberlin also had a black pitcher named Davis. Ban Johnson, later American League president, recollected that Davis "had a wicked inshoot." Fleet Walker, of course, also won his letter in baseball at the University of Michigan.

John L. Harrison became, according to Murdock, the second black student to attend Marietta College, also in Ohio. Harrison, a member of the class of 1887, pitched for the college team, which never lost a game from 1883 through 1887. Harrison later recalled one game in which, reinforced by two professionals from Wheeling, the Marietta team beat nearby Beverly 5–3, after which the players staged such a "hilarious celebration" on the way home that the president, hearing of it, gave three of them "an enforced vacation of two weeks."

Ocania Chalk found that two other blacks played in the West: John Prim for the University of Washington and Frank Armstrong for Cornell College in Iowa. Armstrong, who graduated in 1900, was elected captain his second year, won his varsity letter, and belonged to the college literary society, according to Chalk.

But youths did not need institutions to sponsor their play; they played anywhere they could, as others had in slavery. Spot Poles, born in 1876 in Virginia, played baseball from age six onwards. Lacking equipment, he used a broomstick and a tennis ball. Another youth, Harry J. Morton, came to Hampton Institute in 1896 with the ambition of being a baseball player or a prize fighter but became a bricklayer instead and an active YMCA worker, according to *Southern Workman*. J.F. Gregory, who played college ball in the nineties, said he went through the customary sporting experience of youngsters on the Washington, D.C., sandlots, and that he and his friends formed a league. Another black man, interviewed in 1958 at age 79, when asked if he ever danced as a youth was quoted as saying, "No, but I sure could play baseball and make de home runs!"

In Portsmouth, Ohio, where there was trouble in the late 1880s between black and white children, the black boys had to stay on "their side of town."

But because all the boys, white and black, played baseball, soon the black and white teams began to challenge each other, and, recalled Al Bridwell, later a (white) shortstop for the New York Giants,

> before you knew it we [whites and blacks] were playing each other all the time and not thinking a thing about it. Did away with all that trouble we'd had before and brought us all together. Before long, any kid could go anywhere in town he wanted. I'm not saying baseball did it all. But it helped.

As a writer James Weldon Johnson left more detailed records of his childhood baseball experiences than most black adults have, and his biographers used them extensively. Johnson, born in 1871 in Jacksonville, became a well-known grade school pitcher in that city. He and his younger brother Rosamond gathered with their friends to watch and admire both the black and white semipro teams playing on local fields. Johnson pitched for a team called the Domestics and reputedly had a good curve. He not only practiced whenever possible, he read everything he could on baseball, including *Sporting Life*. His skill even attracted the attention of a pitcher for the professional Cuban Giants, who played and worked as waiters in the winter at one of the big Florida resort hotels. Probably Johnson's biggest thrill came at the time he and his friend, a catcher, were invited to play in a game with Jacksonville's leading black team, the Roman Cities, whose exploits were described in an earlier chapter, against a team from Savannah, Georgia. Most shops closed that Saturday morning, so a large turnout must have been expected. As one of Johnson's biographers describes it, when the two teenagers, Johnson and his catcher, were issued the blue-and-red uniforms of the Roman Cities, they found them much too big, so they went back to town to get their own white flannel suits and caps and black stockings. Another biographer says that when the two boys showed up as team members the crowd laughed, but the laughing stopped when Johnson demonstrated his skill: he struck out sixteen men, and the Roman Cities won by a "ridiculous" score.

Like boys, adults needed no special sponsorship to play ball. They used the opportunities of social affairs for indulging in baseball games as adjuncts to picnics, suppers, fairs, festivals, and excursions, often held by churches. In Savannah, Georgia, for example, blacks enjoyed picnics, games between black teams, and railroad excursions, even out of state. Excursions from New Orleans to St. Louis, Mobile, and Biloxi for picnics often featured baseball games. Excluded from white athletic clubs, blacks also organized their own, some of which fielded baseball teams. The Calumet Wheelmen, formed in 1892 in New York, grew to 250 members and supported a baseball team, as did the Fruition Cake-Walk Society, a dancing club founded in Brooklyn in 1890 to cultivate outdoor sports. Blacks also formed athletic clubs in New Orleans.

Black women were aware of baseball. Laura Hamilton, born in Ohio in

1864, married a man who in 1884 became a Washington, D.C., civil service employee. While awaiting the birth of their first child she lived with her grandmother in Alexandria, Virginia, and her husband visited weekends. Her August 1885 diary has the entry, "Mama [her grandmother] washed two quilts. I helped all I could but baby was bad. Went to see ball game in evening. Quite a crowd. I enjoyed it hugely."

Ida Wells-Barnett began her diary as a twenty-three-year-old teacher and budding journalist in Memphis. At 30, in the 1890s, she would launch in the New York *Age* a nationwide campaign against lynching after three of her friends were lynched. In Memphis in May of 1886 she wrote, "I went to the baseball park and saw a professional game for the first time, but lost my temper and acted in an unladylike way toward those whose company I was in."

Charlotte Forten was a young black woman whose wealthy and cultivated family lived in Philadelphia on the same street as Octavius Catto's Institute for Colored Youth. To her surprise and delight she received an appointment to teach in the public schools of Salem, Massachusetts, where she wrote in her journal on April 30, 1857, "Played ball at recess with the children. 'Tis fine exercise." In 1862 Forten went as a teacher to the South Carolina Sea Islands, and one of the first things she taught the Gullah children there was how to play baseball.

Anita Turner became the first black woman to graduate from Dudley Sargent's summer school in physical training at Harvard. As a pioneer in women's physical training she later changed her classes for women at Howard University from exercise to games.

Some blacks found opportunities to play ball for businesses. In the late 1880s the American Brewing Company in Indianapolis organized a black baseball club to advertise its company with jokes, stunts, and free beer. Then the brewer sold the ball club to a black saloonkeeper. The team eventually became the well-known black professional club called the Indianapolis ABCs. In Kansas City in 1897 a Chinese laundryman, Quong Fong, sponsored a black team called Wall's Laundry Grays, but according to Janet Bruce, the historian of the Kansas City Monarchs, the team became better known for fisticuffs than for ball playing. Hotels had already begun employing blacks to double as waiters and baseball players. In Rockport, Massachusetts, at the new, luxurious Turk's Head Inn the waiters imported from the South in 1890 proved, according to the town historian, "first-rate swatters."

But it was in the military where young black men could, even in the nineteenth century, indulge their growing passion for baseball. Although nearly 200,000 blacks served in the Union and Confederate armies during the Civil War as well as in the Union Navy, and there is some evidence blacks as well as whites played ball during the war, it was the postwar years that offered real opportunities. All-black units, the Ninth and Tenth Cavalry regiments and the 24th and 25th Infantry regiments, fought successfully in the Indian wars and bravely in the Spanish-American War. Even Theodore Roosevelt, no supporter of blacks (as we shall see), claimed in 1904 that the Afro-American soldiers in Cuba had saved his life, adding, "The Rough Riders [contrary to myth, without horses] were in a bad position when the Ninth and Tenth Cavalry came rushing up the hill, carrying all before them."

In the 1870s the black troopers at western forts began to be known among the Indians as the Buffalo Soldiers. Various explanations have been given for the appellation, but it was obviously one of respect. During that same era the Buffalo Soldiers played baseball whenever they could. In the mid-nineties Troop H of the black Tenth Cavalry, stationed at Fort Buford, North Dakota, held the baseball championship of the post, having established a no-loss record by beating companies of the black 25th Infantry and the white 20th Infantry. A team called the Browns, representing the black Ninth Cavalry at Fort Douglas, Utah, in 1897, defeated a team, probably white, from Park City, Utah, that, according to the *Army and Navy Journal*, had been "invincible" and famous all over the state. Two thousand fans reportedly paid fifteen cents each to see the game, in which the Browns excelled in teamwork and "scientific batting." Park City threatened in the ninth with four runs but failed to come up with the fifth, so the Browns won 9–8 in a "hair-raising" finish.

The black 25th Infantry, too, excelled at ball playing. As manager, captain, and acting coach of the 25th's teams from 1894 through 1908, said Master Sergeant Dalbert P. Green, "I spent the happiest days of my life." Green related that before Colonel Andrew S. Burt became the regiment's commanding officer,* there was no regimental team, only company teams, for which players had to furnish their own uniforms and for whose evening practice or Sunday and holiday games they were not excused from any duties. But after Burt took over and saw the baseball players lose 7–0 to a company of the (white) 20th Infantry, Burt said he wanted a regimental team formed. Practicing evenings and playing Sundays, the team began to win, assisted by the colonel's son, Lieutenant R.J. Burt, who had played on the 1895 West Point baseball team.

One crushing defeat in this period did hurt the morale of the 25th's team. The Tacoma, Washington, club, the leading team of the Northwestern League of Organized Baseball, was transferred to represent Toledo, Ohio, in the American Association, a higher league, and sought games en route. Since the 25th had bested all comers, it was challenged by the professionals but endured "the bitterest kind of defeat," after which the new Toledo team went on to win the pennant and send some players to the majors.

When the Spanish-American-Cuban War broke out in the spring of 1898, one company of the 25th moved to Florida and four companies to Chickamauga Park, Georgia. Soon after the four settled in Georgia, Colonel Burt

*Commanding officers of black units were whites.

challenged a local white unit, the 12th Regiment, to a baseball game. The 12th, led by the 25th's former commander, Colonel George L. "Charity" Andrews, had a "practically semipro team" and, displaying no charity, won handily. The black regiment swore to get even for the Chickamauga loss, but retaliation took a long time to accomplish. Meanwhile, several companies of the regiment, sent to Fort Logan, Colorado, in the spring of 1899, organized another team and defeated some of the best college clubs and other strong nines of the state.

Thus it is clear that even while professional black ball players were being ejected in the nineteenth century from the major and minor leagues of Organized Baseball, blacks had been developing, and continued to develop, accomplished young players through the same avenues where white youths found opportunities: sandlots, schools, colleges, social occasions, jobs, and the military.

36

A LONG, ROUGH ROAD STILL TO TRAVEL

The so-called Progressive Era meant little or nothing to American Negroes. In the South Jim Crow legal segregation assured them of hardscrabble lives. The most uncouth, low-lived white ranked above any black. In the North Jim's cousin James Crow confined blacks to a cramped and stunted existence.

The legal segregation of the South and the customary discrimination of the North applied to all aspects of Afro-American life: housing, employment, travel, entertainment, and even burial. Blacks were restricted to certain theatre seats even in Harlem. Baseball parks introduced their own quixotic regulations. For instance, they assigned blacks separate ticket windows, entrances, seating sections, and exits in southern ball parks. In Atlanta, according to John A. Lucas and Ronald A. Smith, amateur baseball teams of different races could not even play within two blocks of each other. And the Sunday church service, as has been said, was the most segregated occasion in American society. "If [a black person] is in a strange city," pointed out Booker T. Washington in 1912, "he does not know in what hotel he will be permitted to stay; he is not certain what seat he may occupy in the theatre [if any], or whether he will be able to obtain a meal in a restaurant." Fleet Walker in his 1908 book, *Our Home Colony,* expressed the bitter truth that "An educated Negro is thrown from a hotel or theatre just as certainly as an ignorant one. Discriminating laws and customs are blind to internal qualifications."

Progressives placed great store by outdoor recreation, but playgrounds and parks limited black children either by law (in the South) or by custom and the threat of trouble (in the North). Separate play facilities, if any, for black children were few in number and poor in quality compared with those available to white children. New York's black Harlem, for instance, contained no parks or playgrounds whatever. In 1911 when a few black boys from St. Cyprian's Parish House came to play baseball and other sports at a borderline park, white boys complained. In Brooklyn the Lincoln Settlement House opened one playground for black children about 1916. Boston's playgrounds were theoretically open to all, but prejudice and discrimination crept into their administration.

The South offered even poorer park and playground facilities for blacks. According to the *Negro Year Book*, cities like Chattanooga and Dallas finally established a few parks and playgrounds in the teens, and Norfolk, Virginia, had two for black children as opposed to four for white. New Orleans had only one, and not until 1916 did Atlanta provide two playgrounds for black children, whereas white children by then had eleven. Black Atlanta women took a hand in the situation and in 1919 arranged for two more city playgrounds. In Jacksonville, Florida, too, black women took action and got men interested in raising the money for playground equipment. Memphis delayed a plan to provide two playgrounds and recreation centers for blacks until the administration saw how the whites would take to their own new recreation centers. Only then did the city hire a black social worker, William Jones, to organize everything and everyone to inaugurate the black centers. In Washington, D.C., with a population about one-third black, individual philanthropists developed only two playgrounds with baseball facilities for black children.

Blacks also created their own commercial recreation facilities. Moses Moore, who had made a fortune speculating in real estate, opened Dahomey Park in Dayton, Ohio, in 1910, with a pro black baseball team, the Dayton Marcos, as one of its attractions. The team, owned by Moore and others, made its home in a stadium on the park grounds. In Mobile, Alabama, a group of blacks formed the National Park Amusement Company, leased the amusement concession from the National Negro Fair Association, and began creating a baseball grounds and grandstand to feature games between the Colored Mobiles and their opponents.

But blacks' attempts to enjoy amusements and recreation, like their attempts to move up the social and economic scale, stirred whites to violence. Their migration to the North in unprecedented numbers after 1915 brought many of them into contact with whites who had similar desires for upward mobility. In Chicago the sudden shift in the city's racial complexion resulted in a riot during the summer of 1919, the worst of a series of outbreaks during the years 1917–19. Two factors ignited the Chicago outburst. First, the big jump in black population caused competition by blacks and whites for recreation space, including space on baseball diamonds in city parks and playgrounds. Second, the mayor, "Big Bill" Thompson, had intimidated the police, who were afraid to arrest the gangs of white youth formed into politico-athletic clubs supported by politicians and stimulated by fear of black encroachment.

During that summer, according to Allan Spear's *Black Chicago* and the post-riot report of the city's own commission, black boys who tried to use the baseball diamonds in Washington Park, a recreation area separating the black belt from a white zone, came under regular attack by white gangs, who also terrorized blacks trying to use the Fuller Park and Armour Square recreation centers near Wentworth Avenue. White gangs like Ragen's Colts, one of whose members was Richard Daley, later Chicago's mayor, often came to play baseball at Washington Park, where they got into fights with black teams over the use of the diamonds. Fights also erupted over interracial games. Frederick M. Thrasher's study of Chicago gangs quotes a white gang member concerning a fight between his own gang and some blacks that erupted during a baseball game with "the colored guys from Lake Street." With the score tied, "the niggers did not want to play no more" because "it was getting dark." A series of three vicious gang fights eventually resulted.

Chicago politicians cultivated and supported the white gangs, called athletic and social clubs. As described in Thomas Philpott's *The Slum and the Ghetto*, such clubs had less to do with athletics than with playing craps, shooting pool, drinking at stag parties, and holding sex orgies. Mayor Thompson, ironically, had cultivated and received support from the black wards. He was himself a good baseball player and an all-star athlete at the Chicago Athletic Club and the Illinois Athletic Club. Once in office, according to his biographers, he did little to fulfill campaign promises to clean up the police department, which backed gangs like Ragen's Colts, the "personal guard" of Cook County Commissioner Frank Ragen, made up mostly of youths 15–22, who on election day strongarmed voters into favoring their sponsors.

Like the summer of 1965 in Watts, the one in 1919 was filled with strife. The main clash of 1919 erupted at a bathing beach when a black boy swam across an imaginary segregation line and was stoned and drowned by white boys. Fighting spread all over the Black Belt, and at the end of thirteen days 38 people, mostly blacks, lay dead, more than 400 suffered injuries, and about 1,000 were left homeless. Other studies of the riot by William Tuttle, Lee E. Williams, and Carl Sandburg, then a young Chicago reporter, agree that the police sympathized with the white rioters and protected Ragen's Colts and other gangs, and that Mayor Thompson allowed the riot to get out of hand before he called on the governor to send in the National Guard. Afterward, Chicago's Commission on Race Relations criticized discrimination in public institutions, praising the YMCA for its services.

The Y itself harbored the virus of discrimination by offering only separate facilities for blacks. And not until 1912 in Atlanta did it appoint its first worker for black boys, although even before the Civil War a Y existed in that city. The most popular form of "colored Y," as it was known, was the type for college students, beginning at Howard University in Washington in 1869, and by the 1880s most black schools and colleges had YMCAs.

By the 1900s the separate black city Y associations sponsored sports, often including baseball. Philadelphia's Southwest branch organized a baseball team in the teens; the Louisville "colored" Y had a team, too. The Carlton "colored" Y opened in Brooklyn, New York, in 1902, and received praise in the *Colored American Magazine* in 1908: "The athletic spirit is much in evidence. The ball players are already in the field, and a good team is being worked out by the enthusiasts. Only members of the branch are eligible." By the teens, according to the New York *Age*, the Carlton Y's team belonged to a Brooklyn YMCA League. Kansas City, Missouri, too, fielded a black Y baseball team which in 1909, according to the *Age*, went undefeated. In Wilmington, Delaware, Webster McDonald, later a black professional baseball manager, played ball at the Y playground around 1910. In East St. Louis not until a full year after a violent riot in 1917 did a local YMCA official get around to recognizing the "need of something for the Colored People of the City" and hire a black school principal to start recreation work for the summer of 1918. In Washington, D.C., Edwin B. Henderson was once ousted from the gallery of the "white YMCA" while watching a basketball game because white spectators objected to the presence of blacks. Henderson responded by helping to organize a black branch of the Y that opened in 1911, and he taught and participated in sports there. Ida Wells-Barnett, the black militant, pointed out long before the Chicago riot the failure of the Y to provide services to black migrants in the Windy City, but not until 1913 did a black Y finally open there.

A few settlement houses accepted blacks, but most preferred that blacks set up their own. Blacks often complied, as they had even in farm country, like rural Alabama in 1892, as well as in cities like Chicago and Washington (1904) and Boston (1908). Some settlements furnished play facilities. By 1910 approximately 10 black settlement houses functioned around the country, and by 1914–15 they numbered about 31. Athletic clubs for boys were organized by settlements like Stillman House in New York and by the Negro Settlement House in Wilmington, Delaware, where Judy Johnson, later a famous black third baseman and manager, played ball and where his father directed athletics.

Even at more restrictive institutions black boys sometimes got a chance to play ball. Beginning in 1897 the aforementioned George Junior Republic in upper New York state admitted blacks. The Republic, known as the poor man's prep school, averred Jack M. Holl in his book on the Republic, compared favorably with Tuskegee College and Hampton Institute. But some white boys resented blacks at the Republic. An article in *Southern Workman* in 1905, in an understatement, said, "It is a hard lesson for the [white] boy from the South to work side by side with a colored boy or, worse yet, to find himself 'in the gang' with a Negro keeper. But the Republic law is no respecter of persons."

At Virginia's Negro Reform School, opened in 1899, the director, J.H. Smyth, a Howard University graduate, permitted baseball. A visitor there in 1904 saw "a dozen or so little blue-bloused, bare-footed chaps . . . at a merry game of ball." Smyth explained that these were "some of our small boys" and that "There is less work for them than for the older ones; but all have their recreation, a squad at a time."

Black adults got to play ball on white teams in prison. The Ohio Pene-
tentiary baseball team of 1919, pictured in *Baseball Magazine,* included at
least three black members. At San Quentin prison the warden, James A.
Johnston, held a baseball-throwing contest one Thanksgiving in which each
competitor tried to throw farther than an excellent black athlete known as
Alabama, who soon beat all twelve of his challengers. Then a prisoner condemned to death, who like Alabama had played ball, asked Warden Johnston
for permission to throw against Alabama. The condemned man's throw surpassed Alabama's, and he had the glory of being announced victor. Later,
Johnston learned that Alabama had held back and had not thrown as far
against the condemned man as he had against the others. "That man," wrote
Johnston of Alabama, "a Negro convict, handicapped by his color, branded
as a felon, stigmatized as an outcast, was with it all and in spite of it all, a
good sport."

The black church represented a carapace and a haven for blacks in an
inhospitable and precarious society. Churches and social organizations often
featured athletic contests as part of outings. Picnics and other gatherings
frequently took place at a park with an athletic field, according to E.B.
Henderson, so that baseball and other sports could be part of the program.
Churches in particular sponsored baseball in the 1900s. When a preacher
in Sedalia, Missouri, organized a baseball team for black boys, Bill Drake,
who would later play for prominent black teams, was mortified to find that
despite his frequent practice he was not a good enough player to make the
team.

In Chicago the Presbyterian Church sponsored an interracial league of
nine white teams and a black one beginning in 1908 and continuing to about
1915. The Chicago *Defender* proudly announced in 1911, 1912, and 1913
that the (black) Grace Church team, composed of high school and college
students, won the league championship, and that when the whites lost they
"took it like sports," with "never a hard word on either side." The "Grace
Base Ball Boys" held parties and picnics, too. Admission to their dance, with
Garfield Wilson's Orchestra playing, in April 1912, cost twenty-five cents,
and the *Defender* urged, "Take a Little Tip from Father and Attend the
Grand Social Given By Grace Base Ball Boys at Union Masonic Hall."

Black churches in other cities sponsored baseball in the 1900s. St. Louis
had an all-black Church Baseball League in the teens. In 1909 in New York,
after the Beckel African Methodist Episcopal church team defeated the
Dunbars of St. Mark's Church and arranged a game against the St. Chris-
topher's team, the New York *Age* reported the players' hope for more church
teams so that a league could be formed. Even black ministers played a six-
inning game at a conference at Glen Cove, Long Island, in July of 1914. In
Washington E.B. Henderson, then a teacher, urged leading churches to
devote more time to sports.

Young black fellows also formed, in New York and other cities, athletic clubs that aped the exclusive clubs of affluent whites. These clubs usually fielded baseball and other sports teams. The Alpha Physical Culture Athletic Club, formed in 1903 in Brooklyn, by 1910 had seventy-three members, including physicians, dentists, lawyers, teachers, musicians, clerks, government employees, realtors, brokers, and students. It also supported what the *Negro Handbook* for 1910 called a first-class base ball team." Its "grand field day" that August, said the New York *Age*, would include a baseball game "for which a silver cup will be won." Another Brooklyn athletic club, the Smart Set, organized in 1905. It supported several sports teams, including baseball, basketball, and track. The Mozart Club, organized in New Jersey in 1908, fielded a baseball club that won many games, but the win that gave the Mozarts the most pleasure was the one over the Alpha Club, at its picnic, where it won that silver cup! The Laetitia Athletic Club of Brooklyn, organized the same year, produced a baseball team, among other sports teams. Philadelphia and Pittsburgh both had black athletic clubs, Philadelphia's boasting a uniformed baseball team.

Important as were all these sponsors of black youth baseball, the most prolific seedbed of adult black players, as with the whites, was the impromptu sandlot game. Like white boys, black boys needed no particular encouragement or sponsorship to play ball. By 1911 baseball enjoyed sufficient popularity among them for *The Crisis*, a publication of the black leader W.E.B. DuBois, to enlist the game as an enticement for them to become salesmen for the magazine. The editors offered boys a complete set of equipment for a team in exchange for selling the magazine. Under the heading "Play ball, boys," the magazine's ad declared,

> Baseball is the most popular sport in this country. In every hamlet, town, and city may be the future "Rube Fosters" [manager of the Chicago American Giants] and "William Matthews" [the outstanding college player] romping over corner lots, batting, pitching, and learning to play the game. Organize your team and get our great baseball outfit for a few hours' work.

The well-known photographer Lewis Hine shot a picture, printed in *Playground* in 1912, called "The Third Strike," showing a black boy of about twelve, in white shirt and knickers, fanning the air with his bat; significantly, the other players and spectators are mostly whites, for in some places, both North and South, the two races played ball together. In the South black and white boys could play ball and other sports together until adolescence, when both groups became more conscious of their different stations.

Even in games, however, distinctions might surface. Rollin Chambers, white, told of his boyhood in a small South Georgia community where the "Negroes were always a little apart. . . . If we were playing ball, they were in the outfield and we did the batting." But more commonly, black boys in the South recalled playing only with other blacks. In Sedalia, Missouri, an interested adult took Bill Drake and other boys out onto the prairie and "threw fly balls up to them." In Louisiana, Dave Malarcher, later to become a famous black pro player and manager, played on a little boys' team called the Baby *T*s. Malarcher told researcher John Holway that older black boys played on a different team, and still older ones on a third. Their mothers made suits for them, and the boys played Saturday afternoons after picking rice in the fields at forty or fifty cents a day. Although the boys were not supposed to play on Sundays, there were three other teams in the vicinity ready to play, so they stole away and played match games with them. Crush Holloway, of Waco, Texas, who later played for the professional Baltimore Black Sox, was not supposed to play on Sundays, either, but he and his friends played two or three games that day, with balls made from twine or with cheap ready-made balls that might last for five or six games. Also playing Sundays in Texas sandlots against parental rules was Jesse Hubbard, later a professional pitcher, who instead of going to Sunday school passed right on to the ball park, then got a whipping when he got home.

Benjamin Brawley, the black novelist, wrote a touching story about a South Carolina black child's longing for a baseball, the crisis in the boy's life coming when his baseball team cannot get up enough money for a ball and he decides to run away. At the end, his mother's hopes for him make him decide to stay after all.

In the North, black boys might play either on black teams or on integrated teams, as Judy Johnson did in Wilmington, Delaware. Ted Page's family was the only black one in his Youngstown, Ohio, neighborhood, so Page, later an excellent hitter with professional black teams, played with boys of other ethnic groups until 1914 when a clubhouse called the Booker T. Washington Settlement opened. Black children in Hackensack, New Jersey, played baseball in a vacant lot because the Y and other community recreation facilities were closed to blacks, and supervised programs carried the invisible sign "Whites Only." In New York's black neighborhoods children played ball in the streets. Harlem had many young black teams. The New York *Age* printed a photo of a group about aged twelve sitting, with serious faces, and only partly uniformed, on a stoop. Written on the photo was "Web's Harlem Tigers, 82 W. 134 St., N.Y.," and the caption reads, "The Undefeated Base Ball Club." Up at 136th Street and Fifth Avenue, the Moon Athletic Club was playing on Olympic Field in 1911 against a white club, the Silver Stars, called Harlem's "hope of the white race," when racial violence broke out. For three innings the Silver Stars had found it nearly impossible to hit past Harry Lyons, the black shortstop, and they soon discovered the reason: according to the Harlem *Home News* Lyons was using "the largest player's glove ever seen . . . fully as large and plump as a good old-fashioned feather pillow." Before the fourth inning the Stars protested to the umpires, who ordered Lyons to remove his glove. He refused. He could not wear a smaller mitt, he said, because he had "powerful big hands." The ensuing argument became a brawl. Both benches emptied and spectators joined in the fray. Fists flew, bottles and other missiles were thrown, and baseball bats were wielded. Lyons threw away his glove, ran from the field, and returned with a razor. When order was restored, according to Jervis Anderson's *This Was Harlem*, more than a dozen people had been hurt, including Lyons, carried off the field unconscious. When he revived, in the hospital, he was arrested and charged with felonious assault. And all because of a glove probably the size of those used today.

Young Afro-American men also continued to organize and play as amateurs and semipros long after strong black professional teams were already touring the country and playing each other as well as white teams. While newsmen often disparaged the black pro clubs by calling them "semipros," they were not, since the team members made their living playing ball. Real semipro and amateur black teams kept forming and playing all over the country, and some eventually turned pro or produced players that became pros.

In the South amateur and semipro clubs could be seen in New Orleans; Washington, D.C.; Donaldson and Union, Louisiana; and Fairfax County and the vicinity of Hampton, Virginia, for instance. In Atlanta, Georgia, according to John Dittmer's *Black Georgia in the Progressive Era*, fans gathered to watch pickup games, such as one in 1913 between black physicians and college professors for the benefit of a center called the Neighborhood Union. *The Age* in 1909 mentioned the McNulty Brothers team's victory over the Savannah Giants on the Ontario Field in Savannah.

Amateur baseball could become something of an annoyance. Illustrative is the complaint of the black newspaper, the St. Louis (Missouri) *Palladium*, in May of 1903,

> Will the police protect the people on Lawton Avenue from baseball fanatics who take [over] Lawton Avenue every evening to play baseball against the wishes of the people and against the laws of the City of St. Louis? The nuisance [extends] from Jefferson avenue to Beaumont street. Chief Desmond ought to send a detective on this route and stop this nuisance.

A year later the same paper told of a baseball game about a mile south of Richmond, Missouri, during which a Jersey cow being followed by a swarm of bumblebees caused a "wild stampede" when scores of people ran against a barbed wire fence in a frantic effort to escape the maddened animal. Worse yet, the bees soon began attacking the crowd. The game was abandoned, and the bees were left in possession of the field.

Outside the South, black amateur and semipro teams formed, for example, in Cincinnati and Athens, Ohio; in Philadelphia; in Washington, D.C.; and in New York and New Jersey. In the Boston area the West Medford Independents organized in 1902, assisted and praised by the town's mayor, Lewis Lovering, who helped the players obtain their first uniforms. The Independents won the 1908 championship of the Greater Boston Colored League, an organization of six suburban nines. A black writer for the Boston

Globe, Robert Teamoh, inspired the league's inception and soon became its president. The league did not last as long as the West Medford Independents, a team that played until 1912, then organized a second club that continued until World War I, after which a third team organized and played through the 1920s. Black teams also appeared in the West. For instance the Eurekas, the Mascots, and the Tigers performed in Denver, Topeka, and Kansas City respectively. The New York *Age* reported many games around the country without always specifying the status of the teams, but from their names and circumstances it is clear that most were amateurs or semipros.

Black women took an interest in sports as well as in social action. The *Defender* in 1912 chided black women fans of the American Giants, a black pro team in Chicago, for "hysteria," most of it on the part of a few members of supposedly exclusive "box parties" who wanted the limelight. But young black women also played ball. The New York *Age* in 1915 carried an ad that read "Girl Ball Players Wanted/Girls wanted to play Base Ball/Saturdays and Sundays. Good Pay./Address C. Gould/1326 54th St., Brooklyn, N.Y."

Young women could play ball at Hampton, too. *Southern Workman* asserted that, despite the attention attracted by a girls' basketball match, the chief interest of the crowd at Thanksgiving Day exercises in 1900 centered upon a girls' baseball game:

> Here was a game that everybody could watch understandingly, and it was played with an accuracy, an energy, and an abandon that repeatedly called forth the applause of the multitude. The oft-repeated assertion that girls cannot throw was quickly disproved. Catching, not throwing, was their weak point. Their batting was excellent and should have to be seen to be appreciated.

After two innings, however, the game was called on account of rain with the score 5 for the black girls to 4 for their Indian opponents.

By the 1900s E.B. Henderson had built school sports in Washington, D.C., into a highly organized state. His biographer, Leon Coursey, rightly describes Henderson as a man of incredible perseverance. He almost single-handedly raised the sports of the capital city schools, both black and white, to the organizational level of New York City's.

Henderson's work in athletics took place in the atmosphere of an academic oasis. M Street School in Washington (renamed Dunbar High School in 1916), became a center for scholars, attracting teachers and students that epitomized the belief of W.E.B. DuBois in the development of the "talented tenth," a select group he believed should furnish the leadership of the race. Unlike Booker T. Washington, DuBois did not advocate "industrial education." He thought blacks of ability should try for the highest development of their intellect. One of the principals at M Street school in this era was W.T.S. Jackson, mentioned earlier as having played college baseball. Jackson aided Henderson in developing intramural sports competition at M Street. Another patron for Henderson in the black schools was Anita Turner, assistant physical training director for the black school system. She had for three summers taken Dudley A. Sargent's Harvard Summer School course in physical training. Henderson, after graduating first in his class at a black normal school, became Washington's first physical training teacher (1904). Then Henderson himself attended Sargent's course, borrowing the $50.00 tuition money and surviving by waiting on Sargent's table in his boarding house.

Henderson's responsibilities in Washington soon expanded into administration. The city of Washington had no formal playgrounds, white or black, until it charged Henderson and Birch Bayh, father of the senator, in 1909 with planning them, Henderson for blacks and Bayh for whites. Yet even in these unorganized times for sport the two black Washington high schools, M Street and Armstrong, played ball, and the *Negro Handbook* printed a photograph of a group of young black men on what looks like the school steps, labeled "Colored High Schools Champion Base Ball Team, 1909, Washington, D.C."

Perhaps the sedulous Henderson's biggest contribution to physical training was his organizing in 1910 a Public Schools Athletic League, like that of New York and other cities, for all black schools of Washington. That fall he invited teachers representing the black elementary and high schools to a meeting one evening at M Street's assembly hall to plan competition in each school for the various sports like baseball, basketball, track, and soccer, with the chance for boys to earn proficiency badges in bronze, silver, and gold. The intramural competition that resulted soon developed into citywide sports trials like those in New York. The New York *Age* reported the aim of Henderson's PSAL as improving the boys' health and especially preventing tuberculosis, which blacks suffered from more than whites. Henderson later stated the purpose of the league as to "help to offset the temptations of city living and to a recognized degree help reduce delinquency." He said, perceptively, that (black) children "find in these organized activities a chance to do some of the things every normal growing boy and some girls want to do."

PSAL baseball began in the black schools of Washington the following spring (1911) when thirty-one elementary schools, organized into divisions, took part in a series of elimination games for the division championships. In the final playoff Lucretia Mott School's team won the city championship. In 1912 Cook School won, and Mott captured it again in 1913. By 1912, the white schools of Washington had copied the black ones and instituted a PSAL of their own.

Meanwhile, Henderson had already set in motion another sports project: forming the black Interscholastic Athletic Association of the Middle Atlantic States among area high school and college students. The *Crisis* announced in 1911 that the purpose of the association was to spread the idea of sound health for colored people. Early members included M Street School, Armstrong Technical School of Washington, Howard University, and two Baltimore institutions: the black high school and Morgan College. *Crisis* declared that the association "has probably done more to build amateur athletics for the race than any other agency." Boys under twenty-one who had never played professionally were eligible, and they could play only for their own institutions.

Henderson's final contribution of the era was getting publicity for black scholastic and collegiate athletics, first by obtaining mention in one of Spalding's athletic handbooks and then by writing and publishing separate black handbooks during the teens. The first such black athletic handbook, published in 1910, sold more than 8,000 copies and reportedly did much to encourage athletics among black school and college students.

Other black schools of the country lagged behind Washington in development of organized athletics, in part because the schools themselves were nonexistent. Some cities had no high schools for blacks. Atlanta had none; Kansas City had one; and the entire state of North Carolina offered only one. Blacks, although they represented eleven percent of the population of the United States, received only two percent of total expenditures for education. And the figures were much worse in the South, where rural schoolhouses were reported by a government worker in 1919 as "miserable beyond all description," the teachers "absolutely untrained," while the whites, by comparison, had "excellent facilities."

Without good schools, black children in general lacked organized school baseball. Even as late as 1915 few black schools had anything more than perhaps a representative team. Only in the border cities of Baltimore, Wilmington, St. Louis, and Louisville did the black school systems organize sports to any degree. Boys did manage to play school ball, though. The New York *Age* published, in the fall of 1911, news of an "unusual game" in Key West, Florida, in which a picked team from the white schools lost an exciting contest, 2–0, to the black team of the Douglass School (doubtless the only black school in the area), during which Pitcher Hepburn of Douglass struck out 18 and allowed only one player to reach first. In Alabama Larry Brown, later a professional catcher, played for his school in Pratt City and Leroy "Satchel" Paige for his Mobile school team.

Out in the Sea Islands off South Carolina, where Charlotte Forten had during the Civil War taught baseball to the Gullah-speaking children, Hampton Institute sent a group of teachers in 1905 to instruct the children. One of the teachers described the tactics used with the children: "We began on baseball, and our Hampton teachers were as engaged [determined] to play with the pupils as to work with them." She found that the children were buoyed in their work by their memories of enjoyable games they had played and the prospect of more. One of her students wrote, "I don't care how hard

I work. I have a baseball game behind me, and I have a baseball game before me on Saturday." The teacher also found improvement in children's behavior after the institution of regular baseball games. She wrote,

> Rules and good spirit soon took their proper place, and quarrels fell off. Self-initiative has made itself felt in their [the children's] play. Small barefooted boys with an old piece of board for a bat and gray moss wound about the catcher's hand for a glove have taken the place of knots of boys pitching into [each other] on the way to school in their need for letting off physical energy.

The teachers thus used baseball to substitute for fighting.

In the North, black children were sometimes prevented from playing on school athletic teams. Before 1900 they could not take part in New York City athletics. By 1915 only 42 of 314 black children interviewed on the city streets said they belonged to the Public Schools Athletic League. Nevertheless, in 1908 a sensational young black PSAL pitcher, Pete Greene, led his team, Commercial High of Brooklyn, to the city championship and received the Brooklyn *Eagle*'s prize as the best high school pitcher of the year. In 1909 he tried to do it again but lost to Morris High School in twelve innings, 3–2, at Washington Park before thousands of spectators. In Boston a black grammar school boy was elected captain of his school's baseball, football, and relay teams and chosen class president as well.

At Holmes School in far western Spokane, Gomez Simpson, son of a retired army sergeant, stood out as the only black among 400 students, and the New York *Age* reported him the school's leading athlete in 1915, excelling in baseball, basketball, and track. By then even the Institute for Colored Youth in Philadelphia, where Octavius Catto had once taught, had its baseball team.

Black higher education was undergoing change for the better. Northern philanthropists had intended the schooling blacks received to be devoted primarily to job training, along the lines Hampton and other "industrial schools" espoused. By and large, Southerners disapproved of any and all black schooling. In 1904 the St. Louis *Palladium* reported Arkansas Governor Jeff Davis as saying in a Texarkana speech that every time you educate a "nigger" you spoil a good field hand. Secretary of War William Howard Taft, speaking as a guest at Tuskegee in 1906, pronounced Negroes to their faces "a people not fit to enjoy or maintain the higher education." Yet more than 1,600 blacks graduated from college in the first decade of the twentieth century, claimed the *Negro Year Book* in 1913. Furthermore, in black colleges baseball was often the leading sport. Students played baseball in at least thirty black colleges of varying quality in the South, most of them in Georgia, Tennessee, and North Carolina. Some of this baseball was intercollegiate, and occasionally a black college team played a white one or a black professional club.

According to the *Southern Workman,* even Hampton Institute in Virginia encouraged practice in field sports, not to develop champions but for recreation. For the most part, Hampton held to that policy. Informal holiday and summertime baseball games were common there. Students played intramural Fourth of July games from 1901 through 1904. In the Labor Day game of 1902, however, the students played a local team that *Southern Workman*, in an attempt at humor, called the Cuban Giants of the neighborhood. In the summer of 1901 fourteen baseball nines played on campus. At first they traveled only as far as the school's farm, to play their fellow students there, but in the second decade of the century the rules loosened, and a Hampton nine played teams like Lincoln University, Virginia Union University, the Hampton Giants, and the Scotland Giants.

At Tuskegee, too, baseball remained informal during the first decade of the century. Working ten hours each weekday on the farm in summer, boys were unable to play until Saturday, when work stopped at five P.M. Yet in the second decade Tuskegee began playing skilled opponents, and after Thomas Jarvies Taylor took over as baseball coach in 1912, the varsity held a high place among southern schools and colleges, according to a Tuskegee archivist. In fact in 1912 the team won 17 out of 18, and the New York *Age* called it "undoubtedly the fastest aggregation of ball players ever in a southern school team."

Atlanta remained a center for black college ball. Morehouse continued to play its local rivals, Clark University, Atlanta University, and Morris Brown College. In 1910 Morehouse, then still called Atlanta Baptist, won an A.G. Spalding trophy for its performance against Morris Brown and Clark. That year Rube Foster's famous professional team, the Chicago Giants, played both Atlanta University and Hampton.

The papers of Atlanta University President Edward T. Ware, examined by John Dittmer, revealed the extent to which the university identified itself with what happened on the baseball grounds. In 1910 several Atlanta University baseball players walked off the field in the middle of a game to protest the insertion into the lineup of a player they regarded as incompetent. Shocked at the students' "breach of loyalty to Atlanta University" as shown by their desertion of their teammates, President Ware decided their behavior "could not be overlooked" and called a faculty meeting that resulted in expulsion of six of the offenders not only from the team but also from the university. Angry alumni protested this "heavy-handed authoritarianism," as Dittmer called it, but Ware and his faculty held fast, including faculty member W.E.B. DuBois, who declared, "This is a time for unfaltering firmness. The suspended boys should leave the campus *today.* . . . Unless this firm stand is taken we shall have trouble." And that evidently ended the controversy.

Howard University, in Washington, D.C., not only sponsored intercollegiate baseball throughout the period against teams like Shaw University and Virginia Union, it formed an athletic council like Harvard's, and in 1916 the team even went south to play. The following year Howard hired its first full-time athletic director. Its prep school, Howard Academy, also supported a baseball team.

Fisk University, in Tennessee, had no athletic association, and the students complained of the lack. Furthermore, it had no training table, no athletic coach, and neither professional players nor any of questionable scholarship, according to Joe M. Richardson's history of the college. President Fayette McKenzie, a Ph.D. and Phi Beta Kappan, discouraged intercollegiate athletics, although the baseball team did play some local institutions.

In Alabama both Selma University and Talledega played ball. In Virginia, Virginia Union maintained a baseball team and an athletic association. South Carolina's Claflin University, at Orangeburg, posted a winning record of 6 and 2 for the 1914 season, according to the New York *Age*. But once it permitted a teacher to play in a game with Atlanta University.

E.B. Henderson's handbooks have preserved photographs of many southern black baseball college teams of the early twentieth century, including, in North Carolina, those for Livingstone College, Biddle University, Mary Potter, National Religious Training School, Kittrel College, and the Agricultural and Mechanical College of Greensboro. Another team of the Tarheel State was Shaw University, which the New York *Age* claimed in 1913 planned a "southern" baseball trip. The *Age* also reported the organization of a North Carolina InterscholasticAssociation, to include some of the above-mentioned institutions and several others. In 1913 the association included only Hampton, Howard, Lincoln University, Shaw, and Virginia Union, because, said Henderson's handbook, other colleges seemed unwilling to accept the association's eligibility rules, especially its four-year rule, as well as being fearful of incurring financial obligations.

Other southern institutions continued baseball. Dave Malarcher, later an outstanding professional, studied at New Orleans University while playing ball for its undefeated team until the military drafted him in 1918. Two West Virginia black colleges, Storer in 1911 and West Virginia Colored Institute in 1913, furnished Henderson with photos and records of opponents. In Florida, Allen Normal, Florida Agricultural and Mechanical, Florida Institute, Apalachicola, and Tallahassee, all played each other. In the West, Arkansas Baptist's team reportedly went undefeated in 1913 against colleges in Mississippi, Tennessee, Arkansas, Texas, and Oklahoma.

In the summer of 1914 Pop Watkins, a Brooklyn promoter, organized a team of black players mostly from southern colleges like Hampton, Tuskegee, Shaw, and Claflin. He made Watertown, in upstate New York, the team's headquarters and took it on tour of the central part of the state. The team won twenty-six straight. Thus black college players, like white, sometimes played summer ball.

Some blacks played baseball for white colleges. Foremost among them was Clarence Matthews of Harvard, class of 1905. He played four years on the Harvard varsity. When in 1902 *Sporting Life* announced Matthews as a new Harvard player it reported that the university was "wildly enthusiastic over him." And well it should have been. In the big game against Yale that spring, Matthews proved his worth to the team. The Cincinnati *Enquirer* described his feat in glowing terms:

> It was none other than their colored right fielder Matthews who cinched the game in the last half of the ninth by a timely single, which caused the partisans of both colleges to tender the plucky descendant of slaves one of the greatest ovations ever given a member of his race. . . .

Matthews came to bat amidst an uproar and, said the reporter,

> demonstrated that he was possessed of a wonderful amount of nerve by smashing out the drop ball pitched by Garvan, Yale's great twirler, sending the winning run across the plate. . . . He has always ranked as a good sticker, but it took the crucial test last Saturday to prove his real merit to his white associates of the club.

Once in a game in April 1902 against Georgetown, the latter team objected to playing against a black, but according to the Boston *Globe* Harvard refused to bench Matthews, and Georgetown backed down and played the game. Again in 1903 when a Virginia team made the same objection in advance of a game, Harvard stood fast, deciding against playing that institution. Matthews, playing shortstop by then, also took part in two Harvard-Yale games in 1903, both of which Harvard won. In the first one he hit a home run. He also played in one of the Yale games of 1904, which Harvard again won.

Once more in 1904 Georgetown objected in advance to Harvard's having Matthews in the lineup. This time, said the Boston *Globe*, "Appreciating that the popular colored player could not make the trip without suffering humiliation from Southern prejudice, the Harvard team stayed in the North." One of Matthews's teammates, Henry V. Greenough, later wrote, "Harvard may have had better shortstops since Matthews, but I can't name them. He was a damn good player and a very decent fellow." Matthews worked his way through Harvard. Summers he worked in hotels or Pullman cars. *McClure's Magazine* asserted in 1905 that he refused offers of $40.00 a week to play summer ball and quoted him as saying that he did not believe in accepting favors; they made you dependent: "Mr. Washington taught us at Tuskegee that the best help a man can get is an opportunity to help himself." In the summer of 1906, after leaving Harvard and before enrolling in law school, Matthews turned pro, playing with a New England summer league. In 1913 he was appointed Assistant United States District Attorney. From 1915 to 1919 he worked as a railroad attorney, and in the twenties he entered politics on Cal Coolidge's side.

Partly because he played for a first-rate college, Matthews attracted considerable notice, but other blacks also played ball on white college baseball teams in the early 1900s. Like Fleet Walker and his brother Weldy in the nineteenth century, Merton Robinson caught for Oberlin for three years, and his brother Howard did the same, according to the 1911 *Crisis*. At Ohio Wesleyan Charlie Thomas played under none other than manager Branch Rickey, who was instrumental later in breaking Organized Baseball's color line. Some of Thomas's fellow players did not welcome him, and at hotels Rickey might have to talk the hotel management into letting Thomas stay with the team. Once at the Oliver Hotel in South Bend, Indiana, in 1904, the club was halted in the lobby. Thomas could not go upstairs. As Arthur Mann, factotum of Rickey and his biographer, tells it, Rickey sent his student manager to check on YMCA vacancies for Thomas and persuaded the manager to permit the black player to wait upstairs in his, Rickey's, room, pending the student's return. There Thomas broke down, tears splashing on his hands as he rubbed them and lamented, "Black skin . . . oh, if I could only make 'em white!"

A well-known black who in these years played for Rutgers University in New Jersey was Paul Robeson, who won a $650.00 state scholarship to attend and earned no fewer than twelve varsity letters, including one for baseball, in 1919.

Industry also offered some opportunity for blacks to play ball. In the 1900s, however, immigrants began replacing blacks in many jobs. Fleet Walker deplored the situation in his book, *Our Home Colony*:

> Even in the common trades of the builder, such as bricklaying, carpentering, etc., the Negro father sees a rapidly fading opportunity for his boy. . . . What Negro parent can have the audacity to hold up before his beloved son the possibility of [his] ever becoming President of the United States?. . . . The whites say, "Educate yourselves, get an industrial education! Very good advice, indeed; but it reminds us of the advice the good old mother gave her son: "Don't go near the water until you have learned to swim." Negroes have been elected to high places . . . yet how singular [that] a colored man . . . finds it next to impossible to get an opportunity to learn how to construct an engine or to build a house.

But in industrial enclaves both North and South, some jobs in heavy industry, at wages double and triple those southern wage blacks could usually earn, were open to them. In Alabama blacks comprised seventy-five percent of the labor force of the big steel and coal companies. In 1907 United States Steel took over and modernized a Birmingham steel company called Tennessee Coal and Iron, thus requiring less unskilled (black) labor, so fewer blacks were hired. After crushing a 1908 strike the company introduced an elaborate welfare program, including recreation, to assure a stable labor force resistant to unionization. It also hired Hampton and Tuskegee graduates to help administer this welfarism for blacks. The company fielded two baseball teams, one for whites, called the big team, and another for blacks, which they referred to as the little "jive" team. Larry Brown, a mule driver for Tennessee Coal and Iron, played on that black team and later became a catcher and manager for many black pro teams.

In Pittsburgh the large steel works also arranged for segregated company-sponsored black athletic teams organized by black welfare workers to keep the labor force docile and anchored to the company. Carnegie-Illinois Steel not only offered employees company ball, according to Rob Ruck it also built baseball facilities for children and employed playground instructors. The Homestead Grays, a first-rate professional black team, eventually grew out of a team made up mostly of black steel workers at Homestead, Pennsylvania. At Buckeye Steel Casting Company of Columbus, Ohio, blacks joined whites on some of their company athletic teams, playing in a league put together by the Y, but they also formed their own all-black teams in baseball and other sports.

Jobs for blacks with railroads often added an opportunity to play ball. The railroad YMCA, which for years had organized amusement for whites, began in the 1900s to furnish (separate) services to blacks as well, and the Baltimore and Ohio Railroad contributed $500.00 to launch the program. Railroad companies continued to hire blacks as redcaps (porters) in the 1900s. A redcap earned $25.00 a month, less than in heavy industry ($12.00 a week), but with tips he could make as much as $100.00 a month. The Pennsylvania Railroad's redcap baseball team became very successful in the teens. By 1915 redcaps had formed an interrailroad baseball league traveling to different cities to play each other. The New York *Age* reported games like the three-cornered affair at Olympic Field, New York, when the Grand Central Station, New York, porters first beat the Pennsylvania Red Caps and then took on those of Washington and defeated them, too. Top Pennsy Railroad officials attended, and afterward the visiting redcaps were entertained at a banquet where debutantes acted as hostesses. The following month the New York, Pittsburgh, and Washington redcap teams went so far as to travel to Philadelphia as guests of the Broad Street Station team, where the New York team won the deciding baseball game. In September porters from Penn Station in New York and in Washington's Union Station split a two-game series at American League Park in Washington.

Almost any group of black employees might form its own team if the owners permitted. In the 1900s some workers on the Fall River Line, a steamship company in Massachusetts, organized a baseball team that became the Commonwealth Giants. Members included Lorenzo Dow Turner, later a University of Chicago linguist, and Frank Forbes, who became a boxing commissioner. Saw mill teams in East Texas and in Louisiana played baseball on Saturdays, attested to by researcher William Rogosin. In a progressive western town, Buxton, Iowa, where black and white coal miners worked side by side, according to Janice Beran the YMCA sponsored athletic teams, including the Buxton Wonders Baseball Team. At first an all-black team, the Wonders eventually became integrated.

Government service opened another opportunity for blacks both to obtain decent jobs and to play ball. In 1903 the St. Louis *Palladium* printed an admiring report of the "sensational plays" and "good material for a strong team" among local post office clerks, who "passed their leisure hours playing base ball." Washington, D.C., in particular teemed with government teams, so to speak. By 1910 black players in various governmental offices and agencies had formed a league, in which, for example, Post Office defeated Agriculture and Interior defeated an unnamed Bureau. Other teams included one representing the War and Navy Departments.

Black vaudeville actors, like the white ones, fielded baseball teams. On a cold May day in 1902 several hundred fans shivered through a game at the Bronx Oval in New York to watch the Cole & Johnson Colts (Cole & Johnson were then playing in the Broadway hit, "Red Moon") repeat their stage success on the diamond by defeating the Colored Vaudeville Association team 9–1, its pitcher striking out twelve men.

Hotels, particularly resort hotels, still hired blacks. There waiters could make about $23.00 to $33.00 a month, captains up to $40.00, and headwaiters $75.00. From at least 1910 on, two resort hotels in Palm Beach, the Breakers and the Royal Poinciana, each hired a group of black professional ball players for the winter season to play each other for the delectation of guests; it is unclear whether they also acted as waiters. In 1910 the Royal Giants played as "the Breakers" and the Leland Giants as "the Poincianas." The following year none other than Sol White managed "the Breakers," and Rube Foster, who would form the Negro American League, captained the team. Outstanding black professionals like Pop Lloyd, Pat Duncan, Bud Petway, Red Wickware, and Home Run Johnson played for these resort hotel teams.

As earlier, opportunity to play ball lay open to Afro-Americans in the four black military regiments of the Regular Army. The segregated Ninth and Tenth Cavalry and 24th and 25th Infantry Regiments continued to excel in baseball, beating many competitors, white and black, military and civilian, amateur and semipro.

The Tenth Regiment's baseball exploits at Fort Riley early in the century were especially noteworthy. In the Department (state or military area) athletic meet held at the fort in 1905, the Tenth defeated not only white teams from Fort Riley but also those from Fort Leavenworth and lost only to the other competing black regimental team, the 25th. Besides supporting a regimental team, the Tenth also ran a kind of intramural league among its units; the team with the best percentage in that league received a pennant.

In 1907 the Army posted the Tenth Regiment to the Philippines, where First Sergeant W.W. Thompson of its G Troop pitched for the team of Fort William McKinley and helped win the pennant for the Fort in the Manila Baseball League of 1906–07. Back in the States, Troop M of the Tenth still remained at Fort Riley, where it captured the championship of the post baseball league of 1908 from fourteen other teams. In July of 1909 the Tenth passed through New York City on its way to a new post, proudly exhibiting a glass punch bowl won in a Manila series and challenging all comers at baseball.

From 1909 through the early teens the Tenth was stationed at Fort Ethan Allen, Vermont, where its baseball team played successfully against local nines like St. Michael's College at Winooski but lost to the University of Vermont and then to the black pro team, the Cuban Stars, in a stiff wind and snow flurries.

Like white soldiers, the black players of the Tenth encountered Sabbatarian objections. According to Marvin Fletcher's *Negro Soldiers and the Army*, about the year 1911 locals made some objections to the soldiers' playing on the Sabbath. One minister wrote the War Department that such games furnished "an attraction for the young people to an environment which is not the best for them." The Tenth's colonel replied curtly that no one was compelled to come to the games. But the Army did respond by banning games between civilians and soldiers, although the commanding officer grumbled that outside the post, "disreputable dives" supplied a lot more vice than those inside it.

By 1913 the Tenth was playing non-military teams again—at Schenectady, where they defeated a black professional team, the Mohawk Giants. A game with the Fifth Infantry (white), stationed at Plattsburg, that year highlighted the Tenth's season. The team hired a steamer for the trip across Lake Champlain. More than 200 men and their families participated in that outing, and the black team won over the white, 11–4. Then the Tenth was transferred from cold Vermont to broiling Ford Huachuca, Arizona, where the baseball team responded to the change by winning 8 out of 10 games played, although it lost 2 out of a 3-game series with the 25th Infantry.

Meanwhile, the 9th Cavalry, another black unit, did well at baseball both in Montana and at the Presidio in California, the team disporting itself in its new yellow-gray uniforms with black socks. Transferred to the Philippines in 1908, the 9th won the athletic meet held by the Department of Luzon. A prominent alumnus of the Ninth, Soldierboy Semmler, in the 1930s would own the professional team called the New York Black Yankees.

At this time black soldier-athletes dominated athletics in the Philippines. In February 1908 the *Army and Navy Journal* pointed out that because three black regiments (the 24th, 25th, and 9th) had won the three departmental athletic meets in Manila, only black athletes would participate in the Division meet and compete for its prizes. To the *Journal's* correspondent, this situation clearly showed the great need for better white recruits!

The 24th was shipped back to the States from the Philippines and stationed at Fort Owego, New York, but some of its units went on to Madison Barracks, in the same state, and when two teams of the 24th from its two locations played each other, according to Fletcher, 2,000 spectators showed up.

The 24th Infantry, although unnamed in the article, is apparently the unit described in 1931 in a *Baseball Magazine* piece by a retired army man recalling an unusual ball game he had seen about twenty years earlier. The black regiment in the game, he said, had just returned from a long tour of service in the Philippines, where its baseball team had enjoyed remarkable success. It was stationed at Madison Barracks, New York, but along with some white units was sent for maneuvers to an upstate camp, where on days off an elimination series of baseball games was played. When only two teams were left at the top, the black team and a white one from Governors' Island, interest and rivalry mounted, and the Fourth of July was set as the day for the deciding contest. That day backers of each team clustered in separate groups, the whites blowing bugles, horns, and other wind instruments, the blacks pounding on pots and pans. The players and their friends on both sides wagered on the game. With the blacks leading 4–3 going into the last half of the ninth, Sergeant Trickey, a "smashing batsman," came up for the whites against Sergeant Richards, a "magnificent" curve baller, pitching for the blacks. With the count two and two on the batter, and two runners on, the black catcher, Corporal Larkin, called for a pitchout, then threw over the third baseman's head, ostensibly to pick off the runner, but he intentionally threw wild into left field. The runner dashed for home, only to be tagged by Larkin with the ball! Pandemonium followed. When the major representing Governors' Island demanded an accounting, Larkin revealed that what he had thrown to the outfield was not a ball but "an ole Irish pertater I'd stuck in my britches, after brekfas', and it was botherin' me." The writer of the story fails to reveal the result of the game, but he does say that in the evening Larkin's colonel sent for him and asked how the catcher so conveniently happened to have such a perfectly shaped potato in his pocket. Larkin replied that he was afraid of scurvy, so at breakfast he had asked the cook to give him his potato raw. "Besides, Sir Colonel, 'tween me an' you, before I was able to get the right kind of pertater we both had to pick over about two barrels of 'em."

Later in the decade the 24th Infantry, by then posted to Houston, got into serious trouble. On August 19, 1917, as reported in the *Army and Navy Journal*, the 24th's crack Company M baseball team challenged the Houston Black Buffalos to a doubleheader at West End Park. But it is not clear whether the games were ever played. During the month of August the soldiers of the 24th Infantry had suffered a series of "unbearable" racial insults from the white residents of Houston, who "treated them like scum," as accounts like that of Professor Robert V. Haynes, *A Night of Violence*, make clear. Several men of the 24th had been reading Robert S. Abbott's Chicago *Defender* and DuBois's *Crisis* and preferred DuBois's concept of racial pride to Booker T. Washington's accommodation. On the night of August 23 about 150 of the soldiers of the regiment, including around 30 of the men from Company M, went to Houston to retaliate. In the ensuing three hours of rioting sixteen whites were killed, among them four policemen. Three separate courts martial pronounced harsh sentences resulting in nineteen soldiers hanged and many others imprisoned for long terms.

Meanwhile, in the Philippines the baseball team of the 25th Infantry Regiment, the fourth all-black regiment, was defeating all comers. "During these days," said the recorder Dalbert Green in the regimental history, "the regiment was busily engaged in policing the territory that was assigned to them of the many insurgent bands that were roaming through the country at that time, but a small matter like that," he added lightly, "never caused a moment of laxity in playing ball." In Bamban, Luzon, the 25th finally got "revenge" against its old rival, the 12th Infantry, which in 1898 had beaten the 25th at Chickamauga Park: the 25th took two games from the 12th. About this time Corporal William Crawford died accidentally in a freak accident during a baseball game against the 41st Volunteers, Dalbert Green reported. Wearing a bolo knife hung at his belt, Corporal Crawford slid into a base; it stuck in his abdomen, and he died a few days later.

In 1901 the 25th went to Manila. The city, said Green, was alive with regimental teams, and the 25th challenged all comers to games for "money, marbles, or chalk, money preferred." In a game for the championship of the islands against Battery H of the 6th Artillery, the 25th won and became champions. Early in 1902 Arlie Pond, a former pitcher for the Baltimore National League Club but at this time a major in the Medical Corps, became manager and coach of the 25th's regimental team, and during its stay at Malabong, Luzon, it won several games.

The following year the Army split up the 25th. Some companies were sent to Fort Reno, Oklahoma, but most were ordered to Fort Niobrara, Nebraska, and shortly reassigned to Fort Riley. The men were directed to march the 254 miles from Niobrara to Norfolk, where they could entrain for Riley, so the regimental team arranged games with local teams all along the line of march, winning every one. On their arrival at Fort Riley the men were in time to plunge into a series of baseball elimination games. "Dopesters" ranking the teams discounted the 25th's Fort Niobrara nine because it had just completed that long march, favoring instead the Regiment's Fort Reno team and the Tenth Cavalry's Fort Robinson team (the Tenth, too, had been split). But the Niobrara team of the 25th beat all comers, including the white Fort Leavenworth and Fort Riley teams. Then it battled the Tenth's Fort Robinson team to a twelve-inning win and the championship.

When some companies of the 25th were moved to Texas, trouble began. As John M. Carroll explained in *The Black Military Experience*, black soldiers were beginning to resent treatment meted out to them in the South, where whites found it impossible to bear the sight of blacks wearing a uniform that represented authority and thus suggested superiority. Several ugly incidents between white Texans and soldiers of the 25th had already occurred, especially in El Paso when after city police arrested two soldiers of the 25th, their comrades marched to the jail and fought a gun battle to rescue them.

Then in Brownsville, near Fort Brown where the 25th was quartered in 1906, citizens made the black soldiers' stay disagreeable. Trouble with brothel managers and saloonkeepers created one of the main problems. Violence in Brownsville commenced when, after a rumor of attempted rape, the men were confined to barracks, where their resentment built until a group of them broke out. In the fray that followed one civilian was killed and another wounded.

Evidence against the soldiers, none of whom could be identified, is inconclusive and mostly circumstantial, whereas considerable evidence, according to Bernard McNalty's and Morris McGregor's book, *Blacks in the Military*, indicates that it was townspeople, using stolen rifles, who rioted. Testimony showed that under ordinary (nonracial) circumstances such local disturbances would have been considered ordinary frontier rows. Nevertheless, President Theodore Roosevelt intervened and arbitrarily ordered three full companies of the 25th, including six holders of the Medal of Honor, dismissed without honor and without any trial. Roosevelt, already embarrassed, according to Professor Haynes, by criticism over having invited Booker T. Washington to the White House for dinner, accepted the assumption that the soldiers were protecting each other and that all were guilty. Washington had urged a more moderate course, but after Roosevelt discharged the soldiers, Washington refused to condemn the president, saying merely that black people felt hurt and disappointed. DuBois's Niagara Movement, on the other hand, responded by attacking Washington. Even the *Army and Navy Journal* criticized the War Department when it removed the 25th from Fort Brown, saying that "public clamor" should not be a reason for transferring troops "on demand," and that the army "should be secure against local caprice or race prejudice." Fleet Walker took note in his book of Roosevelt's dismissal of the soldiers, calling it "ominous."

Roosevelt's response should have been expected. According to Professor Thomas Dyer's *Theodore Roosevelt and the Idea of Race*, Roosevelt believed black soldiers, as members of an "immature race," should behave as directed, that they lacked the capacity for leadership, were superstitious, fearful, and "but a few generations removed from the wildest savagery." But Roosevelt's estimate of blacks was not exceptional in this era. U.B. Philips, the outstanding historian of the South in the early 1900s, represented the usual view of academics in his belief that blacks were inherently childlike. Professor Josiah Royce, a Johns Hopkins Ph.D., wrote in 1908 that the "Negro" was in "his present backward state" not just because of circumstances but because of mental limitations. Other books of the day referred to blacks as "debased," "ignorant," and "akin to the monkey." *Sporting News* showed no hesitancy in using terms like "coon." So Roosevelt was reflecting the opinion of the majority of well-read white people and scholars of the time, who accepted the basic premise of black inferiority and belief in the necessity for paternalism in treating blacks.

After the Brownsville episode the 25th Infantry returned to the Philippines, where again the regimental baseball team won the championship of the Department in 1908, after which it toured the islands, beating most opponents. In the fall of 1909 the Army sent some companies of the 25th to Fort Lawton, Washington state, and some to Fort George H. Wright in the same state. Both units of the regiment formed teams, and the Fort George Wright nine proved strong against semipros around Spokane. When the team at Ford George Wright got a new regimental baseball officer, Lieutenant O.H. Saunders, a star from the West Point team, he was, according to Dalbert Green, "received with the wildest of joy."

In 1913 the 25th moved again, this time to Schofield Barracks, Hawaii, where company teams played to be selected for battalion leagues. After a battalion series the best players were picked for a new regimental team, whose "strategy board" met after each game to review plays. That team won the championship of the post baseball league. "The 25th Infantry," reported the Hawaiian correspondent of the New York *Age*, "is cleaning up in athletics on this island."

Then the 25th's team took the championship of the Honolulu City League by playing the teams of the All-Chinese, the Portuguese, the Asians, and Schofield Barracks. Later it defended its title against stateside visitors like California college teams, Pacific Coast League teams, and picked teams from the majors and minors. When in 1914 Happy Hogan of the Vernon P.C.L. team led an invasion of the island with stars from his team and the majors, Schofield Barracks declared a holiday, and the 25th paraded around the ball park with the visitors, led by the 25th's band. However, Hogan's team, with Death Valley Scott, late of the White Sox, pitching, won that game and others against the 25th, which suffered, Sergeant Dalbert Green wrote, from eagerness, nervousness, and stage fright. But by then banners won in athletics by companies, battalions, and the regiment already covered the walls of the 25th's amusement hall at Schofield.

After Sergeant Green's retirement the 25th's team continued defeating every baseball nine in Hawaii. But why wouldn't it? By then it boasted Bullet Rogan with his masterly pitching, Oscar "Heavy" Johnson, a hard-hitting fielder, Walter "Dobie" Moore, an excellent shortstop, Lemuel Hawkins, first baseman, and Bob Fagan, second baseman. John Holway believes this was probably the finest service team of the era. In 1916 it won forty-two and lost two, not only from military teams but also civilian teams like Santa Clara University, a strong college team, and the Olympic Club of San Francisco, against whom Johnson hit the winning homer in the last half of the ninth.

No wonder when Casey Stengel saw this team playing at Fort Huachuca, Arizona, where part of the 25th had been transferred, he was impressed. Huachuca was an inhospitable place on the edge of the desert where the Buffalo Soldiers had once played a major role in rounding up hostile Indians.

Stengel, barnstorming with the Pittsburgh Pirates in 1919, watched Rogan and recommended him later to J.L. Wilkinson, white owner of the Kansas City Monarchs, who signed the pitcher and the other four as well for his team, where they became highly successful.

A little-known black unit, the United States Cavalry Detachment at West Point, New York, also played ball. In 1909 and 1910 the New York *Age* reported its games and challenges to "colored teams of good standing. . . at home and abroad." During 1915 the newspaper also gave considerable space to the baseball exploits of a black Navy Yard team of Charleston, South Carolina, which won the city championship and then went on tour, beating colleges and pro teams until, winning eighteen out of twenty-two, it claimed the championships of Georgia, Florida, and South Carolina!

When World War I began, approximately 10,000 soldiers were serving in the four black regiments of the Regular Army. Black Americans rushed to join those units, and within two weeks one of the regiments was filled, so the War Department decided that no more black enlistments would be accepted, much to the fury of black citizens who still wanted to join the Army. The Army simply did not know what to do about black soldiers.

Not one of the four black regiments became part of the A.E.F. as a unit during the war, although each had to give up many of its best noncommissioned officers and send them to training camps to be prepared for commands, and many individual soldiers transferred to the newly-set-up black units of the A.E.F., the 92nd and 93rd Divisions. Some blacks went to France with the 92nd. The 93rd was made up of black National Guard units, and several of these units went to France, too. But the 25th was kept in Hawaii and the Tenth, except for a few cadres of troops sent to Europe, stayed at Fort Huachuca.

The onset of the draft settled the matter of whether blacks could enlist in the Army. They were drafted with whites. Negro soldiers often found camp life difficult, for many black draftees trained under white officers who hated their assignments and treated their men with contempt. Moreover, about eighty or ninety percent of blacks were arbitrarily assigned to labor battalions.

In Europe, the British did not want black American troops attached to their army, but the French, who had their own black colonials in the front lines, were glad to have them, so the 369th Infantry Regiment was detached from the black 93rd Division and became part of the French Army, where the black soldiers reportedly received better treatment than from their own countrymen. Europeans accepted blacks without discrimination. The 369th's fighting qualities were so well recognized that the French Army awarded it, along with three other black American units, the Croix de Guerre en masse.

Recreation for black soldiers, who often trained in the South, presented a problem. Secretary of War Baker conferred with Raymond Fosdick, chairman of the Commission on Training Camp Activities, and as a result he and Emmett Scott, a black man who had for eighteen years been secretary to Booker T. Washington, surveyed provisions for black trainees' recreation. Assisted by volunteers in the cities adjoining the camps, the War Camp Community Service gradually organized separate recreation programs for blacks.

The Y provided some camp recreation, too. Although in some camps Y secretaries discriminated against black soldiers, in other camps the two races played games together. Some of the Y's 331 "social secretaries" were directors of physical training, who set up baseball and football teams and scheduled boxing matches. A familiar name on a list of Y secretaries in Emmett Scott's *Official History of the American Negro in the World War* (1919) is none other than J. Francis Gregory, the college baseball player. A few black Y secretaries served in France, and one caught in the trenches during an attack while giving first aid fought with the soldiers for two days. Organizations like the Knights of Columbus, the Federal Council of Churches of Christ, the Red Cross, and the Salvation Army offered blacks some clubs, canteens, and entertainment. In the South, where blacks could not always get into theatres or Y auditoriums, they built their own amusement houses, formed musical bands, and put on shows.

The Army itself furnished competition in baseball and other sports in the combat units, where athletic officers were assigned. Otherwise, commanding officers often failed to recognize the need for athletics among black soldiers. Charles Williams in his 1923 book, *Sidelights on Negro Soldiers*, tells of some exceptions. A black longshoremen's baseball team at Camp Alexandria, Newport News, Virginia, made an enviable record, beating all white and black teams in the area. At Camp Gordon, Atlanta, the Army set aside three fields on which the black soldiers could practice baseball and equipped the battalion teams with uniforms. The battalion teams always formed up and marched to the field for their two games a week before enthusiastic crowds. The Camp Gordon battalion teams also played games with the Atlanta colleges and with the team of the federal prison there. Gerald Patton's *War and Race* mentions a black officers' training camp set up at Fort Des Moines in 1917, where the men played baseball and other sports.

Black labor battalions even played ball in Europe. Once in France in 1918 while longshoremen competed "tooth and nail," according to *Trench and Camp*, rooters suddenly began turning their backs to the game and standing at attention. Then a black soldier called the ball players to attention. A runner who was ten feet off first base spun on his heel, the pitcher dropped the ball and the batter his bat. The "Marsellaise," said the journalist, had hushed the great American game.

But not permanently.

37

TWO STRIKES CALLED BEFORE YOU BAT

The Harlem Renaissance of the 1920s in art, music, and literature brought pulsating black cultural life to the attention of many Americans. To some whites this cultural outpouring revealed that blacks had particular talents; but to most it merely established a new black stereotype—the exotic African, the uninhibited, emotional, irrepressive, immoral, alarmingly phallic stranger. Nativism became a major force, and the Ku Klux Klan revived. One Klavern even tried to get the owner of the Cincinnati Reds to declare Sunday, July 20, 1924, Klan Day at the park and permit the Klan, 40,000 strong in the county and 100,000 in the area, to publicly present flowers to the managers and players of the two teams.

On the other hand, since the twenties marked a decade of prosperity, the needs of black people, including their recreation, received more notice. Their average life expectancy increased by five years, from the pathetic 35 to the slightly less dismal 40, whereas the figure for whites approached 55. Race leaders like Marcus Garvey advanced ethnic pride. Garvey charged his people, "No more fear, no more cringing, no more sycophantic begging and pleading." Although like Fleet Walker before him Garvey advocated emigration to Africa, few blacks responded to the idea. Another wave of black migration to the North added to the gradual development of cohesive black communities in major northern cities.

Blacks felt their lowly status most, said George S. Schuyler in the *American Mercury* in 1929, when they searched for recreation. Two studies of recreation facilities in urban areas showed that cities in the South with public parks often closed them to blacks. Any conveniences available to blacks were inferior to those for whites in the same city. A "colored park" often constituted only a bare tract, with no equipment, often lacking an athletic field; a "colored playground" was smaller, less well equipped, and served by black supervisors paid less than whites. As for amusements, said *Southern Workman*, "the worst types of dives" were usually open to the Negro, although he might have trouble getting a ticket to a Shakespearean play.

Recreation Magazine claimed that the war experience had stimulated pro-

594

vision for recreation for blacks, but that was because the War Camp Community Service clubs for black soldiers had been taken over by black citizens and operated as community centers.

Some cities did set aside separate parks or playgrounds for Afro-Americans. In the South a park might be turned over to blacks on certain days or one afternoon a week. Memphis had a separate 55-acre tract for blacks called Douglass Park, which included ball grounds. Interracial friction in that city dropped from the time the park opened, claimed *Southern Workman*. Beaumont, Texas, finally in 1927 voted the bonds for a long-projected black park. Sports were available there, and baseball proved very popular, even school teams using the diamonds for both practice and match games. Washington, D.C., had a park that the city turned over to blacks temporarily, on Tuesday afternoons. That park's administrator also set aside certain of its baseball diamonds for blacks. Winston-Salem also established two baseball leagues for Negroes in a recreation area, and Orlando, Florida, hired a high school teacher to organize recreation, including a city baseball league, for blacks of both sexes and various ages.

In the North blacks could enjoy the large parks of cities like Philadelphia, New York, and Buffalo, but in those parks with bathing beaches, as in Chicago and Gary, segregation prevailed in order to avoid friction.

In 1920 the Playground Association at long last gave special attention to black needs, and some improvement resulted. Until the appointment of Ernest T. Attwell as head of a separate Bureau of Colored Work, the Association did virtually nothing for the race, although in World War I it had trained black recreation workers in a separate summer school. Attwell, a follower of Booker T. Washington and a Tuskegee graduate, had during the world war been a government worker. After the Playground Association hired him in 1920, his bureau offered field service and training institutes to blacks and biracial groups seeking organized recreation. Attwell also issued progress reports detailing improvements in recreation opportunities as a result of help given by his bureau, including information on the building of baseball fields for black citizens.

In 1921 Attwell reported that a recent Playground Association survey had revealed the shameful fact that only about three percent of American playgrounds welcomed black citizens. Two years later he wrote in *Southern Workman* that since the close of the war the association had introduced recreation programs for blacks in forty-seven cities, giving several examples. Within six years of Attwell's appointment, states Richard Knapp in his dissertation, "Play for America: The National Recreation Association," almost a hundred cities furnished recreation facilities for blacks. In the South, the association soon reported black playgrounds opened in Macon, Georgia; Louisville, Kentucky; and Charleston, West Virginia. Attwell also worked to arrange help for municipalities from foundations and philanthropists.

In the North, friction continued in the public parks and playgrounds of

Chicago. The 1922 report of the Chicago Commission on Race Relations analyzing the 1919 riot and its aftermath showed that racial disturbances over baseball diamonds had not disappeared in the city. Wentworth Avenue was considered the dividing line between white and black Chicago, and Ted Page, later an outfielder for several black professional clubs, told John Holway he played ball "every day" in 1920 at a playground at Wentworth and 33rd. But west of Wentworth, reported the Commission, fear was probably keeping black children out of the parks. The director of the Armour Square playground denied that black boys had been refused permits to play ball there, although she felt it necessary to warn any black team that she could not be responsible for its protection outside the park, since there had been some serious riots just beyond park boundaries. At Robey Playground the Commission learned of a recent fight over a baseball diamond between two black boys aged eleven and a fourteen-year-old white boy. At Washington Park, however, the Commission reported a mingling of races on the ball field, sometimes one team white and the other black, and occasionally both races on one team. Nevertheless, Ragen's Colts remained active in Washington Park and "hatched mischief" in nearby pool rooms. With only one policeman in charge of fifteen ball diamonds, Washington Park remained a potential trouble spot.

Cities were miserly in hiring and paying black play leaders. And such leaders were scarce to begin with. Few took the YMCA's training course, and blacks were not admitted to courses taught by the American College of Physical Education or the Chicago Normal School of Physical Education. To deal with the situation Attwell organized a short training institute for black play leaders in Chicago in July of 1922 and another in Philadelphia, on Lombard Street, in June of 1926.

As for aid to black baseball players from the settlement house movement, it was minimal. The movement never gained great headway among Negroes, although Boston, Minneapolis, Cleveland, Philadelphia, and Pittsburgh did contain black settlements, and black Boy Scouts were strictly segregated. The Scouts' national organization appointed a "Director of Interracial Relations," but his title was a ludicrous misnomer; the last thing the organization wanted was a mingling of black and white Scouts.

The YMCA, too, stayed segregated. Its college branches remained the most numerous among black Ys, active in about 140 to 200 institutions. City branches either excluded or discouraged blacks, so boys had to wait until a separate black branch opened, as one did in 1923 in Pittsburgh, as Bob Ruck reported, forming ball teams on which two future professionals, Ted Page and Josh Gibson, played, as did Wendell Smith and Chester Washington, both future sports writers active in efforts during the 1930s to get black ball players back into Organized Baseball. A black YMCA baseball league operated in St. Louis and another in Cleveland on Central Avenue. Channing Tobias, afterward an alternate United Nations delegate, served for a number of years as the Y's national black service secretary for "colored men and boys."

Of course, blacks could still play ball in prison. The all-black team of the Branch Prison at Marquette in the Upper Peninsula of Michigan, reported the Pittsburgh *Courier* in 1923, rated with the best in the state. When this team played another prison team, the Pirates, for the prison championship on Sunday, August 19, the entire prison population showed up and circled the field to watch.

Schools in the South, and some in the West, continued limited in number and quality and still segregated in the twenties. The photographer Gordon Park grew up in Fort Scott, Kansas, where he had to go to a separate black school and sit in the peanut gallery at the movies. He yearned to be able to have a soda at the drugstore in town, like the white kids. In the mid-twenties the fourteen southern states altogether supported only 209 accredited and 582 nonaccredited black high schools, so many communities simply went without black high schools altogether.

Even in Chicago schools blacks could suffer exclusion from extracurricular activities or be relegated to segregated groups. Some schools accepted integration, however. Bud Harris in Pittsburgh and Chet Brewer in Des Moines both played on integrated teams. Fran Matthews, like Brewer an eventual pro, became the first black captain of the baseball team at the Rindge Technical High School in Cambridge, Massachusetts.

Some black boys had the opportunity of playing on school teams even in the South. Quincy Trouppe's black elementary school in St. Louis, with Trouppe as catcher, "won several banners," Trouppe said. Later he attended one of the only two black high schools in the city. Each year they fought each other for the colored championship in baseball. Trouppe's high school stood right across the park used by the professional black St. Louis Stars, and to Trouppe's delight several famous pro players watched the high school playoffs.

In Washington, D.C., E.B. Henderson kept organizing, this time forming a strictly secondary school association called the South Atlantic High School Athletic Conference, to cover baseball, football, and other sports. Moreover, he worked to present a balanced physical education program in the black schools, not only expanding competitive athletics but improving overall instruction in physical training. According to his biographer, Leon Coursey, Henderson's approach to physical training was superior to that of the physical educators in the white Washington schools, who in 1924 had hired a white ex-professional baseball player, Guy "Doc" White. Under White's direction white Washington teachers failed to improve the physical education programs and continued to be interested only in coaching. In 1928 Henderson presented the city's black physical training teachers with a new course of study that included scales for checking achievement and suggestions for introducing leisure-time activities, although the teachers were so overburdened by large classes that little of the new course could be put into practice. At both black Washington high schools, Dunbar and Armstrong, in these years both boys' and girls' sport included baseball.

In black colleges baseball probably reached its height in the twenties, with only football challenging. Both Hampton and Tuskegee opened athletic fields and played intercollegiate baseball. Hampton's opponents included other Virginia institutions. Tuskegee athletics improved after the administration permitted students to organize and run their own athletic association. In 1924, according to the *Army and Navy Journal*, Tuskegee won a "thrilling tussle" from the 24th Infantry at Fort Benning, beating its nine by one run in the ninth inning.

Howard University baseball expanded its scope in the twenties with southern trips and play against foreigners. In 1924 Howard's baseball team took a six-day southern trip around Virginia, playing local colleges. A more extended trip in 1927 took the team through parts of North Carolina, Pennsylvania, Maryland, and Georgia, according to the university's yearbook. In 1924 came the first of two matches with foreign teams when the team of Meiji University toured the United States, trying its mettle against the nines of institutions like New York University, Princeton, Harvard, and Yale. The Howard nine, as hosts of the Meiji team, boasted the student yearbook, defeated this crack aggregation in ten innings, 4–3. The following year another Japanese team toured the states playing ball, but this one, a strong semipro group called Daimai, composed of the best Japanese college players and backed by an important newspaper, the Osaka *Mainichi*, defeated the Howard team, 10–3.

Howard's President James S. Durkee reported unprecedented success on the part of the institution's sports teams in this era and went so far as to boast that the scholastic standing of athletes stood far above those who did not participate in sports. Even freshmen formed a baseball team in 1922 and played a regular schedule against Dunbar and Armstrong high schools of Washington and Morgan College of Baltimore. That same year the Howard yearbook announced that athletic training had "come to be regarded as a matter of importance in the University curriculum" and that, having long since outgrown its "modest athletic facilities," Howard planned a new athletic field and gym. The university opened that new facility near the end of the decade.

The black colleges also benefited from the assistance of E.B. Henderson. He and others organized the Colored Intercollegiate Athletic Association, which later merged with the North Carolina Intercollegiate Athletic Association. In 1923 the Virginia Normal School team of Petersburg, Virginia, called the Hilltoppers, took the championship of this association by winning over the Virginia Seminary team of Lynchburg. Other members of the association, according to the Pittsburgh *Courier,* included Hampton Institute, Virginia Union, and Lincoln University. Later, other colleges joined. In

1925 the association published an attractive bulletin, reprinted in *Southern Workman*, illustrating its various sports, baseball among them, giving team records along with addresses of members and proceedings of the association's annual meeting.

Henderson's other contributions to black colleges in this period included attempts to raise the status of black athletic officials. As with black playground officials, they numbered few and earned less than did white officials. And, like the pro black clubs, black colleges usually hired white officials, believing players would respect the decisions of white umpires more than they would black. Setting up an organization for black athletic officials, Henderson, according to his biographer, gradually got their fees for officiating increased to the level of the whites'.

A scattering of black baseball players continued to play in white college ball of this era. Henderson knew of some at Boston College, at Springfield, and at the University of Vermont. Researcher John Behee found one at the University of Michigan, and Ocania Chalk discovered a few others. Earl Brown, according to Henderson, pitched successfully for Harvard, throwing a no-hitter against Northeastern College and another against Yale! He went on to pitch for the professional Lincoln Giants.

Black churches of the twenties, particularly in the North, in the estimation of Charles Williams, director of physical education at Hampton, were gradually overcoming an earlier inclination to think of all forms of recreation as instruments of the devil. In 1926 Williams published in *Southern Workman* the results of a survey he made revealing that young church members had in the past been disciplined for teaching boys baseball and playing ball with them. Many ministers still had warped social vision, Williams said, and either opposed community recreation or left it to other organizations like the Y. Some, however, began promoting and encouraging baseball and basketball leagues. Williams asked 80 ministers in four states if they approved of certain types of recreation for children of their community. Out of 79 replies, 72 said yes to baseball. As a model, Williams offered St. John's Congregational Church in Springfield, Massachusetts, where the Reverend Mr. William N. DeBerry, educated at Fisk and Oberlin, believed in the church as a social center. Most boys of DeBerry's church belonged to the Sunday School Athletic League, and in the summer of 1925 his boys' baseball team won 13, lost 5, and tied 1.

Williams might also have used Chicago Sunday schools as a model. T.J. Woofter's *Negro Problems in Cities* found that 300 baseball players from 20 black Sunday schools in Chicago had formed their own baseball league. The black Sunday school clubs had formerly belonged to the (interracial) Cook County Sunday School Association, but after a Negro team won the championship for three successive seasons the Cook County Association tried to shunt the black teams into a separate division, so the blacks withdrew entirely and formed their own league.

Black baseball, like the white, sprang from the play of boys on sandlots and playgrounds. When some of those boys grew old enough and skilled enough to join pro and semipro teams, they in turn affected the next generation of boys by becoming models for the youngsters and thus encouraging boys who wanted to be ball players. Black youths who loved baseball, like the white, not only practiced every chance they got, they also hung around the parks where the black pro clubs played, picking up bats for the players if they could, offering to pitch batting practice or shag balls, and working as groundkeeper, ice boy, or batboy. Ted Radcliffe lived on Wentworth Avenue near the park of Rube Foster's American Giants; Newt Allen worked at the Kansas City Monarchs' park; Buck Leonard hung around the semipro team of Rocky Mount, North Carolina; and Quincy Trouppe, who haunted the park of the pro St. Louis Stars, said he "ate, slept, and breathed baseball." All these boys themselves became pro players in the black leagues.

As fans, blacks in St. Louis, Kansas City, and Birmingham were during the twenties still relegated to separate sections of the parks. Whites could and did attend the Negro League games and sit in roped-off sections among black fans. The behavior of black fans at Negro League games seemed to whites, with their typically more inhibited behavior, to be amazingly unrestrained. An article in *Baseball Magazine* in 1929 described black fans from the white point of view:

> Rooting, at a Negro ball game, begins the moment the home team takes the field for practice. . . . Grandstand spectators howl their appreciation of every bit of strategy. . . . For real fervent, wholehearted rooters go to a Negro ball game. The razzing of the crowd is a never-ending delight. . . . White visitors find colored spectators quite as entertaining as the game itself.

But black fans loved white baseball, too. When a Washington Senator drove out a home run on the club's way to winning the 1924 pennant, according to the *Daily American*, local white and black rooters slapped each other on the back delightedly. Some Cleveland blacks were Boston fans, Manager Bob Quinn wrote his son in 1926, and "Everyone in the world is praying for the Red Sox, even colored folks at the Shrine Church of St. Teresa in Cleveland, so we had better start winning."

Black professional club owners, like the white, sometimes cultivated women fans. The Kansas City Monarchs, for example, held a half-price ladies' day in 1923, Janet Bruce mentioned. Young women also played ball. At Howard University, for instance, the 1920 university yearbook reported on both basketball and baseball teams for the female students, and declared,

> in spite of our warning that the Girls' baseball team can never seriously threaten the championship of the East, Dean Tuck insists that from her immense wealth of material she is able to, and will, produce one of the best aggregations in the country.

Young women committed for crimes to Virginia Industrial School were taught how to play in an attempt to make them physically fit. At both Virginia Industrial School and at Hampton, administrators endorsed sports for women in order to develop healthy, vigorous mothers-to-be. Janice Porter Barrett, a Hampton graduate and superintendent at the industrial school, published an article in *Southern Workman* in 1926 featuring an action photograph of baseball players labeled "A Game of Ball."

During the prosperous 1920s, Afro-Americans at least held their own in northern industry. Most were, however, still only unskilled workers. The Tennessee Coal and Iron Company of Alabama, a United States Steel subsidiary, continued to employ welfare workers to serve blacks: S.C. Johnson of Oberlin and John W. Oveltree of Tuskegee organized recreation and games at four locations for the company's 15,000 black employees. Other southern industrial plants employing many blacks, such as the American Cast Iron Pipe Company, Fairbanks-Morse Scale Company, and the Aluminum Company all provided playgrounds and recreation, according to Ernest Attwell in *Playground*. A periodical for black youth, *The Brownies Book of 1921*, printed a photograph of an industrial club in the usual team pose: the nine of the Dupont Plant at Hopewell, Virginia, most of them in striped uniforms and caps, displaying crossed bats in the foreground.

Chicago was a center for black industrial ball, supported heavily by the big companies, especially the meat packers, who sponsored eight stockyard teams including the Libby-McNeill Giants and the Morris Cadets, all part of a YMCA Industrial Baseball League. Black industrial ball also flourished in Pittsburgh, where, according to the Pittsburgh *Courier*, any club that applied for membership in the Negro Industrial League had to have eighteen amateur players most of whom were industrial workmen. Most black Pittsburgh industrial teams represented steel mills, as Rob Ruck's research shows. The mills hired black welfare workers to organize and supervise employees' athletic teams in order to promote industrial peace and produce stability and adjustment to the community as well as reinforce the color line.

Another such league, the Tandy League, or Colored Industrial League, operated in St. Louis. It was called after the black Army veteran Captain Charlton H. Tandy and organized in 1922 above the Locust Street office of a Spalding sporting goods store. The Tandy League's first clubs represented the Union Electric Company, Scullin Steel Company, Mississippi Valley Tanning Company, and Missouri Press Brick Company. Until the city of St. Louis got around to grading the grounds at Tandy Park, according to sports writer Normal "Tweed" Webb, the young fellows themselves prepared the diamond. At age nineteen Webb played for the Broomer Tailors in that league. His team eventually became the Pullmans, winners of eight Tandy League titles. Kansas City likewise organized a Negro Twilight League in 1922, according to Janet Bruce, and many of its teams represented local industries.

Southern whites thought high wages made blacks "shiftless and irresponsible" and that blacks returning from Army service were receiving consideration they would not normally get. On their part, black soldiers found that their war service really altered nothing in their situation, and whites moved quickly to disabuse them of any notion that as civilians their status had changed. Some returned soldiers were lynched in uniform. After the war even the military gave blacks the cold shoulder. The Marine Corps stayed white, the Navy took blacks only as messmen or stewards, and the War Department, according to Nalty and MacGregor, tried to break up the four black Regular Army units.

A few blacks, like the later pro Dave Malarcher, played ball with Army teams in Europe just after the armistice, before being sent home. At St. Sulpice, France, four companies of the 312th Labor Battalion on duty with the Depot Quartermaster developed a crack colored nine of former pros, according to *Stars and Stripes* in 1919. After the club defeated several good nines, the base officer awarded St. Sulpice the colored championship of Base Section No. 2. Since there was no league for Negro players at the base, said the newspaper, the team had to play independent ball. One of the San Sulpice players, Harold Morris, later played for the Kansas City Monarchs and other important black teams.

Back in the States, baseball continued in the segregated black Regular Army units, the 24th and 25th Infantry Regiments. In 1923 the *Army and Navy Journal* described the 25th as the Army's most athletic infantry regiment. The 24th, said the *Journal* two years later, had one of its most brilliant seasons, taking 19 out of 22 games. Stationed at Fort Benning, Georgia, the 24th Infantry led the post baseball league. One of its players in 1929 was Terris McDuffie, who later played for several important black teams. McDuffie said the regiment's colonel, who wanted winning sports teams, got West Point officers to come to Georgia and coach baseball and other sports. Once the Birmingham Black Barons, who then boasted the superlative pitcher Satchel Paige, went over to Fort Benning to play the 24th Regiment. McDuffie said later that Paige threw so hard that the average hitter could not get his bat around for a full swing.

If the prosperity of the twenties raised black expectations, the depression of the thirties dashed them, especially in the early years of the decade, when many black families depended on public aid not just for recreation but for sustenance as well.

Ernest T. Attwell, still director in the 1930s of the Playground Association's bureau of "colored work," did what he could to improve their lot. Some cities, like Detroit, Cincinnati, and Dayton, increased their services to blacks through playgrounds and recreation centers, but the increase was in part due to the receipt of federal emergency funds.

Recreation available to blacks in northern cities was uneven. In Cleveland the heavily congested black district bounded by Woodland, Center, Central, and Scovill avenues had no public baseball fields, according to Leyton Carter's *A Study of Public Recreation in Cleveland* (1936), and anyone in this black ghetto who wanted to play ball had to walk "long distances" across Euclid Avenue and northward to get to a public baseball diamond. But in Richmond, Indiana, black residents made a community center out of a former firehouse and organized a junior baseball league for sixteen boys, who received uniforms. A study of parks available to blacks in Pittsburgh, according to Ruck, revealed no recreation facilities available in proportions even approaching the recognized standard.

In the South, wrote black historian Carter Woodson, whites were provided for first; often the blacks got nothing. The Playground Association's journal reported only 8 playgrounds for black children in Washington, D.C., in 1932; by the end of the decade, according to the Federal Writers Project study of Washington, the number had risen to 15, but by then the whites had twice that many. Gunnar Myrdal wrote that Winston-Salem, with the largest black population in the state of North Carolina, provided no playgrounds for blacks, and Greenville, South Carolina, denied blacks use of an 18-acre tract between two densely-populated Negro areas chiefly because it was used as a playing field for a white baseball team. Tennessee began developing Booker T. Washington State Park on 350 acres, which would include a play field with a baseball diamond. But Birmingham, Alabama, had no black parks at all. In Waco, Texas, blacks could not use the city's 18 parks but were given 2 playgrounds (whites had 7). Houston's 10-acre park for blacks had been donated to the city by ex-slaves. In Beaumont, Texas, the black residents established their own playground through the Colored Congregational Church with the "encouragement" of the Department of Parks, which contributed some equipment and helped the residents bargain for the rest, as though the Negro population comprised foreigners instead of citizens.

Efforts to improve black recreation facilities in the thirties paid some dividends, however. *Playground Magazine* and other sources indicated an increase in playgrounds for blacks from 135 in 1924 to 361 in 1930 and then to 632 in 1937. The Playground Association also worked to develop more black play leaders. Ernest Attwell got Fisk University to open a special free summer session to train leaders in a three-week course in 1930. But the situation remained dismal; black playground workers in Chicago still received about half to two-thirds the pay of white workers and on top of that had to make do with inadequate equipment.

The New Deal made a difference in black recreation, however, as it did in other aspects of black life in the thirties. During Franklin D. Roosevelt's first term in office he did little for blacks, but during his second term blacks received an improved share of economic aid, jobs, and relief, according to Harvard Sitkoff's *New Deal for Blacks*. In Chicago, for example, the National Youth Administration rehabilitated the South Side Boys Club, located in a black slum, and hired workers to offer and supervise athletics for thousands of boys. One of the supervisors there in 1932 was Richard Wright, later a famous novelist. His wages at the club, he said, came to "just enough to provide a deficient diet." Every day black youths between eight and twenty-five came to draw, read, and play. "Rich people," Wright wrote, were paying him to distract the black boy with games, swimming, marbles, and baseball "in order that he [the boy] might not roam the streets and harm the valuable white property which adjoined the Black Belt."

This cynical view must have had a grain of truth, for it was similar to the theme of an article in *Southern Workman* in 1930 written by a black boys' club director in Philadelphia, the Wissahockon Boys Club. Such clubs as his, the writer said frankly, were needed for keeping boys out of trouble. Stopping boys' crime would go a long way to prevent adult crime, he went on, and boys' clubs were an agency "of proven worth in minimizing juvenile delinquency." Historian John Hope Franklin described another youth program in Philadelphia as an NYA program for black youth where boys were offered athletics through the Colored Playfield Project by the simple expedient of opening vacant lots as play fields. The NYA's final report maintained, however, that young black men employed on NYA projects played on the same athletic teams as whites, except in the South.

In the depression poor white youths could join the Civilian Conservation Corps. So could blacks—or they could try to; black youths had difficulty getting selected. A quota system operated, and fewer blacks than whites got accepted in proportion to their number, according to the research of John Salmond. Nor did black camp officials represent a proportionate percentage of Negro enrollees, wrote Kenneth Holland in *Youth in the CCC* (1942). Moreover, 84 of the camps were separate "Negro camps," 12 of them located in the South; 71 other camps were biracial. Furthermore, Salmond's investigations showed racial prejudice and discrimination by administrators as well as hostility from whites near the camps. Nevertheless, the blacks who gained entrance to the program did have the opportunity of playing ball. In 1935 *The Crisis* printed an interview with a young black who told of his CCC experience. He and others sent to Ford Dix were separated by color, and the segregation was "rigidly maintained." The young black men were then taken to a camp in the upper South. There all sports were encouraged: "We have a baseball team, boxing squad, etc.," under a black athletic director, although all other camp officials were white, he said. In a separate report about black camps, *The Civilian Conservation Corps and Colored Youth*, the United States Government could boast, "Sports are popular in the camps, many companies having their own baseball, basketball, track, and football teams."

Liberal black city churches permitted athletics in the 1930s, Carter Woodson said in a 1934 book, but in a 1930 volume, *The Rural Negro*, he painted a less optimistic picture of nonurban black recreation. Rural churches, he said, were still dominated by conservative ministers who refused to tolerate competitive athletics, declaring, "If you shoot marbles, play croquet, or indulge in baseball your soul will be damned." Yet some young people, he went on, "do not care" and organize athletic teams to compete against others in the district. Baseball, he added, was one of the easiest of recreations to indulge in, because it "may be set up fairly well with merely a bat and a ball."

Besides continuing to be confined to separate "colored branches" of the YMCA, Negroes might be shunted into separate black baseball nines of the American Legion. Quincy Trouppe's team in St. Louis, sponsored by the Tom Powell Post 77, was coached by Bill Donaldson, umpire of the professional black St. Louis Stars, and managed by a man named Gus Lowe. When Trouppe's team won the championship of the Colored Division of the St. Louis Legion posts, Lowe tried to arrange a city championship between the white division winners and Trouppe's team. All he could manage was one four-inning game, which ended in a 3–3 tie.

Even training schools or reform schools, if they were biracial, might separate boys by color on the baseball diamond. The Missouri Training School for Boys at Boonesville set aside one of its baseball diamonds for blacks. The white boys at the Kentucky House of Correction at Greendale used an excellent athletic field for baseball and other team games, but the "colored boys," reported the *Osborne Handbook of Juvenile Institutions*, had to make do with an "unimproved playground." A separate training school for blacks at Pikeville, Tennessee, offered no organized program of recreation and employed no recreation director, but the boys played baseball and other sports on their own.

At least two prisons, Ohio State Penitentiary and Michigan State Penitentiary, allowed opportunities for blacks to play ball. For despite claims that baseball would keep young fellows out of trouble, skill in ball playing failed to keep some accomplished players from landing in prison. A photo of the "Colored All-Stars," a black uniformed team from Ohio State Pen at Columbus, got its picture in *Life Magazine* after the "White All-Stars" defeated the team. But at Michigan State Prison blacks and whites evidently played ball together.

School News, the inmates' own newspaper at Michigan State Prison, acclaimed as potential baseball stars two black players mentioned above:* Napoleon "Kid" Mitchell, left fielder, who hit better than anyone else on the team, and a player named Giles, highly touted in advance of his appearance as having played for the Chicago American Giants and the Indianapolis ABCs, both top-flight black pro teams. Mitchell, in a game against Michigan State College, hit the first pitch "on the beezer," reported the paper, for a three-bagger. Giles, on the other hand, although much was

*See above, Chapter 26

expected of him, appeared only once, pitching against a team called the Hartford Independents, and losing 8–6.

By the thirties the black schools in Washington, D.C., were using athletic games as the basis for physical training classes and employing thirty physical training teachers, some with advanced degrees, to do the job. At the same time, E.B. Henderson traveled around the city on his bicycle visiting the schools, training officials, and teaching the rudiments of many sports. He also earned a B.A. at Howard and an M.A. at Columbia, and in 1939 he published his landmark book, *The Negro in Sports*, written at the suggestion of Carter Woodson. Eleanor Roosevelt aided him in his efforts to get equal treatment for blacks in the District of Columbia schools.

Outside Washington, blacks might not even have access to a high school. In the coal mining area of Alabama where Piper Davis lived, blacks had two elementary schools, whose joint baseball team played a few games each year against teams of other black elementary schools in nearby towns. The lone high school admitted only whites. As Davis told the story to Theodore Rosengarten for the magazine *Southern Exposure*, one year the coach of the white high school arranged a home-and-home series beginning with a game on the white diamond with the joint team of the two black elementary schools, but the best black player refused to go there because he was afraid of whites. The rest of the team went and lost the game. When the whites came to the blacks' diamond to play, the best black player took part, and the blacks won. Then the white high school fired its coach for being too friendly with blacks.

In a suburb of Birmingham, Alabama, Billy Bruton, who eventually achieved a twelve-year career in the majors, attended a high school without a baseball team, so the boys played "wherever we could clear a field."

Baseball facilities sometimes appeared in unexpected places. Near Jackson, Mississippi, Dr. Laurence C. Jones founded Piney Woods Country Life School, beginning with a handful of barefoot boys in a small building. He improved the school and made it into a valuable property. In the depression, said his biographer, Jones laid out a baseball field that was "the envy of the local white community, who used it for their match games." Thereafter, the school developed baseball teams good enough for Jones to send them to compete with outside teams to publicize his school.

Black colleges in the thirties underwent stresses similar to those the white colleges experienced. W.E.B. DuBois, in a Howard University commencement address in 1930, criticized black college students for avoiding hard intellectual pursuits and warned them against spending their time in extracurricular activities, especially "semi-professional athletics." DuBois omitted mentioning that the same thing was being said of the white students of the twenties and thirties. In their attitudes toward study, black college students only acted like their white counterparts. Charles H. Williams, Hampton's physical education director, in a 1933 issue of the *Quarterly Review of Higher*

Education Among Negroes, elaborated upon the problems DuBois referred to. Williams described the evils infecting black colleges, such as permitting outsiders or faculty members to play on teams, seizing on a pretext for forfeiting a losing game, overemphasizing the varsity, failing to fulfill commitments to play, and considering victory more important than clean play. But Williams took a twofold stance on college athletics, implying that the problems he listed had been solved or at least mitigated. He claimed that in the thirties black colleges suffered less from recruiting and saw more sportsmanship on the field. Moreover, he believed athletics contributed to physical fitness and character development, and he optimistically stated that athletic opportunities for interracial contacts could improve race relations.

What Williams and DuBois had to say about shortcomings in black college athletics had much pith. At least three colleges, Virginia State, Edward Waters in Jacksonville, Florida, and Stillman College, are known to have given out either athletic scholarships or jobs for athletes in the thirties. At Stillman, according to the college history, the players got either jobs or loans. Stillman's president believed the varsity baseball team and other athletic teams to be desirable because they helped advertise the institution and attract new students. At Virginia Union the team at least attracted women. When the college's baseball team played and beat Hampton in Richmond in their annual match, the occasion brought out "the fair damsels of Richmond and vicinity bedecked in their Easter regalia," as the Pittsburgh *Courier* described it.

Blacks, though not officially excluded from white college teams, rarely played on them in the thirties. Their scarcity stemmed from the attitude and understanding among athletic directors that only the few very best blacks, those who could immediately break into a team's starting lineup, would be permitted to participate. John P. Davis, author of *The American Negro Reference Book*, laid the infrequency of blacks on white college teams to the reluctance of some athletes to play against a team with a Negro member. A coach would "think twice" before selecting a black for his team, for fear of offending potential rival nines.

If they could not play professionally on white teams and were seldom allowed to participate on white college clubs, blacks could watch ball games, and somehow many managed even in the depression to attend white and black professional games. In the thirties only two major-league clubs still compelled blacks to sit in segregated sections: the two in St. Louis. Not until 1944 did the management of the Browns and Cardinals discontinue restricting blacks to the bleachers and the pavilion.

Black women played ball, too. The *Defender* in 1933 announced the formation of a women's team in Steelton, Pennsylvania, under the leadership of Mrs. Sadie Houston. And in Cleveland the same year a men's team, the Cleveland Giants, featured a female second baseman, Isabelle Baxter. The day her team beat the Canton Clowns she accepted five fielding choices and made her only error when after a spectacular stop of a ball behind first base she pulled the first baseman off the bag with a wide throw. Moreover, she hit safely once and drove two other hard-hit balls to the outfield.

Industrial support for black baseball and other company welfarism lessened in the thirties, just when most needed. At the beginning of the depression, since urban blacks were usually the first to lose jobs during cutbacks, a mass discharge of black industrial workers occurred. But when industrial unions banded together in the C.I.O. to organize the big industries, blacks found themselves included in the movement. Unionism improved their standard of living. As a result many blacks switched their allegiance to the Democrats in the 1936 elections, and in the second part of the decade a federal administration more sympathetic to blacks eased their situation.

Paternalism did continue in some industries. In Birmingham Piper Davis got a job at the American Cast Iron Pipe Company, ACIPCO, mostly because he played ball. A friend working there pointed him out to the recruiter as a ball player, so he was hired at $3.36 a day. The company paid for equipment and uniforms, insured the players, and sent them on tour. At work, players had a second locker for their baseball suits. Davis said that for a ball player, especially for a married man, working and playing for ACIPCO "was a better deal than signing with a traveling club." The company sponsored not only the black team, playing in the city Industrial League on Mondays, Wednesdays, and Saturdays, but also a white team, playing Tuesdays, Thursdays, and Saturdays. The two teams never played each other.

The Tennessee Coal and Iron Company of Alabama continued to sponsor a black ball team. In Memphis, Tennessee, blacks could play in an industrial league. If a company employed no black welfare workers, the Urban League, said Carter Woodson, might help blacks adjust to new communities and even interview employers to learn what provisions could be made for employees' recreation.

In the North, industrial support in Pittsburgh for athletes tailed off, but the "colored Y" helped coordinate a black industrial league. In Milwaukee some blacks played on a team sponsored in 1935 by the Wehr Steel Foundry, which throughout the depression retained a corps of black workers in mainly hot and fatiguing jobs, according to Joe William Trotter's book on black Milwaukee, expecting complete loyalty from them in return, especially during organizing threats from white workers.

Unions formed sports teams, too. In addition, communists wooed the workers in the thirties with sports. Left-wing trade unions, as shown by Mark Naison, involved black athletes in the trade union sports leagues they sponsored in Harlem. These leagues were intentionally integrated, as seen in the *Daily Worker*'s announcement in 1938 that the Meat Cutters' Joint Council would have two Negro players on its baseball team.

The Brotherhood of Sleeping Car Porters, organized by A. Phillip Randolph, joined the A.F. of L. and made their union strong and militant. They even used baseball games as a fund-raising expedient. The railroad men still played ball, judging by the *Defender's* reports of such interracial games as the defeat of the white Oakdale Merchants of Louisville by the black Smalling Red Caps. Great resort hotels might hire black pro teams like the Black Yankees to entertain guests. As for government teams, the Chicago Post Office reputedly had some of the best black ball players in the country. Out in Hollywood, noted the *Defender*, Oscar Smith, a movie lot worker at Paramount, joined the studio's baseball nine, and Richard Arlen, Bing Crosby, and Gary Cooper bought him his uniform, spikes, and glove.

In the military blacks remained segregated; not until 1948 did Truman order the end of discrimination, so the all-black units endured a while longer. The word "colored" stayed as part of the names of the all-black units until the War Department ordered it deleted in 1940. Thus in the 1930s the *Army and Navy Journal* could still report games of the "Colored Detachment" of the Field Artillery at Fort Sill, Oklahoma.

The 24th and 25th Infantries continued to play ball in the thirties, the former at Fort Benning, playing teams like Howard University and Florida Agricultural and Mechanical College of Tallahassee, while the 25th, at Fort Huachuca, Arizona, observed its 67th anniversary celebration with boxing, a baseball game, a dinner, and a dance. In 1940 *Army and Navy Journal* mentioned that the regimental commander of the 25th approved baseball trips for the ball team to Mexico, where, said the journalist optimistically, the players "will no doubt add to the friendly relations with our neighbors south of the border."

Black troops, like blacks generally, might still be thought of as separate and different, and commanders habitually assumed they should have separate recreation facilities. As late as the fall of 1941 Brigadier General F.E. Uh, commander of the Seventh Corps Area, conferred with St. Louis, Missouri, officials about the possibility of establishing a recreation park for Negro soldiers, according to the *Army and Navy Journal*. And citizens of Wilmington, North Carolina, the town closest to Camp Davis, began cooperating to provide separate recreation facilities for the black soldiers there. As writer Waring Cuney wrote in 1937,

> You want to know what it's like
> Being colored?
> Well,
> It's like going to bat
> With two strikes
> Already called on you—

BIBLIOGRAPHICAL NOTE

THE LIST of publications on baseball is enormous. For a long book like this, one that covers so many topics, all sources used over a long period cannot possibly be cited. To save space, certain shortcuts are used here. Reference works and books on general historical background are not listed. Additional sources are mentioned in the text. Where the entire file of a periodical has been used, individual articles are not cited.

Research was carried out at many libraries and other institutions.

LIBRARIES, ARCHIVES, AND COLLECTIONS

The Research Library of the Boston Public Library has an extensive periodical collection. Many of the older periodicals are housed in its storage facility, the New England Depository Library. It also has a good microfilm collection of newspapers, not only Boston papers and those of surrounding towns but also from cities across the country and some abroad. The BPL's Rare Book Collection was also used. The Library owns a collection of the annual reports and proceedings of conventions of the Playground and Recreation Association. It has some reports of the Michigan State Board of Corrections and Charities. It also has the original program of the visit of the White Fleet to Sydney, Australia, August 1908, and it houses catalogs, prospectuses, and yearbooks of some Indian schools, including Haskell, Carlisle, Chilocco, and Chemawa. Some prison wardens' reports for the young men's reformatory at Elmira, New York, and for the Michigan State Board of Corrections are in the BPL. In addition, it has the original reports of the Massachusetts Emergency and Hygiene Association, 1885–1904, an early Boston playground association.

Three other Boston libraries were used. For early religious periodicals I consulted the library of the Congregational Christian Historical Society and the Unitarian Universalist Association, and I also used a private subscription library, the Atheneum.

The Cleveland Public Library has a collection of recreation surveys and local periodicals. It also owns a useful 1907 pamphlet by Earl Cline, "Inter-High-School Athletics," reprinted from the *American Physical Education Review* by the Russell Sage Foundation.

The New York Public Library houses a great collection of old books, periodicals, guidebooks, and newspapers. Foreign books on baseball were found there. The files of the New York Athletic Club *Journal* for the 1890s are in the NYPL, which also has Spalding's baseball guides for 1892–1912 and guides for local groups like the

Intercity and Metropolitan Baseball Associations. NYPL also has several guides for indoor ball and softball published by the A.G. Spalding Company and one published by the physical educators' association.

The Widener Library at Harvard University has a collection of prison documents consisting of the official annual or biennial reports of prison wardens made to their supervising bodies. The reports include information on recreation budgets, equipment, and programs, and evaluations of those programs, and they represent prisons in Michigan, Connecticut, Indiana, Kansas, Massachusetts, New York, and Washington state, often ranging over the years from the 1870s into the 1920s, although the reports for some years are missing. Widener also houses a collection of prison and reformatory newspapers.

Widener's collection includes reports of juvenile institutions, including those of the Minnesota State Reform School at St. Paul, 1869–1888; State Industrial School at Rochester, New York, 1890–1900; Boston House of Reformation, 1898–1912; Massachusetts State Reform School at Boston, 1865, 1879–1899; Lyman School for Boys at Westboro, Massachusetts, 1851–1879; Lancaster School, Massachusetts, 1895–1910; Monson School, Boston, Massachusetts, 1894–1895; Parental School, West Roxbury, Massachusetts, 1902–1904; Massachusetts Training Schools, 1911–1913; Michigan State Reform School at Lansing, 1893, 1912; Boys Industrial School, Topeka, Kansas, 1926–1928; and Washington State Reformatory, 1912–1914. Other documents at Widener include *Proceedings of the Virginia Conference of Charities and Corrections*, Danville, 1913; Annual Reports of the Public Welfare's Recreation Department, Kansas City, Missouri, 1911–1913; Reports of the Michigan State Board of Corrections and Charities for scattered years, 1871–1940; publications of the National Conference of Charity and Corrections, 1901; *Ohio Bulletin of Charities and Corrections*, quarterly 1896–1913; and Annual Reports of the Children's Institutions Department, Boston, Massachusetts, 1897–1920.

The Public Library of Keene, New Hampshire, owns a separate and extensive collection of New England town histories, the John Wright Collection. The Historical Society of Cheshire County, also in Keene, has collections of letters, photos, high school yearbooks, and business records documenting early baseball in Keene and surrounding towns.

The Library of the Baseball Hall of Fame and Museum at Cooperstown, New York, is essential for scholars in the field. I first began doing research there in 1952 in connection with my doctoral dissertation. From a small room housing mostly secondary sources and the August "Garry" Herrmann Papers, it has grown to a large building with multiple files and a variety of useful sources. Its most helpful manuscript collection for this book is the Herrmann Papers, which in part reveals Organized Baseball's relations with independent clubs. The Bob Quinn letters in Cooperstown were also used.

The Burton Historical Collection, a branch of the Detroit Public Library, houses the Ernie Harwell collection, consisting of scrapbooks, pictures, letters, rosters, programs, guides, and books. Some of this material shows Organized Baseball's relations with independent clubs.

The Fiorello H. LaGuardia Papers, in New York City, include letters, reports, clippings, memoranda, newspaper articles, and scrapbooks. The Alfred J. Scully Baseball Collection at the Chicago Historical Society includes some manuscript, newspaper clippings, and questionnaires. The Society also has copies of the Chicago *Tribune* and the *Sporting News*.

The National Archives at the Library of Congress in Washington, D.C., besides furnishing books during my research there, subsequently lent other books through its interlibrary loan service. It also furnished names of foreign-language translators.

The archives of five colleges were examined, those of three women's colleges and two coed institutions. The archives of Mars Hill College, Mars Hill, North Carolina, contain letters, documents, newspaper clippings, minutes of trustees' meetings, photographs, scrapbooks, college publications, and newspapers. The archives at Keene State College, Keene, New Hampshire, include mainly periodicals, college annuals, and reports relating to college sports.

Radcliffe's, Wellesley's, and Mount Holyoke's archives were searched. Radcliffe's archives include reports of the head of the physical education department as well as student newspapers and college yearbooks. Wellesley's include manuscripts, annuals, and periodicals. Mount Holyoke's archives are extensive and include athletic association files and constitutions, letters of alumnae, questionnaires, notebooks, theses, student handbooks, scrapbooks, pamphlets, and memorabilia.

Many college and university archivists generously sent me photocopies of college reports, newsletters, periodicals, alumni publications, student annuals, student newspapers, student theses, programs, schedules, flyers, clippings, and manuscripts. Some also sent long letters analyzing sources they were unable to copy or loan. These colleges and universities include Agnes Scott, Barnard, California, Chicago, Cincinnati, Cornell, Dartmouth, Fordham, Fort Wayne, Georgia, Gettysburg, Goucher, Indiana, Iowa, Maryland, Mills, Missouri, Nebraska, Northwestern, Ohio State, Pennsylvania State, Randolph-Macon, Rutgers, Sacred Heart, Saint Bonaventure, Saint Mary's, Santa Clara, Seton Hall, Simmons, Smith, South Carolina, Vassar, Virginia, Washington State, and Wisconsin. The archivist of Miss Porter's School also furnished information.

The Schomburg Collection of Negro Literature and History, a branch of the New York Public Library, contains clippings and scrapbooks relating to Negro ball. It also owns a copy of *Sol White's Official Baseball Guide* (Philadelphia, 1907), and it houses a collection of black newspapers, such as the Chicago *Defender*.

The Leon Gardiner Collection on Negro History in the Historical Society of Pennsylvania at Philadelphia has papers of the Pythian Baseball Club, 1867–1870, with letters, bills, reports, rules, correspondence, scorecards, programs, and checks. It also owns books and other materials relating to early Philadelphia blacks.

The Asheville, North Carolina, Public Library has the reports of the U.S. Philippine Commission for scattered years 1901–1913.

The Merrimack Valley Textile Museum, North Andover, Massachusetts, owns a collection of New England textile mill house organs that feature employee baseball. These include the *Amoskeag Bulletin* and the *Whitin Spindle*. The director kindly sent many photocopies of such publications.

DOCUMENTS

Federal government documents include Department of Commerce, Bureau of the Census, *Prisoners and Juvenile Delinquency in the United States* (Washington, 1910);

U.S. Bureau of the Census, *Crime and Pauperism* (Washington, 1896), Part I; International Penal and Prison Commission, *The Reformatory System in the United States* (Washington, 1900), in Widener; and Ruth Bloodgood, *The Federal Courts and the Delinquent Child* (Washington, 1922). Such agencies as the NRA, WPA, and CCC also produced useful reports. Several government reports from the Bureau of Labor Statistics were used on recreation activities of employees. Also used were reports of the Commissioner of Indian Affairs and reports of the superintendents of the Indian schools to the Commissioner, a recommended course of study for the Indian schools, two guides for the use of games in such schools, a history of federal Indian policy, and the Indian Reorganization Act of 1934. These documents are all in the BPL.

The federal government's Bureau of Prisons also published a few documents, called *Federal Offenders*, that include reports of federal prison wardens. Biennial volumes of these reports dated 1929–1936 are available, some at Widener and some at BPL. Other federal documents offer prison statistics: *Prisoners and Juvenile Delinquents in the United States, 1910* (1918); *Prisoners 1923; Crime Conditions in the United States as Reflected in Census Statistics of Imprisoned Offenders* (1926); and *Crime and Mental Disease or Deficiency; Statistics (etc.) 1933* (1936). Another federal document used is the Celler Hearings (*Hearings Before the Subcommittee on Study of Monopoly Power of the Committee on the Judiciary*, House of Representatives, 82nd Congr., 1st Sess., 1951; Washington, D.C., 1952).

Reports of national and state agencies include *Reformation, the 66th Annual Report of the New York Prison Association* (New York, 1910); the New York Prison Association's similar 69th report, 1913; and the *New Jersey Prison Inquiry*, 1917, prepared by Harry Elmer Barnes. The Prison Association of New York (State) issued annual reports that often covered recreation at state institutions; BPL has these for 1910–1930. New York State also published a *Prison Survey* in 1912.

City documents were also used. Official recreation surveys undertaken by various municipal governments, such as those of Cleveland, New York, and Chicago, proved useful.

Other available documents include the reports made by official observers representing the National Society for Penal Information, which sent inspectors into state and federal prisons and sometimes reformatories, prison camps, and houses of correction, to report on conditions, including recreation. Although the title varies, these reports, made every few years 1925–1942, are usually called *Handbook of American Prisons*, and are available at BPL.

The American Prison Association held national meetings and published reports that sometimes offered recreation information. Zebulon Brockway's paper, "The Idea of a True Prison System for a State," is in *National Congress on Penitentiary and Reformatory Discipline* (Ohio, 1970), in BPL. A transcript of a tape recorded by Jesse Collyer, a Sing Sing umpire, was obtained through the Ossining, New York, Oral History Project. The Meriam Report, *The Problem of Indian Administration*, was published in 1928 by the Brookings Institution.

BPL has copies of the typewritten records of the Federal Writers Project on interviews with slaves, 1936 and 1938, assembled by the Library of Congress and entitled *Slave Narratives; Folk History of Slavery in the United States from Interviews with Former Slaves*. Similar material is in eighteen volumes of slave testimony prepared from typed interviews by George R. Rawick and entitled *The American*

Slave: A Composite Autobiography (Westport, Connecticut, 1972); Norman R. Yelman, *Voices from Slavery* (New York, 1970); and John Blassingame, *Slave Testimony* (Baton Rouge, 1976).

DISSERTATIONS

In addition to those mentioned in the text, many dissertations were read in connection with this work, although not all of them can be named here. The most useful were dissertations by Melvin Adelman, John R. Betts, Dominick Cavallo, Patricia Click, Leon M. Coursey, Martin E. Dann, Lawrence Finfer, Arnold Flath, Robert H. Freeman, Philip E. Frohlich, Robert L. Goldman, Rosalind Graham, Richard T. Knapp, Thomas W. Nightingale, Timothy O'Hanlon, Brucille Phillips, Roberta B. Powell, William Donn Rogosin, Robert P. Smith, Richard A. Swanson, Stephanie L. Twin, and Harold H. Wolf.

MANUSCRIPTS

Many scholars generously sent me copies of their formal research papers, not all of which were subsequently published. Those written by the following researchers proved especially helpful: Robert K. Barney, Bruce Bennett, Donald Chu, Richard E. Derby, Jr., with Jim Coleman, William H. Freeman, Rudolph Haerle, Jim Harper, Masaru Ikei, Tony Ladd, Guy M. Lewis, Angela Lumpkin, Tracy Mehr, Eugene Murdock, Roberta J. Park, Ben G. Rader, Gerald Redmond, R.W. Reising, Steven A. Riess, John R. Schleppi, Leverett T. Smith, and David Zang.

Other manuscripts used include a copy of a typed report by S.H. Reilly, "The Great White Fleet" (U.S. Navy, May 1973); a typed manuscript, "Baseball in the United Kingdom," by William T. Morgan of London, England (1973); and a copy of an undated, typed manuscript, "History of the Sporting News," all in my collection. I also used a 1916 graduation paper by Harry Kingman on foreign baseball from the Springfield College archives, Springfield, Massachusetts. Professor Ross C. Owens of Tuskegee prepared a manuscript, "History of Baseball [at Tuskegee]," in 1978 for my use. A copy of a typed manuscript, "A Study of Public Recreation in Cleveland" (Cleveland, 1936) is in my files. Two other manuscripts, both by Blanche Trilling, director of physical education at the University of Wisconsin, describe women's sport at her university. Copies of these were sent to me. An anonymous manuscript on Alta Weiss is in the files of the baseball library at Cooperstown.

QUESTIONNAIRES AND LETTERS, WITH INCLUSIONS

Forty-five corporations responded to a questionnaire about their companies' recreation policy and history. Some sent detailed information. Long, helpful letters from Champlin Petroleum Company and the Halliburton Company, for example, detailed their companies' baseball history.

Ten letters from representatives of various national amateur and semipro baseball organizations, responding to my queries, are in my files. Some of these representatives also sent pamphlets, handbooks, and official lists of winners of annual championships.

Letters from representatives of the U.S. Army and the U.S. Navy and from the archivists of the U.S. Military and Naval Academies helped clarify certain questions about use of sports by these institutions. The archivists also kindly sent photocopies of reports, annuals, and team records.

Several prison officials, in response to queries, wrote me in detail describing prison recreation policy: Larry Howard of the United States Department of Justice, Bureau of Prisons; Robert J. Wright, editor of the *American Journal of Corrections;* T.D. Taylor, an officer of the Columbus, Ohio, Facility; and Ralph Masters, former official of the Atlanta Federal Prison.

Representatives of some Indian schools generously sent material. F.H. Klein, formerly of Chemawa, supplied photocopies of pages from the school annual, 1928–1940, and a copy of a 1915 manuscript by Charles Larsen on Chemawa baseball history, the original of which is stored in the Oregon Historical Society at Portland.

Many members of the Society for American Baseball Research (SABR) and the North American Society for Sport History (NASSH) kindly responded by letter to my queries about their research.

Representatives of various black colleges, like Morehouse, Howard, and Hampton Institute, as well as black baseball figures like Tweed Webb, sent information.

Japanese sources proved most forthcoming. Beginning in 1965, Professor Junji Kanda, then assistant to the Japanese baseball commissioner, wrote several times replying to my queries. Both Waseda University and Keio University in Tokyo sent valuable information. At Keio, reference librarians Komei Kato, Masayoshi Higashida, and Keio Taku wrote at different times, and at Waseda, Koichi Yukishima wrote. In addition, Isao Odachi of the Japanese Federation of Amateur Baseball responded by mail to my questions, as did historian Masaru Ikei of Keio University.

INTERVIEWS

In 1971, interpreted by Samuel Ishikawa of the Masaoka-Ishikawa Company, Professor Junji Kanda graciously gave me an interview in New York, answering my questions about early Japanese baseball.

Mrs. Lois Turner, a Chicago teacher interviewed in 1969, furnished information about an amateur team formed by employees of the Fall River Line.

The interview with Mayme Dwyer Seelye took place in Keene, New Hampshire, in 1985.

GUIDES AND HANDBOOKS

Edwin Henderson's son, Dr. J.M.H. Henderson of Tuskegee, kindly lent his collection of photocopies of some of the athletic handbooks published by Henderson and his collaborators. Guidebooks for the national amateur-semipro organizations, NBC, NBF, and ABC, are in my own collection, as are copies of the New York Public Schools Athletic League handbooks for 1913 and 1917.

The BPL has copies of several editions, 1912–1926, of *The Negro Year Book*, an informative handbook prepared by Monroe N. Work.

PAMPHLETS

Copies of the following pamphlets are in my collection: "A History of Company A—314th Engineers 89th Division" (1920); "Haskell Highlights, 1884–1978"; and

Edna Munro, "A History of the Department of Physical Education for Women at Indiana University" (Bloomington, 1971).

RELEASES
Periodic releases of the Associacion Internacional de Beisbol Amateur (AINBA), the current international amateur baseball association, were used.

TRANSLATORS
Kimi Kimura, a Washington translator, translated several Japanese-language books. Marion Tuttle Thomas of Setauket, New York, translated two periodical articles from the French. Enrique Rueda-Puerto of North Shore Community College, Beverly, Massachusetts, translated a Spanish-language book.

NEWSPAPERS
Complete files of *Sporting News* and the New York *Times* through 1941 and selected issues thereafter proved essential. Selected dates of other newspapers were consulted when they could be expected to contribute details on a particular issue.

Widener has the prison newspapers *Our Paper* (Concord, Massachusetts Reformatory, 1885–1897; *The Summary* (Elmira, New York, Reformatory, 1926–27); *The Mentor* (hand-printed, from the Charlestown, Massachusetts, State Prison, 1904–1911); *The Star of Hope*, later *Star-Bulletin* (Sing Sing, New York, Prison, 1899–1907); and *Ohio Penitentiary News* (Columbus, Ohio, Prison, 1935–36). Both Widener and BPL have some issues of *Mutual Welfare News*, from the Naval Prison at Portsmouth, New Hampshire.

For military research I used the complete file, 1863–1941, of the *Army and Navy Journal*. Other useful periodicals in the BPL are *Journal of the Military Service* (1879–1917); *Army and Navy Life* (1906–1909); *Canal Record* (Panama Canal, 1905–1912); *Stars and Stripes* (Paris, France, 1918–1919); *The Salvo* (Boston Navy Yard, 1918–1919); *Trench and Camp* (Camp Jackson, South Carolina, 1918); another edition of *Trench and Camp* (Camp Gordon, Georgia, 1919); *Divisional Review* (Massachusetts National Guard, Camp Devens, Ayer, Massachusetts, 1928–1929); and shorter files of *The Navy, Journal of the Military Service*, and *U.S. Naval Institute Proceedings*.

Newspapers reporting on Indian life include *Wassaja* (1982–1983), in the Newton, Massachusetts, Public Library; *The Indian Sentinel* (1910), *The Red Man* (1910), *World's Fair Bulletin* (1904), *Indian Boys' and Girls' Club News* (1924), *Akwesasne Notes* (1973), and *The Native American* (1910), all in BPL.

Valuable inside information on the operation of recreation at Michigan State Prison at Jackson came from an inmate, who went to the trouble of making photocopies for me of nearly every issue of the prison paper, *School News*, 1931–1935.

The Denver Public Library kindly sent photocopies of stories covering the winners of the Denver *Post* championships.

BPL has microfilmed copies of black newspapers like the New York *Age*, Cleveland *Gazette*, Pittsburgh *Courier*, St. Louis *Palladium*, and *The Crisis*. It also owns a file of the *Daily Worker*.

PERIODICALS

Complete files of *Playground* (later, *Recreation*), the publication of the Playground and Recreation Association, were used, as were complete files of *Baseball Magazine* and the *Athletic Journal*.

Complete files of the publications of the two main sport history associations were also used: those of the Society of American Baseball Research, or SABR (*The National Pastime* and *Baseball Research Journal*) and of the North American Society for Sport History, or NASSH (annual *Proceedings, Journal of Sport History*, and periodical *Bulletins*). The *Journal of Sport History* in particular has published many insightful and well-documented articles, whose authors, I regret, cannot all be credited here individually. I also used the complete file of *Baseball History* as well as that of the Sport Literature Association, *Aethlon* (formerly *Arete*). Complete files of the New York Athletic Club's journal for the 1890s is in NYPL.

Very suggestive were the articles, book reviews, and article listings in the main publication of the Organization of American Historians, the *Journal of American History*, including issues published under its former title, *The Mississippi Valley Historical Review*.

Countless individual periodical articles were used. Evaluations of children's sports literature, for example, are found in such periodicals as the *Journal of Popular Culture, The Saturday Review of Literature, Editor and Publisher, Bookman, The English Journal*, and the *Essex Institute Historical Collection*.

Useful state and local journals published by historical societies and similar journals of folklore include the *Bucks County Historical Society Collections, Wisconsin Magazine of History, Montana the Magazine of Western History, Siskiyou Historical Society Journal, North Carolina Historical Review, North Carolina Folklore Journal, Illinois History, Yearbook of the History Society of Middletown, New York, True West, American Heritage, Journal of American Folklore, Journal of the West, Cheyenne Sun Magazine, Oklahoma Today, Palimpsest, Utah Historical Quarterly, Minnesota History*, and *Apalachee*.

Scholarly sources used on the chapters about boys include periodicals like the *Journal of Social History, Research Quarterly, New-York Historical Society Quarterly, American Quarterly, Social Service Review, North American Review, American Jewish Quarterly, South Atlantic Quarterly, Journal of Ethnic Studies, The School Review, Journal of Educational Sociology, Research Quarterly, National Municipal Review*, and *Pedagogical Seminary*, as well as the journal of the American Health and Physical Education Association, which published under various titles over the years.

Popular magazine articles used for topics in the chapters on boys include *Outing, Nation, Literary Digest, Outlook, Harper's Weekly, Collier's, Popular Science, Atlantic Monthly, American City, Scribner's, Lippincott's, Living Age*, and *School and Society*.

Helpful material on college ball was found in such periodicals as *Quest, American Quarterly, Kenyon College Alumni Bulletin, The Harvard Graduate, The Harvard Alumni Bulletin, The Princeton Alumni Weekly, The University of Chicago Magazine, The University of Virginia Magazine*, the *Union [College] Alumni Monthly, Chicago History*, the *Quarterly Review of Higher Education*, and the *American Journal of Sociology*.

Articles in magazines like *Prison World, Jail Association Journal*, and the *American Journal of Correction* offered some information.

Some women's magazines like *Godey's Lady's Book* and *Ladies' Home Journal* proved helpful. For Indian history, articles in the *Smithsonian* and in the *Indian Historian* were useful.

For business and industrial ball, see such periodicals as *Industrial Management, Nation's Business, International Labor Review, Industrial Sports Journal, Factory and Industrial Management, Illinois Central Magazine*, and *Southern Exposure*. The entire file of the *Boston Typo-Athlete* (1912–1920) and the file of *Fire* (Chicago, 1922–1929) in the Boston Public Library were read. The publicity director of the White Motor Company, Cleveland, Ohio, sent photocopies of *The White-Book* and *The Albatross*, company organs reporting employee baseball, for 1914–1919.

Articles on the popularity of softball appeared in such periodicals as *Saturday Evening Post, Literary Digest*, and *Collier's*. An unusual source is the *SA Journal, Organ Bratrslava CSPS* (Czech Protective Society) for the 1930s.

For military ball, periodical articles included ones in *Scribner's*, the *Hawaiian Journal of History, National Geographic, Scientific American, Alabama Historical Quarterly, Presidential Studies Quarterly*, and *Asia Magazine*. Some of the material on the foreign contacts of national baseball associations is based on William T. Morgan's quarterly, *Baseball Courier* (Cardiff, Wales, 1960s) and *Baseball Mercury* (London, 1970s).

Black periodicals include *Colored American Magazine* and especially the *Southern Workman*, for which I used the complete file (1872–1930).

BOOKS

Information on baseball as used in boys' work may be found in such older works as Charles Stelzle, *Boys of the Street; How to Win Them* (New York, 1904); Frank Erb, *The Development of the Young People's Movement* (Chicago, 1917); W.L. Stone, *The Development of Boys' Work in the United States* (Nashville, Tennessee, 1935); and William E. Ball, *100 Years and Millions of Boys* (New York, 1961). Contemporary books on child-saving include Leonard Benedict, *Waifs of the Slum and Their Way Out* (New York, 1907), and Allen Hoben, *The Minister and the Boy* (Chicago, 1912).

Other useful contemporary sources on boys include William R. George, *The Junior Republic* (New York, 1910); Madeleine Doty, *Society's Misfits* (New York, 1916); John J. Bagley, *Pauperism and Crime in Michigan* (Lansing, 1875); James Hiatt, *The Truant Problem and the Parental School* (Washington, 1915); Henry Barnard, *Reformatory Education* (Hartford, Connecticut, 1857); Homer Folks, *The Care of Destitute, Neglected, and Delinquent Children* (New York, 1902); J.G. Rosengarten, *Reform Schools* (Philadelphia, 1879), and the same author's *Penal and Reformatory Institutions* (Philadelphia, 1880); Catharine M. Sedgewick, *Memoir of Joseph Curtis, A Model Man* (New York, 1858); and Frederick M. Thrasher, *The Gang: A Study of 1,313 Gangs in Chicago* (Chicago, 1927).

Newer sources that proved suggestive for the chapters on boys include the works of the following authors: Leroy Ashby, Willard Gaylin, et al., James Gilbert, Cary Goodman, Herbert Gutman, Joseph Hawes, Jack M. Holl, Joseph Kett, Robert Mennel, David Nasaw, Thomas Philpott, Robert Pickett, Anthony Platt, Neil Postman, David Rothman, Steven Schlossman, Stanley Schultz, and Viviana Zelizer. Books on the progressives by Allen F. Davis, by Paul McBride, and by Ronald G. Walters were used. Steven A. Riess has an excellent book on sports in the progressive era.

Books describing sports for boys include Alfred Rochefort, *Healthful Sports for Boys* (New York, 1910); D.C. Beard, *Outdoor Handy Book* (New York, 1901); Norman W. Bingham, *The Book of Athletics and Out-of-Door Sports* (Boston, 1895); Henry S. Curtis, *Play and Recreation for the Open Country* (Boston, 1914), *Education Through Play* (New York, 1915), and his *The Play Movement and its Significance* (New York, 1917; Joseph Lee, *Play in Education* (New York, 1915); and Everett Mero, *American Playgrounds* (Boston, 1908).

Baseball as it developed as part of parks and public recreation facilities receives treatment in such works as Galen Cranz, *The Politics of Park Design* (Cambridge, Massachusetts, 1982); Stephen Hardy, *How Boston Played* (Boston, 1982); Cynthia Zaitzevsky, *Frederick L. Olmsted and the Boston Park System* (Boston, 1982); and Henry Reed and Sophia Duckworth, *Central Park* (New York, 1972).

Settlements are covered in newer studies, like Paula Todisco, *Boston's First Neighborhood* (Boston, 1976), as well as older sources like Robert A. Woods and Albert Kennedy, *The Settlement Horizon* (New York, 1922). Biographies of settlement workers are also available, such as Barbara Sicherman, *Alice Hamilton* (Boston, 1984), and books by the workers themselves, like Mary Simkhovich, *Neighborhood* (New York, 1938), Jacob Burnes, *West End House* (Boston, 1934), and Lillian Wald, *The House on Henry Street* (New York, 1915.

Descriptions of available recreation facilities include Gustavus Kirby, *The Recreation Movement* (New York, 1911); John A. Krout, *Annals of American Sport* (New Haven, Connecticut, 1929); Jesse F. Steiner, *Americans at Play* (New York, 1933); Foster Rhea Dulles, *America Learns to Play* (New York, 1940); George D. Butler, *Pioneers in Public Recreation* (New York, 1965); Harold Meyer and Charles Brightbill, *Community Recreation* (Boston, 1948); and Richard Kraus, *Recreation and Leisure in Modern Society* (New York, 1971).

A sampling of countless books on leisure and sports would include George B. Cutten, *The Threat of Leisure* (New Haven, 1926); L.B. Jacks, *Education Through Recreation* (New York, 1932); and Frederick Cozens and Florence Stumpf, *Sports in American Life* (Chicago 1953). In addition, general works on sport and on physical education provided useful background; authors of such works include John R. Betts, Fred Leonard and George B. Affleck, John A. Lucas and Ronald A. Smith, Deobold B. Van Dalen and Bruce L. Bennett, and C.W. Hackensmith.

The use of recreation in schools may be checked in such titles as Harriett Marr, *The Old New England Academies* (New York, 1959), and O.J. Kern, *Among Country Schools* (New York, 1906). Boys' baseball in private schools may be found in school histories like August Heckscher, *St. Paul's* (New York, 1980) and Laurence Crosbie, *Phillips Exeter Academy* (Norwood, Massachusetts, 1923), as well as more general works like James McLachlan, *American Boarding Schools* (New York, 1970), and biographies like Millard Kennedy, *Schoolmaster of Yesterday* (New York, 1940), and Martin Fausold, *James W. Wadsworth, Jr.* (New York, 1975).

Studies of recreation in churches include older books like Charles D. Giauque et. al, *Recreation in Church and Community* (New York, 1938); Norman E. Richardson, *The Religious Education of Adolescents* (New York, 1913), and *The Church at Play*

(New York, 1922); Charles Gill and Gifford Pinchot, *The Country Church* (New York, 1913); and H.C. Hayden, *Amusements in the Light of Reason and Scripture* (New York, 1880). A helpful newer study is Aaron Abell, *The Urban Impact on American Protestantism* (Cambridge, Mass., 1943).

For baseball used to prevent delinquency or used in special education, some available titles are Ernest K. Coulter, *The Children in the Shadow* (New York, 1913); William Healy, *The Individual Delinquent* (Montclair, New Jersey, 1915); Ethel Shanas and C.E. Dunning, *Recreation and Delinquency* (Chicago, 1942); Walter Reckless and Mopheus Smith, *Juvenile Delinquency* (New York, 1932); William and Dorothy Thomas, *The Child in America* (New York, 1928); and Peter L. Tyor, *Caring for the Retarded in America* (Westport, Connecticut, 1984).

Studies of American ethnics that mention their playing baseball include Gary Mormico, *Immigrants on the Hill* (Urbana, Illinois, 1986); Humbert Nelli, *The Italians in Chicago* (New York, 1970); and John Bodmar, *The Transplanted* (Bloomington, Indiana, 1985). Memoirs of ethnic players include M. Mark Stolarik, *Growing Up on the South Side* (Lewisburg, Pennsylvania, 1985), and Mary Dearborn, *Love in the Promised Land* (New York, 1988).

For American Legion baseball I depended largely upon Raymond Moley, *The American Legion Story* (New York, 1966); Richard J. Loosbrock, *The History of the Kansas Department of the American Legion* (Topeka, 1968); Richard R. Jones, *A History of the American Legion* (Indianapolis, 1946); and William Gellerman, *The American Legion As Educator* (New York, 1938).

Baseball in New Deal programs is mentioned in works like Betty and Ernest K. Lindley, *A New Deal for Youth* (New York, 1938); Lewis Lorwin, *Youth Work Programs* (Washington, 1941); Donald Howard, *The WPA and Federal Relief Policy* (New York, 1943), and several books on the CCC.

For the YMCA see such works as William Whiteside, *The Boston YMCA and Community Need* (New York, 1951); C. Howard Hopkins, *History of the Y in North America* (New York, 1944); and Richard C. Morse, *My Life with Young Men* (New York, 1918).

To prepare the material on juvenile literature I read, or reread, many baseball books for boys, some of which are in my own collection. They are hard to come by, but the Library of Congress has the Baseball Joe series, and the Library of the Baseball Hall of Fame and Museum at Cooperstown has Noah Brooks's *The Fairport Nine*. Several good books include information on juvenile baseball literature: Christian Messenger, *Sport and the Spirit of Play in American Literature* (New York, 1981); David MacLeod, *Building Character in the American Boy* (Madison, Wisconsin, 1983); Russell Nye, *The Unembarrassed Muse* (New York, 1970); and especially Daniel T. Rodgers, *The Work Ethic in Industrial America* (Chicago, 1974).

Dozens of college histories were examined, sometimes two or three histories about a prominent individual institution. General works on American education, too, contributed bits of information, as did books on sports in college. Samples include William C. Ringenberg, *Taylor University* (Grand Rapids, Michigan, 1973); Charles E. Frank, *Pioneer's Progress: Illinois College, 1829–1979* (Carbondale, Illinois, 1979); and Richard M. Hurd, *A History of Yale Athletics* (New Haven, Connecticut, 1888). For baseball contacts of American college players with Japanese students, I used translation-summaries of two complete books, Takayuki Kubota's *Yakyu Taikan (Baseball in Perspective)*, published in Tokyo in 1949, and his *Koko Yakyu Hyakunen*

(A Hundred Years of Japanese Baseball), as well as partial translation-summaries of several other Japanese-language books on Japanese baseball history.

Some books chronicle town teams. They include Keith Sutton, *Wayne County Sports History, 1871–1972* (Honesdale, Pennsylvania, 1972); W.R. Griffith, *Early History of Amateur Baseball in the State of Maryland, 1858 to 1872* (Baltimore, 1897); and Frank Salvus, *Saint Paul Baseball with the Amateurs and Semipros Prior to 1920* (St. Paul, 1948).

Town histories used include Marshall Swan, *Town on Sandy Bay* (Rockport, Massachusetts, 1980), and the Bedford, New Hampshire, Historical Society, *History of Bedford, New Hampshire, 1737–1971* (Bedford, New Hampshire, 1972). More general books on towns, like John Hudson, *Plains Country Towns* (Minneapolis, 1985), also have information on this topic.

Company and industry histories offer information on baseball and recreation policies. Samples of these are Margaret Byington, *Homestead; the Households of a Mill Town* (New York, 1910); Nicholas Wainwright, *History of the Philadelphia Electric Company, 1881–1961* (Philadelphia, 1961); Gerald Zahavi, *Workers, Managers, and Welfare Capitalism: The Shoeworkers and Tanners of Endicott Johnson, 1890–1950* (Urbana, Illinois, 1988); Robert S. Smith, *Mill on the Dan: A History of Dan River Mills, 1882–1950* (Durham, North Carolina, 1960); Jack T. Kirby, *Rural Worlds* Lost (Baton Rouge, 1987); Harriet Herring, *Welfare Work in Mill Villages* (Chapel Hill, North Carolina, 1929); and Maury Kline, *History of the Louisville & Nashville Railroad* (New York, 1972).

I used studies of business policies that emphasize the use of recreation in dealing with employees, the best of which is Stuart Brandes, *American Welfare Capitalism, 1880–1940* (Chicago, 1976). The work of Robert L. Goldman and Tamara Hareven in this field is also notable. Good collections of industrial sports articles and selections from other books include Eric Larrabee and Rolf Meyersohn, *Mass Leisure* (Glencoe, Illinois, 1958), and Sebastian deGrazia, *Of Time, Work and Leisure* (New York, 1962).

Bruno Beneck, *Il Giocco della Vita* (Milano, 1973) offers information, in Italian, on relations of amateurs with Organized Baseball.

Many books were examined for the chapters on the armed forces, such as biographies and autobiographies of military figures; guides to ships and military units; studies of military forts; histories of the armed services, of the service academies, and of wars and campaigns; reminiscences of servicemen; commentaries on health and recreation at forts and camps; and histories of the agencies that furnished recreation to the services. Some examples of useful sources for the chapters are Joseph Odell, *The New Spirit of the New Army* (New York, 1918); Robert Wooster, *Soldiers, Sutlers, and Settlers; Garrison Life on the Texas Frontier* (College Station, Texas, 1987); W.H. Beehler, *The Cruise of the Brooklyn* (Philadelphia, 1885); William H. Baumer, Jr., *Sports as Taught and Played at West Point* (Harrisburg, Pennsylvania, 1939); Francis Buzzell, *The Great Lakes Training Station: A History* (Boston, 1919); Katherine Mayo, *"That Damn Y," A Record of Overseas Service* (Boston, 1920); Conrad Hoffman, *In the Prison Camps of Germany* (New York, 1920); Roger Batchelder, *Watching and Waiting on the Border* (Boston, 1917); Manuel F. Alfonso and T. Valero Martinez, *Cuba Before the World* (Havana and New York, 1915); Gwenfread Allen, *The YMCA in Hawaii, 1869–1969* (Honolulu, 1969); Edward F. Allen, *Keeping Our Fighters Fit* (New York, 1918); Raul Diez Muro, *Historia de base ball profesional de Cuba* (Havana, 1949); John M. Gates, *Schoolbooks and Krags* (Greenwood, Connecticut, 1973); Richard O'Connor, *The Spirit Soldiers* (New York, 1973); and Games Committee, *Interallied Games, Paris 22nd June to 6th July 1919* (NP, 1921).

A sampling of books useful on indoor ball and softball would include Arthur T. Noren, *Softball* (New York, 1940); Elmer D. Mitchell, ed., *Sports for Recreation and How to Play Them* (New York, 1936); and Morris A. Bealle, *The Softball Story* (Washington, 1957).

Many books on Indians contributed useful information: biographies and autobiographies, tribal histories, reminiscences, evaluations of government Indian policies, and works on the Indian boarding schools and on Hampton Institute. Some samples are Luther Standing Bear, *My People, The Sioux* (New York, 1928); William W. Savage, Jr., ed., *Indian Life: Transforming an American Myth* (Norman, Oklahoma, 1977); Ralph Linton, *Acculturation in Seven American Indian Tribes* (Gloucester, Massachusetts, 1963); Joseph H. Cash and Herbert T. Hoover, *To Be An Indian: An Oral History* (New York, 1971); Charles A. Eastman (Ohiyesa), *The Indian Today* (Garden City, New York, 1915); Theodore Fischbacher, *A Study of the Role of the Federal Government in the Education of the American Indian* (Tempe, Arizona, 1967); Lawrence Schmeckebier, *The Office of Indian Affairs* (Baltimore, 1927); Richard H. Pratt, *Battlefield and Classroom: Four Decades with the American Indian, 1867–1904* (New Haven, Connecticut, 1964); F.W. Blackmar, *Indian Education* (Lawrence, Kansas, 1899); and Robert W. Mardock, *The Reformers and the American Indian* (Columbia, Missouri, 1971).

Books contributed information on prisons. A sampling follows. Memoirs of prison officials include Sanford Bates, *Prisons and Beyond* (Freeport, New York, 1936); James V. Bennett, *I Chose Prison* (New York, 1970); and several books by Thomas Mott Osborne and by Lewis Lawes. Books on prison policy include Corinne Bacon, comp., *Prison Reform* (White Plains, New York, 1917); and Charles R. Henderson, ed., *Correction and Prevention* (New York, 1910). Histories of individual prisons include Robert Park, *History of the Oklahoma State Penitentiary at McAlester, Oklahoma* (McAlester, 1914). General histories of American prisons include Harry Elmer Barnes, *The Story of Punishment* (Boston, 1930). Books by prisoners include Victor Nelson, *Prison Days and Nights* (New York, 1933), and Bill Mills, *25 Years Behind Prison Bars* (Emory, Texas, 1933).

Some books on women and higher education proved helpful, notably Barbara M. Solomon, *In the Company of Educated Women* (New Haven, Connecticut, 1985), and Helen H. Horowitz, *Alma Mater* (New York, 1984). Histories of individual colleges were searched, like Marian C. White, *A History of Barnard College* (New York, 1954); Delavan Leonard, *The Story of Oberlin* (Chicago, 1898); and James Smart, *Striving* (Canaan, New Hampshire, 1984). Books on women and sport include Carl E. Klafs and M. Joan Lyon, *The Female Athlete* (St. Louis, 1973).

Works on women in prisons include Barbara Brenzel, *Daughters of the State* (Cambridge, Massachusetts, 1983); Nicole Rafter, *Partial Justice* (Boston, 1985); and Estelle Freedman, *Their Sisters' Keepers* (Ann Arbor, Michigan, 1981).

Many general books on women's position in society were consulted. They include Vern L. Bullough, *The Subordinate Sex* (Urbana, Illinois, 1974); Barbara Deckard, *The Women's Movement* (New York, 1975); William Chafe, *The American Woman* (New York, 1972); Sheila Rothman, *Woman's Proper Place* (New York, 1978), and

Carl Degler, *At Odds; Women and the Family in America from the Revolution to the Present* (New York, 1980).

On blacks, see Fleet Walker's book, *Our Home Colony; A Treatise on the Past, Present, and Future of the Negro Race in America* (Steubenville, Ohio, 1908), in the Oberlin College Library. Useful memoirs of black players include those of Quincy Trouppe, *Twenty Years Too Soon* (New York, 1977). Books that cover recreation in black communities include Alan H. Spear, *Black Chicago* (Chicago, 1967); Seth M. Scheiner, *Negro Mecca, A History of the Negro in New York City* (New York, 1965); Frances Blascoer, *Colored School Children in New York* (New York, 1915); Wendell Dabney, *Cincinnati's Colored Citizens* (Cincinnati, 1926); Alrutheus Taylor, *The Negro in Tennessee, 1865–1888* (Washington, 1941); David A. Gerber, *Black Ohio and the Color Line, 1960–1915* (Urbana, Illinois, 1976); George C. Wright, *Life Behind a Veil: Blacks in Louisville, Kentucky, 1865–1930* (Baton Rouge, 1985); and Thomas C. Cox, *Blacks in Topeka, Kansas, 1865–1915, A Social History* (Baton Rouge, 1982). One source for black industrial recreation is John W. Bracey, et al., eds., *Black Workers and Organized Labor* (Belmont, California, 1971).

Biographies used for the chapters on blacks include Lloyd Wendt and Herman Kogan, *Big Bill of Chicago* (Indianapolis, 1954), and Constance Webb, *Richard Wright, A Biography* (New York, 1968). One of several sources for the Chicago race riot over recreation is Lee E. Williams and Lee E. Williams III, *Anatomy of Four Race Riots* (Jackson, Mississippi, 1972). Histories of black colleges include Paul W. Terry, ed., *A Study of Stillman Institute* (University, Alabama, 1946).

Some sources for blacks in the military include Emmett J. Scott, ed., *Scott's Official History of the American Negro in the World War* (Chicago, 1919); Marvin E. Fletcher, *The Negro Soldier and the United States Army, 1891–1917* (Madison, Wisconsin, 1968); E.L.N. Glass, *History of the Tenth Cavalry, 1866–1921* (Fort Collins, Colorado, 1972); and J.H. Nankivell, *History of the 25th Regiment of the United States Infantry, 1869–1926* (Denver, 1927).